PSALMS II

51–100

VOLUME 17

THE ANCHOR BIBLE is a fresh approach to the world's greatest classic. Its object is to make the Bible accessible to the modern reader; its method is to arrive at the meaning of biblical literature through exact translation and extended exposition, and to reconstruct the ancient setting of the biblical story, as well as the circumstances of its transcription and the characteristics of its transcribers.

THE ANCHOR BIBLE is a project of international and interfaith scope: Protestant, Catholic, and Jewish scholars from many countries contribute individual volumes. The project is not sponsored by any ecclesiastical organization and is not intended to reflect any particular theological doctrine. Prepared under our joint supervision, THE ANCHOR BIBLE is an effort to make available all the significant historical and linguistic knowledge which bears on the interpretation of the biblical record.

THE ANCHOR BIBLE is aimed at the general reader with no special formal training in biblical studies; yet, it is written with the most exacting standards of scholarship, reflecting the highest technical accomplishment.

This project marks the beginning of a new era of co-operation among scholars in biblical research, thus forming a common body of knowledge to be shared by all.

William Foxwell Albright
David Noel Freedman
GENERAL EDITORS

THE ANCHOR BIBLE

PSALMS II
51–100

INTRODUCTION, TRANSLATION, AND NOTES

BY

MITCHELL DAHOOD, S.J.

YALE

THE ANCHOR YALE BIBLE

Yale University Press

New Haven & London

THE ANCHOR BIBLE
PUBLISHED BY DOUBLEDAY
a division of Bantam Doubleday Dell Publishing Group, Inc.
1540 Broadway, New York, New York10036

THE ANCHOR BIBLE, DOUBLEDAY, and the portrayal of an anchor with the letters AB are trademarks of Doubleday, a division of Bantam Doubleday Dell Publishing Group, Inc.

ISBN 978-0-300-13957-0

Library of Congress Catalog Card Number 66-11766

PRINTED IN THE UNITED STATES OF AMERICA

CONTENTS

PRINCIPAL ABBREVIATIONS

1. Publications

AfO	Archiv für Orientforschung
AJSL	American Journal of Semitic Languages and Literatures
ARW	Archiv für Religionswissenschaft
BA	Biblical Archaeologist
BASOR	Bulletin of the American Schools of Oriental Research
BCCT	*The Bible in Current Catholic Thought,* ed. J. L. McKenzie
BDB	F. Brown, S. R. Driver, and C. A. Briggs, eds., *A Hebrew and English Lexicon of the Old Testament*
BH^3	*Biblia Hebraica,* ed. R. Kittel, 3d ed.
BHS	*Biblia Hebraica Stuttgartensia,* eds. K. Elliger and W. Rudolph
BO	Bibliotheca Orientalis
BP	*The Book of Psalms,* by A. A. Anderson
BSOAS	Bulletin of the School of Oriental African Studies
BZ	Biblische Zeitschrift
BZAW	Beihefte zur Zeitschrift für die alttestamentliche Wissenschaft
CAD	*The Assyrian Dictionary,* Oriental Institute of the University of Chicago
CBQ	Catholic Biblical Quarterly
CECBP	*A Critical and Exegetical Commentary on the Book of Psalms,* by C. A. Briggs
CML	*Canaanite Myths and Legends,* by G. R. Driver
CPBP	*Canaanite Parallels in the Book of Psalms,* by J. H. Patton
CRAIBL	Comptes Rendus de l'Académie des Inscriptions et Belles Lettres
DISO	*Dictionnaire des inscriptions sémitiques de l'ouest,* by Charles F. Jean and Jacob Hoftijzer
EA	*Die El-Amarna Tafeln,* ed. J. Knudtzon
FuF	Forschungen und Fortschritte
GB	Gesenius-Buhl, *Handwörterbuch*
GHB	*Grammaire de l'Hébreu Biblique,* by P. Joüon
GK	*Gesenius' Hebräische Grammatik,* ed. E. Kautzsch
GLECS	Groupe Linguistique d'Études Chamito-Sémitiques
HTR	Harvard Theological Review
HUCA	Hebrew Union College Annual

ICC	International Critical Commentary
IDB	The Interpreter's Dictionary of the Bible
IEJ	Israel Exploration Journal
JAOS	Journal of the American Oriental Society
JBL	Journal of Biblical Literature
JCS	Journal of Cuneiform Studies
JJS	Journal of Jewish Studies
JNES	Journal of Near Eastern Studies
JPOS	Journal of the Palestine Oriental Society
JQR	Jewish Quarterly Review
JRAS	Journal of the Royal Asiatic Society
JSS	Journal of Semitic Studies
JTS	Journal of Theological Studies
KAI	*Kanaanäische und Aramäische Inschriften,* by H. Donner and W. Röllig
KB	L. Koehler and W. Baumgartner, *Lexicon in Veteris Testamenti Libros*
LKK	*The Legend of King Keret,* by H. L. Ginsberg
OLZ	Orientalistische Literaturzeitung
PCTNT	*The Psalms Chronologically Treated with a New Translation,* by M. Buttenwieser
PEQ	Palestine Exploration Quarterly
PNWSP	*Proverbs and Northwest Semitic Philology,* by M. Dahood
PPG	*Phönizisch-Punische Grammatik,* by Johannes Friedrich
1QIs[a]	The St. Mark's Isaiah Scroll, ed. M. Burrows
1QM	Qumran War Scroll
1QS	Qumran Manual of Discipline
11QPs[a]	*The Psalms Scroll of Qumrân Cave 11* (Discoveries in the Judaean Desert of Jordan, IV), ed. James A. Sanders
Rendiconti Lincei	*Atti dell'Accademia Nazionale dei Lincei, Rendiconti della classe di scienze morali, storiche e filologiche*
RHR	Revue de l'histoire des religions
ThR	Theologische Rundschau
TNSI	*A Text-Book of North-Semitic Inscriptions,* by G. A. Cooke
TS	Theological Studies
TSP	*Tempora und Satzstellung in den Psalmen,* by Diethelm Michel
UHP	*Ugaritic-Hebrew Philology,* by M. Dahood
UT	*Ugaritic Textbook,* 4th ed., 1965, of C. H. Gordon's *Ugaritic Grammar*
VT	Vetus Testamentum
VTS	Vetus Testamentum Supplements
WO	Die Welt des Orients

WuS	*Wörterbuch der ugaritischen Sprache,* by Joseph Aistleitner
ZA	Zeitschrift für Assyriologie und vorderasiatische Archäologie
ZAW	Zeitschrift für die alttestamentliche Wissenschaft
ZDMG	Zeitschrift der deutschen morgenländischen Gesellschaft
ZDPV	Zeitschrift des deutschen Palästina-Vereins
ZLH	F. Zorell, *Lexicon Hebraicum*

2. Versions

AB	The Anchor Bible, 1964–
AT	The Bible, an American Translation, 1931
ATD	Das Alte Testament Deutsch
BJ	Bible de Jérusalem, 2d ed.
CCD	Confraternity of Christian Doctrine Version
KJ	The Authorized Version of 1611, or the King James Version
LXX	The Septuagint
LXX^A	Codex Alexandrinus
MT	Masoretic Text
RSV	The Revised Standard Version, 1946, 1952
Symm.	Ancient Greek translation of the Old Testament by Symmachus
Syr.	Syriac version, the Peshitta
Targ.	Aramaic translations or paraphrases
Vulg.	The Vulgate

3. Other Abbreviations

Akk.	Akkadian
Ar.	Arabic
Aram.	Aramaic
Heb.	Hebrew
NT	New Testament
OT	Old Testament
Phoen.	Phoenician
Ugar.	Ugaritic

GLOSSARY OF TERMS

aleph, the first letter of the Phoenician-Hebrew alphabet, whose symbol is ', e.g., *'ādām,* "man."

prothetic aleph, an *aleph* placed before a root or a word to modify its form and/or meaning.

aphel (masc. singular imperative, etc.), a causative conjugation formed by placing an *aleph* before the verb; e.g., *pā'al,* "he did," but *'ap'ēl,* "he caused to do."

primae aleph nouns, nouns whose first consonant is *aleph.*

athnach, a symbol used by the Masoretes to indicate the principal pause in a verse.

asseverative or *kaph veritatis,* the particle *kī* when it emphasizes the following word; e.g., *kī ṭōb,* "truly good."

beth comparativum, the preposition *b^e^* when employed to express comparison; e.g., Ps li 9, *b^e^'āzōb,* "than gushing water."

beth essentiae, the preposition *b^e^* when used to state identity of subject and predicate; e.g., Ps xcix 6, "Moses and Aaron were his priests" (*b^e^kōh^a^nāyw*).

bilabials, consonants such as *b* and *m* that are pronounced by pressing the two lips together.

by-form, an alternate form or spelling of a word.

chiasm or *chiasmus, chiastic,* the arrangement of words in an "x" pattern.

construct, the shortened form that a noun assumes before another noun or verb in the genitive case. E.g. Absolute *dābār,* "word," but in construct *d^e^bar yhwh,* "word of Yahweh."

copulative conjunctions, conjunctions which connect words rather than, say, contrast them.

dativus commodi, the dative of advantage.

dislegomenon, a word or form that occurs only twice.

hapax legomenon, a word or form occurring only once.

haplography, the accidental omission by a scribe of a letter or a word.

hendiadys, literally "one through two," hendiadys is a rhetorical figure using two words to express one idea.

hiphil elative, a causative verb form that is employed to heighten the root idea, e.g., Ps li 9, *'albīn,* "I'll be much whiter."

hiphil energic, a causative verb form ending in *-annāh*.

hithpoel participle, a participle of reflexive conjugation.

ketiv, literally "what is written," *ketiv* is a term of the Masoretes which indicates that what is written in the received text is at variance with their vocalization; see *qere*.

lamedh, the twelfth letter of the Phoenician-Hebrew alphabet, our "l."

merism or *merismus*, a rhetorical figure in which totality is expressed by mentioning the two extremes of a class; e.g., Ps viii 8, "small and large cattle," or xxxvi 8, "gods and men," namely, all creatures dependent upon Yahweh.

nota accusativi, the particle *'ēt*, which introduces the accusative object.

partitive construction, the use of the prepositions *min* or *b^e^* to express the notion of part; e.g., Prov ix 5, "Eat some of my bread" (*b^e^laḥmī*).

piel, the third Hebrew conjugation which often intensifies the root idea of the verb, but which can also express other nuances; see *piel privative*.

piel participle, the participle of the intensive conjugation.

piel privative, the third conjugation of the verb when used to negate the root idea.

postpositive verb, a verb placed at the end of its clause under the influence of an emphatic particle such as *kī*, "indeed."

precative perfect, a verb form, often balanced by an imperative, that states an ardent wish or prayer.

preterit verb, a verb expressing past action.

pual, the passive of the piel or intensive conjugation.

pual participle, the participle of the passive of the intensive verb form.

qal, the light form, that is the simplest form, of the verb; e.g., *rādap*, "to pursue," whereas the intensive or piel form *riddēp* means "to pursue closely."

qal imperfect, the prefixed verb form of the simple (as opposed to the intensive or causative) conjugation.

energic qal imperative, the imperative of the simple conjugation, followed by the ending *-annāh* which serves to intensify the imperative idea.

qere, a term employed by the Masoretes to indicate that their pointing or vocalization is at variance with the consonants of the received text.

qtl verb, the suffixed form of the verb, to be distinguished from the *yqtl* or prefixed verb form.

scriptio defectiva, literally "defective or incomplete spelling," this manner of writing does not indicate long vowels by the use of vowel letters such as *-h*, *w* or *y*; see *scriptio plena*.

scriptio plena, literally "full or complete spelling," this manner of writing employs vowel letters such as *-h*, *w*, and *y* to indicate long vowels.

shaphel causatives, semantically equal to the hiphil conjugation, the shaphel causatives prefix *sh-* to the root to form a causative verb; e.g., *pā'al*, "he did," but *shaph'ēl*, "he caused to do."

stichometric, referring to the division of stichs or cola in a verse.

terminus technicus, literally "a technical expression," often employed in the original language because it has no perfect equivalent in other languages.

waw emphaticum or *emphatic waw,* the particle *w*ᵉ or *wa* used, not as a connecting conjunction, but rather as an emphasizing word.

waw explicativum, a technical expression which means that the particle *w*ᵉ or *wa* explains the preceding word; in English it would usually be rendered by the relative pronoun "who" or "which."

yod, the tenth letter of the Phoenician-Hebrew alphabet, whose symbol is *y*.

primae yod, a root whose first letter is *yod.*

yqtl verb, the prefixed form of the verb, to be distinguished from the *qtl* or suffixed verb form.

LIST OF ANCIENT NEAR EASTERN TEXTS

Arslan Tash Incantation, an eighth-seventh century B.C. Phoenician inscription found in Syria.

El Amarna Correspondence, a corpus of Akkadian letters discovered in 1887 in central Egypt. They were written around 1350 B.C. by kings and princes in Syria-Palestine to the Egyptian Pharaoh, and are of special significance for the biblical scholar because of the numerous Canaanite expressions (Canaanisms) interspersed throughout the letters.

Hadad Inscription, an Aramaic inscription of the eighth century B.C. discovered at Zincirli in southeastern Turkey. Though commonly described as Aramaic, the language of the inscription contains many similarities to Phoenician.

The Keret Legend, one of the important Ugaritic texts preserved in three broken tablets. It tells of a Syrian king who has lost his family and is heartbroken.

Mari texts, a corpus of more than twenty thousand tablets discovered in 1935 in northern Mesopotamia. Written in the Amorite dialect of Akkadian, these tablets date to the period circa 1700 B.C., the era of Hammurapi.

Mesha Inscription, found in 1868 at Diban in Transjordan; also called the Moabite Stone. It was set up by King Mesha of Moab in the ninth century B.C., and contains the longest text in the Moabite dialect discovered till now.

INTRODUCTION

The original plan was to include Psalms 51–150 in this second volume (cf. *Psalms I* [The Anchor Bible, vol. 16; New York, 1966], pp. XVIII, XLIII) but this has not proved feasible. The amount of relevant Northwest Semitic material available for use and citation exceeds earlier expectations; in fact, I had thought it would be possible to translate the remaining psalms with relative dispatch, frequently referring the reader to *Psalms I* for pertinent discussion and documentation of the principles on which the translations would be based. But Psalms 51–100 alone contain enough new problems and ideas which were not discussed in *Psalms I* to rightfully claim a volume for themselves.

To those whose special interests lie in psalms found in the third part of the Psalter, this change of plan will doubtless be disappointing. Some reviewers and correspondents, however, made it clear that three volumes devoted to Psalms would be desirable. They stated their preference for an expanded explanation and proof of certain points fleetingly touched upon in *Psalms I;* and this, in *Psalms II,* I have tried to provide.

In *Psalms I,* p. XLIII, I stated my reluctance to take a stand on a number of critical issues until research on all one hundred and fifty Psalms had been completed. This means that the fuller discussions of dating, literary genre, authorship, *Sitz im Leben,* as well as the planned excursus on grammar and style, will have to be deferred to *Psalms III.* In the present volume, however, some of these questions are discussed in the NOTES to the Psalms, and some conclusions concerning these issues are tentatively drawn. The indexes will help the reader locate these discussions.

A more serious problem concerns the nature of this work. Several reviewers have questioned the inclusion of this commentary in The Anchor Bible, a series addressed to "the general reader with no special formal training in biblical studies." One reviewer writes that as the general reader "wrestles with the infixed *-t-* conjugation, the *nota accusativi,* the enclitic *mem,* the double-duty suffix, the energic mood, *beth essentiae,* and a hundred more technical terms, he may be permitted to wonder whether in this volume the aim was forgotten or the target missed. The scholar, on the other hand, will look for volume II."[1] In self-defense I would plead that, while my unrepentant preference for philological discourse resulted in what may be an overly technical volume, the series does aim at "exact translation" and the "effort to make available all the significant historical and *linguistic* (italics mine) knowledge which bears on the interpretation of the biblical record."

When I agreed to participate in this project, I did not fully appreciate the number or the magnitude of the textual and philological problems that would confront a translator of the Psalter, nor did I envision volumes that would be disproportionately technical. On the other hand, though I was aware that, in the words of the late E. A. Speiser, "Substantive departures from King James are apt to be resented as so many wanton desecrations,"[2] and that consequently a scholar who sets out to improve the translation of a single verse in the Psalter had better have his evidence available, I had no idea that substantive departures from tradition would begin in verse 1 of Ps i and continue, to date, to the final verse of Ps c. If, then, philological evidence must accompany a new translation—and most scholars and not a few general readers find new versions without some justifying notes infuriating—the discussion inevitably becomes technical and may indeed move beyond the ken of the laymen. Who would have foreseen that the "exact translation" of the Psalter would entail so much philological discourse, and that the laudable aims of the entire series would appear so difficult to reconcile with the volumes dedicated to Psalms? Partially to remedy this situation, the writer has in this volume, especially in the introductory NOTES to Pss li–c. devoted more space to questions of greater interest to the non-professional reader, such as dating of psalms, literary genre, and theological content.

[1] Charles L. Taylor in *Religious Education* (November 1966).
[2] *Genesis* (The Anchor Bible, vol. 1; New York, 1964), p. LXXV.

Relationships between Ugaritic and Hebrew

The proper assessment of the relevance of Ugaritic for Psalms research is complicated by the assumed chronological as well as geographical distance between the Ras Shamra tablets and biblical writings. Thus in each of two reviews of recent commentaries about Job, R. Tournay[3] harps on the time differential between the tablets and the Book of Job. What seems to underlie Tournay's diffidence vis-à-vis the Ugaritic material is his assumption that with the destruction of Ugarit circa 1200 B.C. the Canaanite language known from the Ras Shamra tablets also perished. Discoveries of inscriptions employing Ugaritic script from such distant points as Beth Shemesh near Jerusalem, from Mount Tabor and Tell Taanach (in a late twelfth-century archaeological context) in central Palestine, suffice to indicate that what was being written and spoken in Late Bronze and Early Iron Age Palestine did not appreciably differ from the speech of Ugarit. Apart from their intrinsic interest, the Ugaritic alphabetic texts, along with the Canaanisms in the Akkadian tablets from Ras Shamra and El Amarna, prove valuable to the Semitist in his reconstruction of Canaanite spoken in Palestine toward the end of the second millennium.

Hence in recent years I have avoided the term "influence" when describing the rapports between Ugaritic and Biblical Hebrew. It is not so much a question of "influence" or "dependence," as of elucidation. This distinction bears emphasis, particularly in the face of such assertions as the following: "Moreover, ancient Ugarit was destroyed in the 13th century B.C., and the epic texts which Dahood uses were probably composed at least by the 15th century. No direct dependence is thinkable."[4] The Ugaritic texts, in particular the poetry, contain grammatical or lexical data always present in the Hebrew Bible but for one reason or another unrecognized or unappreciated. The occurrence of such phenomena in clear Ugaritic contexts has alerted the Hebraist to search out and to recognize similar usages in the Bible. The first illustration of the point is provided by the Karatepe Phoenician Inscriptions, discovered in 1946 in southeastern Turkey. In these inscriptions the infinitive absolute followed by the

[3] *Revue biblique* 74 (1967), 127–28.
[4] Jared J. Jackson in *Pittsburgh Perspective* 7 (1966), 31.

independent personal pronoun was the normal construction for expressing past time. The analysis of this construction convinced Semitists that their former explanation of this usage in Ugaritic and in Phoenician inscriptions published before 1946 was wrong; the necessary corrections were made and incorporated into subsequent studies. But no one, I believe, is ready to maintain that the Ugaritic construction was due to eighth-century Phoenician influence; this construction was native to Northwest Semitic dialects, and its undoubted appearance in Phoenician merely supplied scholars with the necessary insight to identify this usage in cognate dialects.

The emphatic particle *kī,* which causes the verb to be placed last in its clause, has always been materially present in Old Testament poetry, but no one formally identified it there until clear Ugaritic examples persuaded Hebraists that the biblical poets were no strangers to this stylistic nicety. Then again, Hebrew lexicons and grammars have lumped together four different morphemes under the preposition *l*^{e}, "to, for, from," but the fourfold Ugaritic distinction into the preposition *l,* emphatic *lamedh,* vocative *lamedh,* and negative *lamedh*—all of them orthographically identical—also obtains for Biblical Hebrew so that today the Bible translator must weigh four or five semantic possibilities when he encounters a simple *l*^{e}*!* Finally, the liberal use of the dative suffix in Ugaritic has necessitated a restudy of this syntactic phenomenon in Hebrew. That this usage was often lost on the Masoretes can be illustrated by citing Ps lxxvii 14, *'*^{e}*lōhīm baqqōdeš darkekā mī 'ēl gādōl kē'lōhīm,* reproduced in the Revised Version (1903), "Thy way, O God, is in the sanctuary: Who is a great god like unto God?" The RSV attempts to avoid the insipidity of the second-colon question by inserting an unwarranted *our* in the second colon: "What god is great like our God?" The root of the problem, however, is the Masoretic word division, *gādōl kē'lōhīm,* "great as God." By shifting the purported comparative *k* to the preceding word and pointing it as dative suffix *-kā,* we obtain the reading *g*^{e}*dōl*^{e}*kā '*^{e}*lōhīm,* "greater than you, O God," and this translation of the verse: "O God, your dominion is over the holy ones: What god is greater than you, O God?" (See p. 230.) What lends particular conviction to this new word division and parsing is not only the trenchancy of the second-colon question, but also the emergent rhetorical device known as inclusion. The verse now begins and ends with vocative "O God!"

It seems to me, then, that the problem of Hebrew-Ugaritic relationships has been badly put. Rather than speak of "influence" or "dependence," we shall be better adjusted to advance research in this area if we think in terms of mutual elucidation. Just as Hebrew grammar and lexicography have served—and still do—to explain many of the Ugaritic texts, so too the philological data supplied by the clay tablets can brightly illuminate many obscure corners of biblical philology.

Text-Critical Principles

In his review of *Psalms I*,[5] John L. McKenzie, apropos of my handling of the Hebrew text, concludes with the assertion that "all of this suggests that textual criticism is still one of the most unprincipled disciplines of biblical scholarship." Now it is axiomatic that textual criticism, partly a science and partly an art, when applied to a work of such high literary merit as the Bible, where nuances, allusions, and theological overtones are so numerous, does give the subjective element a certain amount of leeway. But in its present wording McKenzie's statement may cause serious misunderstanding, and therefore, though the professional student of the text will experience no difficulty in identifying the basic text-critical principles underlying this translation, it would nonetheless be wise to spell them out. Simplifying somewhat, I would list them under four headings: (1) preservation of the consonantal text; (2) sense; (3) grammar; (4) prosody.

Consonantal text. The study of the Psalter within the wider ambience of Northwest Semitic so frequently vindicates the consonantal text against its ancient translators and its medieval reworking by the Masoretes that one must concede its primacy. To be sure, in the majority of cases in the Psalter, the consonantal text and the Masoretic pointing are in happy agreement, but where the Masoretic punctuation cannot be coaxed into yielding sense, the textual critic should cut free and chart a course on the linguistic map of Northwest Semitic. The numerous new grammatical and lexical details supplied by the Ras Shamra texts and Phoenician inscriptions enhance the possibility of reaching a clear and coherent translation and exegesis with the consonantal text intact. Adherence to this principle has resulted, for example, in the identification of a new Hebrew morpheme, the third person suffix *-y*, normal in Phoenician and quite common in

[5] In CBQ 29 (1967), 139.

biblical poetry, were its existence, however, was not appreciated by the Masoretes. The dative suffix to express comparison, which was completely lost on the Masoretes in above-cited Ps lxxvii 14, also neatly illustrates the point.

Hence I am unable to follow the reasoning of W. Brueggemann[6] who writes: "The employment of the Ugaritic evidence permits the author to retain the Massoretic reading in many places where it had often been changed in line with the versions, yet in other places he argues that the Massoretes did not understand the text before them and so he is free to make changes on the basis of the non-biblical evidence. This curious having-it-both-ways is concerned primarily with changed pointing and wrong word division." Were a critic to endorse Brueggemann's manner of arguing, he would never be free, say, to adopt a single reading of the LXX without accepting all the readings of the LXX. While I try in each instance to give respectful consideration to Masoretic vocalization, I am not so naïve as to believe that the Masoretes, who came on the scene more than a *thousand* years after the composition of the latest psalms, still understood the fine points of archaic poetry, already unknown to the Jewish translators of the LXX in the third-second centuries B.C. and to the monks of Qumran another century later; for example, the consonantal text of Isaiah contains five enclitic *mems* that have been edited away by the scribes of Qumran who obviously did not understand the function of this particle elucidated only since the Ras Shamra discoveries. The modern textual critic must consequently recover many of the syntactic and lexical treasures of Hebrew poetry from the thicket of Masoretic points. For example, a questioning alertness before the Masoretic vowel points has recovered the composite divine name *yhwh 'ēl* in Pss xxxi 6, xxxix 13, cxli 8, cxliii 1, 7, 9; Jer x 2, xv 15. Aware of the limitations imposed by the Masoretes' linguistic and historical distance from the original text, the critic will hold a brief primarily for the unvoweled consonantal text and only secondarily for MT. My respect for the transmitted text does not require that I always accept the construction placed upon it by the Masoretic schools of the Middle Ages. If this method is called "having it both ways," then let us make the most of it.

The rather negative judgment expressed in *Psalms I* (p. xxiv) concerning the ancient versions unhappily still stands; the evidence

[6] In *Theology and Life* 9 (1966), 176.

presented in this volume suggests an even further devaluation. For instance, in only three of the forty-odd occurrences of vocative *lamedh* detected in the Psalter and elsewhere, did one or other of the versions recognize it as such. Jerome's frequent translation of the *yqtl* form by the present or future in *Juxta Hebraeos* where the intended meaning is the past (as often in Ugaritic), the versional unfamiliarity with the third person suffix *-y* in nearly all of its one hundred and sixty occurrences, and the near total ignorance in all the versions of the widely used precative perfect as a stylistic variant of the imperative, are hard facts which do not inspire confidence in the ancient translators.[7]

SENSE. The principle of the *lectio difficilior,* "the more difficult reading," can be abandoned only when the consonantal text makes no rational sense. In Psalms 51–100 consonantal text and sense rarely conflict—no more than three instances come to mind—so here at least the problem is not acute. But the differences between definitions of "sense" will divide scholarly opinion. Ps lxxvii 14b again may serve as illustration. Should one remain content with conventional "Who is a great god like unto God?"—which does make sense—when "What god is greater than you, O God?" is also syntactically available and further supported by the emergent inclusion? Here the subjective and aesthetic element enters; in other words, at this point textual criticism becomes less a science and more an art.

Or again, though devoid of style in its context, the traditional rendering of Ps lx 3, *'ānaptā teššōbēb lānū,* "Thou hast been angry; oh, restore us" (RSV), is not devoid of sense. But how much better is "You were wrathful, you turned away from us," a version made possible by the recognition that in Ugaritic and Hebrew alike *lānū* can signify "from us."

GRAMMAR. But when the third principle of textual criticism, namely, grammar, comes on the agenda, the confrontation between traditional Hebrew grammarians and the proponents of the Northwest Semitic method is often dramatic. For the traditional grammarians (here again I simplify), if a phenomenon is not formally discussed by the medieval Jewish grammarians or by Gesenius-Kautzsch, its existence in Biblical Hebrew may be seriously questioned. On the other hand, those familiar with the new philological data presented by Ugaritic and Phoenician are convinced that current Hebrew gram-

[7] Cf. further Edwin M. Good, "The Composition of Hosea," in *Svensk exegetisk årsbok* 31 (Lund, 1966), 21–63, especially p. 25.

mars are hopelessly out of date since Biblical Hebrew, especially its poetry, contains many usages not described by the standard grammars.

Ps xxiv 6 illustrates well this conflict between sense and traditional grammar. Context and parallelism demand that consonantal *mbqšy pnyk y'qb* be rendered, "O you who search for the Presence of Jacob." The final consonant of *pnyk,* however, presents a problem. Some simply propose its deletion, but this measure runs counter to the first principle, the preservation of the consonantal text. In *Psalms I,* p. 152, I proposed the explanation of *k* (to be vocalized *kī*) as an emphatic particle inserted in a construct chain, much like enclitic *mī*. At the time, no other instances of this usage were at hand, so that the reader might well have suspended judgment. Since then, however, a good number of examples (e.g., Pss lxviii 25, lxix 30; Judg v 31; Ezek xiii 4, xxvii 8–9, 25; Hos viii 5; Amos viii 14; Zech ix 13) have turned up, thus sustaining the initial observation.

The Phoenician Pyrgi Inscription, discovered in 1964 at Santa Severa, fifty-five kilometers north of Rome, provides another illustration of the collision between sense and traditional concepts of grammar in its final phrase, *km hkkbm 'l.* Faithful to textbook canons, the original editors rendered the phrase "like these stars," but were at a loss to explain what stars the inscriber had in mind. The existence in Isa xiv 13 of the expression *kōkᵉbē 'ēl,* "the stars of El," suggested that the Pyrgi phrase was semantically identical, even though the author put both the article and the enclitic *mem* with the construct noun of the construct chain.[8] This parsing, also valid for phrases in Ps cxv 16 and Num xxi 14, which was recently dismissed as unworthy of further discussion, has already been adopted by at least six orientalists.[9]

Thus the discovery of new grammatical phenomena in Northwest Semitic obliges the Hebraist constantly to review the translation and parsing of biblical poetic books and never to consider the grammar of Gesenius-Kautzsch as definitive.[10]

PROSODY. The general term prosody, the fourth criterion of textual criticism, includes such diverse topics as parallelism, stichometry,

[8] Cf. *Orientalia* 34 (1965), 170–72.

[9] E.g., K. A. Kitchen, *Ancient Orient and Old Testament* (London, 1966), p. 161, n. 33; J. A. Fitzmyer in JAOS 86 (1966), 295–96.

[10] I once heard a lecturer remark that he knew some scholars who, while doubting the inspiration of Holy Scripture, would never question the inspiration of Gesenius-Kautzsch!

syllable counting, breakup of composite divine titles and stereotyped phrases, chiasm, assonance, alliteration, and inclusion. In actual practice, prosody is applied to the text simultaneously with the other three principles, and though prosody does not normally assume priority over these, it can often serve as a check on them. The lack of parallelism and syllabic equilibrium betrays the shortcomings of MT and the versions alike in Ps cxliii 7:

mahēr ʿanēnī yhwh	(3 beats + 7 syllables)
kālᵉtāh rūḥī	(2 beats + 5 syllables)
ʾal tāstēr pānekā mimmennī	(3 beats + 9 syllables)
wᵉnimšaltī ʿim yōrᵉdē bōr	(3 beats + 9 syllables)

RSV Make haste to answer me, O Lord!
My spirit fails!
Hide not thy face from me,
Lest I be like those who go down to the Pit.

The prevalence of the 3+3 meter in this psalm points to a missing word in the second colon; this lack can readily be supplied by transferring MT *ʾal* to this colon and repointing it to the divine name *ʾēl*. Hence the first two cola read:

mahēr ʿanēnī yhwh	(3 beats + 7 syllables)
kālᵉtāh rūḥī ʾēl	(3 beats + 6 syllables)

Hasten to answer me, Yahweh!
My spirit fails, O El!

From this transposition and revocalization comes to light the composite divine name *yhwh ʾēl* (cf. *Psalms I*, p. 64; *Biblica* 46 [1965], 317 f.), whose components are separated and placed in the parallel cola where their grammatical function is identical, namely, that of vocatives. At the same time, this prosodic operation removes the syntactically difficult *ʾal* from the third colon,[11] so that the final two cola read:

tastēr pānekā mimmennī	(3 beats + 8 syllables)
wᵉnimšaltī ʿim yōrᵉdē bōr	(3 beats + 9 syllables)

Should you turn your face from me,
I would resemble those who have descended the Pit.

[11] MT literally translates, "Do not turn your face from me, and I shall resemble those descending the Pit."

The conditional statement *tastīr pānekā,* without the conditional particle *'im,* recurs in Ps civ 29, "Should you turn away your face, they would be dismayed." This example illustrates the value of prosody as a text-critical norm, and at the same time brings out the conflict between consonantal *'l,* to be pointed *'ēl,* and MT *'al,* which creates a grammatically non-viable sentence.

The study of Hebrew versification uncovers a metrical pattern—lost in MT and in the versions—that may be represented by the letters A+B / / C / / Á+B́, where each letter stands for a thought unit. The recognition of this scheme reveals new semantic dimensions in the Psalter. Ps xcviii 2 illustrates this usage very well.

MT	*hōdīaʿ yhwh yešūʿātō*	(3 beats + 8 [9] syllables)
	leʿēnē haggōyīm gillāh ṣidqātō	(4 beats + 11 syllables)

RSV The Lord has made known his victory,
He has revealed his vindication
in the sight of the nations.

Critics have noticed that the second colon is metrically disturbed, and the note in BH[3] suggests that a colon may have fallen out of the text. Metrical and semantic equilibrium can be restored, however, by scanning the line into the A+B / / C / / Á+B́ pattern in which the C member stands metrically independent but semantically belonging to the first and third cola alike.

hōdīaʿ yhwh yešūʿātō
leʿēnē haggōyīm
gillāh ṣidqātō

Yahweh made known his victory
before the eyes of the nations
He revealed his vindication.

Verification of Proposals

Two rather persistent questions about *Psalms I* can be couched roughly in these terms: How can one be sure that this translation of Psalms, which departs so radically not only from the venerable traditions of the MT and the ancient versions, but also from contemporary translations and Psalms scholarship, is sound and reliable? How can one scientifically control these new proposals? Reviewing *Psalms I* in the *Journal of Biblical Literature*,[12] David A. Robertson expresses his deep concern about the potential harm that may accrue from the book. He writes: "The wisdom of presenting this book to the general public must be seriously questioned. Dahood comes up with some really wild interpretations, many of which concern very important theological matters (like the question to what extent the concept of immortality is present in the Psalter), and not even the best-educated layman or minister will be able to assess them properly. In short, most of what this commentary contains should be for scholarly consumption only, and should be transmitted to the public only after intensive evaluation by those best qualified to do so."

The reader will find, I believe, in the present volume satisfactory answers to the questions posed, and a reply to the strictures of Robertson. Employing the same method, *Psalms II* confirms *Psalms I* on point after point, bringing new examples and parallels from the Psalter and other writings in support of the earlier proposals. Here I shall cite but a few instances illustrating how some of the "wilder" ideas fare under further research. At Ps xviii 28 (*Psalms I*, pp. 112 f.) I postulated, on the basis of context alone, the existence of the root *'mm*, "to be strong, wise." In the meantime, the Polish scholar T. Penar has directed my attention to the Hebrew text of Ecclus x 1, *šwpṭ 'm ywsr 'mw*, "A sagacious ruler instructs his people," where Hebrew *'m* is reproduced by both the LXX and Syriac as "wise." No doubt someone will argue that these ancient versions had before them a Hebrew original whose reading was *ḥkm* instead of *'m*, but then the burden of proof is his. Unfortunately for him, however, the Hebrew text is untouchable because the wordplay on *'m*, "sagacious," and *'mw*, "his people," would crumble into dust at the touch of a textual critic. This Late Hebrew testimony is buttressed by Early Canaanite evidence in UT, 51:IV:41–43, *tḥmk il ḥkm ḥkmt 'm 'lm ḥyt ḥẓt tḥmk*, "Your message, O El, is wise: your wisdom is eternal sagacity, felicitous life your message." The inclusion beginning with *tḥmk*, "Your message," and closing with *tḥmk*, "your message," resembles the inclusion cited above in connection with Ps lxxvii 14.

The newly discovered Hebrew root *l'y*, "to prevail," widely attested in Ugaritic and Phoenician, bears a considerable burden in *Psalms I*, especially as the etymology of the divine title *lē'*, "the Victor." A Dutch reader has informed me that in Job xiii 15, consonantal *l'*

[12] Vol. 85 (1966), p. 484.

answers to LXX *ho dynastēs,* "the Omnipotent." Hence the translation of this passage in *Psalms I,* p. 144, "If the Victor should slay me," is sustained by new evidence.

The translation and exegesis of Ps iii 7, "I fear not the shafts of people deployed against me on every side" (contrast RSV, "I am not afraid of ten thousands of people who have set themselves against me round about"), facilitate the translation of Job vi 4, "For Shaddai's arrows are aimed at me, my spirit sucks in their venom, God's terrors are arrayed against me."

Ps xxxi is thick with thorny problems of translation and exegesis, and some of the solutions proposed may look adventurous. Against many critics and the apparent requirements of meter, I upheld the authenticity of vs. 10, *napšī ūbiṭnī,* "my throat and my belly." What I had failed to see at the time was that the Ugaritic description of weeping in 1 Aqht:34–35, *tbky pǵt bm lb tdm' bm kbd,* should be translated with Driver,[13] "Pughat wept from her heart, she shed tears from her liver." For the ancient Canaanites and Israelites the source of tears was the stomach, so that when the psalmist states, "My eye is wasted with sorrow, my throat and my belly," he really means that he is prostrate from weeping. Tears originate in his belly, flow through his throat, and stream out his eyes. This example also illustrates how fidelity to the first principle of biblical text criticism—the retention of the consonantal text—pays good dividends.

Ps xxxi 19, "that speak against the Ancient Just One (*ṣaddīq 'attīq*)," clarifies Job xxxiv 17, *ha'ap śōnē' mišpāṭ yaḥᵃbōš wᵉ'im ṣaddīq kabbīr taršīᵃ',* "Shall the enemy of justice conduct the inquiry, or will you pronounce the Venerable Just One guilty?" Compare RSV, "Shall one who hates justice govern? Will you condemn him who is righteous and mighty?" The translation of Ps xxxi 22, "For he has shown me wondrous kindness from the fortified city," assumes that heaven was imagined and represented as a fortified city, an assumption that is validated by its bearing on Deut i 28 (=ix 1), "It is a people taller and stronger than we (*mimmennū*) are; their cities are larger and more fortified than the heavens (*bᵉṣūrōt baššāmayim*)." From this popular comparison it becomes clear that heaven was considered a fortified city. Commentators who adopt the customary translation, "fortified up to heaven," cannot explain the syntax of *bᵉṣūrōt baššāmayim.* Our version is supported by the balance between comparative *min* and comparative *bᵉ,* precisely as in Ps li 9

[13] CML, p. 59.

and elsewhere. The stress in *Psalms I* on the meaning "from" for b^e, questioned by Jackson,[14] produces excellent results, for example, in Mal ii 8a, *w^e'attem sartem min hadderek hikšaltem rabbīm battōrāh,* "But you yourselves have turned aside from the way; you have caused many to lapse from the law." Compare RSV on the second colon, "You have caused many to stumble by your instruction." But this latter version obviously falls short, because it must insert an unwarranted suffix with *tōrāh,* "your instruction," and destroys the parallelism between *min hadderek,* "from the way," which refers to the way of the commandments, and *battōrāh,* "from the law," which, as in vs. 6, signifies the law of Yahweh. Unlike Levi, who in vs. 6 is described *w^{e}rabbīm hēšīb mē'āwōn,* "and many he converted from sinning," the priests have caused many to fall away from the observance of the law. But all these fine contrasts are lost in the modern versions that are innocent of the fact that b^e, especially when balancing *min,* often signifies "from."

Finally, the repeated recourse in *Psalms I* to the third person suffix *-y* in order to explain recalcitrant texts is upheld by the scores of verses in other biblical books witnessing this suffix. One citation will suffice. Judg xii 7 closes its description of Jephthah's career with these three words: *wayyiqqābēr b^e'ārēy gil'ād.* Here RSV correctly translates, "and was buried in his city in Gilead," with the appended note: "Gk: Heb *in the cities of Gilead.*" On the basis of *Psalms I* methodology, recourse to the LXX becomes superfluous; by repointing MT *'ārēy* to singular *'īrīy,* whose suffix is third person *-y,* syntactically the construct in a construct chain (*Psalms I,* pp. 110, 293), we can arrive at the same translation as RSV without, however, sacrificing the consonantal text.

From these few examples confirming the validity of the method adopted in *Psalms I* one may legitimately argue that this translation and commentary on Psalms presents less danger to the general reading public than the modern translations, such as RSV, CCD, and *The Jerusalem Bible,* which, ignoring or minimizing the grammatical and lexical discoveries of the past forty years, have frequent demonstrable errors of translation and exegesis. Were one to prefer charges against *Psalms I,* one would perhaps be better advised to tax it rather with being too faithful to traditional versions and not sufficiently faithful to its own enunciated principles. Thus its rendition of Ps iii 9, "O

[14] *Pittsburgh Perspective* 7 (1966), 32.

Yahweh, salvation! upon your people your blessing!," failed to take account of the double-duty suffix, which would produce a preferable "O Yahweh, your salvation! upon your people your blessing!" The translation of Ps xviii 40, *takrīaʿ qāmay taḥtāy,* "You felled my assailants beneath me," is much too indebted to traditional "Thou didst make my assailants sink under me" (RSV). Consistency with the remarks at Pss viii 7, xviii 39, xlv 6, on Ugar. *tḥt pʿnh,* "at his feet," would have resulted in "You made my assailants kneel at my feet." The correct understanding of *taḥtāy,* "at my feet," enables the translator to safeguard the precise signification of *takrīaʿ,* which does not mean "to fell" or "to make sink," but simply "to make kneel," in a gesture of homage or adoration. Cf. Job ix 13, *taḥtāw šāḥaḥū ʿōzerē rāhab,* "At his feet the warriors of Rahab prostrated themselves," where *taḥtāw šāḥaḥū* is the Hebrew equivalent of El Amarna *ana šēpē šarri lu ištaḫaḫin,* "At the feet of the king I prostrate myself." Contrast RSV, "Beneath him bowed the helpers of Rahab."

Greater attention to archaic case-endings (*Psalms I,* pp. 51, 303) and following through on the observations about *rab,* "rich" (*Psalms I,* pp. 99, 229) would have prevented the grammatically approximate version of Ps xliv 13, *welōʾ ribbītā bimeḥīrēhem,* "and did not consider them of much value." By repointing to *bimeḥīrīhem,* a singular noun with the genitive ending (the MT plural form is otherwise unattested, whereas Syriac and *Juxta Hebraeos* read the singular), and considering the precise nuance of *ribbītā,* we can translate, "and did not grow rich from their price," an unexceptionable synthetic parallel to first-colon "You sold your people for a trifle."

On the other hand, a number of original suggestions have not found further confirmation and, for the nonce, must remain in the penumbra of uncertainty. But as one reviewer has sagely observed, we are still living with unanswered questions concerning the Psalter, and this is part of the excitement. The number of uncertain proposals, moreover, is no greater than that found, say, in RSV or other current versions.

The translation and exegesis of texts in Psalms 51–100 expressing a belief in immortality (e.g., Pss lxi 3, 5–8, lxv 5–6, lxxiii 24–26, xcii 14, xciii 13–14, xcvii 11) can only serve to aggravate Robertson's consternation at my identifying this doctrine in *Psalms I* (most reviewers take a positive attitude toward my handling of the immortality and afterlife passages). At the same time, it will render more difficult the position of John L. McKenzie,[15] who wants to see this belief validated elsewhere before admitting its presence in the Psalter. Happily, this doctrine can be reasonably established in Proverbs,[16] thanks to Ugaritic which has furnished us with the key words of a *Wortfeld* describing the nature and characteristics of immortality. Among these texts of Proverbs, the mostly widely agreed upon is xii 28.[17]

For those who await the verdict of the academic community on the proposals set forth in these volumes, the period of expectation may prove shorter than is normally the case. Increased interest in Ugaritic and its bearing on the Bible has manifested itself in the surprising number of studies on this subject in, say, the last five years. Journals, which never before opened their pages to this supposedly esoteric discipline, now welcome articles on Ugaritic, and book-review editors try to keep their readers abreast of biblical developments by reviewing or abstracting works on Ugaritic. The increased tempo of Ugaritic-Hebrew research will doubtless help interested scholars decide more quickly, and on the basis of more diversified evidence, whether these volumes "speak what is true or merely seek to phrase something new."

[15] In CBQ 29 (1967), 139.

[16] Consult M. Dahood, *Proverbs and Northwest Semitic Philology* (abbr. PNWSP) (Rome, 1963), pp. 20, 25, 29, 48.

[17] Cf., e.g., R. B. Y. Scott, *Proverbs & Ecclesiastes* (The Anchor Bible, vol. 18; New York, 1965), p. 91; C. T. Fritsch, review of preceding volume, in *Journal of Religion* 46 (1966), 71; Derek Kidner, *Proverbs. An Introduction and Commentary* (London, 1964), p. 100; F. Vattioni, "L'albero della vita," in *Augustinianum* 7 (1967), 133–44. In *Revue biblique* 69 (1962), 497, R. Tournay, unwilling to admit immortality in Prov xii 28, emends the text away, surely the counsel of despair.

SELECTED BIBLIOGRAPHY

Commentaries

Anderson, A. A., *The Book of Psalms* (abbr. BP) (New Century Bible: based on RSV, 2 vols.). London, 1972.

Briggs, C. A., *A Critical and Exegetical Commentary on the Book of Psalms* (abbr. CECBP) (International Critical Commentary, 2 vols.). Edinburgh, 1906.

Buttenwieser, Moses, *The Psalms Chronologically Treated with a New Translation* (abbr. PCTNT). University of Chicago Press, 1938.

Castellino, Giorgio, *Libro dei Salmi*. Torino-Roma, 1955.

Delitzsch, Franz, *Biblischer Kommentar über Die Psalmen*. Leipzig, 5th rev. ed., 1894. Edited by Friedrich Delitzsch.

Gunkel, H., *Die Psalmen* (Handkommentar zum Alten Testament). Göttingen, 1926.

Gunkel, H., and Begrich, J., *Einleitung in Die Psalmen. Die Gattungen der religiösen Lyrik Israels* (Handkommentar zum Alten Testament). Göttingen, 1933.

Kraus, H. J., *Psalmen* (Biblischer Kommentar Altes Testament, 2 vols.). Neukirchen Kreis Moers, 2d ed., 1961.

Mowinckel, Sigmund, *Psalmenstudien*, I–VI. Kristiania, 1921–24.

———, *The Psalms in Israel's Worship. A Translation and Revision of* Offersang og Sangoffer, by D. R. Ap-Thomas. Oxford, 1963. 2 vols.

Nötscher, F., *Die Psalmen* (Echter-Bibel). Würzburg, 1947.

Podechard, E., *Le Psautier. Traduction littérale et explication historique. Psaumes 1–75*. Lyon, 1949. 2 vols.

Schmidt, H., *Die Psalmen* (Handbuch zum Alten Testament). Göttingen, 1934.

Weiser, A., *The Psalms: A Commentary* (Old Testament Library). London-Philadelphia, 1962.

Articles

Albright, W. F., "The Old Testament and Canaanite Literature and Language," CBQ 7 (1945), 5–31.

———, "The Psalm of Habakkuk," *Studies in Old Testament Prophecy. Essays presented to Theodore H. Robinson*, ed. by H. H. Rowley (Edinburgh, 1950), pp. 1–18.

———, "A Catalogue of Early Hebrew Lyric Poems (Psalm LXVIII)," HUCA 23 (1950), 1–39.

———, "Notes on Psalms 68 and 134," *Norsk teologisk Tidsskrift* 56 (1955), 1–12.

Coppens, J., "Les parallèles du Psautier avec les textes de Ras-Shamra-Ougarit," *Muséon* 59 (1946), 113–42.

Cross, F. M., Jr., and Freedman, D. N., "A Royal Song of Thanksgiving: II Samuel 22=Psalm 18," JBL 72 (1953), 15–34.

Dahood, M., "Ugaritic Studies and the Bible," *Gregorianum* 43 (1962), 55–79.

Jirku, A., "Kana'anäische Psalmenfragmente in der vorisraelitischen Zeit Palästinas und Syriens," JBL 52 (1933), 108–20.

Johnson, A. R., "The Psalms," *The Old Testament and Modern Study*, ed. H. H. Rowley (Oxford, 1951), pp. 162–209.

O'Callaghan, Roger T., "Echoes of Canaanite Literature in the Psalms," VT 4 (1954), 164–76.

Robinson, T. H., "Basic Principles of Hebrew Poetic Form," *Festschrift Alfred Bertholet*, ed. W. Baumgartner and others (Tübingen, 1950), pp. 438–50.

Stamm, J. J., "Ein Vierteljahrhundert Psalmenforschung," ThR 23 (1955), 1–68.

PSALMS II

51–100

PSALM 51

(li 1–21)

1 *For the director. A psalm of David,*
2 *when Nathan the prophet came to him,*
as he himself had come to Bathsheba.

3 Have pity on me, O God, in your kindness,
in your immense compassion delete my rebellious acts.
4 Rain down, wash me of my guilt, [2]*
and of my sin clean me.
5 My rebellious acts that face me I know too well, [3]
and my sin is ever before me.
6 Against you alone have I sinned, [4]
and before your eyes committed the crime;
And so you are just when you sentence,
and blameless when you judge.
7 Indeed, I was brought forth in iniquity, [5]
and in sin my mother conceived me.
8 Since you indeed prefer truth [6]
to both cleverness and secret lore,
Teach me Wisdom!
9 Unsin me, I'll indeed be purer than gushing water, [7]
Wash me, and I'll be much whiter than snow.
10 Let me hear songs of joy and gladness, [8]
the bones you crushed rejoice.
11 Turn your face from my sins, [9]
and delete all my crimes.
12 A clean heart, O God, create in me, [10]
and re-create within me a resolute spirit.
13 Do not banish me from your presence, [11]
nor deprive me of your holy spirit.

* Verse numbers in RSV.

14 Give me again your saving joy, [12]
and by your generous spirit sustain me,
15 That I may teach rebels your ways, [13]
and sinners to return to you.
16 Deliver me from the tears of death, [14]
O God, my God;
That my tongue, my Savior,
may loudly sing your goodness.
17 Lord, open my lips [15]
that my mouth may declare your praise.
18 For should you delight in a sacrifice [16]
I would offer it
A holocaust, should you desire.
19 The finest sacrifices are a contrite spirit: [17]
a heart contrite and crushed,
O God, do not spurn.
20 In your benevolence make Zion beautiful, [18]
rebuild the walls of Jerusalem.
21 Then will you wish legitimate sacrifices, [19]
holocaust and whole offering;
Then will young bulls mount your altar.

NOTES

li. An individual's prayer of contrition; a lament. After a heinous crime which the psalm title and tradition identify with King David's sin, the poet prays for moral purification and restoration. If vs. 20 belongs to the original composition, and there is no solid reason for doubting its authenticity, the psalm can hardly be dated earlier than the sixth century B.C. or later than the rebuilding of the walls of Jerusalem under Nehemiah in 444 B.C. (Neh iii 16). The use of *bārā'*, "to create," in vs. 12 may likewise point to the sixth century, since it is in the work of P and Second Isaiah that this verb occurs most frequently.

2. *came to him, as he himself had come.* The wording of the Hebrew seems to reflect the literary-theological law of biblical religion, that for every action there is a corresponding reaction. Nathan's visit to David balances David's visit to Bathsheba.

3. *my rebellious acts.* The traditional rendition of *p*ᵉ*šā'āy* by "my transgressions" (RSV) is, within the context of this psalm and of current American English, altogether too pallid. The fundamental notion

expressed by the verb *pāšaʻ* is "to rebel, revolt." The noun *pšʻ* describes the behavior of Aqhat, a hero of Canaanite legend, when he stubbornly refuses to hand over his magic bow to the importunate goddess Anath. The text is UT, 2 Aqht:VI:43–44, *laqryk bntb pšʻ*, "I'll surely oppose you in the path of rebellion."

The root *pšʻ* can also be connected with covenant violations on the part of a vassal against his suzerain, and are therefore acts of rebellion of the gravest nature. For example, II Kings iii 4–5 describes Mesha, the king of Moab, as a vassal of the Israelite king Ahab. Upon Ahab's death, however, Mesha is said to have rebelled (*wayyipšaʻ*) against the new king of Israel in violation of the convenant oath. We may accordingly assume that when *pšʻ* is mentioned in relation to God, a violation of one of the ten commandments is involved. The latest full study of *pšʻ* and its connotations is by Rolf Knierim, *Die Hauptbegriffe für Sünde im Alten Testament* (Gütersloh, 1965), pp. 113–43.

delete my rebellious acts. Namely, from the criminal records kept by the divine bookkeeper; see the second NOTE on Ps lvi 1.

4. *Rain down.* Reading *hāribbāh* for MT *harbeh* (Ketiv); see *Psalms III*, pp. XXXI f. The energic hiphil *hāribbāh*, "Rain down," from the root from which derives *rᵉbībīm*, "rain," forms an inclusion with the energic hiphil in vs. 20, *hēṭībāh*, "make beautiful." Just as the goddess Anath washed off blood with heavenly spray (ʻnt:II:38–41), so the psalmist asks for divine rain to cleanse himself of sin. See UHP, p. 51.

wash me . . . clean me. A fine example of chiasm and of assonance, with all four words of the chiastic cola ending in *-ī*, the first person singular suffix. This stress on the first person sharpens the contrast with the second person suffix of the person offended in vs. 6.

5. *that face me.* As scholars are unable to explain satisfactorily the presence of the independent pronoun *'ᵃnī*, that serves no palpable emphasizing function in this context, one may propose the pointing *'ōnay*, the plural participle determined by the suffix of the first person singular, from *'ānāh*, "to meet, face." Briggs, CECBP, II, p. 10, simply deletes *'ᵃnī* as an unnecessary gloss, which makes the line too long. A second objection may be entered against MT *'ᵃnī:* it results in the word order, object-subject-verb, a sequence described by GK, § 142, as "very rare." GK cites only four examples in the OT, among them our text, the only example in the Psalter. Thirdly, the balance with *negdī*, "before me," favors such pointing; cf. Job xviii 12, "Let the Hungry One face him (*'ōnō*), with Death stationed at his side" (see M. Dahood, *Psalms I* [The Anchor Bible, vol. 16; New York, 1966], p. 237). Finally, the Masoretes may again mistake *'ōnay* for *'ᵃnī*, in Ps cix 25, "But as for those who meet me (*'ōnāy*, MT *'ᵃnī*), I am an object of scorn to them; they look at me and shake their heads" (cf. Ps xxxi 12 for a similar sentiment). Compare Isa lix 12, "Our

rebellious acts indeed are with us, and our iniquities we know well." This root appears in Ugar. *tant/tint*, "meeting, assignation"; consult W. F. Albright in BASOR 150 (1958), 38, n. 13.

ever before me. Comparing Ps xxxviii 18, "For my iniquity is stationed at my side, my grief is ever before me."

6. *before your eyes*. The Hebrew is capable of being understood thus or, "And done that which is evil in thy sight" (RSV). My preference is based on the assumed parallelism with "against you alone" and on the consideration that "before your eyes" accentuates the defiant nature of the psalmist's sin. In God's very presence he did not hesitate to rebel.

the crime. The use of the definite article in *hāra'* seems to point to a specific crime.

And so. As in Ps lxviii 24 and Prov ii 20, *l^{e}ma'an* expresses consequence rather than purpose. On Amos ii 7, see T. J. Meek in JAOS 58 (1938), 128.

and blameless. No one can bring a legitimate claim against you. In the Akkadian juridical texts from Ras Shamra the verb *zakū* (*tizkeh* in our text) is frequently found, with various nuances as "to be free of every obligation, exempt from service, free from claims." See Jean Nougayrol, *Le palais royal d'Ugarit*, III (Mission de Ras Shamra Tome VI; Paris, 1955), pp. 230–31.

7. *brought forth in iniquity*. All men have a congenital tendency toward evil; this doctrine finds expression in Gen viii 21; I Kings viii 46; Job iv 17, xiv 4, xv 14, xxv 4; Prov xx 9.

Since . . . truth. Contrary to the prevailing scansion of vs. 8 into 3+3, I read the line as 3+2+2, exactly as vs. 3. Since *hēn* receives an accent in vs. 7, it should also be accented here and not deleted as orthographic, as recommended by some.

8. *to both*. Parsing *ba* of *baṭṭūḥōt* and *b^{e}sātūm* as the comparative *beth*, a topic discussed in *Psalms I*, p. 230, which recurs in the following verse.

cleverness. The obscure word *ṭūḥōt*, that appears again in a related context in Job xxxviii 36, derives most satisfactorily from the name of the Egyptian god of knowledge Thoth, "the clever-minded one." For a full discussion, consult Marvin H. Pope, *Job* (AB, vol. 15; New York, 1965), § 37, NOTE *ad loc*. Being derived from Egyptian sources, this cleverness has a pejorative connotation for the psalmist.

and secret lore. Cf. Ezek xxviii 3, "Look, you are wiser than Daniel (a Canaanite sage), and no secret lore (*sātūm*) is too hidden for you." Hence the association of *sātūm* with Daniel, now well known from the Ras Shamra tablets, suggests that *sātūm* refers to Canaanite secret, magical arts. In this light, the psalmist is seen to contrast the "true Wisdom" of the Israelites with the "cleverness" of the Egyptian wizards and the secret arts of the Canaanites.

9. *Unsin me.* A literal reproduction of piel privative *tᵉḥaṭṭᵉʾēnī,* whose imperfect serves as stylistic substitute for the imperative; cf. vs. 8, *tōdīʿēnī,* "Teach me," and vs. 10, *tašmīʿēnī,* "Let me hear." As noticed in *Psalms I,* pp. 29–30, the same usage is frequently met in Ugaritic; cf. also prose usage in UT, 56:35, *tdkn aḥdh,* "Grind them together." One encounters two piel privatives in Ps lii 7; cf. Joüon, GHB, § 52d.

I'll indeed be purer. The *wāw* before *'eṭhār* parses as the emphatic *waw* that often occasions the positioning of the verb at the end of its clause, as noticed in *Psalms I,* pp. 24–25. The emphatic element of *wᵉʾeṭhār* thus matches the intensive nuance expressed by its opposite number, the hiphil elative verb *'albīn,* "I'll be much whiter." New examples of emphatic *waw* include Pss lxii 5, lxix 15, lxxvii 2, lxxxvi 8, cxviii 27, cxxx 5; Exod xv 2, *sūs wᵉrōkēb wᵉrāmāh* (MT *wᵉrōkᵉbō rāmāh*) *bayyām,* "Horse and rider he indeed hurled into the sea"; Isa xxxvii 26, *mīmē qedem wiṣartīhā* (1QIs[a], not grasping function of *w,* simply omitted it), "From days of old indeed I planned it"; xlv 23, *yāṣā' mippī ṣedeq haddābār* (MT *ṣᵉdāqāh dābār*) *wᵉlō' yāšūb,* "Truth has issued from my mouth, the word shall never return"; xlviii 16c (with postposition of underscored substantive), *šᵉlāḥanī wᵉrūḥō,* "He has sent me his very own spirit."

than gushing water. Since the customary "hyssop" (KJ, RSV; a plant, perhaps the origan, whose twigs were used in ceremonial sprinkling), unknown elsewhere in the Psalter, and "snow" make such an ill-matched pair, it is necessary to seek in consonantal *'zwb* another vocable more compatible with *šeleg,* "snow." The stem *zwb,* "to gush, flow," documented in Ugar. *mdb,* "flood" // *ym,* "ocean," and probably in the unpublished personal name *ydb hd,* provides the needed etymology, and Ps lxxviii 20 (also cv 41) the desired nuance: "It was he who struck the rock; water gushed forth (*yāzūbū*) and swept down in torrents." Morphologically, *'zwb,* perhaps to be pointed *'āzōb,* belongs to the class of nouns with prothetic *aleph.* This class of nouns is particularly well represented in the Phoenician dialect; e.g., where other Canaanite dialects such as Hebrew have *gᵉdūd,* "marauding band," Phoenician has *'gdd* with prothetic *aleph;* cf. the place names along the Phoenician coast: *'kšp, 'rwd, 'kzb, 'ršp, 'šqln, 'šdd.* On the last-cited name, see F. M. Cross, Jr., and D. N. Freedman in BASOR 175 (1964), 49. Aware of this morphological tendency, the Hebraist will encounter less difficulty in explaining Job xxxiii 7, *'ekep=kap,* "hand" (see Dahood, *Biblica* 44 [1963], 209); xxxvii 13, *'arṣō,* "his good pleasure" (cf. Pope, *Job,* § 36, NOTE *ad loc.*); xli 24, *'ḥryw* (also Prov xxix 11), "nostrils," from *nḥr*, "to snort," and Prov xxii 13, *'rṣḥ*, "slayer." Consult fifth NOTE on Ps lxviii 22 for another example.

Since *be'āzōb* ostensibly balances *miššeleg*, "than snow," *be* must be comparative; see third NOTE on vs. 8. Arguing that the psalmist would hardly request God to sprinkle him with hyssop, H. Graetz (*Kritischer Commentar zu den Psalmen* [Breslau, 1882], I, p. 350), proposed the emendation of *be'ēzōb* to *mē'ēzōb*, but the well-documented sense of *be*, "from" (consult *Psalms I*, NOTES on Pss ii 4, iii 3, and Indexes of *Psalms I* and *Psalms II*), shows such emendation to be gratuitous. The same comparatives *be* and *min* occur in Prov xxiv 5, "A wise man is superior to a strong one (*bā'ōz*)/And a learned man is better than one who is physically powerful (*mē'ammīṣ kōaḥ*)." See R. B. Y. Scott, *Proverbs & Ecclesiastes* (The Anchor Bible, vol. 18; New York, 1965), § 27, and Dahood, *Biblica* 44 (1963), 299.

I'll be much whiter. Hiphil *'albīn* seems to carry the elative (*Psalms I*, p. 271) or intensifying nuance that renders it a good variant parallel to emphatic *we'eṭhār*.

The poetic sequence brought to light by this grammatical analysis is that commented upon in the NOTES to Pss vi 8, xxxviii 18, and xlvi 6 in *Psalms I*, namely, A+B+C // Á+B́+Ć. Cf. UT, 1 Aqht: 40–42. What is more, the recovery of the congruous metaphor ("gushing water – snow") supports the thesis that though the biblical poets may have occasionally mixed their metaphors, the exegete must proceed on the supposition that the imagery is coherent. Consult the writer's article, "Congruity of Metaphors," in *Festschrift Walter Baumgartner* (Leiden, 1967).

10. *Let me hear.* The frequent emendation of *tašmī'ēnī* to *taśbī'ēnī*, "Sate me," on the strength of Syriac version (see RSV), is unwarranted since the following accusatives, when correctly defined, can be apt objects of "hear."

songs of joy and gladness. This meaning of *śāśōn weśimḥāh* may be inferred from the following texts: Jer xxxi 7, *ronnū leya'aqōb śimḥāh*, "Sing aloud, O Jacob, songs of gladness"; Zeph iii 17, *yāśīś 'ālayik beśimḥāh yaḥarīš be'ahabātō yāgīl 'ālayik berinnāh*, "He will rejoice over you with a glad song, he will compose his love ballad, exult over you with loud singing." The apparent synonymy with *rinnāh*, "loud singing" (RSV), suggests that *śimḥāh* was something audible. Finally, Ps lxviii 7, *mōṣī' 'asīrīm bakkōšārōt*, "who led forth prisoners to music," points to a similar interpretation of Ps cv 43, *wayyōṣī' 'ammō beśāśōn berinnāh 'et beḥīrāyw*, "And he led forth his people with songs of joy, his chosen ones with loud singing." Thus E. R. Dalglish (*Psalm Fifty-one in the Light of Near Eastern Patternism* [Leiden, 1962], p. 141, n. 252) is not fully justified in his stricture of Pierre Bonnard's paraphrase, "Fais-moi (les chants) de joie et de fête, et qu'ils dansent les os que tu broyas" (Pierre E. Bonnard, *Le Psautier selon Jérémie*, Lectio Divina 26 [Paris, 1960]).

the bones you crushed. Nagging doubts cling to this customary rendition of *dikkītā*, "you crushed." That the psalmist has been shattered by remorse is evident (cf. vs. 19), but that God should be said to have caused this remorse needs demonstration. Dalglish's reference (*op. cit.*, p. 143, n. 265) to G. Ernest Wright, *The Old Testament against Its Environment*, pp. 91 f., does not solve the problem. Some commentators, e.g., *The Oxford Annotated Bible*, conclude from this expression that the poet had been smitten by serious sickness, but the psalm provides no further evidence of physical distress. The psalmist's anguish is strictly spiritual.

Since the preceding verse speaks of cleansing and purification, one must consider the possibility that *dikkītā* is a dialectal form of *zikkītā*, "you purified." There is evidence that by the time of the LXX, *dky*, "to be pure," had entered the Hebrew language alongside *zky;* cf. PNWSP, p. 31. That the poet should use both *zky* (vs. 6) and *dky* in the same psalm is no more unusual that the use of *d'k*, "to be extinguished," in Job xvii 1, but *z'k*, with the same meaning in the next chapter, xviii 5. But until a satisfactory explanation of Ps xliv 20, *dikkītānū*, apparently identical with *dky*, has been provided, one may, with misgivings, adopt the traditional version.

11. *Turn your face.* Parsing *hastēr* as an imperative of the infixed *-t-* conjugation of *sūr*, "to turn aside"; cf. *Psalms I*, NOTE on Ps x 11. This analysis renders superfluous the tortuous exegesis of Dalglish (*Psalm Fifty-one*, p. 145), who, deriving the form from *sātar*, "to hide," writes: "'Hide thy face from my sins' can only mean: Turn thy face away from beholding my sins, so that thou wilt no longer see them, regard them, punish concerning them."

12. *create in me.* Some versions (CCD is a recent example) take *lī* as "for me," but the apparent balance with *beqirbī*, literally "in my midst," argues against this interpretation. In Canaanite and biblical poetry, the function of prepositions was very flexible and their choice often depended on considerations beyond their dictionary definitions. In the present context, the desire to avoid two successive words beginning with bilabials (*berā' bī*) may account for the uncommon use of *lī*, "in me." Other examples of *le*, "in," number Pss xvi 10, lxvi 9, lxxxvii 5, xciii 5 (see J. D. Shenkel in *Biblica* 46 [1965], 413–14); Job xv 28, xxxix 26.

14. *by your generous spirit.* The suffix of *yiš'ekā*, "your salvation," also determines parallel *rūaḥ nedībāh* on the principle of the double-duty suffix studied in *Psalms I*, pp. 17 f., NOTE on Ps iii 4. In other words, "your generous spirit" is synonymous with vs. 13, "your holy

spirit"; its bearing on the translation of Ps liv 8 will be discussed there.

The stylistic trait of placing the accusative of means before its verb has been noticed at Ps v 10. In view of the psalmists' fondness for this construction and word order, the version found in CCD, though grammatically defensible, must be judged less probable: "And a willing spirit sustain in me." Compare Ps cxliii 10, *rūḥᵃ kā ṭōbāh tanḥēnī bᵉ'ereṣ mīšōr,* "With your good spirit lead me into the level land."

sustain me. The deployment of the imperfect (*tismᵉkēnī*) as a stylistic variant of the energic imperative (*hāšībāh*) is a hallmark of the psalmist's style that recurs in vs. 20, where the appreciation of this practice is crucial for the grammatical analysis of consonantal *tbnh.* Cf. also *Psalms I,* pp. 29 f., NOTE on Ps v 4.

15. *That I may teach.* Parsing *'ᵃlammᵉdāh* as the subjunctive (not the cohortative) expressing purpose; cf. *Psalms I,* p. 57, and Ps lxix 30–31, "May God's help bulwark me / That I might praise (*'ᵃhalᵉlāh*) God's Name in song."

to return to you. The second colon is not an independent sentence, but a clause dependent upon the subjunctive verb of the first colon. The psalmist asks God for a determined spirit to be able to teach rebels and sinners the way to return to God.

16. *the tears of death.* Pointing *dammīm* for MT *dāmīm,* "blood," and relating the noun to *dāmam,* "to weep," studied in *Psalms I,* p. 24. Cf. likewise UT, Glossary, No. 674, p. 385, where Gordon admits Heb. *dmm,* "to weep." Just as *māwet,* "death," can also denote "the place of death, namely, Sheol" (e.g., Ps vi 6), so *dammīm* may have come to signify the place of tears par excellence. Cf. Matt viii 12, "But those who were born to the kingdom will be driven out into the dark, the place of wailing and grinding of teeth." The poet asks to be rescued from such a place in order to be able to acclaim God's goodness. And as several texts make clear (e.g., Pss vi 6, xxx 10, lxxxviii 11–13), there is no praise of Yahweh in the realm of sorrow. The connection between *dammīm,* "tears," and the nether world has been preserved in a misunderstood verse of Ecclus ix 9, *pn tṭh 'lyh lb wbdmym tṭh 'l šḥt,* "Lest you permit your heart to succumb to her, and in tears you descend to the Pit." Contrast *The Apocrypha of the Old Testament, Revised Standard Version,* ed. Bruce M. Metzger (New York, 1965), p. [140], "Lest your heart turn aside to her, and in blood you be plunged into destruction."

Many commentators, recognizing that *dāmīm,* "blood," comports poorly with the over-all context of Ps li, propose the interpretation "blood-guiltiness," but this definition is unsustained by usage.

my God. Pointing *'ᵉlōhay* for MT *'ᵉlōhēy.*

my Savior. Explaining *tᵉšū'ātī* as an abstract noun used as a divine appellative; see discussion of cognate *yᵉšū'ōt* in *Psalms I*, p. 173, NOTE on Ps xxviii 8. This analysis does not affect the phrase *'ᵉlōhē yiš'ī*, "the God who will save me," in Pss xxv 5 and xxvii 9.

Read and translated thus, vs. 16 scans into 4+4 beats with thirteen syllables in the first half-verse and fourteen in the second. Proposals to delete *'ᵉlōhay* (MT *'ᵉlōhēy*) *tᵉšū'ātī* are therefore to be rejected.

17. *my lips . . . my mouth.* An example of the Ugaritic balance between *p*, "mouth," and *špt*, "lips," is cited in the second NOTE on Ps lix 8, while the fourth NOTE on Ps lvii 8 assesses the value of parallel pairs as a criterion for the linguistic and literary classification of Ugaritic.

18. *should.* Vocalizing *lū'* with the LXX against MT *lō'*.

I would offer it. Repoint MT *wᵉ'ettēnāh* to *wᵉ'ettēnēhū*, and read the line as a tricolon with a 6:5:6 syllable count. The middle colon is a double-duty modifier, that is, it looks both ways. Scanned thus, the line discloses its chiastic structure: A+B//C//B'+A'.

should. As in the first colon, reading *lū'*, "if, should," for MT *lō'*, "not."

19. *The finest sacrifices.* In the phrase *zibḥē 'ᵉlōhīm*, the latter word seems to function as a superlative; consult *Psalms I*, p. 220, NOTE on Ps xxxvi 7 and compare Ps lxxxiii 13, *nᵉ'ōt 'ᵉlōhīm*, which AT has soundly rendered "the very finest meadows." To render *'ᵉlōhīm* as a divine name in this phrase would put God in both the third and the second person in the same verse. To be sure, this is not a fatal objection, but the proposed parsing does permit a smoother translation.

do not spurn. Not "You will not spurn" (CCD). It is characteristic of this poet to use the imperfect form as an imperative; see vss. 8–10, 17, 20.

20. *make Zion beautiful.* This specification of generic *hēṭībāh* proceeds from its pairing with *tibneh*, "rebuild!" In Ps xlviii 3, Zion is apostrophized as "the most beautiful peak."

rebuild. Like Ugar. *bny*, *bānāh* signifies both "to build" and "to rebuild." Hence the poem must be dated after the destruction of Jerusalem by the Babylonians in 586 B.C. and before the restoration of the wall under Nehemiah in 444 B.C.

Both LXX and *Juxta Hebraeos* took consonantal *tbnh* as niphal *tibbānū* with "walls" as the subject, but this reconstruction slights the poet's predilection for employing the imperfect form as a stylistic variant of the imperative; see NOTE on vs. 14.

Those who maintain an historical connection between the title of the psalm and its contents ascribe it to King David, but are in consequence forced to label vss. 20–21 as a later addition, written some time after the destruction of Jerusalem in 586 B.C. As most of the psalm headings are demonstrably late, sound method counsels the retention of these verses as authentic and the ascription of the psalm heading to a later hand.

21. *legitimate sacrifices.* Namely, performed according to ritual prescriptions; for such sacrifices Jerusalem was the only legitimate site.

For this nuance of *ṣedeq*, see *Psalms I*, p. 25, NOTE on Ps iv 6; R. T. O'Callaghan in VT 4 (1954), 170, and James Swetnam, "Some Observations on the Background of *ṣdyq* in Jeremias 23, 5a," in *Biblica* 46 (1965), 29–40.

holocaust and whole offering. There are plenty of versions and commentaries where this phrase is deleted, but its authenticity is sustained by metrical considerations. The line divides into two parts, each introduced by *'āz*, "then." The first part contains four beats and eleven syllables; the second part also numbers four beats and eleven syllables! To delete the phrase in question would destroy the carefully constructed accentual and syllabic balance.

mount. Since MT *ya'ᵃlū* can be parsed either as qal or hiphil imperfect, the more common version, "They shall offer up," is possible though less probable. The latter translation must import an indefinite subject "they" to serve as subject of *ya'ᵃlū*. It is much simpler, and more graphic, to take *pārīm*, "young bulls," as subject with *ya'ᵃlū* its predicate. *The Grail Psalms, a New Translation* (Fontana Books; London, 1963), p, 92, "Then you will be offered young bulls on your alter," is grammatically questionable.

PSALM 52

(lii 1–11)

1 *For the director. A maskil of David.*
2 *When Doeg, the Edomite, came and told Saul, "David has come to Ahimelech's house."*

3 Why do you boast of wickedness, O champion?
O devoted of El, why at all times [2]*
4 do you harbor pernicious thoughts?
Your tongue is like a sharpened razor,
artist of deceit!
5 You love evil rather than good, [3]
lying instead of telling the truth. *Selah*
6 You love all the words [4]
of your destructive deceitful tongue!
7 With a crash may El demolish you, [5]
eternally unchild you!
May he pluck you from your tent,
and snatch your sons alive from the earth! *Selah*
8 The just will look on in dread, [6]
but then will laugh at him:
9 "So this is the man who would not [7]
consider God his refuge,
But trusted in his great wealth,
relied on his perniciousness!"
10 I, for my part, like an olive tree [8]
flourishing in the house of God,
Trust in the love
of the eternal and everlasting God.
11 I will praise you, O Eternal, [9]
because you acted;
And I will proclaim your Name,
so good to your devoted ones!

*** Verse numbers in RSV.**

Notes

lii. Composed in terse graphic language, this poem contrasts the condition and destiny of the pagan who relies on his cunning with that of the just believer who draws his strength from God.

The inability of scholars to fit this psalm into one of the standard literary categories ("The analysis and the determination of the literary type in Ps 52 offer great difficulties"—Hans-Joachim Kraus, *Psalmen* (Biblischer Kommentar Altes Testament; Neukirchen, 1961, 2nd ed.), I, p. 393) does not hinder the understanding and appreciation of a composition marked by sarcasm, invective, and a warm profession of faith in God's goodness.

The poem divides into three strophes: (a) vss. 3–6; (b) vss. 7–9; (c) vss. 10–11. The lack of a fixed stichometric pattern, the recurrence of enjambment, double-duty suffixes and particles create translation difficulties that Northwest Semitic philology only partially resolves.

1. *A maskil.* A sense-giving harmony; it bears a double, intellectual-exegetical and artistic-musical meaning. See M. Gertner, BSOAS 25 (1962), 22–24.

2. *Doeg, the Edomite.* I Sam xxi 8 and xxii 6 ff. relate that Doeg, the chief of Saul's herdsmen, denounced the priest Ahimelech for receiving David into his house and offering him material and spiritual assistance. In reporting David's presence in the house of Ahimelech, Doeg apparently stated the facts correctly, so the psalmist could scarcely have aimed at him this lament that stresses the mendacious nature of his target (vss. 4–6). Hence the superscription bears no demonstrable historical connection with the contents of the psalm, but was added by later liturgists to give the poem a setting.

came . . . has come. As in the superscription of Ps li, the verb *ba'* appears twice; whether this fact has any further significance cannot be made out.

and told Saul. The Hebrew further adds the words "and he said to him," but since this phrase is apparently equivalent to our quotation marks, there is no need to reproduce it *along with* the quotation marks, as is done by AT and some other versions. See first Note on Ps cii 20.

3. *Why . . . why.* As in Pss ii 1, iii 2–3 (cf. Ps lxxiv, 1, 10), the interrogative force of *mah* extends from the first to the second colon. The appreciation of this elliptical poetic usage renders needless the insertion of *mī* in the second colon of Isa xl 13, as recommended by BH^3. Nor does $1QIs^a$ contain a *mī* in the second colon.

do you boast . . . harbor pernicious thoughts. Verse 3 and the first two words of vs. 4 form a bicolon arranged chiastically:

mah tithallēl bᵉrā'āh haggibbōr (4 accents+10 syllables)
ḥᵃsīd 'ēl kol hayyōm hawwōt taḥšōb (4 accents+10 syllables)

O champion. Comparison with Ps cxx 2–4, where lies and slanderous remarks are likened to the sharpened arrows of a *gibbōr,* "warrior, champion," reveals that the much-disputed MT pointing *gibbōr* in our passage may well be correct. The present context is similar to that of Ps cxx 2–4. In vs. 9, however, after the *gibbōr,* "champion," has been cut down to size, he is sarcastically termed a mere *geber,* "man." This irony would be lost were one to adopt the reading *hagbēr ḥassēd 'el,* "increasing the contempt of God," that is sometimes proposed. For another analysis of this verse, see Claus Schedl in BZ 5 (1961), 259–60.

O devoted of El. Vocalizing *ḥᵃsīd 'ēl* for MT *ḥesed 'ēl,* I find another example of this confusion in Ps lxix 17. Since the psalmist wants to contrast the unprincipled scoundrel with the true worshipers of vs. 11, *ḥᵃsīdekā,* "your devoted ones," the term *ḥᵃsīd 'ēl* would be sarcastic. Pretending to be one dedicated to El, the man is really a liar and scoundrel.

4. *harbor pernicious thoughts.* The substantive *hawwōt,* usually rendered "ruin, destruction," carries the nuance "poisonous, pernicious" when describing "tongue" or "speech." Thus Prov xvii 4, *šōqēr* (MT *šeqer*) *mēzīn 'al lᵉšōn hawwōt,* "A liar mulls over pernicious speech." See NOTES below on Pss lv 12, xci 3, and ZLH, p. 187a.

a sharpened razor. With *ta'ar mᵉluṭṭāš* compare Ps vii 13 and UT, 137:32, *ḥrb lṭšt,* "a sharpened sword." The passive pual participle *mᵉluṭṭāš* is more accurately reproduced by "sharpened" than by "sharp" (RSV). The Hebrew passive vocalization makes it highly probable that Ugar. *lṭšt* is a qal passive participle; cf. UT, § 9.24 (2), p. 78. From the point of view of English, *The Jerusalem Bible*'s "Your tongue is razor-sharp" is excellent, but the Hebrew reads "like a sharpened razor"; in keeping with the principles of translation followed in this commentary, I follow the Hebrew as closely as English idiom permits.

In its three occurrences, Ugar. *t'rt* (= Heb. *ta'ar*) signifies "scabbard" by metonymy.

6. *the words of your destructive deceitful tongue.* Usually rendered as a vocative "O deceitful tongue!," *lᵉšōn mirmāh* preferably parses as the genitive of a construct chain beginning with *dibrē,* "the words of." Hence I would read vs. 6 as an instance of enjambment (see below on vs. 10; *Psalms I,* pp. 41, 43, etc.) with two equally balanced cola:

'āhabtā kol dibrē (3 accents+6 syllables)
bela' (MT *bāla'*) *lᵉšōn mirmāh* (3 accents+6 syllables)

In a construct chain, it might be remarked, as many as six genitives can depend upon one construct; cf. Gen xlvii 9 (3 nouns), xli 10 (4 nouns);

Isa xxi 17 (6 nouns), and Joüon, GHB, § 129c. In Ugaritic one finds *ṯpṭ qṣr npš*, literally, "the cause of one short of spirit"; UT, § 8.16.

your . . . tongue. Forming an inclusion with vs. 4, *lᵉšōnᵉkā*, and closing the first strophe, *lᵉšōn* here need not have a formal suffix to justify this translation since it is the name of part of the body; *Psalms I*, pp. 88 f., 95, etc.

7. *With a crash. gam* is to be identified with Ugar. *gm*, "aloud, with a loud voice," and is synonymous with biblical *bᵉqōl*, "aloud, with a crash." Compare Ezek xxvi 15, "Will not the coastlands rock at the crash of your collapse (*miqqōl mappaltēk*)?" This sense of *gam* shows its deletion in Jer li 44 to be mistaken: *gam ḥōmat bābel nāpālāh*, "With a crash the wall of Babylon will fall." Cf. Jer xlix 21, "The earth is rocked by the crash (*miqqōl*) of their fall" (John Bright [The Anchor Bible, vol. 21; New York, 1965], § 42). In Ps lxxxv 13, *gam* describes the sound of thunder: "With a crash (*gam*) will Yahweh give his rain, and our land will give its produce." Cf. also Judg v 4, "The earth rocked, with a crash the heavens dripped, with a crash the clouds dripped with water." Other instances of *gam*, "aloud," may be seen in Pss lxxi 22, 24, cxxxvii 1 (cf. Dahood, CBQ 22 [1960], 402, n. 7); Num xi 4 (see Desmond Beirne, *Biblica* 44 [1963], 201–3); Isa xiii 3, xiv 8, lxvi 8; Jer xlviii 2; Joel i 18, 20; Neh iii 35. Cf. also Dahood, *Biblica* 45 (1964), 399; Thomas F. McDaniel, *Philological Studies in Lamentations* (Johns Hopkins University dissertation, 1966: University Microfilms, Ann Arbor), pp. 16–17, on Lam i 8; UT, Glossary, No. 547.

may El demolish you. Hermann Gunkel (*Die Psalmen* [Göttingen, 1926], p. 230) was correct when breaking with the traditional versions and in analyzing the verb *yittāṣekā* (I read pausal form instead of MT) as expressing a curse rather than a prophecy. Usually predicated of destroying buildings, *nātaṣ*, "to pull down, demolish," refers to the knave's house and family. Since the divergencies in translation stem from the manner in which one analyzes the verse structure, it may be helpful to give the stichometric division adopted here:

> *gam 'ēl yittāṣekā//lāneṣaḥ yᵉḥattēk* (A+B)
> *yissāḥᵃkā mē'ōhel//wᵉšērešᵉkā mē'ereṣ ḥayyīm* (Á+B́)

eternally. The adverbial idea expressed by *lāneṣah* balances adverbial *gam*, "with a crash."

unchild you. Vocalizing *yᵉḥattēk* (MT *yaḥtᵉkā*) and parsing it as a piel privative denominative verb (see first NOTE on Ps li 9) from *ḥtk*, which in Ugaritic denotes either "father" or "son" depending on its vocalization. A. F. Scharf in *Verbum Domini* 38 (1960), 213–22, followed by the writer in *Ugaritic-Hebrew Philology* (abbr. UHP) (Biblica et Orientalia 17; Rome, 1965), p. 58, has translated it "may he unfather you," but the stichometric pattern suggests that *yᵉḥattēk* is synonymous with *šērešᵉkā,* and hence to be derived from *ḥtk* meaning "son" rather than "father." In other words, these two verbs contain imprecations against the scoundrel's children and balance the two verbs that denounce the scoundrel himself. Cf. the Ugaritic denominative verb *aḫt,* "you have become a brother," from *aḫ;* see the fourth NOTE on Ps lxviii 20.

Balancing three verbs with suffix *-kā, yᵉḥattēk* need not need be supplied with its own suffix; since the root already ends in *-k,* the psalmist would be hardly disposed to add the syllable *-kā.* What is more, the proposed vocalization permits the colon *lānesaḥ yᵉḥattēk,* with two accents and six syllables, perfectly to balance *'ēl yittāṣekā,* also numbering two accents and six syllables. The objection of Marvin H. Pope, JBL 85 (1966), 465, to this etymology on the grounds that one would expect an additional *k* for the object suffix bespeaks an unfamiliarity with the widely accepted poetic phenomenon known as the double-duty suffix. Cf. most recently William L. Holladay, JBL 85 (1966), 418, 429, n. 38.

pluck you. The verb is *nāsaḥ,* which appears in tandem with *kārat,* "cut off," in Prov ii 22, "But the wicked shall be cut off from the earth, and the treacherous will be plucked up (vocalizing qal passive *yussᵉḥū*) from it." That *nāsaḥ* belongs to the language of curses is clear from the Aramaic Inscription from Nerab, lines 9–10, *šhr wšmš wnkl wnšk ysḥw šmk w'šrk mn ḥyn,* "May ŠHR, Shamash, Nikkal, and Nusku pluck your name (or offspring) and your house from the living." See Donner and Röllig, KAI, II, p. 275.

from your tent. Suffixless *'ōhel* shares the suffix of its verb "may he pluck you"; cf. above, fourth NOTE to vs. 7.

snatch your sons. Parsing *šērešᵉkā* as precative perfect (*Psalms I,* pp. XXIV, XXXIX, 19 f., etc.) continuing the preceding three jussives; compare Ps iv 2 where a precative serves for stylistic variation amid three imperatives. Etymologically, it is a denominative verb from *šōreš* in its metaphorical meaning "offspring, scion," a meaning put into clearer light by the synonymy of *šrš* and *bn* in UT, 2 Aqht:I:21–22, *bl iṯ bn lh km aḫh wšrš km aryh,* "Surely he, like his brothers, will have a son and, like his brethren, an offspring." Cf. Isa xiv 29; Prov xii 3; Ecclus x 16, and Phoen. *šrš,* "offspring" (Charles F. Jean and Jacob Hoftijzer, *Dictionnaire des inscriptions sémitiques de l'ouest* [abbr. DISO] [Leiden, 1965], p. 321, lines 18–19).

alive. Usually parsed as the genitive after *'ereṣ,* "earth," *ḥayyīm* may well be the adjective modifying the plural antecedent in the verb; cf. Ps lv 16, *yērᵉdū šᵉ'ōl ḥayyīm,* "May they go down to Sheol alive." The psalmist desires that the wicked man's children be snatched away by death while they are still in the full vigor of life; cf. Job's children snatched by death.

8. *look on in dread.* A similar wordplay on *yir'ū* and *yīrā'ū* is noticed in the fourth NOTE on Ps lxiv 5.

but then will laugh. At first awestruck by the vigor of the divine punishment meted out to the impious, the devout worshipers will then rejoice at God's action.

9. *consider God his refuge.* The clause *yāśīm 'ᵉlōhīm mā'ūzzō* is important for the translation and exegesis of Ps xci 9, *'elyōn śamtā mᵉ'ōnekā,* "Consider the Most High your mainstay."

relied. yā'ōz is an imperfect form expressing past time; cf. *Psalms I,* pp. 39, 51, 56.

his perniciousness. The widely adopted emendation by Gunkel (*Die Psalmen,* p. 231) of *hawwātō* to *hōnō,* "his wealth" (so Syr. and Targ.), fails to appreciate that for some biblical writers "rich" ("his great wealth") and "wicked" ("his perniciousness") are correlative concepts, just as the phrase "poor but honest" correlates "poor" and "dishonest." Thus Isa liii 9 pairs *rᵉšā'īm,* "the wicked," with *'āšīr,* "the rich man," while the proposed emendation of *kerem rāšā',* "the vineyard of the wicked man," to *kerem 'āšīr,* "the vineyard of the rich man," in Job xxiv 6 may prove needless. Prov xi 7 associates *'ādām rāšā',* "the wicked man," with *tōḥelet 'ōnīm,* "hope placed in riches," and Eccles viii 8 makes *reša',* "wickedness" connote "riches." Consult *Psalms I,* p. 229, NOTE on Ps xxxvii 16, *rᵉšā'īm rabbīm,* "the wicked rich." The psalmist does not condemn riches as such, but only wealth acquired unjustly or ruthlessly. Hence we must understand "his wealth" and "his perniciousness" as complementary to express the idea of ill-gotten gain. Since few words are precise synonyms, the terms of the second colon are not usually perfect replicas of the corresponding words in the first colon, adding nuances and overtones that complete the total concept the psalmist wishes to express.

10. *I . . . like an olive tree.* Most versions make of vs. 10a an independent sentence, but the poet's use of enjambment in vss. 6 and 10b suggests that vs. 10a is all the subject of *bāṭaḥtī* in vs. 10b.

the love. Like *dibrē,* "the words of," in vs. 6, construct *ḥesed* marks the end of the first colon (2 accents–6 syllables) whose genitive forms the second colon (3 accents–7 syllables); hence another instance of enjambment.

the eternal and everlasting God. As in Ps xlv 7, reading *'ᵉlōhē-m* (with enclitic *mem*) *'ōlām wā'ed,* a genitive governed by the construct *ḥesed* in the first colon. Cf. Pss x 16, xlviii 15, cxlv 1 for cognate composite titles of God.

11. *O Eternal.* Analyzing *lᵉ'ōlām* into the vocative particle, recently studied by me, "Vocative LAMEDH in the Psalter," in VT 16 (1966), 299–311, and the divine appellative, as in Ps xxxi 2. Such parsing

eliminates the need to insert the vocative *yahweh* after *'ōdᵉkā,* as frequently proposed. This analysis makes *'ōdᵉkā lᵉ'ōlām* a fine parallel to *'ᵃqawweh šimᵉkā,* "I will proclaim your Name"; cf. especially Ps lxxxvi 12.

because you acted. By punishing the wicked and saving the just. On the absolute use of *'āśāh,* cf. especially Ps xxxvii 5, "Trust in him and he will act," and *Psalms I,* p. 228, NOTE thereto. Whence RSV gets the object of *'āśītā,* "because thou hast done it," is not immediately evident. See *Psalms I,* p. 241, NOTE on Ps xxxix 10.

I will proclaim. For this meaning of *'ᵃqawweh,* see *Psalms I,* pp. 121 f., NOTE on Ps xix 5. RSV correctly renders it by "proclaim" but needlessly emends the text.

your Name. An hypostasis or person since it is personal subject of the following word *ṭōb;* hence the capitalization. See *Psalms I,* p. 127, and NOTES on Pss liv 9, lxix 31.

so good. The divine Name is portrayed as a person bestowing blessings on those who revere it. In Ps liv 9 the Name of Yahweh is said to have rescued the psalmist from all his adversaries. Here *kī* seems to be emphatic; see *Psalms I,* p. 197.

to. For this nuance of *neged,* cf. Ps lxxxviii 2.

your devoted ones. The genuine worshipers of Yahweh as contrasted with the hypocritical *ḥᵃsīd 'ēl,* "devoted of El," in vs. 3.

PSALM 53

(liii 1–7)

1 *For the director; according to "mahalath." A maskil of David.*

2 The fool thinks in his heart:
"God is not present."
They perform corrupt, abominable deeds;
there is no one who does good.
3 From heaven God looks down [2]*
upon the sons of men,
To see if there be one who ponders,
one who searches for God.
4 Each is miscreant, [3]
together they are depraved;
There is no one who does good,
no, not a single one.
5 Don't they know, all the evildoers, [4]
that they who devour his people,
Devour the grain of God
they did not harvest.
6 See how they marshaled their troops, [5]
but the siege didn't last
because God scattered your besiegers' bones.
You were dismayed till God gathered them.
7 O that from Zion would come Israel's salvation! [6]
When God restores his people's fortunes,
let Jacob rejoice and Israel be happy!

* Verse numbers in RSV.

NOTES

liii. An Elohistic (see *Psalms I*, p. XXXI), Northern edition of a poem appearing in a Yahwistic, Southern edition as Ps xiv. For explanations the reader is referred to the NOTES on Ps xiv; the following comments are mainly limited to the textual variants and to modifications of the earlier translation. Attempts to reconstruct the original poem underlying Pss xiv and liii have proved stillborn because they ignored the fact that the existing variants may reflect two different dialects. Valuable information on the double transmission of a single episode is provided by the Ugaritic doublets UT, Krt:195–206 and 128:III:25–30; 1 Aqht: 61–67 and 68–74, studied by A. Jirku, "Doppelte Überlieferungen im Mythus und im Epos von Ugarit?," in ZDMG 110 (1960), 20–25. Jirku attributes the variants in these Canaanite doublets to the different Canaanite dialects in which the two versions were composed. See also J. A. Montgomery in JAOS 53 (1933), 110.

1. *mahalath.* A technical term of uncertain meaning that recurs in the superscription to Ps lxxxviii.

A maskil. See first NOTE on Ps lii.

2. *thinks.* Though "says" (as *Psalms I*, p. 80) is quite defensible, "thinks" is a more satisfactory rendition of *'āmar* when it occurs in a sentence of the type known as *Hoffartsmonolog*, "insolence monologue." On this literary genre, cf. the brief remarks of G. von Rad, *Theologie des Alten Testaments* (München, 1962), II, p. 190, n. 10, and the following texts: Isa x 7–8, xxxvii 24, xlvii 7–8; Ezek xxviii 2, xxix 3, 9; Obad 3. Cf. especially Ezek xxviii 3, "And you thought, 'I am a god.'" In the light of these texts, it becomes clear that Ps x 13, *'āmar b*^{e}*libbō lō' tidrōš*, is to be rendered, "Thinking to himself, 'You will not requite,'" and Ps xxx 7, *wa'*^{a}*nī 'āmartī b*^{e}*šalwī bal 'emmōṭ l*^{e}*'ōlām*, "I thought in my insouciance, 'I will never stumble,'" belong to the genre of *Hoffartsmonolog*. See also *Psalms I*, p. 191, NOTE on Ps xxxi 23 with the bibliographical reference there.

God is not present. More correct rendition of *'ēn '*^{e}*lōhīm* than "There is no God" (*Psalms I*, p. 80); consult *op. cit.*, p. 117, NOTE on Ps xviii 42, "But the Savior was not there."

deeds. Where Ps xiv 1 reads *'*^{a}*līlāh*, "deed," our passage has *'āwel*, "iniquity." Perhaps we should vocalize *'āl* or *'ōl*, a Northern by-form of *'*^{a}*līlāh*. Cf. Prov xiv 14, *midd*^{e}*rākāyw yiśba' sūg lēb ūmē'ālāyw 'īš ṭōb*, "The miscreant will have the full measure of his conduct, and the good man of his deeds." The standard emendation of *'ālāyw* to *ma'*^{a}*lālāw*, "for his [good] deeds" (so R. B. Y. Scott [The Anchor Bible, vol. 18], § 15) may now be questioned. Prov xvi 23, *lēb ḥākām* *yaśkīl pīhū w*ᵉ*'al ś*ᵉ*pātāyw yōsīp leqaḥ*, "The mind of the wise man imparts intelligence to his speech, and the action of his lips increases persuasiveness." The emendation of *'al* to *ba'al*, "the master of," on the basis of LXX and Syr. becomes difficult to defend. Prov xvi 27, *'īš b*ᵉ*līyya'al kōreh rā'āh w*ᵉ*'al ś*ᵉ*pātāyw k*ᵉ*'ēš ṣārabet*, "A depraved man concocts (see Dahood, PNWSP, p. 37, for this sense of *kōreh*) evil, and the action of his lips is like a scorching fire." Cf. also Prov xvi 22.

Morphologically, the relation of *'al* (or *'ōl*) to *'*ᵃ*līlāh* is analogous to that between *'ūl*, "suckling," and *'ōlāl* or *'ōlēh*, "child." It may be remarked here that the occurrence of *'ōl* or *'āl*, "deed, action," in Ps liii and in Proverbs links the Psalm more closely to the genre of Wisdom Literature; cf. *Psalms I*, p. 80.

4. *Each. kullō* is a stylistic variant of *hakkōl* found in Ps xiv 3; not infrequently the pronominal suffix and the article substitute for one another. Cf. the balance between *hassūs*, "his horse," and *ḥēlō*, "his military might," in Ps xxxiii 17. Cf. Joüon, GHB, § 137f 2), p. 422; the NOTES on Pss lv 23, lvi 5, and Ps iii 9 where *birkātekā*, "your blessing," indicates that *hay*ᵉ*šū'āh* should be rendered "your salvation"; a correction to *Psalms I*, p. 15.

miscreant. For *sāg* Ps xiv 3 reads *sār;* both words are synonyms and to emend one into the other slights the principle of double transmission discussed in the introductory NOTE to this psalm. The value of this principle for textual criticism will be further examined at Ps lv 23.

5. *devour his people.* Comparing Jer ii 3, "Israel was Yahweh's own portion / His harvest's first yield. / All eating of it will perish; / Punishment will overtake them—Yahweh's word" (Bright, The Anchor Bible, vol. 21, with modifications of mine).

6. *marshaled their troops.* The mention of *ḥōnāk*, "besiegers," lacking in Ps xiv 5, from *ḥānāh*, "to encamp," suggests that the nuance borne by *pāḥ*ᵃ*dū paḥad* is military; compare *Psalms I*, p. 82. The psalmist, as in the historical psalms (lxxviii, cv), may be alluding to an historical event, such as Sennacherib's siege of Jerusalem, described in II Kings xviii–xix.

God scattered . . . bones. Cf. Ps cxli 7, "May their bones be scattered at the entrance of Sheol." In II Kings xix 35 it is reported, "And that night the angel of Yahweh went forth, and slew five thousand one hundred and eighty in the camp of Assyrians." For this translation of the number, S. H. Horn, *Andrews University Seminary Bulletin* 4 (1966), 27–28.

your besiegers. Explaining *ḥōnāk* as collective singular participle *ḥōnē* followed by the suffix of the second person singular masculine, whose antecedent is "people" in vs. 5, or analyzing consonantal *ḥnk* as *scriptio defectiva* (*Psalms I*, p. 328) for *ḥōnekā*. Cf. Ps cxl 9–10, *sollāh* (MT *selāh*) *rō'š mesibbāy*, "Heap high the heads of those who encompass me."

You were dismayed. Namely, the people of Israel. For this nuance of *hebīšōtāh*, cf. Jer ii 26 and Bright (The Anchor Bible, vol. 21), textual note[h–h].

gathered them. Namely, the besiegers. Since MT *me'āsām*, "rejected them," is not particularly meaningful in this context (this particular form of *mā'as* is a hapax legomenon), I tentatively vocalize *me'assēm* from **'āsam*, the root preserved in Ugar.-Heb. *'āsām*, "granary." The sense would be euphemistic, "to gather in death," like *'āsap* in certain contexts. Thus the poet would be playing on the words "harvest" (vs. 5), "scatter" and "gather" (vs. 6).

7. *from Zion.* Briggs, CECBP, I, pp. 108 f., has remarked that "here is an entirely different situation from that of v. 2 [v. 3], where salvation comes from Yahweh in heaven." This observation, however, may not be correct. In Canaanite mythology, Mount Zaphon, with its roots in the earth but its peak in the clouds, was considered both a terrestrial and celestial mountain; sometimes it is difficult to determine which is meant. Just as *hēkāl* in the Psalter can denote either the temple in Jerusalem or God's heavenly temple (*Psalms I*, p. 179), and *qōdeš* the sanctuary on earth or the heavenly shrine (Pss lxiii 3, cl 1), so Zion may also refer to his celestial mountain. This observation casts new light on the exegesis of Ps xx 3, "May he send you help from his sanctuary, from Zion sustain you." The sanctuary and the Zion in heaven are clearly intended because vs. 7 explicitly states, "Now I know that Yahweh has given his anointed victory / Has granted him triumph from his sacred heaven / And from his fortress has given victory with his right hand." Cf. Heb xii 22, "But you have come up to Mount Zion, to the city of the living God, the heavenly Jerusalem, to countless angels, to the solemn gathering of all God's elder sons etc." Consult first NOTE on Ps xcix 2.

salvation. Apparently plural *yešū'ōt* should not be altered to the singular form of Ps xiv 7. The ending *-ōt* may well be the Phoenician singular ending discussed in *Psalms I*, pp. 275, 299. Here then would be further evidence for the Northern provenance of Ps liii. New instances of the feminine singular absolute ending *-ōt* include Pss x 7, *mirmōt* (the three closely parallel synonyms are all singular), lxviii 12, *mebaśśerōt*, lxxviii 15, *tehōmōt*, 72, *tebūnōt*, lxxxviii 9, *tō'ēbōt;* Josh xv 6, *lebā'ōt* (DISO, p. 29), I Sam ii 3, *dē'ōt;* Job xiii 6, *rībōt*, xxi 30, *'abārōt*, xxxi 36, *'aṭārōt*, xxxviii 32, *mazzārōt;* Prov xxii 14, *zārōt*. Recent bibliography includes G. Levi Della Vida, *Oriens Antiquus* 2 (1963), 91, and J. T. Milik, *Revue biblique* 73 (1966), 101. See also the fifth NOTE on Ps lxxiii 18 and the writer's study, "The Phoenician Contribution to Biblical Wisdom Literature," in the

Centennial Volume of the American University of Beirut (Beirut, 1968).

let Jacob rejoice. In the final colon the poet has chosen his words carefully, adding assonance to alliteration: *yāgel ya'ᵃqōb yiśmaḥ yiśrā'ēl.* Thus all four words begin with *yod,* but the first two have *ya-,* while the last two begin with *yi-.*

PSALM 54

(liv 1–9)

1 *For the director; with stringed instruments. A maskil of David,*
2 *when the Ziphites came and told Saul, "Look, David is hiding among us."*

3 O God, save me through your Name,
and by your might defend me.
4 O God, hear my prayer, [2]*
give ear to the words of my mouth;
5 Because foreigners have risen against me, [3]
and barbarians seek my life;
But they are not aware that God is my Leader. *Selah*
6 See how God became my helper, [4]
the Lord the true Sustainer of my life!
7 He made the evil recoil on my defamers, [5]
in his fidelity he annihilated them completely.
8 For your nobility I will sacrifice to you, [6]
I will praise your Name, Yahweh, truly good,
9 Because from all my adversaries he rescued me, [7]
and my eye feasted on my foes.

* Verse numbers in RSV.

NOTES

liv. Usually classified as the lament of an individual, this poem, upon comparison with royal Pss xx and lxxxvi, distinctly emerges as the supplication of a king for deliverance from his foreign enemies. The verbal and conceptual similarities that point to such a classification will be registered in the philological NOTES.

Balance characterizes the structure of the psalm. Verses 3–4 contain the plea for help, with vs. 5 giving the reason for the supplication.

Verses 6–7 describe God's response to the poet's plea, vs. 8 tells how the psalmist reacts to God's intervention while vs. 9 states the reason for the reaction of the psalmist.

1. *maskil.* See first NOTE on Ps lii.

2. *Ziphites.* This incident is recounted in I Sam xxiii 19.

Look. *h*^{a}*lō'* in a number of passages cited by BDB, p. 520a, Zorell, ZLH, p. 191a, and Joüon, GHB, § 161c, equals *hinnēh,* "Behold!," and is to be identified with Ugar. *hl,* "Behold!" Compare Ps cxxxix 21, *h*^{a}*lō',* with Ps xcii 10, *hinnēh.* In Ezek xxviii 3, MT reads *hinnēh,* "Behold!," but the LXX must have translated from a Hebrew text reading *h*^{a}*lō',* "Behold!" This, however, was mistranslated by the LXX as the interrogative particle *mē,* "Are you not (wiser, etc.)?" The reading of the LXX's *Vorlage* must be judged original and MT contaminated. Cf. first NOTE on Ps lx 12.

3. *your Name.* Consult fourth NOTE on Ps lii 11. Just as the suppliant expects his deliverance to come through the divine Name, to which he ascribes a certain subsistence, so at the end of the poem (vs. 9) the psalmist attributes his rescue to the intervention of this divine being. The mention of Name in the opening colon begins the rhetorical figure of inclusion (*Psalms I,* p. 5) that closes in vs. 9a, where the Name is the subject of the verb "rescued me."

A significant clue to the person of the suppliant is found in the observation that in royal Ps xx 2, the Name of Jacob's God is besought on behalf of the king.

save me . . . defend me. The imperative-imperfect sequence is an element of style with antecedents in Ugaritic poetry, as noticed in *Psalms I,* pp. 29 f., 31, 65, 261.

4. *give ear.* Imperative *ha'*^{a}*zīnāh* recurs in royal Ps lxxxvi 6.

5. *foreigners.* Though the doublet in Ps lxxxvi 14 matches *'ārīṣīm* with *zēdīm,* "arrogant men," the present reading *zārīm* may be defended because Isa xxv 2–3 and 5 witness the same parallelism between *zārīm* and *'ārīṣīm.* But even in the Isaian passages some critics (e.g., Gunkel) would find on the strength of the LXX further misspellings of *zārīm* for *zēdīm.* But 1QIs^{a}, both times reading *zrym//'ryṣym,* makes against them; hence MT in the psalm passage stands.

God is my Leader. A comparison of *lō' śāmū '*^{e}*lōhīm lngdm* with Ps lii 9, *lō' yāśīm '*^{e}*lōhīm mā'ūzzō,* "who would not consider God his refuge," casts doubt upon the accuracy of traditional "They do not set God before them" (RSV). Hence I tentatively propose (also in Ps lxxxvi 14) the vocalization *lin*^{e}*gīdī-m,* with enclitic *mem.* The divine epithet *nāgīd* may well be present in two other psalms: xvi 8, *šiwwītī yhwh lin*^{e}*gīdī* (MT *l*^{e}*negdī*) *tāmīd,* "I have chosen Yahweh as my perpetual Leader," a version that seems preferable to that of *Psalms I,* p. 86; since biblical writers call God their *melek,* "king," or *šōpēṭ*, "ruler," the title *nāgīd* seems eminently appropriate, especially in view of vs. 8, *n^edābāh,* discussed below. Ps xxii 26, "One hundred times will I repeat to you my song of praise/in the great congregation/I will fulfill my vows, O Prince" (reading *nāgīd* for MT *neged*). See *Psalms III*, third NOTE on Ps cix 14.

6. *Hinnēh,* "Look! Behold!", introduces the second strophe, which describes God's response to the psalmist's plea.

the true Sustainer of my life. The grammatical analysis of the expression *b^esōm^ekē napšī* has been a matter of spirited controversy. Arguing from the Phoenician phrase in Kilamuwa 13–14, *wmy bbny 'š,* "And whoever (is *the* son) among my sons who . . . ," Gevirtz in VT 11 (1961), 141, n. 3, argues that the bibilical phrase should be rendered, "The Lord is (*the* supporter) among the supporters of me (my soul/life)."

Given the relative frequency of the emphatic *b* in the Psalter (*Psalms I*, p. 177), one might also identify this particle in *b^esōm^ekē* with the plural form of the participle understood as the plural of majesty since its subject is "the Lord." Cf. the discussion of synonymous *haššōlēk* in Ps lv 23.

7. *He made . . . recoil.* Vocalizing with the Qere *yāšīb* and parsing it as a past narrative form balancing the preterit verb *hiṣmītām;* see *Psalms I*, p. 56, and NOTE on Ps lv 13. In Ugaritic poetry by far the commonest way of expressing past time is by *yqtl,* i.e., *yāšīb* in present instance; cf. UT, § 13.32. For the thought, Ps vii 17.

my defamers. The king was the preferred target of the verbal shafts of his foreign (and also domestic) enemies; consult *Psalms I*, p. 117, for the exegesis of royal Pss xviii 44 and lxxxix 51.

A re-examination of its five occurrences (Pss v 9, xxvii 11, liv 7, lvi 3, lix 11) discloses that *šōrēr,* generally translated "enemy" (RSV), more specifically denotes "defamer, slanderer." GB, p. 817a, is content to define the term as *Feind,* "enemy, foe," even though it correctly refers the reader to El Amarna usage where the verb *šāru* means *verleumden,* "to slander, defame." This Canaanism, which glosses Akk. *i-ka-lu karṣiya,* "to denounce, slander," has been studied by W. F. Albright in BASOR 89 (1943), 30, n. 13, who parses *širtī* as the qal passive preterit of the root that appears in Hebrew as *šūr* "to trick, betray." He renders the sentence in which *širti* appears, "I have been slandered (treated disloyally) before the king, my lord." This too is the biblical nuance. In Ps v 9, *šōr^eray* are evidently the same persons as vs. 7, *dōb^erē kāzāb,* "those who tell lies." Accordingly read in vs. 9, "my defamers" for "my rivals" (*Psalms I*, p. 28). In Ps xxvii 11, the *šōr^erāy* find themselves in approximate company with vs. 12, *'ēdē šeqer,* "false witnesses." The Amarna nuance is manifest here. In

Pss lvi 3 and lix 11 the substantive is found in contexts lamenting sins of the tongue, that will be examined subsequently.

in his fidelity. Reading *ba'ᵃmittō* (with defective spelling of *-ō*) for MT *ba'ᵃmittᵉkā*, whose suffix *-kā* should be detached and pointed *kī*, the emphatic conjunction. Gunkel (*Die Psalmen*, p. 236) has remarked that the psalmist could properly ascribe his deliverance to God's loyalty, but hardly the annihilation of his enemies. He accordingly proposed the emendation "in your wrath," but this proves needless when the poem is understood as the supplication of a king. A special bond existed between Yahweh and his king, and in self-imposed fidelity to the king, Yahweh was obliged both to defend him and to rout his foes. This motif finds its most sustained articulation in royal Ps lxxxix. As a corollary, the retention of *'ᵉmet*, "fidelity," here safeguards the text of Ps cxliii 12, where the correlative term *ḥesed* has often been emended: *ūbᵉḥasdᵉkā taṣmīd 'ōyᵉbāy*, "And in your kindness annihilate my foes."

annihilated them. Punctuating *hiṣmītām*, third person masculine singular perfect followed by plural suffix *-ām*, in place of MT imperative *haṣmītēm*. The final position of the verb is probably due to the emphatic *kī*, which often causes postposition; see Ps xlix 16 and NOTE thereto (*Psalms I*, p. 301). For this same verb preceded by an emphatic *waw*, cf. II Sam xxii 41, *mᵉśanᵉ'ay wā'aṣmītēm*, and Ps cxviii 10, *bᵉšēm yhwh kī 'āmīlēm*, "By Yahweh's name I surely had them circumcised." In brief, the proposed vocalization of vs. 7:

yāšīb hāra' lᵉšōrᵉrāy (8 syllables+3 beats)
ba'ᵃmittō kī hiṣmītām (8 syllables+3 beats)

completely. Answers to emphatic *kī*, misconstrued by MT as the pronominal suffix *-kā*; see preceding NOTE and *Psalms I*, p. 301. For other instances of Masoretic confusion between the pronominal suffix *-kā* and emphatic *kī*, written defectively, see *Psalms I*, p. 197, and the NOTES on Pss lvi 13, lix 10, lxiii 2, lxviii 36, lxxxix 2–3, cxix 161, cxxvi 1, cxliii 9.

8. *For your nobility.* The phrase *binᵉdābāh* is a hapax legomenon that must therefore be interpreted on its own merits. Suffixless *nᵉdābāh* receives its determination from the suffixes of *lāk*, "to you," and *šimᵉkā*, "your Name," whose referent is God; hence the generosity or nobility in question is not the psalmist's as heretofore interpreted. The poetic use of the double-duty suffix (*Psalms I*, pp. 17 f.) seems the occasion of a similar misunderstanding in Ps cxix 7, *'ōdᵉkā bᵉyōšer lēbāb bᵉlomdī mišpᵉṭē ṣidqekā*, "I praise you for your upright heart as I learn your just ordinances." Since *ṣidqekā* refers to God's justice, its frequently parallel word *yōšer*, "uprightness," should also be at-

tributed to Yahweh rather than to the psalmist. Other texts ascribing *nᵉdābāh* to God include Ps li 14, "And by your generous spirit sustain me"; Deut xxiii 24, "You must observe and do that which you have vowed to Yahweh, your generous God." For the syntax of the final phrase *'ᵉlōhekā nᵉdābāh,* with a suffix intervening in a construct chain, see *Psalms I,* p. 110. The root *ndb* occurs in the Ugaritic personal names *ndbhd* and *ndbd,* both meaning, "Hadd is generous," and in *ndbdn,* "the judge is generous."

I will praise. Cf. royal Ps lxxxvi 12, "I will honor your Name, O Eternal."

your Name. Consult first NOTE on vs. 3.

truly good. kī ṭōb modifies "your Name"; cf. Ps lii 11.

9. *he rescued me.* The subject of the third person *hiṣṣīlānī* is the hypostasized, or personalized, Name of Yahweh. Thus the literary figure of inclusion begun in vs. 3a is closed here. There is no basis in the Hebrew original for the customary rendering, "For thou hast delivered me" (RSV). Such a version derives from the LXX and Syr. which were unable to account for the sudden change from the second person ("to you . . . your Name") in vs. 8 to the third person in vs. 9a. What these ancient versions and their modern followers failed to appreciate is the independent activity of the hypostasized Name of Yahweh expressed by the third person *hiṣṣīlānī,* "He rescued me." Here there is question of more than a striking example of personification for a poetic effect.

The Name is conceived as an attribute of Yahweh endowed with a personal identity. This theological development will bear on the dispute whether Wisdom in the Book of Proverbs was an hypostasis with an independent existence and activity. Consult Scott (The Anchor Bible, vol. 18), § 9, introductory NOTE to Prov viii 1–36.

my adversaries . . . my foes. Abstract *ṣārāh,* "adversity," assumes a concrete denotation by reason of its balance with plural concrete *'ōyᵉbay,* "my foes." Consult *Psalms I,* pp. 32 f., and the similar usage in UT, 'nt:IV:48, *mnm ib yp' lb'l ṣrt lrkb 'rpt,* "What foe has risen up against Baal, what adversary against the Mounter of the Clouds?" Cf. Pss cxxxviii 7 and cxliii 11, and Anderson, BP, I, pp. 411–12. The bearing of parallel words on the question of Ugaritic-Hebrew linguistic and literary relationships is discussed in the fourth NOTE on Ps lvii 8.

feasted. With the phrase *bᵉ'ōyᵉbay rā'ᵃtāh 'ēnī* may be compared the expression in the Moabite Inscription of King Mesha (ninth century B.C.), line 4, *hr'ny bkl śn'y,* "He (namely, the god Chemosh) let me gloat over all my enemies." Cf. Pss cxii 8, cxviii 7.

PSALM 55

(lv 1–24)

1 *For the director; with stringed instruments. A maskil of David.*

2 Give ear, O God, to my prayer,
and feign no ignorance of my plea.
3 Heed me and answer me, [2]*
descend at my complaint.
4 I shudder at the voice of the foe, [3]
at the stare of the wicked;
For they heap invective upon me,
and slander me to my face.
5 My heart's fluttering in my breast, [4]
and Death's terrors assail me;
6 Fear and terror assault me, [5]
and shudders overcome me.
7 "Had I but pinions like a dove, [6]
to fly away and be at rest,
8 Far away would be my flight, [7]
in the wilderness would I settle! *Selah*
9 To my haven would I hasten, [8]
out of the sweeping wind and tempest."
10 Destroy, O Lord, their forked tongue! [9]
For I see violence and strife in the city,
11 making their rounds day and night; [10]
upon its walls are both malice and mischief!
12 From its center, pernicious deeds, [11]
From its center, they never leave,
From its square, oppression and fraud!
13 It was not a rival [12]
who heaped on me the insults that I bear;

* Verse numbers in RSV.

It was not my enemy who defamed me,
that I should hide from him.
14 But you, a man of my rank, [13]
my companion and confidant:
15 We used to take sweet counsel together— [14]
in God's house—
We used to mingle among the throngs.
16 May death overcome them, [15]
may they go down to Sheol alive;
For venomous words proceed
from their throat and breast.
17 But I called to God, [16]
and Yahweh saved me.
18 Even, morn, and noon, [17]
I complained and moaned;
And the Ransomer heard my voice,
19 making payment for my life. [18]
He drew near to me
when full many were against me.
20 El heard me and answered, [19]
the Primeval One sent his reply *Selah*
because in him there is no variation.
But they did not fear God.
21 He stretched out his hands [20]
against his closest ally,
and violated his covenant.
22 Smoother than cream was his speech, [21]
but hostility was in his heart,
His words were softer than oil,
but they were sharpened swords.
23 Your Provider is the Most High Yahweh, [22]
your Benefactor who will sustain you;
Never will he allow the just man to stumble.
24 But you, O God, will make them descend [23]
to the sludgy Pit.
Let not men of idols and figurines
live out half their days.
For my part, I trust in you.

NOTES

lv. The lament of an individual who is dejected because of the open hostility of his fellow citizens, and especially because of his betrayal by a close friend.

The psalm departs from the classic patterns of individual laments with the insertion of a three-line lyric (vss. 7–9) that closely resembles Jer ix 1. This similarity alone does not, however, permit the inference drawn by R. Tournay, *Les Psaumes* (*Bible de Jérusalem* [abbr. BJ], 2d ed.; Paris, 1955), p. 227, that the psalm has been inspired by Jeremiah. In these three lines the presence of an uncommon parallelism, documented in Ugaritic, suggests the possibility, if not the probability, that both Jeremiah and the psalmist are beneficiaries of a common literary treasure. Thus we are robbed of a possible criterion for dating the lament.

Nor need we suppose with Tournay (*ibid.*) and most commentators that "le texte semble parfois altéré et en désordre" ["Now and then the text seems distorted and in disorder"]. The application to difficult passages of grammatical principles revealed or elucidated by the Northwest Semitic texts (*Psalms I*, pp. XXVII ff.), to supplement the rules listed in standard grammars of Biblical Hebrew, shows the consonantal text to be markedly sound and the verses logically arranged. What has made the logical sequence difficult to follow has been the misconstruing of the verbal tenses (e.g., vs. 17) by translators and exegetes.

Gunkel (*Die Psalmen*, p. 238) has plausibly suggested that the psalm was composed by an Israelite resident in a heathen city. The betrayer who is denounced in vss. 13–15 would thus be a fellow Jew with whom the poet had made a pilgrimage to Jerusalem. This proposal of Gunkel is corroborated by the translation proposed below for vs. 24, "men of idols and figurines," a description of pagans, and by the extrinsic consideration that several of the OT books were composed on non-Israelite soil. For example, the arguments for the composition of the Book of Ecclesiastes by a Jew living in a Phoenician city-state daily become more impressive; see the new material on this subject in Dahood, "The Phoenician Background of Qoheleth," *Biblica* 47 (1966), 264–82.

2. *Give ear . . . my prayer.* The invocation *ha'^{a}zīnāh '^{e}lōhīm t^{e}pillātī* will figure in the argument for reading in Ps cxliii 1, *ha'^{a}zīnāh 'ēl* (MT *'el*) *taḥ^{a}nūnay*, "Give ear, O El, to my plea for mercy."

feign no ignorance. Preferable to RSV "Hide not thyself." For this nuance of *'ālam*, see *Psalms I*, p. 162; Eccles iii 11, *'lm* (pointing uncertain), "ignorance" (Dahood, *Biblica* 33 [1952], 206), and Job xxii 15, *'ōraḥ 'lm,* "the path of ignorance" (Pope, *Job,* NOTE *ad loc.*). Cf. now Jer xviii 15, *šᵉbīlē 'lm,* "bypaths of ignorance/darkness."

The hithpael form *tit'allam* is employed to bring out the notion of pretending or feigning, as in *hit'aššēr,* "to feign oneself rich"; GK, § 54e. Consequently, the phrase *hit'allamtā mēhem* in Deut xxii 1, 3, 4 should be rendered "You shall not feign ignorance of them," and not "withhold your help" (RSV). For example, Deut xxii 1 should be translated, "You shall not watch your brother's ox or his sheep go astray and feign ignorance of them; you shall take them back to your brother." A recognition of this nuance elicits sense out of the puzzling command in Isa lviii 7b, *kī tir'eh 'ārōm wᵉkissītō ūmibbᵉśārᵉkā lō' tit'allām,* "When you see someone naked, clothe him; and do not feign ignorance of your flesh." Our charity, in the thought of the prophet, should be based on the consideration that our fellow man is part of our own flesh.

3. *descend.* For unexplained MT *'ārīd,* vocalizing *'ōrēd* (or possibly archaic *'ōrid*), the aphel masculine singular imperative from *yārad.* Literally *'ōrēd* means "bring yourself down," the causative form expressing an inner object. Compare Ps x 1, *ta'līm.* "(Why) do you hide yourself?" One reads a similar sentiment in UT, 2 Aqht:I:17–18, *yqrb b'l bḥnth abynt* [*d*]*nil mt rpi,* "Baal draws near because of his pleading, because of (note double-duty preposition) the wretchedness of Daniel the Raphite." In UT, Krt:77, King Kirta is commanded: *šrd b'l bdbḥk,* "With your sacrifice make Baal descend," while in Krt:35–36, *wbḥlmh il yrd,* El is said to descend while Kirta dreams.

The occurrence of aphel forms in Ugaritic alongside the normal shaphel causatives (see Dahood, UHP, pp. 24 f.) makes it highly probable that a number of misunderstood—and hence often emended—forms are aphel causatives in Hebrew. Elsewhere in the OT, the following are the more probable instances: Ps cv 22, *'sr;* Gen xli 43, *'brk;* I Sam ii 33, *'dyb;* Isa xix 6, *h'znyḥw* (read *'znyḥw;* 1QIsᵃ reads hiphil *hznyḥw*), xxviii 28, *'dwš* (1QIsᵃ *hdš*), xlvii 3, *'pg',* li 19, *'nḥmk* (1QIsᵃ *ynḥmk*), lvii 17, *hstr w'qṣp* (1QIsᵃ *'hstr w'qṣwph*); lxiii 3, *'g'lty* (1QIsᵃ *g'lty*); Jer xxv 3, *'škym* (see Hans Bauer and Pontus Leander, *Historische Grammatik der hebräischen Sprache des Alten Testaments* [Hildesheim; reprinted 1962], p. 333g); Job xiii 17, *'ḥwty;* Eccles v 16, *y'kl* (Dahood, *Biblica* 47 [1966], 272).

at my complaint. Compare UT, Krt:37–38, *wyqrb bšal krt,* "And he (namely El) drew near at the request of Kirta."

4. *at the voice.* As in vs. 13, *mimmennū,* "by him," *min* expresses agency or cause in *mīqqōl.*

the stare. Identifying the disputed hapax legomenon *'āqat* with Ugar.

'q, "eyeball," in UT, Krt:294–95, *d'qh ib iqni 'p'ph sp ṯrml*, "Whose eyeballs are the pureness of lapis, whose pupils the gleam of *ṯrml*." The Canaanite pairing with *'p'p*, "pupil" (cf. *Psalms I*, p. 70), and the biblical balance with *qōl*, "voice," permit a measure of confidence in defining *'q;* cf. Ginsberg, LKK, p. 39, and T. L. Fenton, *Ugarit-Forschungen* 1 (1969), 66–67.

they heap. For this sense of *yāmīṭū*, Ps cxl 11, *yāmīṭū* (MT *yimmiṭū*) *'ᵃlēhem geḥālīm*, "May he (*Psalms I*, pp. 61 f., on third person singular *yaqtulu*) heap hot coals upon them."

invective. This specification of generic *'āwen*, "iniquity, trouble," derives from its association with *śāṭan*, "to slander."

slander me. For a discussion of *śāṭan*, see *Psalms I*, p. 237.

to my face. Apparently in tandem with the preposition *'ālay*, "upon me," *bᵉ'ap* is preferably interpreted as a prepositional phrase sharing the suffix of *'ālay* (*Psalms I*, pp. 17 f.), rather than "in anger" (RSV). Cf. Deut xxxiii 10b, *yāśīmū qᵉṭōrāh bᵉ'appekā wᵉkālīl 'al mizbᵉḥekā*, "They shall put incense before you, and whole offerings upon your altar." The balance between *bᵉ'appekā* and *'al* is that which I propose to find in the psalm. In the "Apostrophe to Zion," a non-canonical composition from Qumran (11QPsᵃ Zion [14]/11–12) appears the verse *'rbh b'p tšbḥtk ṣywn m'lh lkwl tbl*, which the editor, J. A. Sanders, translates, "Praise from thee is pleasing to God, O Zion, ascending through all the world." This free translation should cede to a more literal and more meaningful rendition: "May your praise, O Zion, enter into his presence, exaltation from all the world." See J. A. Sanders, *The Psalms Scroll of Qumrân Cave 11 (11QPsᵃ)* (Discoveries in the Judaean Desert of Jordan, IV; Oxford, 1965), p. 87. Gordon, UT, pp. 94, n. 1, 362, No. 264, would find this sense in 55:5, *wyṣq baph*, "And pour it in front of him," but for another interpretation, cf. Dahood, UHP, p. 3.

5. *assail me*. For the military shade of meaning in *nāpᵉlū*, see *Psalms I*, p. 231, while the stylistic variation between the imperfect *yāḥīl* and perfect *nāpᵉlū* has been noted on pp. 39, 51, 56, etc. Cf. Job vi 4, "God's terrors stand arrayed against me," and xx 25, "Terrors (*'ēmīm*) shall march against him."

7. *"Had* . . . 8. *settle*. The quotation mark reproduces the verb *wā'ōmar*, normally rendered, "And I said"; cf. the second NOTE on Ps lii 2.

The similarity of vss. 7–8 to Jer ix 1 has been remarked in the introductory NOTE; and the assumed literary dependence of the psalmist upon the prophet has been questioned. The following observations suggest that both may have drawn from a common source.

be at rest . . . 8. *wilderness*. The association of *'eškᵉnāh* with *midbār* re-echoes UT, Krt:103–5, *kirby tškn šd km ḥsn pat mdbr*, "Like locusts they come to rest on the steppe, like grasshoppers on the borders of the wilderness."

I would settle. The root of *'ālīn* is found in UT, 2 Aqht:II:18–19, *grš d 'šy ln,* "One who will drive away the abusers of my night guest."

9. *I would hasten.* Parsing *'āḥīšāh* as subjunctive or volitive; *Psalms I,* pp. 240 f., and the first NOTE on Ps li 15.

to my haven. Understanding *miplāṭ* as an accusative of place with verb of motion, "hasten"; GK, § 118d–f. This specification of the sense *miplāṭ* is afforded by Ps cxliv 2 where *miplāṭī* (MT *m^epal^eṭī*) stands fourth in a series of nouns denoting fortress or refuge. Hence Ps xviii 3 should be corrected (*Psalms I,* p. 101) to read: *miplāṭī 'ēlī,* "My God is my haven."

sweeping. The hapax legomenon *sō'āh* is apparently related to Ugar. *s't* in UT, Krt:214, *s't bšdm ḥṭb,* "He swept from the fields the woodcutter," as rendered by Ginsberg, LKK, p. 19.

10. *their forked tongue.* Repointing *peleg l^ešōnām,* literally "the cleft of their tongue," for MT imperative *pallag l^ešōnām,* "Cleave their tongue," and parsing it as direct object of imperative *balla'.* With their vocalization *pallag,* the Masoretes created a rather ridiculous situation, because as far as the maligned psalmist was concerned, the tongues of his enemies were already as cleft and venomous as those of vipers. Under such conditions, the psalmist was hardly disposed to request that God divide the tongues of his detractors. In Ps iii 8 the beleaguered poet prays God to "smash the teeth" of his calumniators.

11. *making their rounds.* Literally "They go around it." The psalmist ironically describes violence and strife as the city watchmen, and malice and mischief as the sentinels on the walls.

12. *From its center . . . oppression and fraud.* The translation of vss. 11–12 owes much to D. N. Freedman, who suggested the stichometry followed here.

b^eqirbāh hawwōt (A+B)
b^eqirbāh w^elō' yāmīš (A+C)
mēr^eḥōbāh tōk ūmirmāh (Á+B́)

In the repeated expression *b^eqirbāh,* "from its center," the preposition *b^e* denotes "from," as frequently noted in *Psalms I,* p. 320. Here it is synonymous with *min* of *mēr^eḥōbāh,* "square," a parallelism noticed in *Psalms I,* p. 128. Other examples of *b//min* that might be cited include Pss vi 8, xviii 9, li 9, lix 13, lxviii 35, lxxxix 34, xciii 4, cxviii 5; Deut i 28, ix 1; Isa liii 10–11; Jer x 13; Ezek xxvi 15, xxvii 18, xxviii 18; Hos vii 16; Job vii 14, xv 30; Prov xxiv 5; Ecclus vi 11; 1QS 3:19.

pernicious deeds. For this nuance of *hawwōt,* see NOTE on Ps lii 3.

Expressing a collective idea, *hawwōt* is used with a singular verb *yāmīš*, as in Ps lvii 2.

never leave. The *waw* of *welō'* parses as emphatic and helps explain the postposition of the verb; cf. the second NOTE on Ps li 9 and Ps lxxx 19, *welō' nāsōg*, "We have never turned away."

13. *not a rival.* Here the negative particle negates a noun exactly as in UT, 'nt:IV:49–50, *lib yp' lb'l*, "No foe has risen up against Baal."

heaped on me the insults that I bear. The syntax of *yeḥārepēnī we'eśśā'* remains elusive because of its elliptical quality, but a case can be made for seeing in the first verb the implicit noun, namely, "insults," that forms the object of *'eśśā'*. Syntactically, *we* of *we'eśśā'* serves as a relative pronoun; see *Psalms I*, p. 18.

There is no need to alter the imperfect form *yeḥārepēnī* to the perfect, as advised by BH³, since in poetry this is a normal form for expressing the past; cf. *Psalms I*, p. 56, NOTE on Ps liv 7, and below on vs. 20.

who defamed me. Psalms I, p. 73, examines the idiom *'ālay higdīl*. The parallelism between *ḥērēp*, "taunt," and *'alay higdīl* appears to elucidate Zeph ii 8b, *ḥērepū 'et 'ammī wayyagdīlū 'al gebūlī-m* (first person singular suffix followed by enclitic *mem* for MT *gebūlām*), "They taunted my people and slandered my territory"; Zeph ii 10, *kī ḥērepū wayyagdīlū 'al 'am yhwh ṣebā'ōt*, "Because they taunted and slandered the people of Yahweh of Hosts." In this latter text, the close association with *ḥērepū* reveals the synonymy of *wayyagdīlū 'al*.

14. For the sudden change from the third to the second person, in talking about one's "enemy" here, also sometimes encountered in Northwest Semitic curses, consult *Psalms I*, pp. 34 f., 134.

15. *in God's house.* The phrase *bebēt 'elōhīm* is suspended between *namtīq sōd* and *nehallēk berāgeš*, being parallel to neither and yet belonging to both cola. This curious structure will be taken up again at Ps lvii 5.

the throngs. Psalms I, p. 7, cites the evidence for this definition of *rāgeš*.

16. *overcome them.* Dividing MT *yaššimāwet* into two words, *yēšēy* plus *māwet*, "death," and parsing *yēšēy* (vocalization tentative) as the jussive form of the verb **wašaya* (= Heb. *wāšāh*) that underlies Ugar. *tšyt*, Heb. *tūšiyyāh*, "victory, success." For a recent discussion of this word, see Pope, *Job*, NOTE on xii 16a.

go down to Sheol alive. Comparing Ps lii 7, "and snatch your sons alive from the earth!"

The sudden shift from the singular subject in vss. 13–15 to the plural in vs. 16 is a characteristic of imprecations that is commented upon, with a listing of texts, in *Psalms I*, pp. 34 f., 134.

venomous words. Just as the adjective or passive participle *petīḥōt* in vs. 22 connotes "drawn swords," so here the feminine plural adjective *rā'ōt* seems to connote "venomous words." This nuance of *ra'* can be felt in Ps lxiv 6; Ezek v 16 (compare Deut xxxii 24).

from their throat. Understanding *b^{e}* as "from" (first NOTE on vs. 12), and relating *māgūr/māgor* to the root *gwr* preserved in *gāron*, "throat," and *gargeret*, "throat, neck." In other terms, the phrase *bim^{e}gūrām b^{e}qirbām* collocates the same roots and ideas that appear in parallelism in Ps v 10, *qirbō-m . . . g^{e}rōnām*.

17. *I called. 'eqrā'* expresses past action; see second NOTE on vs. 13.

God . . . Yahweh. For the sequence *'^{e}lōhīm // yhwh*, cf. Ps xlvii 6 (*Psalms I*, p. 283); Pss lvi 11, lxviii 27, etc.

saved me. Balancing *'eqrā'*, "I called," *yōšī'ēnī* also expresses past time.

18. *And . . . heard.* MT *wayyišma'*, with consecutive *waw*, confirms the analysis of the preceding *yqtl* forms as referring to past action.

the Ransomer. Since the metrical pattern 3+2 recurs in vss. 17, 18a, 19b, 20a, 20b, 21, 22a, 22b, it seems that 18b–19a (our verse) should also read 3+2: *wayyišma' qōlī* (19) *pōdeh* (*MT pādāh*) // *b^{e}šālōm napšī-m* (with enclitic *mem*).

Participial *pōdeh* describes divine activity in Ps xxxiv 23, *pōdeh yhwh nepeš '^{a}bādāyw*, "Yahweh ransoms the life of his servants," and Deut xiii 6, *happōd^{e}kā*, "who ransomed you." Here *pōdeh* is a divine appellative, another addition to this impressive list of divine epithets disclosed in the Psalter; cf. *Psalms I*, p. 325, and below, NOTE on vs. 23.

19. *making payment.* Vocalizing piel infinitive construct *b^{e}šallēm* instead of MT *b^{e}šālōm;* the version given in *Psalms I*, p. 177, stands in need of correction. To judge from the related context of Ps xxxiv 23 (*Psalms I*, p. 207), God made payment to Death to save the life of the psalmist.

for my life. napšī-m is the objective genitive after construct *šallēm*. Reading *napšī-m* whose enclitic *mem* has been detached from *mqrb* to permit a grammatical analysis of the latter; cf. *Psalms I*, p. 327. Numerous new examples of enclitic *mem* attached to a pronominal suffix, as in Ugaritic (cf. Horace D. Hummel in JBL 76 [1957], 91), have materialized in recent years and have been confirmed as such in several texts of Isaiah, where the offending *mem* was expelled by the scribes of Qumran, who did not understand the presence of this intruder; e.g., Isa xl 17, *negdō-m 'epes* appears in 1QIs^{a} as *ngdw wk'ps*, and lxiii 3, *'ammī-m*, "my people," is read *'my* by 1QIs^{a}. Cf. further Jer xiii 20, *ś^{e}'ī 'ēnayik-m ūr^{e}'ī*, "Lift up your eyes and see," where singular *ś^{e}'ī* and *r^{e}'ī* prove that the Masoretes did not understand this enclitic; see *Psalms I*, pp. XXII f. Had they grasped its nature, they would not have pointed *'ēnēkem* with the second person plural suffix.

A similar blunder can be seen in Jer xlviii 12 *niblēhem,* which is grammatically anomalous; read *niblēhū-m,* "his vessels."

He drew near. Reading *qārab* (MT *miqq*ᵃ*rab,* see foregoing NOTE) and comparing Ps lxix 19, "Draw near, O El." It will be noticed that *'ēl* occurs in the next verse. This phrase harks back to vs. 3 where the psalmist beseeches God to descend at his prayer.

full many. Breaking down *b*ᵉ*rabbīm* into the *beth emphaticum* and *rabbīm,* discussed in *Psalms I,* p. 177. Compare Ps lvi 3, "How many (*rabbīm*) are battling against me!" and Anderson, BP, I, p. 417.

20. *El heard me.* The verb *yišma'* borrows its suffix object from the suffix of immediately preceding *'immādī,* "against me." Thus far, seven examples of the verb *šāma'* without its own suffix have been identified. To those listed in *Psalms I,* p. 24, might be added Ps lix 8. See also C. H. W. Brekelmans, *Jaarbericht . . . Ex Oriente Lux* 17 (1963), 205, n. 2, and GK, § 117f, who observes that after *šāma'* the suffix is often omitted.

and answered. Vocalizing *wayya'an-m,* with enclitic *mem* (see second NOTE on vs. 19), for MT *w*ᵉ*ya'*ᵃ*nēm,* "and answered them."

the Primeval One. qedem is the second part of the divine composite name semantically equal to Deut xxxiii 27, *'*ᵉ*lōhē qedem,* "the Primeval God." The relationship between these two divine titles is analogous to that between *'ōlām,* "the Eternal One," and Isa xl 28, *'*ᵉ*lōhē 'ōlām,* "the Eternal God." This abbreviated title recurs almost certainly in Prov viii 22, *yhwh qānānī rē'šīt d*ᵉ*rākō* (MT *darkō*) *qedem mip'ālāyw,* "Yahweh created me in the beginning, the Primeval One directed (with *dativus commodi*) his works." Cf. CBQ 30 (1968), 513. This separation of the composite divine title *'ēl qedem,* with one component in each of the parallel cola, exemplifies the poetic practice noticed in *Psalms I,* pp. 104 f., 242, 280, etc.; see below, NOTE on Ps lxii 11–12.

in him. Understanding *lāmō* as referring to God, not to the foes of the psalmist as traditionally interpreted. Though *lāmō* does mean "for, in them," in some texts, there are also clear passages where it denotes "for, in him," e.g. Gen ix 26; Isa xliv 15, liii 8. Perhaps consonantal *lmw* should be vocalized *lammū,* from *lamhū;* cf. *Psalms I,* p. 285, NOTE on Ps xlvii 5, *lannū,* "for himself." Hebrew grammars and lexicons recognize that *lmw* is an alternate form of *lō* in Gen ix 26 f.; Isa xliv 15, liii 8. Besides the present verse, I would add to this list Pss lxiv 6, lxvi 7, cxxix 3 (translated in *Psalms I,* p. XLII).

there is no variation. Unlike the Canaanite deities, the Primeval One of Israel is not a capricious God. Yesterday, today, and the same forever. Cognizant of God's immutable attributes, the Hebrew poet was confident that Yahweh would answer a legitimate request. For statements on God's immutability, Ps cii 27–28, *kal*ᵉ*būš taḥlīpēm wĕyaḥlōpū w*ᵉ*'attāh hū',* "You change them like a garment, and they pass away;

but you remain the same," and James i 17, "With him there is no variation, no play of passing shadows." In fact, the first part of this sentence appears in C. D. Ginsburg's Hebrew New Testament (Trinitarian Bible Society Edition; London, 1944) as, *'ᵃšer 'ēn ḥᵃlīpōt lō*. Given that *lō* and *lmw* can both refer to the third person singular, one would be justified in using the psalm reading as it stands to translate the Greek of the Epistle of James.

But they. Namely, the "full many" of vs. 19 as well as the treacherous friend mentioned in the next verse.

21. *his closest ally.* Namely, the psalmist. The plural form *šᵉlūmāyw* (cf. *Psalms I*, pp. 42–43, for this vocalization) may be a plural of intensity, like plural *'ōyᵉbay*, "my archfoe," in Ps xviii 4, 49. D. N. Freedman suggests the possibility that *bšlmyw* may parse as the genitive case followed by the singular suffix: *īhū*>*īw*.

22. *Smoother.* Deriving from the root *ḥlq*, "to be smooth," is the substantive in Ps xvi 5, *ḥelqī*, "my smooth wine."

than cream. Reading *mēḥem'ōt* for MT *maḥmā'ōt*, and explaining *ḥem'ōt* as the Phoenician form of Jerusalem dialect *ḥem'āh*, "butter, cream." In Ugaritic the substantive is *ḫmat // ḥlb*, "milk." The anomalous MT reading is probably to be traced to the Masoretic unfamiliarity with Phoenician feminine singular substantives that terminate in *-ōt*, even in the absolute state. Other examples of such forms are given in the second NOTE on Ps liii 7. That consonantal *ḥm't* contains the word denoting "cream" is clear from its balance with *miššemen*, "than oil," a parallelism that recurs in Job xxix 6, *birḥōṣ hᵃlīkay bēḥēmāh wᵉṣōrī ṣōq* (MT *wᵉṣūr yāṣūq*) *'ᵃmūday* (MT *'immādī*) *palgē šāmen*, "When my feet were bathed with cream and balsam, when rivers of oil flowed over my legs." For further details on Joban verse, see Dahood, UHP, p. 60.

but hostility was in his heart. Though MT *ūqᵃrāb libbō*, "but his intention was war," is passable, *ūqᵉrī bᵉlibbō* furnishes a more elegant reading while entailing no consonantal changes. The present MT lection apparently stems from a consonantal text employing no vowel letters. The noun *qᵉrī*, "hostility," is well attested in Hebrew and the verb *qry*, "to oppose, encounter hostilely," appears four times in Ugaritic.

sharpened swords. Ps lix 8 depicts slanderers emitting daggers from their lips, while iii 7 describes detractors as archers deployed about their victim. Hence it seems necessary to derive *pᵉtīḥōt*, usually rendered "drawn swords," from *ptḥ* II, "to incise, engrave," hence "to sharpen."

23. *Your Provider.* The translation of this line—*toto caelo* different from traditional, "Cast your burden on the Lord, and he will sustain you" (RSV)—strikingly illustrates the results produced by the application of Northwest Semitic methods and texts to biblical poetry. Cf.

vs. 18, *pōdeh,* "the Ransomer," and the two other new divine titles in vs. 23.

The root sense of *šlk* is quickly and firmly established. Its association with *y*ᵉ*kalk*ᵉ*lekā,* "He will sustain me," is the first clue. The second is afforded by Ps lxxi 6, *'ālekā nismaktī mibbeṭen,* "By you have I been supported from the womb," and Ps xxii 11, *'ālekā hošlaktī mērāḥem* "By you have I been nourished from birth." What scholars, including the writer (see *Psalms I,* p. 136), have failed to recognize is that *hošlaktī* is a synonym of *nismaktī,* whose sense is undoubted. The parallelism in the present verse with *y*ᵉ*kalkēl,* whose meaning is also established, settles the signification of *šlk* II, to be distinguished from *šlk* I, "to cast." The root *šlk* II, "to nourish, provide," happily supplies the lacking etymology for Phoenician *šlk,* frequent in personal names such as *b'lšlk, šmššlk, 'šmnšlk, šlkb'l;* see Z. S. Harris, *A Grammar of the Phoenician Language* (New Haven, 1936), p. 150.

Because of its syntactic balance with the suffix of *yōhēb*ᵉ*kā,* "your Benefactor," the article of *haššōlēk* functions as a suffix, hence "Your Provider." Consult *Psalms I,* p. 203; Ps iii 9, *hay*ᵉ*šū'āh,* "your salvation," parallel to *birkāteka,* "your blessing," and Eccles vii 1, *hammāwet // hiwwāl*ᵉ*dō.* Cf. likewise the first NOTE on Ps liii 4.

Most High Yahweh. Identifying *'al yhwh* as the composite divine title studied in *Psalms I,* p. 117. Cf. also Ps cxli 3, *šītāh yhwh šomrāh l*ᵉ*pī niṣṣ*ᵉ*rāh 'al dal ś*ᵉ*pātāy,* "Put, O Yahweh, a muzzle on my mouth; guard, O Most High, the door of my lips." This analysis of divine names brings to light the poetic sequence A+B+C // Á+B́+Ć. Other examples of *'al,* "Most High," will be noted at Pss lxii 8, lxviii 30, 35, cxxxix 14, cxlvi 5.

The appositeness of calling *'al* the Provider lies in the fact that he is closely associated with rain in I Sam ii 10, an association probably received from the Canaanites who relate *'ly* (a by-form of *'l*) to rainfall in UT, 126:III:7–8, *n'm larṣ mṭr b'*[*l*] *wlšd mṭr 'ly,* "Sweet to the earth was the rain of Baal, and to the field the rain of the Most High."

your Benefactor. MT *y*ᵉ*hāb*ᵉ*kā,* emended by RSV, "your burden," but with the note, "Or *what he has given you,"* is a substantive that is hapax legomenon, which should be repointed as the qal participle *yōhēb,* followed by the pronominal suffix. Verb forms of *yāhab* are well attested from Genesis on, and are found in the Psalter. Thus in *yōhēb* we have a synonym of Ps xviii 33, *yōtēn,* "the Bestower," a divine title commented upon in *Psalms I,* p. 114.

to stumble. mōṭ has a gravid sense, connoting stumbling into the nether world; consult *Psalms I,* pp. 78 f. The lot of the just contrasts with that of the wicked, said in the following verse to be destined for the Pit. In vss. 18–19 the psalmist implies that Yahweh paid ransom money to save the life of his servant; hence the psalmist speaks from experience when insisting that God will never permit the just to perish.

24. *will make them descend.* The psalmist enunciates his belief in divine retribution in the nether world; cf. Dahood, PNWSP, pp. 25 f.

Structurally, hiphil *tōrīdēm,* occurring in the final verse of the lament, forms an inclusion (*Psalms I,* p. 327) or "envelope figure" with vs. 3 aphel *'ōrēd,* "descend." The benign effects of God's descent from heaven during the psalmist's prayer contrast with the malefic state of the wicked when they must descend from earth into Sheol.

sludgy Pit. The apparently tautological expression *b^{e}'ēr šaḥat* (RSV, "the lowest pit"; BJ, *les puits du gouffre*) yields a pellucid image when *šaḥat* is dissociated from the homonym meaning "pit"—*b^{e}'ēr* adequately expresses that concept and is used of Sheol in Ps lxix 16—and identified with the vocable *šaḥat,* "filth, sludge." Hence *b^{e}'ēr šaḥat* literally reads "the pit of sludge." Such a version perfectly accords with the frequently recurring motif that Sheol is a slimy place (*Psalms I,* pp. 34, 43, 140, 184, 278 f.), and enjoys good analogues in Ugaritic poetry where Death's city is termed *hmry,* "miry or slushy," and his realm called *ḫḫ arṣ,* "infernal filth" (UT, 51:VIII:11–13). For a fully documented study of *šaḥat,* "filth," in Job ix 31, see Marvin H. Pope, "The Word *šaḥat* in Job 9:31," in JBL 83 (1964), 269–78, and J. van der Ploeg, *De Psalmen* (Roermond, 1963), p. 128, who renders our phrase "the pit of dissolution."

men of idols and figurines. The arguments for this rendition of *'anšē dāmīm ūmirmāh,* customarily translated "bloody and deceitful men" (KJ), are given in *Psalms I,* pp. 31 f. The poet equates his detractors with polytheists, but he may have meant this phrase in a literal sense since this psalm gives indications of having been composed on heathen soil, as suggested by Gunkel, *Die Psalmen,* p. 238. See introductory NOTE.

live out half their days. In addition to punishment in the future life, the psalmist asks for a retribution of the wicked during their earthly days.

The more common derivation of the verb *yeḥ^{e}ṣū* from the fraction *ḥ^{a}ṣī,* "half," Ugar. *ḫṣt,* is sustained by the Canaanite penchant, so amply demonstrated in the Ugaritic texts (UT, § 7.73), for coining verbs from numerals. Consult *Psalms I,* pp. XLI, 142. Koehler's unfortunate and unwarranted emendation of *yeḥ^{e}ṣū* to *yāqēṣṣū* (KB, p. 324a) will hopefully not be included in the third edition of the *Lexicon,* now in preparation.

PSALM 56

(lvi 1–14)

1 *For the director; according to "The Dove of the Distant Gods."*
A miktam of David, when the Philistines seized him in Gath.

2 Have pity on me, God!
How men hound me!
All day long they harass me
with both jaws.
3 My defamers hound me [2]*
all day long.
How many are battling against me!
4 Exalted One, when I have fears, [3]
I put my trust in you.
5 Of God do I boast, O slanderer. [4]
In God I put my trust,
I fear not,
What can flesh do to me?
6 All day long my slanderers vex me, [5]
against me are all their plans.
7 Evilly they conspire, conceal themselves, [6]
see how my maligners watch!
Lurking like a footpad for my life.
8 From their malice deliver us, [7]
in your anger subject the peoples, O God!
9 Write down my lament yourself, [8]
list my tears on your parchment,
my hardships on your scroll.
10 If my foes draw back, [9]
recoiling when I cry out,
Then will I know
that God is for me.

* Verse numbers in RSV.

11 Of God do I boast, O slanderer, [10]
Of Yahweh do I boast, O slanderer!
12 In God I put my trust, [11]
I fear not,
What can man do to me?
13 Indeed will I, God Most High, [12]
pay my vows with praises to you.
14 Would that you rescue me from Death, [13]
keeping my feet distant from Banishment,
That I might walk before God
in the field of life.

Notes

lvi. The lament of a king who prays for deliverance from slanderers. Throughout the mental sufferings brought on by malicious tongues, the king's trust in God remains unshaken. This refrain recurs in vss. 4–5 and 11–12. Nonetheless, in vs. 10 he makes it clear that he would like to see this trust confirmed by a positive response from God.

Though most modern commentators classify the psalm as the lament of an individual, there is no agreement concerning the status of this individual. Several hitherto unrecognized similarities between phrases in vss. 2, 3, 7, 8 and other royal psalms corroborate the view of those identifying the suppliant as a king. Thus the psalm is pre-Exilic, though nothing more specific regarding the date can be inferred from its contents and language. The language is admittedly difficult, but this fact in itself does not warrant the generous emendations to which the text has been subjected.

1. *The Dove of the Distant Gods* (pointing *'ēlīm*, "gods," for MT *'ēlem*, "muteness"). A doubtful translation of what seems to be the title of a song to which the music of this psalm was set. The "Dove" may be a reference to Yahweh, who in Ps lxviii 14; Jer xxv 38, xlvi 16, l 16 is called *yōnāh*, "Dove."

miktam. The definition "an inscription on a stone slab" (*Psalms I*, p. 87) is now supported by Jer ii 22, *niktām 'ᵃwōnēk lᵉpānay*, "(Though you scrub yourself with lye / And use as much soap as you wish,) your guilt remains inscribed before me." MT hapax legomenon *niktām*, usually rendered "the stain (of your guilt)," is preferably read as niphal perfect *niktam*, from **kātam*, "to inscribe." This translation accords with the well-documented motif of the divine bookkeeper in Pss xxxii 2, li 3, lxix 28–29, lxxix 8, lxxxvii 6, cxxx 3, cxxxix 16, in vs. 9 of the present psalm, and Exod xxxii 32–33.

when the Philistines seized him in Gath. Cf. I Sam xxvii.

2. *Have pity on me, God! ḥonnēnī 'ᵉlōhīm* forms an independent unit distinct from the following 3+3 cola.

How. Explaining *kī* as an interjection (as in vs. 3) rather than as the conjunction "for, because," which is how the versions interpret it.

men. Singular *'ᵉnōš* has a collective meaning. In vs. 4 the poet employs the synonym *bāśār,* "flesh," and in vs. 12 the synonym *'ādām,* "men."

hound me. Though many critics have related *šᵉ'āpanī* to *šā'ap* II, "to crush, trample upon," a derivation from *šā'ap* I, "to pant after," better comports with the activity of slanderers that is described in vs. 7.

All day long . . . 3a *all day long.* The psalmist achieves structural interlocking of vss. 2b and 3a not only by using the inclusion "All day long . . . all day long," but also by pairing *lᵉḥēm,* "with both jaws," and *šōrᵉray,* "my defamers," and by balancing the *yqtl* verb *yilḥāṣēnī,* "harass me," with *qtl šā'ᵃpū,* "hound me," that shares the suffix of its counterpart.

harass me. Cf. preceding NOTE as well as Ps lv 13 where *yqtl* and *qtl* verb forms are in tandem.

with both jaws. Instead of MT *lōḥēm,* reading *leḥēm,* a contracted Northern dual form of *lᵉḥī,* "jaw, cheek." On Northern duals, see *Psalms I,* pp. XXXVIII, 70, 88, 95, 279. Grammatically, *leḥēm* is an accusative of means, while its position before its verb is a stylistic trait of the psalmists noticed in *Psalms I,* pp. 35 f., 97, 115 f., 211, 309. Its appositeness in this genre of psalm is indicated by its presence in singular form in Ps iii 8, also a royal lament against personal slanderers. Thus the frequent emendation of consonantal *lḥm* to *lāḥōṣ,* "to oppress," may prove groundless. To be sure, one meets *lōḥᵃmīm,* "those battling," in vs. 3b, but there may be an intended play on words, just as vs. 7, *'ōqᵉbay,* "my maligners," is meant to evoke the "heels" of the psalmist who is dogged by his enemies.

3. *My defamers.* Consult NOTE on Ps liv 7. Gunkel (*Die Psalmen,* p. 243) rightly observes that *šōrᵉrīm* really means *Verleumder,* "slanderers, defamers," but inexplicably opts for *Feinde,* "enemies," in his translation.

How many. Explaining *kī* (also in vs. 2) as the exclamatory and interrogative particle—occurring in the Ugaritic, El Amarna, and Mari texts—that has been studied by W. F. Albright, "The Refrain 'And God saw *kī ṭōb*' in Genesis," in *Mélanges bibliques rédigés en l'honneur de André Robert* (Paris, 1957), pp. 22–26. On Jer xxii 22, *kī* (usually deleted by critics) *'āz tēbōšī,* "Ah, but then you'll be shamed," see Bright (The Anchor Bible, vol. 21), § 18. The phrase *kī rabbīm* is thus synonymous with *mah rabbū* in Ps iii 2, which the present writer now sees to be a royal lament as proposed by A. Bentzen, *Messias, Moses redivivus, Menschensohn* (Zürich, 1948), p. 20.

are battling. Consult the seventh NOTE on vs. 2 for the probable wordplay involving *lōḥᵃmīm*, "those battling," and *lᵉḥēm*, "jaws."

4. *Exalted One*. Transposing *mārōm* from the end of vs. 3 to the beginning of vs. 4. As a result, vs. 3 divides into two cola 3+3, and so does vs. 4 once *mārōm* is joined to it. The divine appellative *mārōm* is examined in *Psalms I*, pp. 44 f. Unable to account for *mārōm*, which he finds "*unverständlich*" ["unintelligible"], Kraus, *Psalmen*, I, p. 407, chastises its recalcitrancy by declaring it counterfeit. Compare the lament Ps xli 8 (*Psalms I*, p. 251) where *'ēlī*, "Most High," is invoked by the psalmist to protect him against his foes.

when I have fears. Often subjected to emendation, *yōm 'īrā'* proves its integrity when, with *mārōm*, it forms a three-beat colon perfectly balancing *'ᵃnī 'ēlekā 'ebṭāḥ*.

5. *Of God do I boast*. The apparent identity of this phrase with Ps xliv 9, *bē'lōhīm hillalnū* indicates that traditional "In God I will praise his word" has missed the sense of this affirmation. What is more, *bē'lōhīm 'ᵃhāllēl* appears to be synonymous with *be'lōhīm bāṭaḥtī*, "In God I put my trust."

O slanderer. Reading *dōbᵉrō* for MT *dᵉbārō*, and parsing the suffix as a stylistic surrogate for the article functioning as the vocative particle. For the article as vocative, cf. GK, § 126e, and for the suffix as a substitute for the article, see the first NOTE on Ps liii 4 and *Psalms I*, pp. 98, 191, 298. The nuance "to gossip, slander" of *dibbēr* has been noted in *Psalms I*, p. 251; to the texts cited there might be added Pss l 20, cxvi 10, cxix 23, cxx 7; Isa lviii 13.

I fear not. The last three cola of vs. 5 syllabically number 6+3+6; this suggests that the middle phrase *lō' 'īrā'*, "I fear not," belongs to both cola, this being the arrangement cited at Ps lv 15 and discussed in the first NOTE on Ps lvii 5.

6. *my slanderers*. Reading *dōbᵉray* for MT *dᵉbāray;* see vs. 5.

vex me. The accusative suffix of *yᵉ'aṣṣᵉbū* is supplied from the preceding word on the principle of the double-duty suffix.

7. *they conspire*. Lexicographers are at variance in defining and deriving *yāgūrū*, but the pairing here with *yaṣpīnū*, "conceal themselves," with *'ārᵉbū*, "They lie in wait," in Ps lix 4, and with *ḥāšᵉbū*, "They plan," in Ps cxl 3 suggests "to conspire, plot" as its meaning. Jerome's *Juxta Hebraeos, congregabuntur*, "They will gather," points in the same direction. A derivation from *gwr*, the root found in *gārōn*, *gargeret*, and *māgōr* (see NOTE on Ps lv 16), "throat, gullet," is semantically feasible. Compare "ruminate" from Latin *rumen*, "throat, gullet."

conceal themselves. Vocalizing consonantal *yṣpynw* as *yaṣpīnū*, the internal hiphil (GK, § 53d) form of *ṣāpan*, "to hide, conceal." The most relevant analogue is Job xviii 3, *niṭmīnū beʻēnekā-m* (MT *beʻēnēkem*), "(Why) must we hide ourselves from your sight?" (Cf. Job xxix 8, "The young men saw me and hid.")

see. Identifying *hemmāh* with Ugar. *hmt,* "Look, behold!," discussed in *Psalms I,* p. 56. Gunkel's emendation of *hemmāh* to *hinnēh* on the basis of Ps lix 4 (*Die Psalmen,* p. 244) confirms the proposed identification and at the same time points up the futility of the textual emendation. Anderson, BP, I, p. 422, also prefers "Look, behold!"

my maligners. In vs. 3 they are termed "my defamers," and in vs. 6, "my slanderers." Within such a context, *ʻaqēbay* can scarcely mean "my heels"—the phrase *ʻaqēbay yišmōrū* does not occur elsewhere—but must have the denominative sense "to malign, slander," examined in *Psalms I,* pp. 251 f. Hence vocalize *ʻōqebay.*

like a footpad. Pointing *keʼōšēr* (MT *kaʼašer*), the qal participle of *ʼāšar,* "to proceed, march." While piel *ʼiššēr* is the more common conjugation, qal *ʼāšar* is attested in Phoenicianizing Prov ix 6. The verbal form is probably denominative from *ʼašūr,* "foot, leg" (*Psalms I,* p. 95). To be sure, piel forms of denominative verbs from names of parts of the body are more frequent, but there are some clear examples of the qal conjugation in the Ugaritic participle *ṭkmt,* "who shoulders," in *rāgal,* "to foot it," *pāʻam,* "to thrust," *kāraʻ,* "to bow down," from *keraʻ,* "knee," and Deut xxxiii 2, *ʼōšedōt,* "those striding," from Ugar. *išd,* Heb. *ʼešed,* "leg, foundation," as proposed by Dahood, UHP, pp. 52 f.

One need not search long to find comparable similes. Prov vi 11 and xxiv 34, "And poverty will come upon thee like a vagabond (*mithallēk*), and want like a beggar" (see W. F. Albright, VTS 3 [1955], 9 f.), and Prov xxiii 28, "For she lies in wait like a robber, and snatches cloaks from men" (cf. Dahood, *Biblica* 42 [1961], 363).

8. *From their malice.* In their present collocation, the four seemingly simple words *ʻal ʼāwen palleṭ lāmō* create a host of difficulties that the proposed version does not claim to surmount. Since a normal usage is *pālaṭ min,* "to deliver from," *ʻal* may be assumed to denote "from," a meaning studied in *Psalms I,* p. 26.

deliver us. Apparently parallel to imperative *hōrēd,* whose subject is God, *palleṭ* may also be parsed as an imperative (piel) addressed to the deity.

Finally, *lāmō,* "us," becomes less troublesome when understood as containing the suffix of the first person plural, as proposed in *Psalms I,* p. 173. The construction *pālaṭ le* may be compared with, say, Ps cxvi 6, *welī yehōšīaʻ,* "He saved me."

To whom does "us" refer? Probably to the king and his people; see Pss iii 9, xxviii 8–9.

in your anger. KJ renders *b*[a]*'ap,* "in *thine* anger," but *thine* need not be in italics since in Canaanite and Hebrew poetry no suffix is required with names of parts of the body (*'ap* literally means "nostril, nose, face"); consult *Psalms I,* pp. 89, 95, 184, 271, 284. Cf. Lam ii 3, *gāda' bāḥ°rī 'ap kōl qeren yiśrā'ēl,* "He has cut down in his fierce anger all the might of Israel," and Job xl 24, *b*[e]*mōq*[e]*šīm yinqob 'āp,* "Can he pierce his nose with barbs?" Other examples of suffixless *'ap,* "his anger," appear in Lam iii 43 and Pss lxxvii 10, lxxxix 44. By the same token, there is no need to emend *raglayim,* "his feet," to *raglāyw* in Prov xxvi 6, as proposed by Scott (The Anchor Bible, vol. 18), § 30, textual note[a].

subject. In his philological commentary on Phoenician Karatepe I: 19–20, *w'nk 'ztwd 'ntnm yrdm 'nk,* "But I, Azitawaddu, subdued them, I subjected them," M. Dunand in *Bulletin du Musée de Beyrouth* 8 (1946–48), 27, correctly cited the sense of *hōrēd,* "subject," in our present passage to elucidate the meaning of the Phoenician causative form *yrdm.* Cf. Ps lix 12.

the peoples. The mention of *'ammīm* in this psalm becomes intelligible only if the supplicant be a king or leader of his people. Why a private person should take it upon himself to imprecate foreign nations has not been adequately explained. R. Tournay, *Les Psaumes,* p. 233, n. [h], states the problem clearly: "This reference is surprising; some omit it as an addition; others think that the author of the psalm is a Jew of the diaspora or that he suffers in Judea from the presence of foreigners. This stich of four beats could be a liturgical addition placed on the lips of David and of the community." However, within the context of a royal psalm such a reference is perfectly normal and accords with the other evidence for this classification listed in the introductory NOTE.

9. *Write down.* Following the imperatives *palleṭ,* "deliver," and *hōrēd,* "subject," and balancing the energic imperative *śīmāh,* "list," *sāpartāh,* with the full spelling (cf. *Psalms I,* p. 26) must be a precative perfect. Consult *Psalms I,* p. 20, and note the related imagery in Ezek ii 9–10, "And I looked, and lo! there was a hand stretched out to me; and lo! there was in it a scroll. And he unrolled it before me, and it was covered with writing on both sides—words of lamentation, mourning, and woe were written on it."

yourself. On the emphasizing function of the independent pronoun *'attāh,* see *Psalms I,* pp. 19 f.

my lament. Paired with *dimā'tī,* "my tears," *nōdī* is most reasonably derived from *nūd* in the sense of "to grieve, lament"; cf. the NOTE on Ps lxix 21 and Jer xxii 10 where *nūd* is synonymous with *bākāh,* "to weep." The word was doubtless chosen for the sake of the pun with *nō'd*[e]*kā,* "your parchment."

The presence of a pun in a lugubrious context accords fully with Northwest Semitic literary practice. For example, this pun issues from the dying lips of King Kirta: *al tkl bnqr 'nk my rišk udm't*, "Do not consume your eyes with flowing, the waters of your head with tears" (UT, 125:25–28). Ginsberg, LKK, p. 45, has noticed the wordplay here and in the similar context of Jer viii 23; in both passages there is a pun on the word *'ēnu/'ayin*, which means both "eye" and "fountain," while the root of Ugar. *nqr* is that of *māqōr*, "spring, fountain," in Jer viii 23. In *Rivista biblica italiana* 8 (1960), 364 f., the present writer has called attention to the paronomasia in the sorrowful context of Lam i 16, *'ēnē 'ēnay* (MT *'ēnī*) *yōr^edāh mmayim*, "The fountains of my eyes stream with water." The form *yōr^edāh* preserves the archaic feminine dual and plural ending *-āh;* cf. I Sam iv 15, *w^e'ēnāyw qāmāh*, "And his eyes were set." Consult further GK, § 145k, n. 2; UT, p. 70, n. 3; *Psalms I*, p. 98.

list. Literally "Place!," *śīmāh* more specifically denotes "to put in writing." See Job xxxviii 33; Prov viii 29, and Dahood, "The Metaphor in Job xxii 22," in *Biblica* 47 (1966), 108–9, where *qaḥ-nā' mippīū tōrāh w^eśīm 'amārāyw bil^ebābekā* is rendered, "Take instruction from his mouth, and write down his words in your heart." In Ugaritic, *št*, a synonym of *śīm*, specifically means "to write, list," in UT, 2106:3, *b spr l št*, "They were not listed on the tablet," and in 2060:34–35, *aṯr iṯ bqṯ wštn ly*, "Find out what is going on and write to me!"

your parchment. Traditional and quaint "Put thou my tears in thy bottle" (RSV) lacks both an archaeological and a philological foundation. J. L. Kelso, *The Ceramic Vocabulary of the Old Testament* (New Haven, 1948), p. 43, writes: "*Nō(')d* in Ps 56:9(8) is usually translated 'tear bottle,' but there is no archaeological evidence for the 'tear bottle' in Old Testament times. In this passage the word doubtless has one of its normal usages 'a waterskin.' "

In all its other biblical occurrences, *nō'd* refers to a container made of animal skin, but here the parallelism with *siprāh*, "a scroll," and its collocation with two verbs denoting "to write" leave but little doubt that *nō'd* means a skin for writing, namely a "parchment."

The motif of the divine bookkeeper is documented in the second NOTE on vs. 1.

my hardships. Describing *h^alō'* as erroneous punctuation for *hal'ē*, the hiphil infinitive absolute of *lā'āh*, "be weary," from which derives the substantive *t^elā'āh*, "hardship." Its suffix is supplied by that of "my tears" and "my lament"; cf. *Psalms I*, pp. 17 f.

your scroll. The genuineness of the feminine hapax legomenon *siprāh*—masculine *sēper* being the standard form—need not be questioned. In the Northwest Semitic dialects, a noun common to all or some of them might appear in masculine or feminine forms. Thus Heb.

ta'ar, "razor," appears as Ugar. *t'rt* (NOTE on Ps lii 4); Heb. *ḥermeš*, "sickle," equals Ugar. *ḫrmtt*, and Heb. *laḥaš*, "incantation," is morphologically feminine in Phoen. *lḥšt*. Unique *siprāh* is thus evidence of dialect mixing in the Psalter.

10. *If*. With this nuance of *'āz* compare Ar. *'idā*, "in that case, when," and see A. S. van der Woude in *Jaarbericht . . . Ex Oriente Lux* 18 (1964), 312–13. This sense is also found in UT, 2005:1, *id yph*, "When /if he sees"; see UT, Glossary, No. 71a, p. 351, and Charles Virolleaud, *Le palais royal d'Ugarit*, V (Mission de Ras Shamra Tome XI; Paris, 1965), p. 11.

draw back, recoiling. Dividing vs. 10a into two 3+3 cola instead of scanning it 4+2; hence read: *'āz yāšūbū 'ōyebāy//'āḥōr beyōm 'eqrā'*. As in vs. 4, *yōm 'īrā'*, the genuineness of *beyōm 'eqrā'* is vindicated against those who propose its deletion.

recoiling. Parsing *'āḥōr* as qal infinitive absolute, continuing the action of *yāšūbū*. In fact, we have here a variation on the oft-mentioned breakup of stereotyped phrases (cf. Ps lv 20) whereby the expression *šūb 'āḥōr* (cf. Ps ix 4) is split up. Though usually an adverb, *'āḥōr* can also morphologically be a qal infinitive absolute; on *hallō'*, see fifth NOTE on vs. 14 below.

Then. This signification of *zeh*, touched upon in *Psalms I*, p. 153, can now receive fuller documentation. On Gen xii 18, see Speiser, *Genesis*, § 15, NOTE *ad loc.*, and for the usage in Job xxvii 12, Pope (The Anchor BIble, vol. 15), § 26. Other examples are listed in Joüon, GHB, § 143g.

For all his protestations of trust in God, the psalmist would nonetheless welcome some concrete evidence of divine protection.

is for me. Cf. Ps xxxi 3, "Be mine, O mountain of refuge," and Hos i 9, "And I am not yours."

13. *Indeed will I*. With no consonantal changes, I would propose this reading of vs. 13: *'ēlī* (MT *'ālay*) *'elōhīm nedāray kī* (MT *nedārekā*) *'ašallēm tōdōt lekā*. The meter is 2+2+2, as in vs. 8.

The reading *kī 'ašallēm* is analyzed into emphatic *kī* and its postpositive verb, a construction examined in *Psalms I*, p. 301. Other instances of the Masoretic confusion between the pronominal suffix *kā* and the emphatic particle *kī* have been listed in the fifth NOTE on Ps liv 7. The appositeness of emphatic *kī* in a promise is self-evident; cf. Ps lxxi 23.

God Most High. *'ēlī* (MT *'ālay*) *'elōhīm* is the equivalent of Pss vii 11, lxii 8, *'al 'elōhīm* (*Psalms I*, pp. 45 f.), and Ps lvii 3, *'elōhīm 'elyōn*. This title forms an inclusion with vs. 3, *mārōm*, "Exalted One!"

pay my vows. Not least among the considerations that led to the stichometric division proposed in the first NOTE on this verse is the fact that MT *'ᵃšallēm tōdōt,* "I will render thank offerings," is a hapax legomenon, whereas *šillēm neder* is a well-attested biblical expression; e.g., Ps cxvi 14, *nᵉdāray lyhwh 'ᵃšallēm,* "I will pay my vows to Yahweh." What is more, MT *nᵉdārekā,* "your (i.e., God's) vows" creates problems that many have sought to avoid by emending to *nᵉdārīm.*

14. *Would that.* Precative *kī* is studied in *Psalms I,* p. 19.

you rescue me. Parsing *hiṣṣaltā* as precative perfect; consult *Psalms I,* p. 20. Recurring, with variations, in Ps cxvi 8–9, and having no organic relationship with the contents of the psalm, vs. 14 is best interpreted as a prayer for a direct transition from terrestrial life to life with God in Paradise. In Ps cxvi 8–9, this prayer has no direct connection with the immediate context; thus our exegesis of vs. 14 here, as an independent unity not growing out of the preceding thoughts, is warranted.

For other expressions of the belief in the direct transition from temporal to eternal life without the intervening experience of death, cf. Pss xvi 10–11, xlix 16, lxxiii 24, and *Psalms I,* pp. 91, 301.

from Death. As in Ps vi 6 (BDB, p. 560b; *Psalms I,* p. 38), *māwet* is understood as the name of a place, specifically the nether world or Sheol. This interpretation is tied up with the exegesis of the following phrase.

keeping my feet distant. Consonantal *hl' rgly* awaits a fully satisfactory explanation, but a measure of coherency is gained with the punctualization *hallō' raglay* and the parsing of *hallō'* as the piel infinitive absolute of the root preserved in Mic iv 7, *hannahᵃlā'āh,* defined by GB, p. 180a, *die weit Entfernten* ["the one far removed"]. In our passage, such a definition accords with "rescue." Cf. the use of infinitive absolute in vs. 10.

from Banishment. A poetic name for the infernal regions, from the verb *dāḥāh,* "to hurl, thrust, banish." A hapax legomenon, the substantive *deḥī* is customarily rendered as the common noun "stumbling," but the pairing with *māwet* as the name of a place indicates that *deḥī* is a place name. As has been noted in *Psalms I,* p. 224, *dāḥāh* connotes "hurling" with special reference to Sheol.

field of life. The phrase *'ūr* (MT *'ōr*) *haḥayyīm* is treated in *Psalms I,* pp. 222 f. In the doublet of this verse in Ps cxvi 9, the equivalent of *'ūr haḥayyīm* is *'arṣōt haḥayyīm,* "the lands/fields of life." Faithful to the principle discussed in the introductory NOTE to Ps liii and in the first NOTE on Ps lv 23, namely, that variants found in doublets are wont to be rather precise synonyms, we are able to establish the synonymy of *'ūr* and *'arṣōt,* a synonymy that is sustained by other texts cited in *Psalms I,* pp. 222 f.

PSALM 57

(lvii 1–12)

1 *For the director: "Destroy not!" A miktam of David, when he fled from Saul into the cave.*

2 Have pity on me, O God,
have pity on me;
For my soul takes refuge in you.
In the shadow of your wings I take refuge,
till the scourge pass by.
3 I call to God, Most High, [2]*
to the Avenger El, Most High.
4 He will send from heaven to save me [3]
from the taunts of those who hound me. *Selah*
God will send his kindness and fidelity.
5 Myself amid lions [4]
I must lie
Amid those raging for human prey.
Their teeth are spear and arrows,
their tongue a sword that is sharp.
6 Your stature is above the heavens, [5]
over all the earth your glory.
7 They spread a net for my feet, [6]
a noose for my neck;
They dug a pit for my face,
may they fall into it! *Selah*
8 Firm is my resolve, [7]
O God,
Firm is my resolve;
I will sing and chant.
9 Awake, my heart. [8]

* Verse numbers in RSV.

Awake, O harp and lyre!
that I might awake Dawn!
10 I will thank you among peoples, O Lord,
I will sing to you among nations, O truly Great One!
11 For your kindness towers to the heavens, [10]
your fidelity to the sky.
12 Your stature is above the heavens, O God, [11]
over all the earth your glory.

NOTES

lvii. The lament of a king, harassed by malicious slanderers. The royal classification has been recently contested by Kraus (*Psalmen*, I, p. 412), who argues that motifs of royal psalms were frequently taken over by private, unknown supplicants. On the level of mere phraseology this is quite possible, but Kraus fails to appreciate that the spirit of the present lament is of a piece with royal psalms liv, lvi, lviii, lix. Moreover, *'al tašḥēt*, "destroy not," in the superscription, which to Kraus remains "unexplained," is evidently connected with the prayer of Moses in Deut ix 26, so that the liturgist responsible for the psalm heading must have ascribed this lament to the king or to a religious leader of Israel.

The structure of the poem deserves brief comment. After his cry for help (vs. 2), the psalmist expresses his confidence that God will intervene on his behalf. Verse 5 describes his situation, a description resumed in vs. 7, after being interrupted by a refrain in vs. 6 that recurs in the final verse. Verses 8–11 contain the customary vow in the form of a thanksgiving hymn intended to move God to deliver the psalmist from his present distress.

1. *Destroy not!* Probably the opening words of a song to whose music the present lament was to be set. Cf. Deut ix 26, "And I (namely, Moses) prayed to Yahweh, 'O Lord God, destroy not (*'al tašḥēt*) your people and your patrimony, whom you have redeemed through your greatness, whom you have brought out of Egypt with a mighty hand."

miktam. See second NOTE on Ps lvi 1.

of David. The superscription relates the psalm to events narrated in I Sam xxii 1 ff. and xxiv 1 ff.

2. *takes refuge*. *ḥāsāyāh* for normal *ḥās*^{e}*tāh* (GK, § 75u) preserves the third original consonant *yod*, as in Ugar. *mĝyt*, "She arrived," and ancient Phoenician of Byblos (tenth century B.C.) *'ly*, "He went up" (Heb. *'ālāh*). See the third NOTE on Ps xci 9.

shadow of your wings. For this imagery, *Psalms I,* pp. 107 f. and Ps xci 4, where the context is similar to ours.

the scourge. Kindred nuances of *hawwōt* are discussed in NOTES to Pss lii 4 and lv 12. BJ renders *le fléau,* "scourge, calamity."

pass by. As in Ps lv 12, formally plural *hawwōt* is construed with a singular verb.

3. *Avenger El.* On the divine name *gōmēr 'ēl,* consult Dahood, "The Root GMR in the Psalms," in TS 14 (1953), 595–97, and *Psalms I,* p. 45. Anderson, BP, I, p. 426, adopts this definition of *gōmēr.* The poet returns to the thought of divine retribution in vs. 7, "May they fall into it!"

Most High. Pointing *'ēlī* (MT *'ālāy*); see *Psalms I,* p. 45.

4. *He will send.* Similar language is found in the royal hymn of thanksgiving, Ps xviii 17.

from the taunts. For MT *ḥērēp* pointing *ḥārēp,* the piel infinitive construct that is governed by the preposition of *miššāmayim,* "from heaven." Two other clear examples of the double-duty preposition can be seen in vss. 5 and 7, while further instances are listed in *Psalms I,* pp. 201–2. For this phenomenon in Job xix 24, consult J. J. Stamm in ZAW 64 (1953), 302, and in Job xxix 6 (with infinitive construct); see Dahood, UHP, p. 60. Cf. Jer xviii 15b, *wayyikkašᵉlū-m* (MT *wayyakšīlūm*) *bᵉdarkēhem šᵉbīlē 'ōlām,* "And they stumbled in their ways, *in* bypaths of darkness." On *'ōlām,* "darkness, ignorance," see Pope, *Job,* NOTE on, xxii 15.

those who hound me. For MT singular *šō'ᵃpī* reading plural *šō'ᵃpāy,* whose definition is considered in the second NOTE on Ps lvi 2. The occurrence of *šā'ap,* "hound," in both these psalms is another indication that they belong to the same literary type, namely, royal psalms.

kindness and fidelity. Personified as two attendants to lead the poet to safety; cf. *Psalms I,* pp. 148, 247, and NOTE on Ps lxxxix 15. Since in Canaanite mythology the gods or dignitaries are often accompanied by two attendants, the present personification may tell us something about the identity of the supplicant. According to Philo of Byblos (see Eusebius, *Praeparatio evangelica,* I, 10, 13), "justice" and "rectitude" were gods in the Phoenician pantheon. We may infer that "kindness" and "fidelity" also belonged to the larger Canaanite pantheon, but in Hebrew theology they were demythologized and reduced to attendants of Yahweh.

5. *Myself amid lions.* This line has never yielded to satisfactory translation or syntactic analysis, but a measure of coherence is gained by observing its structure. It consists of seven words: the first three, numbering seven syllables, belong to the first colon; the last three, also numbering seven syllables, form the second, and the fourth word, the verb *'eškᵉbāh,* is the pivot word predicated of both cola. A similar arrangement of words is commented upon at Ps vii 3, where *kᵉ'aryēh,* "like a lion," links the

two halves of the verse. Other texts exhibiting this prosodic pattern include vss. 8 and 10; Pss vi 11, lv 15, lvi 5, 12, lxxiii 25, lxxxiii 18, lxxxiv 3, lxxxvi 12, lxxxviii 6, 18, xcviii 2, 9, cxix 62, 142, 144, 160, 166, 169, 174, cxxi 6, 7; Job xxii 23; Prov vii 18.

amid lions. The prepositional phrase *bᵉtōk* extends its governing force to parallel *lōhᵃṭīm* in the second colon, a stylistic phenomenon noted in vs. 4 and to be noted in vs. 7.

MT *lᵉbā'īm* is often considered erroneous pointing for *lᵉbī'īm* (Briggs, CECBP, II, p. 41), since the commonly attested singular is *lābī'*. But the Canaanite personal name *laba'ya* from **lab'u*, Ar. *lab'ah*, "lioness," suggests the existence in Northwest Semitic of *lebe'*, "lion," alongside *lābī'*; hence MT *lᵉbā'īm* is quite defensible. Consult W. F. Albright in BASOR 89 (1943), 16, n. 51a, and Bauer and Leander, *Historische Grammatik*, p. 579, n. 1. In Ugaritic both *lbu* and *lbit* occur.

The comparison of calumniators and backbiters to lions recurs in Ps lviii 7. Hence it is difficult to credit the suggestion of B. Mazar in VT 13 (1963), 312, that the poet has in mind mercenaries called *lᵉbā'īm* whose emblem was the lioness-goddess.

Amid. To have the second colon syllabically match the first with seven syllables, the poet did not repeat the prepositional phrase *bᵉtōk;* see second NOTE on vs. 5.

those raging. Literally "those blazing," *lōhᵃṭīm* is a participle modifying first-colon *lᵉbā'īm*, "lions." The poet graphically describes his plight by placing the verb *'eškᵉbāh* between "the lions" and "the blazing ones."

human prey. Syntactically, *bᵉnē 'ādām* is an accusative of specification.

spear and arrows. The mythopoeic origin of the psalmist's language is suggested by the occurrence of the parallelism between singular "spear" and plural "arrows" in highly mythologizing Hab iii 11, "At the light of your arrows as they sped, at the flash of your glittering spear."

a sword that is sharp. Compare Ps lii 4, "Your tongue is like a sharpened razor."

6. *Your stature.* Usually parsed as energic qal imperative, *rūmāh* is better understood as a substantive (note the place name *rūmāh* in II Kings xxiii 36; Judg ix 41), with a signification similar to masculine *rūm*, "height." Such a substantive properly balances *kᵉbōdᵉkā*, "your glory," from which it receives its modifying suffix according to the poetic technique studied in *Psalms I*, pp. 17 f. J. Halévy, (*Recherches bibliques* [Paris, 1905], III, p. 164) has correctly observed that neither *rūmāh*, "Be exalted," or Graetz's emendation *rōmᵉmāh*, "Arise!," give a satisfactory sense. He proposed to read *rūmᵉkā*, "your elevation, your glory," parallel to *kᵉbōdᵉkā*. But the psalmists' extensive use of the double-duty suffix proves this emendation superfluous. Were the psalmist to modify *rūmāh* by a suffix—*rūmātᵉkā*—he would have added two extra

syllables to the first colon, unduly unbalancing the two halves of the verse. On the validity of syllable-counting as a textual criterion, see D. N. Freedman in ZAW 72 (1960), 102, and *Psalms I,* p. 13.

There is literary evidence that ancient Semitic criteria for the qualifications of the supreme deity paralleled their conception of the ideal king. Primitive usage required that the king be above average height; Saul was chosen king by reason of his "countenance and tallness of stature" (I Sam xvi 7). In Canaanite myth, the god Athtar's claim to occupy the vacant throne of Baal is rejected because he is physically too small: "He takes his seat on the throne of Victor Baal. But his feet do not reach the footstool, his head does not reach the top" (UT, 49:I:30–33). Consult the excellent treatment of this motif in Gaster, *Thespis,* 1961, pp. 218 f. Yahweh's stature, however, towers above the heavens, and his glory extends over the breadth of the earth.

7. *a net.* Though unwitnessed in other Semitic languages, Heb. *rešet* appears in the Canaanite dialect of Ugarit as *rṯt,* "net." Cf. Dahood in *Biblica* 47 (1966), 404–5.

a noose. Identifying consonantal *kpp* with Akk. *kippu(m),* "noose, snare," from *kapāpu,* "to bend." Cf. W. G. Lambert, *Babylonian Wisdom Literature* (Oxford, 1960), p. 130, line 90, *kun-na-aš-su kip-pu zi-ru,* "A nasty snare is prepared for him." Names of instruments are among the most common Akkadian loanwords in Hebrew. Thus the parallelism between *rešet,* "net," and *kpp,* "noose," may be compared with Job xviii 8–9 where *rešet* appears in context with *ṣammîm,* "nooses." For this definition of *ṣammîm,* see G. R. Driver in JBL 73 (1954), 133, n. 47.

for my neck. The preposition of *lip'āmay,* "for my feet," also governs parallel *nepeš,* an ellipsis that has been noticed in vss. 4–5. On *nepeš,* "neck," see *Psalms I,* p. 321, and O. Sander, "Leib-Seele-Dualismus im Alten Testament," ZAW 77 (1965), 329–32. Ps cv 18, balancing *napšō* with *raglāyw,* "his feet," presents the equivalent parallelism; cf. also Jer ii 25.

a pit. Less frequent than synonymous *šaḥat* and *šûḥāh, šīḥāh* is morphologically the feminine of the qal passive participle. Cf. Ps ii 1, *rīq,* "troops" (*Psalms I,* pp. 7 f.), Ps l 23, *śīm,* "who is set" (*Psalms I,* p. 310). To this formation also belongs Ps cxxvi 1, *šībat ṣiyyōn,* "the repatriated of Zion"; *šībāh* is the feminine passive participle of *šūb,* an abstract form understood concretely.

for my face. That he might fall face first into the pit. Following "feet" and "neck," *pānay* of *lᵉpānay* seems to bear its literal sense. J. Halévy, *Recherches bibliques,* III, p. 164, has seen that *lᵉpānay* does not fit the context, but his emendation to *lᵉraglay,* "for my feet," is not the correct solution. It is sufficient to give *lᵉpānay* its literal, physical meaning.

may they fall. Parsing *nāpᵉlū* as precative perfect, a topic discussed in

Psalms I, p. 20. Compare Ps cxli 10, "May the wicked themselves fall (*yipp^elū*) together into the net."

8. *Firm . . . resolve.* Verse 8a is a five-word line whose third word, vocative *'^elōhīm*, "God," belongs to both cola and joins them as the pivot word, a word arrangement that has been noted in vs. 5a and that recurs in vs. 10.

my resolve. Cf. NOTE on Ps lv 22.

O God. Vocative *'^elōhīm* is to be understood with both cola comprising this line, functioning exactly as vocative *'^adōnay* in vs. 10. See the first NOTE on vs. 5.

sing and chant. Parsing *'āšīrāh* and *'^azamm^erāh* as subjunctives or volitives dependent upon "my resolve." *Psalms I*, pp. 57, 240 f., considers some aspects of the subjunctive mode in Northwest Semitic. The pair of synonyms *šīr* and *zāmar* is duplicated in the unpublished Ugaritic tablet RŠ 24.253:3–4, *dyšr wyḏmr bknr wṯlb*, "Who sings and chants with lyre and lute." In his discussion of paired synonyms in Ugaritic and Hebrew, Gordon (UT, § 14.3) rightly observes that "Nowhere does the proximity of Heb. and Ugar. manifest itself more plainly than in the pairs of synonyms used parallelistically in both languages." Writing in *Peake's Commentary on the Bible* (London, 1962), § 49b, p. 62, Albright states: "So far nearly a hundred examples of pairs of words in parallelism have been found to be common to biblical Hebrew and Ugaritic." The present writer's file now contains 240 pairs of such parallel words, an increase of 115 since UHP (pp. 43 f.) was published. In these we have another valuable criterion for the linguistic and literary classification of Ugaritic.

9. *my heart.* Literally "my liver." The parallelism with *libbī*, also witnessed in Ugar. *lb//kbd*, supports the reading, *k^ebēdī* (MT *k^ebōdī*, "my glory"). Other instances of Masoretic confusion between "my glory" and "my liver" are noted in *Psalms I*, pp. 43, 184. This mispointing demonstrates the Masoretic limitations vis-à-vis archaic poetry and its pairs of parallel words; cf. *Psalms I*, p. XXII.

The sentiment expressed here might be compared with Song of Sol v 2, *libbī 'ēr*, "My heart is awake." Since both *lb* and *kbd* are considered the seat of both sorrow and joy (cf. UT, 1 Aqht:34–35, "Pughat cries from her heart, she weeps from her liver," and 75:I:12–13, "El laughs from his heart and chuckles from his liver"), the psalmist needs rouse his heart and liver if he is to sing and chant with brio. Cf. Ps xxx 13, "So that my heart (*kābēd*) might sing to you, and weep no more."

lyre. On Ugar. *knr*, see *Psalms I*, p. 297, and text quoted above in final NOTE on vs. 8.

I might awake. Parsing *'ā'īrāh* as subjunctive; cf. last NOTE on vs. 8. By his heartfelt song the psalmist intends to hasten the moment of daybreak, when God was thought to answer a suppliant's prayer; cf. *Psalms I*, pp. 280–81, and the second NOTE on Ps lxxxviii 14.

Dawn. Probably an allusion to the Canaanite god of dawn, *šḥr*, whose birth is celebrated in the Ugaritic myth of *šḥr* and *šlm* "Sunset." That biblical poets were familiar with this myth may be inferred from the occurrence of both roots *šḥr* and *šlm* in Song of Sol i 5, as well as from Isa xiv 12. Ovid, *Metamorphoses* XI, 597, ascribes the rousing of Dawn (*evocat Auroram*) to the crowing of the cock.

10. *I . . . nations.* The structure of this line is identical with that of vs. 8a and similar to the word arrangement of vs. 5a. In this five-word line, the third word—vocative *'adōnāy*—belongs to both halves of the line.

among peoples . . . among nations. Such a promise to praise God in foreign countries suggests that the vower is no mere private citizen, but rather a person of rank on whose lips such a promise would not sound extravagant. Of course, one might object that the language employed is highly stylized, but there are other clues in this poem pointing to the royal character of the psalmist; cf. introductory NOTE.

O truly Great One! As in Ps cviii 4, *kī gādōl* is transposed from the following verse and interpreted as a divine epithet in the vocative case balancing "O Lord!" Consult the first NOTE on Ps cviii 4.

I will sing to you. Though in several texts *zāmar* does govern an accusative object, the psalmists most often employ the construction *zāmar le*. So there is solid probability that the suffix of *'azammerekā* expresses the dative rather than the accusative, as normally described by the lexicons; consult *Psalms I*, p. 326.

12. *Your stature.* See first NOTE on vs. 6.

PSALM 58

(lviii 1–12)

1 *For the director: "Destroy not!" A miktam of David.*

2 O counselors, leaders, may you pronounce just verdicts,
govern men with equity.
3 But no, you act with a heart of malice, [2]*
with lawless caprice you balance your hands.
4 The wicked are loathsome from the womb, [3]
liars are wayward from birth.
5 Their venom is like the venom of a serpent, [4]
like that of a deaf adder that stops its ear;
6 Which does not hear the voice of charmers, [5]
of the cunning weaver of spells.
7 O God, rip their teeth from their mouths, [6]
knock out the fangs of the lion's whelps, Yahweh!
8 May they ebb like water that flows swiftly, [7]
may he shoot his arrows like the emaciated;
9 Like one ravaged by consumption, [8]
may he pass away;
Like a woman's stillbirth,
may they never see the sun.
10 . . . . , [9]
. . . .
11 The just man will rejoice [10]
when he beholds his victory;
He will wash his feet
of the blood of the wicked
12 And men will say:
"Surely the just man has a reward, [11]
Surely there is a God who governs on the earth."

* Verse numbers in RSV.

Notes

lviii. Sorely maligned, the psalmist brings a libel suit against his calumniators. Receiving no satisfaction from the unjust judges, he excoriates them (vss. 2–3) and then imprecates his defamers in verses containing some of the most difficult phrases in the Psalter (vss. 4–10). The poet, however, is able to recompose his soul through his conviction that God still governs the world and will vindicate the just man.

1. *Destroy not!* See first NOTE on Ps lvii 1.

miktam. Cf. second NOTE on Ps lvi 1.

2. *O counselors.* Explaining *h'mnm* as defective spelling (see next NOTE) for *hā'ᵃmūnīm* and identifying *'ᵃmūnīm* with the *'ammounēis* of Philo Byblius, who were learned priests attached to the court. This term has been studied by W. F. Albright in JBL 60 (1941), 210; BASOR 94 (1944), 18, n. 28; and identified by me, UHP, p. 30, in Job xii 20, where this substantive stands parallel to *zᵉqēnīm*, "the elders." Though assuming a different etymology for the word in question, Pope, *Job*, NOTE *ad loc.* reaches a similar conclusion when writing, "The 'confident' may refer to royal counselors who need to be ever ready with some word of advice."

leaders. Defective spelling (see preceding NOTE) for *'ēlīm*, literally "rams" but metaphorically "leaders, lieutenants." For the metaphorical use of this term, see *Psalms I*, pp. 9 f. on Ps ii 5, where the word is also written defectively. Many moderns interpret *'ēlīm* as "gods," for rulers, but this usage is not documented, whereas *'ēlīm*, "rams=leaders," is well attested. Cf. BDB, p. 18a, and Jer iv 22, where LXX correctly reads *'ēlē*, "rulers," for MT *'ᵉwīl*.

pronounce. Parsing *tᵉdabbērūn* as an energic imperfect form functioning as an imperative; consult NOTES on Ps li 8–10. On Ugar. *dbr*, "to manage," cf. UT, Glossary, No. 641, p. 384.

just verdicts . . . with equity. For the Ugaritic and Phoenician pairing of the roots *ṣdq* and *yšr*, see W. F. Albright, JAOS 67 (1947), 157, n. 36, and UT, Krt:12–13, *aṯt ṣdqh lypq mtrḫt yšrh*, "His legitimate wife he truly found, his lawful spouse," and Phoenician Yeḥawmilk, 6–7, *kmlk ṣdq wmlk yšr lpn 'l gbl qdšm*, "For he is a legitimate king and a lawful king through the favor of the holy gods of Byblos."

govern. *tišpᵉṭū* parses as an imperfect with imperative function; see next to last NOTE. As noted in *Psalms I*, p. 13, the basic meaning of *špṭ* is "to exercise authority." In UT, 127:43–47 can be seen the association of the verbs *dbr* and *ṯpṭ=špṭ*.

3. *But no.* The adversative force of *'ap* here corroborates the translation of Ps xliv 10 (*Psalms I*, p. 266) and the comment thereon. In both

texts the proposed emendation of *'ap* to *'ak*, "surely, but," proves gratuitous.

heart of malice. Understood as such by Targ. and Syr., and emended by many to *'āwel*, "malice," MT *'ōlōt* (also in Ps lxiv 7) can readily be defended and explained within the framework of Northwest Semitic. Masoretic *'ōlōt* is the Phoenician pronunciation for classical Heb. *'awlāh*, "injustice, malice." In Phoenician, the diphthong of the first syllable *aw* contracts to *ō* (Friedrich, PPG, § 86), while the Hebrew feminine ending *-āh* appears in Phoenician as *-ōt*. Hence *'ōlōt* is the genuine Phoenician form of Heb. *'awlāh;* cf. *Psalms I*, p. 275, and NOTE on Ps lv 22. Compare Ps xcii 16, Job v 16, *'ōlātāh*, and Isa lxi 8, *'ōlāh*, in which *aw* of the first syllable contracts to *ō*, as in Phoenician and Ugaritic. The Ugaritic form is written *ǵlt*, pronounced *ǵōlatu;* cf. Dahood, UHP, p. 8.

with lawless caprice. An instance of hendiadys, literally "with caprice, lawlessness"; *Psalms I*, p. 326. MT *bā'āreṣ ḥ^{a}mas* is repointed *ba'^{a}reṣ ḥāmās*, with the substantive *'āreṣ*, whose vocalization is uncertain, derived from *rāṣāh*, "to be pleased with." In other words, *'āreṣ*, with prothetic *aleph*, is synonymous with *rāṣōn*, with afformative *nun*, "goodwill, pleasure, caprice." For a discussion of forms with prothetic *aleph*, consult NOTE on Ps li 9, and for *rāṣōn*, "caprice, whim," see Gen xlix 6, "and maimed oxen at their whim" (Speiser [The Anchor Bible, vol. 1], § 61, last NOTE *ad loc.*

Two convincing instances of this noun recur in Job xxxvii 12b–13, "Everything that he ordains (*y^{e}ṣawwe-m*, with enclitic *mem;* MT *y^{e}ṣawwēm*) upon the earth is his good pleasure (*'arṣāh*). Whether for discipline, or for his good pleasure (*l^{e}arṣō*), or for mercy, he makes it find its mark." Consult Pope, *Job*, § 36, NOTE on xxxvii 13a, and compare Prov viii 31. Several scholars have recognized this vocable in the Hadad Inscription, line 13, *'rqy='rṣy*, "my pleasure." About this form J. A. Montgomery, JAOS 54 (1934), 421, writes: "Cooke correctly, 'probably some part of the *verb rqy=rṣy*'.' It is actually the first stem of the verb with prosthetic *aleph*, of which there are numerous examples for the same root *r'h* in early Syriac."

For *ḥāmās*, "lawlessness," see Stanley B. Marrow, "Ḥāmās ('violentia') in Jer 20, 8," in *Verbum Domini* 43 (1965), 241–55; Speiser (The Anchor Bible, vol. 1), § 19, first NOTE on Gen xvi 5.

you balance your hands. This seems to be the plain sense of *y^{e}dēkem t^{e}pallēsūn*. The root *pls*, "to level, smooth," is found in Ugaritic and Phoenician personal names.

The picture drawn by the poet recalls Ps xxvi 10, "In whose left hand are idols, and whose right hand is full of bribes," while the presence of both *'ōlōt*, "malice," and *y^{e}dēkem*, "your hands," is documented in a similar context of UT, 127:32–33, *šqlt bǵlt ydk ltdn dn almnt*, "You have let your hands fall into malice. You do not judge the cause of the widow." Ginsberg, LKK, p. 49, has justly compared *šqlt bǵlt ydk* with Ps cxxv 3, "Lest the just stretch forth their hands into malice."

4. *are loathsome.* Deriving *zōrū* (GK, § 72n, for vocalization) from *zūr,* "to be loathsome," Akk. *zēru,* "to dislike." The nuance expressed here resembles that in Hos v 7, *b^eyhwh bāgādū kī bānīm zārīm yūlādū* (MT *yālādū*), "They have been faithless to Yahweh, because they were born loathsome children." Cf. Phoenician Karatepe III:16, *wyp'l lš'r zr,* "And should do damage to the gate." Donner and Röllig, KAI, II, p. 42, approach the correct sense when translating "und tut an meinem Tore etwas Fremdes=Böses" ["And should do something strange=evil to my gate"]. The proper solution would be to dissociate *zr* from *zwr* I, "to be strange," and to derive it from *zwr* II, "to be loathsome, evil, nasty." Cf. also Akk. *kippu ziru,* "a nasty snare," quoted in the second NOTE on Ps lvii 7.

The psalmist's opinion regarding the incorrigibility of the wicked corroborates the translation and exegesis of Ps xxxvi 4, "Too crass is he to act prudently, to do good." Consult *Psalms I,* p. 219.

are wayward. By following MT and keeping *tā'ū* in the second colon (against BH^3) we have the desired predicate and, at the same time, obviate the need for emending *dōb^erē kāzāb* to *dibb^erū kāzāb,* as found in the LXX. What is more, by preserving MT *dōb^erē kāzāb,* "liars," we can more clearly point to whom vs. 7 *k^epīrīm,* "lions," alludes, since in Ps lvii 5 slanderers are also termed "lions" (*l^ebā'īm*).

wayward from birth. In contrast to the devout psalmist, who may properly be described in the words of Ps xxii 11, "By you have I been nourished (see NOTE on Ps lv 23 for this sense of *hošlaktī*) from birth, from my mother's womb you are my God."

5. *Their venom.* Usually parsed as a construct form dependent upon the preposition *lāmō* (GK, § 130a), *ḥmt* may also be analyzed as a feminine absolute form ending in *-t,* as in Ugaritic and Phoenician (*Psalms I,* p. 167). Hence vocalize *ḥēmāt* (MT *ḥ^amat*). In an unpublished incantation from Ugarit (RŠ 24.244), *ḥmt,* "venom," occurs repeatedly.

like . . . like. The prepositional sequence *k^e* (*kid^emūt*) . . . *k^emō* occurs in UT, Krt:103–5, *kirby . . . km ḥsn,* "like locusts . . . like grasshoppers." Cf. Job xxxviii 14.

venom of a serpent. nāḥāš equals Ugar. *nḥš,* while the balance between *nāḥāš* and *peten* is now documented in the unpublished tablet RŠ 24.244, *ytt nḥšm mhrk bn bṯnm itnnk,* "A present of serpents is your dowry, your gift a brood of adders." On the importance of parallel words for assessing the literary and linguistic relationships between Hebrew and Ugaritic, cf. fourth NOTE on Ps lvii 8, and for the interchange between *b* and *p* in *bṯn=peten*, *Psalms I*, pp. 90, 141, 206.

like that of a deaf adder. Verse 5 has lent itself to many diverse versions and interpretations because of the phrase *kᵉmō peten*, which is elliptical for *kᵉmō ḥᵃmat peten*, "like the venom of an adder." The proximity of *kidᵉmūt ḥᵃmat nāḥāš*, "like the venom of a serpent," allows the poet to forgo a word that a prose writer would have included. Cf. Isa xlii 2 where *qōlō* in the second colon is also the implied object of *yiśśā'* in the first colon.

The point the psalmist wants to make is that the depravity of the congenitally wicked resembles the poison of a deaf adder, which cannot be charmed to permit the enchanter to remove its venom. The rulers and judges are so corrupt that no amount of pleading, however just and right, can dissuade them from their iniquitous behavior.

adder. *peten* equals Ugar. *bṯn*, "dragon, adder," Akk. *bašmu*, "viper, serpent." Consult W. F. Albright, HUCA 23 (1950–51), 27.

that stops. The root of *'āṭam*, "to stop," is possibly found in the incantatory text, UT, 1001:6–7, *ḥw bṯnm uḫd b'lm* [*a*]*ṭm prṯl lrišh*, "a brood of adders trained by wizards, an iron stopper upon its head." On UT, 67:I:5–6, *uṭm ḏrqm*, "The red blood is stopped," see W. F. Albright in BASOR 83 (1941), 41, n. 13.

6. *charmers*. The hapax legomenon piel participle *mᵉlaḥᵉšīm* appears in the singular form *mlḫš* in the unpublished tablet RŠ 24.244; cf. *Psalms I*, p. 251, where *lḫšt*, "charm, spell," and *mlḫš*, "charmer," should be read for typographically erroneous *lḥšt* and *mlḥš*, respectively. See C. Virolleaud in CRAIBL, 1962 (appeared 1963), 107, and C. F. A. Schaeffer in AfO 20 (1963), 213.

weaver of spells. The root and meaning of *ḥōbēr ḥᵃbārīm* appear in a recently published Phoenician inscription from Spain, dating from the seventh century B.C. Certain persons are here described as *bny š'l l'štrt ḥbry tnt*, "mediums of Astarte and spell-casters of Tinnit." Cf. Deut xviii 11, *ḥōber ḥāber wᵉšō'ēl 'ōb*, "a weaver of spells and a consulter of ghosts," and M. Solá-Solé, "Nueva inscripción fenicia de España," in *Rivista degli studi orientali* 41 (1966), 97–108, who, however, completely misses the sense of *ḥbry tnt* when construing it as an appositive of Astarte and translating the entire phrase "oracle priests of Astarte, the companion of Tanit." Cf. F. Vattioni in *Orientalia* 36 (1967), 178–80.

7. *O God . . . Yahweh!* This inclusion formed by two vocatives resembles Ps lxxvii 14 where vocative *'ᵉlōhīm* at the beginning and end of the verse creates the inclusion.

from their mouths. The preposition *bᵉ* of *bᵉpīmō* denotes "from," as correctly seen by *Juxta Hebraeos*, *"Deus excute dentes eorum ex ore eorum."* See *Psalms I*, p. 319, for examples of *bᵉ*, "from."

knock out. *n^e^tōṣ* is related to the hapax legomenon in Job iv 10, *šinnē k^e^pīrīm nittā'ū*, "But the young lions' teeth are broken."

the fangs. The hapax legomenon *maltā'ōt* probably derives from *nāta'*, "to break, knock out," cited in the preceding NOTE. The following development seems to have occurred: **mantā'ōt* becomes *maltā'ōt* by dissimilation, while *m^e^tall^e^'ōt*, also "fangs," seems to be the result of metathesis. See Dahood, "The Etymology of MALTA'OT (Ps 58, 7)," in CBQ 17 (1955), 300–3, where he proposed the reading in UT, 51:VIII:17–20, *al y'dbkm kimr bph klli bṯbr nt'nh tḫtan*, "lest he put you two like a lamb into his mouth, lest like a lambkin you be crushed by his grinding fangs." Thus the balance here between *ph*, "his mouth," and *nt'nh*, "his fangs," resembles the collocation *b^e^pīmō malt^e^'ōt* in our verse.

lion's whelps. In another connection, Speiser (*Genesis*, § 61, second NOTE on xlix 9) has remarked, "The several biblical synonyms for 'lion' designate various breeds (e.g., the Asiatic as opposed to the African) or stages of growth. It so happens that no direct synonym is available in English." Some scholars, however, deny that *k^e^pīrīm*, usually rendered "young lions" or "lion's whelps," is demonstrably distinguishable from the other general designations of "lion." In poetical parallelism, they maintain, *k^e^pīrīm* may be only a synonym for the different word for "lion" in the other colon.

As in Ps lvii 5, the psalmist labels his slanderers (the "liars" of vs. 4) "lion's whelps" because of their efficiency in tearing their victims to pieces. Cf. Ps xxxv 17 and *Psalms I*, p. 214. The transition from "adder" to "lion" has been commented upon by some exegetes; here might be cited a similar association in Ps xci 13, "Upon the lion and the adder will you tread, you will trample on the young lion and the serpent." For the apparent cognates in Semitic which mean "lion" in one dialect and "serpent" in another, consult Pope, *Job*, § 27, NOTE on xxviii 8b.

8. *that flows swiftly.* The construction of *hālak* with *dativus commodi lāmō* serves to clarify the reading and translation of Deut xxxiii 2, *w^e^'ittō-m r^e^bībōt qōdeš mīmīnō 'ōš^e^dōt lāmō*, "And with him myriads of saints, marching apace at his right side." For details, Dahood, UHP, p. 52.

may he shoot his arrows. Singular *yidrōk ḥiṣṣāw* makes vs. 8b chiastically balance vs. 9a singular *yah^a^lōk*, while in vss. 8a and 9b the corresponding verbs are plural. As remarked in *Psalms I*, pp. 34–35, the sudden shift from the singular to the plural, or vice versa, is a hallmark of biblical and Northwest Semitic curses.

like the emaciated. I understand *k^e^mō yitmōlālū* as an elliptical relative clause of the type discussed in *Psalms I*, pp. 213–14; see below NOTE on Ps lxxv 9. Of course, the outcome of a battle between the emaciated and the strong is a foregone conclusion. In Canaanite myth the god Athtar, being *dq anm*, "one of little vigor," and unable to poise a lance like Baal, is rejected as the successor of puissant Baal. Cf. UT, 49:I:22–24.

9. *ravaged.* With some manuscripts reading *šaklūl* (MT *šablūl*) and parsing it as a shaphel formation of *kālāh*, "to be spent, destroyed." The form *šaklēl* in Ps xxxv 12 is discussed in *Psalms I*, p. 213.

by consumption. MT *temes*, probably to be pointed *tāmās* from *māsas*, "to dissolve, waste away," is an accusative of means. Thus the phrase *šaklūl temes* collocates the two roots found in parallelism in Isa x 18, *minnepeš 'ad bāśār yekalleh wehāyāh kimesōs nōsēs*, "And he will ravage from throat to genitals, and it shall be like the wasting of a consumptive." For this version of *minnepeš 'ad bāśār*, see O. Sander, ZAW 77 (1965), 329–32.

may he pass away. For this nuance of *yahalōk*, cf. Gen xv 2 (UHP, p. 65); Job x 21, xiv 20 (Pope, *Job*, NOTE on xiv 20a), xix 10; BDB, p. 234a. Singular *yahalōk* forms a chiasm with vs. 8b, *yidrōk*.

Like a. Understanding the force of *kemō* in the first colon as extending to the second; *Psalms I*, pp. 201 f., 220. So it is strictly not necessary to assume the omission of one *k* (though this may not be ruled out) in UT, 49:II:22–23, *'dbnn ank imr* (Gordon, <*k*>*imr*) *bpy klli bṯbr nt'y* (CBQ 17 [1955], 182 f.) *ḫtu hw*, "I put him like a lamb into my mouth, like a lambkin he was crushed by my grinding fangs." Cf. also A. Herdner, *Corpus des tablettes en cunéiformes alphabétiques découvertes à Ras Shamra–Ugarit de 1929 à 1939* (Mission de Ras Shamra, Tome X; Paris, 1963), p. 40, n. 5. The preposition of *klli*, "like a lambkin," in the second colon may also be understood with parallel *imr*, "lamb," in the first colon.

woman's stillbirth. Though normal in the construct state, *'ēšet* is not infrequent in the absolute form: Deut xxi 11; I Sam xxviii 7; Jer xiii 21; Prov ix 13. Cf. *Psalms I*, pp. 62, 167, and Scott (AB, vol. 18, § 10, textual note c.) who correctly parses *'ēšet* in Prov ix 13 as the Canaanite absolute form, the equivalent of *'iššāh*.

A similar comparison is used in Job iii 16 and Eccles vi 3–5.

may they never see. Parsing *bal ḥāzū* as a negative precative perfect; this is a stylistic variant of the jussive expressed by *yahalōk*. Consult *Psalms I*, p. 20, for precative usage, and Joüon, GHB, § 160m, on *bal* as poetic synonym of *lō'*. As noticed above, *ḥāzū* chiastically pairs with the plural verb in vs. 8a.

10. . . . . . . The Hebrew of this verse is unintelligible to me. The RSV, without the benefit of a note that the Hebrew is unclear, or that its version rests upon emendation, reads, "Sooner than your pots

can feel the heat of thorns, whether green or ablaze, may he sweep them away!"

11. *will rejoice.* There are several indications that the psalmist has adapted here an old motif of Canaanite mythology. The just man's exultation in victory over the wicked sounds not unlike UT, 'nt:II:24–27, *tḫtṣb wtḥdy 'nt tǵdd kbdh bṣḥq ymlu lbh bšmḫt kbd 'nt tšyt,* "Anath battles and beholds: her liver swells with laughter, her heart fills up with joy, Anath's liver with victory." On *tšyt* in the final colon, see Pope, *Job,* NOTE on xii 16a.

he beholds. The verb *ḥāzāh* occurs as *tḥdy* in the Ugaritic text quoted in the preceding NOTE.

his victory. Preferable to RSV "the vengeance." The suffix of *nāqām* is forthcoming from *pe'āmāyw,* "his feet," by virtue of the double-duty suffix (*Psalms I,* pp. 17 f.); *nāqām,* "victory," occurs in Ps xviii 48. The nuance "deliverance" is commented upon by Bright, *Jeremiah,* second NOTE on xi 20, while Amarna *naqāmu,* "to save," is the point of departure for Albright's discussion in *History, Archaeology and Christian Humanism* (New York, 1964), p. 96, n. 28. Albright notes that Heb. NQM seldom means "avenge" but rather "save."

He will wash his feet. After her gory triumph over her enemies, the goddess Anath is described in cognate terms. UT, 'nt:II:34–35, [*t*]*rḥṣ ydh bdm ḏmr* [*u*]*ṣb'th bmm' mhrm,* "She washes her hands of the blood of warriors, her fingers of the gore of troops." This Canaanite parallel suggests that there is a solid basis for the LXX, Vulg., and Syr. reading *kappāyw,* "(he will wash) his hands," as against MT *pe'āmāyw,* "his feet."

of the blood. Not "in the blood" as traditionally rendered. Compare *yirḥaṣ bedam* with UT, 127:10, *trḥṣ nn bd't,* "She washes him clean of sweat." For other instances of *be,* "from," NOTE on Ps lv 12 and *Psalms I,* p. 319. Hence Gen xlix 11, *kibbēs bayyayin lebūšō ubedam 'anābīm sūtóh,* should be rendered, "*Of* wine he washes his garments, his robes *of* the blood of grapes," rather than, "In wine he washes his garments / His robes in the blood of grapes" (Speiser, The Anchor Bible, vol. 1). This line poetically states that the grape harvest is so abundant that Judah must wash his clothes of the juice and wine with which they are soaked. These interpretations are confirmed by lQM 14:2–3, *wbbwqr ykbsw bgdyhm wrḥṣw mdm pgry h'šmh,* "And in the morning they shall launder their garments and wash themselves clean of the blood of the guilty corpses." Here the phrase *rḥṣw mdm,* "wash themselves clean of the blood," employing the preposition *min,* "from," equals our phrase *yirḥaṣ bedam,* "he will wash [his feet] of the blood," where the psalmist uses the preposition *be,* "from." I am indebted to T. Penar for this parallel.

12. *men . . . just man . . . God who governs.* By using the words *'ādām, ṣaddīq, 'ᵉlōhīm* and *šōpᵉṭīm,* the psalmist creates a fourfold inclusion with vs. 2. So men and God, justice and equity are the main themes of the poem.

reward. Consisting of his victory over the wicked. For this sense of *pᵉrī,* see Prov xi 30, "The reward of the just man is the tree of life."

who governs. The plural participle *šōpᵉṭīm* agreeing with the plural of majesty *'ᵉlōhīm* reflects a usage documented in *Psalms I,* p. 280. In contrasting the governance of God with the governing of the unjust rulers in vs. 2, the poet continues the inclusion mentioned in the first NOTE on vs. 12.

PSALM 59

(lix 1–18)

1 *For the director: "Destroy not!" A miktam of David, when Saul sent to watch the house to kill him.*

2 Rescue me, God, from my foes,
against my attackers be my bulwark.
3 Rescue me from evildoers, [2]*
and from men of idols save me.
4 For see how they lurk for my life, [3]
how powerful men conspire against me.
For no guilt of mine,
for no sin of mine, Yahweh,
5 For no misdeed of mine [4]
they charge and take positions.
Rouse yourself for my encounter,
and see for yourself,
6 Yahweh, God of Hosts, God of Israel! [5]
Awake to punish all the nations,
show no mercy to wicked traitors. *Selah*
7 They wait till evening, [6]
then growling like dogs they prowl the city.
8 See how they belch from their mouth [7]
swords from their lips.
"For who will hear us?"
9 But you, Yahweh, will laugh at them, [8]
making sport of all the nations.
10 My God is a fortress, [9]
truly am I protected;
God himself is my bulwark,

* Verse numbers in RSV.

11 a rampart is my God. [10]
God will go before me,
will let me gloat over my defamers.
12 O El, slay them lest my people falter; [11]
send them staggering from your bastion,
and bring them down,
O our Suzerain Lord!
13 By the sin of their mouth, [12]
the gossip from their lips,
Let them be caught;
for their presumption, curses, and lies
Let them be proscribed.
14 In your rage exterminate them, [13]
exterminate and annihilate them,
That they might know that God
rules from Jacob to the edges of the earth. *Selah*
15 They wait till evening,
then growling like dogs they prowl the city. [14]
16 Growling they roam for prey, [15]
if not sated, they retire not.
17 But I will sing your strength, [16]
sing aloud each morning your firmness;
Because you have been my bulwark,
my refuge when besieged.
18 My God is my fortress, [17]
truly am I safeguarded;
God himself is my bulwark,
my rampart is my God.

Notes

lix. Accurately described by Briggs, CECBP, II, p. 50, as "antique in language and style, and exceedingly difficult," this psalm has in recent decades been classified as either a national or an individual lament. A more precise rendition of some of its obscure phrases and their correlation to expressions in royal psalms points rather to a classification among the royal laments. The king complains to God about his foreign enemies, described as nations in battle array (vs. 5), and protests against his domestic defamers (vss. 8, 11), whom he compares, in a singular simile, to a pack of prowling dogs (vss. 7, 16).

The psalmist's twofold denunciation of these two groups results in an intertwining of motifs that has baffled commentators; W. O. E. Oesterley, for example, finds the structure of the poem curious. An awareness that two different categories of foes are the target of the psalmist's invective facilitates an appreciation of the lament's structure and metaphors.

1. *Destroy not!* Consult first NOTE on Ps lvii 1.

miktam. Cf. second NOTE on Ps lvi 1.

when Saul. Though this reference to the story of David's escape by night from the messengers of Saul (I Sam xix 8 ff.) coincides with the contents of the poem only in part, the attribution to the Davidic period does accord with the archaic quality of the language and the martial quality of much of its phraseology.

sent. The object, "messengers," explicit in I Sam xix 11, is here to be mentally supplied. This usage further illustrates the elliptic nature of biblical poetry.

2. *God.* Reading *'elōhīm* (MT *'elōhāy*) with one manuscript, LXX, and Syr., the final *mem* being taken from the following congeries *mmtqwmmy.*

my foes . . . my attackers. The parallelism between *'ōyebay* and *(m)teqōmemay* bears comparison with UT, 76:II:24–25, *nṭ'n barṣ iby wb'pr qm aḫk,* "We have planted my foes in the nether world, and the attackers of your brother in the mud." For the treatment of synonymous pairs in Ugaritic and Hebrew poetry, see the fourth NOTE on Ps lvii 8.

against my attackers. Literally "from those who rise up against me." Once the initial *mem* of consonantal *mmtqwmmy* is attached to preceding word (see first NOTE on vs. 2), the textual critic is left with two alternatives: he may analyze *mtqwmmy* into the preposition *min* followed by the substantive *teqōmēm* (Ps cxxxix 21), or he may assume the hithpoel participle *mitqōmemay* (Ps xvii 7), supplying the preposition from the parallel word *mē'ōyebay,* on the basis of the principle examined in *Psalms I,* pp. 201 f. A preference for the first explanation will secure the reading in Ps cxxxix 21, which has been questioned and will be challenged anew because of the reading in 11QPs^a, *wmmtqwmmykh.*

be my bulwark. Cf. *Psalms I,* p. 127. The pairing of the imperfect form *teśaggebēnī* with the imperative *haṣṣīlēnī* is a technique of stylistic variation that biblical poets have inherited from their Canaanite predecessors; *Psalms I,* pp. 65 f. The military expression *teśaggebēnī* forms an *inclusio* (*Psalms I,* p. 327, and below on vs. 12) or "envelope figure" with vs. 18, *miśgabbī* "my bulwark."

3. *men of idols.* The heathen "nations" of vs. 6; cf. NOTE on Ps lv 24 and *Psalms I,* p. 163.

4. *see how they lurk.* Compare Pss iii 3 and lvi 7. Gunkel's appeal to the phrase *hinnēh 'ārebū* to emend Ps lvi 7 *hēmmāh* to *hinnēh,*

"Look! Behold!" (*Die Psalmen*, p. 244), is invalidated by Ugar. *hm*, "See, behold!"

powerful men. Comparing *'ōyᵉbī 'ōz*, "my powerful Foe," in royal Ps xviii 18.

conspire. On *yāgūrū*, NOTE on Ps lvi 7.

no guilt of mine . . . no sin of mine. For the grammar of *piš'ī* and *ḥaṭṭa'tī*, see NOTE on Ps xvii 3 (*Psalms I*, p. 94). Cf. also Ps cxv 7, *yᵉdēhem wᵉlō' yᵉmīšūn*, "They have hands, but do not feel."

5. *no misdeed of mine*. Suffixless *'āwōn* shares the suffixes of synonymous *piš'ī* and *ḥaṭṭā'tī*; *Psalms I*, pp. 17 f. The Israelite king feels he has done nothing to invite an attack by foreign powers.

they charge. This military nuance of *rūṣ* recurs in royal Ps xviii 30; Job xv 26, xvi 14. The last passage is cited in *Psalms I*, p. 308, but the conjunction *pā* has been omitted through an oversight. The correct reading: *yiprᵉṣēnī pereṣ 'al pānāy pā-rōṣ* (MT *'al pᵉnē pereṣ*) *yārūṣ 'ālay kᵉgibbōr*. A closely cognate nuance can be seen also in UT, 49:I:22–24, *dq anm lyrẓ 'm b'l ly'db mrḥ 'm bn dgn*, "One of little vigor cannot charge like Baal, wield a spear like Dagan's son."

take positions. The usual parsing of *yikkōnānū* as an assimilated form of hithpael *yitkōnānū* is sustained by 1QIsª which reads *ttkwnny* for MT *tikkōnānī* in Isa liv 14. For the military sense of this verb, Nah ii 6, "His captains are strong, they hurtle in their march, they speed toward the wall, and the mantelet is positioned (*hūkan*)."

Rouse yourself. *'ūrāh liqrā'tī* is profitably compared with Ps xxxv 2, *qūmāh bᵉ'ezrātī*, "Rise to my battle."

for my encounter. Namely, with my enemies. Not "Come to my help" (RSV). The translation and exegesis are afforded by the similar context of Ps xxxv 3, "Ready the spear and the javelin to confront (*liqra't*) my pursuers."

and see for yourself. Metrical considerations indicate that the first two words of vs. 6, *wᵉ'attāh* should be attached to vs. 5, which now scans into 2+2//2+2. If the *wᵉ* of *wᵉ'attāh* is original, and not the product of faulty word division, it may be parsed as *waw emphaticum* (*Psalms I*, p. 329) strengthening the independent pronoun, which in turn emphasizes the imperative. An analogous use of the personal pronoun to stress the imperative idea is noticed in Pss iii 8 and x 14, *rā'ītāh kī 'attāh*, "See for yourself." Cf. NOTES below on Pss lxix 19–20 and cxxxix 1–2.

Yahweh, God of Hosts. Recurring in Pss lxxx 15, 20, lxxxiv 9, grammatically difficult MT *yhwh 'ᵉlōhīm ṣᵉbā'ōt* is no longer to be explained as the result of the mechanical substitution of *'ᵉlōhīm* for *yhwh* (so GK, § 125h), but rather as a construct chain with an interposed enclitic *mem*. Hence vocalize *'ᵉlōhē-m ṣᵉbā'ōt*, as proposed by

Hummel, JBL 76 (1957), 97. A familiarity with the scores of examples in Ugaritic and Hebrew of an enclitic *mem* in a construct chain—not counting the several hundred instances of this enclitic attached to words in other combinations—would have exorcised the doubts expressed by M. Tsevat in HUCA 36 (1965), p. 50, n. 11. The fact that *'ᵉlōhē ṣᵉbā'ōt* occurs eighteen times no more forbids the insertion of an enclitic *mem* in this formula than does the standard expression *šᵉmē šāmayim,* "the highest heaven," prevent the psalmist from writing *haššᵉmēy-m* (MT *haššāmayim*) *šāmayim,* "the highest heaven," in Ps cxv 16. Syntactically, *'ᵉlōhē-m ṣᵉbā'ōt* is identical with Jer x 10, *'ᵉlōhē-m 'ᵉmet,* "the true God" (= II Chron xv 3, *'ᵉlōhē 'ᵉmet*).

Of course, the use of this divine title is particularly apt in the military context of vss. 5–6.

to punish. pqd is found once in Ugaritic, but with the probable denotation "to give orders."

wicked traitors. Synonymous with "the nations" who have violated their pact with the Israelite king. For this nuance of *bōgēd,* see *Psalms I,* p. 156.

7. *They wait.* Referring to the king's domestic enemies. Since a derivation from *šūb,* "to return," yields no viable translation, relate *yāšūbū* to *šūb,* "to sit, wait," a by-form of *yāšab,* discussed in *Psalms I,* pp. 44, 148, 213. Of course, this version accurately describes the behavior of wild dogs or jackals, which usually stay in their dens during the day and issue forth after dusk in search of prey. See NOTE on Ps xci 5, *paḥad laylāh,* "the pack of night." Gen xlix 27 describes how a wolf passes the daylight hours in his lair: "Benjamin is a ravenous wolf, devouring prey from morning (*babbōqer*) and dividing spoil till evening (*lā'ereb*)." For details, cf. Dahood, UHP, p. 27.

like dogs. Wild dogs or jackals are meant.

prowl the city. Cf. first NOTE on Ps lv 11.

8. *they belch.* Probably represented in the Ugaritic personal name *nb'm, nāba'* has a pejorative connotation when predicated of the wicked or arrogant, as in Prov xv 28 and Ps xciv 4. Here its object, "swords," does not appear until the second colon, an instance of enjambment (*Psalms I,* p. 326). In prose one would write, "From their mouth and lips they belch swords." RSV needlessly resorts to conjecture in the second colon: "and snarling with their lips."

from their mouth . . . from their lips. On *bᵉ*, "from," see *Psalms I,* p. 319, and UT, 1 Aqht:141–42, *bph rgm lyṣa bšpth hwth,* "From his mouth his word had not gone forth, from his lips his utterance." This text illustrates the double-duty suffix (*rgm//hwth*), a usage that serves to elucidate numerous biblical passages (*Psalms I,* p. 326), as well as the pair *p//špt,* as in our verse. Compare *bᵉpīhem* with Ps lviii 7, *bᵉpīmō,* and *bᵉśipᵉtōtēhem* with Ps xlv 3, "Charm flows from your lips (*b^e^šip^e^tōtekā*)." Another instance of *b^e^*, "from," leads to a new translation and interpretation of vs. 12 below. See also Dahood, *Biblica* 52 (1971), 355–56.

swords. If one prefers, with some commentators, "reproaches" to "swords," the projected emendation of consonantal *ḥrbwt* to *ḥrpwt* would prove needless, given the numerous instances of the interchange of *b* and *p* (*Psalms I*, pp. 90, 141, 206). However, such a reinterpretation is not counseled because in Ps lv 22 words are termed "drawn swords," in lii 4, the tongue is called a "sharpened razor," and in lvii 5 "a sword that is sharp." These figures of speech, it may be remarked, further point up the unity of Pss lii–lix and help explain their grouping in the Psalter. Pss iii 7, xviii 44, and lxxxix 51 liken sarcastic remarks to shafts or arrows.

who will hear us. Other instances of *šāma'* with unexpressed accusative suffix are given in *Psalms I*, p. 24, and in NOTES on Pss lv 20 and lxvi 18. This attitude of the psalmist's maligners is termed "presumption" in vs. 13.

9\. *will laugh . . . making sport of.* Compare the similar context and phraseology in Ps ii 4. This similarity of language conspires with other considerations to suggest a tenth-century date for this psalm, the period when Ps ii was composed.

at them . . . the nations. The former might refer to the royal poet's internal enemies, the latter to his foreign foes.

10\. *My God is a fortress.* Reading *'uzzū 'ēlī kī* instead of MT *'uzzō 'ēleykā*, "O strength, to you." This lection uncovers the composite divine name *'ēl 'elōhīm* (*Psalms I*, p. 305 f.), whose elements are separated and placed in the parallel cola (*Psalms I*, p. 325). New instances of this composite name are registered in Pss lxii 2, 11–12, lxxvii 2, lxxxiv 8.

The form *'uzzū*, parallel to *ḥasdū* in next verse, preserves the archaic nominative ending *-u*, lengthened to *-ū* under the accent. One may retain MT *'uzzō* and adopt the usual explanation given to related forms such as *ḥay^e^tō 'āreṣ;* cf. Bauer and Leander, *Historische Grammatik*, § 65h, p. 524. I suspect, however, that MT *ḥay^e^tō* is erroneous; here too, *ḥay^e^tū* would preserve the nominative ending as in Ugaritic.

This denotation of *'uzzū*, which neatly comports with the military metaphors throughout the psalm and, more immediately, with "my bulwark" and vs. 11, "rampart," is examined in *Psalms I*, p. 50. In Ps lxii 7–8 "fortress" and "bulwark" are again associated.

truly. The emphasizing *kī* materializes with the separation of MT *'ēleykā* into *'ēlī+kī*. It thus balances the emphatic *kī* in the following colon. As in Ugaritic, this particle often causes the verb to be thrown to the end of its clause; see *Psalms I*, p. 301, and cf. third NOTE on Ps liv 7, where MT again mistakes defectively written *kī* for the suffix *-kā*.

am I protected. Punctuating niphal *'eššāmērāh* for MT qal *'ešmōrāh.*

The doublet in vs. 18 reads synonymous *'ezzāmērāh* (MT *'ᵃzammērāh*), "am I safeguarded."

God himself. Parsing *kī* as asseverative, emphasizing the subject *'ᵉlōhīm*. For other instances, *Psalms I*, p. 65, where examples of *kī* intensifying the subject *'attāh* are cited, and Robert Gordis, "The Asseverative *Kaph* in Ugaritic and Hebrew," in JAOS 63 (1943), 176–78.

In this verse, it may be noted, suffixed *miśgabbī*, "my bulwark," is paired with suffixless *'uzzū*, "fortress," suffixed *'ēlī*, "my God," balances suffixless *'ᵉlōhīm*, "God," just as in vs. 11, suffixed *'ᵉlōhay* is paired with suffixless *'ᵉlōhīm*. Verse 10 thus scans into 2+2+2 and suggests that the following verse contains the same metrical pattern.

11. *a rampart.* Like *'uzzū*, "fortress," in preceding verse, *ḥasdū* preserves an archaic nominative ending. In recent years several scholars have noticed that in a number of texts *ḥesed*, "piety, kindness," connotes "strength." In IDB, III, p. 915b, D. Napier correctly observes that *ḥsd* in its root sense conveys the quality of sustaining strength, strength in duration, while L. J. Kuyper, in his study, "The Meaning of *ḥsdw* ISA XL 6," in VT 13 (1963), 489–92, cites a number of texts where this connotation is predominant. The relevant texts number Ps cxliv 2; II Chron xxxii 32 (cf. II Kings xx 20); Jon ii 9. For the present purpose, the most instructive is Ps cxliv 2: *ḥasdī ūmᵉṣūdātī miśgabbī ūmiplāṭī* (MT *ūmᵉpalᵉṭī*) *lī*, "my rampart and my fastness, my bulwark and my haven."

my God. Pointing *'ᵉlōhay* (MT *'ᵉlōhēy*) with two manuscripts and the LXX.

God will go before me. In royal Ps cx 5, God is pictured waging battle at the king's right hand, but here he is described as preceding the psalmist (probably the king) into combat. Whereas the preceding cola show the psalmist ensconced in his fortress, the present line depicts him sallying forth behind God to inflict defeat upon his adversaries.

Our stichometric division, 2+2+2, diverges from the traditional interpretation, which reads the line as a 3+3 bicolon. The metrical pattern of vs. 11 is thus identical with that of vs. 10, a 2+2+2 tricolon.

will let me gloat. Cf. Pss liv 9 and cxviii 7.

my defamers. See NOTE on Ps liv 7.

12. *O El.* Pointing *'ēl* (MT *'al*), the divine name also found in vs. 10. Cf. *Psalms I*, p. 64. The same Masoretic confusion between the negative imperative particle *'al* and the divine name *'ēl* recurs in Pss lxii 11, cxliii 7, and Jer xv 15, *yhwh zokrēnī ūpoqdēnī wᵉhinnāqēm lī mērōdᵉpay 'ēl* (MT *'al*), "Remember me, Yahweh! Take note of me! Deliver me from those that harass me, O El!"

slay them. In balance with imperatives *hᵃnī'ēmō*, "send them staggering," and *hōrīdēmō*, "bring them down," *taharᵉgēm* is an imperfect functioning as an imperative; consult NOTE on Ps li 8. The root *hrg* occurs in UT, 6:5, but the insufficiency of context precludes certain identification with our verb; see UT, Glossary, No. 792. The sequence, imperfect —imperative, is but one of numerous devices employed by the biblical poets to create stylistic variety, as remarked in fourth NOTE on vs. 2.

my people. A further indication that the supplicant is a king, who here prays that the morale of his subjects be sustained. Cf. introductory NOTE and second NOTE on vs. 11.

falter. Deriving *yiškeḥū* from *šākaḥ* II, "to shrivel, flag," discussed in *Psalms I,* p. 190. Compare Isa xxiii 16, *zōnāh niškāḥāh,* "O worn-out whore!," with Ezek xxiii 43, *bālāh ni'ūppīm,* "consumed by adultery."

send them staggering. After praying God that his people will not flag, the king asks the contrary for his military opponents, since this is the literal sense of *hanī'ēmō,* hiphil imperative of *nūa',* "to waver, stagger."

from your bastion. As above in vs. 8, giving *be* its frequent sense of "from" (*Psalms I,* p. 319), and identifying *ḥēl* with the vocable designating "rampart, bastion," not, as tradition has done, with *ḥayil,* "strength," though this latter derivation is not peremptorily excluded. In Ps cxxii 7, "Peace be within your bastions (*beḥēlēk*), and tranquility within your citadels," some of the ancient versions (LXX, Vulg., Syr.) again prove misleading when translating *ḥēlēk,* "your strength." Thus the association of *ḥēl,* "bastion," with vs. 10 *'uzzū,* "fortress," resembles that of Isa xxvi 1b, *'īr 'ōz* (MT *'oz,* but 1QIs[a] *'wz*) *lānū yešū'āh yāšīt ḥōmōt wāḥēl,* "A fortress-city is ours, the walls and ramparts provide safety." (Cf. also Ps xlviii 14.) This substantive is probably represented by the Ugaritic place name *ḥl* in UT, 113:40.

bring them down. Namely, to Sheol. In other terms, *hōrīdēmō* is synonymous with "slay them." Cf. Pss lv 24; BDB, p. 434a, and Isa lxiii 6, *we'ōrīd lā'āreṣ niṣḥām,* "And I brought their glory down to the nether world."

O our Suzerain Lord! The Ugaritic balance *adn,* "lord" // *mgn,* "suzerain" (UT, 125:44–45), now leads me to opt for the reading considered in an earlier edition where I wrote, "I do not discount, however, the possibility that *mgnnw* might here signify 'our Suzerain.'" See also R. C. Hanson, *The Psalms in Modern Speech* (Philadelphia, 1968), II, p. 29.

13. *their mouth . . . their lips.* Consult second NOTE on vs. 8.

gossip. Because of its pairing with "sin," *dābār* here carries a pejorative connotation that is discussed in the second NOTE on Ps lvi 5. Both *ḥaṭṭa't pīmō,* "sin of their mouth," and *debar śepātēmō,* "gossip from their lips," are accusatives of means preceding the verb, a characteristic of the psalmists' style (*Psalms I,* p. 325).

Let them be caught. Analyzing the *waw* preceding the verb *yillākēdū* (pausal form ending the clause, MT *yillākedū*) as emphatic. As observed in *Psalms I*, pp. 24 f., the *waw emphaticum* often causes the verb to be placed last in its clause. Ignorance of this usage goes far toward explaining the diverse stichometric divisions of vs. 13 witnessed in the versions.

for their presumption. Which consists in thinking that God does not hear them (fourth NOTE on vs. 8) and will not intervene on the psalmist's behalf. The preposition *b* of *bigᵉ'ōnām* balances *min* in the two following substantives; *Psalms I*, p. 128, and third NOTE on Ps lv 12.

Let them be proscribed. Vocalizing niphal *yissāpērū* (MT piel *yᵉsappērū*) to balance niphal *yillākēdū*, "be caught." Though uncertain, this version may partially be clarified by Jer xvii 13, *yᵉsūrēy* (MT *yᵉsūray*), *bā'āreṣ yikkātēbū*, "Those who turn from him shall be inscribed in the nether world." Thus *yissāpērū* may here be elliptical for *yissāpērū bā'āreṣ*.

14. *In your rage*. Like suffixless Ps lvi 8, *bᵉ'ap*, "in your anger" (see NOTE), *bᵉḥēmāh*, "in rage," needs no further determination since it is also a part of the body (*bᵉ'ap* means literally "nostrils, nose, face").

exterminate them. The accusative suffix of *kallēh* is forthcoming from parallel *'ayyēnēmō*, "annihilate them," on the principle treated in *Psalms I*, pp. 17 f. The verb *kly* is frequent in the Ras Shamra tablets. Here the Hebrew reads *kallēh beḥēmāh kallēh*, "Exterminate them in your rage, exterminate them."

annihilate them. Vocalizing piel imperative **'ayyēnēmō* (MT *'ēynēmō*), to balance piel imperative *kallēh*; see Dahood, *Biblica* 44 (1963), 293.

they might know. Namely, in Sheol. Cf. Ps xxii 30, "Before him shall bend the knee of all who have gone down to the mud."

from Jacob. As in vss. 8, 12, and 13, *bᵉ* denotes "from." God's governance of the world emanates from Israel to the ends of the world, a probable allusion to the navel-of-the-earth motif; cf. *Psalms I*, pp. 142 f., 290. UT, 49:I:32–33, *rišh lymǵy apsh*, "His head did not reach its (throne's) edge," sharply contrasts with the biblical description of Yahweh's dominion reaching to the *'apsē hā'āreṣ*, "ends of the earth."

to the edges. The sequence *bᵉ*, "from," . . . *lᵉ*, "to," recurs in Gen xlix 27, and Eccles xi 6, *babbōqer . . . lā'āreb*, "from morning . . . till evening"; cf. Dahood, UHP, pp. 26 f.

15. *They wait*. See first NOTE on vs. 7.

16. *Growling*. Since the independent pronoun *hēmmāh* (MT) has no clear function here, perhaps the infinitive absolute *hāmōh* is to be read. The frequency of infinitives absolute in El Amarna Akkadian, Ugaritic, and Phoenician has taught us to seek more of these than MT discloses; *Psalms I*, p. 214.

they roam for prey. Compare I Pet v 8, "Your enemy the devil, like a roaring lion, prowls round looking for someone to devour."

they retire not. The phrase *lō' yiśbᵉ'ū wayyālīnū* still baffles, but the discovery of new examples of double-duty negatives (*Psalms I,* p. 326) supports the interpretation of the Syriac version, which puts a negative before each of the two verbs: "if they are *not* sated, they do *not* retire." Ibn Esra follows the Syriac.

17. *sing your strength.* The construction *'āšīr 'uzzekā* is now matched in the unpublished tablet RŠ 24.245, *tšr* (*'nt*) *dd al*[*iyn*] *b'l,* "(Anath) sings the love of Victor Baal."

your firmness. A cognate nuance of *ḥesed* is examined in first NOTE on vs. 11.

when besieged. Generic *ṣar,* "distress," acquires a more specific denotation by reason of context; *Psalms I,* p. 127.

18. *My God is my fortress.* First NOTE on vs. 10.

truly. Second NOTE on vs. 10.

am I safeguarded. Since the doublet in vs. 10 reads *'eššāmērāh, 'ezzāmērāh* (MT *'ᵃzammērāh*) evidently equals Ugar. *ḏmr,* "sentinel, guard" (UT, Glossary, No. 727). This root has been recognized in Exod xv 2 and II Sam xxiii 1 by F. M. Cross, Jr., and D. N. Freedman in JNES 14 (1955), 243, and by H. Cazelles in *Mélanges A. Robert,* pp. 135 f. Cf. Isa xii 2, xxv 5; Ps cxviii 14; Job xxxv 10, and Nahum Sarna, "Ezechiel 8:17: A Fresh Examination," in HTR 57 (1964), 347–52.

God himself. Consult third NOTE on vs. 10.

my rampart. First NOTE on vs. 11. The fact that the last two cola of vs. 11—*yᵉqaddᵉmēnī 'ᵉlōhīm yar'ēnī bᵉšōrᵉrāy*—do not appear here supports the stichometric division proposed for vs. 11, namely that the first colon—*'ᵉlōhay ḥasdū*—belongs semantically to vs. 10.

my God. Cf. second NOTE on vs. 11.

PSALM 60

(lx 1–14)

1 *For the director; according to "Lilies." A solemn commandment.*
2 *A miktam of David, to be taught; when he strove with Aram-Naharaim and with Aram-Zobah, and Joab returned and smote of Edom in the Valley of Salt twelve thousand.*

3 O God, you were angry with us,
and you ran from us;
You were wrathful,
you turned away from us.
4 You shook the land, [2]*
and it went to pieces;
Weak from its fractures,
much did it totter.
5 You made your people drain the cup, [3]
you made us drink a wine that dazed us.
6 To those who fear you, give a banner [4]
to which to rally against the bowmen. *Selah*
7 That your beloved may be delivered, [5]
give us victory with your right hand,
and grant us triumph!
8 God spoke from his sanctuary: [6]
"Exultant, I will make Shechem my portion,
and measure off the Valley of Succoth.
9 Gilead is mine, and Manasseh is mine; [7]
Ephraim is my helmet,
Judah my commander's staff.

* Verse numbers in RSV.

10 Moab is my washbasin, [8]
upon Edom will I plant my sandal,
over Philistia will be my cry of conquest."
11 Who will bring me the Rock City? [9]
Who will offer me Edom's throne?
12 But you, O God—will you be angry with us, [10]
and go forth no more, O God, with our armies?
13 Grant us liberation from the adversary, [11]
since the aid of man is futile.
14 With God we'll achieve victory, [12]
he himself will trample on our adversaries.

Notes

lx. Like Ps xliv, this is a national lament in which the community, probably in the person of the king (cf. vss. 7, 9), prays for deliverance from its adversaries. To place the psalm historically with any degree of certainty is beyond the reach of present scholarship, but the superscription, language, and contents permit a tentative dating in the Davidic period. If, however, vs. 7 *y^{e}dīdekā*, "your beloved," alludes to King Solomon, who was also named *y^{e}dīdyāh* (II Sam xii 25), the psalm would belong to the Solomonic period.

The lament presents a rather curious structure. Verses 3–5 describe a shattering national defeat that is likened to a cosmic catastrophe. A prayer for liberation is the burden of vss. 6–7, while vss. 8–10, consisting of 3+3+3 tricola—all other verses are 3+3 bicola—transmit the oracle that answers the prayer of the preceding two verses. The final verses (11–14) are a prayer for victory.

Verses 7–14 recur, with minor variations, in Ps cviii 7–14.

1. *Lilies.* A musical term of uncertain meaning recurring in Pss xlv 1, and lxix 1.

A solemn commandment . . . to be taught. With *'ēdūt . . . l^{e}lammēd* might be compared royal Ps cxxxii 12, *b^{e}rītī w^{e}'ēdōtī zō '^{a}lamm^{e}dēm,* "My covenant and my solemn commandment which I shall teach them." For this definition of *'ēdūt,* see R. de Vaux in *Mélanges Eugène Tisserant,* I (Vatican City, 1964), p. 127.

2. *miktam.* Consult NOTE on Ps lvi 1.

when he strove . . . . Cf. II Sam viii 2, 3, 13; I Chron xviii 2, 3, 12, which narrate that David (with Joab commanding the army) slew eighteen thousand Edomites in the Valley of Salt, near the Dead Sea. But the connection between the superscription and the contents of the psalm is obscure on a number of points, such as the mention of Aram-Naharaim, an area of northern Mesopotamia important as the home of the Hebrew patriarchs, in the superscription but not in text of the psalm.

3. *you were angry with us.* The writer's hesitation in accepting the definition of *zānaḥ,* "to be angry," in Ps xliv 10 (*Psalms I,* p. 266) stemmed from insufficiently clear parallelism, but here the balance with *'ānaptā,* "You were wrathful," permits no indecisiveness. However, I would dissent from R. Yaron in VT 13 (1963), 238, who terms the present usage "transitive"; the suffix of *zānaḥtānī* is not accusative, but dative (*Psalms I,* p. 326). Yaron arrived at his definition of *zānaḥ,* usually rendered "to reject," through Akk. *zenû,* "to be angry," but it may be of historical interest to cite the nineteenth-century observation of E. F. C. Rosenmüller, *Scholia in Vetus Testamentum in compendium redacta* (Lipsiae, 1831), III, p. 377: "Verbum *znḥ* proprie *rancidum esse,* hinc, ad animum translatum, significat *iram, indignationem, odium,* praesertim grave, diuturnum, et inveteratum" ["The verb *znḥ,* properly *to be rancid,* whence transferred to the mind, signifies *wrath, indignation, hatred,* that is especially serious, lasting, and deep-seated"].

and you ran from us. If strict parallelism marks the members of this verse, consonantal *prṣtnw* should express something akin to "You turned away from us." Hence I would break down *prṣtnw* into the conjunction *p^e^,* "and" (*Psalms I,* pp. 307 f.), *raṣtā* from *rwṣ,* "to run," predicated of God in Ps xl 14, and the dative suffix *-nū* (see preceding NOTE). Compare Jer x 20, *bānay y^e^ṣā'ūnī,* "My sons have issued from me," and Ps lxxiii 27, *r^e^ḥēqekā,* "those who go far from you." Hence when God is angry, he is pictured as going far from his people. This gives rise to the prayer *šūbēnū,* "Return to us!," recited to appease the wrathful deity; cf. Ps lxxxv 5–6.

You were wrathful. Being a denominative verb from *'ap,* "nostril, wrath," *'ānaptā* belongs to that growing list of Northwest Semitic verbs derived from names of the parts of the body; cf. the NOTE on Ps lxxiii 6 and *Psalms I,* pp. 84, 118, 164.

you turned away from us. The construction *t^e^šōbēb lānū* finds an apt illustration in UT, 2 Aqht:VI:42, *ṯb ly,* "Turn away from me," as correctly translated by W. F. Albright in BASOR 94 (1944), 34, n. 22, who compares *ṯb ly* with Heb. *šūb mimmennī*. For other instances of *lᵉ*, "from," cf. *Psalms I*, p. 321; UHP, p. 29, and *Biblica* 47 (1966), 406, while the intransitive use of polel *šōbēb* can be seen in Jer viii 5, "Why does this people turn away (*šōbᵉbāh*)?"

4. *the land*. Palestine is intended, since the next verse mentions "your people."

and it went to pieces. MT *pᵉṣamtāh* is a hapax legomenon of uncertain meaning. The consonants *pṣmth* are capable of another analysis: conjunction *pᵉ*, "and" (see second NOTE on vs. 3), followed by *ṣūmᵉtāh*, third person feminine singular, qal passive, of *ṣāmat*, "to destroy, annihilate," Ugar. *ṣmt//mḫṣ*. One may also vocalize *ṣāmattāh*, "you destroyed her."

Weak. Traditionally explained as an alternate spelling of imperative *rᵉpā'*, "Heal!," consonantal *rph* becomes syntactically viable when vocalized as the feminine adjective *rāpāh* (MT *rᵉpāh*), modified by the accusative of instrumentality *šᵉbārehā;* see the next NOTE.

from its fractures. Parsing *šᵉbārehā* as instrumental accusative, and for the thought comparing UT, 'nt:III:30, *b'dn ksl tṯbr*, "Behind, her loins do break." The vocable *šᵉbārehā*, collocated with *rāpāh*, is significantly telltale: the motif delineated in vs. 4 is that of a person—here Palestine personified—collapsing or going to pieces on receiving bad news. By abandoning his people during a battle, God was considered responsible for Palestine's debilitation when the nation learned of the military rout. This motif has been touched upon in *Psalms I*, p. 281. To the bibliography given there may be added D. R. Hillers, "A Convention in Hebrew Literature: The Reaction to Bad News," in ZAW 77 (1965), 86–90, where the four essential elements are examined. Of the key words that figure in this motif, four appear in our verse: *hir'aštāh*, "you shook," *rāpāh*, "weak," *šᵉbārehā*, "her fractures," and *māṭāh*, "did it totter."

much did it totter. Explaining *kī* as emphatic with the resulting postposition of the verb; *Psalms I*, p. 301, and below on Pss lxxxix 2–3, xc 4.

5. *You made your people drain*. Vocalizing *hōrē'tāh* (MT *hir'ītāh*) and deriving the verb from *yr'* II, "to drink deeply," studied in *Psalms I*, p. 206.

the cup. Namely, the cup of divine wrath; cf. Ps lxxv 9, where *māṣāh*, "to drain," is used of the chalice prepared by God, and Isa li 17–18, which describes Jerusalem's condition as the result of imbibing divine indignation.

MT *qāšāh* is parsed as the accusative of *qāš*, "cup," found in UT, 'nt:v:41–42, *klnyy qšh nbln klnyy nbl ksh*, "All of us carry his cup, all of us carry his chalice." The apparent synonymy here with *ks*, "chalice," and the parallelism with *yayin*, "wine," in the psalm adequately indicate the sense of biblical *qāšāh*. It is evidently related to Heb. *qaśwāh*, "jar," Ar. *qaśwatu*, "basket." This uncommon poetic word forms a wordplay with immediately following *hišqītānū*, "You made us drink." In laments such play on words is, paradoxically, quite common; e.g., Pss v 10, vii 16, xliv 19, lvi 9, lxix 30, lxxiv 19, lxxx 10, lxxxvi 1, lxxxviii 10, 16, 18, cxxxvii 5; Lam i 16. In this practice the biblical poets are maintaining a Canaanite tradition of the Late Bronze Age (1500–1200 B.C.); see NOTE on "my lament," Ps lvi 9, and W. L. Holladay, VT 20 (1970), 156.

that dazed us. In view of the Hebrew personal name *rᵉʿēlāyāh*, it seems probable that the root of *tarʿēlāh*, "reeling, dazed condition," is represented in the incomplete Ugaritic personal name *rʿl* [ ], whose missing element is a divine name such as *il* or *bʿl*.

6. *give*. Parsing *nātattāh* as precative perfect, with full writing of the final syllable, commented upon in *Psalms I*, p. 26. Cf. Ps iv 8, *nātattāh*, "Put!"

a banner. MT *nēs* is preferable to the reading *nūs*, "refuge," adopted by some scholars. The several striking verbal similarities between our psalm and Ps 20 permit one to argue that MT *nēs*, "banner," supports the rendition of Ps xx 6, *nᵉdaggēl*, "We hold high the banners" (*Psalms I*, p. 128).

bowmen. Explaining *qōšeṭ* as an abstract form, "archery," here understood concretely, whose final *ṭ* resulted from the partial assimilation to emphatic *qoph*. No longer is it necessary to resort to Aramaic influence for an explanation of the form, since partial assimilation is already witnessed in UT, 1005:4; 1010:14, *ṣṭq* (=*ṣdq*) *šlm;* UT, § 5.24.

7. *your beloved*. Probably the king; cf. the introductory NOTE. The plural form *yᵉdīdekā* would be a plural of majesty, similar to plural *ʿᵃbādekā*, "your servant," a reference to the king in Ps lxxxix 51.

give us victory. For this nuance of *hōšīʿāh*, whose object suffix is forthcoming from parallel and synonymous *ʿᵃnēnū* (cf. *Psalms I*, pp. 17 f.), see *Psalms I*, p. 128.

with your right hand. As in Pss xviii 36, cxxxviii 7, *yᵉmīnᵉkā* is an accusative of means.

grant us triumph. Consult *Psalms I*, pp. 116, 128, on *ʿnw*, "to triumph." The Ketib reads *ʿᵃnēnū*, but the Qere has *ʿᵃnēnī*, "grant me triumph," whose singular suffix could well accord with "your beloved" understood of the king.

8. *God spoke*. These words introduce the oracle given in reply to the community's supplication. A priest or prophet has received divine as-

surance that God is still the master of nations and will intervene on Israel's behalf; cf. *Psalms I*, p. 128, on Ps xx 7.

from his sanctuary. As in Pss xx 3 (cf. first NOTE on Ps liii 7), lxiii 3, lxviii 25, cxxxiv 2, cl 1, *qōdeš* refers to the heavenly sanctuary, while the phrase *dibber beqodšō* is syntactically similar to Ps xcix 7, *be'ammūd 'ānān yedabbēr*, "He spoke from the pillar of the cloud." Other examples of *be*, "from," are given in *Psalms I*, p. 319. RSV renders our phrase, "God has spoken in his sanctuary," with the appended note, "Or *by his holiness*." Neither alternative seems correct. *The Grail Psalms, A New Translation* (see *Psalms I*, p. 16), has grasped the true force of the preposition, rendering: "From his holy place God has made this promise." In UT, 'nt:III:27, *qdš* doubtless refers to Baal's heavenly sanctuary.

Exultant, I will make Shechem my portion. A case of hendiadys, the text literally reading, "I will exult and I will make Shechem my portion."

Shechem. A city in central Palestine, belonging to the tribe of Ephraim.

Valley of Succoth. In central Transjordan, in the territory of the tribe of Gad. Nelson Glueck (*Explorations in Eastern Palestine* [New Haven, 1951], IV, p. 308 and Fig. 101) proposed to identify biblical Succoth with Deir 'Alla in the Jordan Valley, but recent excavations at this site have led the excavator, H. J. Franken, to query this identification, without, however, wishing to deny categorically such an equation.

9. *Gilead . . . Manasseh . . . Ephraim . . . Judah*. All Hebrew territories or parts of the Hebrew empire under the United Monarchy.

10. *Moab*. A kingdom east of the Dead Sea, in what is now Jordan. Moab, Edom, and Philistia were also attached to the United Monarchy, either as provinces or as vassal states. The whole list thus gives a fairly good impression of the United Monarchy, though no rapport can now plausibly be established between the objects listed and the various nations.

my washbasin. Fine specimens of footbaths were discovered during the excavations of Samaria in central Palestine and have been published by J. W. Crowfoot, *The Objects from Samaria. Samaria-Sebaste* (London, 1957), Pl. xvii 16, Fig. 29, and p. 187, for discussion.

Edom. A traditional enemy of Israel, occupying the region between the Dead Sea and the Gulf of Aqaba.

will I plant. Deriving *'ašlīk* from *šlk* II, "to nourish, support, rest," discussed in the first NOTE on Ps lv 23. The oracle pictures God, the conquering warrior, resting his foot on the neck of Edom's king as a sign of vanquishment. *Psalms I*, p. 116, discusses this motif in connection with Ps xviii 41. Though it related *'ašlīk* to *šlk* I, "to cast," the

Targ. took the phrase as referring to the custom of placing the foot on the neck of the vanquished. Hence the widely held interpretation of the phrase in a juridical sense (with the usual citation of Ruth iv 7—most recently by G. M. Tucker in CBQ 28 [1966], 44) may have to go by the board.

my sandal. Among the products of the artisan-god Kothar's skill that are listed in UT, 51:I:26–44, figure *n'l il* (line 37), "El's sandals," and during the twenty-third archaeological campaign at Ras Shamra (1960) was found a bronze statue of El, whose open sandals were overlaid with gold. Cf. Schaeffer in AfO 20 (1963), 206–7, Fig. 21.

over. Reading *'ªlē* (MT *'ālay*), as in geminate phrase of Ps cviii 10.

my cry of conquest. Parsing *hitrō'ā'ī* as hithpoel infinitive construct, followed by the first person singular suffix. The doublet in Ps cviii 10 reads the finite verb *'etrō'ā'*, "I give a cry of conquest."

11. *Who will bring me.* That is, as tribute. The speaker here is probably the king. M. Bogaert in *Biblica* 45 (1964), 236 f., has explained the suffix of *yōbīlēnī* as datival, precisely as in UT, 51:v:93–94, *tblk ǵrm mid ksp,* "The mountains will bring you much silver."

Rock City. Another name for Petra ("rock"), the famous capital of the Nabataeans. Whether *ṣōr* is identical with biblical Sela because of the identical meaning of the names is still disputed. With Hummel in JBL 76 (1957), 97; P. J. Calderone in *Biblica* 42 (1961), 431, and Bogaert in *Biblica* 45 (1964), 237, I read *'īr-m* (*mem* enclitic) *ṣōr* for MT *'īr māṣōr.* Cf. J. Starcky, *Pétra et la Nabatène,* in *Supplément au Dictionnaire de la Bible,* ed. by H. Cazelles and A. Feuillet, Fasc. 39 (Paris, 1964), cols. 886–1017.

will offer me. There is no need to read imperfect *yanḥēnī* as suggested by BH³ and BHS because given the frequent *yqtl//qtl* sequence, perfect *nāḥanī* makes an unexceptionable sequent to imperfect *yōbīlēnī,* "will bring me." See the second NOTE on Ps cviii 11. Should *yanḥēnī* prove to be the preferred reading, it would still be unnecessary to assume the haplography of a *yod.* There is ample evidence that when the same consonant ended one word and began the next, it was written but once; it was a consonant shared by two words. Cf. Wilfred Watson, "Shared Consonants in Northwest Semitic," *Biblica* 50 (1969), 525–33.

Edom's throne. Identifying *'ad* (pointing uncertain) with Ugar. *'d* in UT, 127:22–24, *yṯb krt l'dh yṯb lksi mlk lnḫt lkḥṯ drkt,* "Kirta sits upon his seat, he sits upon his royal throne, upon the peaceful bench of his authority." Other biblical texts with *'d,* "seat, chair," number Pss lxxxix 30, 38, xciii 5 (see J. D. Shenkel in *Biblica* 46 [1965], 404–9), xciv 15, cx 1; Isa xlvii 7, lvii 15; Jer xxii 30; Zeph iii 8. Consult M. Dahood in *Sacra Pagina,* eds. J. Coppens et al. (Paris-Gembloux, 1959), I, pp. 276–

78; *Biblica* 44 (1963), 300, n. 3; UHP, p. 67; Georg Sauer, *Die Sprüche Agurs* (Stuttgart, 1963), p. 36, n. 3.

12. *But you.* Parsing *hᵃlō'* as the interjection "Behold!" discussed in the second NOTE on Ps liv 2, not as the interrogative particle.

be angry with us. Understanding the suffix of *zānaḥtānū* as the dative of disadvantage; cf. first NOTE on vs. 3.

13. *liberation from the adversary.* See the NOTE on Ps cviii 13 for the explanation of *'ezrat miṣṣār,* rendered "help against the adversary" in earlier printings.

14. *will trample on our adversaries.* Cf. Pss xliv 6 and cx 5, "The Lord at your right hand will smite kings on the day of his wrath."

PSALM 61

(lxi 1–9)

1 *For the director; upon a stringed instrument. Of David.*

2 Hear, O God, my cry,
listen to my prayer!
3 From the brink of the nether world [2]*
to you I call
As faint grows my heart.
From it lead me
to the Lofty Mountain.
4 O that you would be my refuge, [3]
a towered fortress against the Foe!
5 That I might dwell in your eternal tent, [4]
find refuge under the shelter of your wings. *Selah*
6 O that you yourself, O God, would hear my vows, [5]
would grant the request of him who fears your name.
7 Add days to the king's days, [6]
turning his years into endless generations.
8 Let him sit enthroned before God forever, [7]
may kindness and fidelity be appointed to safeguard him.
9 Then will I always hymn your name, [8]
fulfilling my vows day by day.

* Verse numbers in RSV.

NOTES

lxi. If with most modern scholars we classify this psalm as an individual lament composed by a member of the Old Testament community (cf. Kraus, *Psalmen*, I, p. 433), we shall find it difficult to account for the prayer for the king in vss. 7–8. With Gunkel and Kraus we shall be forced to describe these two verses as the misplaced work of a later hand. If, however, we assume that the suppliant is a king, no such problem arises. The one question that is raised—the shift from the first (vss. 2–6, 9) to the third (vss. 7–8) person—can satisfactorily be explained as *Hofstil* ("court style"). For our purpose, the most lucid parallel is the fifteen-line Phoenician Inscription of King Yeḥawmilk of Byblos dating to the fifth-century B.C. Throughout the first eight and one half lines Yeḥawmilk speaks of himself in the first person ("And I made for my lady, mistress of Gebal, this altar of bronze . . ."), but at the end of line 8 he unexpectedly shifts to the third person: "May the mistress of Gebal bless Yeḥawmilk, king of Gebal, and grant him life, and prolong his days and his years over Gebal, for he is the legitimate king. . . ." Hence this psalm is most coherently interpreted as a royal supplication for deliverance from death (vss. 2–4) and admittance to the celestial dwelling of God where the king might eternally praise the name of God in his immediate presence (vss. 5–9).

1. *a stringed instrument.* Scholars are wont to repoint singular *n^egînat,* which is hapax legomenon, to plural *n^egînôt,* which is normally found (e.g., Pss iv 1, vi 1, liv 1). But since it is the more difficult reading, *n^egînat* should be preserved and explained as a feminine absolute form in *-at,* as in Ugaritic; see first NOTE on Ps lx 13.

3. *the brink of the nether world.* For the exegesis of this phrase, cf. Christoph Barth, *Die Errettung vom Tode in den individuellen Klage- und Dankliedern des Alten Testaments* (Basel, 1947), p. 83, and for a listing of texts with *'ereṣ,* "nether world," *Psalms I,* p. 106. The phrase *miq^eṣēh hā'āreṣ* recurs in Jer x 13 where, as here, it has been taken as "bounds of the earth." Once it is recognized, however, that in Jer x 12 *'ereṣ* also refers to the underworld, the sense of *'ereṣ* in Jer x 13 becomes clearer. These two verses would read: "Who made the nether world by his power, established the earth by his wisdom, and by his skill stretched out the heavens. At his thunder masses of water pour down from heaven, and he brings up vapors from the brink of the nether world" (cf. Gen ii 6). Verse 12 articulates the tripartite division of the cosmos (cf. NOTE on Ps lxxvii 19), while vs. 13 depicts God causing the two extremities of the cosmos—heaven and the nether world—to supply man, occupying the center of the universe, with the water he needs.

The psalmist is here describing the human condition in existentialist terms: man constantly stands at the edge of the abyss, and only divine assistance can prevent his falling into it. Ecclus li 9 voices a related idea: *w'rym m'rṣ qwly wmš'ry š'wl šw'ty,* "And I raised my voice from the City, and from the gates of Sheol my cry."

to you I call. The first part of vs. 3 is preferably scanned as a tricolon with *'ēlekā 'eqrā',* "to you I call," serving as a double-duty modifier or two-way middle. It is thus preceded by a prepositional phrase describing the place, "From the brink of the nether world," and followed by a prepositional phrase stating the time, "As faint grows my heart." The line now scans as a 6:5:5 tricolon rather than a 11:5 bicolon.

It may be pointed out here that the parallelism between *'ereṣ* "nether world," and *ṣûr,* "mountain," can be identified in UT, 'nt:III:25–26, *hmlt arṣ,* "the multitude of the nether world," parallel to *ģry il,* "my towering mountain."

From it. Namely, from the edge of Sheol. Explaining the suffix *mimmennī* as third person singular masculine; cf. *Psalms I,* pp. 10 f., and Eccles ii 25, *ḥûṣ mimmennī,* "apart from him," as translated and parsed in *Biblica* 43 (1962), 353.

lead me. Parsing *tanḥēnī* as a jussive form with imperative meaning, thus forming an inclusion with imperative *šim'āh,* "hear," in vs. 2; *Psalms I,* pp. 29 f.

The psalmist uses *tanḥēnī* in a double sense: to lead from the rim of annihilation and to lead into Paradise. *Psalms I,* pp. 33, 147, examines several texts (Pss v 9, xxiii 3, lxxiii 24, cxxxix 24) where *nāḥāh* is a *terminus technicus* for ushering one into eternal mansions.

Lofty Mountain. Parsing *yārūm* as the passive participle of the root *yrm,* discussed in *Psalms I,* p. 118 (under *yāram* in the Index, p. 48 should be corrected to 118). Usually rendered "rock," *ṣûr* has more the Ugaritic meaning of *ģr//gb',* "mountain." Compare Ps xviii 47. Cf. UT, 76:III:12–13, *y'l b'l bģ[r] wbn dgn bš[mm?],* "Baal went up to the mountain, and Dagan's son into heaven." The restoration *bģ[r]* is now sustained by the reading of Herdner, *Corpus des tablettes,* p. 51, but the completion of *bš[mm]* is conjecture.

"The Lofty Mountain" is apparently a poetic name of God's heavenly abode, like *ṣiyyôn* in Ps liii 7 (see NOTE thereto). In other words, the psalmist's request resembles the prayer of Ps xliii 3, "Let them bring me to your holy mountain (*har qodšekā*) and to your dwelling." I am now inclined to interpret this latter prayer as a request for admittance to God's celestial abode rather than to his temple in Jerusalem. Compare Ps cxxi 1, *'eśśā' 'ēnay 'el hehārīm,* "I raise my eyes to the mountain," with Ps cxxiii 1, *'ēlekā nāśa'tī 'et 'ēnay hayyōšᵉbī baššāmayim,* "To you I raise my eyes, O you who sit enthroned in the heavens!" From this comparison it becomes reasonably clear that *hārīm* is a plural of majesty denoting the heavenly mountain.

4. *O that. Psalms I,* pp. 19 f.

a towered fortress. Analyzing *migdal 'ōz* (also in Judg ix 51; Prov xviii 10), customarily translated "a strong tower" (RSV), as a composite noun (*Psalms I,* p. 325) comprised of *migdāl,* "tower," and *'ōz,* "fortress" (*Psalms I,* p. 50). Though few, the composite words in Ugaritic are sufficient to indicate that Hebrew lexicographers have underestimated their number in the OT. Compare Isa xxvi 1 *'īr 'ōz,* translated "fortress-city" in *Psalms I,* p. 173.

the Foe. Referring to the enemy par excellence, Death; cf. *Psalms I,* pp. 77, 105. With *'ereṣ,* "nether world," in vs. 3, *'ōyēb* at the end of vs.

4 forms an inclusion (*Psalms I*, p. 327). The association of *'ōyēb* with *'ereṣ*, "nether world," and *'āpār*, "mud," in Ps vii 6 makes it very probable that the term there also refers to Death; this identification was not explicitly made in *Psalms I*, p. 43, though it is found on p. 105.

Canaanite imagery shows through this plea that God become a towered-fortress against Death. In UT, 51:v:121–27, Baal pleads with the artisan-god Kothar not to put windows in his palace. The motive is not altogether clear, but several scholars believe that the reason is to be found in Jer ix 20, "For Death has come up through our windows, has entered our castles." Hence to ward off Death, a fortress with towers is needed.

5. *That I might dwell.* Parsing *'āgūrāh* as subjunctive; cf. Ps ix 15, and *Psalms I*, p. 57.

your eternal tent. Parsing *be'oholekā 'ōlāmīm* as a construct chain with the pronominal suffix *-kā* interposed; consult *Psalms I*, pp. XXXIX f., 110, and UHP, p. 15, where UT, 'nt:III:26, *btk ǵry il ṣpn* is rendered, "in the midst of my towering mountain Zaphon." Stylistically, this construct chain balances the construct chain *beséter kenāpekā*, "under the shelter of your wings." New examples of this poetic syntax number Deut xxiii 24, *'elōhekā nedābāh*, "your generous God"; Job xv 10, *kabbīr mē'ābīkā yāmīm*, "older than your aged father," xviii 14, *yinnātēq mē'oholō mibṭāḥō*, "He is snatched from his comfortable tent" (Pope, The Anchor Bible, vol. 15). New bibliography includes A. A. Wieder in JBL 84 (1965), 164, n. 30.

As in Ps xxviii 5, *'ōhel* designates God's celestial habitation, and as in Ps xxvii 4, the psalmist is requesting eternal union with God in the afterlife. Thus there is greater reason to believe that "your tent" and "your holy mountain" in Ps xv 1 refer to those in heaven, and that Ps xv is a liturgy specifying the requisite moral qualities for admission to Paradise.

your wings. This imagery is treated in *Psalms I*, pp. 107 f.

6. *O that.* See first NOTE on vs. 4.

you yourself. Cf. *Psalms I*, pp. 20, 241, for *kī 'attāh* with the precative perfect.

would hear. Parsing *šāma'tā* as precative perfect; cf. *Psalms I*, p. 20.

would grant. Parsing *nātattā*, as in Ps lx 6, as precative perfect.

the request. Explaining *yerešet* (MT *yeruššat*) as a by-form of royal Ps xxi 3, *'arešet;* cf. *Psalms I*, p. 95, for other examples of interchange between *primae yod* and *primae aleph* nouns. There may even be a third by-form in unexplained Job xvii 11, *mōrāšē lebābī*, "my cherished desires," literally "the requests of my heart."

of him who fears your name. Parsing *yir'ē šemekā* as a plural of majesty designating the king, just as plural *'abādekā*, "your servant," refers to the king in Ps lxxxix 51. Traditional "those who fear your name" is difficult to fit into the context of the psalm. As in Ps xiii (see *Psalms I*, third NOTE on Ps xiii 5), there appear to be but three *personae dramatis* in this poem: God, Death, and the psalmist. Representing in his person the community of believers, the king may appropriately use the plural form.

7. *Add.* In balance with precative *šām'atā*, "hear," and *nātattā*, "grant," in vs. 6, imperfect *tōsīp* functions as an imperative; cf. *Psalms I*, pp. 29 f., and above on vs. 3.

days to the king's days. The king speaks of himself in the third person; the use of *'ebed* as a substitute for the first person singular pronoun (*Psalms I*, p. 124) may be cited to illustrate the practice of using a third person substantive as a surrogate for the first person.

Since this is a prayer for immortality, *yāmīm*, "days," does not mean the days of a man on earth, but his days with God in the afterlife, in other words, divine days. Cf. Job x 5, "Are your days as the days of a mortal? / Your years as men's years?" (Pope, The Anchor Bible, vol. 15).

The wording of this prayer affects the translation and exegesis of Prov ix 10–11, "The beginning of wisdom is reverence for Yahweh, and knowledge of the Holy One is understanding, because through him (the suffix of *bī* is third person singular) your days will be multiplied, and he will increase for you the years of your life." In this passage, to explain "days" and "years" as purely terrestrial would be much too restrictive.

turning. The lifeless second colon needs a verb which is forthcoming when often-emended MT *k*^{e}*mō* is vocalized *kammō*, the piel infinitive absolute of **kimmā*, "to make like," a verb coined from the adverb *k*^{e}*mō*, "like, as."

his years. When the goddess Anath promises Aqhat immortality, she assures him: *ašsprk 'm b'l šnt* (2 Aqht:VI:28–29), "I will make you number years like Baal." (For Ugar.-Heb. *'m*, "like," see M. Held in JBL 84 [1965], 280, n. 36.)

The biblical parallelism between *yāmīm* and *šānōt* equals that of UT, 1019:4–5, *alp ymm wrbt šnt*, "a thousand days, ten thousand years." Parallel pairs of words are discussed in the fourth NOTE on Ps lvii 8.

endless generations. This request bears comparison with that made by the king of Pyrgi in Etruria on behalf of the statue of the goddess Astarte: *wšnt lm'š 'lm bbty šnt km hkkbm 'l*, "And may the years of the statue of the goddess in her grave be as the years of the stars of El." Consult P. Nober, "Scavi nel santuario etrusco di Pyrgi," in *Verbum Domini* 43 (1965), 198–205.

Heb. *dōr wādōr* equals Ugar. *dr dr*. The biblical association of *melek* and *dōr wādōr* is a reminiscence of UT, 68:10, *tqḥ mlk 'lmk drkt dt drdrk*, "You will receive your eternal kingship, your everlasting dominion." Cf. Exod iii 15.

8. *sit enthroned*. The pregnant sense of *yēšēb* is discussed on pp. 7 f. of *Psalms I*.

before God. Enjoying the beatific vision; cf. especially royal Ps xxi 7 and its exegesis in *Psalms I*, p. 133; also p. 99 on Ps xvii 15. The third person reference to God belongs to court style.

forever. The lack of the preposition *l*[e] with *'ōlām* (notice *lā'ad* in the following verse) is disturbing, and the possibility that *'ōlām*, "eternity," by metonymy denotes "eternal seat" is not excluded. Jer xlviii 18, *r*[e]*dī mikkābōd*, correctly rendered "Come down from your throne of glory" by AT, supplies an instructive analogy. Cf. also Ps xi 4.

kindness and fidelity. These divine attributes here, as in Pss lxxxv 11, lxxxix 15 and lvii 4, are personified as two attendants appointed to insure the king's safety. Consult *Psalms I*, pp. 148, 247, and NOTE on Ps lxxxix 15.

be appointed. Explaining consonantal *mn* as defective spelling for *mūnū*, precative perfect, qal passive. Many commentators, in the steps of GK, § 75cc, adopt MT *man*, and parse it as an apocopated piel imperative. This transition from third person *yēšēb* to second person *man* is stylistically harsh, whereas our analysis preserves the third person in both parts of the verse. Another misunderstood qal passive from *mānāh*, "to number, appoint," appears in Job vii 3, "Thus I am allotted empty months, / Weary nights are appointed (reading qal passive *mūnū* for MT *minnū*) me" (Pope, The Anchor Bible, vol. 15).

9. *hymn*. As noticed at Ps lvii 8, the root of Heb. *zāmar* appears in Ugaritic as *ḏmr*.

fulfilling. Parsing *l*[e]*šall*[e]*mī* as a circumstantial infinitive; GK, § 114o, and *Psalms I*, p. 167.

day by day. *yōm yōm* equals Ugar. *ymym*, "every day."

PSALM 62

(lxii 1–13)

1 *For the director; according to Jeduthun. A psalm of David.*

2 The God of gods alone
is my mighty castle;
My soul, from him will my triumph come.
3 He alone is my mountain of triumph, [2]*
my bulwark:
I will not stumble into the Dragnet.
4 How long will you bluster, [3]
indulge in gossip about a man?
All of you are like a leaning wall,
a sagging fence.
5 Craft alone do they propose, [4]
to ruin they indulge in lies;
With their mouth indeed they bless,
but in their heart they curse. *Selah*
6 God himself alone [5]
is my castle;
My soul, from him truly comes my hope.
7 He alone is my mountain of triumph, [6]
my bulwark:
I will not stumble.
8 The Most High God is my triumph, [7]
my Glorious One is my mountain-fortress,
God himself my refuge.
9 Trust in him, at all times the Strong One. [8]
Pour out your hearts before him,
for God is our refuge. *Selah*
10 Men of lowly birth are mere vapor, [9]
those of high degree a delusion.

* Verse numbers in RSV.

On scales they are lighter than leaves,
  together lighter than vapor.
11 Rely not on criminal extortion, [10]
  do not idolize wealth;
When God enounces, pay attention!
12 One thing has God spoken, [11]
  only two have I heard:
13 "Strength belongs to God, [12]
  and to you, O Lord, firmness;
You repay each man according to his deeds."

NOTES

lxii. A psalm of trust. This type of psalm may have developed from the laments, in which expressions of confidence are a common feature (see *Psalms I*, p. 68, introductory NOTE on Ps xi). The poet professes his absolute confidence in God's protection. Filled with this assurance of divine shelter, the psalmist instructs those who share his belief to place their trust in God rather than in extortion or wealth. There are several didactic elements in the poem (vss. 10–12), but not in sufficient number of justify BJ's classification as *psaume didactique*.

The psalm abounds in textual obscurities and ambiguities, so that the above version may not have consistently grasped the poet's intentions. The following NOTES indicate where the uncertainties lie.

1. *Jeduthun*. The name of a member of a musical guild instituted by King David; cf. W. F. Albright, *Archaeology and the Religion of Israel*, 2d ed. (Baltimore, 1946), p. 127. The name recurs in the superscriptions of Pss xxxix and lxxvii.

2. *The God of gods*. Reading *'ēl* (MT *'el*) *'ᵉlōhīm*, a title discussed in *Psalms I*, pp. 305 f. This composite appellative recurs in vss. 11–12, where its two components are separated in the parallel cola. Cf. NOTE on Ps lxxxiv 8, and Isa xlii 5, *hā'ēl yhwh*, but *h'l h'lwhym* in 1QIsᵃ.

alone. Taking *'ak* in a restrictive rather than in an asseverative sense. All five occurrences of *'ak* (vss. 2, 5, 6, 7, 10) in this psalm lend themselves to the restrictive interpretation.

my mighty castle. Identifying *dūmiyyāh* as a masculine form (see vs. 6) of Ugar. *dmt*, Akk. *dimtu*, "castle, fortress." Dahood in *Biblica* 45 (1964), 83–84, has identified *dūmāh*, "fortress," in Ezek xxvii 32, *mī kᵉṣūr kᵉdūmāh bᵉtōk hayyām*, "Who is like Tyre, like the fortress in the midst of the sea?" Ezekiel's collocation of *ṣūr* and *dūmāh* resembles the psalmist's balancing of *dūmiyyāh* with *ṣūrī*, "my mountain," in the next verse, where synonymous *miśgabbī*, "my bulwark," also appears. The final *-yāh* of *dūmiyyāh*, which recurs in Ps lxv 2, where it is parallel to *ṣiyyōn*, "the (heavenly) Zion," is the superlative or intensifying morpheme discussed in *Psalms I*, p. 240. (Cf. also Jer ii 31, *'ereṣ ma'pēlyāh*, "land of total darkness," a name for Sheol.) As remarked above, *dūmī*, without the superlative ending, appears in vs. 6, associated with *ṣūrī*, "my mountain," in vs. 7.

My soul. Shifting the *athnach* so as to put "my soul" in the second colon. *Psalms I*, p. 257, NOTE on Ps xlii 6, cites other texts containing the motif known as "the dialogue of a man with his soul."

my triumph. Or "my salvation." See *Psalms I*, p. 131.

3. *alone*. Cf. second NOTE on vs. 2.

my mountain. *ṣūr* equal Ugar. *ģr*, *"mountain,"//gb'*, "hill," an appellative of Baal, as noticed in *Psalms I*, p. 105. See W. F. Albright, "Baal-Zephon," in *Festschrift Alfred Bertholet*, ed. O. Eissfeldt et al. (Tübingen, 1950), pp. 1–4.

my mountain of triumph. Literally "my mountain and my triumph," a case of hendiadys. An analogous phrase appears in UT, 'nt:III:23, *bgb' tliyt*, "on my hill of victory," parallel to line 22, *bģr nḥlty*, "on my mountain of dominion."

I will not stumble. Concerning the pregnant sense of *lō' 'emmōṭ*, "I will stumble into Sheol," see *Psalms I*, pp. 78 f., and the fourth NOTE on Ps lv 23.

into the Dragnet. Unexplained *rabbāh* is tentatively identified with Ugar. *rbt* in UT, 51:II:32–33, *qḥ rṯt bdk* [ ] *rbt 'l ydm*, "Take the net in your hand, the dragnet upon both hands." In the Canaanite passage there can be little doubt about the general sense of *rbt*, a synonym of well-known *rṯt*, but whether it answers to the biblical vocable enjoys less certainty. But the pregnant sense of *'emmōṭ* in other passages, where it connotes "to stumble into Sheol," permits the inference that "Dragnet" is another of the many poetic designations of the nether world. The motif of Sheol as a place of nets receives brief comment in *Psalms I*, p. 258, and appears in Ps xviii 6 and Job v 5.

4. *will you bluster*. Deriving the hapax legomenon *tᵉhōtᵉtū* from the root underlying Ugar. *hwt*, "word." Pope (The Anchor Bible, vol. 15), discusses Job vi 30b, *hāwōt*, "words." Cf. also Dahood, UHP, p. 56, and Ps lii 3, "Why do you boast of evil?"

indulge in gossip. Literally "indulge your palate." An uncertain version stemming from the proposed reading *tirṣū ḥēk kullᵉkem* for MT *tᵉroṣṣᵉḥū kullᵉkem*. The phrase *tirṣū ḥēk* thus would compare with Ps xlix 14, *bᵉpīhem yirṣū*, "who indulged their taste." The verb *yirṣū* recurs in the following verse of our psalm.

All of you . . . sagging fence. Figurative for "You are a menace to the community."

5. *Craft alone.* With Gunkel (*Die Psalmen*, p. 264), reading *maššū'ōt* (MT *miśśe'ētō*) from *nāšā'*, "to beguile, deceive," and attaching the final *waw* to the following verb.

do they propose. Reading *weyā'aṣū* (see preceding NOTE), and parsing the *waw* as emphatic (*Psalms I*, p. 24).

to ruin. To bring about the downfall of the just. Our absolute translation reflects the Hebrew transitive infinitive *haddīaḥ*, the only known instance of its use without an accusative object.

they indulge in lies. The construction *yirṣū kāzāb*, "indulge in lies," resembles vs. 4, *tirṣū hēk*, "indulge in gossip."

With their mouth. Reading *bepī* (MT *bepīw*), and attaching the final letter to the following verb as emphatic *waw*. Since it counterbalances suffixed *qirbām*, "their heart," pī needs no suffix on the strength of the principle discussed in *Psalms I*, pp. 17 f. Or one may appeal to the practice, mentioned in *Psalms I*, p. 89, whereby the suffix may be omitted with names of parts of the body.

indeed they bless. Reading *wībārēkū* (MT *yebārēkū*; see preceding NOTE), and parsing the initial *waw* as emphatic (*Psalms I*, p. 24). As in the first colon of this verse, the emphatic particle may be responsible for the postposition of the verb.

they curse. Comparing *yeqallelū* with Ras Shamra Akk. *tu-qa-*[*l*]*i-il* in *Le palais royal d'Ugarit*, III, 16.270:27, p. 43.

6. *God himself.* Parsing the *lamedh* of *lē'lōhīm* as emphatic (*Psalms I*, p. 143), and comparing Ps lxxxix 19, *lyhwh*, "Yahweh himself."

alone. As throughout this poem, *'ak* bears a restrictive connotation; consult second NOTE on vs. 2.

my castle. Consult third NOTE on vs. 2.

My soul. As in vs. 2, *napšī* is shifted to the second colon.

7. *my mountain of triumph.* The third NOTE on vs. 3 comments on this hendiadys.

I will not stumble. See fourth NOTE on vs. 3.

8. *The Most High God. Psalms I*, pp. 45 f., examines the composite divine name *'al 'elōhīm*. Attention might be directed to the corresponding divine name *'l yhwh*, "the Most High Yahweh," in Pss xviii 42 and lv 23.

my Glorious One. This divine title *kebōdī* receives comment in *Psalms I*, p. 18, NOTE on Ps iii 4.

mountain-fortress. Comparing vs. 2, "my mighty castle." Rendered "my mighty rock" by RSV, *ṣūr 'uzzī* preferably parses as a composite noun like *migdal 'ōz*, "a towered fortress," in Ps lxi 4. In view of these examples, Ps xxxi 3, *leṣūr mā'ōz* perhaps denotes "O mountain-refuge!" rather than "O mountain of refuge!"

God himself. Though customarily parsed as *beth essentiae*, the initial consonant of *bē'lōhīm* might also be identified as the particle of emphasis studied in *Psalms I*, p. 177. In other words, *bē'lōhīm* and *lē'lōhīm* (vs. 6) express the same idea.

9. *the Strong One.* Deriving *'ām* from *'mm*, "to be strong," studied in *Psalms I*, pp. 112 f. The context suggests, however, that *'ām* might here denote "the fortress" (compare *'āz*, "strong," and *'ōz*, "fortress"), as in Nah iii 12, "All your fortifications (*mibṣārayik*) are fig trees, your fortress (*'ām*, MT *'im*) first-ripe figs," and UT, 2063:9–12, *'bdk b lwsnd [y?]bṣr 'm mlk*, "Your servant in LWSND has reinforced the royal fortress."

10. *lighter than leaves.* A doubtful rendering of unexplained *l'lwt*, which I would break down into comparative *lamedh* (*Psalms I*, p. 183) and *'lwt*, an assumed feminine plural of *'āleh*, "leaf."

lighter than vapor. The occurrence of *moznayim*, "scales," and *hebel*, "vapor," in the same line may impinge on the translation of disputed Isa xl 15, *hēn gōyīm kᵉmar mdly ūkᵉšaḥaq mō'znayim neḥšābū*, "Look, the nations are like a drop from a cloud (see Dahood, *Biblica* 47 [1966], 414–15), and they are evaluated like mist on scales." The unique singular form *šaḥaq*, from which root derives the plural form *šᵉḥāqīm*, "clouds, heaven," may well denote "mist," since the relationship between "mist" and "clouds" is apparent. Cf. *nᵉśī'īm*, "vapors" that form clouds and portend rain; BDB, p. 672a.

11. *criminal extortion.* Departing from the traditional verse-division, I attach *ūbᵉgāzēl*, "crime," to the first colon where with *bᵉ'ōšeq*, "extortion," it forms an hendiadys (*Psalms I*, p. 326).

do not idolize. Explaining *tehbālū*, usually rendered "set no vain hopes," as a denominative (piel pointing may be indicated) verb from *hebel* in the specific sense of "idol" (cf. BDB, p. 211a, and *Psalms I*, pp. 151, 188). Cf. Jer ii 5, *wayyēlᵉkū 'aḥᵃrē hahebel wayyehbālū*, "And they went after idols and worshiped them," and II Kings xvii 15. This analysis brings out the appositeness of balancing *tehbālū* with *tibṭᵉḥū*, "rely," which often denotes to trust in divinity. The psalmist warns against divinizing either just or unjust acquisitions.

wealth. Attaching *ḥayil* to the second colon of vs. 11, where it balances "criminal extortion." By *ḥayil* the poet doubtless intends to mean legitimate wealth as opposed to "criminal extortion."

When God enounces. Reading *kī yānūb 'ēl* (MT *'al*). Other instances of Masoretic confusion between *'al* and *'ēl* are documented in the first NOTE on Ps lix 12. That *nwb* expresses a labial action emerges from the following poetic texts: Prov x 31, *pī ṣaddīq yānūb ḥokmāh*, "The mouth of the just man enounces wisdom" (a slightly different version was proposed by Dahood, PNWSP, pp. 20 f.); Isa lvii 19, *bōrē' nwb śᵉpātīm*, "who creates the utterance of the lips"; Zech ix 17, *tîrôš yenōbēb betûlōt,* "New wine makes the maidens talkative" (cf. Joel iii 1); Prov v 20, *welāmmāh tišgeh benīb zārāh* (MT *benī bezārāh*), "Lest you be enticed by the seductive words of the harlot." This root appears in the Ugaritic substantive *nbt* (equals Heb. *nōpet*), "honey," and as a passive participle in UT, 51:II:32, *kt il nbt bksp,* "a gorgeous dais cast of silver." The primitive sense of the root is probably "to flow." In the psalm context, the synonymy with *dibber* accords with the usage in the cited biblical passages.

pay attention! Parsing *tāšītū* as an imperfect with imperative function; cf. Joüon, GHB, § 113m, and *Psalms I,* p. 306.

12. *One thing.* Comparing *'aḥat dibber* with Ps xxvii 4, *'aḥat šā'altī,* "One thing I have asked."

has God spoken. 'elōhīm is the component of the composite divine name *'ēl 'elōhīm,* whose previous occurrence in this poem has been remarked in the second NOTE on vs. 2. The psalmist here employs the well-documented (*Psalms I,* p. 325) poetic practice known as the breakup of stereotyped phrases, placing *'ēl* in vs. 11c and *'elōhīm* in vs. 12a.

only two. Though the numerical sequence x/x+1 is a poetic device common in the Semitic languages and literatures, the biblical bards were doubtless immediately indebted for it to their poetic predecessors in Canaan. This "numerical ladder" device does not always follow strict logic. The "one thing" and "only two" are mentioned in vs. 13. Consult W. M. W. Roth, "The Numerical Sequence x/x+1 in the Old Testament," in VT 12 (1962), 300–11, and Georg Sauer, *Die Sprüche Agurs,* pp. 87–112.

13. *firmness.* Since this poem stresses mainly God's power—witness the metaphors in vss. 3, 7, 8 and the parallelism here with *'ōz*—*ḥesed* probably bears the connotation examined in the NOTES on Ps lix 11 and 17. In warning men that God will repay them according to their behavior, the psalmist would be inclined to emphasize divine power and determination rather than mercy.

PSALM 63

(lxiii 1–12)

1 *A psalm of David, when he was in the Wilderness of Judah.*

2 O God, my God, for you I long,
my soul ardently thirsts for you,
my body pines for you
More than parched earth yearns for drops of water.
3 So in your sanctuary may I gaze upon you, [2]*
beholding your power and glory.
4 How much sweeter your kindness [3]
than my life and lips that praise you!
5 So may I bless you throughout my life eternal, [4]
in your heaven raise my hands.
6 Yonder with milk and fatness [5]
may my desire be satisfied;
While my lips shout for joy,
my mouth will praise you.
7 When on my couch I think of you, [6]
and through my vigils muse on you—
8 "O that you would be my help, [7]
that I might find refuge
in the shadow of your wings.
9 May my soul cling fast to you, [8]
your right hand grasp me."
10 But they who murderously seek my life, [9]
may they go to the nether world's depths.
11 May they be smitten by him [10]
with the edges of the sword,
Become the portion of jackals.
12 But the king will rejoice in God; [11]
all who swear by him will glory,
While the mouth of those telling lies will be shut.

* Verse numbers in RSV.

NOTES

lxiii. A king's prayer for the beatific vision in the heavenly sanctuary. Scholars, who generally classify this poem as a lament or a song of trust (vss. 9–10), are wont to describe vs. 12, which mentions the king, as a secondary addition. This judgment, however, fails to appreciate the literary practice whereby the poet-king might speak of himself in the first person in one part of the psalm and in the third person in another. See NOTE on vs. 12 and introductory NOTE to Ps lxi.

Form critics usually depict the author of this poem as a Levite in exile passionately yearning to participate in the temple service in Jerusalem. This reconstruction of the *Sitz im Leben* or "situation in life" stems from a misinterpretation of ambivalent *qōdeš*, "sanctuary," in vs. 3. If, as maintained in the apposite NOTE, *qōdeš* designates the celestial abode of God, we must assume another situation in life. Maligned by enemies (vs. 12) and threatened by foes (vs. 10), the desolate king, in language similar to that of Philip i 23, prays for deliverance from this life's vicissitudes in order to repose in the shadow of God's wings (vs. 8).

1. *Wilderness of Judah.* An allusion to events narrated in I Sam xxii 5, xxiii 14 ff.

2. *O God . . . drops of water.* This verse presents the interesting metrical arrangement A+B // B́+Á in which B—*kī* (see below) *ṣāmeʾāh lekā napšī*—and B́—*kāmah lekā beśārī*—are structurally very similar and semantically akin. These shorter cola are set between the longer cola A and Á that provide the framework of a long simile.

for you. Parsing *'attāh* as the independent pronoun serving as the direct object of the verb. Cf. UT, § 6.4, for examples such as *kbd hwt* ('nt:VI:20), "Honor him!"; UHP, p. 10, concerning Job xli 26; *Biblica* 47 (1966), 275 f., regarding Job xxxii 8, *rūaḥ hī'*, "the spirit of her," and Eccles vii 26, *'aššūrē hī'*, "the feet of her." For the present purpose the most relevant text is Ps cxxxvii 6, *'im lō' 'a'aleh 'att* (MT *'et*) *yerūšālāim 'al rō'š šimḥātī*, "If I do not extol you, O Jerusalem, above my keenest joy." The advantage of this parsing is that Jerusalem, addressed in the second person in vs. 6a, "If I do not remember you," remains in the second person.

I long. Reading *'ašaḥēr* and detaching the final *k* of consonantal *'šḥrk;* see next NOTE. This denominative verb from *šḥr*, "dawn," connotes to seek with one's whole heart. Ugar. *šḥr* denotes the common noun "dawn" as well as being the name of the divinity Dawn. Our version "for you I long" is sustained by the LXX *pròs sè 'orthrízo,* "For you I awake at dawn." Thus the syntax and the word order of the phrase *'attāh 'ᵃšaḥēr* closely compare with the syntax and word order of UT, 1 Aqht:15–16, *hwt l aḥw,* "But I will surely revive him."

ardently. The suffix of MT *'ᵃšaḥᵃrekkā* has been detached (previous NOTE) and pointed as defectively written *kī,* the emphatic conjunction; cf. fourth NOTE on Ps liv 7. This reading and parsing discloses a verse consisting of two five-syllable feet (*'ᵉlōhīm 'ēlī+'attāh 'ᵃšaḥēr*) followed by two four-syllable feet (*kī ṣāmᵉāh+lᵉkā napšī*). This scansion, it may be noted, points up the gratuitousness of deleting one word in the first two cola, as recommended by numerous scholars and registered in the critical apparatus of BH³.

thirsts. Heb. *ṣāmā'* equals Ugar. *ǵm'.*

More than. Parsing *bᵉ* of *bᵉ'ereṣ* as comparative; cf. NOTES on Ps li 8–9.

yearns. Since MT *'āyēp,* "faint, weary," does not agree with the gender of *'ereṣ,* "earth," I tentatively propose the infinitive absolute pointing *'āyōp,* while omitting the conjunction *wᵉ* as secondary. This vocalization resolves the problem of gender and accords with the conclusion reached on the evidence of Northwest Semitic discoveries, especially in the last twenty years (i.e., since the discovery of the long eighth-century Phoenician inscriptions at Karatepe in southeastern Turkey), that biblical poets employed the infinitive absolute much more frequently than the Masoretic pointing suggests. Consult *Psalms I,* p. 214.

drops of water. The hapax legomenon *bᵉli māyim,* "without water," is extremely banal in this verse of passionate language. Many commentators simply delete it as an explanatory gloss making the line too long; cf. Briggs, CECBP, II, p. 75. Accordingly, I propose reading *ballē* or *bullē māyim,* from *bālal,* which in Arabic denotes "to soak, to moisten (with water)," and in Hebrew and Akkadian, "to mix." Phoen. *bll* is the name of a sacrifice, while UT, 56:22, *bln qṭ yṣq baph* might well signify, "Pour the drops of *qṭ* into his nostrils." Cf. Job xxxvi 27, *niṭpē māyim,* "waterdrops."

3. *So.* My yearning to see God is like the longing of parched earth for water.

your sanctuary. Consult second NOTE on Ps lx 8 for *qōdeš,* "heavenly sanctuary." Suffixless *qdš* shares the suffix of the following word; *Psalms I,* pp. 17 f. Another example of this usage recurs in vs. 7.

may I gaze on you. Explaining *ḥᵃzītīkā* as precative perfect (*Psalms I,* p. 20) and as a technical term for gazing on the face of God in the future life; cf. *Psalms I,* pp. 99, 167.

beholding. Taking *lir'ōt* as a circumstantial infinitive (*Psalms I,* p. 50), not an infinitive to express purpose, as construed by CCD, "Thus have I gazed toward you in the sanctuary to see your power and your glory."

4. *How much.* For this meaning of *kī,* see *Psalms I,* p. 197.

sweeter. This nuance of *ṭōb* is discussed in *Psalms I*, pp. 206, 270. Cf. further Jer xii 6, xxxi 14, and for Akk. *ṭābu*, "sweet," R. D. Biggs in JCS 19 (1965), 97.

than my life. Reading *mēḥayyāy* for MT *mēḥayyīm*, whose final *mem* should be attached to the next word, as suggested by D. N. Freedman.

and lips. Attaching the final *mem* of preceding word to read *miśśᵉpātay*. This reading has the advantage of making masculine "life" and feminine "lips" the subject of the masculine verb, whereas in the traditional interpretation feminine *śᵉpātāy* is discordantly construed with the masculine verb; the discordance is even greater when the subject precedes the verb, as here.

Since adequate praise of God's goodness is beyond the psalmist's power in this life, he hopes to be able to extol God in the heavenly afterlife.

that praise you. The reading proposed in the two preceding NOTES safeguards the rule of agreement in gender between the subject and predicate. After subjects of different genders the predicate is put in the masculine plural (GK, § 146d). In view, moreover, of the Ugaritic personal name *bn ašbḥ*, one must be more cautious in terming *yᵉšabbᵉḥūnᵉkā* an Aramaism, as done by Briggs and more recently by Max Wagner, *Die lexikalischen und grammatikalischen Aramaismen im alttestamentlichen Hebräisch* (Berlin, 1966), p. 111. On the supposed Aramaicity of *plṭ*, see *Psalms I*, pp. 261 f.

5. *So*. See the first NOTE on vs. 3.

my life eternal. *Psalms I*, p. 320, lists the places where this gravid sense of *ḥayyīm*, Ugar. *ḥym*, is explained.

The intricate pattern of suffixes in this verse merits comment. There is the usual chiasmus with the verbs at the beginning and end of the bicolon, with the prepositional phrase in the middle: *'ᵃbārekᵉkā// 'eśśā' kappāy* and *bᵉḥayyāy//bᵉšāmekā*. Thus the order of suffixes is *-kā . . . -āy//-kā . . . -āy*, but that in the first colon *-kā* is attached to the verb, and to the prepositional phrase in the second. On the other hand, the suffix *-āy* is attached to the prepositional phrase in the first colon, and to the verbal phrase at the end of the second.

in your heaven. Since MT *bᵉšimᵉkā*, "in your name," does not issue in any significant assertion and receives no adequate explanation (cf. the attempts of Kraus, *Psalmen*, I, p. 448, to wrest meaning from the expression), one may propose the reading *bᵉšāmekā*, "in your heaven." *Psalms I*, p. 292, records an identical Masoretic mispointing in Ps xlviii 11, and new instances will be registered in Pss lxviii 5, cxliii 11. Thus the association here of "your heaven" with "your sanctuary" in vs. 3 compares with the parallelism in Ps cl 1, "Praise God in his sanctuary, praise him in his vaulted fortress," where "vaulted fortress" is a poetic name for heaven.

raise my hands. In a gesture of adoration.

6. *Yonder.* Namely, in Paradise with God. Generally rendered "as with," consonantal *kmw* (MT *k^{e}mō*) is probably to be identified with Akk. *kīmū*, "instead of," and pointed *kīmō* or *kīmū*. This definition yields considerable dividends in these passages: Ps cxli 7, *kīmō* (MT *k^{e}mō*) *pūl^{e}ḥū ūbūq^{e}'ū* (MT *pōlē^{a}ḥ ūbōqē^{a}'*) *bā'āreṣ*, "Yonder in the nether world may they be cleaved and split"; II Sam i 21, *'al ṭal w^{e}'al m^{e}ṭar 'ēlī* (= UT, 126:III:6, *mṭr 'ly;* contrast MT) *kīmō* (MT *k^{e}mō*) *šōd yeter ūmōt* (MT *ūś^{e}dēy t^{e}rūmōt*), "Let there be no dew, and let there be no rain of the Most High! Yonder may there be violence to excess and death."

milk. In the Masoretic phrase *ḥēleb wādešen*, "fat and fatness," the latter is often deleted here as contributing little to the thought and disrupting the meter. The difficulty can be resolved by the vocalization *ḥālāb*, "milk," and the observation that in Joel iii 18 and Isa lv 1 (*dešen* appears in following verse), *ḥālāb*, "milk," is figurative for the abundance of the eschatological age. Since our context presumably pictures the celestial banquet of the afterlife, "milk" would be entirely appropriate. In UT, 128:II:26, the royal offspring is described as *ynq ḥlb a[ṯ]rt*, "Sucking the milk of Asherah."

and fatness. dešen forms part of the messianic banquet depicted in Ps xxxvi 9, "They are sated with the fatness (*dešen*) of your estate/ from the stream of your delicacies/you give them to drink." Cf. Ps xxiii 5.

my desire. Concerning this nuance of *napšī*, cf. Pss x 3, xlix 19; UT, 127:11, *npšh llḥm tpth*, "She whets his appetite for food," and 49:II: 17–18, *npš ḫsrt bn nšm*, "Desire was lacking in men."

be satisfied. See third NOTE on Ps lxv 5.

my lips. Vocalizing *ś^{e}pātay*, as in vs. 4, for MT construct *śiptē*, "lips of," which creates syntactic difficulties.

shout for joy. Instead of MT *r^{e}nānōt*, a plural hapax legomenon, I read feminine plural participle *rōn^{e}nōt*.

7. *my vigils.* Suffixless *'ašmūrōt* receives its determination from parallel *y^{e}ṣū'āy*, "my couch," by reason of the principle documented in *Psalms I*, pp. 17 f.; see second NOTE on vs. 3.

8–9. *O that . . . grasp me.* Verses 8–9 record the nocturnal prayer of the psalmist.

O that. Concerning *kī* as a precative particle, *Psalms I*, p. 19, and second NOTE on Ps lv 10.

you would be. Parsing *hāyītā* as precative perfect; consult third NOTE on vs. 3.

find refuge. This sense of *'^{a}rannēn* is discussed at some length in *Psalms I*, p. 196, NOTE on Ps xxxii 7.

shadow of your wings. Cf. especially Ps xxxvi 8, "Gods and men find refuge in the shadow of your wings," a description of the security of the afterlife in heaven, for which the psalmist prays.

9. *my soul*. *napšī* may here be no more than a surrogate for the personal pronoun "I" (cf. AT, "I have clung close to you"), but the proposed version better accords with the theme struck in vs. 2.

cling fast. Since vss. 8–9 are interpreted as prayers, *dāb*ᵉ*qāh* parses as precative perfect; see third NOTE on vs. 3.

grasp me. Precative *tām*ᵉ*kā* is a synonym of *lāqaḥ*, the technical term for "assume" into heaven, as proposed in *Psalms I*, p. 252. As in Ps xli 13, *tāmak* occurs in a prayer for union with God in the afterlife.

10. *But they*. *w*ᵉ*hēmmāh* expresses emphatic antithesis.

who. As in Pss 1 8, lxxi 18, lxxxv 9, the relative pronoun *'ᵃšer* is to be understood; see *Psalms I*, pp. 113, 213 f., 307.

murderously. That is, with murderous intent. Explaining disputed *l*ᵉ*šō'āh* as a prepositional phrase whose root *š'y* probably equals *š'y* in UT, 3 Aqht:23–25, *špk km šiy dm km šḫṭ lbrkh*, "Like a murderer pour out his blood (notice that *dm* shares the suffix of *brkh*, "his knees"), like a slaughterer upon his knees." The balance with *šḫṭ*, "to slaughter," brings out the force of *šiy*. In this sense *Juxta Hebraeos* understood the phrase: "*Ipsi vero interficere quaerunt animam meam*" ["They, however, seek to slay my soul"]. Cf. Gen xlix 3, *yeter š't* (MT *śᵉ'ēt*) *w*ᵉ*yeter 'āz*, "an excess of murder, and an excess of violence"; Ezek xxxix 2; Lam iii 47. Ps xl 3, *bōr šā'ōn* is rendered "pit of Destruction" (*Psalms I*, p. 243).

may they go. Parsing *yābō'ū* as jussive mode rather than indicative "They shall go" (RSV). The several precatives in the poem prompt this interpretation.

nether world's depths. While asking Paradise for himself, the poet would consign his mortal foes to Sheol. As so frequently in Psalms, *'ereṣ* here denotes the nether regions (*Psalms I*, p. 106). In other terms, *taḥtiyyōt hā'āreṣ*, "the nether world's depths," is synonymous with Ps lxxxvi 13, *š*ᵉ*'ōl taḥtiyyāh*, "deepest Sheol." Cf. Eph iv 9, "Now the word 'ascended' implies that he also descended to the lowest level, down to the nether world."

11. *May they be smitten by him*. Bogaert, *Biblica* 45 (1964), 241, n. 2, correctly explains consonantal *ygyrhw* as containing a passive form (so LXX and Syr.), followed by a suffix expressing dative of agency. The agent is Sheol, as may be inferred from Ps cxli 7, and from the apt parallel in UT, 49:II:35–37, "She seizes the godly Mot, with sword she cleaves him, with blade she hacks him." The root *ngr*, "to smite," is studied in *Psalms I*, pp. 241 f. A recently recognized dative of agency

results in a new version of Eccles v 5, *lipnē himmālē'ᵃkā* (MT *hammal'āk*), "before it has been fulfilled by you"; cf. *Biblica* 47 (1966), 282; the third NOTE on Ps lxix 36; the seventh NOTE on Ps lxxii 17; the second NOTE on Ps lxxiii 26, and third NOTE on Ps lxxiv 19.

edges of the sword. Cf. Jer xviii 21, *haggīrēm 'al yᵉdē ḥāreb,* "Smite them with the edges of the sword."

portion. Gunkel's (*Die Psalmen,* p. 268) description of *mᵉnāt* as an Aramaism (see third NOTE on vs. 4) can scarcely be sustained in view of UT, 2 Aqht:II:33, *mnth,* "his portion" (consult Gaster, *Thespis,* 1961, p. 338, and Herdner, *Corpus des tablettes,* p. 80, n. 4), and 49:II:35–36, *ltikl 'ṣrm mnth,* "The birds consume his portions."

jackals. Heb. *šū'āl* equals Ugar. *ṯ'l.* The ancients dreaded the lack of proper burial so much that the Phoenician kings Tabnit and Eshmunazor, for example, curse those who would disturb their graves in these terms: "May they not have a burial place with the shades, nor be buried in a grave!" Cf. Gevirtz in VT 11 (1961), 149.

12. *But the king.* Just as adversative *wᵉhēmmāh* marks the transition from the psalmist (vss. 2–9) to the psalmist's enemies (vss. 10–11), so adversative *wᵉhammelek* indicates the shift from the adversaries to the person evidently identical with the speaker in vss. 2–9, namely the psalmist himself. Similar usage is remarked in the second NOTE on Ps lxi 7, and can be more fully illustrated by Canaanite practice in UT, 2 Aqht:VI:18–19, *wtn qštk [ly tq]ḥ qṣ'tk ybmmt limm,* "But give me your bow, let the creatress of the peoples take your arrows." Though the reading *ly* is not above doubt, the goddess Anath seems, in the first colon, to speak of herself in the first person, and in the second colon refers to herself in the third person ("the creatress of the peoples"). Similar indirection characterizes UT, 76:II:24–25, *nṭ'n barṣ iby wb'pr qmaḫk,* "We have planted my foes in the nether world, and in the mud those who rose up against your brother." Here "my foes" (first person) are identified with "those who rose up against your brother" (third person).

will rejoice. Cf. royal Ps xxi 2. Victory over his opponents will be the motive of his joy, as in Ps xxi.

swear by him. Namely, by God, as maintained by Friedrich Baethgen, *Die Psalmen* (Göttingen, 1904), p. 191. "All who swear by him" is a poetic description of the Israelites. The widely held view that the antecedent of *bō* is the king, i.e., "those who swear by the king," is grammatically unobjectionable, but the position of *bē'lōhīm* and *bō*—each at the end of its colon—suggests a parallelism of thought and an identity of persons. The LXX agrees.

the mouth of those telling lies. Regarding the king as the chief butt of criticism, consult the second NOTE on Ps liv 7.

will be shut. Namely, in Sheol, the land of silence; the poet resumes the thought of vss. 10–11. According to Canaanite mores, one of the duties of a loyal son was to silence the slanderers of his father. The text is UT, 2 Aqht:I:29–30, cited in *Psalms I,* pp. 20 f.

PSALM 64
(lxiv 1–11)

1 *For the director. A psalm of David.*

2 Hear my voice, O God, when I complain;
from the hostile pack protect my life.
3 Shelter me from the council of the wicked, [2]*
from the gathering of evildoers;
4 Who sharpen their tongue like a sword, [3]
aim their poisonous remark like an arrow
5 To shoot from ambush at the innocent; [4]
they shoot at him suddenly and fearlessly.
6 They fortify for him venomous substance, [5]
carefully conceal their snares,
Thinking, "Who looks down upon us?
7 Who can investigate our perfect crime?" [6]
But the Investigator will investigate
the innermost man,
even the depths of the heart.
8 Exalted be the God of the Arrow! [7]
double be their wounds!
9 The Most High shall make slanderers stumble, [8]
all the arrogant will be brought low.
10 Every man will stand in awe, [9]
and proclaim the deed of God,
and ponder what he has done.
11 Let the just man rejoice in Yahweh, [10]
and fly to him for refuge!
Let the upright in heart glory!

* Verse numbers in RSV.

NOTES

lxiv. An individual lament in which the maligned psalmist prays for deliverance from personal enemies. This psalm, which develops the thought of the final line in Ps lxiii, "While the mouth of those telling lies will be shut," inculcates the doctrine of *lex talionis*, the law of retaliation. The poisoned shafts of calumniators will be their undoing. Several wordplays mark the style of the poem (vss. 3, 5, 6, 9).

2. *the hostile pack*. Literally "the pack of foes." Traditionally rendered "dread," *paḥad* is preferably identified with Ugar. *pḫd*, "flock," discussed in *Psalms I*, pp. 81 f. The parallelism with vs. 3, *sōd mᵉrēʿīm*, "the council of the wicked," and *rigšat pōʿᵃlē ʾāwen*, "the concourse of evildoers," is convincing. For the nuance "pack," see Ps xci 5 and Song of Sol iii 8. The proposal of J. H. Tigay, JBL 92 (1973), 517–22, to emend *paḥad* to **pōḥar* must be declined since it requires a consonantal emendation.

protect. On the sequence imperative-jussive (*šᵉmaʿ–tiṣṣōr*), *Psalms I*, pp. 65 f.

3. *Shelter me*. *tastīrēnī* contains the first pun of the psalm. The poet needs shelter because his enemies operate from a *mistārīm*, "a sheltered or hidden place," rendered "from ambush" in vs. 5.

the gathering. For this meaning of *rigšat*, which RSV renders "the scheming," see *Psalms I*, p. 7.

4. *sharpen their tongue*. Cf. Pss lii 3, lv 22, lvii 5, lix 8.

their poisonous remark. This definition of *dābār mār*, cited in *Psalms I*, p. 251, at Ps xli 9 to illustrate *dᵉbar bᵉliyyaʿal*, "a lethal substance," finds further support in Job xx 14, *mᵉrōrat pᵉtānīm*, "vipers' venom," and in the hendiadys of Gen xlix 23, *wayᵉmārᵃrūhū wārōbbū*, "And they shot poisoned arrows at him." The substantive *rōʾš*, "bitterness, poison," presents an instructive analogy to *mar*, "bitter, poisonous."

Though recent commentators miss the allusion, Rosenmüller (*Scholia in Psalmos* [1831], p. 390) cites the view of earlier scholars who saw in *mar* the word for "poison" and in the verse a reference to the use of poisoned arrows. Hence Pope's comment on Job vi 4 (AB, vol. 15) that "The present passage plainly refers to poisoned arrows, which are not mentioned elsewhere in the OT" requires modification.

like an arrow. As noticed in the second NOTE on Ps cxx 4, *ḥiṣṣām* parses as an adverbial accusative stylistically balancing the preposition of *kaḥereb*, "like a sword."

5. *from ambush*. In the phrase *bammistārīm*, *ba* has the meaning "from"; *Psalms I*, p. 319.

they shoot. Briggs, CECBP, II, p. 79, cites this hiphil form *yōrūhū* to impugn the accuracy of the infinitive *lirōt*, "to shoot," in this same verse, alleging that the use of qal in the same psalm as two hiphils (cf. vs. 8) with the same meaning is improbable. This objection slights, however, the three instances from Psalms cited in *Psalms I*, p. 177; cf. further GK, § 113w, and Exod xix 13; I Sam xxiii 22; Mic vi 14; Job vi 2, xxii 30; Eccles iii 5, and the second NOTE on Ps lxix 15.

suddenly. For the stylistic balance between adverbial *pit'ōm* and the prepositional phrase *bammistārīm*, "from ambush," consult *Psalms I*, p. 259, where Ugaritic analogues are cited.

fearlessly. Namely, with no fear of being punished by God. Cf. Ps x 4, 11, 13. There is a wordplay on *yōrūhū*, "they shoot," and *yiyrā'ū*, which would be lost were one to adopt the ill-conceived suggestion of the BH³ critical apparatus that *yōrūhū* be deleted, *metri causa*. Many commentators follow Syr., reading *w^elō' yērā'ū*, "but they are not seen," for MT *w^elō' yiyrā'ū*, on the grounds of better parallelism with *bammistārīm*, "from ambush," but the second NOTE to this verse observes that the parallel of *bammistārīm* is adverbial *pit'ōm*, "suddenly." The verb *yiyrā'ū*, "they (do not) fear," forms a further wordplay with vs. 6, *yir'eh*, much as in Ps lii 8, *w^eyir'ū ṣaddīqīm w^eyiyrā'ū*, "The just will look on in dread." Consult the second NOTE on Ps cxii 8.

6. *for him*. The sixth NOTE on Ps lv 20 examines *lāmō*, "for him, in him"; cf. Ps lxvi 7.

venomous substance. Consult the second NOTE on Ps lv 16, and compare *dābār mār*, "poisonous substance," discussed above in the second NOTE on vs. 4. To make sure that the poisoned arrow achieves its mission, the psalmist's enemies apply a stronger solution.

carefully conceal. An uncertain version of *y^esapp^erū liṭmōn*, literally "They count while concealing," which I take as hendiadys for "They carefully conceal."

Thinking. Cf. first NOTE on Ps liii 2 on *'āmar*, introducing the *Hoffartsmonolog* ["monologue of insolence"].

Who looks down upon us? The unexampled construction *yir'eh lāmō* (I Sam xvi 7, *yir'eh la'ēnayim* means "He sees according to appearances") suggests that *yir'eh* here has the sense of *šāqap*, "to look down upon." Compare the related context of Ps liii 2–3, *'āmar nābal b^elibbō*, "The fool thinks in his heart," . . . *'^elōhīm miššāmayim hišqīp 'al b^enē 'ādām*, "From heaven God looks down upon the sons of men." For the wordplay on *yir'eh* and vs. 5, *yiyrā'ū*, see NOTE to latter.

The evidence marshaled in *Psalms I*, p. 173, for *lmw* (probably vocalized *lammū*), "for us, upon us," renders superfluous the emendation to *lānū*, supported by Syr. and *Juxta Hebraeos*.

7. *Who can investigate*. An example of double-duty interrogative *mī*; *Psalms I*, pp. 8, 16, and cf. BJ. The seeming plural form *yaḥp^eśū* is parsed as third person masculine singular with the archaic indicative ending; see *Psalms I*, pp. 61 f., 78, and NOTE below on vs. 9.

our perfect crime. Reading *'ōlōt tummēnū*, literally "the crime of our perfection," for unexplained MT *'ōlōt tam^enū*, literally "the crime in which they are perfect." The second NOTE on Ps lviii 3 explains the Phoenician feminine singular form *'ōlōt.*

the Investigator. Pointing *m^{e}ḥappēś*, the piel participle, instead of the MT pual *m^{e}ḥuppāś*. This divine appellative belongs to the category of Ps xxxiii 15, *hammēbīn*, "the Observer," and Ps cxxxix 11, *'ōmēr* (MT *'ōmar*), "the Seer."

will investigate the innermost man. Compare Prov xx 27, *nēr yhwh nišmat 'ādām ḥōpēś kol ḥadrē bāṭen*, "With a lamp Yahweh searches the breath of man, all the inward parts," and Zeph i 12, *'^{a}ḥappēś 'et y^{e}rūšālāim bannērōt*, "I (Yahweh) will search Jerusalem with lamps."

even. Taking the *w^e* of *w^{e}leb* as emphatic rather than conjunctive.

the depths of the heart. Literally "the deep heart."

8. *Exalted.* The LXX and Syr. saw in consonantal *yrm* the root *rwm*, "to be high," but I prefer a derivation from its by-form *yrm*, discussed in *Psalms I*, p. 118, and the reading *yārūm*, the passive qal participle of *yrm*. Cf. Ps lxi 3.

the God of the Arrow. Reading the construct chain with interposed *mem* (*Psalms I*, p. XL), *'^{e}lōhē-m ḥēṣ* (MT *'^{e}lōhīm ḥēṣ*), and comparing *yārūm '^{e}lōhē-m ḥēṣ* here with Ps xviii 47, *yārūm '^{e}lōhē yiš'ī*, "Exalted the God of my triumph," and Jer x 10, *w^{e}yhwh '^{e}lōhē-m '^{e}met*, "For Yahweh is the God of truth." In Ugaritic mythology the archer-god of pestilence Resheph receives the epithet *b'l ḥẓ ršp*, "Lord of the Arrow Resheph," and in Phoenician religion he was known as *ršp ḥṣ*, "Resheph of the Arrow." Compare Job xxxiv 6, *'ānūš ḥiṣṣī b^{e}lī pāša'*, "diseased by his arrow (with third person singular suffix *-y*), though sinless."

double. Analyzing consonantal *pt'm* (MT *pit'ōm*) into the conjunction *pa* (*Psalms I*, p. 293) and *tō'ēm*, the qal participle of *tā'am*, "to be double." For the syntax of a masculine singular predicate (*tō'ēm*) followed by a feminine plural subject (*makkōtām*), see GK, § 145o.

be. Parsing *hāyū* as precative perfect; *Psalms I*, p. 20.

9. *The Most High.* For MT *'ālēmō* reading *'ēlī* (*Psalms I*, p. 45), and attaching *mem* to following word. Thus the parallelism between vs. 8, *yārūm*, and vs. 9, *'ēlī*, exhibits the two roots found in the Ugaritic personal name *yrm'l* (UT, 2106:4).

shall make . . . stumble. Parsing MT *yakšīlūhū* as hiphil third person singular masculine with archaic indicative ending *-ū;* cf. first NOTE on vs. 7. The suffix *-hū* would be *dativus commodi*. The juxtaposition of the roots *kšl*, "to stumble," and *'ly*, "to be high," heightens the theological paronomasia (*Psalms I*, p. 285), much as in Ps lxxxvi 13, where *'ēlī* (MT *'ālāy*) contrasts with *š^e'ōl taḥtiyyāh*, "deepest Sheol."

slanderers. Reading *m^{e}lašš^{e}nīm* for MT *l^{e}šōnām;* the initial *mem* has been detached from preceding MT *'ālēmō*, as indicated in the first NOTE to vs. 9. The Masoretes betray a certain unsteadiness vis-à-vis the verb *liššēn*, "to slander," Ugar. *lšn*, as can be observed in Ps ci 5, *m^e^lōš^e^nī*, and Prov xxx 10, *'al talšēn*, where purported hiphil is preferably read as piel, as in Ugaritic.

the arrogant. Who presume that God is too much the Exalted One (see *Psalms I*, p. 62, on Ps x 4) to see what goes on upon earth (vs. 6) or to vindicate his commandment forbidding calumny. I propose the lection *rō'hēbīm* (MT *rō'ēh bām*), qal participle of *rāhab*, "to act stormily, arrogantly." The pointing *ro'hbām* (cf. Ps xc 10), "their arrogance," also merits consideration.

will be brought low. Psalms I, p. 257, examines the root *ndd*, "to bow down," from which *yitnōd^a^dū* is here tentatively derived. Such an etymology nicely squares with synonymous *kāšal*. Isa xvii 11, *nd qāṣīr* may be a further attestation of this root. Cf. the second NOTE on Ps lxviii 13.

10. *will stand in awe.* Namely, at the vigor of the divine intervention on behalf of the maligned but innocent psalmist.

11. *fly to him for refuge.* Describing *ḥāsāh*, "fly for refuge," as a precative perfect balancing jussive *yiśmaḥ*, "rejoice"; *Psalms I*, pp. 20, 250. The proposal to delete *ḥāsāh bō* as overloading the line ignores the metrical pattern 3+2+3 witnessed in Pss x 15, 18, lxxi 3, lxxv 2, lxxvii 3, xcvii 5, cxl 11.

PSALM 65

(lxv 1–14)

1 *For the director; a psalm of David. A song.*

2 Praise to you in the mighty castle,
O God in Zion.
And vows shall be paid to you,
3 because you hear prayers. [2]*
To you must all flesh bring
4 its sinful deeds. [3]
Beyond number are our rebellious acts,
forgive them!
5 How blest is he whom you choose [4]
and bring near,
That he might dwell in your court.
May we be fully imbued
with the beauty of your house,
the holiness of your temple.
6 At the vindication, our triumphant God, [5]
show us your wondrous deeds;
Who pacified all the ends of the earth
and of the distant sea.
7 Who stabilized the mountains with his strength, [6]
being girded with might.
8 Who silenced the roaring of the seas, [7]
the roaring of their waves,
the turmoil of the peoples,
9 While denizens of the earth's ends [8]
stood in awe at your signs.
Make the twinkling stars of dawn and dusk
shout for joy!

* Verse numbers in RSV.

10 Visit the earth, [9]
    make her skip with mirth,
    make her fruitful with your rain.
With water fill the heavenly channel,
    provide her grain;
For this you brought her into being.
11 Drench her furrows, [10]
    her ridges soak down;
Soften her with copious showers,
    bless her growth!
12 Crown the peaks with your rain, [11]
    and may your pastures drip fatness;
13 May the boundless meadows drip fatness; [12]
    gird the hills with exultation!
14 May the hollows be dressed in flocks, [13]
    and the valleys mantled in wheat.
May they jubilate and sing!

Notes

lxv. The customary classification of this psalm as a hymn of public thanksgiving for a bountiful harvest (cf. Mowinckel, *The Psalms in Israel's Worship* [see Selected Bibliography], I, pp. 119 f.) results from construing the *qatal* verb forms in vss. 10, 12, 14 as expressing past time. The presence of imperatives in vs. 11, however, and of jussives in vss. 13 and 14, rather clearly indicates that the *qatal* forms are precative perfects (*Psalms I*, pp. 19 f., 23, where several criteria for detecting the precative mood are enumerated), and that the second part of the psalm (vss. 9–14) is a prayer for rain (*Psalms I*, pp. 23, 25), not a hymn of thanksgiving. The bearing of Northwest Semitic philological discoveries on the question of literary genre in the Psalter (briefly treated in *Psalms I*, pp. xxxii f.) is clearly manifest in this poem. When applied to the first section of the poem (vss. 2–8), the new philological and stylistic principles disclose that vss. 2–6a contain a prayer for admittance to God's heavenly abode after death, while vss. 6b–8 describe God's victory in primeval times over the watery forces of chaos and destruction. Thus the psalm looks to the eschatological future, to the primeval past, and to the needs of the present.

2. *in the mighty castle.* A poetic name for heaven; compare Pss xi 4, *hēkāl,* "the heavenly temple," viii 3, *'ōz,* "the celestial fortress," xx 7, g^{e}*būrōt,* "fortress in heaven" (also in Ps lxvi 7). The preposition in the

phrase *b^eṣiyyōn*, "in Zion," also governs parallel *dūmiyyāh* on the strength of the literary usage known as the double-duty preposition (*Psalms I*, p. 326). The third NOTE on Ps lxii 2 discusses the meaning and morphology of *dūmiyyāh*, "mighty castle."

in Zion. Referring to the heavenly Mountain Zion, as will become clearer upon consideration of the terms *ḥāṣēr*, "court," *bēt*, "house," and *hēkāl*, "temple," in vs. 5. Cf. the first NOTE on Ps liii 7 for other texts where *ṣiyyōn*, "Zion," denotes primarily the empyrean mountain where God dwells, and note especially Ps l 2.

3. *because*. Though not formally expressed in the text, the juxtaposition of *neder*, "vow," and *šōmē^a'*, "hear," suggests this logical connection of the two thoughts.

must all flesh bring. Namely, to the final judgment, the eschatological day when God will reward or punish each man according to his deeds. Compare Ps l 2, 4, "Out of Zion, the perfection of beauty, / God shone forth . . . He summoned the heaven above,/and the earth, to the trial of his people." In this text which speaks of a trial, God is represented as coming from his heavenly Zion preceded by a raging fire. Cf. Pss i 5, vii 7–8, cxliii 3.

The proposal to read hiphil *yābī'ū* for MT qal *yābō'ū* founders on the observation that in nine texts, listed in *Psalms I*, p. 262, the qal of *bw'* means "to bring."

4. *Beyond number*. Literally *gāb^erū m^enī* (MT *mennī*) means "They are too numerous to be counted." Like *rābab*, "to be many, great," *'āṣam*, "to be mighty, numerous," so *gābar*, "to be mighty," denotes here "to be numerous." This nuance permits a clearer version of Ps cxii 2, *gibbōr bā'āreṣ yihyeh zar'ō*, "His progeny will be numerous upon the earth." Consonantal *mny*, tentatively pointed *m^enī*, parses as an archaic infinitive construct of *mānāh*, "to count," morphologically identical with the Ugaritic infinitives construct *bm bkyh*, "while he wept" (UT, Krt: 31), *lšty ṣḥtkm*, "I have called you to drink" (UT, 128:IV:27; cf. UT, § 9.52, p. 89).

For a kindred sentiment, compare Isa i 18, "Though your sins are like scarlet, they shall be white as snow."

forgive them. As in vs. 9, *tarnīn*, the imperfect has imperative force.

5. *How blest*. Comparing Ps lxxxiv 5, *'ašrē yōš^ebē bētekā 'ōd y^ehal^elūka*, "How blest are those who dwell in your house (i.e., in heaven), eternally singing your praise!" Syntactically, *'ašrē* is a construct before the finite verb *tibḥar*, "you choose" (GK, § 130d), a usage witnessed in UT, 52:64, *aṯt itrḫ*, "the two wives I have wed." See UT, § 8.16, and the third NOTE on Ps lxxi 18.

and bring near. Piel *t^eqārēb* might be compared with UT, 77:27, *aqrbk abh b'l*, literally "I shall bring near to you her father Baal," i.e., "I shall introduce to you her father Baal."

your court. That is, the court of the "mighty castle" (vs. 2). Though some manuscripts read singular *ḥṣrk,* MT plural *ḥaṣērekā* may be singular in meaning in keeping with Canaanite poetic practice of using a plural form of names of buildings to express the singular; see UT, § 13:17, and *Psalms I,* p. 262. As here, Ugar. *ḥẓr* (also dialectal *ḥṭr*) balances *bt,* "house," and *hkl,* "temple."

May we be fully imbued. In several passages describing eternal life and the beatific (notice vs. 5a, "How blest") vision, the root of *niśbeʻāh* plays an important role; cf. Pss xvi 11, xvii 15, lxiii 6, xci 16, ciii 5.

the beauty of your house. Referring to God's celestial abode, the archetype of his temple in Jerusalem, just as the temple of Baal discovered at Ugarit was considered a replica of its heavenly archetype. On the latter question see Norman C. Habel, *Yahweh versus Baal: A Conflict of Religious Cultures* (New York, 1964), p. 78. On *ṭūb,* "beauty," see *Psalms I,* p. 170, while pp. 148 f. list several texts where *bayit* designates the heavenly habitation of Yahweh.

the holiness of your temple. Again referring to God's dwelling in heaven. The principle of the double-duty preposition, touched upon in the first NOTE on vs. 2, permits *qedōš* (perhaps vocalize *qōdeš*), "holiness," to share the preposition of parallel *beṭūb.* On *hēkāl,* "heavenly temple," see *Psalms I,* pp. 106, 148 f., 179.

6. *At the vindication.* Namely, the day of final judgment alluded to in vss. 3–4. Here *beṣedeq* bears the same nuance as in Ps xvii 15, where it is parallel to "at the resurrection."

our triumphant God. The phrase *'elōhē yišʻēnū* introduces the following lines (vss. 6b–9a) depicting Yahweh's conquest of Chaos in primeval times. Because of this victory, God will be able to display new wonders to his elect after the day of final judgment.

show us. Parsing consonantal *tʻnnw* as hiphil imperfect of *ʻyn,* "to see," attested in I Sam ii 32, xviii 9; Ecclus xiv 10; Ugar. *ʻyn* II, and Ar. *ʻāyana.* See below on Ps xci 8. Here it might be apposite to cite a passage from Canaanite mythology evincing kindred language and ideas: UT, ʻnt:III:23–28, *abn brq dl tdʻ šmm rgm ltdʻ nšm wltbn hmlt arṣ atm wank ibǵyh btk ǵry il ṣpn bqdš bǵr nḥlty bnʻm bgbʻ tliyt,* "I understand lightning that the heavens know not, thunder that men know not, nor the multitudes of the nether world understand. Come, and I will show it in the midst of my towering Mount Zaphon, in my sanctuary upon my mountain of dominion, in my pleasance upon my mountain of victory." Here Baal is described leading the goddess Anath to his celestial Mount Zaphon (compare vs. 2 on celestial Zion) where he will show her spectacular phenomena unknown to the gods or to men, alive or dead. The balance in lines 27–28 between *bqdš* and *bnʻm* associates ideas expressed by the psalmist's *ṭūb,* "beauty," and *qōdeš,* "sanctity."

Who pacified. Reading hiphil participle *mabṭīaḥ* (MT *mibṭaḥ*), which balances hiphil participle *mēkīn*, "stabilized" (vs. 7), and *mašbīaḥ*, "silenced" (vs. 8). This nuance of *mabṭīaḥ* is discussed in *Psalms I*, second NOTE on Ps xxii 10, where Yahweh is termed *mabṭīḥī 'al šedē 'immī*, "(who) made me tranquil (or, 'my pacifier') upon my mother's breast."

ends of the earth. Comparing *qaṣwē 'ereṣ* with UT, 126:III:3, *lqṣm arṣ*, "to the ends of the earth," cited in *Psalms I*, p. 281. The high incidence of mythical terms in vss. 6–9 suggests that *qaṣwē 'ereṣ* is a demythologized expression originally designating personalized forces of chaos that had to be subdued by Yahweh before he could begin the ordering of chaos. Cf. Loren R. Fisher, "Creation at Ugarit and the Old Testament," in VT 15 (1965), 313–24.

and of the distant sea. Reading *weyam reḥōqī-m*, with *mem* enclitic, for MT *weyām reḥōqīm*, which is grammatically dissonant. The phrase parses as a genitive determining *qaṣwē*, "ends." Compare the genitive ending in Ps xliv 13, *welō' ribbītā bimeḥīrīhem*, "Nor did you grow rich from their price," where the MT hapax legomenon plural *meḥīrēhem* is the result of confusing singular *meḥir* followed by the genitive ending with the construct plural; contrast *Psalms I*, p. 264. With this analysis the grammatical incongruity vanishes from Job xviii 5, *gam 'ōr rešā'ī-m* (MT *rešā'īm*) *yid'āk welō' yiggah šebīb 'iššō*, "Surely the light of the wicked man is put out, and the flame of his fire does not shine." The usual emendation of purported plural *rš'm* to singular *rš'* becomes disposable. Other instances of the genitive ending (apart from those given in GK, § 90l), well documented in the Ras Shamra tablets, recur in Pss lxix 27, lxxxiii 4 (?), lxxxiv 11, cv 27, cxxiii 1, cxxxviii 6; Num xxiii 10; II Sam xxii 44; Ezek v 3; Hos xi 4, xiii 2 (cf. *Biblica* 44 [1963], 296); Job xxiv 3; Prov iii 28, vii 7, xvi 13, xxii 17, xxiv 17; Song of Sol i 9; Lam ii 17.

7. *Who stabilized the mountains.* Comparing Ps xxx 8, "more stable than the mighty mountains."

being girded with might. With the phrase *ne'zār bigebūrāh* compares *'ōz hit'azzār* in Ps xciii 1, a hymn that has been adapted from an older Canaanite composition. Nonetheless, the phrase carries little conviction; perhaps one should read *ne'zārū bigebūrāh*, "They (i.e., the mountains) are girded with his might" (cf. vs. 13). Suffixless *gebūrāh* is modified by determined *kōḥō*, "his strength" (*Psalms I*, pp. 17 f.). The high mountains of Syria and Anatolia were considered gods or invested with divine qualities.

8. *Who silenced.* Related to *šābat*, "to cease," *šābam*, "to muzzle" (cf. the fifth NOTE on Ps lxviii 23), the root of *mašbīaḥ* occurs in UT, 'nt:III:37, *išbḥnh*, in parallelism with *lištbm tnn*, "I indeed muzzled Tannin." As maintained in UHP, p. 20, and *Orientalia* 34 (1965), 392, Gordon's reading in UT, p. 254, *išbm[n]h* is orthographically improbable

and phonetically objectionable, since it slights the Barth-Ginsberg law, according to which the second or third consonant of the root must be a laryngal when the vowel of the preformative is *i*. The root *šbḥ* II, "to silence," recurs in the cognate epic passage of Ps lxxxix 10.

the peoples. The association of *le'ummīm*, "peoples," with *yammīm*, "seas," reflects the Canaanite motif of UT, 'nt:II:7–8, *tmḫṣ lim ḫp y[m?] tṣmt adm ṣat špš*, "She (i.e., the goddess Anath) smote the peoples of the seashore, she annihilated the men of the rising sun." Hence one must discount the observation of Briggs, CECBP, II, p. 82, that the phrase *hamōn le'ummīm* is the work of a later editor, and of Kraus, *Psalmen*, I, p. 452, that it is an addition to be put in brackets, *metri causa*. In the cognate epic verses of Ps xlvi 3–7, "Nations tremble, kingdoms totter" (vs. 7) is a constitutive phrase which validates the presence of our phrase in a mythological context.

9. *earth's ends.* The psalmist stresses the cosmic nature of God's victory over the oceanic forces.

your signs. Just as the primordial peoples were awed by Yahweh's exploits, so may we see his awe-inspiring deeds at the final judgment. Stylistically, *'ōtōtekā* forms an inclusion (*Psalms I*, p. 327) with vs. 6, *nōrā'ōt*, "wondrous deeds."

the twinkling stars. Deriving *mōṣā'ē* from *yāṣā'*, "to shine," studied in *Psalms I*, pp. 93 f., 228, 306, and comparing this colon with Job xxxviii 7, *beron yaḥad kōkebē bōqer*, "when the morning stars together shouted for joy." This etymology considerably clarifies Song of Sol viii 10, *'āz hāyītī be'ēnāyw kemōṣ'ēt šālōm*, "Who (*'āz* is the Phoenician relative pronoun) have become in his eyes like the evening (*šālōm* equals Ugar. *šlm* in the myth of *šḥr w šlm*, "Dawn and Dusk") star. Cf. Neh iv 15, *'ad ṣe't hakkōkābīm*, "until the stars began to shine," and *Biblica* 47 (1966), 416.

dawn and dusk. Biblical *bōqer wā'ereb* semantically correspond to Canaanite *šḥr w šlm;* cf. the preceding NOTE.

shout for joy. Parsing *tarnīn* as an imperfect with the function of an imperative; this well-documented feature of the psalmists' style receives comment in the second NOTE on Ps li 14. Its alternation with precative perfect *pāqadtā*, "visit," in vs. 10 earmarks the mode of *tarnīn*, whose root is attested in UT, 1001:5, *brnk*, "when you shout," and 1001:6, *arnn*, "I shall shout."

With this colon begins the second part of the psalm, namely the prayer for rain. By asking God to make the stars shout for joy, the poet asks for rain in mythopoeic terms. Thought of as sources of rain (UT, 'nt:II:41, *rbb tskh kbkbm*, "With showers the stars anoint her"; Judg v 20–21; Gaster, *Thespis*, 1961, p. 237), the stars would exult to supply the Israelites with rain. In Ps lxviii 12 the Lord's thunder is said to gladden the army of stars.

10. *Visit.* Moses Buttenwieser, *The Psalms Chronologically Treated with a New Translation* (abbr. PCTNT) (Chicago, 1938), p. 51, has correctly seen that *pāqadtā*, *'iṭṭartā*, "Crown" (vs. 12), and *lābᵉšū*, "be dressed" (vs. 14) are all precatives expressing a wish. Their alternation with imperfects and imperatives (vs. 11, *rawwēh*, "Drench," and *naḥēt*, "Soften") leaves little doubt concerning the mood of these perfect forms. The verb *pqd*, probably "to give orders," occurs in UT, 127:14, while the prayer *pāqadtā hā'āreṣ* is semantically equivalent to the opening words of the prayer for rain in Ps lxxxv 2, *rāṣītā yhwh 'arṣekā*, "Favor your land, Yahweh!" The presence of *pāqad* in our verse reveals that Ps lxxx 15, *pᵉqōd gepen zō't*, "Visit this vine," is a prayer for rain.

make her skip with mirth. Explaining the hapax legomenon *witᵉšōqᵉqehā* (MT *wattᵉšōqᵉqehā*, with *waw consecutivum* erroneously took *pāqadtā* as referring to past time) as a denominative verb from *šōq*, "thigh." As observed in *Psalms I*, pp. 84, 118, 164, Ugaritic and Hebrew evince a strong tendency to coin verbs from names of parts of the body. Ugar. *šq ymm* equals Exod xxix 22, *šōq hayyāmīn*, "the right thigh." Cf. Ps cxiv 6–8, "Why, O mountains, do you skip (*tirqᵉdū*) like rams, O hills, like lambs? Dance (*ḥūlī*), O earth, at the presence of the Lord, at the presence of Jacob's God, who turns the rock into a pool of water, the flint into a spring of water."

make her fruitful with your rain. Literally "Rain down, enrich her." Reading *hᵃribbōtā* (MT *rabbat*), from the root preserved in *rᵉbībīm*, "showers." The initial *he* of *hrbt* is supplied by the final *he* of preceding *tšqqh* on basis of the orthographic practice examined in the third NOTE on Ps lx 11. Cf. especially Ps civ 17–18; Prov vii 10, xxix 22. In vs. 11, it might be noted, occurs *rᵉbībīm*, "showers," to which we would relate the precative perfect *hᵃribbōtā*.

fill. Vocalizing piel imperative *mallē'* for MT *mālē'*.

the heavenly channel. Namely, the conduit leading from the freshwater ocean above the heaven to earth. Hence it is called *peleg 'ᵉlōhīm*, "the divine channel." An empty channel means drought upon the earth. Similar imagery appears in Job xxviii 26, "When he made a groove (*ḥōq*) for the rain, / A path for the thundershower," and xxxviii 25, "Who cleft a channel (*tᵉ'ālāh*) for the downpour, / A path for the thundershower?" (Pope, The Anchor Bible, vol. 15). Cf. also Gen vii 11, viii 2. The noun *plg*//*nḫl* (cf. Job xx 17) occurs in the Ugaritic tablet RŠ 24.244:69.

provide. Understanding *tākīn* as an imperfect with imperative meaning, in balance with imperative *mallē'*, "fill." This stylistic variant receives comment in the second NOTE on vs. 4, and fourth NOTE on vs. 9.

her grain. Vocalizing *dagna-m* (MT *d^{e}gānām*), the accusative singular followed by the enclitic *mem.* Compare *nbtm,* "honey," with enclitic *mem,* in UT, 49:II:7. The function of the enclitic would be to balance the suffix of *t^{e}kīnehā,* "into being," a stylistic usage noticed in *Psalms I,* pp. 34, 64 f., 75. Some ancient versions translate "her grain," but this does not mean that we must read *d^{e}gānāh.* One must not, however, exclude the possibility that *dgnm* is defective spelling for **d^{e}gānīm,* like *ḥiṭṭīm,* "wheat." In Ugaritic, *dgn* is both a common noun, "grain," and the name of the god Dagan.

you brought her into being. A doubtful translation. Usually considered corrupt, the colon *tākīn dagnām kī kēn t^{e}kīnehā* by its very sound suggests that the poet is playing on words. The first *tākīn* denotes "to prepare," as elsewhere in Hebrew, but *t^{e}kīnehā* may rather carry the Ugaritic-Phoenician sense of *kwn,* "to be." Hence the causative form here would denote "to bring into being, create." Since God created the earth to yield food for man (Gen i 29), so the psalmist reasons, he should provide the rain necessary for the earth to discharge its function.

11. *Drench.* Piel imperative *rawwēh* (not piel infinitive absolute as maintained by many, e.g., Gunkel, *Die Psalmen,* p. 275) earmarks the mode of the preceding (vs. 10) and following (vss. 12, 14) perfects, which are precative. Cf. in particular Ps iv 2, where, for stylistic variation, the poet inserts a precative perfect among three imperatives. In our verse, two imperatives (*rawwēh,* "drench," and *naḥēt,* "soften") perfectly balance two imperfects (*t^{e}mōg^{e}gennāh,* "soften," and *t^{e}bārēk,* "bless"). The root of *rawwēh* doubtless occurs in the Ugaritic personal name (*bn*) *rwy,* the root meaning of which is "to be saturated," and a new biblical occurrence has been recognized in Prov v 18; see UHP, p. 26.

her furrows. t^{e}lāmehā equals Ugar. *tlm.*

her ridges. Better manuscripts read *gdwdh,* with *scriptio defectiva* of penultimate syllable.

soak down. The piel imperative *naḥēt* literally means "Make descend!" Since the lowering of the ridges between the furrows is to be achieved by rainfall, "soak down" fairly represents its meaning. In the Maronite breviary for vespers of Tuesday there is the prayer: *'aḥēt mōr meṭrē daḥnōnōk,* "Make descend, O Lord, the rains of your mercy." The chiasm *t^{e}lāmehā rawwēh naḥēt g^{e}dūdehā* much resembles that of Ps xlvi 10; cf. *Psalms I,* p. 325.

with copious showers. The defective spelling *rbybm* found in some manuscripts appears preferable to the full spelling adopted by BH^3. See vss. 6, *mbṭḥ,* 10, *t'šrnh,* 11, *gdwdh,* for other instances of *scriptio defectiva.* Heb. *rᵉbībīm* equals Ugar. *rb* and *rbb,* "copious showers, rain," whose root is purportedly found in vs. 10, *hᵃribbōtā.*

12. *Crown.* Parsing *'iṭṭartā* as precative perfect; see first NOTE on vs. 10. The construction of *'iṭṭēr* with two accusatives is commented upon in the second NOTE on Ps viii 6, where Phoenician usage is also cited. UT, 126:III, a text describing the coming of the rains after the summer drought, contains in line 11 the congeries *'ṭrṭrm,* whose first three consonants materially answer to our root. Cf. also UT, 127:8, *'ṭrptm//rišh,* hence possibly signifying "crown of the head."

the peaks. The chiastic arrangement of vss. 12b and 13a suggests that vs. 12a chiastically balances vs. 13b. Hence consonantal *šnt* (the defective spelling, as in vs. 11 *gdwdh* and *rbybm,* should be noticed) should be synonymous with vs. 13b, *gᵉbā'ōt,* "hills." Ar. *saniya,* "become high, exalted," supplies the etymology, and Ugar. *šnt* in UT, 127:57–58, *tqln bgbl šntk,* "May your arrogance be humbled on the hill," may be a Northwest Semitic attestation of the root; cf. Aistleitner, WuS, No. 2650, p. 312. For biblical occurrences of this root in Prov xxiv 21b, consult D. Winton Thomas in ZAW 52 (1934), 236–38; L. Kopf in VT 9 (1959), 280–83. On Ecclus xxxiii 13, D. Winton Thomas in VT 10 (1960), 456. Cf. 11QPsᵃ Creat. (the "Hymn to the Creator" of the Psalms Scroll) 6 (13), *m'ṭr hrym tnwbwt,* "crowning the mountains with fruit."

with your rain. Masculine *ṭōb,* "rain," is documented in *Psalms I,* p. 25, while feminine *ṭōbāh* recurs with this denotation in Ps lxviii 11, where it is associated with vs. 10, *gešem,* "rain." In our context it is preceded by *rᵉbībīm,* "copious showers," and followed by *dešen,* "fatness."

your pastures. The land of Israel belongs to Yahweh; hence it is accurately termed "yours." For this definition of *ma'gālekā, Psalms I,* p. 146.

drip fatness. Comparing *yir'ᵃpūn dāšen* with UT, 49:III:6–7, *šmm šmn tmṭrn nḫlm tlk nbtm,* "The heavens rain oil, the wadis flow with honey." Of the biblical phrase Buttenwieser, PCTNT, p. 50, writes: "There is nothing so primitive as this anywhere else in the Psalter." The cited Ugaritic verses show that the biblical poet is beneficiary of a lush Canaanite tradition; cf. first NOTE on Ps xlv 9.

The roots that are paired in biblical *ṭōbātekā,* "your rain," and *dāšen,* "fatness," are parallel in the unpublished tablet RŠ 24.252:5–6, *bmrqdm dšn b ḥbr kṯr ṭbm,* "among the plump dancers, among the merry companions of Kothar."

13. *the boundless meadows.* Since the fixed phrase *nᵉ'ōt midbār,* usually translated "meadows in the wilderness," has received no clear, satisfactory definition, I suspect that the genitive *midbār* merely serves as a superlative, like *'ēl, 'ᵉlōhīm, mōt,* signifying "vast, boundless." In

other words, *nᵉʾōt midbār* is synonymous with Ps lxxxiii 13, *nᵉʾōt ʾᵉlōhīm,* "the vast meadows," or, with AT, "the very finest meadows."

drip fatness. Metrical considerations (3+3) precluding the insertion of another word, the poet makes the final word of vs. 12, *dāšen,* also limit the verb of vs. 13a on the principle of the double-duty noun. Cf. fourth NOTE on Ps lviii 5.

gird the hills. The chiastic structure of vss. 12–13 points to God as the subject of consonantal *tḥgrnh,* which apparently balances the precative perfect *ʿiṭṭartā,* "Crown!," whose subject is God. Hence vocalize *taḥgōrannāh* (MT *taḥgōrnāh*), the second person singular of the energic mode; *Psalms I,* p. 326.

with exultation. Comparing vs. 10, "Make her (i.e., the earth) skip with mirth." The stylistic trait of placing the accusative of means before the verb is remarked in *Psalms I,* p. 35, where Canaanite antecedents are cited.

14. *the hollows. Psalms I,* p. 230, examines the meaning and etymology of *kārīm,* "hollows." This definition has been accepted by John S. Kselman, CBQ 32 (1970), 581, n. 13. He has identified the construct feminine plural by-form *kᵉrōt,* "hollows," in Zeph ii 7. The parallelism there with *nᵉwōt,* "pastures," and *gidrōt,* "folds," along with the collocation with *ṣōʾn,* "flock," in the same verse, sustains this definition.

be dressed. Interpreting (contrary to the version in *Psalms I,* p. 230) *lābᵉšū* as precative perfect, continuing the prayer begun in vs. 9b. See first NOTE on vs. 10, *pāqadtā,* "Visit!"

in flocks. The parallelism suggests, however, that *ṣʾn* might be cognate to Isa xxxiv 1, *ṣeʾᵉṣāʾ,* "produce," and Job xxxviii 27, *mōṣāʾ deše',* "green grass."

and. On *ʾap* as the equivalent of the simple copulative conjunction, see *Psalms I,* p. 89.

PSALM 66

(lxvi 1–20)

1 *For the director; a song. A psalm.*

Cry out to God with joy, all the earth!
2 Sing his glorious name,
  indite his glorious praise!
3 Say: "O God, so terrifying by your deeds!
So great is your strength,
  that your foes cringe before you.
4 All the earth worships you,
  sings to you and sings your name!" *Selah*
5 Come and see the works of God,
  terrifying in action before men.
6 He turned the sea into dry land,
  they passed through the river dry-shod.
Come, let us rejoice in him!
7 He rules from his eternal fortress;
  his eyes keep watch on the nations
  lest the rebels rise up against him. *Selah*
8 Bless our God, O peoples,
  with full voice proclaim his praise!
9 Who placed us among the living,
  and did not put our foot in the Quagmire.
10 But you tested us, O God,
  you refined us as silver is refined.
11 You brought us into the wilderness,
  put ulcers on our thighs;
12 You made sickness ride our head;
  we went through fire and through water,
After you had led us out of abundance.
13 I shall enter your house with my burnt offerings,
  shall pay to you my vows,

14 Which my lips pronounced
and in my distress my mouth expressed.
15 I shall offer you burnt offerings of fatlings,
together with the smoke of burning rams;
I shall prepare an ox and goats. *Selah*
16 Come, listen, all you who revere God,
while I tell what he has done for me.
17 To him I cried with my mouth,
and sounds of music were on my tongue.
18 Had I been conscious of guilt in my heart,
my Lord would not have heard me.
19 But God did hear me,
he heeded my voice in prayer.
20 Blessed be God!
Because he did not dismiss my prayer,
his kindness will I retell a hundred times.

Notes

lxvi. This psalm is comprised of two sections. The first part (vss. 1–12) is a hymn in praise of God's might and his care for his people throughout its history, especially at the Exodus (vss. 5–9) and during the wanderings in the desert (vss. 10–12). The second part (vss. 13–20) is the thanksgiving hymn of an affluent individual fulfilling his vows in the temple (vss. 13–15) and recounting the story of his experience.

Many scholars maintain that the two parts of the psalm were originally two independent hymns, but if that were so, the first part would have no appropriate ending, and the beginning of the second section would be unduly abrupt. Moreover, mere fortuity does not explain the collocation of the natural pair of verbs, *tōṣī'ēnī,* "You led us out," in the last clause of vs. 12 and *'ābō',* "I shall enter," which begins the individual's hymn of praise in vs. 13. In the present state of inquiry, however, we are unable to reconstruct the original *Sitz im Leben* of this psalm.

2. *Sing.* As noticed at Ps lvii 8, Heb. *zāmar* equals Ugar. *ḏmr.*
indite. The ostensible A+B+C//Á+B́+Ć word arrangement suggests, as pointed out to me by D. N. Freedman (unpublished), that *śīmū* answers to *zammᵉrū.* The documentation of *śīm,* "to list, compose," in the fourth Note to Ps lvi 9 supplies a credible etymology.

3. *O God.* Parsing the initial *lamedh* of *lē'lōhīm* as vocative (cf. Pss xvi 2, cxl 7), and comparing the numerous examples listed in *Psalms I,* p. 21, and in Dahood, "Vocative LAMEDH in the Psalter," VT 16 (1966), 299–311.

so terrifying by your deeds. The current translation of *mahn norā' ma'aśekā,* "How terrible are thy deeds!" (RSV), disregards the lack of agreement in number between singular *nōrā'* and plural *ma'aśekā.* Comparison with vs. 5, *nōrā' 'alīlāh* reveals that in our phrase singular *nōrā'* describes God while plural *ma'aśekā* parses as an accusative specifying why God inspires awe. This grammatical analysis bears on the reading and translation of Ps cxxxix 14, *'ōdekā 'al kī nōrā'* (*')attā* (MT *nōrā'ōt*) *nāpaltī* (MT *niplētī*) *nāpōl 'āyōm* (MT *niplā'īm*) *ma'aśekā,* "I praise you, Most High, because you are awesome; I fall in adoration before you, so dreadful in your deeds."

4. *All the earth.* The psalmist conceives of Yahweh as the God of the whole world and of all peoples. This universalism can no longer be used as a criterion for dating this hymn since in the Late Bronze Age (1500–1200 B.C.) the Canaanite high gods were considered cosmic deities. For instance, Baal, the storm-god, was thought to rule over the world from his home in the northern heavens. He alone reigned over gods and men; his kingdom was "eternal, to all generations."

5. *the works of God.* Hummel in JBL 76 (1957), 103, may be correct in moving back the purported preformative *mēm* to the previous word as enclitic *mem;* likewise in Ps xlvi 9, "the works of Yahweh" (*Psalms I,* p. 277).

before men. Cf. *Psalms I,* pp. 146, 257, 307, for *'al,* "before, in the presence of." For a parallel to the sentiment expressed here, see, e.g., Ps xcviii 2. On *'al,* see also Pío Suárez in *Verbum Domini* 42 (1964), 71–80.

6. *He turned . . . they passed.* The sequence perfect (*hāpak,* "he turned")—imperfect (*ya'aberū,* "they passed") to express past narrative is a hallmark of Canaanite poetry; *Psalms I,* pp. 24, 56. This stylistic observation, while not precluding the LXX reading *hōpēk,* strengthens the case for the Masoretic preterit pointing.

the sea . . . the river. Commentators generally take *yām* to refer to the Sea of Reeds and the crossing during the Exodus, and *nāhār* as the Jordan that was forded in the time of Joshua. However, a study of Ugaritic poetic pairs of words suggests that *yām and nāhār are* synonyms; the psalmist thus alludes to only one event in Israel's history, namely, the Exodus. When Baal is instructed to *mr ym lksih nhr lkḥṯ drkth,* "Drive Sea from his throne, River from his seat of dominion" (UT, 68:19–20), he must unseat but one rival identified by the two poetic synonyms *ym* and *nhr.* Since vss. 9–12 are a reprise of the

Exodus theme and the subsequent wanderings in the wilderness of Sinai, and since there is no further mention of the supposed crossing of the Jordan, we must conclude that the psalmist, like the Canaanite bard, intends *yām* and *nāhār* as poetic alternates. This exegesis, one might remark, deprives Kraus, *Psalmen*, I, p. 457, of a key text for his reconstruction of the Gilgal feast near the Jordan when the passage through the Sea of Reeds was liturgically celebrated.

Come. Identifying *šām* with El Amarna *šumma*, "Behold!," studied in *Psalms I*, pp. 81, 291.

7. *from his eternal fortress.* For the syntax of *g^ebūrātō 'ōlām*, cf. *Psalms I*, pp. 110, 214, 293, and Ps lxi 5, *'ohol^ekā 'ōlāmīm*, "your eternal tent." The fourth NOTE on Ps xx 7 (*Psalms I*, p. 128) sets forth the evidence for *g^ebūrāh*, "fortress," as well as citing texts where *b^e*, as here, denotes "from."

his eyes keep watch. The psalmist here portrays God as the sentinel of the universe, a motif preserved in the epithet *zmrwt yiśrā'ēl*, "the Sentinel of Israel," in II Sam xxiii 1; cf. the third NOTE on Ps lix 18. The root of *tiṣpenāh*, "keep watch," probably occurs in UT, Krt:149, *bṣp 'nh*, "in the gaze of her eyes," a phrase apparently collocating the roots of our phrase *'ēnāyw baggōyīm tispenāh.*

lest. God keeps careful watch over the heathen to put down any incipient rebellion. *Psalms I*, pp. 59, 215, cite the evidence for this translation of *'al*. Stylistically noteworthy is the position of *'al* after the subject; normally it heads its clause, but this inversion is of a piece with vs. 18, where the conditional particle *'im*, contrary to standard practice, does not stand first in its clause. Cf. UT, 1 Aqht:159–60, *šršk barṣ al yp'*, "Your root grow not in the earth!," and Krt:116–17, *ḥẓk al tš'l qrth*, "Your arrows discharge not toward the city!"

rise up. The implicit object of hiphil *yārīmū* is probably "themselves." Notice a similar construction in Ps lv 3 where aphel causative *'ōrēd* governs an inner object. Cf. Nah i 9, *lō' tāqūm pa'^amayim ṣārāh*, "No adversaries shall rise up twice." However, in view of Ps lxxv 6 (cited in the next NOTE) and the Ugaritic-Hebrew penchant for ellipsis, the object to be supplied after *yārīmū* might be *qeren*, "horn," or *rō'š*, "head."

against him. Analyzing *lāmō* as an alternate form of *lō*, as proposed at Ps lv 20, and comparing Ps lxxv 6, *'al tārīmū lammārōm qarn^ekem*, "Raise not your horn against the Exalted One."

8. *with full voice.* Parsing *qōl* as adverbial, like vs. 17, *pī*, "with my mouth."

9. *Who placed us.* As a nation among the other nations of the earth.

among the living. By guiding the Israelites safely through the Sea of Reeds, God kept them from becoming denizens of the underworld.

the Quagmire. This poetic name for Sheol is discussed in *Psalms I*, pp. 78 f., NOTE on Ps xiii 5. The Masoretic punctuation *lammōṭ*, "Quagmire," shows that they understood *mōṭ* as a substantive. Cf. Ps cxxi 3, where MT again reads *lammōṭ*. KB's proposal (p. 502a) to read *lāmūṭ* in both verses does not commend itself. Of course, this version neatly comports with the translation proposed for Ps xxxi 9, "You did not put me into the hand of the Foe, / nor set my feet in the broad domain," where *merḥāb* is taken as a poetic name of Sheol.

10. *tested us.* During the long period of wandering in the Sinai desert. The metallurgical term *bāḥantānū*, "you tested us," paired with *ṣ^e^raptānū*, "you refined us," evokes the image of the torrid desert.

as silver is refined. Comparing *kiṣ^e^rop kāsep* with El Amarna 37:18, *kaspa ṣarpa*, "refined silver."

11–12. *You brought us . . . you had led us.* These two verses contain five cola, the first four of which are chiastically arranged A+B // B́+Á. Thus A and Á begin with verb forms of *bw'*, "to come," consist of verb with suffixed object and prepositional phrase, and each numbers eight syllables. The B and B́ cola are equally well matched: each contains verb+object+prepositional phrase, and the syllable count is 9:9. Verse 12c, on the other hand, is comprised of suffixed verb and prepositional phrase, and accordingly forms an inclusion with vs. 11a, i.e., the A colon.

11. *the wilderness.* Generally translated "net," *m^e^ṣūdāh* is in this context more meaningfully derived from the root *ṣwd*, "to range, wander," found in the hithpael form in Judg ix 12 and in the common nouns *ṣayid* and *ṣēdāh*, "provisions for a journey." The recognition of this root neatly resolves the textual problem in Lam iv 18, *ṣādū ṣ^e^'ādēnū milleket bir^e^ḥōbōtēnū*, "Our feet have ranged far without coming into our squares." This clause collocates the roots *ṣwd* (or *ṣyd*) and *hlk* that appear in parallelism in, e.g., UT, 52:67–68, *ttlkn šd tṣdn pat mdbr*, "They (the twin gods Dawn and Dusk) walk continually through the field, they range the confines of the steppe." The employment of the verb *tṣdn* to describe the wandering of the gods in the steppe, and the fact that in the unpublished tablet RŠ 24:244 the place whither the god Ḥoron turns is called *mṣd(h)*, sustain the proposed definition of biblical *m^e^ṣūdāh* as "wilderness, steppe." In CRAIBL, 1962 (appeared 1963), 108, Virolleaud reports that a fragment from Ras Shamra describes the banishment of the god Ḥoron into the wilderness where he planted a tree called *'r'r;* Jer xvii 6 uses the simile *k^e^'ar'ār bā'^a^rābāh*, "like a tamarisk in the desert." Cf. also Ezek xix 9; Dahood in *Gregorianum* 43 (1962), 72; *Biblica* 44 (1963), 548.

ulcers. If *m^e^ṣūdāh* is correctly defined "wilderness," the undefined hapax legomenon *mū'āqāh* might well allude to an effect of the plague which ravaged the Israelites during their sojourn in the desert (Num xi 33). Afflicting the thighs, the *mū'āqāh* might be considered a synonym of *šeḥīn*, "boil, inflammation"; consult the second NOTE on Ps xliv 20 (*Psalms I*, p. 267). No convincing etymology presents itself, though a connection with Ugar. *'qqm//aklm*, "devourers," in UT, 75:I:27, 37, might be considered. On this hypothesis *mū'āqāh* would signify something like "wasting, consumption, gnawing."

This definition finds confirmation in the word arrangement of vss. 11–12; *mw'qh* is meant to be the counterpart of vs. 12a *'nwš*, "sickness."

12. *sickness.* Relating consonantal *'nwš* (perhaps defective spelling for *'enūšāh*, cf. Ps lxix 21) to *'ānaš*, "to be sick, mortally ill." The traditional version, "Thou didst let men ride over our heads" (RSV), does not lend itself to easy exegesis, and GB, p. 759b, correctly describes the present passage "unclear," *pace* S. Mowinckel in VT 12 (1962), 285, who understands it as, "Thou hast let men drive their chariots over our heads," and writes, "The passage is quite clear."

Another unrecognized substantive from this root occurs in I Sam ii 33, *wekol marbīt bēteka yāmūtū 'anūšīm* (MT *'anāšīm*), "And all the increase of your house will die of the pest." A number of texts mention the head as the seat of illness: Isa i 5, *kol rō'š lā'ḥolī*, "The whole head is sickness itself" (the *lamedh* is emphatic); II Kings iv 19, *rō'šī rō'šī*, literally "my head, my head!," but really "I'm very sick"; UT, 127:9–10, *zbln 'l rišh wtṯb*, "She completely repelled the malady from his head"; J. Nougayrol, *Le palais royal d'Ugarit*, IV, 17.159:7 (p. 126), *ma-ru-uṣ qaqqadi-šu*, "the sickness of his head."

through fire and through water. A summary statement of the trials experienced; cf. Isa xliii 2. The repetition of the preposition in Hebrew (*bā'ēš ūbammayim*) is emphatic and should be reproduced in translation; cf. *Psalms I*, p. 8, NOTE on Ps ii 2, and contrast CCD, "We went through fire and water."

out of abundance. Referring to the relative abundance the Israelites enjoyed in Egypt; cf. Num xi 5, "O that we had flesh to eat! We remember the fish that we used to eat for nothing in Egypt, the cucumbers, the melons, the leeks, the onions, and the garlic; but now we are hungry, and there is not a thing, except that we have the manna to look at."

The fourth NOTE on Ps lx 3 cites bibliography for *le*, "from." The phrase *wattōṣī'ēnū lārewāyāh*, "After you had led us out of abundance," syntactically resembles Ps lxviii 21, *lammāwet tōṣā'ōt*, "escape from death," as understood by W. F. Albright in HUCA 23 (1950–51), 38. This analysis, one may note, renders superfluous the emendation, based on the ancient versions, of *lārewāyāh* to *lārewāḥāh*; cf. *Psalms I*, pp. xxiv ff., for a reassessment of the ancient versions as guides to the meaning of the Hebrew original.

The first part of the psalm ends in vs. 12; its structure as a tricolon underlines this fact.

13. *I shall enter your house.* Comparing the syntax of *'ābō' bēt^e^kā* with UT, 128:IV:21, *bt krt tbun*, "They entered Kirta's house," and with Phoenician Arslan Tash, lines 5–6, *bt 'b' bl tb'n*, "The house I enter you shall not enter."

The shift from plural "we" in vss. 9–13 to singular "I" in vss. 13–20 creates a problem that still awaits solution. Some scholars maintain that the nation is speaking in its unity, but more probably the speaker of these verses is a prominent individual of the Israelite community. To judge from his offerings, he was evidently a wealthy person.

with my burnt offerings. The suffix of *n^e^dārāy*, "my vows," in the second colon, also modifies parallel *'ōlōt;* cf. Brekelmans in *Jaarbericht . . . Ex Oriente Lux* 17 (1963), 204; *Psalms I*, pp. 17 f.

14. *my lips . . . my mouth.* For the Ugaritic parallelism between *p*, "mouth," and *špt*, "lips," see the second NOTE on Ps lix 8, and for the importance of parallel pairs as a criterion for the classification of Ugaritic, the fourth NOTE on Ps lvii 8.

16. *while I tell.* Though it belongs with the third colon of this verse, the verb *'^a^sapp^e^rāh* is, for metrical reasons, placed by the poet at the end of the first colon. A similar case of inversion is noticed in the NOTE to Ps xl 17. The mode of *'^a^sapp^e^rāh* is subjunctive; cf. the first NOTE on Ps lxi 5.

17. *I cried with my mouth.* As observed in NOTE on Ps v 10 (*Psalms I*, p. 35), the practice of placing the accusative of means (*pī*) before its verb characterizes the style of the psalmists.

Gunkel (*Die Psalmen*, p. 279) has compared the present phraseology with El Amarna 107:10–11, *ù pu-ya a-wa-te^meš^ aq-bu a-na šarri^ri^ ki-ta-ma*, "And my mouth, the words I spoke to the king, are truth."

my mouth . . . my tongue. The balance between *pī* and *l^e^šōnī* is attested in Virolleaud, *Palais royal d'Ugarit*, V, 124:2–3, *bpy t'lgt blšny ģr*, "from her mouth stammering, from her tongue mooing." See UT, Glossary, No. 1854a and above NOTE on vs.14.

sounds of music. Disputed MT *rōmam* probably equals Ugar. *rm*, "sound (of music)," in such phrases as *rm tph*, "the sound of his drum," and *rm ṯlbm*, "the sound of strings (?)." Cf. UT, Glossary, No. 2333. Hence vocalize as plural *rōmīm* or *rāmīm*.

on my tongue. Prima facie, taḥat l^e^šōnī seems to say "under my tongue," but the meaning of *taḥat* is not limited to "under"; cf. the third NOTE on Ps viii 7, *taḥat raglāyw*, "at his feet."

18. *Had I.* The inversion (NOTE on vs. 16) of *'im* in the phrase *'āwen 'im rā'ītī* sustains the version proffered for the final colon of vs. 7.

would not have heard me. Concerning the lack of an explicit suffix with *yišma'*, see *Psalms I*, p. 24, and the NOTES on Pss lv 20 and lix 8.

19. *did hear me.* Cf. preceding NOTE. By foregoing the use of the accusative suffix with *šāma'* (*šᵉmā'anī*), the psalmist could keep the first colon shorter (seven syllables) than the second colon (eight syllables). Had he employed the suffix, the first half of the verse would have numbered nine syllables; Hebrew prosody *normally* discountenances a first colon longer than the second.

20. *Because.* As the relative pronoun "who," *'ašer* is sometimes understandably deleted. As a causal conjunction "because" it acquires a *raison d'être*, and hence no longer subject to deletion. For this causal force, see the first NOTE on Ps cxix 38.

will I retell a hundred times. When consonantal *m'ty* is seen to form an inclusion with vs. 13, *'ašallēm*, "I shall pay," we recognize the same two verbs that stand parallel in Ps xxii 26, "One hundred times will I repeat to you (*m'tk*) my song of praise/in the great congregation/I will fulfill my vows (*'ašallēm*), O Prince!" For the scansion of Ps xxii 26 as containing a double-duty modifier or two-way middle, see *Psalms III*, p. 441. Hence in our verse repoint MT *mē'ittī*, "from me," to *mī'ētī*, "will I retell a hundred times."

PSALM 67

(lxvii 1–8)

1 *For the director; with stringed instruments. A psalm; a song.*

2 May God have pity on us and bless us;
may he cause his face to shine,
may he come to us. *Selah*
3 If your dominion is known upon the earth, [2]*
your victory among the nations,
4 The peoples will praise you, O God, [3]
the peoples will praise you all together.
5 The nations will be happy, [4]
and will shout for joy,
because you are the ruler.
You will lead nations into the plain,
and peoples into the land. *Selah*
6 The peoples will praise you, O God, [5]
the peoples will praise you one and all.
7 May the earth yield her produce, [6]
may God, our God, bless us.
8 May God bless us, [7]
all the ends of the earth revere him.

* Verse numbers in RSV.

Notes

lxvii. Usually classified as a harvest song sung during the Feast of Tabernacles (Kraus, *Psalmen*, I, p. 462), or a hymn of public thanksgiving for the crops of the earth (so Mowinckel in VT 5 [1955], 29), this psalm assumes a different aspect with the recognition that vs. 7, *nātenāh*, "may . . . yield," in tandem with the jussive verb *yebārekēnu*, "May he bless us," is a precative perfect. Hence this poem expresses a wish, a prayer. Cf. Anderson, BP, I, p. 480. A comparison of its vocabulary and idioms with Pss iv, lxv, lxxxv—all prayers for rain—discloses that the present poem specifically prays for rain, even though this term does not explicitly appear in its eight verses. Consult *Psalms I*, pp. 23, 26 f., and the introductory NOTE to Ps lxv.

The poem divides into three parts. Verse 2, with three jussives followed by one precative perfect—all in the third person singular—expresses the request. Verses 3–6, employing direct addresses in the second person singular, set forth the reasons why God should accede to the supplication of the people. Concealing one of the most subtle and sophisticated examples of chiasm in which one precative perfect is followed by three jussive forms in the third person, vss. 7–8 balance the three jussives and one precative perfect of vs. 2, and render explicit the request obliquely stated in vs. 2.

2. *have pity on us.* Comparing jussive *y^eḥonnēnū* with imperative *ḥonnēnī* in the prayer for rain Ps iv 2.

bless us. See second NOTE on vs. 7.

may he cause . . . to shine. For the exegesis of the phrase *yā'ēr pānay(w)*, see the second and third NOTES on Ps iv 7 (*Psalms I*, p. 26), where pertinent El Amarna and Ugaritic parallels are cited.

may he come to us. Reading *'ātānū* for MT *'ittānū;* the construction *yā'ēr 'ittānū* has never been satisfactorily explained. The related expression in Num vi 24 reads *'ēlekā;* cf. the sage observations of Rosenmüller, *Scholia in Vetus Testamentum,* III, p. 400. By reading *'ātānū* (there is impressive evidence that the Masoretes did not understand dative suffixes), we recover the third masculine singular of the precative perfect *'ātā,* followed by the dative suffix *-nū.* To the one example of *'ātāh,* "to come," followed by a dative suffix in Job iii 25, cited by Bogaert in *Biblica* 45 (1964), 239, may be added another in Mic vi 2, "Hear, you mountains, the controversy of Yahweh, and come before me (reading niphal imperative *hē'ātūnī-m* for MT *hā'ētānīm*), you foundations of the earth." Compare Isa xli 5. The stylistic advantage of such a punctuation arises first, from its disclosing a second verb in the final colon of vs. 2 to balance the two verbs of the first colon, and second, as remarked in the introductory NOTE, it shows that this verse with three jussive verbs and one precative perfect chiastically balances vss. 7–8 with one precative perfect and three jussive verbs.

The prayer "May he come to us" probably has its origin in the belief that God's absence is the cause of drought in the land. In Canaanite belief, the death of the storm-god Baal and his sojourn in the underworld produced drought and sterility upon the earth. Herein probably lies the exegesis of the request in Ps lxxxv 5—also a prayer for rain—*šûbēnû 'elōhê yiš'ēnû*, "Return to us, O God of our prosperity."

3. *your dominion.* Seeing in *darkekā* the nuance of Ugar. *drk* "dominion." Consult *Psalms I*, p. 2; *Biblica* 38 (1957), 320, n. 1; C. H. W. Brekelmans, *Ras Sjamra en Oude Testament* (Nijmegen, 1962), pp. 16 f., and Anderson, BP, I, p. 480.

your victory. Over the unruly forces of chaos in primordial times. This triumph gave Yahweh full governance over the cosmos, with complete control over rainfall and fertility; consult the second NOTE on Ps lxv 6.

For this nuance of *y*e*šû'āh*, which is suggested by its pairing with "your dominion," see the listing in BDB, p. 447b, and especially Pss xx 6, xxi 2, lxv 6. Ps lxxx 3, in pairing *g*e*bûrāh*, "might," with *y*e*šû'ātāh*, associates two ideas similar to those I propose to find in the present verse.

By appealing to the motive of praise from all the nations who will see God's intervention on behalf of his people, the poet seeks to induce Yahweh to send the desired rain.

4. *The peoples.* In view of the observation made in the first NOTE on Ps lxvi 4, one can no longer subscribe to Mowinckel's opinion (VT 5 [1955], 29) that the worldwide universalism expressed by this psalm indicates relatively late times. Israelite universalism in the flowering of nascent Canaanite universalism documented in the Ras Shamra tablets.

will praise you . . . will praise you. The refrain in this verse, repeated in vs. 6, presents the metrical pattern A+B+C // A+B+D. The Canaanite antecedents of this poetic pattern can be seen in such texts as UT, 52:8–9, *bdh ḫṭ ṯkl* (A+B+C) *bdh ḫṭ ulmn* (A+B+D), "In his hand is the staff of bereavement, in his hand the staff of widowhood." See W. F. Albright in *Studies in Old Testament Prophecy*, T. H. Robinson Volume, ed. H. H. Rowley (Edinburgh, 1950), p. 6.

5. *will be happy.* The note of joy also figures in the prayers for rain, Pss iv 8, *śimḥāh*, "happiness," and lxxxv 7, *w*e*'amm*e*kā yiśm*e*ḥû bāk*, "that your people might rejoice in you."

and will shout for joy. Comparing *y*e*rann*e*nû* with *tarnîn* in the petition for rain found in Ps lxv 9.

because you are the ruler. For this nuance of *tišpōṭ* consult *Psalms I*, p. 13. Scanning vs. 5a into 3+2 meter and vs. 5b into 2+3, thus disclosing a chiastic arrangement:

> *yiśm*e*ḥû wîrann*e*nû l*e*'ummîm//kî tišpōṭ* (3+2)
> *'ammîm mîšōr//ûl*e*'ummîm bā'āreṣ tanḥēm* (2+3)

You will lead. The verb *tanḥēm*, whose final *mem* is probably enclitic rather than the accusative suffix, since its objects are already expressed, is a double-duty verb serving both parallel cola. The metrical scheme is thus climatic: A+B // Á+B́+C, or in grammatical terms, object+prepositional phrase//object+prepositional phrase+verb.

As noted in *Psalms I*, pp. 33, 147, 262, the verb *nāḥāh* connotes "to lead into Paradise."

into the plain . . . into the land. Comparison with Ps cxliii 10, "With your good spirit *tanḥēnī bᵉ'ereṣ mīšōr*, 'lead me into the level land,'" discloses that in our verse *mīšōr* and *bā'āreṣ*, though separated in the parallel cola, express one composite idea. Hence the preposition of *bā'āreṣ* should also modify *mīšōr*, just as the one verb really belongs to both parts of the verse. And since in Ps cxliii 10 the terms are eschatological, referring to the induction into Paradise, we must assume a similar connotation here. Once the heathen nations witness Yahweh's miraculous intervention on behalf of his own people, they too will be converted to his praise, thus rendering themselves fit subjects for salvation.

6. *will praise you . . . will praise you.* Cf. the second NOTE on vs. 4.

7–8. *the earth . . . the earth.* *'ereṣ* at beginning of vs. 7 and at end of vs. 8 forms a fine inclusion.

yield her produce. Explaining *nātᵉnāh* as precative perfect parallel to jussive *yᵉbārᵉkēnū*, "May (God) bless us." Cf. the introductory NOTE for the chiasm between *nātᵉnāh* and precative perfect *'ātānū* in vs. 2; *Psalms I*, pp. 20, 26 f., and the first NOTE on Ps lx 6, *nātattāh*, "Give!" A fine parallel to this prayer comes in Ps lxxxv 13, *wᵉ'arṣēnū tittēn yᵉbūlāh*, "And our land will give her produce!" With the phrase *'ereṣ . . . yᵉbūlāh* might be compared UT, 67:II:5, *ybl arṣ*, "produce of the earth," while the stylistic balance between precative perfect and jussive may be attested in UT, 77:38–39, *ar yrḫ wyrḫ yark*, "Let shine the moon, and let the moon shine for you."

bless us. Namely, with rain. Cf. Mal iii 10, "And thereby put me to the test, says Yahweh of Hosts, if I will not open the windows of heaven for you and pour down for you overflowing blessing."

8. *bless us.* *yᵉbārᵉkēnū* forms an inclusion (*Psalms I*, p. 327) with the same verb in vs. 2.

ends of the earth revere him. Comparing Ps lxv 9, "While the denizens of the earth's ends stood in awe at your signs."

PSALM 68

(lxviii 1–36)

1 *For the director. A psalm of David, a song.*

2 When God arises,
his foes scatter,
and his enemies flee before him.
3 Like drifting smoke they are driven, [2]*
like melting wax before the fire;
At the sight of God the wicked disappear.
4 But the just will rejoice, [3]
they will exult at the sight of God,
they will jubilate with joyful song.
5 Sing, O gods, chant, O his heavens, [4]
pave the highway for the Rider of the Clouds!
Delight in Yahweh,
and exult before him!
6 Father of the fatherless, [5]
and defender of the widows
Is God from his holy habitation.
7 God who established a home for the solitary, [6]
led forth the prisoners to music;
But the stubborn were entombed in the Wasteland.
8 O God, when you went out [7]
before your people,
When you marched across the desert, *Selah*
9 The earth quaked and the heavens sprinkled [8]
at the sight of God,
The One of Sinai;
at the sight of God,
The God of Israel.

* Verse numbers in RSV.

10 Your generous rain pour down, O God, [9]
your patrimony and dominion yourself restore!
11 Provide for your family that dwells in it, [10]
with your rain sustain its inhabitants, O God.
12 Let the Lord send forth the word [11]
rejoicing a numerous host.
13 May the kings of the hosts bow themselves, bow themselves, [12]
the country's pasture land share the boon;
14 O that they would empty out between the sheepfolds! [13]
The wings of the dove are plated with silver,
and her pinions with yellow gold.
15 When Shaddai covered the kings, [14]
then snow fell on Zalmon.
16 O mighty mountain, mountain Bashan, [15]
O many-peaked mountain, mountain Bashan!
17 Why do you look with envy, [16]
O many-peaked mountain,
At the mountain God desired for his abode,
where Yahweh will dwell forever?
18 God's chariots were twice ten thousand, [17]
thousands the archers of the Lord,
who created Sinai as his sanctuary.
19 You ascended the heights, [18]
you took captives,
you received gifts from their hands.
But Yahweh God completely entombed the stubborn.
20 Blessed be the Lord day by day, [19]
El himself, our Savior, unburdened us.
21 El himself is for us the El of salvation, [20]
since to the Lord Yahweh we owe our escape from death.
22 God indeed smote the heads of his foes, [21]
split their skulls
as he marched forth from his heavens.
23 The Lord said: [22]
"I stifled the Serpent,
muzzled the Deep Sea."
24 Thus your foot crushed their limbs, [23]
The tongues of your dogs—
your foes were their portion.

25 Behold the marches of God, [24]
the marches of my God,
of my King from his sanctuary.
26 The singers in front, [25]
the musicians last,
In the middle, maidens beating tambours.
27 Bless God in the congregation, [26]
Yahweh in the convocation of Israel.
28 Look, little Benjamin leads them: [27]
the princes of Judah in double file,
the princes of Zebulun,
the princes of Naphtali.
29 Send, my God, your strength, [28]
strengthen, O God, what you have built for us.
30 Your temple, Most High, is Jerusalem, [29]
kings will bring gifts to you.
31 Rebuke the beast of the reed thicket, [30]
the herd of wild bulls with its calves;
Who trampled on peoples in his lust for silver,
delighting in battle, scattered peoples.
32 Let Egyptian merchants bring blue cloth, [31]
Cush speed his wares to God.
33 O kings of the earth, sing, [32]
O gods, sing praises to the Lord! *Selah*
34 Behold the Rider of his heavens, [33]
the primeval heavens;
Hark, he sends forth his voice,
the mighty voice!
35 Give praise to God, [34]
the Most High of Israel;
Whose majesty and might
are too great for heaven;
36 Too awesome is God for his sanctuary! [35]
Truly is he the God of Israel,
who gives victory and valor.
O people, bless God!

Notes

lxviii. Widely admitted as textually and exegetically the most difficult and obscure of all the psalms, this composition began to yield some of its secrets in 1950 when W. F. Albright brought to bear upon its manifold problems the new grammatical and stylistic principles unfolded by the Ras Shamra tablets. This justly famous article, "A Catalogue of Early Hebrew Lyric Poems (Psalm LXVIII)," in HUCA 23 (1950–51), 1–39, remains basic not only for the resolution of the numerous problems besetting this psalm, but also for an understanding of the background against which the archaic poems of the Psalter must be studied. The translation and NOTES offered here owe more to this pioneer study than the explicit credits might suggest.

Albright analyzed this composition as a collection of thirty incipits or beginnings of poems that were written down in the Solomonic period. He based his dating on the fact that the psalm swarms with instances of misunderstood defective spelling at the ends of words, in accordance with the characteristic fully defective orthography of Phoenicia and early Israel, which was replaced by the standard spelling of the Divided Monarchy in the course of the ninth century B.C. The present writer extends the use of this principle (see the NOTES, e.g., on vss. 5, 23, 25, 35) and applies other grammatical and poetic principles that have been elucidated by the Ugaritic-Phoenician discoveries since 1950, such as the third person singular suffix *-y* (vss. 11, 31, 34, 36), vocative *lamedh* (vss. 5, 33, 36), precative perfect (vs. 10), Phoenician ending of feminine singular nouns (vss. 12, 21, 36), double-duty suffixes (vss. 10, 21, 24).

The recognition of these various elements results in a translation often differing from Albright's and disclosing much greater conceptual unity throughout the composition than his analysis allows. In fact, this psalm may be fairly classified as a triumphal hymn (much like Exod xv, the Song of Moses) which, in mythopoeic language and mythological motifs that are sometimes historicized, celebrates the defeat of the Egyptians and the deliverance of the Israelites (vss. 2–7), the escape into the wilderness and the theophany of Sinai (vss. 2–9), and finally the settlement in Canaan implied by the prayer for rain (vss. 10–15). The rest of the poem plays variations on these principal themes. Thus vss. 16–19 are a reprise of the Sinai theme; vss. 20–24 allude in highly mythical language to the defeat, at the Sea of Reeds, of Egypt (another name for Leviathan who is Egypt in Isa xxvii 1; Ezek xxix 2, xxxii 2); vss. 25–28 describe a solemn procession into the assembly where the community, recalling the previous deliverance from Egypt, prays (vss. 29–31) for help against a new threat from Egypt, here termed "the beast of the reed thicket." The closing verses (32–36) are a summons to praise, inviting the heathen nations, including the Egyptians (32), to hymn the Most High of Israel. For a review of other attempts to classify this composition, see Samuel Iwry,, "Notes on Psalm 68," in JBL 71 (1952), 161–65.

2. *When God arises.* Namely, in a theophany. Since the marching song of the ark begins with similar phraseology (Num x 35), many commentators have concluded that the present psalm begins with the march from Horeb. Unlike Num x 35, our verses do not mention the *'ārōn*, "the ark." The first historical allusion comes in vs. 7, so that there is no real basis for the view that the opening verses describe the manifestation of God's presence with the ark. What we have here is simply a celestial theophany; the reasons will be given in the NOTES that immediately follow.

Briggs, CECBP, II, p. 105, is surely correct in parsing this verse as a temporal clause and apodosis without the conjunction, as is frequent in poetry. The Masoretic pointing of all three verbs as qal imperfect indicative, not jussive with ancient and modern versions, sustains his analysis. For other instances of temporal or conditional clauses without the morphological indicator, see *Psalms I*, pp. 19, 168, and PNWSP, p. 6, where Prov i 23, *tāšūbū lᵉtōkaḥtī hinnēh 'abbī'āh lākem rūḥī*, "If you heed my warning, behold I will pour out my spirit upon you," is illustrated by UT, 1019:12–14, *ttn wtn wlttn wal ttn*, "If you give, give; if you don't give, don't give!" With the recognition that the morphological indicator has been omitted, the warning on the lid of the Aḥiram sarcophagus becomes intelligible: *ld't hn ypd lk tḥt zn*, "Warning! Behold you will meet misfortune if you smash this!" Cf. Dahood, *Orientalia* 34 (1965), 85.

his foes scatter . . . his enemies flee. When the Canaanite weather-god Baal makes his voice reverberate throughout the vault of heaven, panic seizes his enemies: UT, 51:VII:35–37, *ib b'l tiḫd y'rm šnu hd gpt ǵr*, "The foes of Baal seize the forests, those who hate Hadd the ridges of the mountain." Of course, the parallel synonyms *ib* and *šnu* contain the same roots as *'ōyᵉbāyw*, "his foes," and *mᵉśānᵉ'āyw*, "his enemies"; consult the fourth NOTE on Ps lvii 8.

flee. The verb *nūs*, "to flee," probably appears in UT, 2063:14–15, *mlk syr ns*, "The king retreated, fled." Consult Michael C. Astour, "New Evidence on the Last Days of Ugarit," *American Journal of Archaeology* 69 (1965), 253–58, especially p. 257. UT, Glossary, No. 1660, p. 444, tentatively terms *ns* a place name.

3. *Like . . . smoke.* Cf. Ps xxxvii 20, "More quickly than smoke shall they vanish."

drifting. Reading niphal *hinnādēp* (MT *hindōp*) to match *tinnādēpū.*

they are driven. Vocalizing *tinnādēpū* (MT *tindōp*), niphal third person masculine plural. In Ugaritic, the imperfect form with preformative *t-* often replaces the form with preformative *y-* when the subject is masculine plural; UT, § 9.14. W. F. Albright in HUCA 23 (1950–51), 12, 17, prefers the singular pointing *tinnādēp,* explaining the plural subject "foes" as collective in meaning. While his analysis is possible, the El Amarna evidence points to a plural vocalization of the *tqtl* form in Ugaritic when the subject is formally masculine; cf. W. L. Moran in *The Bible and the Ancient Near East: Essays in Honor of William Foxwell Albright,* ed. G. Ernest Wright (Garden City, N.Y., 1961) pp. 62 f. See likewise the second NOTE on vs. 14 below.

4. *rejoice . . . exult . . . jubilate.* With D. N. Freedman I scan vs. 4 as a tricolon rather than a bicolon, as construed by some versions.

they will exult. Briggs and others would delete *ya'al^{e}ṣū* as metrically disruptive and as an improbable variation of vs. 5, *'il^{e}zū,* "they will exult," but one may counter the second objection by pointing to Job xviii 5, *d'k,* "to extinguish," but in the preceding chapter, xvii 1, *z'k,* also "to extinguish." See below on vs. 22, *'šmyw,* "his heavens." What is more, the chiastic arrangement of A and B (i.e., subject-verb // verb-prepositional phrase) guarantees the authenticity of *ya'al^{e}ṣū,* while the syllable count 7:8:7 shows that Briggs' objection on metrical grounds is unwarranted.

joyful song. The second NOTE on Ps li 10 records some evidence for this definition of *śimḥāh.*

5. *Sing . . . chant.* The Ugaritic text pairing the verbs *šr* and *ḏmr* (=Heb. *zāmar*) is cited in the fourth NOTE to Ps lvii 8.

O gods. In Canaanite religion the gods were considered sons of El and formed part of the pantheon. In the Old Testament the term often refers to angels or spiritual beings who are members of Yahweh's court; cf. *Psalms I,* p. 175, where relevant passages are listed.

This translation, which radically departs from tradition, results from parsing *l* of *lē'lōhīm* as the vocative *lamedh* (*Psalms I,* p. 21), an analysis suggested by vs. 33, where the balance with vocative "O kings of the earth" leaves little doubt as to the function of *l* in *lē'lōhīm.* Compare Ps xlvii 7, *zamm^{e}rū '^{e}lōhīm zamm^{e}rū,* "Sing praises, you gods, sing praises." The most recent bibliography of *lamedh vocativum* appears in *Biblica* 47 (1966), 407; in Dahood, "Vocative LAMEDH in the Psalter," VT 16 (1966), 299–311, and T. Penar, "'Lamedh Vocativi' exempla biblico-hebraica," in *Verbum Domini* 45 (1967), 32–46, with an index of all the biblical passages discussed.

O his heavens. Vocalizing *šāmāw* (MT *š^{e}mō*) and consulting the third NOTE on Ps lxiii 5 where texts attesting similar confusion between "name" and "heavens" are listed. Defective spelling can readily account for the confusion. Both the gods and the heavens are invited to prepare a highway for the Rider of the Clouds. From this vocalization, it might be noticed, emerges the association of "his heavens" with "Rider of the Clouds," an association with a Canaanite counterpart in UT, 'nt:II:39–40, [ṭ]l *šmm šmn arṣ rbb rkb 'rpt*, "dew of heaven, oil of earth, showers of the Rider of the Clouds." In vs. 34, "his heavens" is expressed with the third person suffix *-y*, *šmy*. Cf. vs. 22, *ba'ašāmāyw*, "from his heavens."

pave the highway. Comparing *sollū* with Isa xl 3, *yaššerū ba'arābāh mesillāh lē'lōhēnū*, "Make straight in the desert a highway for our God," and Judg v 20, "From heaven fought the stars, from their courses (*mesillōtām*) they fought against Sisera." Cf. W. F. Albright in *Studies in Old Testament Prophecy*, p. 14, n.[t]. Gunkel (*Die Psalmen*, p. 288) correctly objects that men cannot build a highway for the approaching God, and logically infers that *sollū* must here have another meaning. What he did not take into account, however, was the fact that, as in Isa xl 3, gods and heaven, not men, are invited to pave the highway for the advent of the Lord. Hence his objection to this translation of *sollū* (cf. Isa lvii 14, lxii 10) is invalid.

Rider of the Clouds. Or, "the Mounter of the Clouds." This expression has rightly been recognized from the beginning of Ugaritic studies as identical with *rkb 'rpt*, a standing Ugaritic appellation of the Canaanite storm-god Baal. Nor is it necessary to emend biblical *'rbt* to *'rpt*, since there are numerous instances of non-phonemic interchange between *b* and *p* in Northwest Semitic, as noticed in PNWSP, pp. 10, 32 f., 43; *Psalms I*, pp. 90, 141, 206, and the third NOTE on Ps lviii 5. Moreover, the proposal to delete one *b* as dittographic in *rkb b'rbt* (cf. Ugar. *rkb 'rpt*) leaves out of account vs. 34, *rkb bšmy*, "the Rider of his heavens." D. N. Freedman has called my attention to the fact that the pattern in vs. 4 (7:8:7) corresponds to the syllable count of vs. 5 (10:9:10). Hence the insertion of *b* in *rkb b'rbt* may be due to metrical considerations, since without it the colon would be too short syllabically.

Delight. A doubtful translation of consonantal *šmw* (MT *šemō*) which I would read *śemū*, qal masculine plural imperative of **yśm*, "to be pleasant, beautiful," Ugar. *ysm//n'm*, "pleasant." This root very probably recurs in Ps lxxxv 14. Of course, this etymology yields a sense in perfect accord with *'ilezū*, "Exult!" (at the same time disclosing a fine example of chiasm) and resolves the syntactical problems attending MT *beyāh šemō*, which makes no sense as it stands.

6. *fatherless . . . widows*. Comparing UT, 2 Aqht:v:7–8, *ydn dn almnt yṯpṭ ṯpṭ ytm*, "He judges the case of the widow, defends the cause of the fatherless."

from his holy habitation. The heavenly abode, as in Deut xxvi 15;

Jer xxv 30; Zech ii 17. In rendering the preposition *b*^{e}, "from," rather than "in," we uncover a description of divine intervention on behalf of the helpless resembling that of Ps xviii 10, where God is said to descend from heaven to rescue the afflicted psalmist. Cf. also Ps xxxi 22, "For he has shown me wondrous kindness from the fortified city (*b*^{e}*'īr māṣōr*), and 1QS 3:19, *bm'n 'wr twldwt h'mt wmmqwr ḥwšk twldwt h'wl,* "From the habitation of light are the origins of truth, and from the fountain of darkness the origins of perversity."

7. *a home.* Probably referring to the land of Canaan to be settled by the Israelites after their deliverance from Egypt. Cf. Jer xii 7; Hos viii 1 and ix 15, where the land of Ephraim is termed *bēt yhwh* and *bētī,* respectively (cf. ix 3, *'ereṣ yhwh*). See below on vs. 13, *n*^{e}*wat bayit;* GB, p. 96b, 7, and F. I. Andersen in *Orientalia* 35 (1966), 118, for this possible meaning of *bt* in the Mesha Inscription.

The form *baytāh,* with the archaic accusative ending (see the sixth NOTE on Ps lxv 10 and *Psalms I,* p. 51), is the second accusative governed by the hiphil participle *mōšīb.* Cf. UT, 127:37–38, *rd lmlk amlk ldrktk aṯbnn,* "Come down from your royal throne that I might rule, from the seat of your dominion that I might sit thereon," where *aṯbnn,* "that I might sit thereon," is apparently used transitively, with the final *-n* the pronominal object; UT, § 9.11, p. 73. Since vs. 7 numbers 10:9:10 syllables, the preservation of the accusative ending in *baytāh* may be due to metrical considerations.

the solitary. As some commentators (e.g., Rosenmüller) have observed, the term *y*^{e}*ḥīdīm,* "solitary ones," here denotes those in exile from their home or fatherland. In the present context it denotes the Israelites in Egypt. In HUCA 23 (1950–51), 19, W. F. Albright has compared this colon with UT, Krt:96–98, *yḥd bth sgr almnt škr tškr,* "The solitary one closed his house, the widow hired herself out."

prisoners. The Israelites who were in bondage in Egypt.

to music. Several scholars (Ginsberg, Gordon, Albright, Mowinckel) have identified the hapax legomenon *bakkōšārōt* with Ugar. *kṯrt,* "female singers," but here employed with the nuance "music." This interpretation comports nicely with the description of the Israelite exodus from Egypt in Ps cv 43, "So he led forth his people with joy, his chosen ones with singing." The grammar of *bakkōšārōt* finds a close parallel in Isa xxiv 9, *baššīr lō' yištū yāyin,* "They will not drink wine to song."

But. On the adversative sense of *'ak,* see N. H. Snaith, "The Meaning of Hebrew *'ak,*" VT 14 (1964), 221–25.

the stubborn. Probably referring to the Pharaoh and the Egyptians who, having seen the miracles worked by Moses (Exod xiii 15), stubbornly refused to let the Israelites go. As a result, the Lord slew the first-born of the land of Egypt. The poet may also have had in mind the rebellious Israelites, such as Korah, Dathan, and Abiram (Num xvi), or those labeled *dōr sōrēr,* "a stubborn generation," in Ps lxxviii 8.

were entombed. Literally "dwell," but *šākan* also bears the gravid sense "to dwell in the tomb" in Ps xciv 17; Isa xxvi 19; Nah iii 18, while in Ps xlix 12 and Isa xxii 16 *miškān* specifically refers to the tomb. This nuance probably occurs in Hatra Aramaic *mškn',* as proposed by J. Pirenne in GLECS 7, p. 113. See below NOTE on vs. 19.

in the Wasteland. Interpreting the hapax legomenon *ṣᵉḥīḥāh,* usually defined "scorched land," as another of the thirty-odd biblical names for the underworld. Texts describing Sheol as a waterless waste include Jer ii 31; Joel ii 20; Job xii 24 f., and as a place of thirst Isa v 13; Jer xvii 13b; Job x 22; Luke xvi 24. Concerning the latter motif, consult Gaster, *Thespis,* 1961, pp. 204 f. Of course, "the wasteland" can also be understood literally, i.e., the howling wilderness in which the Egyptians perished and were entombed; cf. Deut xxxii 10.

The LXX interestingly renders *šākᵉnū ṣᵉḥīḥāh* as *toùs katoikoũntas 'en táphois,* "(the rebellious) who dwell in tombs."

A touch of irony in fact marks the present choice of the poetic term for Sheol because Exod xiv 28 records that "The waters returned and covered the chariots and the horsemen and all the army of Pharaoh that followed them into the sea," while the next verse relates that "The people of Israel walked on dry ground through the sea."

It might be noted here that the lexicons list the substantive *ṣᵉḥīḥāh,* but this form is the accusative, the object of *šakᵉnū;* the nominative form is thus **ṣāḥīḥ,* "glaring surface," preserved in Ezek xxiv 7, 8, etc. As in Pss lxv 5, xciv 17; UT, Krt:103–4, *kirby tškn šd,* "like locusts that dwell on the field," *šākan* takes a direct object; see NOTE above on *yāšab* with the accusative.

9. *the heavens sprinkled.* Just as a person breaks out into a sweat at the sight of an unexpected caller (PNWSP, pp. 29 f.; D. R. Hillers in ZAW 77 [1965], 86–90; fourth NOTE on Ps lx 4), so the heavens drip rain when God suddenly appears in a theophany. The appearance of the storm-God Yahweh causes rain even in the desert. This fact serves as an introduction to the prayer for rain embedded in vss. 10–15 and as a motive why God should send rain to his patrimony in Palestine.

E. Vogt in *Biblica* 46 (1965), 207–9, proposes the emendation of *nāṭᵉpū* to *nāṭāyū,* "tottered," since elsewhere *nāṭap* is modified by the accusative of material with which the subject drips, but in Ps lxv 13 synonymous *yirʿᵃpū* is used absolutely, though contiguous *dešen* in the preceding colon makes it quite clear how the poet intends the verb to be modified. In the present verse the explicit accusative *mayim,* "water," is omitted for metrical reasons, as in Ps lxv 13. What is more, the proposed emendation slights the underlying metaphor that describes the reaction of a person to a surprise visitor, which consists in the shattering (*rā'ăšāh* in first phrase of vs. 9) of the loins and the sweating of the forehead.

The One of Sinai. Because he created Sinai as his sanctuary (vs. 18), and because he appeared there to Moses at the momentous point in Israelite history, Yahweh received the epithet *zeh sīnay* (also in Judg v 5). The grammar of this has been clarified by the standing Ugaritic epithet *il dpid*, "El the merciful one," literally "El the one of heart," and by Mari *zu-ḫatni(m)*. Compare Pss lxxv 8 and civ 25, *zeh hayyām*, "the One of the Sea." To the bibliography given in *Psalms I*, p. 152, should be added Dahood, *Biblica* 45 (1964), 405; N. C. Habel, *Yahweh versus Baal*, p. 90, n. 39; T. J. Meek, *The Bible Translator* 16 (1965), 144–45 (reprinted from JBL 79 [1960], 331–32), who writes: "I am finally persuaded that Grimme was right in his contention that *zê sînai* in Judges 5:5 is to be translated 'the One of Sinai.'" Accordingly, the deletion of this epithet as a gloss, lately sustained by I. L. Seeligmann in VT 14 (1964), 80, n. 1, and E. Vogt in *Biblica* 46 (1965), 208, disregards both Northwest Semitic usage and metrical exigencies, since vs. 9 now scans into 2+2+2//2+2+2. On Proto-Sinaitic *'l d 'lm*, "El (god) of eternity," see most recently W. F. Albright, *The Proto-Sinaitic Inscriptions and Their Decipherment* (Harvard Theological Studies, XXII; Cambridge, 1966), p. 24.

10. *Your generous rain.* This phrase begins the prayer for rain (vss. 10–15). The pronominal suffix "your" is supplied from the parallel colon; *Psalms I*, pp. 17 f. Unwitnessed in the other Semitic languages, *gešem*, "rain," now appears in Ugaritic as *gšm*, whose palatal sibilant *š* authorizes the Hebrew lexicographer to omit several false etymologies that have found their way into Hebrew lexicons under this entry. In fact, the biblical expression *gešem nᵉdābōt* (see the first NOTE on Ps liv 8) bears semantic comparison with UT, 2059:14, *gšm adr*, "a mighty downpour."

pour down. Parsing *tānīp* as an imperfect form with imperative sense; cf. the second NOTE on Ps li 14 and E. Vogt, *Biblica* 46 (1965), 361, n. 1. Its balance with the precative perfect *kōnantā* accords with this analysis.

your patrimony and dominion. Namely, the land of Canaan where Yahweh settled his people. The often-emended expression with a double-duty suffix *nāḥᵃlātᵉkā wᵉnil'āh* (cf. most recently E. Vogt, "'Regen in Fülle' (Psalm 68, 10–11)," in *Biblica* 46 [1965], 359–61) neatly points up the foolhardiness of emending a difficult text. The same two roots appear in parallelism in UT, 'nt:III:27–28, *bqdš bǵr nḥlty bn'm bgb' tliyt*, "in the sanctuary upon the mountain of my patrimony, in the pleasance upon the hill of my dominion/victory." Not only does the Canaanite passage pair the root *nḥl* with *liy*, but it also makes use of the double-duty suffix (as in the biblical phrase), since that of *nḥlty* serves to determine its counterpart *tliyt*.

Psalms I, p. 13, discusses *nāḥᵃlāh*, "patrimony," while the biblical occurrences of the root *l'y*, "to prevail," are listed on pp. 46, 144, and in *Biblica* 47 (1966), 408; cf. also E. Lipiński in *Syria* 42 (1965), 68, n. 3.

yourself. As noticed in *Psalms I*, pp. 19 f., and the second NOTE on Ps lxi 6, the use of the independent pronoun *'attāh* with the precative perfect is rather frequent.

restore. With the refreshing rain revive the scorched and moribund land. Parsing *kōnantāh*, "restore!" as the precative perfect (cf. the preceding NOTE) balancing *tānīp*, an imperfect functioning as an imperative.

11. *Provide*. Like *tānīp* in vs. 10, *tākīn* is an imperfect serving as an imperative. The mention of *gešem*, "rain," in the preceding verse suffices to specify in what sense God should provide for his people. After all, Yahweh is, in the words of Ps cxlvii 8, *hammēkīn lā'āreṣ māṭār*, "the one who prepares rain for the earth." Notice the occurrence of *tākīn* in the rain context of Ps lxv 10.

your family. Relating *ḥayyātᵉkā* to Ugar. *ḥwt*, "house, dynasty, realm," and comparing II Sam xxiii 13, *ḥayyat pᵉlištīm* with I Chron xi 15, *maḥᵃneh pᵉlištīm*.

that dwells. A relative clause without the relative pronoun; cf. *Psalms I*, p. 113; GK, § 155f.

in it. The antecedent of *bāh* being "your patrimony and dominion."

with your rain. Reading *bᵉṭōb* (MT *bᵉṭōbātᵉkā;* see the next NOTE), and referring to *Psalms I*, pp. 25 f., for *ṭōb*, "rain."

sustain. Detaching the final two letters of *bṭwbtk* and the first letter of *l'ny* to read *tākīl*, the hiphil imperfect of *kwl*, "to support, sustain," cited to explain Ps xli 4. A similar derivation has been proposed by W. L. Moran *apud* Albright, "Notes on Psalms 68 and 134," in *Norsk teologisk tidsskrift* 56 (1955), 2. The correctness of the reading *tākīl* is virtually assured by parallel *tākīn;* such assonance and alliteration can scarcely be accidental.

its inhabitants. Reading *'ānēy* (MT *le'ānīy;* see preceding NOTE), the qal plural participle with the third person suffix *-y* (*Psalms I*, pp. 10 f.) from *'wn*, "to inhabit, dwell," examined in the first NOTE on Ps xxvi 8. Cf. also Pss lxxvi 4, lxxxvii 7, and NOTE below on vs. 31.

In summary, the proposed reading of the second colon: *bᵉṭōb tākīl 'ānēy 'ᵉlōhīm*.

12. *send forth*. Parsing *yittēn* as jussive rather than indicative.

the word. Like Akk. *rigmu*, "word" but also "thunder," *'imrāh* (MT *'ōmer h-*), "utterance, speech, word," in this context denotes "thunder." Cf. Ps lxxxv 13.

rejoicing. Reading *'imrāh mᵉbaśśᵉrōt* for MT *'ōmer hamᵉbaśśᵉrōt* and parsing *mᵉbaśśᵉrōt* as the piel feminine participle modifying feminine *'imrāh*. The apparently plural ending *-ōt* is in reality the Phoenician feminine singular ending, as noticed in *Psalms I*, p. 275; in the second NOTE on Ps lviii 3, and the second NOTE on vs. 21 below. For this nuance of *bśr*, cf. UT, 51:v:88–89, *tbšr b'l bšrtk yblt*, "Rejoice, O Baal; I bring you glad tidings," and R. Dussaud, *Revue de l'histoire des religions* 111 (1935), 21.

numerous host. Referring to the stars. Being a source of rain, the stars rejoice at hearing Yahweh's thunder; consult the fifth NOTE on Ps lxv 9. To be sure, *ṣābā'* in a number of texts signifies the stars; GB, p. 671a.

13. *kings of the hosts*. Probably a poetic name for the brighter stars. Cf. Amos v 26, "You shall take up Sakkuth your king," where Sakkuth designates a divine star or planet. Several scholars (e.g., Gaster, *Thespis*, 1961, p. 412) have recognized a Semitic myth about the stars in the words of Ps lxxxii 7, *ūkᵉ'aḥad haśśārīm tippōlū*, "And like one of the Princes you shall fall!" Ps cxxxix 17 becomes more intelligible with the recognition that *rā'šēhem* refers to the leaders of the stars, while Job xxii 12, *rō'š* (perhaps read plural *rā'šē*) *kōkābīm* doubtless alludes to some of the brighter stars.

bow themselves, bow themselves. To empty their contents upon Palestine. Cf. Ps cxliv 5, *haṭ šāmekā*, "Bow your heavens!" Judg v 20–21 poetically relate that the stars participated in the defeat of the Canaanite kings at Taanach-Megiddo by inundating the area, making it impossible for the Canaanite chariots to maneuver.

Psalms I, p. 257, and the fifth NOTE on Ps lxiv 9 present the evidence for *ndd*, "to bow down, incline," the root presumably underlying MT *yiddōdūn*.

the country's. See the first NOTE on vs. 7 for this definition of *bayit*.

pasture land. W. F. Albright, HUCA 23 (1950–51), 22, and A. Malamat, JAOS 82 (1962), 146, discuss this meaning of *nāweh*, Mari *nawūm*.

boon. Literally *šālāl* denotes "prey, spoil, booty," but since the stars are also warriors (e.g., Judg v 20–21), the term is apposite.

14. *O that*. This nuance of *'im* is documented in the first NOTE on Ps vii 13 (*Psalms I*, p. 46).

they would empty out. A doubtful translation of consonantal *tškbwn*, to which I attach a meaning cognate to that found in Job xxxviii 37, *wᵉniblē šāmayim mī yaškīb*, "Who tilts the water jars of heaven?" Compare, however, Judg v 16. Concerning the preformative *t-* of *tškbwn*, see NOTE on vs. 3.

The wings . . . gold. This line presents no material difficulties of translation, but its interpretation is anything but clear. Perhaps the line alludes to the motif of the winged sun-disk; see comments on the next verse.

are plated. The ending of *neḥpāh* is parsed as dual; cf. *Psalms I,* pp. 97–98, 274, and I Sam iv 15, *'ēnāyw qāmāh,* "His gaze was fixed"; I Kings xiv 6, *raglehā bā'āh bappetaḥ,* literally "Her feet entered the door"; Lam i 16, *'ēnē 'ānay* (MT *'ēnī 'ēnī*) *yōr^edāh māyim,* "The fountains of my eyes stream with water." Cf. also Gillis Gerleman, *Ruth: Das Hohelied* (Neukirchen, 1965), p. 191; the second NOTE on Ps lxxii 2, and first NOTE on Ps lxxxviii 10.

silver . . . yellow gold. The Canaanite origin of this line is further evidenced by the pairing of *kesep* with *y^eraqraq ḥārūṣ,* as in UT, Krt:138, *ksp wyrq ḫrṣ.*

15. *Shaddai.* The most recent discussions of this ancient Canaanite and Amorite divine name are those of F. M. Cross, Jr., in HTR 55 (1962), 244–50, and Pope, *Job,* NOTE on v 17b.

covered. Namely, with his clouds, as in Job xxvi 9.

the kings. A certain constellation or group of stars; cf. the first NOTE on vs. 13.

then. Relating *bāh* to *bāhem,* "then, thereupon" (*Psalms I,* p. 122), and identifying it with Ugar. *bh* in UT, 'nt:III:29–30, *hlm 'nt tph ilm bh p'nm tṭṭ,* "As soon as Anath espies the two gods, then her feet stumble."

Zalmon. As recognized by many modern commentators, this mountain is Djebel Hawran (Druz), the (A)salmanos of Ptolemy. As Albright has observed (HUCA 23 [1950–51], 23), the name, etymologically "Dark One," refers to the volcanic character of its rock, so different from the limestone of Lebanon ("White One").

16. *Bashan.* A fertile tableland east of the Jordan; it was bounded on the north by Mount Hermon, Jebel Druze on the east and the hills east of the Sea of Galilee on the west.

O many-peaked mountain. A comparison of *hr gbnnym* with vs. 17, *hrym gbnnym,* reveals in the latter a case of enclitic *mem* in the middle of a construct chain.

17. *look with envy.* Because Yahweh did not choose Bashan as his dwelling.

18. *twice ten thousand.* The hapax legomenon dual *ribbōtayim* is found in UT, 51:I:31, *kt il dt rbtm,* "A gorgeous dais (or the dais of El) worth twice ten thousand (shekels)." In fact, the Ugaritic verse counsels us not to exclude the possibility that biblical *rekeb 'elōhīm ribbōtayim* might signify, "The chariot of God was worth twice ten thousand (shekels)."

archers. As noticed by Albright, *Norsk teologisk tidsskrift* 56 (1955), 2–4, *šn'n* is to be identified with Ugar. *ṯnn,* Alalakh *šanānu,* "archer," New Egyptian *snn,* "officer." Cf. also UT, Glossary, No. 2708, and

W. A. Ward in JNES 20 (1961), 39. The pairing of "myriads" and "thousands" compares with UT, Krt:92–93, *hlk lalpm ḫdd wlrbt kmyr.*

The chariots and the charioteer archers probably form the retinue of Yahweh as he ascends to Mount Sinai, which he created as his holy abode. Deut xxxiii 2–3 articulate a related theme: "Yahweh came from Sinai, and dawned from Seir upon us; he arose from Mount Paran. And with him were myriads (*rbbt*) of saints, marching apace at his right side" (UHP, p. 52).

the Lord, who created. Reading *'ādōn* (cf. Ps xcvii 5) *yābam* for MT *'ᵃdōnāy bām,* and identifying *yābam* with Ugar. *ybm* in the epithet of the Canaanite goddess Anath *ybmt limm,* "the creatress of the peoples," as interpreted by Albright *apud* Millar Burrows, BASOR 77 (1940), 7–8. UT, Glossary, No. 1065, defines *ybmt* as "progenitress," but "beget" and "create" are closely related concepts; cf. *qānāh,* "to create" and also "to beget."

19. *You ascended.* In order to sit on the throne of Sinai; cf. Ps xlvii 6.

the heights. Probably refers to Mount Sinai rather than to Mount Zion, as maintained by many commentators. The mention in vs. 18 of Sinai and later on in the present verse of *sōrᵉrīm,* "the stubborn" (consult the fifth NOTE on vs. 7), suggests that the events described here precede the entry into Canaan.

from their hands. Gaster (*Thespis,* 1950, p. 458) approached the correct sense when writing, "*ba-'adam* is a false interpretation of original BDM=*miyyadam,* as in Ugaritic." Now that the existence of *'d,* "hand," and *ba,* "from," is firmly established in Hebrew (*Psalms I,* p. 95), Gaster's emendation no longer commends itself. Consonantal *b'dm,* probably to be vocalized *bā'ādēm,* conceals a Northern contracted dual form (*Psalms I,* pp. 70, 88 f.).

completely entombed. Parsing *lškn* as *lamedh emphaticum* plus piel perfect *šikkēn* (MT *liškōn*); for this nuance of *škn,* see the sixth NOTE on vs. 7. Another example of emphatic *lamedh* with *škn* occurs in Ps lxxxv 10.

the stubborn. Cf. the fifth NOTE on vs. 7.

20. *day by day. yōm yōm* is documented in UT, 2062:A:11, *wymym,* misconstrued as the plural (written *ymm* in the same tablet) by Virolleaud, *Palais royal d'Ugarit,* V, p. 150.

El himself. This translation attempts to bring out the force of the article in *hā'ēl.*

our Savior. Who rescued us from the Egyptians. Though the versions understand *yᵉšū'ātēnū* as "our salvation," I prefer to understand this abstract noun concretely, as in Ps lxxxviii 2; cf. *Psalms I,* p. 173.

unburdened us. Pointing *yᵉ'ammēs* (MT *ya'ᵃmos*) and parsing it as a piel privative; consult the third NOTE on Ps lii 7. This analysis has been suggested by F. Nivard (private communication). Literally *y[e]'ammēs lānū* reads, "He removed from us the burden," with *lānū* expressing "from us," as noted at Ps lx 3. Quite frequent in Ugaritic, *'ms* now appears in an unpublished passage with El as its subject; see UT, Glossary, No. 1872.

This phrase refers to the delivery of the Israelites from the Egyptian corvée, described in Exod 11–14, and alluded to again in Ps lxxxi 7, "I removed the burden on his shoulder, his hands were freed from the basket."

21. *El himself.* Consult the second NOTE on vs. 20

our escape. Namely, from death in Egypt or when pursued by the Egyptians. Parsing the plural hapax legomenon (the singular occurs a number of times) *tōṣā'ōt,* whose suffix "our" is forthcoming from the first colon, as the Phoenician feminine singular; consult the preceding NOTE. Important for our present purpose is the Phoenician feminine singular form in Ezek xxvii 3, *m[e]bō'ōt yām,* "the gateway to the sea," where such a form neatly comports with the context—the lament over Tyre. Consequently, the emendation to masculine singular *m[e]bō' hayyām,* "gateway of the sea," endorsed by the apparatus of BH^3, can be disposed of without qualms; see F. L. Moriarty in *Gregorianum* 46 (1965), 86.

from death. Namely, in Egypt. As so frequently in Ugaritic (cf. *Psalms I,* p. 321; *Biblica* 47 [1966], 406), *l* here denotes "from" as rightly interpreted by Albright, HUCA 23 (1950–51), 26. Gunkel's tentative emendation (*Die Psalmen,* p. 291) of *lammāwet* to *mimmāwet* becomes quite unnecessary.

22. *smote.* As pointed out by Helen Jefferson in JBL 73 (1954), 154, *māḥaṣ* is an ancient poetic verb, extremely frequent in Ugaritic. Here predicated of the Israelite God, in UT, 68:9, *tmḫṣ ibk.* "You will smite your foe," it is predicated of the Canaanite Baal. As often in Ugaritic and Hebrew poetry, the imperfect form (*yimḥaṣ*) expresses past time; *Psalms I,* p. 56, and the first NOTE on Ps liv 7.

the heads. Further evidence for the antiquity of the psalm is proffered by the collective meaning of *rō'š,* recurring in Pss cx 6, cxl 10; Num xxiv 18; Hab iii 13, and in Canaanite UT, 'nt:II:9–10, *tḥth kkdrt ri[š] 'lh kirbym kp,* "Beneath her, heads like balls; above her, hands like locusts." Cf. UT, § 13.16, and UHP, p. 37.

The Ugaritic-Hebrew brace *r'š//qdqd* has been commented upon in *Psalms I,* p. 47; cf. also the fourth NOTE on Ps lvii 8.

split. Reading perfect *šā'ar* (in balance with imperfect *yimḥaṣ,* "smote"), Ar. *ṯaǵara,* "to split, break," the root of Ugar. *ṯǵr,* Heb. *ša'ar, "gate."* KB, p. 1002a, correctly renders Jer xxix 17, *katt[e]'ēnīm haššō'ārīm,* "like the burst-open figs" (Bright [The Anchor Bible, vol.

21], § 28, renders "putrid figs" with the comment, "Or perhaps 'bruised, mashed' "), but unnecessarily posits a second root, *š'r* II, since it recognizes that the root meaning of *ša'ar*, "gate," is "split."

as he marched. This theme will be resumed in vs. 25, *h^alīkōt 'ēlī*, "the marches of my God."

from his heavens. Accepting MT *ba'^ašāmāyw*, explaining *ba* as "from" (consult the third NOTE on Ps lv 12) and *'^ašāmāyw* as the word for "heavens" with prothetic *aleph*. The third NOTE on Ps li 9 cites numerous instances of nouns with prothetic *aleph*, a nominal formation that characterizes the Phoenician dialect, to judge from the names of cities along the Phoenician littoral. That the psalmist should employ both *šāmayim* (vs. 9) and *'^ašāmayim* is no more unusual than, say, Jer xxi 5, *bizrō^a'*, but *b^e'ezrō^a'* in xxxii 21; Job xxxviii 15, *z^erō^a'*, but *'ezrō'ī* in xxxi 22. Is the hapax legomenon in Isa lix 10, *'ašmannīm* (1QIs^a *'šmwnym*) an elative form or merely *š^emēnīm*, "stout ones," with prothetic *aleph?*

23. *The Lord.* Reading *'^adōnay-m*, with enclitic *mem* (*Psalms I*, p. 327), having detached the *mem* from following *mbšn*. Compare Ugar. *b'lm*, with enclitic *mem*.

I stifled. A doubtful translation of consonantal *'šyb*, which I would vocalize *'aššīb*, the hiphil imperfect of *nāšab*, "to blow, breathe." Syriac *nāšūbā* means "the proboscis of an animal"; given that the parallel verb is *šbm*, "to muzzle," such an etymology commends itself. The force of hiphil *'aššīb* would be privative, a topic discussed in *Psalms I*, pp. 158, 265; cf. also P. Haupt, ZAW 29 (1909), 282, who cites the Ethiopic privative causative form *alhaya*.

Like *yimḥaṣ* in vs. 22 (fourth NOTE), *'aššīb* is an imperfect expressing past time.

the Serpent. Reading *bāšān* (MT *mibbāšān*), the initial *mem* having been joined to the preceding word as enclitic, and identifying it with Ugar. *bṯn*, Akk. *bašmu*, "serpent, dragon." Full discussion can be found in Albright, HUCA 23 (1950–51), 27.

To whom does "the Serpent" historically refer? Since *bāšān* is another name for Leviathan, as appears from UT, 67:I:1–2, *ktmḫṣ ltn bṯn brḥ tkly bṯn 'qltn*, "When you smote Lotan, the primeval serpent, destroyed the twisting serpent," one may, in the light of Isa xxvii 1 where Leviathan refers to Egypt, and in view of the several other mentions of Egypt in the psalm, conclude that the psalmist is describing in poetic terms what Exod i–xiv sets forth in prose. Cf. the second NOTE on vs. 31.

muzzled the Deep Sea. With no emendation of the purely consonantal text (i.e., *'šbm;* MT *'āšīb m-*) reading *'ešbōm m^eṣūlōt yām*, literally "I muzzled the depths of the Sea." When one compares this verse with UT, 'nt:III:37–38, *lištbm tnn išbḥnh* (UHP, p. 20) *mḫšt bṯn 'qltn*, "I indeed muzzled Tannin, I silenced him; I smashed the twisting Serpent," one realizes that the remarks of A. R. Johnson, *Sacral Kingship in Ancient Israel* (Cardiff, 1955), p. 73, n. 8, are mistaken: "The writer can find no justification for the proposal to see in the Hebrew *bāšān* of this stichos the equivalent of the Ugaritic *bṯn*, 'serpent,' and in the line as a whole a reference to the mythical monster of the Deep. . . . This suggestion again fails to do justice to the context (cf. verse 16), and it exaggerates the significance of the parallelism." Contrast Dahood, "MIŠMĀR 'Muzzle' in Job 7, 12," in JBL 80 (1961), 271–72; Pope, *Job*, NOTE on vii 12b; Patrick D. Miller, Jr., in HTR 57 (1964), 240. The theme of muzzling Pharaoh, the great dragon, reappears in Ezek xxix 2–4, "Son of man, set your face against Pharaoh king of Egypt, and prophesy against him and against all Egypt; speak and say, Thus says the Lord God: 'Behold, I am against you, Pharaoh king of Egypt, the great dragon that lies in the midst of his streams . . . I will put hooks in your jaws.'"

24. *Thus*. *lᵉma'an* here expresses result rather than purpose; see the fourth NOTE on Ps li 6.

their limbs. Repoint MT *bᵉdam*, "in blood," to *baddīm*, "limbs."

In Job xli 4, *baddāyw* designates the limbs of the wondrous beast that God created; our verse describes the primordial monsters vanquished by God.

The tongues of your dogs. Probably referring to metaphorical language to God the hunter who hunts with dogs. Consult the second NOTE on Ps lxiv 8.

John L. McKenzie (*Dictionary of the Bible* [Milwaukee, 1965], p. 202) assures us that "In the ancient Near East, much as in the modern Near East, the dog is not kept as a pet nor is he employed for hunting or as a watch dog." This sentence contains no fewer than three erroneous assertions. That the dog was sometimes kept as a pet as early as ca. 1700 B.C. may be inferred from the Kirta Legend; cf. UT, 125:15–16, *kklb bbtk n'tq*. While its sense is not perfectly clear, the association of *klb*, "dog," with *bt*, "house," suggests that dogs were kept in the house. The second assertion that dogs were not employed for hunting is belied by the representation of at least three magnificent "Assyrian hunting dogs" placed directly under McKenzie's statement! Cf. Louis Hartman in CBQ 28 (1966), 253, and the famous golden bowl of Ras Shamra (fourteenth century B.C.) depicting a hunting scene with hunting dogs. See C. F. A. Schaeffer, *Ugaritica II* (Mission de Ras Shamra V; Paris, 1949), Pl. I–VIII and p. 18, where Schaeffer discusses "le chien de chasse," and p. 29, Fig. 8, for the use of hunting dogs in Egypt at the time of Tutankhamen (ca. 1353–1344 B.C.). Our biblical verse joins the archaeological evidence to discredit the claim that in the ancient Near East dogs were not used for hunting.

That the ancients used watchdogs is perfectly clear from Job xxx 1, "Whose fathers I had disdained / To put with the dogs of my flock," and tolerably clear from UT, Krt:122–23, *zġt klb ṣpr*, "the howling of the watch-dog," as rendered by Ginsberg, LKK, pp. 16, 38, and Dahood, *Orientalia* 29 (1960), 348.

your foes. Suffixless *'ōyᵉbīm* receives its determination from parallel "your vilifiers" on the basis of the poetic usage documented in *Psalms I*, pp. 17 f. The initial *mem* of MT *mē'ōyᵉbīm* belongs to the preceding word as an enclitic following a pronominal suffix; to the list of examples given by Hummel in JBL 76 (1957), 99 f., might be added Pss lxviii 29–30, lxix 8–9, cii 9, cxi 10; Isa xl 12, *š'lw-m ym*, 17, *ngdw-m 'ps*, lii 5, *šmy-m nō'āṣ*, lix 2, *pny-m*, "his face"; Jer xiii 20, *'ynyk-m*, xlviii 12, *nblyh-m;* Mic i 11, *lk-m*.

their portion. Comparing UT, 49:II:35–37, *širh ltikl 'ṣrm mnth ltkly npr*, "The birds devour his flesh, the fowl consume his parts."

25. *Behold.* Vocalizing qal imperative *rᵉ'ū* (MT *rā'ū*). Pss lxix 33 and xcviii 3 afford evidence of similar Masoretic confusion between perfect *rā'ū* and imperative *rᵉ'ū*. The poet invites the religious assembly to behold in spirit the theophany described in vss. 2, 8–9.

the marches of God. Probably referring to God's going forth from heaven (vs. 5) to assist his people. A comparison of *hᵃlīkōtekā 'ᵉlōhīm* with *hᵃlīkōt 'ēlī* in the parallel colon virtually compels the grammarian to see in the purported second person suffix *-kā* of *hᵃlīkōtekā* the emphatic *kī* interposed in the construct chain, like enclitic *mi*. The writer resorted to this explanation to account for the translation of Ps xxiv 6 and now is able to point to further examples in Ps lxix 30; Judg v 31; Ezek xiii 4, xxvii 25; Hos viii 5; Obad 9; Zech ix 13. Ezek xxvii 8–9 provide the most instructive instance since *yōšᵉbē ṣīdōn*, "the inhabitants of Sidon," and *ziqnē gᵉbal*, "the elders of Byblos," are evidently meant to balance *ḥkmyk ṣōr*, which should be pointed *ḥokmē-kī ṣōr* and translated "the wise men of Tyre."

from his sanctuary. Vocalizing *bᵉqodšō* (in defective orthography *bqdš;* MT *baqqōdeš*) and comparing vs. 6, *bimᵉ'ōn qodšō*, "from his holy habitation." Either Sinai (vs. 9), or heaven (vs. 6) (or both) are intended.

26. *The singers in front.* This verse apparently describes the procession into the temple where the deliverance from Egypt will be commemorated.

In the middle. Absolute *tōk* is a pure Canaanite (i.e., Ugaritic-Phoenician) form in which the diphthong *aw* becomes *ō*, regardless of position. Hence the widely received emendation of MT *tōk* to *tāwek* cannot be allowed; cf. UHP, p. 8, and the third NOTE on Ps lv 5.

maidens. *'ᵃlāmōt* equals Ugar. *ġlmt*, Phoen. *'lmt*.

beating tambours. *tōpēpōt* is a denominative participle from ***tōp***, "drum, tambour," Ugar. *tp*, cited in UT, Glossary, No. 1274.

27. *in the congregation.* Assembled to commemorate the miraculous deliverance from Egypt. MT *bᵉmaqhēlōt,* a hapax legomenon in the plural form, has lent itself to differing morphological explanations. Albright, HUCA 23 (1950–51), 30, proposes to divide and read *bᵉmō qᵉhillōt,* an analysis endorsed by me in UHP, p. 27. But the presence in this psalm of several Phoenician feminine singular forms ending in *-ōt* (vss. 11, 21) and the place name *maqhēlōt,* one of the stations of Israel during the Exodus (Num xxxiii 25, 26), lead one to think that *maqhēlōt* is a feminine singular of the Phoenician type. The synonymous parallel *māqōr,* "convocation," it will be noticed, is singular.

in the convocation. Being parallel to *bᵉ,* "in," of *bᵉmaqhēlōt, min* of *mimmᵉqōr* also denotes "in," a meaning documented in *Psalms I,* p. 106, and now capable of further documentation in Isa xliv 2, lviii 13; Jer ix 18, xviii 22; Ezek iii 12, xxvii 34; Job xxiii 12; Prov xvii 23 (cf. xxi 14), and the Mesha Inscription, line 11, *w'hrg 't kl h'm[m]hqr,* "And I slew all the people *in* the village."

The substantive *māqōr,* "convocation," derives from the root *qwr,* "to call, convoke," studied by Manfred Weippert in ZAW 73 (1961), 97–99, who finds this root in Isa xxii 5 on the strength of UT, Krt: 119–20, *lqr ṯigt ibrh lql nhqt ḥmrh,* "till the noise of his stallion's neighing, till the sound of the braying of his ass." Gordon, UT, § 11.7, p. 104, renders 1001:5, *hm tqrm lmt,* "If thou sayest to Mot," and the obscure line 1001:rev:10, *p]ḫrk ygršk qr btk ygršk* should probably be rendered "Your own family will drive you out, the assembly in your house will drive you out." Thus the consonantal text of Num xxiii 16 proves sound: *wayyāqor* (MT *wayyiqqār*) *yhwh 'el bil'ām wayyāśem dābār bᵉpīū,* "And Yahweh called Balaam and put the word into his mouth," and Ps cxlvii 17 might now be rendered "Who can stand before his thunder (*qārātō*)?" Cf. also Prov xviii 4, "The words of a man's mouth are deep waters, a gurgling stream the utterance of Wisdom (*qōr ḥokmāh*)," and viii 3, *lᵉyad šᵉ'ārīm lᵉpī qārāt* (MT *qāret*) *mᵉbō' pᵉtāḥīm tārōnnāh,* "Beside the gates she calls with full voice, at the approach to the portals she cries aloud." The prepositional phrase *lᵉpī* and the *qtl* verb *qrt,* with the archaic feminine ending *-t,* form the semantic counterpart of the energic verb *tārōnnāh* (PNWSP, pp. 3–4). In other terms, the verse follows the pattern A+B//Á+B́. In the following verse, it will be noted, the presence of *qōlī,* "my voice," recalls the Ugaritic parallelism of *qr* and *ql.*

The biblical brace *maqhēlōt* and *māqōr* virtually exhibit the same roots found in the Ugaritic pair *qr-ql* (cited above), since, as Albright, VTS 4 (1957), 256, has shown, *qōl,* "voice," goes back to *qahlu,* "call," from *qhl,* "to call, assemble."

28. *Look.* This meaning of *šām* is discussed in *Psalms I,* pp. 81, 292. The verse resumes the description of the procession begun in vs. 26.

in double file. A doubtful version of much-contested *rgmtm,* which I parse as a feminine dual form like Ugar. *thmtm. Juxta Hebraeos* translates it *in purpura sua,* "in their purple robes," a version that merits consideration in view of the Northwest Semitic evidence for nouns appearing with or without prothetic *aleph;* cf. the second NOTE on Ps li 9. Thus in addition to *'argāmān,* Ugar. *agrmn,* there may have been a feminine doublet **rgmt.*

the princes of Zebulun, the princes of Naphtali. The leaders of the Israelite tribes of Zebulun and Naphtali in Galilee.

29. *Send.* Reading piel imperative *ṣawwēh* for piel preterit *ṣiwwāh* of MT. For other texts illustrating this nuance of the verb, see *Psalms I,* p. 259. Stylistically, imperative *ṣawwēh* balances imperative *gᵉ'ar,* "rebuke," of vs. 31.

my God. Reading *'ᵉlōhay* (MT *'ᵉlōhekā*), having detached the purported suffix *-kā;* see the next NOTE.

your strength. Reading *kā'uzzekā* (see the preceding NOTE) and parsing *kā-* as the asseverative kaph emphasizing the substantive. Consult the remarks of G. R. Driver in JTS 15 (1964), 341, on the *kaph veritatis* in Lam i 20, *kammāwet,* "death itself," and those of R. Gordis in JAOS 63 (1943), 176–78, who diagnosed Lam i 20 in the same manner.

what you have built. Namely, Jerusalem, as suggested by the next verse. Albright, HUCA 23 (1950–51), 31, correctly compares *zū pā'altā* with Phoenician *zp'l* in the tenth-century B.C. Phoenician inscriptions of Aḥiram and Eliba'al.

for us. Reading *lānū-m* (MT *lānū mēhēkālekā*) *hēkālekā,* and consulting the sixth NOTE on vs. 24 for other cases of enclitic *mem* appended to suffixes. Hummel, JBL 76 (1957), 105, proposes the reading *lānū-m* in Ps cxxxvii 3, *šīrū lānū-m šīr ṣiyyōn,* "Sing us Zion's song"; but cf. *Psalms I,* p. 173.

30. *Your temple.* Consult the preceding NOTE.

Most High. Interpreting *'al* as the divine appellative studied in *Psalms* I, p. 117, and in the NOTES on Pss lv 23 and lxii 8. This appellative recurs below in vs. 35.

kings. Since Israel's God is the Most High of all the gods, the pagan kings will bear tribute to Jerusalem, his temple.

31. *Rebuke.* Imperative *gᵉ'ar* matches imperative *ṣawwēh,* "send," in vs. 29. Cf. Ps cvi 9, "He rebuked (*wayyig'ar*) the Sea of Reeds, and it became dry," and UT, 137:24, *bhm yg'r b'l,* "Baal rebuked them."

the beast of the reed thicket. Another allusion to Egypt (see the third NOTE on vs. 23), which is called Leviathan in Isa xxvii 1, while Ezek xxix 3 and xxxii 2 term Pharaoh *tnn,* "the Dragon." Since Leviathan possessed many features of a crocodile (cf. Job xl 25 and Pope [The Anchor Bible, vol. 15], pp. 277 f.), "the beast of the reed thicket" would aptly describe Egypt or the Pharaoh, especially since vs. 23 refers to Egypt as "the Serpent," a synonym of Leviathan.

the herd of wild bulls. For this nuance of *'ēdāh*, "herd," cf. *Psalms I*, p. 140. UT, 76:III:21–22, shows that *ibr* (Heb. *'abbīr*) is a synonym of *rum*, "wild buffalo," while 76:II:9 places the *rumm*, "wild buffaloes," in a reed-marsh (*aḫ*).

Who are intended by the "wild bulls"? The well-attested Canaanite-Hebrew practice of using animal names to designate military personnel (*Psalms I*, pp. 9 f.) suggests that the "bulls" are Pharaoh's generals while the "calves" are the soldiers.

with its calves. Namely, with its soldiers; see preceding NOTE. I parse *'eglē* as the plural noun followed by the third person singular suffix *-y* (*Psalms I*, pp. 10 f., and the seventh NOTE on vs. 11) whose antecedent is *'ēdāh*, "herd," or possibly *ḥayyat qāneh*, referring to Pharaoh.

Who trampled on. Extremely significant for the exegesis of this verse is the fact that this rare verb *rāpas* (here *mitrappēs*) is predicated of Pharaoh in Ezek xxxii 2, *wattirpōs nahᵃrōtām*, "You fouled your river by trampling."

peoples. As in vss. 10, 19, 22, the object (*'ammīm*) precedes the predicate (*mitrappēs*); cf. Ps viii 3; Isa xxiii 9; Job xxiii 9; UT, 76:II:6, *qšthn aḫd bydh*, "He took his bow in his left hand."

in his lust. Explaining consonantal *rṣy* as the qal infinitive construct (compare Ugar. *bbk*, "while weeping"; UT, § 9.52) followed by the third person singular suffix *-y* (cf. the fourth NOTE on this verse). Consult the analysis of Prov v 18, *brwk*, proposed by me, UHP, p. 26.

delighting. Parsing *yeḥpāṣū* as the imperfect third person masculine singular with the archaic indicative ending; cf. the first NOTE on Ps lxiv 7.

32. *Egyptian merchants.* A doubtful version. Vocalizing *mōnē* (MT *minnī*) *miṣrāyim*, with *mōnē* the construct plural participle of *mānāh*, "to count," hence "counters (of money)"; cf. II Kings xii 11 and Ezek xxvii 17, *mnyt*, probably to be pointed *mānītā*, "you exchanged."

bring. Reading hiphil jussive for MT qal *ye'tāyū*. Following the two imperatives *ṣawwēh*, "send," and *gᵉ'ar*, "rebuke," the verbs of vs. 32 yield better sense as jussives. Note the two imperatives in the next verse.

blue cloth. *ḥašmannīm* equals Akk. *ḫašmānu*(*m*) but *ḫušmānu* in Ras Shamra Akkadian; cf. Albright in *Norsk teologisk tidsskrift* 56 (1955), 4 f., and CAD, VI, p. 142.

Cush. The biblical name of the territory south of Egypt, corresponding roughly to modern Sudan; in many versions Heb. *kūš* is translated "Ethiopia."

speed. Punctuating hiphil jussive *tārēṣ* (MT *tārīṣ*) from *rūṣ*, "to run, hasten." Parallelism with "bring" makes a verb of motion desirable in the second colon rather than an identification of *trṣ yd* with Akk. *qāta tarāṣu,* "to stretch forth the hand."

his wares. Just as *z^e^rō'ōt,* "arms," connotes "resources" in Ps xxxvii 17 and Job xxii 8–9, so here *yādāyw,* "his hands," seems to connote "the products of his hands, his wares." Cf. Deut xxxiii 7, *yādāyw rabbe* (MT *rab*) *lō,* "Increase his forces for him"; Ezek xxvii 15, *s^e^ḥōrat yādēk qarnōt šēn,* "The profit from your wares was ivory tusks"; cf. Job xx 10 and G. Rinaldi in *Bibbia e Oriente* 6 (1964), 246, who discusses related meanings of *yād.*

Isa lx 1–6, with their description of the wealth of nations pouring into Jerusalem, provides background for the exegesis of our verse.

33. *O kings of the earth.* That *maml^e^kōt* here bears the Phoenician meaning "king" is today widely accepted and needs no further demonstration. It is sufficient here to refer to ZLH, p. 455a, which lists the following passages where *mamlākāh* denotes "king": I Sam x 18; I Kings x 20; II Chron ix 19, xii 8; Isa xlvii 5; Jer i 15, xxv 26; Pss lxviii 33, lxxix 6, cii 23, cxxxv 11. Cf. also W. L. Moran in BCCT, pp. 7–20 for a complete discussion of this meaning, and *Psalms I,* p. 143, where the semantic bond between "kingdom" and "king" is cited to illustrate the definition of *m^e^lūkāh,* "king," in Ps xxii 29.

sing . . . sing praises. The fourth NOTE on Ps lvii 8 cites the Ugaritic text *dyšr wyḏmr,* which juxtaposes the two verbs here found in parallelism: *šīrū . . . zamm^e^rū.*

O gods. Balancing vocative *maml^e^kōt hā'āreṣ,* "O kings of the earth," *lē'lōhīm* (as in vs. 5) must also be in the vocative case; hence the initial *lamedh* is vocative as proposed also for *lā'am* in vs. 36. The verse thus scans into 3+3 meter. Cf. *Psalms I,* p. 21, and Ps xlvii 7, "Sing praises, you gods, sing praises,/sing praises to our king, sing praises." The present verse, along with the next line, resumes the theme of vs. 5.

34. *Behold.* The initial syllable of *lārōkēb* does not readily parse, but the carefully balanced elements of vss. 33–34 suggest that *lā* is the opposite number of *hēn,* "Hark!," heading the second colon.

of his heavens. Identifying the *-y* of *šāmēy* as the third person singular suffix, discussed in the NOTES to vss. 11 and 31. This explanation discloses the balance of "his heavens" with *qōlō,* "his voice," in the second colon.

the primeval heavens. š^e^mē qedem balances *qōl 'ōz,* "the mighty voice," of the second colon.

35. *praise.* Comparing Ps xxix 1, "Give Yahweh glory and praise (*'ōz*)."

the Most High of Israel. Consult the second NOTE on vs. 30.

too great for heaven. Parsing *ba* of *bašš^e^ḥāqīm* as comparative (*Psalms I,* p. 230, and the second NOTE on Ps li 8), and comparing the sentiment with I Kings viii 27, "Behold, heaven and highest heaven cannot contain you." Since heaven cannot contain him, Israel's God came upon the earth to dwell in Jerusalem. On *šeḥāqīm*, "heaven," see Zorell, ZLH, p. 834.

As in Ps li 9, comparative *ba* stylistically matches comparative *min* of *mimmiqdāšekā* in the parallel colon.

36. *for his sanctuary.* Reading *mimmiqdāšey* (MT *mimmiqdāšekā*; see the following NOTE), a plural substantive followed by the third person singular suffix *-y*, as in vss. 11, 31 (twice), 34. Though plural in form, the noun is translated as singular in keeping with the practice discussed in *Psalms I*, pp. 128, 262, 290. Cf. Ps lxxiii 17 and Ezek xxi 7, where the frequent emendation of MT *miqdāšīm*, "the sanctuary," to morphologically singular *miqdāšām*, "their sanctuary," appears ill-conceived.

Like *qōdeš*, "heavenly sanctuary" (consult the second NOTE on Ps lx 8), *miqdāšēy* refers to the celestial shrine; its pairing with *šeḥāqīm*, "heaven," allows little doubt as to the psalmist's intention. It also refers to the heavenly sanctuary in Ps lxxiii 17.

Truly. Detaching the Masoretic suffix *-kā* from the preceding word and vocalizing it as the emphatic particle *kī*, discussed in the fourth NOTE on Ps liv 7 where other instances of the confusion between *-kā* and *kī* are cited. In the present verse the *scriptio defectiva* of the original text would serve to explain the confusion.

Thus analyzed, this line turns out to be a profession of faith; cf. *Psalms I*, p. 87.

victory. Comparing Ps xxix 11, "Yahweh will give his people victory." *Psalms I*, pp. 131, 180, discuss this nuance of *'ōz*.

valor. The hapax legomenon *ta'aṣūmōt* may well be the feminine singular of Phoenician tyoe, like vs. 21, *tōṣā'ōt*. The root appears in Ugaritic as *'ẓm;* notice the personal name *'ẓmt* in UT, 2095:7.

O people. Metrical considerations favor the attachment of *lā'ām* to the last colon of the psalm so that it contains three beats (*lā'ām bārēk 'elōhīm*) to balance three-beat vs. 35a, *tenū 'ōz lē'lōhīm*). At the same time, this stichometric division will establish a better syllabic equilibrium between vs. 36b (*kī 'ēl yiśrā'ēl hū'*—six syllables) and vs. 36c (*nōtēn 'ōz weta'aṣūmōt*—eight syllables). Hence Albright's deletion of *'ōz* as metrically and stylistically superfluous can no longer be sustained on merely metrical grounds.

On this hypothesis, *lā* of *lā'ām* would parse as the vocative particle; cf. the third NOTE on vs. 33.

bless God! Vocalizing singular *bārēk* or plural *bārekū* as in vs. 27; in tenth-century *scriptio defectiva* both forms would be written *brk*.

PSALM 69

(lxix 1–37)

1 *For the director. According to "Lilies." Of David.*

2 Save me, O God,
for the waters have reached my neck.
3 I have sunk into the abysmal mire [2]*
where there is no footing;
I have entered the bottomless waters
where the vortex engulfs me.
4 I am wearied by my crying, [3]
my throat is parched;
My eyes grow bleary
as I wait, O my God!
5 More numerous than the hairs on my head [4]
are my stealthy enemies;
Many more than my locks
are my deceitful foes.
What I did not steal,
this must I restore?
6 O God, you know my folly, [5]
and my faults are not hidden from you.
7 May they who hope in you not be humiliated [6]
through me, Lord Yahweh of Hosts;
May they who seek you not be disgraced
through me, O God of Israel.
8 Because of you I have suffered abuse, [7]
and disgrace has covered my face.
9 And I have become a stranger to my brothers, [8]
an alien to my mother's sons.
10 For zeal for your house has eaten me up, [9]

* Verse numbers in RSV.

and the insults of those who insult you
have fallen upon me.
11 So I poured out my soul while fasting, [10]
and abuse itself was mine.
12 And I made sackcloth my garb, [11]
and became a joke to them.
13 The feasters and the drunkards [12]
compose mocking songs about me.
14 But I—my prayer is to you, Yahweh, [13]
favor me now, O God!
In your great kindness
answer me
With your faithful help.
15 Rescue me from the mire [14]
lest I be submerged.
Let me be rescued from my Enemy,
and from the bottomless waters.
16 Let not the vortex of the sea engulf me, [15]
or the abyss swallow me,
or the Pit close its mouth over me.
17 Answer me, Yahweh, [16]
for your love is bounteous;
As befits your abundant mercy,
turn your face toward me.
18 Turn not your face from your servant; [17]
because distress is mine, quickly answer me.
19 Draw near, O El, redeem me; [18]
ransom me from the abode of my Foe.
20 You know my abuse, [19]
my shame and my disgrace are before you.
21 Abuse has wasted my inmost parts, [20]
rank disease crushed my heart.
I looked for a comforter, but there was none,
and for consolers, but I found none.
22 They put poison in my food, [21]
and for my thirst they gave me vinegar to drink.
23 May their table before them be a trap, [22]
even their companions a snare.
24 May their eyes grow too dim to see, [23]
and make their thighs continually shake.

25 Pour out upon them your indignation, [24]
and let your raging fury overtake them.
26 Let their encampment become desolate, [25]
in their tents may there be no inhabitant.
27 Because they persecuted the one you smote, [26]
and told stories about the pain of him you wounded.
28 Charge them with crime upon crime, [27]
lest they enter your meadow.
29 Let them be erased from the scroll of life eternal, [28]
and not enrolled among the just.
30 But I am afflicted and in pain; [29]
may God's help bulwark me,
31 That I might praise God's Name in song, [30]
and extol it with hymns of thanks;
32 For this will please Yahweh more than a bull, [31]
than an ox with horns and hoofs.
33 Behold, O you oppressed, [32]
let those who seek God rejoice;
May your courage revive!
34 For El hears his poor, [33]
Yahweh does not despise those bound to him.
35 Let heaven and earth praise him, [34]
the seas and all that stirs in them.
36 Surely God will save Zion, [35]
and rebuild the cities of Judah.
Those expelled from it will there return.
37 The progeny of his servants will inherit it, [36]
they shall live there and possess it.

Notes

lxix. The lament of an individual who prays for deliverance from his personal enemies and especially from his archenemy, Death. Kraus (*Psalmen*, I, p. 480) rightly notes that the text of this lament is excellently preserved, but this of itself does not permit the inference that the traditional translations have necessarily grasped the thought of the psalmist. This composition, no less than the psalms exhibiting a poorer state of preservation, yields new translations and images when Northwest Semitic grammatical and stylistic principles are applied to its well-preserved text.

Since there is no sound reason for questioning the authenticity of the final two verses—stylistic and syntactic traits remarked in the comments on these lines caution against their attribution to a later hand—the psalmist was a member of a Jewish community in exile, perhaps in Babylon. A sixth-century B.C. date thus appears most probable.

1. *According to "Lilies."* See the first NOTE on Ps lx 1.

2. *Save me. hōšī'ēnī* forms an inclusion with vs. 36 *yōšīaʿ*, as noticed by Leon J. Liebreich in HUCA 27 (1956–57), 190–92. This stylistic observation can be used to counter the contention that vss. 36–37, as Ps li 20–21, are later additions foretelling the restoration of Israel from exile in Babylon; cf. CCD's introductory note on Ps 68 (69).

the waters. Namely, of Sheol. The stricken psalmist is on the verge of death; cf. Ps xviii 5; Jon ii 6.

my neck. For this meaning of *nepeš*, see the third NOTE on Ps lvii 7. Failure to recognize this sense of *nepeš*, pointed out in 1926 by L. Dürr and later confirmed by Ugaritic usage, has led CCD into an unnecessarily free (and indefensible) translation of *bā'ū mayim 'ad nepeš*, "The waters threaten my life." The lack of a suffix in *nepeš* conforms to the widespread Ugaritic-Hebrew practice of omitting suffixes with nouns designating parts of the body; cf. the third NOTE on Ps lvi 8.

3. *into the abysmal mire.* Comparing *bīwēn meṣūlāh* with Ps xl 3, *miṭṭīṭ hayyāwēn*, "from the miry bog." Both expressions are variations on the theme of Sheol as a place of muck; cf. the second NOTE on Ps lv 24.

the vortex. Basing this connotation of *šibbōlet* upon the root idea of *šbl*, "to twist, whirl," discussed by me in ZAW 74 (1962), 209.

4. *my throat is parched.* The verbal root of *niḥar* appears as *ḥrr* in Ugaritic. Despite the fact that the waters of Sheol have reached the psalmist's neck, the poet's throat burns and is hoarse from crying to God for help.

My eyes grow bleary. Comparing *kālū 'ēnay* with UT, 125:26–27, *al tkl bnqr 'nk*, "Do not consume your eyes with flowing."

as I wait. MT *meyaḥēl* is a piel participle that stands in apposition to the person designated by the suffix. Many grammarians and commentators prefer to alter the pointing to read, with LXX and Targ., *miyyaḥēl*, the preposition followed by the piel infinitive construct, which modifies the verb *kālū*. The former construction appears preferable and sheds light upon Pss lxxxvi 11, *ba'amittekā yāḥīd* (MT *yāḥēd*), "in fidelity to you alone"; lxxxviii 18, *hiqqīpū 'ālay yāḥīd*, "They close in on me alone"; Prov viii 30, *wā'ehyeh 'eṣlō 'āmōn*, "And I was beside him, the Master Architect." Cf. also Ps lxxxviii 9; Lam iii 11, and GK, § 131n.

O my God. Parsing the *lamedh* of *lē'lōhāy* as vocative (*Psalms I*, p. 21). This analysis discloses a neat instance of inclusion begun by vocative *'ᵉlōhīm* in vs. 2. See the first NOTE on vs. 2 for another instance of inclusion in this psalm.

5. *my stealthy enemies.* The meaning and the grammar of this phrase *śōnᵉ'ē ḥnm* (MT *ḥinnām*), are studied in *Psalms I*, p. 214.

Many more. Comparing Ps xl 13, "They are more numerous (*'āṣᵉmū*) than the hairs of my head."

than my locks. The long-standing proposal to read *miṣṣammātī* (MT *maṣmītay*), the preposition *min* plus *ṣammātī* (cf. Isa xlvii 2; Song of Sol iv 1, 3, vi 7), finds support in an analysis of the word order and the parallel elements. In both cola the word order is verb-prepositional phrase-subject, and the parallel elements can be schematically represented A+B+C//Á+B́+Ć. Similar considerations produce a new version in vs. 21 and in Ps xlvi 5.

my deceitful foes. 'ōyᵉbay šeqer is a construct chain with interposed pronominal suffix, as set forth in *Psalms I*, p. 110; cf. also UHP, p. 15.

did not steal. The psalmist has been maliciously accused of theft by his enemies.

this. Progress in the study of the Northwest Semitic dialects and their interrelationships confirms Paul Ruben's identification (JQR 10 [1898], 544, n. 2) of *'āz* with the Phoenician demonstrative pronoun *'z* in Eccles ii 15 was reached independently, while the second NOTE On Song of Sol viii 10, see the third NOTE on Ps lxv 9, and Dahood, *Biblica* 47 (1966), 268, where the identification of *'āz* with Phoenician *'z*, which he correctly recognizes also in Prov xx 14 and Eccles ii 15. on Ps li 9 lists some nouns with prothetic *aleph*.

6. *my faults.* The psalmist admits his own sinfulness, but denies that he is guilty of the crimes with which his accusers charge him.

8. *because of you . . . .* Comparing *'ālekā nāśā'tī ḥerpāh* with UT, 49:v:11–12, *'lk b'lm pht qlt*, "Because of you, O Baal, I have experienced (literally "seen") disgrace."

disgrace has covered my face. Briggs, CECBP, II, p. 121, labels suspicious the word order of *kissᵉtāh kᵉlimmāh pānāy*, maintaining that the earlier order was *kissᵉtanī kᵉlimmat pānāy*. But his contention runs counter to several Ugaritic examples of the sequence: verb-subject-object; cf. e.g., UT, 127:55–56, *yṯbr ḥrn rišk*, "May Ḥoron break your head!" Since Canaanite possessed case endings till about 1200 B.C., the Canaanite poets enjoyed considerable freedom in the matter of sentence or word order. The Hebrew poets (as opposed to prose writers) did not, however, completely surrender this freedom enjoyed by their predecessors in Canaan.

9. *And I have become a stranger.* Reading (vs. 8) *pānāy-m*, "my face" (vs. 9) *wᵉzār hāyītī* for MT (vs. 8) *pānāy* (vs. 9) *mūzār hāyītī*. Concerning enclitic *mem* following pronominal suffixes, see the sixth NOTE on Ps lxviii 24. This analysis eliminates the hapax legomenon

mūzār and restores the parallelism between *zār*, "stranger," and *nokrū*, "alien," that occurs in such texts as Job xix 15, which closely compares with the thought of the present verse.

my brothers . . . my mother's sons. The Ugaritic parallelism between *aḫ* and *bn um* is cited in the second NOTE on Ps l 20.

10. *zeal for your house.* The thought of *qin'at bēteḵā* might be compared with UT, 52:21–22, *iqnu šmt [b]n šrm*, "I am zealous for the names of the Princes."

has eaten me up. Like a devouring flame, since *'ākal* in both Ugaritic and Hebrew is frequently predicated of fire. This text is cited in the future tense as a prophecy in John ii 17; cf. Raymond E. Brown, *The Gospel According to John* (I–XII) (The Anchor Bible, vol. 29; New York, 1966), pp. 123 f.

have fallen upon me. Like burning coals, as suggested by the verb *nāpelū* (cf. Ps cxl 11) and by the imagery of Ps cxx 3–4, where lies are likened to burning coals.

11. *So I poured out.* Repointing MT *wā'ebkeh* to read *wā'ebbōkāh* from **nābak*, a dialectal variant of **nāpak*, "to pour, gush forth." In Ugaritic one encounters both *nbk* and *npk*, substantives denoting "well, source"; cf. UT, Glossary, Nos. 1597 and 1675; Albright, *Archaeology and the Religion of Israel* (2d ed.; Baltimore, 1946), pp. 194 f.; George M. Landes, "The Fountain at Jazer," in BASOR 144 (1956), 30–37, especially pp. 31–34; Dahood, UHP, pp. 65 f. A psalm fragment from Qumran (4QPsa) reads *'k*, "also," for MT *'bkh*, but this is manifestly an inferior reading since it leaves the first colon without a verb. See P. W. Skehan, VTS 4 (1957), p. 154.

In other words, the phrase *'ebbōkāh napšī*, "I poured out my soul," is synonymous with I Sam i 15, *wā'ešpōk 'et napšī*, "And I poured out my soul"; cf. also Pss lxii 9, cii 1; Lam ii 19.

while fasting. For other collocations of the two ideas of prayer and fasting, see Ps xxxv 13, "I afflicted myself through fasting,/ and my prayer rested upon my bosom," and Mark ix 29, "There is no means of casting out this sort but prayer and fasting."

abuse itself. Parsing *la* of *laḥarāpōt* as the emphatic *lamedh* discussed in *Psalms I*, p. 143, and which presumably recurs in vs. 23. Instructive parallels present themselves in Ps cxx 7, *'anī šālōm . . . wehēmmāh lammilḥāmāh*, "I was peace . . . but they were warfare itself"; Isa i 5, *kol rō'š lāḥolī*, "The whole head is sickness itself." The recognition of an emphatic *lamedh* enables H. Neil Richardson to propose a convincing translation of the famous crux in Amos vii 14 in JBL 85 (1966), 89.

12. *And I made sackcloth my garb.* The syntax of *wā'ettenāh lebūšī śāq* is, save for the consecutive *waw*, identical with UT, 77:22, *atn šdh krmm*, "I shall make her field a vineyard."

13. *The feasters and the drunkards.* The psalmist contrasts his own fasting and praying with the feasting and ribaldry of his revilers. The syntax and translation of this verse become intelligible with the recognition of enjambment: the direct object of the verb *yāśīḥū,* "compose," in the first colon is *nᵉgīnōt,* "mocking songs," in the second colon, while the two subjects are *yōšᵉbē š'r,* "feasters" (MT *ša'ar*), in the first half-verse and *šōtē šēkār,* "drunkards," in the second. Similar instances of enjambment can be seen in Pss xxxii 5 and lix 8.

The translation of *yōšᵉbē š'r,* "the feasters," stems from its parallelism with *šōtē šēkār,* while its etymological basis is provided by Ugar. *ṯ'r,* "to arrange, serve food." Cf. UT, 'nt:I:4–5, *yṯ'r w yšlḥmnh,* "He served food and fed him," and John Gray, *The Legacy of Canaan,* VTS, V, 2d ed. (Leiden, 1965), p. 266, who proposes to identify this root in Prov xxiii 7, where its collocation with *tilḥam 'et leḥem* (vs. 6) recalls the Ugaritic concurrence of the two roots. Cf. also Judg v 8 and II Kings xxiii 7. The multiple alliteration and assonance between *yōšᵉbē šā'ar* and *šōtē šēkār* also argues for a similarity in meaning as well. Cf. Ps cxxii 6.

compose. This nuance of *yāśīḥū,* as noted by Briggs, CECBP, II, p. 122, appears in Ps cv 2 and Judg v 10.

mocking songs. Comparing this sense of *nᵉgīnōt* in Job xxx 9 and Lam iii 14.

14. *favor me now.* Reading *'attā rᵉṣēnī* for syntactically difficult *'ēt rāṣōn.* The resulting balance of imperative *rᵉṣēnī* with imperative *'ᵃnēnī* is effective. *Psalms I,* p. 27, cites other texts where MT confused *'ēt,* "time," and *'attā,* "now"; to those texts might now be added Ezek xxiii 43. Cf. *'t,* "now," in the Lachish Letters (F. M. Cross, Jr., and D. N. Freedman, *Early Hebrew Orthography* [New Haven, 1952], pp. 52–53) and in the Hebrew ostracon from Arad (ca. 597–587 B.C.), published by Y. Aharoni in IEJ 16 (1966), 2.

answer me. For the revised scansion of this verse, see the fourth NOTE on Ps cxliii 1.

15. *lest.* Explaining the *wᵉ* of *wᵉ'al* as emphatic (*Psalms I,* p. 329) and comparing the word order of *miṭṭīṭ wᵉ'al 'eṭbā'āh* with Ps lxvi 7, *hassōrᵉrīm 'al yārīmū lāmō,* "Lest the rebels rise up against him." *Psalms I,* p. 59, cites Ugaritic and biblical texts in which *'al* is to be rendered "lest." Another example has materialized in Job xxxvi 21, *hiššāmēr 'al tēpen 'el 'āwen,* well phrased by Pope (The Anchor Bible, vol. 15), "Beware, lest you turn to evil." See below the third NOTE on vs. 28.

Let me be rescued. The frequent proposal to delete niphal *'innāṣᵉlāh* because of the improbability that a poet would use both hiphil (*haṣṣīlēnī*) and niphal of the same verb in the same verse has been discredited by the Ras Shamra tablets, which show the Canaanite poets doing just that. Cf. M. Held in JBL 84 (1965), 272 ff., who cites UT, 51:v:113–16, vi:31–35; 2 Aqht vi:26–29 to illustrate this practice, the third NOTE on Ps lxiv 5 and the first NOTE on Ps lxxvii 12.

from my Enemy. Namely, the enemy par excellence, Death. *Psalms I,* p. 57, proposes this explanation of plural *śōnᵉʾay.* The parallelism with *ṭîṭ,* "mire," *maʿᵃmaqqē mayim,* "the bottomless waters," *šibbōlet,* "the vortex," *mᵉṣūlāh,* "the depth," and *bᵉʾēr,* "the pit"—all poetic terms for the underworld—hardly permits *śōnᵉʾay* to designate here the psalmist's human enemies.

16. *the vortex.* See the second NOTE on vs. 3.

of the sea. In vs. 3 we have *šibbōlet* alone, but here *šibbōlet mayim* with essentially the same meaning; see the following NOTE on *mᵉṣūlāh,* "the depth, sea," and *mᵉṣūlōt yām.* Hence the preferred reading would be *šibbōlet-m yām,* with an intervening *mem* in the construct chain (courtesy D. N. Freedman).

the abyss swallow. That *mᵉṣūlāh,* "the depth," had jaws is also evident from Ps lxviii 23, where the Lord announces that he muzzled *mᵉṣūlōt yām,* "the deep sea," another term for *mᵉṣūlāh.*

the Pit. Namely, the pit of Sheol; cf. the second NOTE on Ps lv 24.

its mouth. Comparing UT, 67:ii:4–5, *bph yrd kḫrr zt,* "He descends into his (Death's) mouth like an olive cake."

17. *for your love is bounteous.* Comparing Ps cix 21.

18. *Turn not.* Parsing *tastēr* as the infixed -t- form of *sūr,* "to turn away"; cf. *Psalms I,* p. 64. Thus *tastēr* expresses the opposite idea of vs. 17, *pᵉnēh ʾēlāy,* "turn your face toward me."

from your servant. Namely, the psalmist himself, since *ʿebed* often substitutes for the personal pronoun or pronominal suffix; cf. *Psalms I,* p. 124.

distress is mine. A literal translation of *ṣar lī;* compare vs. 11, "And abuse itself was mine."

quickly answer me. mahēr ʿᵃnēnī is an instance of hendiadys.

19. *Draw near.* The psalmist possibly alludes to the divine appellative *qārōb,* "the Near One," to be discussed at Ps lxxv 2. The phrase *qorᵉbāh ʾēl* evokes UT, Krt:35–38, *wbḥlmh il yrd . . . wyqrb bšal krt,* "And in his dream El descends . . . And he draws near at Kirta's request."

O El. As in vs. 34, the Masoretes vocalize *ʾl* as the preposition *ʾel;* the pointing *ʾēl,* however, results in much better sense and stichometric division. Cf. the first NOTES on Pss lix 12 and lxii 2, and *Psalms I,* p. 242.

redeem me. Reading *napšī goʾlāh,* the latter being pointed as the emphatic imperative instead of MT imperative plus feminine accusative suffix *-āh.* Just as *ʿabdekā,* "your servant," in the preceding verse is a polite substitute for the pronoun, so here *napšī,* literally "my soul," fulfills a similar function.

from the abode. Since MT *lᵉma'an,* "because, of," yields little sense here (CCD is alive to the problem, rendering "as an answer for my enemies"), I tentatively vocalize *limᵉ'ōn,* from *mā'ōn,* "abode." The "abode of my Foe" refers, of course, to Sheol; though the psalmist is not yet there (vs. 16), he is virtually there (vss. 2–3). According to Ps xlix 8, man cannot redeem himself from Death, but in vs. 16 the psalmist assures us, "But God will ransom me, / from the hand of Sheol / Will he surely snatch me."

my Foe. Plural *'ōyᵉbay,* like *śōnᵉ'ay* in vs. 15, refers to Death, as noticed in *Psalms I,* p. 105. Compare Job v 20, *bᵉrā'āb pādᵉkā mimmāwet,* "In famine he will ransom you from death."

20. *before you.* The two words that follow in MT are transposed to the next verse.

21. *has wasted.* With no consonantal changes, reading piel preterit *killā* (Ugar. *kly*) for MT *kol.* This verb makes a fine parallel to *šābᵉrāh,* "crushed," in the second colon.

my inmost parts. Identifying *ṣōrᵉray* with Ugar. *ṣrrt,* "heart, inwards," discussed at Ps vi 8. In the present passage, its association with *libbī,* "my heart," sustains such an equation. From this word division and vocalization springs the metrical pattern A+B+C//Á+B́+Ć, a sequence noted above in vs. 5 and which, significantly, is the word pattern of Ps vi 8, a verse conceptually akin to the present text. The proposed reading:

killā ṣōrᵉray ḥerpāh (3 beats)
šābᵉrāh libbī wa'ᵃnūšāh (3 beats)

rank. An attempt to reproduce the *wa* before *wa'ᵃnūšāh,* which I take to be emphatic, as suggested by the final position of the word that it accentuates; cf. the second NOTE on Ps li 9.

disease. Parsing *'ᵃnūšāh* (*'ānūšāh*) as a feminine substantive from *'nš,* "to be sick." Its apparent balance with the feminine noun *ḥerpāh,* as well as the feminine verb *šābᵉrāh* suggest this analysis. It is thus related to the masculine substantive *'ānūš* that is found in Isa xvii 11; Jer xvii 9, 16, xxx 12, 15, 16. To be sure, the commentators and lexicographers usually parse *'ānūš* in these texts as a passive qal participle, but an examination of the passages in question shows a noun *'ānūš* (if this be the correct vocalization) to be syntactically more viable; e.g., Jer xvii 16, *wᵉyōm 'ānūš lō' hit'awwētī,* "Nor have I desired the day of disease" (cf. Isa xvii 11, *yōm naḥᵃlāh,* "day of blight"), and xvii 9, *'āqōb hallēb mikkol wᵉ'ānūš hū' mī yēdā'ennū,* "The most devious of all is the heart, and its disease (see the first NOTE on Ps lxiii 2 for the syntax of *ānūš hū'*)—who can diagnose it?"

a comforter. Reading consonantal *nwd* as the qal participle of *nūd*, "to grieve, lament," studied in the third NOTE on Ps lvi 9. Many scholars favor the vocalization *nād*, but MT *nūd* suggests that their *Vorlage* read *nwd* which could be the correct writing of the masculine participle in the Phoenician dialect in which *ā* became *ō;* cf. the second NOTE on Ps lviii 3.

22. *They put poison in my food.* Comparing Ps xli 9, "Pour a lethal substance into him." From the standpoint of Hebrew grammar, this version of vs. 22a appears preferable to RSV, "They gave me poison for my food," which needlessly assumes that *bᵉbārūtī* contains the *beth essentiae* construction. The biblical sentence *wayyittᵉnū bᵉbārūtī rōʾš*, "They put poison in my food," grammatically compares with, say, UT, 2 Aqht:v:26–27, *bd dnil ytnn qšt,* "He put the bow into the hands of Daniel." Cf. also Jer i 9, *nātattī dᵉbāray bᵉpīkā,* "I have put my words in your mouth."

they gave me vinegar to drink. Instead of wine, they offer the psalmist vinegar. *yašqūnī ḥōmeṣ* bears syntactic comparison with UT, 1 Aqht:215, *qḥn wtšqyn yn,* "Receive her and give her wine to drink." Biblical *ḥōmeṣ*, "vinegar," appears in Ugaritic economic texts as *ḥmṣ* and in conjunction with *yn*, "wine."

23. *even their companions.* Reading *lišᵉlūmīm*) for this vocalization see *Psalms I*, pp. 42 f.; MT *lišᵉlōmīm*) and parsing the *lamedh* as emphatic, as above in vs. 11. That the *lamedh* is emphatic may be inferred not only from internal considerations, but also from a related verse in Ps xli 10, *gam ʾīš šᵉlōmī,* "even my colleague." Contrast the treatment of this *lamedh* by E. Vogt in *Biblica* 43 (1962), 79. The suffix in the translation "their allies" is forthcoming from the suffix of *lipnēhem,* on the merits of the principle examined in *Psalms I,* pp. 17 f.

24. *too dim to see.* To curse the enemy with blindness enjoys numerous parallels in ancient Near Eastern literature; e.g., UT, 1 Aqht:167, *ʿwr yštk bʿl,* "May Baal make you blind" (not "one-eyed" as in UT, Glossary, No. 1834).

thighs continually shake. See *Psalms I,* pp. 267, 281.

25. *Pour out.* The metaphor being that of a torrential rain.

your indignation. God's wrath was thought to cause sickness; cf. Ps xxxiii 4, "There is no soundness in my flesh,/because of your indignation."

raging fury. An attempt to preserve the metaphor suggested by the two verbs in this verse; *ḥᵃrōn ʾappᵉkā* is normally rendered "thy burning anger" (RSV).

overtake them. Like a flood or like a flash flood, the latter not infrequently occurring in Palestine. In the spring of 1963, the well-known biblical scholar Jean Steinmann, together with more than twenty French pilgrims, lost his life in a flash flood at Petra in southern Palestine. In Job xxvii 20 the verb *nāśag* is predicated of a flood: *taśśīgēhū kammayim ballāhōt laylāh genābattū sūpāh,* "Terrors will overtake him like a flood, Night will kidnap him like a tempest." Contrast, however, Pope (*Job,* § 26, NOTE *ad loc.*), whose position is weakened by the exegesis of *yaśśīgēm* in the psalm verse, and by the observations that in the Job passage *kammayim* is parallel to *sūpāh* that is governed by the double-duty preposition, and that "Terrors" and "Night" are poetic names for death.

27. *they persecuted.* By gossiping about the stricken psalmist. The verb *rādap* bears this nuance in Jer xx 11 (cf. preceding verse) and Ps cxix 86, *šeqer redāpūnī,* "They persecute me with falsehood."

the one. For MT *'attāh* reading *'ōtōh,* the *nota accusativi* followed by the third person masculine singular suffix written as *-ōh,* as often in early Hebrew orthography (F. M. Cross, Jr., and D. N. Freedman, *Early Hebrew Orthography,* p. 57) and in Moabite; cf. Bauer and Leander, *Historische Grammatik,* § 29k, p. 252. This analysis of consonantal *'th* would eliminate the grating shift from the second to the third person in Ps xxvii 4, *yhwh 'ōtōh* (MT *'ōtāh*) *'abaqqēš,* "Yahweh himself do I seek" (contrast *Psalms I,* p. 165). The following verses (N.B. *sukkōh,* "his abode," in vs. 5) speak of Yahweh in the third person.

and told stories. Since for most Israelites the relation of sin to sickness was one of cause and effect, the psalmist's enemies seized the occasion of his illness to speculate and gossip about the crime he must have committed to draw down upon himself such punishment. See the second NOTE on Ps xli 7, wherein the psalmist complains of similar gossip by his enemies. The substantive *mispār,* Ugar. *mspr,* "tale," further illustrates the nuance of verbal *yesappērū,* while Ps ii 7 witnesses the construction *yesappērū 'el.* Stylistically, imperfect *yesappērū* balances perfect *rādāpū,* "persecuted," a trait that also marks Canaanite poetry; *Psalms I,* p. 327, and the fourth NOTE on Ps lvi 2.

of him you wounded. Parsing *ḥllyk* (MT *ḥalālekā*) as the singular noun *ḥālāl* with the genitive ending *-y(ī)* and the suffix *-kā;* hence vocalize *ḥalālīkā,* "(about) the one wounded by you." The sixth NOTE on Ps lxv 6 lists other examples of genitive endings, while Ps xxxviii 3–4 picture God causing sickness with his arrows.

28. *Charge them.* Put down on the debit side of the ledger; the metaphor is that of the divine bookkeeper discussed in the second NOTE on Ps lvi 1. This nuance of *nātan,* "to give, put," but here "to write down, charge," finds a good analogy in *śām,* "to put," but also "to put in writing," as proposed in the fourth NOTE to Ps lvi 9.

crime upon crime. Comparing Jer ii 22, "Your guilt remains inscribed before me," as proposed in the second NOTE on Ps lvi 1.

lest. See the first NOTE on vs. 15.

they enter. When the following word *ṣidqāteka* is correctly defined as "your meadow," the proposal to emend *yābō'ū* to *yir'ū,* "they see" (so Gunkel, Graetz, Stade) loses its *raison d'être.*

your meadow. *ṣ*[e]*dāqāh* is a name for Paradise discussed in *Psalms I,* pp. 33 f. The special character of the meadow, aside from its location and appearance, is indicated by its inhabitants, the *ṣaddīqīm* (vs. 29), who influence the selection of the term *ṣidqāteka.*

29. *be erased.* Comparing niphal *yimmāḥū* with Phoenician Aḥiram 2, *wh' ymḥ sprh,* "And as for him, may his inscription be erased."

from the scroll. The construction *yimmāḥū missēper* supports this translation of Phoenician Karatepe III:13–14, *'š ymḥ šm 'ztwd bš'r z,* "who shall blot out the name of Azitawaddu *from* this gate," as against "in this gate," as translated by a number of scholars.

scroll . . . enrolled. The roots of *sēper* and *yikkātēbū* appear juxtaposed in UT, 1005:8–9, *nqmd mlk ugrt ktb spr hnd,* "Niqmad, king of Ugarit, has written this letter."

the scroll of life eternal. Since the context is eschatological, *ḥayyīm* here, as well as in the texts cited in *Psalms I,* p. 91, refers to everlasting afterlife. This may also be inferred from the consideration that the two components of the hapax legomenon phrase *sēper ḥayyīm* appear in the Ugaritic text describing immortality, 2 Aqht:VI:26–29, cited in *Psalms I,* p. 91. Hence Briggs, CECBP, II, p. 120, is correct when describing *sēper ḥayyīm* as recording the names of those who share in everlasting life.

enrolled among the just. Jer xvii 13 provides illuminating commentary on the imprecation: *y*[e]*sūrēy* (MT *y*[e]*sūray*) *bā'āreṣ yikkātēbū,* "Those who turn from him shall be inscribed in the nether world."

among the just. Namely, among the righteous in heaven.

30. *I am afflicted.* Gunkel (*Die Psalmen,* p. 299) has directed attention to the wordplay in *'*[a]*nī 'ōnī,* while the second NOTE on Ps lx 5 tries to show that puns were not out of place in Canaanite-Hebrew laments. Another pun recurs in vss. 31–32.

God's help. Since all the verses of this strophe (30–37) introduced by our verse speak of God in the third person, consonantal *yšw'tk 'lhym* best parses as a construct chain with the interposed emphatic particle *kī,* noticed in *Psalms I,* p. 152, but more fully documented in the second NOTE on Ps lxviii 25.

31. *That I might praise.* Parsing *'*[a]*hal*[e]*lāh* as the subjunctive expressing purpose; cf. the NOTE on Ps li 15.

God's Name. Considered as having independent subsistence; hence the capitalization. See the next NOTE and the first NOTES on Ps liv 3 and 9.

extol it. Though the ancient versions and virtually all modern translations take *'*[e]*lōhīm,* "God," as the antecedent of the accusative suffix of *'ᵃgaddᵉlennū,* the parallelism here and texts such as Pss xx 2, lii 11, liv 8–9, which reveal the Name of God as an hypostasis or person acting alongside of God, make it more probable that the suffix in question refers to *šēm* rather than to *'ᵉlōhīm.*

The balance in this verse between the concepts "to praise" and "to extol" supplies an argument for the new reading and translation proposed at Ps lxxv 10.

32. *than a bull. miššōr* forms a wordplay with vs. 31, *bᵉšīr,* "with song"; see the first NOTE on vs. 30.

than an ox. pār shares the preposition of *miššōr,* a fine example of the practice discussed in *Psalms I,* pp. 201 f., NOTE on xxxiii 7.

33. *Behold.* Reading *rᵉ'ū* (MT *rā'ū*) and consulting the first NOTE on Ps lxviii 25. The psalmist, delivered from his persecutors, invites humble believers to witness the divine intervention and be reassured.

let those who seek God rejoice. Dividing the verse into three cola (contrast RSV with two cola) with the metrical arrangement of 2+3+2 that also occurs in Pss lxxvii 6 and lxxxii 8.

34. *El hears.* Reading *šōmēᵃ' 'ēl* for MT *šōmēᵃ' 'el,* as proposed by R. G. Boling in JSS 5 (1960), 247. A similar Masoretic confusion between *'el* and *'ēl* was noticed above in vs. 19.

his poor. Suffixless *'ebyōnīm* shares the suffix of its counterpart *'ᵃsīrāyw,* "those bound to him," in the second colon, by virtue of the frequently cited double-duty suffix. Brekelmans, *Jaarbericht . . . Ex Oriente Lux* 17 (1963), 204, also directs attention to this passage.

those bound to him. Namely, by special religious ties. Usually translated "his prisoners," and occasionally emended to *ḥᵃsīdāyw,* "his devoted ones," *'ᵃsīrāyw* yields fully satisfactory sense when its suffix is analyzed as an objective genitive. In other words the *'ᵃsīrāyw* are synonymous with "his poor" of the parallel colon and with vs. 37, "his servants."

In his commentary on the phrase *b'sry yśr'l,* "When I bound Israel," in the Mesha Inscription, F. I. Andersen, *Orientalia* 35 (1966), 107–8, has remarked that *'sr* is used in a figurative sense to describe persons bound by an obligation, and has cited Num xxx 1–15 where the verb and the noun *'issār* are employed to describe self-imposed vows. A cognate nuance appears in UT, 137:36–37, *'bdk b'l y ymm 'bdk b'l* [ ] *m bn dgn asrkm hw ybl argmnk,* "Baal is your servant, O Yamm, Baal is your servant; [ ] the son of Dagan your bondman. He himself will bring you tribute." As in our biblical passage, *asr* is synonymous with *'bd.* The fact that Baal will be able to bring tribute to his vanquisher Yamm indicates that *asr* does not designate "prisoner" in a physical sense but rather in a moral sense; Baal is bound by the terms imposed by Yamm. Cf. also UT, 1002:22–23.

One can recognize a similar semantic development in *ṣāmad,* "to bind, yoke," but in Ps cvi 28 "to attach oneself to (Baal Peor)," i.e., "to adopt his worship."

36. *will save. yōšīaʿ* forms an inclusion with vs. 2, *hōšīʿēnī,* "save me." Such careful structuring discounts the possibility that vs. 36 is a later addition to the poem; see the first NOTE on vs. 2.

37. *they shall live there.* Some suspect that this line is a variation on vs. 37 and should be deleted. But the recognition of the chiasmus in vss. 36c–37 would seem to put the text above suspicion.

live there and possess it. The parallelism of the verbs *yšb* and *yrš* in Isa liv 3; Jer xlix 1 and UT, Krt:23+25 shows that the version proposed in an earlier edition was ill advised.

PSALM 70

(lxx 1–6)

1 *For the director; of David. For remembrance.*

2 O God, rescue me!
O Yahweh, make haste to help me!
3 Let those who seek my life [2]*
be humiliated and put to confusion;
Let those who desire my ruin
recoil in disgrace.
4 For their shameful slander [3]
may they turn back
Who say to me, "Aha, Aha!"
5 May all who seek you [4]
rejoice and be glad in you;
May they who love your salvation ever say,
"God is great."
6 But I am afflicted and poor, [5]
O God, hasten to me!
My helper and my deliverer are you,
O Yahweh, do not tarry!

* Verse numbers in RSV.

Notes

lxx. An individual lament which, save for a couple of interesting variants, is identical with Ps xl 14–18. For philological and exegetical details the reader is referred to *Psalms I*, p. 247. The following observations supplement the analysis of Ps xl 14–18.

As remarked in the introductory Note to Ps liii, the repetition of the same strophe in the Ugaritic texts is sometimes done with sufficiently significant variants to caution the overzealous biblical scholar not to attempt a perfect harmonization of the divergent readings that may appear in a psalm transmitted twice.

2. *O God, rescue me!* Since its duplicate Ps xl 14 reads "Run, O Yahweh, to rescue me," many versions and commentaries assume that through some mishap the imperative "Run!" has fallen out of the verse. However, by parsing *l^ehaṣṣîlēnî* as an emphatic *lamedh* followed by the hiphil imperative, a construction identical with Pss xxxi 3, lxxi 3; Isa xxxviii 20, *l^ehôšî'ēnî*, "Save me!," one has a semantically and syntactically viable prayer that need not assume an imperative has fallen out of the text. We are simply presented with two different recensions, both of which make sense. It may further be noticed that the syllabic count in MT is 8:8; one can scarcely improve on that!

make haste. ḥûšāh forms an inclusion with vs. 6, *ḥûšāh lî* and with the final phrase of the psalm, *'al t^e'aḥar*, "Do not tarry"; cf. the first NOTE on Ps lxix 2.

3. *be humiliated and put to confusion.* The jussives *yēbōšû w^eyaḥp^erû* express the same sentiments articulated by the precative perfects *kî bōšû kî ḥāp^erû* in Ps lxxi 24.

4. *For their shameful slander.* The phrase *'al 'ēqeb boštām*, occurring here and in Ps xl 16 where it is rendered "over their shame," presents a problem. Interpreted as a prepositional phrase, *'al 'ēqeb* is redundant since each of its components denotes "because"; cf. BDB, p. 784a, who label the expression "pleonastic" and translate and interpret it "*according to the consequence of* their shame, i.e., in consequence of the disgrace falling upon them." Now that the existence of the denominative verb *'āqab*, "to slander," is fairly well established in Northwest Semitic (*Psalms I*, pp. 251 f.), one may tentatively propose the analysis of *'qb* as a substantive from this verb. Hence vocalize *'al '^aqab boštām*, "for their shameful slander." This definition might serve as commentary on vs. 3, *ḥ^apēṣē rā'ātî*, "those who desire my ruin." Since *rā'ātî* is itself a generic word, the proposed definition of *'qb* helps to specify in what sense the poet's enemies seek to ruin him.

may they turn back. In a military sense, i.e., "retreat." The parallel text in Ps xl 16 reads *yāšōmmû*, "may they be desolated," but since this verb can also be used in a military sense, *yāšûbû* and *yāšōmmû* may well be synonyms denoting a military setback. Hence no emendation seems necessary.

Aha, Aha! An exclamation expressing the mockery of the psalmist's foes.

6. *But.* The poet contrasts his wretchedness to God's greatness.

I am afflicted. The wordplay *'^anî 'ānî* is noticed in the first NOTE on Ps lxix 30.

hasten . . . do not tarry. In addition to forming an inclusion with *ḥûšāh* in vs. 2, imperative *ḥûšāh* balances the negative jussive *'al t^e'aḥar.*

This pairing of the roots *ḥwš* and *'ḥr* proves text-critically valuable in determining the correct reading of UT, 2009:10–12, *aḥš*, "I shall hasten," . . . *iḫr*, "I shall tarry." Virolleaud, *Palais royal d'Ugarit,* V, p. 16, reads *ig(?)r*, but Gordon, Glossary, No. 138, correctly reads *iḫr* and compares Gen xxxii 5, *'ēḥar*. On the importance of parallel pairs for determining the linguistic and literary relationships between Ugaritic and Hebrew, see the fourth NOTE on Ps lvii 8.

my helper. Literally "my help," *'ezrī* acquires a more concrete denotation by reason of its association with concrete "my deliverer." Thus the suggested emendation *'ōzᵉrī*, "my helper," becomes expendable; see *Psalms I,* p. 247.

are you. The revised wording aims to bring out the chiasmus and to sharpen the contrast between *wa'ᵃnī*, "But I," and *'attāh*, "you." A similar parallelism of *at//an*, "you//I," occurs in UT, 3 Aqht:rev.:24.

PSALM 71

(lxxi 1–24)

1 In you, O Yahweh, have I trusted,
  let me not be humiliated, O Eternal One!
2 In your fidelity deliver me and rescue me!
Incline your ear to me and save me!
3 Be mine, O mountain of succor!
You promised to come at any time,
  save me!
For you are my crag and my fortress.
4 Free me, O my God, from the hand of the wicked,
  from the grip of the criminal and robber.
5 For you, O Lord, are my hope,
  my trust, O Yahweh, from my youth.
6 By you have I been supported from the womb,
  from my mother's bosom you have been my sustainer,
  of you is my perpetual praise.
7 I have been like a target for archers,
  but you have been my fortress of refuge.
8 My mouth has been filled with your praise,
  and with your glorious deeds throughout the day.
9 Do not cast me off in my old age,
  as my strength fails, forsake me not;
10 Because my foes eye me,
  and those who watch for my life consult together,
11 Thinking: "God has forsaken him;
    pursue and seize him
    for there is none to rescue."
12 My God, be not far from me,
  my God, make haste to help me.
13 May my slanderers be utterly humiliated;
  may they be robed with ignominy and disgrace
  those who seek my ruin.

14 But I will always hope
and ever add to all your praise.
15 My mouth would count your faithful deeds,
throughout the day your saving acts,
even though I knew no numbers.
16 I shall enter your mighty house, O Lord;
I shall proclaim your fidelity,
yours alone, O Yahweh.
17 O God, you have taught me from my youth,
and till now I have recounted your wondrous deeds.
18 So even to hoary old age
do not forsake me, O God;
Till I tell of your power to the assembly,
to each one who enters your mighty house.
19 Your fidelity, O God, reaches heaven,
because you have done great things;
O God, who is like you?
20 Though you made me see
full many tribulations, quarrels, and wrongs,
You will restore me to life;
and from the depths of the nether world
You will raise me once more.
21 Consider precious my large head of cattle,
and enfold me with your comfort.
22 With full voice I will praise you on the harp,
your faithfulness, O my God;
I will sing to you with the lyre,
O Holy One of Israel.
23 My lips will resound with joy—
indeed will I sing to you—
My soul also, which you ransomed.
24 Aloud my tongue will number
throughout the day your faithful deeds.
O that they would be humiliated!
O that they would be put to confusion!
those who seek my ruin.

NOTES

lxxi. The lament of an old man who prays for deliverance from personal enemies. God's protective care since infancy convinces the psalmist that he will not abandon him in the afflictions brought on both by old age and by jeering opponents. To judge from his offering (vs. 21), the aged poet, like the supplicant in Ps lxvi 13–15 (see the first NOTE on lxvi 13), was a man of means. From vss. 22–24 we further learn that he was gifted with musical ability.

1. *O Eternal One.* Verses 1–3 equal Ps xxxi 2–4a with slight variations; only the variations will receive attention here.

2. *deliver me. taṣṣīlēnī* is an imperfect balancing imperative *haṭṭēh*, "incline," a stylistic feature discussed in the second NOTE on Ps li 14 and *Psalms I*, pp. 29 f. Ps xxxi 3 reads imperative *pallᵉṭēnī*, a variant that illustrates the liberty biblical poets enjoyed when adapting a common theme, and points up the gratuitousness of trying to reduce doublets with variant readings to perfect conformity; cf. the introductory NOTE on Ps liii.

rescue me. Imperfect *tᵉpallᵉṭēnī*, with imperative function, answers to Ps xxxi 3 imperative *haṣṣīlēnī*, "Deliver me," but which appears in a separate colon.

3. *O mountain of succor.* In view of the variations cited in the two preceding NOTES, there is no compelling reason to label *lᵉṣūr mā'ōn* an inferior reading that must yield to Ps xxxi 3, *lᵉṣūr mā'ōz*, "O mountain of refuge." Zorell, ZLH, p. 455a, has correctly seen that here and in Pss xc 1, xci 9, *mā'ōn* derives from the root *'wn* which in Arabic *'āna* denotes "to aid, give succor," and hence to be distinguished from *mā'ōn*, "habitation, abode." In these three texts, GB, 443b, ill-conceivedly recommends the emendation of *mā'ōn* to *mā'ōz*. Since *mā'ōn* II and *mā'ōz* are synonyms, there is no need for emendation.

You promised. For this sense of *ṣiwwitā* see Ps cxxxiii 3.

to come at any time. Some critics see in *ṣiwwītā lābō' tāmīd* a corruption of Ps xxxi 3, *lᵉbēt mᵉṣūdōt*, "O fortified citadel," but the practice of free adaptation discussed in the first NOTE on vs. 2 liberates the scholar from such questionable expedients.

4. *robber.* Although it is usually identified as a by-form of *ḥōmēs*, "oppressor," the hapax legomenon *ḥōmēṣ* compares more favorably with the frequent Akkadian verb *ḫamāṣu*, "to despoil, rob." The fact that the psalmist was a rich man (cf. vs. 21) suggests that he has in mind a swindler trying to fleece him of his possessions.

5. *O Lord . . . O Yahweh.* The distribution of the components of

the composite divine name into the parallel cola strongly suggests that the poet intends the same distribution in vs. 16 where, however, many translators do not break up the composite name.

6. *have I been supported.* As noticed in the first NOTE on Ps lv 23, *nismaktī* bears importantly on the definition of *šlk* II, "to nourish," found in the parallel verse, Ps xxii 11.

my sustainer. gōzī remains an unsolved puzzle. Cognate Ps xxii 10 reads *gōḥī* which, unfortunately, is equally obscure. Though 4QPs[a] and Targ. read *'uzzī*, "my strength," for MT *gōḥī*, the sound textual principle that the more difficult reading is to be preferred counsels against seeking such an easy way out of the difficulty. Contrast "The Masoretic text in the Light of Qumran," VTS 9 (1962), pp. 305–21, where Menahem Mansoor, on p. 313, finds the reading *'uzzī* both appropriate and in line with the parallelism.

my perpetual praise. Parsing *tᵉhillātī tāmīd* as a construct chain with interposed pronominal suffix; see the third NOTE on vs. 7.

7. *a target.* As may be deduced from the frequent formula *'ōtōt ūmōpᵉtīm*, "signs and wonders," *mōpēt* is a synonym of *'ōt*, "a sign, mark"; here its more specific sense depends upon the denotation of *rabbīm*, "archers." The traditional version, "I have been as a portent to many" (RSV), scarcely fits the context and has sometimes been described as a false insertion (so BH[3]). Cf. Job vii 20, "Why have you made me your target (*mipgā'*)?," and xvi 12–13. Most relevant, however, is Job xvii 6, *wᵉhiṣṣīganī limšal* (MT *limšōl*) *'ammīm wᵉtōpet lᵉpānīm 'ehyeh*, "He has made me the butt of peoples, and I have become a target before them," where *tōpet*, a by-form of *mōpet*, parallels *māšāl*, "the butt" (cf. the two senses of "butt" in English: object of ridicule as well as a wall of earth behind the targets of a target range). That *māšāl* denotes a concrete object follows from the predicate *hiṣṣīganī* which denotes "to set, fix." In other words, the pair *māšāl* and *tōpet* semantically equals Ezek xiv 8, *lᵉ'ōt ūlimᵉšālī-m*, "for a mark and a butt."

archers. For this meaning of *rabbīm* see *Psalms I*, p. 19. Verse 13 mentions *śōṭᵉnē napšī*, "my slanderers," while Gen xlix 23 juxtaposes *rōbbū* and the related root *yisṭᵉmūhū*, cited in *Psalms I*, p. 19, NOTE on Ps iii 7.

my fortress of refuge. Rendered "my refuge of strength" in *Psalms I*, p. XL, *maḥᵃsī 'ōz* might also be analyzed as a composite term like Ps lxi 4, *migdal 'ōz*, "a towered fortress," parallel to *maḥseh lī*, "my refuge." The second NOTE on Ps lxi 5 examines the syntax of construct chains with interposed pronominal suffixes, a usage noticed above in vs. 6.

Needless to remark, when the military metaphor is identified in the first part of this verse, the appositeness of calling God a "fortress of refuge" becomes evident.

8. *has been filled.* Throughout the period of his persecution the psalmist never ceased to praise God. The preterit verb *hāyītī*, "I have been," in vs. 7 indicates that *yimmālē'* expresses past narrative; see the first NOTE on vs. 17.

9. *in my old age.* As in Ps lxix 34, the balancing member of the first colon (*l^e'ēt ziqnāh*) borrows the suffix of second-colon *kiklōt kōḥī*, "as my strength fails." The verse also contains a fine instance of chiasm: verb-prepositional phrase//prepositional phrase-verb.

10. *eye me.* Recognizing in *'am^erū* the Ugaritic sense of *'mr*, "to see," discussed in *Psalms I*, p. 16. In fact, Gunkel (*Die Psalmen*, p. 302), adopts Lagarde's emendation of *'ām^erū* to *'ār^ebū*, "they lie in wait," a textual alteration that Ugaritic usage renders dispensable.

11. *Thinking.* This nuance of *lē'mōr* receives comment in the first NOTE on Ps liii 2. The verse thus belongs to the genre known as "monologue of insolence," so that proposals to delete *lē'mōr* may safely be discarded.

12. *My God . . . my God.* Suffixless *'^elōhīm* is specified by the suffix of second-colon *'^elōhay;* identical usage has received comment at vs. 9.

13. *slanderers. Psalms I*, p. 237, cites the evidence for this nuance of *śāṭan*.

be utterly humiliated. Seeing in *yēbōšū yiklū*, literally "May they be humiliated, finished," an instance of hendiadys (cf. vss. 18, 21). This analysis makes the frequent emendation of *yiklū* to *yikkāl^emū* gratuitous.

robed with ignominy and disgrace. Pointing qal passive *yū'^aṭū* (MT *ya'^aṭū*) and parsing *ḥerpāh ūk^elimmāh* as accusatives of means.

15. *would count.* The conditional mode of *y^esāppēr* follows from the exegesis of the final colon; see the next NOTE. The phrase *pī y^esappēr*, it might be observed, collocates the two roots that are juxtaposed in UT, 77:45–46, *bpy sprhn*, "In my mouth is their story," and begins an inclusion that closes in vs. 24.

even though. BDB, p. 473b, lists texts employing concessive *kī*.

I knew no numbers. The considerable musical talents of the psalmist (vss. 22–24) sharply diminish the likelihood that *lō' yāda'tī s^epārōt* states a fact; the psalmist's words express a hypothesis. The hapax legomenon feminine plural form *s^epārōt* (elsewhere always *s^epārīm*) creates no morphological difficulties within the larger ambience of Northwest Semitic morphology; for example, Ugar. *'lmt*, the plural of *'lm*, "eternity," plays an important role in determining the reading and translation of Ps xlviii *'lmwt*, as noted in *Psalms I*, p. 293, and Heb. *marbaddīm*, "coverlets," appears as Ugaritic plural *mrbdt*.

16. *your mighty house.* Namely, the temple. For the cognate definition of *g^e^būrāh,* "fortress," see the first NOTE on Ps lxvi 7. The plural form *g^e^būrōt* conforms to the Canaanite practice of using plural forms for names of buildings; cf. the third NOTE on Ps lxv 5. By virtue of the double-duty suffix (*Psalms I,* pp. 17 f.), *g^e^būrōt* becomes specified by the second person singular suffixes of the second colon.

In the Akkadian text from Ras Shamra 15.86:8, 18, *gu₆-bu-ri* is a Canaanite word glossing Akk. *bîtum,* "house," which J. Nougayrol, *Palais royal d'Ugarit,* III, pp. 51, 218, 220, renders *maison-forte.*

O Lord . . . O Yahweh. See the first NOTE on vs. 5.

17. *I have recounted.* Imperfect *'aggīd,* balancing preterit *limmadtanī,* "you have taught me," expresses past time; consult the first NOTE on Ps lxvi 6. According to pre-Ugaritic principles of Northwest Semitic poetry, Briggs, CECBP, II, p. 130, could not be blamed for writing, "Hiph. impf. *ngd* is unsuited to *'d hnh.* It has come up by txt. err. from v. 18."

18. *hoary old age.* Explaining *ziqnāh w^e^śēbāh* as a case of hendiadys, to be compared with UT, 51:v:66, *šbt dqnk,* literally "the hoariness of your beard," but to be rendered "your hoary beard." Other examples of hendiadys are noticed in vss. 13 and 21.

to the assembly. Psalms I, p. 82, studies this meaning of *dōr,* Ugar.-Phoen. *dr,* "assembly." This definition, it might be observed, helps to establish the *Sitz im Leben* of this psalm. Cf. Ps xxii 26, "One hundred times will I repeat to you/my song of praise in the great congregation."

each one. For the distributive sense of *kōl, Psalms I,* p. 241. In the clause *l^e^kol yābō',* *kol* stands as a construct before the finite verb *yābō',* "enters," a usage examined in the first NOTE on Ps lxv 5.

who enters. As in Gen xxiii 10 and xlix 6, *yābō'* is used of participation in a council; consult Speiser (The Anchor Bible, vol. 1), § 30, second NOTE on xxiii 10, and § 61, first NOTE on xlix 6.

your mighty house. See the first NOTE on vs. 16. With vs. 16, *'ābō' big^e^būrōt,* vs. 18, *yābō' g^e^būrātēkā,* forms an inclusion (*Psalms I,* p. 327). That *'ābō'* is used with a preposition in vs. 16 but with the accusative here is stylistically identical with Ps xxxiii 15 where *yaḥde,* "inspects," governs the accusative in the first colon and a preposition in the second. This usage resembles the employment of one verb with two different prepositions in the same verse, a practice documented in the second NOTE on Ps lv 11.

20. *Though.* As in Pss cvi 34, cxxxix 15; I Kings viii 31, etc. (cf. BDB, p. 83b), *'^a^šer* carries a concessive meaning. Analyzed thus, *'^a^šer* serves a distinct function in the sentence and will resist deletion, too often its fate in the past; see BH³ apparatus.

made me see. Reading with Qere *hir'ītani* (*scriptio defectiva* of suffix) and attaching the final *waw* of consonantal *hr'ytnw* to the next word.

full many. Reading *wᵉṣārōt* (MT *ṣārōt;* see preceding NOTE) and explaining the *waw* as emphatic; see the first NOTE on Ps lxix 15. During his long life the psalmist has seen more than his share of tribulations.

quarrels. Reading *rībōt* (MT *rabbōt*), a plural form of *rīb* attested in Deut xvii 8 and Job xiii 6 and doubtless chosen here for the sake of assonance with *ṣārōt,* "full many," and *rā'ōt,* "wrong." Compare the rhyming sequence *ḥokmōt, hāgōt,* and *tᵉbūnōt* (*Psalms I,* p. 297), and Ps xc 15 where the uncommon plural *yᵉmōt,* "days," was probably chosen to favor the assonance with its counterpart *šᵉnōt,* "years." The unusual plural *sᵉpārōt,* "letters," in vs. 16 falls in with this analysis of *rībōt.*

wrongs. The reading *rībōt* (see preceding NOTE) shows that *rā'ōt* belongs to the rhyming triad and should not be deleted, as frequently proposed.

You will restore me to life. Cf. Ps xxx 4, "O Yahweh, you lifted me from Sheol,/you restored me to life/as I was descending the Pit."

the depths of the nether world. The phrase *tᵉhōmōt hā'āreṣ* recalls the juxtaposition in UT, 'nt:III:21–22, *tant šmm 'm arṣ thmt 'mn kbkbm,* "the meeting of heaven with the nether world, of the depths with the stars." For *'ereṣ,* "nether world," see *Psalms I,* pp. 43, 106, 144, and for *'ereṣ* balancing *tᵉhōmōt,* Ps cxlviii 7.

You will raise me. The Israelite considered any diminution of vital force an approach to the condition of Sheol where existence is minimal and man is strengthless (Ps lxxxviii 5). Weakened both by the advance of years and the afflictions brought on by his enemies, the psalmist pictures himself in the lowest circle of Sheol from which he is confident God will raise him. The poet in Ps lxi 3 was considerably better off since he stood only at the edge of the nether world.

once more. The poet asks to be created anew. According to Ps cxxxix 15, man was fashioned in the depths of the nether regions (*bᵉtaḥtiyyōt 'āreṣ*), and the present verse informs us that the psalmist through his sufferings has been reduced to the condition of those in the lowest part of the underworld (*tᵉhōmōt hā'āreṣ*). This verse thus sheds light on the translation and exegesis of Ps xxx 4 which is preferably rendered, "O Yahweh, you lifted me from Sheol,/you restored me to life/having descended (*Psalms I,* p. 181, 'descending') the Pit."

21. *Consider precious.* Recognizing in *tereb* the nuance discussed at Ps xxxvii 16 (*Psalms I,* p. 239), and comparing Ps xx 4, *'ōlātekā yᵉdaššanāh,* "May he consider your burnt offering generous." In *Psalms I,* p. 266, where the present verse is quoted to illustrate Ps xliv 13, *tereb* is wrongly translated as third person "he."

my large head of cattle. Repointing *g^e^dālāñ* (MT *g^e^dullāñ,* "my greatness") and identifying it with Ugar. *gdlt,* "a female head of large cattle (for sacrifice)," a noun occurring in sacrificial texts (see UT, Glossary, No. 562). In UT, 9:4, *gdlt* contrasts with *dqt,* "a female head of small cattle (for sacrifice)." See T. H. Gaster in IDB, IV, p. 155, and Baruch Levine, "Ugaritic Descriptive Rituals," in JCS 17 (1963), 105–11. Just as the wealthy supplicant of Ps lxvi 15 offered an ox and goats along with fatlings and rams, so the affluent psalmist here promises to sacrifice a cow or a heifer in thanksgiving for his deliverance.

enfold me with your comfort. While his enemies are robed with ignominy (vs. 13). An hendiadys construction, *tissōb t^e^naḥ^a^mēnī* literally reads "You will enfold, you will comfort me." Other instances of hendiadys are noticed in vss. 13, 18, while Ps xxxii 7, *t^e^sōb^e^bēnī,* and xxxii 10, *ḥesed y^e^sōb^e^bennū,* "with love will he enfold him," illustrate the sense of *tissōb,* whose meaning completely escaped the LXX, Syr., and *Juxta Hebraeos.* These read *tāšūb.*

22. *With full voice.* For this Canaanite sense of *gam* see the first NOTE on Ps lii 7. This nuance recurs in vs. 24 where the apparent synonymy with vs. 23, "My lips will resound with joy," is significant. For all his years, the grateful psalmist promises to laud Yahweh with "full-throated ease."

with the lyre. On Ugar. *knr,* see *Psalms I,* p. 297.

23. *indeed.* Parsing *kī* as emphatic or asseverative and comparing the first NOTE on Ps lvi 13.

24. *Aloud.* Cf. the first NOTE on vs. 22.

will number. For this nuance of *tehgeh,* consult *Psalms I,* p. 7. Stylistically, *tehgeh ṣidqātekā* forms an inclusion with vs. 15, *pī y^e^sappēr ṣidqātekā.* That *tehgeh* and *y^e^sappēr* are synonyms follows from the parallelism in UT, Krt:90–91, *ḫpṯ dbl spr ṯnn dbl hg,* "serfs beyond counting, archers beyond numbers." Another inclusion is registered in the NOTE after the next.

O that. Concerning the use of *kī* with precative perfects, *Psalms I,* p. 19, and the second NOTE on Ps lvi 14.

would be humiliated. Precative perfect *bōšū* forms an inclusion with jussive *yēbōšū* in vs. 13 where the object of the imprecation is as here, "those who seek my ruin."

O that. See penultimate NOTE.

would be put to confusion. Parsing *ḥāp^e^rū* as a precative perfect and comparing Ps lxx 3, *yēbōšū w^e^yaḥp^e^rū m^e^baq^e^šē napšī,* "Let those who seek my life be humiliated and put to confusion."

PSALM 72

(lxxii 1–20)

1 *Of Solomon.*

With your judgment, God, endow the king,
and with your justice, the king's son,
2 That he may govern your people with justice,
and your oppressed with judgment.
3 May the mountains bring peace to your people,
and the hills justice!
4 May he defend the oppressed of the people,
save the children of the needy,
and crush the extortioner!
5 May he revere you as long as the sun,
and till the moon be extinguished—
ages without end!
6 May he descend like rain upon the mown grass,
like showers upon the scorched lands!
7 May the just man flourish in his days,
and peace distill till the moon be no more!
8 And may he rule from sea to sea,
and from the River to the ends of the earth!
9 Before him may the desert tribes bow down,
and his foes lick the dust!
10 May the kings of Tarshish and the islands
render tribute,
The kings of Sheba and Seba offer gifts!
11 And may all kings prostrate themselves before him,
and may all nations serve him!
12 If he rescues the needy crying for aid,
and the oppressed who has no helper;
13 If he takes pity on the poor and needy,
and saves the lives of the needy;

14 If he redeems their lives from lawless oppression,
and their blood is precious in his eyes;
15 Then may he live long,
and gold from Sheba be given to him!
Then let perpetual prayer be made for him,
blessings invoked on him throughout the day!
16 Let there be a very mantle of wheat upon the land,
suckling on the mountain tops.
Let his fruit blossom like Lebanon,
flourishing like the grass of the earth.
17 Let his progeny last forever,
bear offspring till the sun be extinguished.
Let his progeny be blessed through him,
by him all nations made happy.
18 Blessed be the God Yahweh,
the God of Israel,
Who alone works wonders!
19 And blessed be his glorious name forever!
May all the earth be filled with his glory!
Amen and Amen.
20 The prayers of David, the son of Jesse, are ended.

Notes

lxxii. A prayer for God's blessing on the king, perhaps composed originally for the coronation ceremonies of an Israelite king. Since some of the verses cannot be understood of any earthly monarch except as pure hyperbole, Christian tradition has generally treated this psalm as messianic, that is, as finding its fulfillment in Christ. In recent decades, however, scholars have tended to give up the strictly messianic exegesis. They prefer to class the poem among the royal psalms (see *Psalms I*, introductory Note to Ps ii), admitting only an indirect reference to the Messiah. Cf. P. Veugelers, "Le Psaume LXXII, poème messianique?," in *Ephemerides Theologicae Lovanienses* 49 (1965), 317–43. Of course, the psalm is pre-Exilic, its chief concern being the welfare of the king.

1. *Of Solomon.* Or, "For Solomon." This prayer may well have been composed by a functionary of the Solomonic court. The language

is in some verses very archaic, while vss. 1, 8, 10, 15 can all be applied to King Solomon.

the king . . . the king's son. Referring to the same individual, namely, Solomon, who was the son of King David.

2. *That he may govern.* Explaining the consonants *ydyn* (MT *yādīn*) as defective spelling of the final syllable of subjunctive *yādīnā.* That the verb expresses purpose is clear from the context, from LXX *krínein* which critics needlessly assume derives from a *Vorlage* reading *lādīn.* Cf. the first NOTE on Ps lxi 5. Thus the sequence of imperative *tēn* followed by subjunctive *yādīnā* equals that of UT, 2 Aqht:VI:24, *tn lkṯr wḫss yb'l qšt l'nt,* "Give them to Skillful and Cunning that he might make a bow for Anath."

3. *May the mountains bring peace.* The dispute whether *yiśᵉ'ū* denotes "to bear (fruit)" (so BDB, p. 671a; Gunkel, *Die Psalmen,* p. 308), or "to bring (as messengers)" (so Briggs, CECBP, II, p. 137; BJ) moves toward resolution with the citation of UT, 51:v:100–1, *yblnn ǵrm mid ksp gb'm lḥmd ḥrṣ,* "The mountains did bring him much silver, the hills the choicest gold."

justice. Stylistically noteworthy is the use of *yiśᵉ'ū* with the accusative object in the first colon, but governed by a preposition in the second. Consult the comment on Ps lxvi 20.

your people. With *'ām* sharing the suffix of vs. 2, *'ammᵉkā.*

4. *and crush the extortioner.* Namely, of the poor. Proposals to delete the phrase founder upon comparison with a cognate passage in the Kirta Legend where Prince Yaṣṣib taxes his father with failure to drive out the exploiters of the poor: UT, 127:47–48, *ltdy ṯšm 'l dl,* "You did not drive out those who prey upon the poor." Heb. *dākā'* is a by-form of *dākāh* which appears in the Ugaritic phrase *tdkn aḥdh,* "Crush them together."

5. *May he revere you.* Personal piety, as well as social justice, is required of the king. Often emended with the LXX to *ya'ᵃrīk,* "may he prolong," MT *yiyrā'ūkā* can satisfactorily be parsed as the third person singular imperfect ending in *-u* (*yaqtulu*), which in the Masoretic tradition is lengthened to *-ū* under the accent. The form may also be parsed as a plural of majesty as a sign of respect for the king. Verse 16b, *yāṣīṣū,* parses in the same manner, and the first NOTE on Ps lxiv 7 cites other examples.

as long as. R. Tournay, "Le Psaume LXXII, 16, et le réveil de Melquart," in *Ecole des langues orientales anciennes de l'Institut Catholique de Paris. Mémorial du cinquantenaire 1914–1964* (Paris, 1964), 97–104, concludes from this value of *'im* that the psalm is a late composition, but the closely related meaning of *'im,* "like, on a par with," in the Ras Shamra tablets casts doubt upon the worth of his inference. Cf. UT, 2 Aqht:VI:28–29, *ašsprk 'm b'l šnt,* "I will make you count years like Baal"; H. L. Ginsberg, *Koheleth Interpreted* (Jerusalem, 1961), p. 70; Dahood, *Biblica* 47 (1966), 269, and the second NOTE on Ps lxxiii 5.

be extinguished. Explaining *lpny* as an infinitive construct of *pānāh*, Ar. *faniya*, "to pass away, come to an end," that occurs in Ps xc 9; Jer vi 4, *pānāh hayyōm*, "The daylight is waning." See below on vs. 17. The writing *lpny* corresponds to the Ugaritic infinitive construct *bbkyh*, "while he wept," and *lšty*, "for drinking." Cf. UT, § 9.52, and Ps lxviii 31, *brṣy ksp*, "in his lust for silver."

6. *upon the mown grass.* May the influence of the king be felt in all the cultivated regions of the world. For this meaning of *gēz*, see Amos vii 1, and for related imagery compare UT, 1 Aqht:41–42, *ṭl yṭl lǵnbm*, "the dew that bedews upon the grapes."

like showers. The parallelism between *kᵉmāṭār* and *kirᵉbībīm* re-echoes the association (not the strict parallelism) of these roots in UT, 1 Aqht:41, *tmṭr*, . . . 44, *rbb*.

upon. The preposition of the phrase *'al gēz* extends its force to the presumably parallel *zarzīp* on the strength of the principle mentioned in the second NOTE on Ps lvii 4.

scorched lands. The means to unriddle the hapax legomenon *zarzīp* are still lacking, but a grammatically viable (not necessarily the correct one) solution would be to explain *zarzīp* as a reduplicated noun from *zārab*, defined by BDB, p. 279b, "to be burnt, scorched," and by KB, p. 265b, "become waterless." Either definition proves serviceable; the final *p* of *zarzīp* may be the result of the dissimilation of sonant *b* (**zarzīb*) to mute *p* in the presence of the three sonants *z-r-z*. The noun is probably plural, to be vocalized *zarzīpē 'āreṣ*, meant to balance *'apsē 'āreṣ* in vs. 8.

What the poet prays for is that the king's power extend over both the cultivated and the desert regions of the earth. The motif of "the Desert and the Sown" may also elucidate the textual difficulty of *ṣiyyīm*, "desert tribes," in vs. 9.

7. *the just man.* And not the *'ōšēq*, "the extortioner," of vs. 4. In the light of this exegesis, the frequent alteration of MT *ṣaddīq* to abstract *ṣedeq*, "justice," becomes less cogent.

flourish. The root of *yipraḥ* probably underlies the Ugaritic personal name *prḫ*.

distill. Parsing *wrb* as a contraction of *wyrb* (cf. Ugar. *wld* from *wyld; Psalms I*, p. 148) from *rbb*, found in *rᵉbībīm*, "showers," in the preceding verse. Other occurrences of this verb are discussed in the third NOTE to Ps lxv 10. Uncontracted *yrb* would be either a qal or, more probably, a hiphil imperfect.

till the moon be no more. A reprise of vs. 5, "till the moon be extinguished."

8. *sea . . . River.* Cf. the second NOTE on Ps lxvi 6.

the River. Namely, the Euphrates. Cf. I Kings v 1 (RSV iv 21), "Solomon ruled over all the kingdoms from the Euphrates (*hannāhār*) to the land of the Philistines and to the border of Egypt. They brought tribute and served Solomon all the days of his life."

ends of the earth. The poet may have intended *'apsē 'āreṣ* to balance vs. 6, *zarzīpē 'āreṣ,* "the scorched lands," just as the first word of the present verse, *yērd,* recalls the first word of vs. 6, *yērēd.*

9. *the desert tribes.* Once the motif of "the Desert and the Sown" is identified in vs. 6, the radical association of *ṣiyyīm* with *ṣiyyāh,* "arid region, desert," assumes a new cogency, while the frequent emendation of *ṣiyyīm* to *ṣārīm,* "adversaries," is drained of whatever probability it had. The *ṣiyyīm* thus contrast with the similar ending, *'iyyīm,* "the islands," of the next verse.

10. *Tarshish.* Tarshish has long been identified with Tartessos in southern Spain, but in recent decades a case for situating it in Sardinia has been presented. Cf. *Psalms I,* pp. 291 f.

the islands. The term *'iyyīm,* in addition to designating the islands in the Mediterranean, probably includes the trading colonies that dotted the Mediterranean coasts.

tribute. Feminine *minḥāh* appears in Arabic and Ugaritic as *mnḥ.* The best background for interpreting this verse appears to be the passage relating to Solomon's kingdom in I Kings v 1 (quoted in the second NOTE on vs. 8) and to his dealings with the Queen of Sheba in I Kings x 1, 22.

Sheba and Seba. Kingdoms in South Arabia.

gifts. *'eškār* equals Akk. *iškaru,* "finished products, (a kind of) tax."

12. *If.* Scholars dispute the precise nuance of *kī* (BJ simply omits to translate it), some seeing a causal nexus with the preceding verse, while others deny it all causal value. I prefer to interpret *kī* as introducing the protasis extending over vss. 12–14, with the apodosis beginning in vs. 15. The spiritual and material gifts that the king receives from God are not absolute; if he is unfaithful to his royal obligations, God's blessings will be taken away.

he rescues. On the use of the imperfect (*yaṣṣīl*) in conditional sentences, see GK, § 107x. In the following verse, the conditional idea is expressed by the jussive *yāḥōs,* "take pity." The verb *ynṣl* appears in the unclear context of UT, 2005:rev:8.

crying for aid. In the dispute whether MT *m^e^šawwē^a^'* is to be preferred to *miššō^a^',* "from the noble/rich," no one seems to have invoked the argument from style that supports the Masoretic pointing. When it is allowed that the second colon, *w^e^'ānī w^e^'ēn 'ōzēr lō,* consists of the substantive *'ōnī* modified by a relative clause (as in Job xxix 12), MT *'ebyōn m^e^šawwē^a^'* turns out to be the superior reading. Other instances of explicative or appositional *waw*, as in *wᵉʾēn*, are discussed in *Psalms I*, p. 18, and the third NOTE on Ps lxix 36.

the oppressed who has no helper. Consult the preceding NOTE and compare Job xxix 12, *yātōm wᵉlōʾ ʿōzēr lō*, "the orphan who had no helper" (Pope, The Anchor Bible, vol. 15).

13. *If he takes pity.* Jussive *yāḥōs* expresses a condition.

on the poor. Contrasting the thought of *yāḥōs ʿal dal* with UT, 127:48, *ṯšm ʿl dl*, "those who prey upon the poor."

14. *from lawless oppression.* Literally "from oppression and from lawlessness," *mittōk ūmēḥāmās* is a case of hendiadys. Concerning *ḥāmās*, "lawlessness," see the fourth NOTE on Ps lv 10; the explanation of the two synonyms by hendiadys counters the argument, based on reasons of measure, of those who would delete one term.

their lives . . . their blood. The close association of *dm*, "blood," and *npš*, "soul," in UT, 3 Aqht:obv:24–25 supplies another argument against the adoption of the reading *šᵉmām*, "their name," that is found in the LXX and Theodotion in place of MT *dāmām*.

15. *Then may he live long.* *wīḥī* introduces the apodosis of the conditions stated in vss. 12–14.

gold from Sheba. The verb *nātan* is employed with partitive *min*. Hummel in JBL 76 (1957), 105, proposes to read *lāmō zᵉhab* for MT *lō mizzᵉhab*, but the partitive construction in vs. 1 would seem to militate against this reading.

be given. Pointing qal passive *yuttān* (MT *yitten*) and comparing with the construction *yuttān lō*, UT, 1107:6–8, *b bt mlk mlbš ytn lhm*, "From the palace clothing was given to them."

16. *a very mantle.* The consonants *pst* present the most refractory textual difficulty in this poem. One possibility would be to take *p* as the conjunction "and, even" (*Psalms I*, p. 293), and to identify *st* with Gen xlix 11, *sūtōh*, "his robe/mantle," parallel to *lᵉbūšō*, "his garment." Cf. Phoen. *swt*. The emergent image is genuinely biblical: Ps lxv 14, "May the hollows be dressed in flocks, and the valleys mantled in wheat." See the second NOTE on Ps lxxiv 3.

wheat. A relationship between Heb. *bar* and Mari *burrum*, "a kind of grain," appears likely; cf. CAD, II (B), p. 330b.

suckling. An uncertain version of *yirʿaš*, which I derive from the Ugaritic root *rǵṯ*, "to suck," Ar. *raǵaṯa*. May the grass crops on the mountain tops (Ps cxlvii 8; Isa xlii 15) be so abundant that the flocks might pasture there and suckle their young. Briggs, CECBP, II, p. 131, translates "on the top of the mountains (sheep)," reading (p. 139) *yēraʿ śeh*, "may sheep pasture." He is correct when maintaining (p. 136) that we would expect cattle to be associated with vegetation in the prosperity of the land, but MT *yirʿaš* provides this sense when derived from *rġt*, "to suck." Compare the association of "wheat" and "sheep" in Ps lxv 14.

mountain. The balance between *'ereṣ*, "land," and *hārīm*, "mountain," now finds its counterpart in the unpublished Ras Shamra tablet cited in UT, Glossary, No. 1989a, which reads *isp špš l hrm ġrpl 'l arṣ*, "the obscuring of the sun on the mountains, dark clouds upon the earth."

his fruit. That is, fruit of the womb. Cf. Ps xxi 11; Gen xxx 2; and Lam ii 20.

blossom. Breaking down *wᵉyāṣīṣū* into emphatic *waw* (cf. the sixth NOTE on Ps lxii 5) and imperfect singular with the archaic ending *-ū*, discussed in the first NOTE on vs. 5. In Ps xcii 8, *yāṣīṣū* is predicated of evildoers.

like Lebanon. Comparing Hos xiv 6–7, and adopting the exegesis of Gunkel (*Die Psalmen*, p. 310), who notes that Lebanon, by metonymy, denotes a lofty tree that sinks deep roots. The relevant texts include Isa x 34; Ecclus xxxix 14, 18. That Lebanon belongs to the third colon of vs. 16, and not to the second as in *The Grail Psalms, A New Translation*, is clear from the chiastic arrangement of the four cola comprising vs. 16. Thus *'ereṣ*, "land," in colon A matches *'ereṣ*, "earth," in colon D, while *hārīm*, "mountain," in colon B balances *lᵉbānōn*, "Lebanon," in colon C.

flourishing. A host of difficulties appears when MT *mē'īr* must be explained. I tentatively assume an original consonantal text *m'r*, whose initial letter belongs to the preceding verb as enclitic (*Psalms I*, p. 327, under *mem encliticum*) and whose remaining two consonants are vocalized *'ārō*, the infinitive absolute of **'ārāh*, "to flourish," a root found in the related context of Ps xxxvii 35, *mit'āreh kᵉ'ezrāḥ ra'ᵃnān*, "flourishing like a luxuriant native tree."

grass. Harks back to vs. 6, *'al gēz*, "upon the mown grass."

17. *his progeny*. For this nuance of *šēm*, consult *Psalms I*, p. 250, the second NOTE on Ps xli 6, and note Akk. *šumu*, "name," but also "son."

forever . . . the sun. The concurrence of *'ōlām* and *šemeš* in the same sentence recalls the name of the Canaanite divinity *špš 'lm* (UT, 2008:7) and the Phoenician god *šmš 'lm* (Karatepe III:19).

bear offspring. Pointing piel *yᵉnayyēn* (MT *yinnyōn*), a denominative verb from *nīn*, "offspring, posterity." An instructive analogy is afforded by Gen xvi 2, *'ūlay 'ibbāneh mimmennāh*, "It may be that I may obtain children by her" (KJ), where *'ibbāneh* is a denominative verb from *bēn*, "son." Cf. S. Kardimon, JSS 3 (1958), 123–26, and compare Heb. *bikkēr*, "to bear a first-born," Ugar. *bkr*. On the relative frequency of denominative verbs in Northwest Semitic, *Psalms I*, pp. 84, 237. With *yᵉnayyēn* the last word of the second colon of vs. 17 (contrast BH³), we have three words in the first colon numbering six syllables, and also three words in the second colon that add up to seven syllables.

be extinguished. See the third NOTE on vs. 5.

his progeny. Making *šᵉmō* the first word of the third colon, and consulting the first NOTE on this verse for its definition.

be blessed. If it be original, the initial *waw* of *wᵉyitbārᵉkū* could be explained as emphatic; see the sixth NOTE on vs. 16. Placed in the third colon of vs. 17, *šᵉmō* supplies the third word to balance the three words of the fourth colon and the counterpoise to *gōyim*.

by him . . . made happy. Sense and balance with the passive *yitbārᵉkū*, "be blessed," are better served when consonantal *y'šrhw* is vocalized as pual *yᵉ'uššᵉrūhū* (MT *yᵉ'aššᵉrūhū*) and the suffix *-hū* parsed as a dative of agency, a usage discussed in the first NOTE on Ps lxiii 11 and the third NOTE on Ps lxix 36. By expressing agency, the dative suffix *-hū*, "by him," semantically pairs with *bō*, "through him," in the first colon.

18–19. *Blessed . . . Amen*. Verses 18–19 are a doxology closing the second book of the Psalter; cf. the NOTE on Ps xli 14.

19. *be filled with his glory*. As in Num xiv 21, niphal *timmālē'* governs two accusative objects, both *kᵉbōdō*, "with his glory," and *'et kōl hā'āreṣ*, "all the earth," being accusatives. Cf. Joüon, GHB, § 128c, n. 1, p. 385, who, undeservedly it would seem, describes this construction "strange."

20. *The prayers . . . are ended*. An editor's comment to the effect that this psalm closed the prayer book of David.

PSALM 73

(lxxiii 1–28)

1 *A psalm of Asaph.*

How good God is, O Israel,
to those who are pure of heart!
2 Yet my feet had almost stumbled,
my legs were nearly gone,
3 When I envied the boasters,
begrudged the prosperity of the wicked.
4 For them there are no struggles,
their body is sound and sleek.
5 Theirs is not the toil of mortals,
they are not buffeted like others.
6 And so pride serves as their necklace,
the robe of injustice covers them.
7 Their eyes glisten more than milk,
the fancies of their heart exceed all bounds.
8 They scoff and speak against the Evil One,
they speak against the oppression from the Exalted.
9 They set their mouth against heaven,
and their tongue swished through the nether world.
10 And so they quickly gorged themselves,
and sucked up the waters of the full sea.
11 And they say, "How can God know?
Is there knowledge in the Most High?"
12 Such, then, are the wicked,
who, heedless of the Eternal, increased their wealth.
13 Quite in vain have I kept my heart clean
and washed my hands in innocence,
14 Become one buffeted all day long,
and chastised each morning anew.

15 If I had said, "I will speak thus,"
I would have betrayed the assembly of your sons.
16 And when I strove to understand this,
the injustice of it with my mind;
17 Until I should enter God's sanctuary
and perceive their final destiny.
18 Surely to Perdition will you transplant them,
making them fall into Desolation.
19 How quickly they will belong to Devastation,
utterly swept away by Terrors!
20 Like a dream after awaking, O Lord,
you will value them lightly in the city of phantoms.
21 But when my mind had soured,
and when my emotions had dried up,
22 I became a stupid fool without understanding,
a mere beast in your sight.
23 But I will always be with you.
Take hold of my right hand,
24 Into your council lead me,
and with glory take me to yourself.
25 What shall I lack in heaven
with you
I desire nothing on earth.
26 My flesh and my heart may waste away, O Mountain,
but my heart and my body, God, will be eternal,
27 While those who go far from you will perish.
Annihilate everyone who deserts you!
28 Myself, the nearness of God will be my happiness.
I have put my trust in the Lord Yahweh,
telling of all your works.

Notes

lxxiii. A Wisdom psalm in which the psalmist, before the religious assembly, reflects on the justice of God. Like the author of the Book of Job, the psalmist poses this problem: How can one reconcile the justice of God with the inequities in his government of the world? The poet finds the solution of the problem in the final punishment of the wicked (vss. 18–19) and the eternal union of the just with God in heaven (vss. 23–26). Pss xxxvii and xlix consider the same problem, and their authors reach the same solution as the present poet.

1. *Asaph.* The founder of one of the three chief guilds of Levite temple musicians, the "sons of Asaph" (I Chron xxv 1–2, 6–9). Pss 1, lxxiii–lxxxiii contain ascriptions to Asaph in their titles, but whether these ascriptions indicate a tradition of his authorship of them, or a style peculiar to them and originated by Asaph, remains to be determined. See W. F. Albright, *Archaeology and the Religion of Israel*, pp. 126 f.

O Israel. Parsing the initial *lamedh* of *l^eyiśrā'ēl* as the vocative particle; cf. *Psalms I*, p. xxi, and VT 16 (1966), 308. The name Israel is preceded by the vocative particle also in Pss lxxxi 5 and cxxii 4b. From this grammatical analysis emerges a fine example of enjambment (cf. vs. 25 and the first NOTE on Ps lix 8) and a strong argument against the widely held emendation of *l^eyiśrā'ēl* to *layyāšār 'ēl*, "God to the upright," first proposed by Graetz, *Kritischer Commentar zu den Psalmen*, I, p. 437.

This translation reveals the *Sitz im Leben* (a similar case is pointed out at Ps xlv 2 in *Psalms I*, p. 270) of the psalm: the psalmist is directly addressing the religious assembly of Israelites. Before unfolding his doubts to the congregation (vss. 2–12), he reassures his listeners of God's unmistakable goodness (*'ak ṭōb*) toward men of integrity. Notwithstanding all appearances and everything that might be said to the contrary, God will punish the wicked and reward the righteous in the hereafter.

2. *my legs.* This definition of *'ašūrāy*, usually translated "my steps," is discussed in *Psalms I*, p. 95, and more recently, in *Biblica* 47 (1966), 276, on Eccles vii 26.

were nearly gone. Literally "were poured out," i.e., became as unstable as water. Biblical idiom predicates *šāpak*, "to pour out," of *lēb*, "heart," *kābēd*, "liver," so one may properly use it of *'ašūrāy*, "my legs," but hardly of "my steps," as in the versions. The Masoretic pual vocalization *šupp^ekāh* (also in Num xxxv 33; Zeph i 17) can scarcely be correct since this frequent root nowhere exhibits a piel form; hence one should point it as qal passive, a conjugation unknown to the Masoretes, as argued in *Psalms I*, p. 97.

The ending of *šūp^ekāh* represents the archaic third person feminine dual (or plural) ending; cf. the fourth NOTE on Ps lxviii 14.

The psalmist confesses that when he beheld the prosperity of the wicked he almost fell away from God in apostasy.

3. *the boasters.* This term probably refers to the pagan Canaanites; see *Psalms I*, p. 31.

begrudged. Psalms I, p. 302, examines this nuance of *rā'āh*, "to see." Here the imperfect form *'er'eh* balances perfect *qinnē'tī*, a stylistic usage recurring in vss. 9, 18; see the third NOTE on Ps lxxi 17.

4. *no struggles.* Much-disputed *ḥarṣubbōt* (the versions differ sharply) can viably be derived from **ḥṣb* (see Hos vi 5), Ugar. *ḫṣb*, "to struggle," with the *r* explained as a secondary addition. For example, Ugar. *qrdm*, "ax," has been identified by some with Ar. *qadūm*, "hatchet, ax." Cf. GK, § 30q; Bauer and Leander, *Historische Grammatik*, § 61e[e], pp. 484 f. Note also the alternate forms *dmśq* and *drmśq*, "Damascus."

their body. Literally "their strength." Ginsberg, LKK, p. 37, rightly identifies *'ūl* with Ugar. *ul* in UT, Krt:88, *ṣbuk ul mad*, "Your troops are a mighty force." Consult *Psalms I*, first NOTE on Ps xxii 20 and Aistleitner, WuS, No. 183, p. 18. The Glossary of UT inexplicably fails to make this equation.

sound and sleek. With most modern scholars reading *lāmō tām ūbārī'* for MT *l*[e]*mōtām ūbārī'*, "for their death, and sleek."

5. *not buffeted.* Unlike the psalmist who was buffeted (*nāgūa'*) all day long (vs. 14).

like. For this meaning of *'im*, see the second NOTE on Ps lxxii 5 and BDB, pp. 767b–68a.

6. *serves as their necklace.* As a denominative verb from *'ănāq*, "neck," Ugar. *'nq*, *'ănāqatemō* belongs to the long list of Northwest Semitic verbs derived from names of parts of the body; see the third NOTE on Ps lx 3.

7. *glisten. Psalms I*, pp. 93 f., examine this denotation of *yāṣā'*. This well-documented meaning of *yāṣā'* in Hebrew, Ugaritic, and Arabic renders superfluous Gunkel's emendation to *yēṣaḥ*, "It shines." The disagreement of gender in *yāṣā'* and *'ēnēmō* can be resolved by pointing *yṣ'* as the infinitive absolute *yāṣō'*.

than milk. Repointing *mēḥālāb* (MT *mēḥēleb*, "than fat") and comparing Gen xlix 12, "His eyes are darker than wine, /And his teeth are whiter than milk."

their heart. lēbāb requires no possessive suffix either because it is a part of the body (*Psalms I*, p. 89), or because it balances suffixed *'ēnēmō*, "their eyes" (*Psalms I*, pp. 17 f.). Cf. especially UT, 1 Aqht:34, *tbky pǵt bm lb*, "Pughat weeps from her heart."

8. *speak against.* The construction *y*[e]*dabb*[e]*rū b*[e] recurs in Ps lxxv 6, *t*[e]*dabb*[e]*rū b*[e]*ṣū'r 'attīq*, "nor speak against the Ancient Mountain."

the Evil One. In the mind of unbelievers, Yahweh is the cause of evil upon the earth and hence the Evil One.

the Exalted. Psalms I, pp. 44 f., examines the evidence for this divine appellation; see below on Ps lxxv 6. Since oppression comes from on high, the scoffers set their lip of protest against heaven (vs. 9).

speak . . . speak. Gunkel (*Die Psalmen*, p. 317) notes that the repetition of the same verb in the second colon offends Hebrew style, but this fact alone cannot justify an emendation (Gunkel does not emend the text) because Ugaritic exhibits a number of texts employing identical verbs in parallel cola. For example, UT, 2 Aqht:v:31–33, *tbʻ kṯr lahlh hyn tbʻ lmšknth,* "Kothar departs for his tent, Hayyin departs for his habitation." Cf. also UT, 2 Aqht:vi:42–43; 49:v:2–3; 126:iii:7–8.

9. *They set their mouth.* This bizarre piece of imagery finds splendid clarification in UT, 67:ii:2–3, *[špt la]rṣ špt lšmm [l]šn lkbkbm,* "a lip against the nether world, a lip against heaven, the tongue against the stars," and 52:61–63, *št špt larṣ špt lšmm wlʻrb bphm ʻṣr šmm wdg bym,* "They (i.e., the gods Dawn and Sunset) set one lip against the nether world, the other lip against heaven. The birds of heaven and the fish from the sea entered their mouths." The psalmist likens the prosperous unbelievers to the monstrous voracious gods who devour everything in sight and yet are not sated (line 64, *wl tšbʻn*). This mythological allusion has eluded many versions, e.g., the CCD renders, "They set their mouthings in place of heaven, and their pronouncements roam the earth." Cf. H. Ringgren, VT 3 (1953), 265–72, especially p. 267, and the obscure text UT, 1003:4–8, which evidently describes a cognate scene.

swished. As in vss. 3 and 18, an imperfect form (*tihᵃlak*) balances a perfect verb (*šattū,* "they set").

the nether world. That *'ereṣ* here denotes the underworld (*Psalms I,* p. 106) is clear from the Ugaritic description where *arṣ* must refer to a region beneath the sea, as recognized by Gaster, *Thespis,* 1961, p. 433. Thus the Ugaritic parallelism between *arṣ,* "nether world," and *šmm,* "heaven," supplies another instance of identical parallel nouns in Ugaritic and Hebrew; cf. the fourth NOTE on Ps lvii 8.

10. *they quickly gorged themselves.* Usually considered corrupt, vs. 10 will yield a measure of coherency if we keep an eye on the *Wortfeld* of the mythological motifs of UT, 52:61–64 and 67:ii:2–4 (cited under vs. 9). Key words found there include *št* (vs. 9, *šattū*), *šmm* (vs. 9, *šāmayim*), *ph,* "his mouth" (vs. 9, *pīhem*), *lšn* (vs. 9, *lᵉšōnām*), *arṣ* (vs. 9, *'āreṣ*). Among the remaining Ugaritic words not represented in the Masoretic text are *šbʻ,* "to be sated," and *ym,* "sea."

Accordingly, for MT *yāšīb ʻammō* I would read *yiśbᵉʻū-m* (with enclitic *mem*). The Masoretic unfamiliarity with the enclitic *mem* can readily account for the faulty division of consonants in MT. In Isa lxvi 11 one finds *śᵉbaʻtem* parallel to *tāmōṣṣū,* the same balancing of roots that I propose to find here.

sucked up. Reading *yāmōṣṣū* for MT *yimmāṣū* and comparing Isa lxvi 11. Cf. Ugar. *mṣṣ,* "to suck." Like the mythical monsters, the voracious rich swallow the ocean, leaving nothing for others.

the full sea. Since there has been no explicit mention of *yam,* "sea," as in the Ugaritic text, one suspects that *mālē',* "the full one," is a poetic synonym for the ocean. The use of an adjective to denote a substantive is witnessed in many languages, and Ugaritic provides three good examples in *rḥbt,* "a wide jar, vat" (cf. Ezek xxiii 32), *rbt,* "a large net" (cf. the fifth NOTE on Ps lxii 3), while in the Ugaritic economic texts the adjective *kbd* alone denotes "heavy shekel" or "heavy jar" according to the context.

An unpublished Ugaritic tablet cited by Virolleaud, CRAIBL, 1962, 97, contains the expression *ym mlat,* a phrase reminiscent of Ps xcviii 7 and Eccles i 7; cf. Dahood, *Biblica* 47 (1966), 266.

12. *who.* Other instances of relative or explicative w^e are cited in the third NOTE on Ps lxxii 12.

heedless of the Eternal. A comparison of the hapax legomenon phrase *šalwē 'ōlām* with Ps ix 18, *šekēḥē 'elōhīm,* "that ignore God," and Job viii 13, *šōkeḥē 'ēl,* suggests that *'ōlām* is the divine title studied in *Psalms I,* pp. 152 f., 187, etc. In Targumic Aramaic *šl'* is used of neglecting God. If this parsing is correct, we have in vss. 11–12 three names of God: *'ēl, 'elyōn,* and *'ōlām.*

13. *washed my hands.* In JSS 3 (1958), 116, Loren Fisher compares this phrase with the symbolic action mentioned in a juridical text from Ras Shamra. *Le palais royal d'Ugarit,* III, 15.92, p. 55, states that if an adopted son desires freedom, he must wash his hands, which seems to be a symbolic act of "clearing" oneself. Through this action he becomes free and clear of his previous relationship. Cf. Matt xxvii 24 which describes a similar action of Pilate.

14. *buffeted.* Unlike the wicked who were spared such blows (vs. 5). The psalmist employs the same verb *nāga'* in both verses.

chastised. Grammarians and lexicographers are wont to parse *tōkaḥtī* as a suffixed form of the noun *tōkaḥat,* "reproof," but several scholars (e.g., Bertholet, Gunkel) have felt the need of a verb in this sentence position and have accordingly proposed the emendation *hūkaḥtī,* "I have been chastised." Such an emendation can no longer be sustained in view of the examples of the *taqaṭṭal* (Arabic fifth form) conjugation found in Ugaritic (UT, § 9.32) and which scholars have identified in Deut xxxiii 16; I Sam xxv 34; II Kings vi 8; Job xxii 21. Cf. Anton Jirku in FuF 32 (1958), 212. Hence repoint *tewakkaḥtī.*

15. *thus.* Identifying *kemō* (perhaps read **kimmō* < **kinmō*) with Ugar. *km,* "thus," in UT, 49:II:28–30, *klb arḫ l'glh klb ṯat limrh km lb 'nt aṯr b'l,* "Like the heart of a wild cow toward her calf, like the heart of a wild ewe toward her lamb, thus was the heart of Anath toward Baal."

I would have betrayed. Were the psalmist to speak and endorse the thoughts of the wicked (vs. 11), he would have been unfaithful to the Israelite congregation.

the assembly of your sons. Comparing *dōr bānekā* with Ugar. and Phoen. *dr bn il,* "the assembly of El's sons"; cf. F. J. Neuberg in JNES 9 (1950), 217.

your sons. The Israelites. The poet, as in vss. 18 ff., directly addresses God rather than the congregation that is present.

16. *this.* Namely, why the wicked prosper and the just suffer.

the injustice of it. This translation results when *'āmāl hī'* is parsed as a noun followed by the independent pronoun in the oblique case, a surrogate construction for noun plus suffix. For other instances of this usage, see Dahood, CBQ 32 (1970), 86–90.

17. *God's sanctuary.* Plural *miqdeše* conforms to the frequent Canaanite practice of employing plural forms for names of dwellings; cf. the third NOTE on Ps lxv 5. Canaanite usage thus confirms the explanation of plural *miqdāšekā* in Ezek xxviii 18 proposed by G. A. Cooke, *The Book of Ezekiel* (Edinburgh, 1936), p. 324. He recognized that the plural may denote a single sanctuary with the precincts.

As rightly observed by CCD, "God's sanctuary" refers to heaven; see the first NOTE on Ps liii 7, where I propose a new exegesis of Ps xx 3. At present too difficult for his understanding, the glaring inconsistencies of this life will become intelligible to the psalmist in the hereafter. The poet, it will be seen, repeats his belief in a blessed existence after death in vss. 23–26. In Ps lxviii 36, *miqdāšīm,* parallel to *šeḥāqīm,* "heaven," clearly refers to the celestial sanctuary.

their final destiny. On *'aḥarīt* as a *terminus technicus* for the eschatological destiny, consult *Psalms I,* p. 232, and C. T. Fritsch in *The Journal of Religion* 46 (1966), 72.

18. *Surely. 'ak* emphasizes the psalmist's conviction that the wicked will be punished in the afterlife.

Perdition. Deriving *ḥalāqōt* from *ḥlq,* "to die, perish," a root studied in *Psalms I,* pp. 35, 207, 211. Rendered "Destruction" on p. 211, *ḥalāqōt,* an intensive plural form or singular with the Phoenician ending, is preferably translated "Perdition." Cf. also Dahood, *Biblica* 45 (1964), 408, where it is noted that Patton, CPBP, pp. 38 f., recognized the presence of *ḥlq,* "to perish," in this verse, but he attempted no translation.

will you transplant them. Reading *tištelēmō* (MT *tāšīt lāmō*), from *šātal,* "to transplant," whose eschatological connotations were noticed at Ps i 3. In *Psalms I,* p. 3, this line was rendered as a curse, but now I would interpret it as stating the psalmist's belief more than his wish.

making them fall. As in vss. 3 and 9, the poet balances a perfect form (*hippaltām*) with an imperfect verb (*tištelēmō,* "transplant them").

Desolation. Recognizing in *maššū'ōt* (perhaps to be vocalized *mešō'ōt;* cf. *mešō'āh,* "desolation") a poetic name for the nether world. More than thirty names for the underworld have been thus far identified (not all have been published) in the poetic books of the Hebrew Bible; see *Psalms I,* p. 299. Like its counterpoise *ḥalāqōt, maššū'ōt* may be either an intensive plural or a feminine singular of the Phoenician type ending in *-ōt;* cf. the second NOTE on Ps liii 7.

19. *quickly*. Comparing Job xxi 13, "And they quickly go down to Sheol."

belong to. Parsing *lᵉ* of *lᵉšammāh* as the *lamedh* of ownership; cf. Ps lxviii 21, "To the Lord Yahweh we owe our escape from death."

Devastation. That the psalmist intends the common noun *šommāh*, "waste, devastation," as a metaphor for Sheol follows from its parallelism with *ballāhōt*, "Terrors"; see below.

utterly swept away. Understanding *sāpū tammū* as an instance of hendiadys, and repointing MT *sāpū* as *sūpū*, the qal passive of *sāpāh*, "to sweep or snatch away." Many versions derive MT *sāpū* from *sūp*, "to come to an end," but a cognate text from Job (see the next NOTE) supports an etymology from *sāpāh*. The wicked rich will leave no trace upon the earth.

Terrors. *ballāhōt* is another poetic designation for the abode of the dead, a place of fear and chaos, as may be deduced from the eschatological context and from Job xviii 14, "He is snatched from his comfortable tent / And haled before the King of Terrors" (Pope, The Anchor Bible, vol. 15). As Pope has correctly observed, *melek ballāhōt* is an epithet of Mot, the god of death and the nether world. RSV's "swept away utterly by terrors" transmits no clear picture, while CCD's "They are completely wasted away amid horrors" is grammatically questionable as a translation of the Hebrew.

This understanding of *ballāhōt* neatly solves the textual difficulty in Job xxvii 20, *taššīgēhū kᵉmayim* (MT *kammayim*) *ballāhōt laylāh gᵉnābattū sūpāh*, "Terrors will overtake him like a flood, Night will kidnap him like a tempest." The personification of Night will be discussed at Ps cxxxix 11, while the reading "like a tempest" flows from recognizing the double-duty operation of *kᵉ* in *kᵉmayim* so as to determine counterpoised *sūpāh*.

20. *a dream*. Well documented in Ugaritic, *ḥlm*, "dream," occurs only here in the Psalter.

after awaking. Analyzing *mēhāqīṣ* into *min*, "after," as in Ps lxxviii 65; I Kings viii 54; Jer xxxi 13; Hos vi 2, vii 5, and the hiphil infinitive construct of *qīṣ*, "to awake."

you will value them lightly. Usually rendered "despise, spurn," *tibzeh* here denotes rather "to slight, treat as of slight importance," pretty much as one normally regards a dream after awaking. Thus Esau was said to have undervalued (Gen xxv 34, *wayyibez*) his birthright; cf. CCD, "Thus lightly did Esau value his birthright," and Speiser, The Anchor Bible, vol. 1, "Thus did Esau misprize his birthright." One of the most poignant sorrows of the dead was their consciousness of being forgotten by God and cut off from his love; cf. Ps lxxxviii 6.

the city of phantoms. Repointing *bᵉʿīr ṣᵉlāmīm* for unexplained MT *bāʿīr ṣalmām* and comparing Ps xxxix 7 for this nuance of *ṣelem*.

Among the numerous texts which depict the realm of the dead as a city with gates (Isa xxxviii 10; Job xxiv 12, xxxviii 17: Ecclus li 9; Wisd of Sol xvi 13; Matt xvi 18), the most pertinent for our purpose is misunderstood Job xxiv 12, *mē'īr mētīm* (MT *mᵉtīm*) *yin'āqū wᵉnepeš ḥᵃlālīm tᵉšawwēᵃ'*, "From the City the dead groan, and the throats of the slain cry out." In his *Primitive Conceptions of Death and the Nether World in the Old Testament* (Rome, 1969), Ch. 3, Nicolas J. Tromp studies the motif of the nether world as "City."

In Canaanite mythology, Death's subterranean domain is termed *qrt*, "city" (UT, 51:VIII:11), while the name of the Tyrian god Melqart is often explained as "king of the (nether) city."

21. *had soured*. Preserving the root sense of *yitḥammēṣ*, which in the simple conjugation means "to be sour." This common Sematic root is found in the Ugaritic noun *ḥmṣ*, "vinegar," as remarked in the second NOTE on Ps lxix 22. The sight of the wicked's prosperity, while the God-fearing met nothing but adversity, had soured the psalmist.

my emotions. kilyōtay literally means "my kidneys, viscera," considered to be the seat of the affections.

had dried up. The hapax legomenon *'eštōnān* has been translated in manifold ways and derived from various roots, but a measure of consistency in the metaphor begun by *yitḥammēs*, "had soured," can be gained by relating *'eštōnān* to *yāšan*, "to dry up, become old." Just as milk, when it begins to sour, coagulates and hardens, so the psalmist became hardhearted once his mind had soured. The form *'eštōnān* would parse as the first person imperfect of an infixed *-t-* conjugation, with the reduplication of the final consonant. In Ecclus xi 18 the hithpael *hityaššēn*, "Grow old!," is correctly restored from fragmentary *hty-*; see Zorell, ZLH p. 337b. This root occurs in the Ugaritic phrase *ṣmqm yṯnm*, "dried raisins." Cf. Ps lxxvii 11.

22. *a mere beast*. Like *ḥᵃlāqōt*, "Perdition," and *maššū'ōt*, "Desolation," in vs. 18, *bᵉhēmōt* may be explained either as an intensive plural form with singular meaning, or as belonging to the Phoenician type of feminine singular that ends in *-ōt*. In no case are we to emend *bᵉhēmōt* to *bᵉhēmāh*, as recommended by the critical apparatus of BH³ or the textual note of CCD. Cf. Ugar. *bhmt* and *Psalms I*, p. 52.

23. *But I. wa'ᵃnī* opens the final strophe which proclaims the psalmist's belief in eternal union with God in the future life.

Take hold. Parsing *'āḥaztā* as a precative perfect (*Psalms I*, p. 20), and comparing Ps lxiii 9, "(May) your right hand grasp me," which likewise employs a precative perfect, *tāmᵉkāh*. The modal sequence of this verse—indicative followed by precative—corresponds to the sequence found in vs. 27.

24. *your council*. This meaning of *'ᵃṣātᵉkā* is examined in *Psalms I*, pp. 1 f. Here the poet refers to the heavenly council.

lead me. Analyzing *tanḥēnī* as an imperfect form with imperative function (see the second NOTE on Ps liv 3), and recognizing in *nāhāh* the *terminus technicus,* "to lead into Paradise," discussed in *Psalms I,* p. 33, and the third NOTE on Ps lxi 3. Cf. Ps cxxxix 24, *n*ᵉ*ḥēnī b*ᵉ*derek 'ōlām,* "Lead me into the eternal assembly."

with glory. In view of Ugar.-Heb. *'aḥar/'aḥ*ᵃ*rē,* "with," documented in *Psalms I,* p. 302, one may no longer subscribe to the opinion of Briggs, CECBP, II, p. 149, who discounted LXX *metà dóxēs* and Vulg. *cum gloria* on the grounds that "*'ḥr* as prep. nowhere has this sense." Recent bibliography of *'aḥar,* "with," lists UT, Glossary, No. 138; O. Loretz, *Qohelet und der Alte Orient* (Freiburg, 1964), p. 189, n. 220; F. Vattioni, *Oriens Antiquus* 4 (1965), 146; C. T. Fritsch, *The Journal of Religion* 46 (1966), 71.

take me to yourself. Parsing *tiqqāḥēnī* as an imperfect serving the function of an imperative, and interpreting it as technical word to signify "to take to oneself, to assume." As noticed in *Psalms I,* p. 301, *lāqaḥ* is the verb used by biblical writers to signify "assumption." Cf. Zorell, ZLH, p. 401b. Hence the version of this colon proposed in *Psalms I,* p. 2, should now be couched to conform to the present translation.

As many commentators have seen, the psalmist uses terms that allude to the story of the assumption of Enoch in Gen v 24. He requests the same privilege that was granted Enoch and Elijah (II Kings ii 11). The meaning is evident enough; the psalmist finds the solution to the inconsistencies of this life in the final reward of the righteous after death; cf. *Psalms I,* pp. 90 f., 252 f.

25. *What shall I lack. mī lī* is an idiom that does not readily yield its meaning, but a comparison with Ruth iii 16, *mī 'att bittī,* "What ails you, my daughter?" and UT, Krt:38–39, *mn krt kybky,* "What ails Kirta that he should cry?" suggests the present version. On *mī,* "what?," see Speiser, The Anchor Bible, vol. 1, on Gen xxxiii 8, where he cites Judg xiii 17 and Mic i 5 in support of his version, and C. C. Torrey, *The Second Isaiah* (Edinburgh, 1928), p. 400. Consult also Job xxi 15, *mah šadday,* "What need has Shaddai," as proposed by me in BCCT, p. 65.

*with you. 'imm*ᵉ*kā* is the fourth word in a seven-word line. Does it belong to the first three, or should it be attached to the second colon? As far as sense is concerned, it goes equally well with both. So perhaps we should analyze it as a kind of swivel, or form of enjambment, linking both cola, a metrical device noticed in *Psalms I,* p. 41, and the first NOTE on Ps lvii 5.

26. *O Mountain.* If this eight-word verse divides into two cola of four words each, it becomes apparent that *ṣūr* balances vocative *'*ᵉ*lōhīm* in the

second colon, and hence to be identified with the divine appellative studied in the fifth NOTE on Ps lxxv 6 (courtesy D. N. Freedman).

my heart and my body. Namely, the new heart and body that God will fashion for the psalmist after death. Sentence symmetry suggests that *l^ebābī w^eḥelqī* should match *še'ērī ūl^ebābī,* "my flesh and my heart." Granted this, *ḥelqī* should be synonymous with *še'ērī,* "my flesh," a verifiable assumption in the light of Ugar. *ḥlqm,* parallel to *brkm,* "knees," in UT, 'nt:II:14, 28. From the Canaanite context and parallelism it is clear that *ḥlqm* denotes a part of the body (cf. Ar. *ḥalqu,* "throat, gullet"), and the biblical juxtaposition points to the same conclusion. If Ugar. *ḥlq* denotes "neck," as indicated by UT, Glossary, No. 867, its biblical sense would approach that of *še'ērī;* in other words, an instance of metonymy, with "neck" being used to designate the whole body.

The doctrine of the creation of a new body for the afterlife also finds expression in Job xix 26, *m^ebuššārī* (MT *mibb^eśārī*) *'eḥ^ezeh '^elōah,* "Refleshed by him, I will gaze upon God." The suffix of the pual participle *m^ebuššārī* represents the third person singular (*Psalms I,* pp. 10–11), functioning as the dative of agency (see the first NOTE on Ps lxiii 11). Cf. Ps li 12.

eternal. l^e'ōlām forms an inclusion with vs. 23, *tāmīd,* "always."

27. *those who go far from you.* Parsing the suffix of *r^eḥēqekā* as datival, and consulting the second NOTE on Ps lx 3.

will perish. This assertion resumes the thought of vs. 18.

Annihilate. hiṣmattāh, with the full writing of the final syllable (consult the second NOTE on Ps lvi 9), is best understood as a precative perfect. The structure of this verse, with an indicative followed by a precative mode, closely resembles the modal sequence of vs. 23.

28. *the nearness of God.* The phrase *qirbat '^elōhīm,* which recurs in Isa lviii 2, probably refers to the future life and repeats the thought of vs. 25, *'imm^ekā,* "with you."

will be. If the first colon of vs. 28 conceptually contrasts the lot of the psalmist with that of the apostates who shall perish (*yō'bēdū,* vs. 27), we must conclude that the poet is referring to his future happiness in heaven.

I have put. RSV, "I have made the Lord God my refuge," violates the grammar of the Hebrew text, which reads *šattī b^e,* "I have put in. . . ."

The basis for the psalmist's trust lies in his conviction that God is good (vs. 1). The goodness of God guarantees a reward in heaven for those who are faithful to him.

telling. Namely, to the Israelite assembly; cf. vs. 1. Parsing *l^esappēr* as a circumstantial infinitive; cf. the third NOTE on Ps lxiii 3.

your works. Somewhat jarring is the unexpected shift from the third person in the preceding colon to the second person here, but a similar phenomenon can be seen in Pss xxii 26, 28, cii 16; see *Psalms I*, p. 143. These may all be examples of court style; see the introductory NOTE to Ps lxi.

PSALM 74

(lxxiv 1–23)

1 *A maskil of Asaph.*

Why, O God, are you eternally angry?
Why do your nostrils smoke
against the sheep of your pasture?
2 Remember your flock you acquired of old.
Redeem with your club your patrimony,
Mount Zion where you abode.
3 Raise up your own people
from the total ruins;
The foe has damaged everything in your sanctuary.
4 Your adversaries roared amid your assembly,
they set up emblems by the hundreds.
5 They set fire to the upper entrance,
while axes hacked at the paneling.
6 They cut down all its doors,
they battered with hatchets and mattocks.
7 They set your sanctuary on fire,
they utterly desecrated your name's abode.
8 They said in their hearts,
"Let all their progeny be burned,
all the divine assemblies in the land."
9 Signs for us we do not see,
there is no prophet now;
No one who understands the evidence has come to us.
10 How long, O God, will the adversary blaspheme you,
the foe revile your name, O Conqueror?
11 Why do you draw back your left hand,
and bring your right hand near your bosom?
12 Destroy, O God, the kings from the East,
achieve victory in the middle of the earth!

13 It was you who shattered the Sea with your strength,
who smashed the heads of Tannin,
surging from the sea.
14 It was you who crushed the heads of Leviathan,
who gave him as food
to be gathered by desert tribes.
15 It was you who released springs and brooks,
it was you who turned primordial rivers into dry land.
16 Yours is the day and yours the night,
it was you who caused the moon and sun to be.
17 It was you who fixed the zones of the earth,
you who made summer and winter.
18 Remember the insults of the foe
who blasphemed you, Yahweh,
And the foolish people that reviled your name.
19 Deliver not to wild beasts
those taught by you;
The lives of your afflicted
do not ignore, O Conqueror!
20 Look down upon your temple;
the city is filled with darkness,
the countryside with violence.
21 Let not the downtrodden sit in shame,
rather let the poor and needy praise your name.
22 Arise, O God, champion your cause!
Remember how fools blaspheme you all day long!
23 Do not ignore the clamor of your adversaries,
the ever-ascending uproar of your assailants.

Notes

lxxiv. A national lament (cf. *Psalms I,* the introductory Note on Ps xliv). In this lamentation many commentators find a description of the destruction of the temple by the Babylonians in 586 B.C., and a date shortly after 586 seems most probable for the composition of this psalm. A Maccabean date, favored by some critics, is now ruled out by the discovery at Qumran of substantial Psalms' texts belonging to the first century B.C. On the other hand, the arguments of Julian Morgenstern, "Jerusalem–485 B.C.," in HUCA 27 (1956), 101–79, especially pp. 130 f., that this national lament alludes to the defilement and devastation of the temple by the Edomites in ca. 485 B.C., merit serious consideration.

Save for vss. 5–6, the consonantal text appears to be sound but in many verses its sense has been mangled by the Masoretic pointing and division of clauses. The principal textual difficulties stem from the numerous words and phrases that are hapax legomena.

1. *are you eternally angry*. The first NOTE on Ps lx 3 examines this sense of *zānaḥtā*, which most versions render "cast us off," inserting the accusative "us" for which there is no textual warrant.

Why. The force of *lāmāh* in the first colon extends to the parallel colon, in keeping with the poetic usage discussed in the NOTES to Pss iii 1–2 (*Psalms I*, p. 16) and lii 3. Its omission enables the poet to counterpoise the parallel cola with eleven syllables each.

do your nostrils smoke. A vivid anthropomorphism that is obscured by such translations as "Why does thy anger smoke? (RSV). Which is to say that *ye'šan 'appekā* semantically equals Ps xviii 9, *'ālāh 'āšān be'appō*, "Smoke rose from his nostrils." Cf. UT, 3 Aqht:obv:25–26, *km qṭr baph*, "like smoke from his nostrils."

against. The second NOTE on Ps xxxiv 17 (*Psalms I*, p. 207) cites other texts with *be* in a hostile sense.

2. *Remember*. Found as a Canaanite gloss in J. Knudtzon, *Die El-Amarna Tafeln* (Leipzig, 1915) (abbr. EA) 228:19, *yazkurmi*, the root *zkr* now probably appears in the Ugaritic personal names *d̲kr* (UT, 2011:37) and *d̲kry* (2017:4).

your flock. The metaphorical use of *ṣō'n*, "sheep," to designate the Jews (as the Israelites are called in the post-Exilic period) in the preceding colon suggests that *'adātekā*, literally "your assembly," here metaphorically denotes "your flock." See the first NOTE on Ps xxii 17 (*Psalms I*, p. 140). The metaphor continues into the next colon.

you acquired. The omission of the relative pronoun characterizes the style of this psalmist; cf. vss. 18, 19.

Redeem. Apparently balancing imperative *zekōr*, "remember," *gā'altā* should be parsed as precative perfect (*Psalms I*, pp. 20 ff.). See Ps lxxvii 16.

with your club. Parsing *šēbeṭ* as an accusative of means sharing the pronominal suffix of the following word; *Psalms I*, pp. 17 f. Cf. Ps xxiii 4 and Mic vii 14, *re'ēh 'ammekā bešibṭekā ṣō'n naḥalātekā*, "Shepherd your people with your club, the sheep of your patrimony." The psalmist asks God to smite the invaders with the shepherd's club.

your patrimony. See *Psalms I*, p. 13, for this translation of *naḥalātekā*.

Mount Zion. The collocation of *naḥalātekā*, "your patrimony," and *har ṣiyyōn*, "Mount Zion," is reminiscent of UT, 'nt:III:27, *bǵr nḥlty*, "on the mountain of my patrimony."

where you abode. *zeh šākantā bō* literally reads "which you abode upon it," with relative *zeh* corresponding to the Ugaritic relative pronoun *d;* cf. UT, § 6.24, and Phoenician Aḥiram Inscription, *'rn z p'l 'tb'l,* "the sarcophagus which Ittobaal made."

3. *Raise up. hārīmāh* forms an inclusion with vs. 22, *qūmāh,* "arise," and bears on the pointing and translation of vs. 21, *yēšeb,* "sit."

your own people. Since MT *pe'āmekā,* "your feet," yields no sense, I assume a consonantal original *p'mk,* to be analyzed into the conjunction *pa,* "and," but here serving an emphasizing function like *waw emphaticum* (*Psalms I,* p. 329), followed by *'ammekā,* "your people." Hence vocalize the complete expression *pe'ammekā,* and compare the Syriac reading "your servants." The faulty Masoretic pointing traces back to their complete unfamiliarity with *pa,* "and, but," as can be ascertained by examining the Masoretic vocalization of the passages listed in *Psalms I,* p. 293. For present purposes the most apposite parallel is Amos i 11, *wayyiṭṭōr pelā'ad* (MT *wayyiṭrōp lā'ad*) *'appō we'ebrātō šāmerāh* (MT *šemārāh*) *neṣaḥ,* "And he kept his wrath perpetually, and cherished his fury forever." The emergent parallelism between the verbs *nāṭar* and *šāmar* reappears in Jer iii 5 and supports the analysis of *pe* as emphasizing *lā'ad.* My former colleague W. L. Moran first recognized the conjunction *pe* in the Amos passage. Cf. the first NOTE on Ps lxxii 16 for another possible instance of this particle. Of course, "your people" makes a fine counterpart to "your sanctuary."

from the total ruins. le in *lemaššū'ōt* bears the frequent Ugaritic-Hebrew sense "from"; cf. the fourth NOTE on Ps lx 3. Though the text literally reads "perpetual ruins," some translators (e.g., CCD) see in *neṣaḥ* a superlative element stressing the totality of the destruction rather than its duration. A similar expression of the superlative is noted in v. 7.

your sanctuary. Suffixless *qōdeš,* Ugar. *qdš,* shares the determining force of the suffix in *'ammekā,* "your people," in the first colon; cf. the second NOTE on Ps lxiii 3. Verses 2, 10, and 18 exhibit other instances of double-duty suffixes.

4. *roared.* Namely, like lions since in biblical idiom *šā'agū* is usually predicated of lions, or used in similes comparing a sound to a lion's roar. The choice of verb here may help identify "the wild beasts" in vs. 19. Ugar. *ṯigt,* however, denotes the neighing of a horse.

assembly. Heb. *mō'ēd* equals Ugar. *m'd* in the phrase *pḫr m'd,* "those gathered in assembly," and Phoen. *mw'd* in the Egyptian story of Wen-Amon. Consult John A. Wilson, "The Assembly of a Phoenician City," in JNES 4 (1945), 245.

emblems by the hundreds. Probably the standards of the units of the invading army. Cf. Y. Yadin, *The Scroll of the War of the Sons of Light against the Sons of Darkness.* Redividing the consonants to read *'ōtōt me'ātōt* (MT *'ōtōtām 'ōtōt*), and explaining *me'ātōt* as a form with two feminine endings, like *qešātōt*, "bows," *śepātōt*, "lips." On the position of the numeral as a genitive following its noun, cf. e.g., I Kings xvi 10; Deut xv 9, and GK, § 134o.

5. *They set fire.* Verses 5 and 6 are among the most obscure and difficult of the entire Psalter, and what is proposed here remains in the realm of conjecture.

By reading *yad'īkū* for MT *yiwwāda' ke* comparing Ps cxviii 12, *d'kw ke'ēš qōṣīm*, "They blazed like a fire of thorns," we can extract a coherent translation from the consonantal text. Normally denoting "to extinguish," *dā'ak* in the hiphil (or piel) may have also carried an opposite meaning; cf. *Psalms I*, pp. 158, 265.

axes. qardummōt probably equals Ugar. *qrdm* in the divine title *aliy qrdm.*

hacked. Assuming some such meaning for *sbk* in the hapax legomenon phrase *bisabōk 'ēṣ.*

6. *They cut down.* Consonantal *'tt* may well preserve a verb whose meaning is no longer known. Given the large number of hapax legomena in the psalm, an emendation to *yigde'ū* (LXX), "They cut down," should be discountenanced.

its doors. Vocalizing *petāḥehā* (LXX, Symmachus) for MT *pittūḥehā*, "its carvings."

7. *utterly.* Literally "to the nether world," *lā'āreṣ* is an expression of the superlative, much like *še'ōl*, "Sheol," and *māwet*, "death," which in certain phrases express the superlative. Cf. D. Winton Thomas, "A Consideration of Some Unusual Ways of Expressing the Superlative in Hebrew," in VT 3 (1953), 209–24. Another instance may be present in Ps lxxxix 40, *ḥillaltā lā'āreṣ nizrō*, "You utterly desecrated his crown."

8. *their progeny.* MT *nīnām* is correct; it is the subject of the qal passive verb *śūrāpū*, as explained in the next NOTE. A denominative verb from *nīn is* studied in the third NOTE to Ps lxxiii 17.

be burned. Joining *śūrāpū* to the middle colon which now reads *nīnām yaḥad śūrāpū*, and parsing *śūrāpū* (MT *śārepū*) as the pausal form of the qal passive. Since it expresses design ("They said in their heart"), *śūrāpū* must be a precative perfect; *Psalms I*, pp. 19 ff.

9. *Signs for us.* The suffix of *'ōtōtēnū* is objective; GK, § 135m. The psalmist thinks of his time as characterized by the absence alike of miracles ("signs") and prophecy.

no prophet now. Comparing Ps lxxvii 9, "Have visions from him come to an end?"

the evidence. Reading *'ēdīm* (MT *'ad māh*, "How long?"), the plural of *'ēd*, "witness, testimony, evidence." This reading uncovers an instance of inclusion begun by the first word in the verse, *'ōtōtēnū*, "signs for us," which recalls the juxtaposition in Isa xix 20, *le'ōt ūle'ēd*, "for a sign and for a witness."

has come to us. Vocalizing *'ātānū* (MT *'ittānū*), the verb *'ātā* followed by the dative suffix *-nū.* In *Biblica* 45 (1964), 239, M. Bogaert has identified in Job iii 25 another instance of this verb followed by a dative suffix. Cf. the syntax of synonymous *bā',* "to come," in Pss xxxv 8, xxxvi 12, xliv 18, cix 17, cxix 41.

10. *the adversary . . . the foe.* For the Ugaritic pairing of the root *ṣrr* with *'ōyēb,* see *Psalms I,* pp. 139 ff., and the second NOTE on Ps liv 9.

blaspheme you. Commentators maintain that here and in vs. 18 *yeḥārep* is used absolutely, and while this is formally true, it is in reality incorrect because *yeḥārep* shares the suffix of *šimekā,* "your name," on the principle of the double-duty suffix. Consult the fourth NOTE on vs. 3. By forgoing the suffix, the poet could number ten syllables in the first colon and eleven in the second; had he used it, the first colon would have been top-heavy with twelve syllables.

revile. The verb *yenā'ēṣ* appears in UT, 2 Aqht:I:29–30, *ṭbq lḥt niṣh,* "who will shut the jaws of his detractors."

O Conqueror. Parsing *lāneṣaḥ* as the vocative *lamedh* (see the second NOTE on Ps lxxiii 1) followed by the divine appellative *neṣaḥ.* The standard Hebrew lexicons recognize this appellative in I Sam xv 29, *nēṣaḥ yiśrā'ēl,* but differ in its rendition. Some give "Eminence of Israel," while others prefer "Glory of Israel." In I Sam xv 29 the Vulg. reads *triumphator,* which fits the present context very well since it deals with military foes. In Late Hebrew *nāṣaḥ* means "to conquer." Stylistically, vocative "O Conqueror" matches vocative "O God" in the first colon. From this analysis it becomes quite clear that Ps xliv 24, *lāneṣaḥ,* parallel to vocative *'adōnay,* should now be analyzed in the same manner. Hence translate, "Arise! Why do you sleep, O Lord? / Awake! Be not angry, O Conqueror!" It might be remarked that Ps xliv, like the present poem, is a national lament.

11. *draw back . . . bring near.* The poet depicts Yahweh as idly seated, folding his hands upon his lap.

your left hand. For this definition of *yād, Psalms I,* p. 163, and *Biblica* 47 (1966), 315–16. Another instance of conditioned meaning is commented upon in vs. 16. The first colon ends with *yādekā* and not with the following word, as read by MT. Hence the verse scans into 3+3.

bring your right hand near. Vocalizing a hiphil participle *maqrīb* (MT *miqqereb*). The Ugaritic texts balancing *yd* and *ymn,* as here, are given in the references cited in the preceding NOTE.

your bosom. Reading pausal *ḥēqekā,* since this word ends vs. 11. The double-accusative construction *wīmīnekā maqrīb ḥēqekā* may be compared with UT, 77:27, *aqrbk abh b'l,* "I shall have you approach her father Baal."

12. *Destroy*. Attaching *kallēh* to vs. 12, and parsing it as piel imperative. This transposition leaves vs. 11 with six balanced words in a 3+3 pattern and effects a perfect balancing in vs. 12, which now has eight words that scan into 4 (or 2+2) +4 (or 2+2) meter.

In choosing *kallēh*, the psalmist employs a word that is frequent in mythical texts (see the first NOTE on vs. 13) and hence gravid with mythological overtones. Just as this verb describes the destruction of cosmic foes in mythical contexts, so may God destroy his historical adversaries who have sacked Jerusalem.

O God. If original, the *waw* of *wē'lōhīm* may be parsed as a vocative particle as in Ps lxxv 2 and Jer xi 20. It might be compared with Ar. *wa*, a particle expressing either admiration or grief. Cf. also UT, 52:13, *wšd šd ilm šd aṯrt wrḥm*, "O fields, divine fields, fields of Asherah and the Maiden!"

the kings from the East. Pointing *malkē* (MT *malkī*) *miqqedem*, whose grammar compares with that of, say, Ezek xxi 17, *meqūrē 'el ḥereb* (GK, § 130a), or reading *malkē-m* (with enclitic *mem*) *qedem* "kings of the East." Hummel in JBL 76 (1957), 97, has argued the incorrectness of *malkī*, "my king," rightly noting that nowhere else in the psalm is the first person used.

These "kings from the East" would be the rulers of the the Moabites, Edomites, often called *benē qedem*, "dwellers in the East," and the Ammonites, also an Eastern people.

This new reading bears on the translation and exegesis of Isa xix 11, "How can you say to Pharaoh, 'I am a son of wise men, *ben malkē qedem'?"* Usually translated "a son of ancient kings," *ben malkē qedem* makes much better sense when rendered "a son of Eastern kings," namely, one schooled in Eastern or Edomite wisdom, which was famous in biblical times; cf. Jer xlix 7; Obad 8; I Kings v 10 f.; Job i 3; Prov xxx 1, and Robert Pfeiffer, ZAW 3 (1926), 13–25.

achieve. Balancing imperative *kallēh*, "destroy," the participle *pō'ēl* functions as a surrogate for the imperative. Other instances of this stylistic variation are noticed at Pss ix 14, xvii 14, lxxx 2.

victory. As in Ps liii 7, *yešū'ōt* is a feminine singular form of the Phoenician type. The pervasive military language indicates that "victory" (RSV "salvation") is the nuance borne by *yešū'ōt;* cf. the third NOTE on Ps lxvii 3. In fact, the mention of "victory" here prepares for vss. 13–17, which describe Yahweh's signal triumph over the powers of chaos.

in the middle of the earth. Namely, in Jerusalem which was regarded as the navel of the earth; see *Psalms I*, pp. 142 f., 290. Since, however, Jerusalem stands west of *qedem*, the psalmist may also be alluding in vss. 11–12 to the motif of the four cardinal points discussed in

Psalms I, pp. 291 f. Thus *yādekā*, "left hand," connotes the north, *yemīnekā*, "right hand," the south, *qedem* denotes "east," and if *qereb hā'āreṣ* refers to Jerusalem, we have the fourth direction. And if this explanation is misguided, one can find the missing point of the compass in the first colon of vs. 13, *yām*, "sea," but often denoting "west." This motif recurs in Pss xlviii 3, 8, 11, cxxxix 9–11; Isa xliii 5–6; Job xxiii 8–9; on the last passage consult Pope (The Anchor Bible, vol. 15), NOTE *ad loc.*

13. *It was you.* In his efforts to convince God that he should intervene on behalf of Jerusalem, the psalmist appeals to Yahweh's victory over the forces of chaos and evil before he created the universe. The poet describes this triumph in mythical language taken over from the Canaanites, as we know from Ugaritic literature. UT, 67:I:1–3, contains the following message addressed to the god Baal, who represents the forces of good: *ktmḫṣ ltn bṯn brḥ tkly bṯn 'qltn šlyṭ ḏ šb't rašm*, "When you smite Lotan [=Leviathan], the primeval dragon, when you destroy the twisting dragon, the mighty one of the seven heads." Cf. also UT, 'nt:III:34–44.

It should be remarked that in vss. 13–17 the psalmist uses the independent pronoun *'attāh*, "you," seven times. The subtle artistry of the poet appears more clearly with the knowledge that Yahweh's rival Leviathan had seven heads. Yahweh by himself was able to crush the seven heads of the dragon.

who shattered. The frequent translation of *pōrartā* as "divide" has been influenced by the assumption that the psalmist is here describing the division of waters during the passage through the Sea of Reeds (Exod xiv 21). Thus KJ reads, "Thou didst divide the sea by thy strength," with the marginal note that the Hebrew text reads "break" instead of "divide." The Ugaritic parallels show that vss. 13–14 do not describe historical events but rather primeval happenings. This copious use of mythological motifs does not, however, warrant the conclusion of Folker Willesen in VT 2 (1952), 289–306, that this psalm has no relation whatever to any historical occurrence, but is completely cultic. For him this is not a national psalm of lamentation but originally a ritual lament with a fixed position in the cult drama of the New Year Festival. Willesen unfortunately overlooks those historical psalms, such as Ps lxxxix, which intersperse the description of historical occurrences with mythological motifs. See below on vs. 20.

the Sea with your strength. One catches the overtones when comparing the phrase *be'ozzekā yām* with UT, 68:17, *nhr 'z ym lymk*, "River is strong, Sea does not collapse." Though he may have held his own in the combat with Baal, Sea did collapse under the crushing blows of Yahweh.

who smashed. Here predicated of Yahweh, in Canaanite myth *šib-*

bartā describes the action of Baal in UT, 1 Aqht:114, and of the god Ḥoron in 127:55–56, *yṯbr ḥrn rišk*, "May Ḥoron smash your head!" The biblical phrase *šibbartā rā'šē tannīnī* closely resembles Ugaritic *yṯbr . . . rišk*.

the heads of Tannin. Reading *rā'šē tannīnī* and attaching the final *mem* of MT to the next word. The final vowel of *tannīnī* would be the genitive ending examined in the sixth NOTE on Ps lxv 6. Another example is cited in vs. 20.

The heads of the monster Tannin, another name for Sea, were seven in number as appears from UT, 67:3, *d šb't rašm*, "the one of seven heads," Rev xiii 1, and from the stylistic observation made in the first NOTE to this verse. Mesopotamian cylinder seals also depict seven-headed dragons being attacked by gods; see J. B. Pritchard, *The Ancient Near East in Pictures Relating to the Old Testament* (Princeton, 1954), No. 691, p. 221; Anna Maria Bisi, "L'Idra; Antecedenti figurativi orientali di un mito greco," in *Mélanges de Carthage* (=*Cahiers de Byrsa* X; Paris, 1964–65), pp. 21–42, especially Pl. IV, No. 1.

surging from the sea. Repoint MT *'al hammāyīm*, "upon the waters," to *'ōleh miyyām*, and compare vs. 23, *'ōleh tāmīd*, "the ever-ascending (uproar)." For this reading I am indebted to Liudger Sabottka (private communication). The construing of the plural of majesty *tannīnīm* with singular participle *'ōleh* is *ad sensum* and grammatically unexceptionable.

14. *Leviathan*. Heb. *liwyātān* equals Ugar. *ltn*, "Leviathan," one of the names of the primeval dragons subdued by Yahweh at the dawn of creation.

who gave him. The psalmist plays on the final two syllables of *liwyātān*, which sound like the verb *ytn*, "to give," in Ugaritic, and *tittnennū*. Two other puns are commented upon in vss. 18 and 19. The pairing of perfect *riṣṣaṣtā* "You crushed," with imperfect *tittnennū*, "You gave," exhibits a characteristic of Canaanite poetry commented upon in the first NOTE to Ps liv 7.

to be gathered. A doubtful translation based on reading the infinitive construct *la'ᵃmōl* (MT *lᵉ'ām lᵉ-*), and on the assumption that *'āmal*, "to labor, make," covers the same semantic spectrum as *'āśāh*, "to make," but also "to collect," or *pā'al*, "to make," but in Phoenician also "to collect."

by desert tribes. The defeat of Sea will be so complete that the ocean will become a desert. With this description the psalmist foreshadows the thought of vs. 15b. On *ṣiyyīm*, see the first NOTE to Ps lxxii 9.

16. *caused . . . to be*. Occurring in a description which the psalmist has adapted from Canaanite literature, *hᵃkīnōtā* probably bears the

Ugaritic-Phoenician denotation of *kwn,* "to be, exist," mentioned in the seventh NOTE on Ps lxv 10.

the moon and the sun. The phrase *mā'ōr wāšāmeš* illustrates the poetic usage examined in vs. 11, where *yādekā* denotes specifically "left hand" by reason of being paired with *yᵉmīnekā,* "right hand." In other texts *mā'ōr,* "luminary," may denote either the moon or the sun, but here, because it is conditioned by *šemeš,* it bears the conditioned meaning "moon." Cf. UT, 77:38–39, *ar yrḫ wyrḫ yark,* "Let shine the moon, and may the moon shine for/upon you!"

17. *the zones.* As several commentators have observed, *gᵉbūlōt,* "limits, boundaries," here associated with "summer and winter," specifically refers to the temperature zones.

18. *the insults. Psalms I,* p. 42, collects the evidence for this meaning *zō't.*

the foe who blasphemed you. As noticed in the third NOTE on vs. 2, the psalmist tends to omit the relative pronoun, with the Hebrew reading *'ōyēb ḥērēp.* As noticed in the second NOTE on vs. 10 *'ōyēb,* "foe," shares the suffix of *šimekā,* "your name," in the second colon. As in vs. 10, moreover, metrical considerations led to the omission of the suffix after *ḥērēp.*

19. *to wild beasts.* Reading *ḥayyāt* (MT *ḥayyat*) and explaining the form as feminine absolute ending in *-at;* GK, § 80g, and the second NOTE on Ps lviii 9. Here the singular form expresses a collective idea. Verse 4, *šā'ᵃgū,* usually predicated of lions by biblical writers, provides a clue to the identification of these "wild beasts." Cf. Ps vii 3, "Rescue me lest he tear me (*napšī*) apart like a lion."

those. Literally "souls, persons."

taught by you. Usually rendered "dove" (RSV), or emended to *tōdekā,* "those who praise you," consonantal *twrk* lends itself to a satisfactory parsing according to the principles of Northwest Semitic grammar. Once the suffix *-kā* is identified as a dative employed to express agency, the imperfect passive form of hiphil *hōrāh,* "to teach," comes to light. Hence vocalize *tūrekā,* "taught by you," whose subject is feminine *nepeš,* "those." As in vss. 2 and 18, the poet omits the relative pronoun. The first NOTE on Ps lxiii 11 examines other instances of dative suffixes with passive verbs. Certainly, "those taught by you" (cf. Isa liv 13, *limmūdē yhwh*) makes a fine parallel to "your afflicted." Note the chiastic arrangement of verbs and objects in the two cola: verb-object//object-verb.

The lives. The psalmist continues his punning (see vss. 14 and 18), using *ḥayyat* to denote both "wild beasts" and "lives." The second NOTE on Ps lx 5 points out that the Hebrew poets, when resorting to puns in laments, follow their Canaanite predecessors.

O Conqueror. See the fourth NOTE on vs. 10.

20. *upon your temple*. Reading *l^{e}bîrātekā* (MT *labb^{e}rît kī*), the suffixed form of *bīrāh*, Akk. *birtu*, "citadel, castle," but which specifically denotes "temple" in I Chron xxix 1, 19; see J. M. Myers (The Anchor Bible, vol. 12; New York, 1965). In the Bible *bīrāh* occurs seventeen times, but only in post-Exilic books; this fact and the employment of *bīrāh* by I Chronicles to designate the temple of Jerusalem provide us with a valuable piece of philological evidence for dating this psalm to the post-Exilic period. In the Nabataean inscriptions *byr'* also denotes "temple"; cf. Jean-Hoftijzer, DISO, p. 35, lines 6–7.

the city. Namely, Jerusalem. As in some Phoenician inscriptions, *'ereṣ* here denotes "city" in contrast to *bīrāh*, "the temple," and *n^{e}'ōt*, "the countryside." When describing the open conduits that carried water to a pool within Jerusalem, II Chron xxxii 4 uses the expression *b^{e}tōk hā'āreṣ*, correctly rendered by LXX *dià tēs póleōs*, "through the city." The present writer has studied other biblical texts where *'ereṣ* denotes "city, city-state," in PNWSP, pp. 62 f., and *Biblica* 47 (1966), 280. On II Chron xxxii 4, see W. G. E. Watson, VT 20 (1970), 502, n. 6; *Biblica* 53 (1972), 192–93.

is filled. Detaching the *yod* from MT *ky* and prefixing it to the verb to read *yiml^{e}'ū* (MT *mal^{e}'ū*).

with darkness. Vocalizing *mēḥōšēkī* (MT *maḥ^{a}šakkē*). For the construction *mālē' min*, see Ps cxxvii 5; Jer li 34; Ezek xxxii 6; Eccles i 8. As in vs. 13, *tannīnī*, "Tannin," the final vowel of *ḥōšēkī* is taken as the genitive ending.

the countryside. The poet makes a threefold division: the temple, the city, the countryside.

21. *sit*. With the Syriac, reading *yēšeb* (MT *yāšōb*) and interpreting the action as part of the mourning ritual during which the vanquished sat upon the ground. Cf. Neh i 4, "When I heard these words, I sat down and wept"; Lam ii 10, "The elders of Daughter Zion sit upon the ground and weep." Consult Desmond Beirne, "A Note on Numbers 11, 4," in *Biblica* 44 (1963), 201–3.

This prayer apparently harks back to vs. 3, *hārīmāh p^{e}'amm^{e}kā*, "Raise up your people!"

22. *how fools blaspheme you*. Literally *ḥerpāt^{e}kā minnī nābāl* reads "your blasphemy by fools."

PSALM 75

(lxxv 1–11)

1 *For the director. "Destroy not!" A psalm of Asaph, a song.*

2 We give you thanks, O God,
we give you thanks, O Near One!
Your heavens proclaim your wondrous deeds.
3 Indeed, I will summon the assembly, [2]*
I will judge with equity.
4 When the earth totters, [3]
and all who dwell in it,
It is I who will steady its pillars. *Selah*
5 I say, "O boastful, do not boast, [4]
O wicked, do not raise your horn!
6 Raise not your horn against the Exalted One, [5]
nor speak against the Ancient Mountain!"
7 For he is the Victor from the East and from the West, [6]
he is the Victor from the desert to the mountains.
8 For God is the ruler, [7]
the one who brings down,
and the one who raises up.
9 For in Yahweh's hand is a cup, [8]
and with wine the bowl is filled;
he will draw and pour from this.
Ah, its dregs will they drain,
all the wicked of the earth will drink.
10 But I shall extol the Eternal, [9]
I shall sing to the God of Jacob.
11 I shall break off all the horns of the wicked, [10]
but the horns of the Just One will be exalted.

* Verse numbers in RSV.

NOTES

lxxv. Because of its unusual structure and diversified contents, this psalm cannot be readily classified within the standard types of psalms. In vs. 2 the community on earth, as well as the heavens, give thanks to God for his nearness and, as will be seen from the contents of the poem, for his just governance of the universe. Verses 3–6 are a divine oracle, spoken by a prophet or priest, warning the wicked against the sin of arrogance and of the impending universal judgment. In vss. 7–9 the psalmist describes God's supreme dominion, and depicts a scene of the final judgment, while vs. 10, probably uttered by the king on behalf of the community, is an act of praise. The final verse contains another divine oracle announcing the final discomfiture of the wicked and the triumph of the Just One.

This brief poem, composed in archaic language that resembles the wording of the Song of Hannah (I Sam ii 1–10), contains twelve divine names—hence more titles and names than the number of verses—five of which have cropped up by applying the principles of Northwest Semitic grammar and lexicography.

1. *Destroy not!* Cf. the first NOTE on Ps lvii 1.

2. *O Near One!* Parsing *wᵉqārōb* as the vocative particle examined in the second NOTE on Ps lxxiv 12 followed by the divine title *qārōb*, cited in the first NOTE on Ps lxix 19. Cf. Ps cxix 151, *qārōb 'attāh yhwh*, "You are near, O Yahweh," and Jer xii 2, xxiii 23. In the Koran, *qarīb* and *'aqrab* figure among the numerous divine titles; cf. Y. Moubarac, "Les noms, titres et attributs divins dans le Coran," in *Muséon* 68 (1955), 94–135; 325–68, especially p. 340.

The point of this title is to refute the deistic belief of the wicked that God is too distant to take much interest in human behavior; cf. *Psalms I*, pp. 62, 69.

Your heavens. The problems created by *šᵉmekā*, "your name," can be resolved by the pointing *šāmekā*, "your heavens." The resultant sentiment evokes Ps xix 2, "The heavens are proclaiming the glory of God."

3. *Indeed.* Identifying *kī* as the emphatic introduction of the divine oracle; cf. the fourth NOTE on Ps liv 7.

I will summon. For this sense of *'eqqaḥ,* see Num xxiii 11; Judg xi 5; I Sam xvi 11, and BDB, p. 543b 6.

the assembly. Customarily translated "appointed time," *mō'ēd* bears rather the meaning discussed at Ps lxxiv 4. The oracle speaks of the final judgment when all men will be summoned before the divine tribunal. Cf. Ps lxv 3–4; Joel iii 12; Hab ii 3.

with equity. In distributive justice, giving equitable punishment to the wicked and vindication to the just; cf. Pss vii 7–9, xcviii 9. Plural *mēšārīm* probably occurs in the Ugaritic personal name *bn mšrm.*

4. *totters.* Zorell's (ZLH, p. 416a) discussion of the root *mūg,* "to tremble, totter," is quite superior to that of BDB. The interpretation of this metaphor is linked to that of Ps xi 3, "When (the) foundations are being torn down, what is the Just One doing?" The undermining of justice on earth connotes the undermining of the earth's foundations. Cf. also Ps lxxxii 5.

It is I. As in vs. 3, the independent pronoun adds emphasis. The use of *'ᵃnī* in vs. 3 and *'ānōkī* here led Briggs, CECBP, II, p. 164, to comment that the full form probably betrays another hand. This assessment, however, is overtaken not only by biblical usage (e.g., Job xxxiii 9), but also by Ugaritic practice. Numerous texts (e.g., UT, 49, 51, 67, Aqht) manifest both forms, sometimes in the same couplet; e.g., UT, 51:IV:59–60, *p'db an 'nn aṯrt p'db ank aḫd ulṯ,* "Am I to act as a lackey of Asherah, and am I to act like the holder of a trowel?" Cf. UT, § 6.2.

who will steady. As in vs. 9, *māsak,* "will draw," the perfect form *tikkantī* expresses future action by reason of its balance with future forms *'eqqaḥ* and *'ešpōṭ* in vs. 3, and in vs. 4 with the present participle *nᵉmōgīm.* The root of *tikkantī* occurs in I Sam ii 3, *wᵉlē'ōn tōkᵉnū* (MT *wᵉlō' nitkᵉnū*) *'ᵃlīlōt,* "And the Victor is the weigher (i.e., he holds in equilibrium) of actions." See the second NOTE on vs. 7.

its pillars. Cf. Ps xxiv 2; Job xxxviii 4, and I Sam ii 8, "For the pillars of the earth are Yahweh's, and on them he has set the world."

5. *O boastful.* Analyzing *lahōlᵉlīm* into vocative *lamedh* (see *Psalms I,* Ps xvi 2, and VT 16 [1966], 310), and the substantive whose pagan connotations are commented upon at Pss v 6 and lxxiii 3.

O wicked. See preceding NOTE.

your horn. qāren requires no suffix since it is part of the body; see the third NOTE on Ps lvi 8. The psalmist curiously employs all three numbers of *qeren:* here and in vs, 6 the form is singular, while in vs. 11 we find both the dual *qarnē* and the plural *qar*e*nōt*. In our verse, the singular form was probably dictated by metrical considerations, each colon numbering eleven syllables. A dual or plural form would have upset this balance by adding an extra syllable to the second colon.

As is clear from the parallelism, "to raise one's horn" is figurative for "to become arrogant."

6. *Raise not . . . against the Exalted One.* The phrase *'al tārīmū lammārōm* contains the figure of speech known as theological word-play, a subject examined in *Psalms I*, pp. XXIX, 17, 113, 285. Cf. also the second NOTE on Ps lxiv 9, and Pss xcvii 7, cxxxix 24, cxl 9–10, cxlvii 6; Job xxii 25.

the Exalted One. See *Psalms I*, pp. 44 f.

nor. Negative *'al* in the first colon also negatives the second colon; *Psalms I*, p. 58, and the third NOTE on Ps lix 16. Cf. also Ps cxxi 1–2; Isa lxiii 13–14; Jer xxii 30; Job xxii 11; Prov xxvii 24. A new instance of the double-duty negative appears in Ps xc 3.

speak. Or "charge," i.e., like a bull. *Psalms I*, p. 9, discusses some cognate meanings of *dibbēr*.

the Ancient Mountain. Psalms I, pp. 45 and 118, 191, give differing translations of this phrase, but that found on pp. 118, 191 seems favored by the fact that many of the ancient versions (Aquila, Quinta of Origen, *Juxta Hebraeos*, Syr., Targ.) understand *'ātāq* as an attribute of *ṣawwār*, "neck," and not as a modifier of the verb *t*e*dabb*e*rū*, "speak." With the LXX and Vulg. I would read *ṣū'r* (with intrusive *aleph*), a divine appellative cited in *Psalms I*, pp. 105, 118, 191. By reading the adjective *'attīq* (*Juxta Hebraeos* reads *cervice veteri*, "with an old neck"), as in Ps xxxi 19, we recognize in *ṣū'r 'attīq* the semantic equivalent of Isa xxvi 4, *ṣūr 'ōlāmīm*, "the Everlasting Mountain," or if one prefers, "the Rock of Ages." Cf. Job ix 5, *hamma'tīq hārīm*, rendered by LXX, "who makes the mountains grow old," and xiv 18. The resultant parallelism between *mārōm*, which literally means "height," and *ṣū'r*, literally "mountain, rock," is unexceptionable.

As in Ps xxxi 19, the psalmist seems to be engaging in a theological wordplay on *'attīq* and *'ātāq*, "arrogant," because the clause *t*e*dabb*e*rū b*e*ṣū'r 'attīq* is reminiscent of Ps xciv 4, *y*e*dabb*e*rū 'ātāq*, "They speak arrogantly."

7. *For. kī* evidently indicates the transition from the words of the divine oracle to those of the psalmist who gives the reasons why insolence is foolhardy.

the Victor. Vocalizing *lē'* (MT *lō'*), an adjective or stative participle of the frequent Northwest Semitic root *l'y*, "to prevail," and comparing the Hebrew feminine personal name *lē'āh*. See *Psalms I*, pp. 46, 144, and more recently *Biblica* 47 (1966), 408, with bibliography. Another divine title manifesting a similar stative formation is *'ēm*, "the Awe-Inspirer" (contrast the active form *'āyōm*, "dreadful," much like Ugar. *ib*, "foe," and Heb. *'ōyēb*) in Num xii 6, *šimeʻū-nā' dibrē 'ēm* (MT *debāräy 'im*) *yihyeh nebī'akem yhwh*, "Listen carefully to the words of the Awe-Inspirer; Yahweh will be your prophet." Cf. also Lam v 22.

The close association of the divine titles *ṣū'r 'atīq*, "the Ancient Mountain," and *lē'*, "the Victor," may serve to clarify Job xxxvi 5, *hen 'ēl kabbīr welē'* (MT *welō'*) *yim'as kabbīr kōaḥ lēb*, "Though El is the Old One, he is still the Victor; the Old One detests stubbornness."

East . . . West . . . desert . . . mountains. The motif of the four cardinal points, considered in the fourth NOTE to Ps lxxiv 12.

from the East . . . from the West. Comparing dialectal Phoenician Panamuwa 13, *mn mwq' šmš w'd m'rb*, "from the East even to the West."

from the desert. Namely, from the southern quarter.

to the mountains. Parsing *hārīm* as an accusative of place in answer to the question whither; GK, § 118d-f, and UT, 2059:10–11, *any kn dt likt mṣrm*, "The sturdy ship which you sent to Egypt." Here the poet has in mind the mountains of Lebanon, or the North, for as Briggs has remarked (*ad loc.*), if the author lived in middle Palestine or Galilee, "the mountains" would be the North. This analysis of the phrase *mimmidbār* (MT *mimmidbar*) *hārīm* entails a new translation of a phrase in Deut xi 24, "Every place on which the sole of your foot treads shall be yours; your territory shall be *min hammidbār wehallebānōn min hannāhār nehar perāt weʻad hayyām hā'aḥarōn yihyeh gebūlekem*, "From the desert right to Lebanon (RSV 'from the wilderness and Lebanon'), and from the River, the river Euphrates, right to the western sea shall be your territory."

8. *the ruler.* Consult *Psalms I*, p. 13, first NOTE on Ps ii 10 for this denotation of *šōpēṭ*. In Ps vii 12–13 one again finds *šōpēṭ* associated with *lē'*, "the Victor," as well as in UT, 51:IV–V:43–44, *mlkn aliy[n] b'l ṯpṭn win d'lnh*, "Our king is Victor Baal, our ruler; there is none above him."

the one who. Parsing *zeh*, not as the indefinite pronoun, but rather as the determinative-relative discussed in *Psalms I*, p. 152, and in the second NOTE on Ps lxviii 9.

brings down. Namely, to Sheol, the realm of the dead. As remarked in *Psalms I*, pp. 46 f., the divine appellative *lē'*, "the Victor," crops up in a surprising number of texts dealing with questions of life and death. Being the supreme ruler who has conquered death (cf. Hab i

10), Yahweh has absolute dominion over life and death. Cf. I Sam ii 6, "Yahweh kills and restores to life, he brings down to Sheol and raises up," and Ps cxlvii 6, *mašpīl rešā'īm 'adē 'āreṣ,* "who brings the wicked down to the nether world." *Psalms I,* p. 106, documents *'ereṣ,* "nether world."

the one who. See above the second NOTE to vs. 8.

raises up. That is, from the gates of the underworld. Cf. Ps ix 14, *merōmemī* (our text, *yārīm*) *miššaʿarē māwet,* "Raise me up from the gates of Death."

9. *a cup.* Consult the second NOTES on Pss xvi 5 (*Psalms I*) and lx 5. The metaphor of God's cup of wrath given to the wicked to drink is quite common in the OT; cf. Isa li 17 ff., Jer xxv 15 ff., xlix 12 ff.

the bowl. Pointing *ḥōmer* (MT *ḥāmar*), and equating it with Ugar. *ḫmr,* "wine-bowl, vat." The vocalizing is suggested by *ḥōmer,* "clay, mortar," which in Jer xviii 4, 6, specifically refers to the material from which vessels are made. Though most Ugaritic specialists define *ḫmr* as "wine" (cf. most recently C. H. Gordon, *Ugarit and Minoan Crete* [New York, 1966], p. 49), a re-examination of the relevant texts reveals that "bowl" or "vat" is the correct meaning. Cf. UT, 'nt:I: 15–17, *alp kd yqḥ bḫmr rbt ymsk bmskh,* "A thousand pitchers he took from his bowl, ten thousand he drew from his vat"; 52:6 *šty bḫmr yn ay,* "Drink from the bowl any wine!"; 1081:22, *ḫmrm ṯṯ krm*[*m*] is unclear, but the plural form favors "vats" over "wines," which normally appears in the singular. Deut xxxii 14c, *dam 'ēnāb tišteh ḥōmer* (MT *ḥāmer*), "The blood of the grape you will drink by the bowl."

with wine. yayin is an accusative of material preceding the verb, a stylistic trait of the psalmists noticed in *Psalms I* at Ps v 10. Ps civ 15 supplies the most instructive parallel: *weyayin yeśammaḥ lebab 'enōš,* "And with wine he gladdens the heart of man."

is filled. mālē', which forms an assonance with the last word of the first colon *yahweh,* ends the second colon, which becomes a three-beat colon balancing the first and third three-beat cola.

he will draw. Reading the verb *māsak* (MT *mesek*), which, as pointed out by Graetz in the last century and endorsed by Zorell, ZLH, p. 452a, denotes "to draw, pour." Ditto for Ugaritic where it is parallel to *yqḥ,* "he takes," in UT, 'nt:I:16–17, cited in second NOTE to this verse. Consult UHP, p. 64, and Scott (The Anchor Bible, vol. 18), § 10, which renders Prov ix 2, *māsekāh yēnāh,* "She has poured out her wine." As in vs. 4, *tikkantī,* "I will steady," the perfect form *māsak,* in a series of verbs expressing present or future time, refers to a future event.

and pour. Deriving *yaggēr* from *nāgar,* "to pour out," as in II Sam xiv 14 and Lam iii 49.

from this. The antecedent of *zeh* being masculine *ḥōmer*, "bowl," and not feminine *kōs*, as explained by many commentators. Notice the assonance in the final words of the three cola: *yahweh, mālē', zeh.*

Ah. Vocalizing *'ēk* (the defective spelling is noteworthy; MT *'āk*). Compare Jon ii 5, where the Masoretes again confound *'ak* and *'ēk*, and GB, p. 34a. Used either as an exclamation of lamentation or of satisfaction, *'ēk* here expresses the gratification of the just over the imminent and deserved punishment of the wicked.

its dregs. The antecedent of the feminine suffix in *šᵉmārehā* being *kōs*, "cup," which is usually feminine.

the wicked of the earth. The poet voices his belief in universalism (all men and nations are governed by God); see the first NOTE on Ps lxvi 4. All the inhabitants of the world who defy God must answer for their insolence on the day of judgment.

will drink. Many commentators are wont to drop *yištū*, but this deletion disrupts the meter of vs. 9 which numbers five 3-beat cola that are finely balanced.

10. *I shall extol.* Since hiphil *'aggīd* normally governs an accusative, I propose a redivision of consonants to read *'ᵃgaddēl*, "I shall extol." Cf. Ps lxix 31, *wa'ᵃgaddᵉlennū bᵉtōdāh*, "and extol it with hymns of thanksgiving." Cf. *Biblica* 45 (1964), 397, and F. M. Cross, Jr., in HTR 55 (1962), 234.

the Eternal. Attaching the initial *lamedh* of MT *lᵉ'ōlām* to the preceding word, and identifying *'ōlām* as the divine appellative discussed in *Psalms I*, pp. 151, 153. The psalmist evokes the tradition, preserved in Gen xxi 33, which names the God of Abraham *'ēl 'ōlām*, "El the Eternal." In our text we have further proof that some of God's archaic titles were lost on the Masoretes. The title *'ōlām* antedates written biblical traditions, being found in a Sinai (Serabit el Ḫadem) Canaanite inscription that dates to the period 1550–1450 B.C. F. M. Cross, Jr., in HTR 55 (1962), 238 ff., has recognized there the phrase *'l ḏ 'lm*,

"El, the One of Eternity," on which the new readings and translations in Pss xii 8 and xxiv 6 (*Psalms I*) are partially based. Ps xxiv 6, it might be noted, associates "the One of Eternity" with "the Presence of Jacob."

the God of Jacob. Since the image of the bull's horns recurs throughout this psalm, the toned-down title *'elōhē ya'aqōb* has probably displaced on older reading *'abīr ya'aqōb,* "the Bull of Jacob" (Gen xlix 24; Isa i 24, xlix 26, lx 16; Ps cxxxii 2, 5).

11. *I shall break off.* The speaker remains the psalmist, who introduces himself in vs. 10 with *wa'anī,* "But I." With *'agaddēl,* "I shall extol," *'agaddēa',* "I shall break off," forms an effective theological wordplay. The psalmist will see to it that the Just God triumph over the powers of evil!

horns . . . horns. The use of dual *qarnē* in the first colon but plural *qarnōt* in the second is very curious; the latter perhaps implies more than two horns.

the Just One. The poet apparently contrasts plural *rešā'īm,* "the wicked," with singular *ṣaddīq,* who is God himself. To reward the just and punish the sinners constitutes one of the Supreme Ruler's (*ṣōpēṭ* in vs. 8) principal duties. Hence the psalmist's legitimate expostulation in Ps xi 3, "When (the) foundations are being torn down, what is the Just One (*ṣaddīq*) doing?" Being the psalm's final word, *ṣaddīq* forms an inclusion with vs. 3, also spoken by God, *'anī mēšārīm 'ešpōṭ,* "I shall judge with equity."

PSALM 76

(lxxvi 1–13)

1 *For the director; with stringed instruments. A psalm of Asaph, a song.*

2 In Judah God has shown himself,
his name is great in Israel.
3 His covert was in Salem, [2]*
and his lair in Zion.
4 There with his thunderbolts he shattered the bow, [3]
shield, and sword, and weapons of war. *Selah*
5 O Luminous One, you are majestic! [4]
6 The mountains of the Lion they tried to plunder, [5]
but the warriors slept their last sleep,
and were found no more;
Soldiers with their prowess perished.
7 At your roar, O God of Jacob, [6]
both chariot and horse lay stunned.
8 You, you alone strike terror, [7]
and who will be able to face your fury,
your wrath of old?
9 From heaven you will sound the sentence, [8]
the earth will shudder and fall still;
10 When you arise for the judgment, O God, [9]
to save all the meek of the earth, *Selah*
11 Truly will they praise you [10]
for your rage with other men;
The survivors of your rage will encircle you.
12 Make and fulfill your vows to Yahweh your God, [11]
let all those around him
bring gifts to the One Who Sees,
13 Who fathoms the mind of princes, [12]
who should be feared by the kings of the earth.

* Verse numbers in RSV.

NOTES

lxxvi. A song of Zion, resembling Pss xlvi and xlviii, which celebrates God's victory over the nations. The psalm moves on two levels: it hymns the destruction through divine intervention of historical foes who sought to plunder Jerusalem, and at the same time announces the eschatological defeat of the nations at the last judgment. Though presenting some difficulties, the text does not deserve Gunkel's description, "repeatedly very corrupt." In fact, several (vss. 3, 6, 7) of the obscurities are cleared away by the recognition of a simple metaphor.

2. *has shown himself.* Reading niphal perfect *nōda'* for MT niphal participle *nōdā'*, and comparing Ps xlviii 4. Both these texts allude to an historic occasion which cannot be determined with certitude.

3. *His covert . . . his lair.* The observation of Briggs, CECBP, II, p. 166, that the poet probably intended these terms in a literal sense, conceiving of God as the Lion of Judah, is sustained by the reading proposed in vs. 5. A number of texts liken God to a lion: Ps l 22; Isa xxxi 4; Jer xxv 38; Hos v 14, xiii 7; Job x 16, xvi 9; Lam iii 10.

Salem. An ancient name of Jerusalem (Gen xiv 18; Heb vii 1–2).

4. *with his thunderbolts.* Parsing *rišepēy* as an accusative of means; the suffix of consonantal *ršpy* is that of the third person masculine singular following a plural substantive, discussed in the seventh NOTE on Ps lxviii 11. See below on Ps lxxviii 9. The lexicons recognize *rešāpīm*, "thunderbolts," in Ps lxxviii 48.

This interpretation calls for a reconsideration of the cognate verse Ps xlvi 10, "The bow he breaks, and snaps the spear, the shields he burns with fire." In view of our passage and the specific denotation of "lightning" that *'ēš* bears in Pss xviii 13, 14, cxlviii 3; Exod ix 23, 24, etc., one may propose rendering *'agālōt yiśrōp bā'ēš*, "the war chariots he burns with lightning." See the second NOTE on vs. 7 for *'agālōt*, "war chariots."

weapons of war. Literally "war," *milḥāmāh* by metonymy here denotes "weapons of war," as long admitted by numerous scholars; Zorell, ZLH, p. 441a, cites Isa iii 25, xxi 15, xxii 2; Hos i 7, ii 18, as well as our passage. See *Psalms I*, p. 167, for similar instances of metonymy in Ps xxvii 3.

5. *O Luminous One.* *nā'ōr* evidently harks back to vs. 4, "his thunderbolts." Being enveloped with light, God from time to time makes his light flash upon the earth.

majestic. Detaching the initial letter of *mēharerē* and joining it to *'addīr* to read the plural of excellence *'addīrīm,* as in Pss xvi 3, xciii 4, and Judg v 25.

6. *The mountains.* For the reading *harᵉrē,* see preceding NOTE.

of the Lion. Critics usually ascribe MT *ṭārep,* "prey, booty," to a blunder on the part of the poet who misinterpreted the phrase *harᵉrē 'ad,* "eternal mountains" (Gen xlix 26; Deut xxxiii 15; Hab iii 6) as "mountains of prey," confusing the homonyms *'ad,* "eternity," and *'ad,* "prey." This is possible, but given the metaphor of the lion in vs. 3, *sukkō,* "covert," and *mᵉ'ōnātō,* "lair," which properly denote the den of a lion, a simpler solution would be the repointing *ṭōrēp,* "the render," a poetic designation of the lion alluded to in vs. 3. In attacking the mountains of Judah, the pagan foes were in reality invading the mountains of the Lion of Judah. Biblical poets predicate *ṭārap* of God in Ps l 22; Hos v 14, vi 1; Job xvi 9, while Job xxxviii 39–40, in collocating *ṭerep, mᵉ'ōnōt,* and *sukkāh,* shows that *ṭōrēp* in our verse does not derive from the psalmist's incompetence.

they tried to plunder. The respectable number of aphel forms in Ugaritic and Hebrew (see the first NOTE on Ps lv 3) makes it unlikely that the usual description of *'eštōlālū* (MT *'eštōlᵉlū*) as an Aramaism is correct; see, e.g., Bauer and Leander, *Historische Grammatik,* p. 439p. At a very early period Hebrew employed verbal forms with both *hē* and *aleph* preformatives.

slept their last sleep. The expression *nāmū šᵉnātām* recalls the parallelism of UT, Krt:31–32, *bm bkyh wyšn bdm'h nhmmt,* "While he weeps, there is sleep; as he cries, slumber." Scholars commonly agree that *yšn,* "sleep," and *nhmmt,* "slumber," answer to biblical *yāšēn* and *nūm.*

and were found no more. Vocalizing qal passive *mūṣā'ū* (MT *māṣᵉ'ū*) and reading *wᵉlō' mūṣā'ū* as an independent clause. D. N. Freedman, ZAW 64 (1952), 191, studies the qal passive of this verb in Gen ii 20, and in *Biblica* 47 (1966), 278, the present writer proposes the same analysis of the form in Eccles ix 15. Cf. Ps xxxvii 36, "But he passed away and, lo, he was no more; I sought him but he could not be found (*nimṣā'*)," and see BDB, p. 594a.

their prowess. For this nuance of *yᵉdēhem,* consult BDB, p. 390a; Ps lxxviii 42; Exod xiv 31, and G. Rinaldi, *Bibbia e Oriente* 6 (1964), 246.

perished. Usually deleted because it overloads the verse and contributes little to the sense, consonantal *kl* acquires a *raison d'être* when pointed *kālū. Psalms I,* p. 58, proposes to find a similar instance of defective spelling of *kālū* in Ps ix 18, and the third NOTE to Ps lxxiv 8 also recommends this analysis.

7. *At your roar.* Customarily translated "your rebuke," *ga'ᵃrātekā,* in the context of comparing God to a lion, rather bears this meaning,

documented in *Psalms I*, p. 110. As in Pss xviii 16, civ 7, Yahweh's roar refers to the thunder, so that this verse resumes the thought of vs. 4 mentioning the divine thunderbolts as the weapons of destruction. Though no biblical text predicates *g'r* of a lion, the hippiatric text UT, 56:23, *k yg'r* [*ssw*], "If the horse roars," asserts it of a horse.

chariot and horse. rekeb wesūs juxtaposes the two roots juxtaposed in UT, Krt:128, *ṯlṯ sswm mrkbt*, "three horses, a chariot." If MT *rekeb* is correct (many would read *rōkēb*, "rider"), the dispute concerning Ps xlvi 10, *'agālōt*, is settled favoring the translation "war chariots" over "shields."

8. *your fury*. Namely, the fury of a lion. *Psalms I*, pp. 55, 97, 113 f., 207, investigates this meaning of *pānīm*. Compare Ps xvii 9 where *pānīm*, describes the "fury" of pursuing wolves.

your wrath of old. Stands in apposition with *pānekā*, "your fury." The poet probably inverted the word order (one would expect *'appekā mē'āz*) to avoid the harsh sequence *lepānekā 'appekā*. Here the psalmist asserts that God's wrath on the day of judgment will resemble his primeval fury when he annihilated the monsters representing the forces of chaos (Ps lxxiv 13–15; Isa li 9–10, etc.). The frequent emendation of *mē'āz* to *mē'ōz*, it may be remarked, is invalidated by the observation that this expression (in dialectal form) appears in Ps xlvi 2, a poem belonging to the same literary genus as Ps lxxvi.

9. *you will sound*. Parsing *hišma'tā* as prophetic perfect (GK, § 106n; Joüon, GHB, § 112h), referring to the judgment of the latter days.

10. *When you arise*. Suffixless *beqūm* is determined by the suffix of vs. 11, *tōdekkā*, "will they praise you." Without this suffix, vs. 10a numbers eight syllables, while vs. 10b counts nine; had the poet used it, the first colon would have ten syllables, thus making it too long for the second.

all the meek. Namely, the humbly patient or submissive, as under provocation from others. Not only those of Israel, but also of the whole world. Other expressions of universalism are noted at Pss lxvi 4, lxviii 4, lxxv 9.

11. *Truly*. Parsing *kī* as the emphatic particle, and consulting the first NOTE on Ps lxxv 3.

will they praise you. The subject of *tōdekkā*, "will they praise you," being the collective expression *kol 'anwē 'ereṣ*, "all the meek of the earth." Cf. Jer xii 4; Joel i 20; Job xii 12, and GK, § 145k–1.

your rage with other men. A conjectural translation based on the explanation of *ḥamat 'ādām* as an accusative of cause stating the reason; e.g., Isa vii 25, "You will not be able to go there *yir'at šāmīr*, for fear of briars." Cf. GK, § 118l. As in Ps lxxiii 5, *'ādām* refers to "other men"; see BDB, p. 9a–b. In a number of texts (e.g., Isa xxvii 4, lxiii 5), *ḥēmāh,* "rage," is predicated of God. Here it denotes his fury with sinners at the last judgment.

will encircle you. The verb *taḥgōr* shares the accusative suffix of *tōdekkā,* "will they praise you," by reason of the double-duty suffix, investigated in *Psalms I,* pp. 17 ff. The saved will form the heavenly court around Yahweh. In the next verse the worshipers of Yahweh are termed *s^ebîbāyw,* "those around him," and it may be significant that in Ps lxxxix 8 the members of the celestial court are called *s^ebîbāyw.*

12. *Make and fulfill your vows.* The Hebrew text juxtaposes the two imperatives, "Make your vows, and fulfill them," and follows with the two divine names, "Yahweh your God." Cf. Pss xxvii 2, xxxv 23, cxliv 7; Isa xxv 12, li 17; Jer xiii 18; Job x 21. This is also a stylistic argument against the deletion of *yhwh,* recommended by some critics.

The psalmist invites the Israelites to manifest their gratitude for their deliverance from the invaders by fulfilling their vows and bringing gifts.

vows . . . gifts. The arrangement of *nid^arū* and *šay* in the same verse contributes to the interpretation of UT, 117:14, *bm ṯy ndr,* "With a gift it was vowed."

all those around him. In contrast to the prevailing exegesis, I take *s^ebîbāyw* as referring to the Israelites, not to the surrounding nations. Those who surround Yahweh on earth will form his heavenly entourage.

bring gifts. Comparing *yōbîlū šay* with Ps lxviii 38; Isa xviii 7, and Gen xlix 10, as read and explained by W. L. Moran in *Biblica* 39 (1958), 405–16.

to the One Who Sees. Reading *l^emō rō'ē* for unexplained MT *lammōrā',* and comparing the balance between *la* (*layhwh*) and *l^emō* with UT, Krt:101–3, *yb'r lṯn aṯṯh lm nkr mddth,* "Let him lead his wife to another, to a stranger his well-beloved." See Pss xc 8, cxxix 3; Job xxxiii 22; *Psalms I,* p. 164, and the second NOTE on Ps lviii 5.

For the appellative *rō'ē,* cf. Gen xvi 13, *'ēl r^o'î,* "El the Seer," and *rō'î;* Jer xx 12, *rō'eh k^elāyōt wālēb,* "the One Who Sees the heart and mind"; Job xxii 12, as pointed and translated in *Psalms I,* p. 62.

The point of this appellative, which forms an inclusion with vs. 2, *nōda',* "show" (the verbs *yāda',* "he knows," and *rā'āh,* "he sees," are often found in parallelism), seems to be that the Lion of Judah keeps careful watch over his people and comes to their aid when they are threatened.

13. *Who fathoms.* Deriving much-disputed *yibṣōr* from *bāṣar,* "to inspect, observe, assay," Ar. *baṣira,* identified by B. Duhm in Jer vi 27, *m^ebaṣṣēr,* "assayer" (see GB, p. 110b), and now attested in UT, 2067:3, *bṣr abn špšyn,* "Shapshiyan, the assayer of stones," and 3 Aqht:obv:31, *ybṣr ḥbl diy*[*m*], "The flock of vultures peers down." Cf. Aistleitner, WuS, p. 57, No. 564, and Driver, CML, p. 164a. Of course, this

etymology neatly accords with the proposed reading *rō'ē* in the preceding verse.

princes. Briggs' assertion that *nāgīd* appears nowhere else in the Psalter may need modification in view of the reading submitted at Pss liv 5 and lxxxvi 14.

who should be feared. Because God can read their thoughts.

PSALM 77

(lxxvii 1–21)

1 *For the director, according to Jeduthun. A psalm of Asaph.*

2 With my voice, O God of gods,
I desperately cry;
To my voice, O God of gods,
give ear at once.
3 When I implore my God, [2]*
and seek my Lord,
His hand attacks at night
and does not slacken;
His mind refuses to relent.
4 I think of God and groan, [3]
I speak and my spirit faints. *Selah*
5 My eyes are accustomed to vigils, [4]
I pace the floor and do not recline.
6 I consider the days of old, [5]
I remember the years long past.
7 Through the night I play the lyre, [6]
with my heart I commune
That my spirit might be healed.
8 Will the Lord be angry forever, [7]
and no longer show favor again?
9 Has his kindness ceased forever, [8]
have visions from him come to an end?
10 Have the inmost parts of God dried up, [9]
or his bosom shrunk in his anger? *Selah*
11 Perhaps his sickness is this: [10]
the right hand of the Most High has withered.
12 I will recite your magnificent deeds, [11]
indeed will I recite your marvels of old;

* Verse numbers in RSV.

13 And I will number your works completely, [12]
and speak of your mighty deeds.
14 O God, your dominion is over the holy ones: [13]
What god is greater than you, O God?
15 Come, O God, worker of miracles, [14]
manifest your strength among the peoples.
16 With your powerful arm [15]
redeem the sons of Jacob and Joseph. *Selah*
17 When the waters saw you, O God, [16]
When the waters saw you, they trembled,
even the depths shook with fear.
18 The massed clouds streamed with water, [17]
the heaven echoed your voice,
and your arrows shot back and forth.
19 Your pealing thunder was in the dome of heaven, [18]
your lightning bolts lit up the world,
the nether world quaked and shook.
20 Upon the sea was your passage, [19]
your train upon the cosmic waters,
and so your heels were not seen.
21 Lead your people like sheep, [20]
by the hand of a Moses and an Aaron.

Notes

lxxvii. A psalm of mixed type; vss. 2–13 are a lamentation in which the psalmist bewails a miserable situation. He does not specify the nature of the misfortune, but it would seem that he laments not his own reverses but rather the abandonment of his nation by God. Verses 14–20 are a hymn of praise recounting God's glorious deeds of the past as motivation for his intervention in the present; see the first NOTE on Ps lxxiv 13. Verses 17–20, however, seem to be an ancient poem inserted into the psalm; these are composed of tricola whereas most of the other verses are bicola.

As may be gathered from the philological notes, the language is very archaic throughout; in addition, vss. 17–20 exhibit a marked resemblance to Ps xviii 8–16, while vss. 14–16 recall Exod xv 11–13. Thus a tenth-century date for this composite psalm does not seem unlikely; see the first NOTE on vs. 17.

1. *Jeduthun*. The name of a member of a musical guild instituted by King David. Consult the first NOTE on Ps lxii 1.

2. *With my voice. qōlī* is an accusative of means preceding its verb; see the fourth NOTE on Ps lxxv 9. The urgency of the psalmist's plea in Hebrew can hardly be reproduced in English; *qōlī* is emphatic by position, the intensity of the verb is accentuated by the *waw* of reinforcement which precedes it, while the addressee, *'ēl 'elōhīm,* stands between these highly charged words.

O God of gods. Reading *'ēl* (MT *'el*) *'elōhīm,* literally "God of gods," and consulting the first NOTES on Pss l 1 and lxii 2. In vs. 14 we find again the components of this divine title, while in Ps cxviii 28 and Job v 8 its elements are counterpoised in the parallel cola. The versions, both ancient and modern, are innocent of this composite name in our verse where it stands in the vocative case.

I desperately cry. As recognized by Leo Prijs, BZ 8 (1964), 107, the *waw* preceding the verb *'eṣ'āqāh* emphasizes it; hence the final position of the verb, as often with emphatic *kī* and *lamedh.* See *Psalms I,* pp. 24 f., and the second and fifth NOTES on Ps lxii 5.

In the pre-Ugaritic stage of Hebrew grammatical studies, the observation of Briggs, CECBP, II, p. 176, is quite understandable: "*Waw* with Qal cohort. not capable of good explanation. *Waw,* not in G (LXX), J (*Juxta Hebraeos*), is doubtless txt. err."

O God of gods. Again reading *'ēl* (MT *'el*) *'elōhīm,* and parsing it as vocative; consult above the second NOTE on vs. 2.

give ear. Grammarians puzzle over MT *ha'azīn,* which they describe as an abnormal pointing of the hiphil perfect *he'ezīn;* cf. Bauer and Leander, *Historische Grammatik,* p. 348k. Parsed as hiphil imperative, *ha'azīn* presents no problem of punctuation. The direct object of the imperative is *qōlī,* "my voice."

at once. Explaining the *waw* preceding imperative *ha'azīn* as emphatic; see the third NOTE on this verse. This grammatical analysis results in two three-beat cola, each of which contains ten syllables. The final word *'ēlāy,* "to me," belongs to the next verse. Compare Ps cxlii 2, *qōlī 'ēl* (MT *'el*) *yhwh 'ez'āq qōlī 'ēl* (MT *'el*) *yhwh 'etḥannān,* "With my voice, O God Yahweh, I cry; with my voice, O God Yahweh, I plead for mercy," and Ps xxxix 13, *wešaw'ātī ha'azīnāh 'ēl,* "And give ear to my cry, O El."

3. *When.* According to August Fischer, ZDMG 56 (1902), 800–9, *beyōm* should be translated "when" in some seventy biblical passages. See also Dahood, *Biblica* 33 (1952), 213, on Eccles xii 3, and for Ugar. *bym,* "when," Albright in BASOR 94 (1944), 35, n. 39.

I implore. Pointing *ṣartī* (MT *ṣārātī*) from the root *ṣw/yr,* preserved in *ṣīr,* "messenger" (perhaps originally "beckoner"), and in two passages of Jeremiah: iv 31, *kī qōl keḥōlāh šāma'tī ṣārāh kemabkīrāh,* "Ah, a cry I have heard like a woman's in labor, / A screaming like hers who is bearing her first" (Bright, The Anchor Bible, vol. 21). To arrive at the translation "a screaming," Bright emends *ṣārāh* to **ṣeraḥ*, but such an emendation now becomes unnecessary. Here the parallelism between *qōl*, "voice," and *ṣārāh*, "implore," resembles the association of *qōlī* and *ṣarfī* in vss. 2–3 of our psalm. The probable existence of such a root requires the re-examination of Jer i 5, *beṭerem 'ṣwrk babbeṭen yeda'tīkā ūbeṭerem tēṣē' mēreḥem hiqdaštīkā*, "Before I beckoned you from the womb I knew you; before you came forth from the bosom I set you apart." The Masoretic uncertainty with *'ṣwrk* (MT *'eṣṣawrekā*) and a comparison with Isa xlix 1, "Yahweh called me from the womb, from the body of my mother he named my name," strongly suggest that the root of *'ṣwrk* (vocalize *'eṣūrekā*) is synonymous with *qārā'*, "to call." Such also might be the root attested in UT, 68:6–7, *wttn gh yǵr tḥt ksi zbl ym*, "And his voice was given forth, he screamed beneath the throne of Prince Yamm," and C. Virolleaud in *Le palais royal d'Ugarit*, V, 124:1–3, *arḫ td rgm bǵr bpy t'lgt blšny ǵr*, "The wild cow throws her voice by mooing; from her mouth comes stammering, from her tongue, mooing." But cf. UHP, p. 68.

my God. Reading *'ēlay* (MT pausal *'ēlāy*) which is not the preposition as supposed by MT, but the substantive *'ēlīm*, "God," determined by the first person singular suffix, as in Ps vii 7. Cf. Jer ii 19, cited below in NOTE on "my Lord."

and seek. The verb *dāraš* occurs in the damaged text UT, 8:5, *hlkt tdrš*, "She went to seek."

my Lord. The balance between the plurals of majesty *'ēlīm* and *'adōnay* recurs in Jer ii 19, *welō' pāḥadty* (MT *pāḥadtī*) *'ēlayik ne'ūm 'adōnay yhwh ṣebā'ōt*, "And you did not fear your God; word of the Lord Yahweh of Hosts." This version now takes precedence over that proposed in UHP, p. 21.

His hand . . . His mind. The suffixes of *yādī* and *napšī* are third person singular masculine and refer to Yahweh; *Psalms I*, pp. 10 f. This suffix recurs in vs. 11. The Syriac version saw that the suffix of *yādī* referred to God, while in Job xxiii 2, both LXX and Syr. recognize the third person suffix in *yādī* or at least translate it thus. In Ps xxiv 4, *napšī*, it has been noted, denotes "his mind."

attacks. Comparing *yādī . . . niggarāh* with Ps xxxix 11 (*Psalms I*), *mittigrat yādekā*, "by the club in your hand," and the accompanying discussion of *ngr*, "to smite, attack." Cf. also the first NOTE on Ps lxiii 11, and for the thought, Job xxiii 2, *yādī kābedāh 'al 'anḥātī*, "His hand is heavy despite my groaning," where the suffix of *yādī* expresses the third person. Hence Pope's emendation, *yādō*, "his hand" (*Job*, NOTE on xxiii 2b), does not commend itself. Cf. also UT, 54:11–13, translated in *Psalms I*, p. 194.

to relent. For this meaning of *hinnāḥēm*, see Ps cx 4; Gen vi 6, 7 ([AB, vol. 1], § 8, NOTE *ad loc.*); Num xxiii 19; I Sam xv 29; Jer iv

28 ("For I've spoken and not relented"—Bright, The Anchor Bible, vol. 21. Thus vs. 3 scans into five cola forming the sequence 3+2//3+2+3. Cf. Ps lxiv 10b–11.

5. *are accustomed.* Vocalizing *'^{a}ḥūzōt* (MT *'āḥaztā*) and assigning to this defectively written passive participle the meaning found in Akk. *aḫāzu,* "to learn," and in Song of Sol iii 8, *'^{a}ḥūzē ḥereb m^{e}lumm^{e}dē milḥamāh,* "skilled with the sword and expert in war." Cf. J. C. Greenfield in *Biblica* 45 (1964), 532 f., and UT, 1129:8–9, *ṯlṯ alp ṣpr dt aḫd ḥrṯh,* probably to be rendered, "three oxen of ṢPR that are skilled in plowing."

vigils. Identifying the hapax legomenon *š^{e}mūrōt,* usually rendered "eyelids" (see, e.g., A. Weiser, *The Psalms* [English translation of *Die Psalmen,* 5th rev. ed.; Göttingen, 1959, London, 1962], p. 529), with *'ašmūrāh,* "watch, vigil," occurring in Pss lxiii 7, xc 4, cxix 148, etc. Compare *z^{e}rō^{a}'* and *'ezrō^{a}',* "arm," *š^{e}'ōl,* "Sheol," but at Ps cxli 7, 11QPs^{a} reads *'š'wl,* with prothetic *aleph.* Our vocable is also related to Exod xii 42, *šimmūrīm,* "vigils." See GK, § 85b, and S. Moscati, ed., *An Introduction to the Comparative Grammar of the Semitic Languages* (Wiesbaden, 1964), § 12.14, p. 80.

I pace the floor. Elsewhere in the OT the verb *pā'am* occurs four times: qal in Judg xiii 25; niphal in Gen xli 8 and Dan ii 3, and hithpael in Dan ii 1. In every instance, save ours, the subject is *rū^{a}ḥ,* "spirit." This leads one to think that *nip'amtī* derives its sense more immediately from the idea expressed in Hebrew and Ugar.-Phoen. *p'm,* "foot." The Northwest Semitic penchant for coining denominative verbs from names of parts of the body is most recently remarked in the NOTE on Ps lxxiii 6. The graphic description in Prov vii 12 conveys by means of the noun *pa'am* what the psalmist expresses through the denominative verb: *pa'am baḥūṣ pa'am bar^{e}ḥōbōt w^{e}'ēṣel kol pinnāh te'^{e}rōb,* "A foot in the street, a foot in the square, she lurks at every corner."

do not recline. For the various nuances of the denominative verb *dbr,* "back," see I. E. Eitan in JQR 14 (1923), 39–41; Dahood in *Biblica* 45 (1964), 401, and *Psalms I,* p. 118. Ethiopic *tadabara* denotes "to lie on one's back." In this verse the psalmist mentions his eyes specifically and alludes to his feet and back in the two denominative verbs. See the first NOTE on Ps cvii 9 and 2 Aqht:VI:36–37.

6. *I consider . . . I remember.* Another indication of the archaic quality of the psalmist's language is his stylistic balance of the *qatal* form *ḥiššabtī* with *yiqtol 'ezk^{e}rāh;* cf. Ps lxiii 7 and the second NOTE on Ps lxxiv 14, and below on vs. 17.

the days . . . the years. For the Ugaritic parallelism between *ymm* and *šnt,* see the third NOTE on Ps lxi 7.

7. *I play the lyre.* Vocalizing piel *niggantī* instead of the MT noun

neginātī, "my stringed music." This colon needs a verb, which can be provided by positing an original text using the defective spelling *ngnty*. As in the preceding line, a perfect form (*nigganti*) balances an imperfect verb (*'āśīḥāh*, "I commune").

This reading and analysis lead to a 2+3+2 scansion of the line, a metrical scheme noticed at Pss lxix 33 and lxxxii 8.

That. For a final clause introduced by *we*, see Joüon, GHB, § 116e; Lam i 19, *weyāšībū 'et napšām*, "that they might refresh themselves," and Lam iii 26. For Ugaritic usage in such texts as UT, 127:17–18, *ṭbḫ imr wilḥm*, "Slaughter a lamb that I may eat," see UT, § 13.67.

my spirit might be healed. The hapax legomenon expression *wayeḥappēś rūḥī* awaits a viable explanation, but a tentative solution would be to identify consonantal *ḥpś* as a dialectal form of *ḥābaš*, "to bind up," but here with the figurative sense "to comfort, heal," that is found in Isa lxi 1; Ezek xxxiv 4; Hos vi 1. For the interchange of *b* and *p*, consult *Psalms I*, pp. 90, 141, 206. Hence vocalize as pual *yeḥuppaš*. Since in pre-Masoretic Hebrew texts there was no orthographic distinction between *ś* and *š*, the proposed reading involves no consonantal emendation.

8. *be angry.* On *zānaḥ*, "be angry," see the first NOTE on Ps lx 3.

no longer . . . again. The tautology is in the original Hebrew.

9. *visions from him.* Assigning to *'ōmer*, "visions," which shares the suffix of its opposite number *ḥasdō*, "his kindness" (cf. *Psalms I*, pp. 17 f.), the meaning investigated in *Psalms I*, pp. 16 and 179. For a similar thought, Ps lxxiv 9.

10. *the inmost parts.* The purported infinitive *ḥannōt* from *ḥnn*, "to show favor," is a hapax legomenon which produces another unique construction in the following *šākaḥ*, "dried up," nowhere else followed directly by an infinitive construct. Thus one looks for another vocable in the consonants *ḥnwt*, and their apparent balance with *rāḥmāyw*, literally "his bowels, bosom," suggests that *ḥnwt* answers to Phoen. *ḥn*, "vulva"; Jean and Hoftijzer, DISO, p. 92, line 7. In Job xix 17, MT *ḥannōtī* complements *rūḥī*, "my spirit," and hence denotes "my body" by metonymy. The vocalization of *ḥnwt* remains unknown, though its root may provide the etymology of *ḥnm*, "stealthily, secretly," examined at Ps xxxv 7 (*Psalms I*).

dried up. With Patton, CPBP, p. 27, dissociating *šākaḥ* from the root "to forget" and relating it to Ugar. *ṯkḥ*, "to shrivel, dry up," documented in *Psalms I*, p. 190, with bibliography, and at Ps lix 12. This derivation also supplies a much better parallel to *qāpaṣ*, "to draw together, shrink." Cf. also M. H. Pope in JSS 11 (1966), 240.

his bosom shrunk. The parallelism between the components of the two cola stands forth more clearly when *raḥamāyw*, "his bosom," rather than

God, is parsed as the subject of the verb to be pointed qal passive *qūpaṣ*. Cf. Job xxiv 24, where niphal *yiqqāpᵉṣūn*, "They draw themselves together" (of contraction in death), balances *yimmālū*, "They wither."

For a cognate sentiment, see Ps lxxiii 21, *kilyōtay 'eštōnān*, literally "As to my kidneys, I had become dry." In these graphic, physical terms the psalmist wants to know whether God's affections have dried up.

in his anger. For the lack of suffix with *'ap*, see the third NOTE on Ps lvi 8.

11. *Perhaps*. Literally "And I said."

his sickness. Reading *ḥᵃlōtī* (MT mispoints to *ḥallōtī*), the qal infinitive construct of *ḥālāh*, "to be sick," followed by the third person singular suffix *-ī*, as in vs. 3, *yādī*, "his hand," and *napšī*, "his mind." In other terms, *ḥᵃlōtī* is the semantic equivalent of Isa xxxviii 9, *ḥᵃlōtō*. In light of this pointing Ps xxxv 13 should read *wa'ᵃnī baḥᵃlōtī-m* (with enclitic *mem;* MT *baḥᵃlōtām*) *lᵉbūšī śāq*, "But when I was sick, my garment was sackcloth" (contrast *Psalms I*, p. 209; *dies diem docet*).

has withered. Pointing *šenet* (MT *šᵉnōt* probably traces back to purely consonantal writing *šnt*), the infinitive construct from *yāšan*, "to be old, withered," studied in the third NOTE on Ps lxxiii 21. Compare *šebet* from *yāšab*, *redet* from *yārad*, etc.

Semantically, *šenet yᵉmīn 'elyōn*, literally "the shriveling of the right hand of the Most High," which stands in apposition to *hī'*, resembles the thought of Ps cxxxvii 5, "If I should forget you, Jerusalem, may my right hand wither up (*tiškaḥ yᵉmīnī*)." In vss. 10–11, the psalmist employs three synonyms: *šākaḥ*, *qāpaṣ*, and *šenet*, all conveying the literal idea of "drying up" but metaphorically expressing the thought that God's compassion and power have become ineffectual.

12. *I will recite . . . will I recite*. Reading with the Ketiv hiphil *'azkīr* in the first colon and qal *'ezkᵉrāh* with MT in the second. *Psalms I*, p. 152, and the second NOTE on Ps lxix 15 comment on the stylistic variation of different conjugations of the same verb in parallel cola. Gunkel (*Die Psalmen*, p. 336) would emend *'ezkᵉrāh* to *'addīr* on the grounds that Hebrew stylistic practice forbids the use of the same word *zkr* in parallel cola, but his argument is upset by Ugaritic poetic practice, to say nothing of numerous biblical passages using the same word or root in balancing members of the verse.

Through his song about God's primordial deeds the psalmist hopes to persuade God to repeat such feats on Israel's behalf.

your magnificent deeds. Parsing *yāh* of *ma'alᵉlē -yāh* as a superlative element like *'ēl;* see *Psalms I*, p. 240; Ps cxxxix 6, and Jer ii 31. The pronominal determination "your" comes from parallel *pil'ekā* on the principle of the double-duty suffix discussed in *Psalms I*, pp. 17 f. Cf. Pss lxxxiv 2–3, lxxxix 2, and Prov v 16.

indeed. Understanding *kī* as emphatic and comparing Ps lxxi 23, *kī ʾ^{a}zamm^{e}rāh llāk*, "Indeed will I sing to you." Gunkel (*Die Psalmen*, p. 336) finds *kī* in this context surprising and consequently emends the following verb that is emphasized by *kī* into the adjective *ʾaddīr*, a glaring example of criticism that will hopefully disappear with the advance of Ugaritic-Hebrew comparative studies.

13. *I will number*. For this signification of Ugar.-Heb. *hāgāh*, consult *Psalms I*, p. 7.

completely. Identifying *b^{e}kōl* (MT *b^{e}kol*) with Ugar. *bkl*, "completely, entirely," in UT, 1153:5; cf. UT, Glossary, No. 1240, where 1153:7 is a typographical error for 1153:5.

and speak. Usually read "muse," *ʾaśīḥāh* here has rather the Late Hebrew and Aramaic meaning "speak"; cf. *Juxta Hebraeos, loquar*. In other words, the verbs in vss. 12–13 all describe audible activity.

14. *O God . . . O God*. These two vocatives form an inclusion; cf. Pss lviii 7 and lxxxiii 2.

your dominion. *Psalms I*, p. 2, gives the basic bibliography for this meaning of *derek*, Ugar. *drkt;* cf. also the first NOTE on Ps lxvii 3, and Ps cxxxviii 5 where *derek* and *gādōl*, "great," are associated, as here, and J. D. Shenkel in *Biblica* 46 (1965), 413.

the holy ones. Namely, the gods or celestial beings comprising Yahweh's divine council; see *Psalms I*, p. 175. For this collective meaning of *qōdeš*, which recurs in Ps xciii 5; Exod xv 11; Deut xxxiii 2, see Shenkel in *Biblica* 46 (1965), 412 f., with bibliography. The version proposed in *Psalms I*, p. 127, should be corrected accordingly.

greater than you. Reading *g^{e}dōl^{e}kā ʾ^{e}lōhīm* (MT *gādōl kēʾlōhīm*), and parsing the suffix *-kā* as the second term of a comparison. Not being conversant with the dative functions of pronominal suffixes, the Masoretes so divided the consonants as to produce the insipid reading "What god is great like God," whose flatness RSV tries to avoid by following the LXX, which too failed to understand the functions of dative suffixes, "Which god is great like our God?" The LXX gratuitously inserts the suffix of "our God." In his study of dative suffixes Bogaert cites three examples of the dative expressing comparison: Jer xx 7 (cf. Vulg. "*fortior me fuisti*" ["You were stronger than I"]); Isa lxv 5; Ezek xvi 15 (*Biblica* 45 [1964]), 242–43.

For a cognate sentiment, see Ps xcix 2 in this translation.

O God. Reading *ʾ^{e}lōhīm* with the initial *kaph* affixed to the preceding word, as proposed in preceding NOTE.

15. *Come, O God*. Repointing MT *ʾattāh*, "you," to imperative *ʾ^{a}tēh*, "Come!" In *hāʾēl* the article functions as vocative.

manifest. Perfect *hōdaʿtā* functions as the precative following imperative *ʾ^{a}tēh*, "Come!"

your strength among the peoples. Cf. Ps lxvii 3, "If your dominion is known upon the earth, your victory among the nations."

16. *With your powerful arm.* Literally "with the arm of your power," a construct chain whose genitive *'amm^{e}kā* stems from the root investigated in *Psalms I*, pp. 112 f. That is, it continues the thought of *'uzzekā*, "your strength," in vs. 15, and semantically equals Ps lxxxix 11, *z^{e}rōa' 'uzz^{e}kā*, "your strong arm," and Isa lxii 8. This verse nicely illustrates enjambment, which is lost in the traditional versions where "the sons of Jacob and Joseph," in apposition to "your people," makes a very prosaic ending to a vigorous poem.

redeem. Analyzing *gā'altā* as a precative perfect, precisely as in Ps lxxiv 2, *gā'altā*, whose precative nature is indicated by its parallelism with imperative *z^{e}kōr*, "Remember!" Cf. also Lam iii 58. It forms an inclusion with precative *nāḥītāh* in vs. 21. Unfortunately, the psalmist gives no hints about the critical situation from which he sought deliverance for the Israelites.

17. *When the waters.* The psalmist inserts an ancient poem comprised of tricola—most of the verses in the rest of the psalm are bicola—which glorifies the Creator whose victory over Tehom, the primeval flood, and Sea is a prototype of his victory over the enemies of Israel. Verse 17 is a stairlike triplet with the metrical pattern A+B+C//A+B+D//E+F+G, a pattern repeated in Ps xcii 10. Many commentators have remarked the similarity of vs. 17 to Hab iii 10, and Albright in *Studies in Old Testament Prophecy*, p. 9, has rightly inferred that Ps lxxvii must be older than Hab iii since it preserves the Canaanite metrical pattern which no longer appears in Hab iii. He also notes that Ps lxxvii is connected by the heading with the Canaanite musical tradition of Jeduthun, which might be taken to favor a tenth-century date for the oldest Israelite form of the poem.

they trembled. The *yqtl* form *yāḥīlū* expresses past time; as often in Ugaritic and Hebrew poetry, the *yqtl* and *qtl* forms are merely stylistic variants; see the first NOTE on vs. 6.

the depths. Ugar. *thm*, dual *thmtm*, plural *thmt* show that *t^{e}hōmōt* is not a Mesopotamian borrowing in the Bible, as held by an earlier generation of scholars. In fact, such outstanding biblical scholars as Eissfeldt and von Rad still maintain an *"unstreitbare Zusammenhang"* ["an incontestable connection"] between Babylonian Tiamat and the *t^{e}hōm* of Gen i, meaning a mythological and not only a philological connection. But as W. G. Lambert has shown in his article "A New Look at the Babylonian Background of Genesis," in JTS 16 (1965), 287–300, it was the Amorites who introduced from the West the flood-accounts of Babylonian cosmology. The full repercussions of the Ras Shamra discoveries are clearly still to be felt.

shook. yirg^{e}zū is another *yqtl* form expressing past time.

18. *The massed clouds streamed with water.* The sentence *zōr^{e}mū mayim 'ābōt* is amenable to several grammatical analyses (cf., e.g., R. T. O'Callaghan in VT 4 [1954], 171), but comparison with cognate phraseology in Num xxiv 7 indicates that *'ābōt,* which has both masculine (*'ābīm* in II Sam xxiii 4) and feminine plurals, is the subject; *zōr^{e}mū,* which denotes "to pour forth in floods," is the predicate, with *mayim* an accusative of material-with-which. For an analysis of Num xxiv 7, *w^{e}zār 'āb(ō) mayim rabbīm,* "And his cloud-mass overflows with abundant water," see Dahood, *Biblica* 47 (1966), 415.

your voice. Poetic for thunder, as in Pss xviii 14, xxix 3, etc. The suffix of parallel "your arrows" also determines its counterpart *qōl;* cf. the fourth Note on Ps lxxiv 3. Hence one might take exception to CCD, "The skies gave forth their voice." Cf. Ps xviii 14; UT, 51:v:70, *wtn qlh b'rpt,* "And he (namely, Baal) gave forth his voice from the clouds."

your arrows. Mythological for flashes of lightning.

shot back and forth. As in the preceding verse, the *yqtl* form expresses the past.

19. *the dome of heaven.* Usually translated "whirlwind," *galgal* has rather a meaning derived from that found in Eccles xii 6, namely, "pitcher, vase," as in Phoenician. Cf. *Biblica* 33 (1952), 399; O. Loretz, *Qohelet und der Alte Orient,* p. 190, n. 233. As can be deduced from biblical *gulgōlet,* Akk. *gulgullu,* "skull, a container shaped like a human skull," *galgal* here refers to something domed or vaulted. What is more, the parallelism with *tēbēl,* "earth," and *'ereṣ,* "nether world," suggests that the psalmist is portraying the tripartite division of the universe—heaven, earth, and underworld. Jer x 12 proves exegetically helpful: *'ōśēh 'ereṣ b^{e}kōḥō mēkīn tēbel b^{e}ḥokmātō ūbit^{e}būnātō nāṭāh šāmāyim,* "Who made the nether world by his power, established the world by his wisdom, by his skill stretched out the heavens." Cf. also UT, 51:vii:49–52 and 'nt:iii:23–25, *abn brq dl td' šmm rgm ltd' nšm wltbn hmlt arṣ,* "I have created lightning which the heavens do not know, thunder that men do not know, nor the multitudes in the nether world understand." In JQR 37 (1946–47), 288, T. H. Gaster has translated UT, 128:ii:7, *'dt ilm ṯlṯh,* "the company of the gods in its tripartite division," with the commentary that Baal and Yariḫ are gods of heaven; Resheph is a god of the nether world and Kothar is associated with the sea. Cf. Philip ii 10, "At the name of Jesus every knee should bow, in heaven, on earth and under the earth (Vulg. *caelestium, terrestrium et infernorum*)." Cf. UHP, p. 39, and the fourth Note on Ps cxv 16.

your lightning bolts. Suffixless *b^{e}rāqīm* shares in the determination effected by *qōl ra'am^{e}kā,* "your pealing thunder." The fact that some ancient versions translated "your lightning bolts" does not mean that the suffix stood in their text or warrant the emendation of MT *b^{e}rāqīm* to *b^{e}rāqekā*, because the idiom of the languages into which they translated did not tolerate what is to Western eyes such an intolerable ellipse. A very illuminating cognate, employing similar language and a double-duty suffix, appears in UT, 51:v:70–71, *wtn qlh b'rpt šrh larṣ brqm*, "And he gave forth his voice from the clouds, his lightning bolts flashed upon the earth." The suffix of *qlh* also qualifies *brqm*.

the nether world. For this sense of *'ereṣ*, see *Psalms I*, p. 106, and the third NOTE on Ps lxxiii 9.

quaked. Comparing *rāg^{e}zāh . . . hā'āreṣ* with Isa xiv 9, *š^{e}'ōl mittaḥat rāg^{e}zāh l^{e}kā*, "Sheol below is all astir for you."

20. *sea*. A demythologized allusion to the Canaanite sea-god Yamm.

your passage. As a sign of dominion over the waves. Perhaps our passage should be numbered among those, such as Jer ii 23; Job xxiii 10; Prov xii 28, where the verbal element of *derek* is more prominent than the nominal. Cf. the cognate text Hab iii 15, *dāraktā bayyām sūsekā*, "You made your horses trample Sea."

your train. Reading *š^{e}bālekā* (MT *š^{e}bīlekā*), the plural of *šōbel*, which in Isa xlvii 2 denotes "flowing skirt, train," (BDB, p. 987b), and is related to *šūlāyw* (notice that 1QIs^{a} changes *šblk* to *šwlyk* in xlvii 2) in Isa vi 1, "I saw Yahweh seated on a high and lofty throne, with the train of his garment (*šūlāyw*) filling the temple." The psalmist portrays the victorious God of Israel, robed in a flowing garment, traversing the ocean. The train of his garment explains why his heels were not seen, as stated by the next colon. Similar imagery underlies the obscure text Deut xxxiii 3, *yiššā'ū* (MT *yiššā'*) *mdbrtyk*, "They carry your train," deriving *mdbrtyk* from *dbr*, "to follow," and comparing *dōb^{e}rōt*, "rafts."

your heels were not seen. Literally "were not known, manifested"; the poet states in the preceding colon the reason why they could not be seen. A parallelism equivalent to ours occurs in Jer xiii 22, *niglū šūlayik neḥm^{e}sū '^{a}qēbāyik*, "Your skirts are raised, your limbs (literally "heels") ravished."

21. *Lead*. Explaining *nāḥītāh* as precative perfect, forming an inclusion with vs. 16, *gā'altā*, "Redeem!" It is much more likely that a lament would end with a prayer than by stating an historic fact. Cf., e.g., the ending of the national lament Ps xliv 27, *qūmāh 'āzartā llānū*, "Rise up, help us!"

a Moses and an Aaron. This expectation of two new deliverers can be illustrated by the scrolls of Qumran; the men of Qumran are now known to have expected two Messiahs, one a king, the other a priest. See G. Vermès, *The Dead Sea Scrolls in English* (Middlesex, 1962), pp. 47–52; E. A. Wcela, "The Messiah(s) of Qumran," in CBQ 26 (1964), 340–49; Reinhard Deichgräber, "Zur Messiaserwartung der Damaskusschrift," in ZAW 78 (1966), 333–42.

PSALM 78

(lxxviii 1–72)

1 *A maskil of Asaph.*

Give ear, my people, to my teaching,
incline your ear to the words of my mouth.
2 I will open my mouth in a parable,
I will reveal riddles of old.
3 What we have heard and know,
what our fathers have told us
4 We will not hide from their grandchildren,
but will tell to the next generation:
The glorious deeds of Yahweh and his triumph,
and his miracles that he has wrought.
5 He set up a decree in Jacob
and established a law in Israel,
That what he commanded our fathers,
they should make known to their sons;
6 So that the next generation might know,
the children yet unborn
Might arise and tell them to their children;
7 That they might put their hope in God,
and never forget the deeds of El;
That they might ever keep his commands,
8 and not be like their fathers:
a wayward and rebellious generation,
a generation whose heart was not firm,
whose spirit was unfaithful to God.
9 The sons of Ephraim were his bowmen,
his treacherous archers
who turned tail on the day of battle.
10 They failed to keep the covenant with God,
and refused to walk according to his law.

11 They forgot his deeds,
the wonders that he had shown them.
12 In the sight of their fathers he worked marvels,
in the land of Egypt, in the plain of Zoan.
13 He split the sea and brought them through,
he made the waters stand like a dike.
14 He led them by a cloud by day,
and through the night by light of fire.
15 He split the rock in the wilderness,
and watered the vast wasteland itself.
16 He made streams come out of the crag,
and caused waters to run down like rivers.
17 Yet they continued to sin against him,
to defy the Most High in the arid stretch.
18 They tested God in their heart
by asking food for their gullet.
19 They spoke against God, saying,
"Can God prepare a table in the wilderness?
20 Even though he struck the rock,
so that the water gushed forth,
and streams swept down in torrents,
Can he also give bread
or provide meat for his people?"
21 So when Yahweh heard them
he was full of wrath;
His fire blazed up against Jacob,
and his anger rose against Israel;
22 Because they had no faith in God,
and did not trust his saving power.
23 Yet he commanded the skies above,
and opened the doors of heaven.
24 He rained down upon them manna to eat,
and gave them the grain of heaven.
25 Mere man ate the food of angels,
he sent them provisions in abundance.
26 He let loose the east wind from heaven,
and led forth the south wind from his fortress.
27 And he rained flesh upon them like dust,
winged fowl like the ocean sands.

28 He made them fall in the midst of their camp,
round about their dwellings.
29 So they ate and had their fill,
he brought them what they craved.
30 They did not desist from their complaining
with their food still in their mouth.
31 God's anger rose against them;
he slew their sturdiest,
and cut down the flower of Israel.
32 In spite of all this they went on sinning,
and believed not in his wonders.
33 Their days he made vanish more quickly than vapor,
and their years more quickly than a fleeting phantom.
34 When he slew them they sought him,
they repented and sought God in earnest.
35 They remembered that God was their Mountain,
and the Most High God their Redeemer.
36 But they flattered him with their mouth,
while they lied to him with their tongue.
37 Their heart was not steadfast toward him,
they believed not in his covenant.
38 But he the Merciful forgave their sin,
and did not destroy them.
He restrained his anger often,
and nurtured none of his rage.
39 He remembered that they were but flesh,
a passing breath that never returns.
40 How often they defied him in the wilderness,
and grieved him in the desert!
41 Again and again they tempted God,
and provoked the Holy One of Israel.
42 They did not remember his power,
the day when he ransomed them from the adversary;
43 When he wrought his miracles in Egypt,
and his prodigies in the plain of Zoan;
44 When he turned into blood their rivers,
their streams so that they could not drink.
45 He sent flies against them to devour them,
and frogs to destroy them.

46 He gave their crops to the grasshopper,
the fruit of their labor to the locust.
47 He killed their vines with hail,
and their sycamores with frost.
48 He handed over their cattle to hail,
and their flocks to thunderbolts.
49 He sent against them his blazing anger,
fury, rage, and havoc;
An escort of his pestiferous angels
50 to smooth his path before him.
He did not spare them from death,
but handed over their lives to the plague.
51 He smote all the first-born of Egypt,
the first fruit of their vigor in the tents of Ham.
52 Then he led forth his people like sheep,
and like a flock guided them through the wilderness.
53 He guided them securely and unafraid,
while the sea engulfed their foes.
54 He brought them to his holy mount,
the mountain that his right hand had won.
55 He drove out the nations before them,
and felled them on their upland patrimony;
He settled the tribes of Israel in their tents.
56 But they defiantly tempted God,
the Most High and his commandments they did not heed.
57 They turned away and broke faith like their fathers,
they recoiled like a treacherous bow.
58 They angered him with their hillsite shrines,
and with their idols roused his jealousy.
59 God heard them and was enraged,
and the Grand rejected Israel.
60 He abandoned his dwelling in Shiloh,
the tent he pitched among men.
61 He gave his fortress to the captors,
his glorious ark into the hand of the adversary.
62 He handed over his people to the sword,
and vented his wrath on his patrimony.
63 Fire devoured their young men,
and their maidens were not praised in wedding song.

64 Their priests fell by the sword,
and their widows sang no dirges.
65 Then the Lord awoke like one who had slept,
like a warrior resting after wine.
66 He smote his adversaries on the rear,
he covered them with everlasting shame.
67 He rejected the tents of Joseph,
and chose not the tribe of Ephraim.
68 But he chose the tribe of Judah,
Mount Zion which he loved.
69 And he built his sanctuary like the high heavens,
like the earth he established from eternity.
70 And he chose David his servant,
and took him from the sheepfolds.
71 From following ewes he brought him
to shepherd Jacob his people,
and Israel his patrimony.
72 He tended them with blameless heart,
and with skillful hands he guided them.

Notes

lxxviii. A didactic psalm, drawing salutary lessons from Israel's history, composed for use at the major festivals; cf. Pss cvi, cvii. After an elaborate eight-verse introduction stressing the importance of handing down the history of God's dealings with his people, the psalmist emphasizes the disobedience and ingratitude of the people, singling out the defection of the Ephraimites or the Northern Kingdom (vss. 9–11), which led God to reject them in favor of Judah or the Southern Kingdom (vss. 67–69). The psalmist further polemicizes against the Northern Kingdom in vss. 56–64, maintaining that the defeat at Shiloh resulted from God's rejection of Ephraim because of her idolatry. These historical references point to the composition of the psalm between 922–721 B.C., in the period from the breakup of the Davidic United Monarchy in ca. 922 B.C. to the destruction of the Northern Kingdom by the Assyrians in 721 B.C.

The linguistic evidence corroborates this inference. No psalm, it would seem, employs as many *yqtl* forms to express past time; see vss. 15, 26, 29, 38 (thrice), 40 (twice), 45, 47, 49, 58, 64, 72. Since the *yqtl* was the normal form of expressing past events in Ugaritic poetry and, to a lesser extent, in early biblical poems, one may use this linguistic feature as a criterion for the early dating of the psalm. Another linguistic trait of this composition—though without chronological implications as far as can be made out—is the frequent use of irony, wordplay, and play on roots; see the comments on vss. 1, 9, 18, 19, 29–30, 33, 49, 63, 66. The omission of suffixes also marks the style of the psalmist; see vss. 6, 21, 28, 38 (twice), 51, 59.

1. *Give ear . . . your ear.* The first play on roots involves the denominative verb *ha'ᵃzīnū* and the substantive *'ozneᵉkem;* others recur in vss. 19, 49.

2. *parable.* The Hebrew word *māšāl* signifies properly "a comparison," then any proverb (see Ps xlix 5) or saying in which some deeper meaning lies, to be gleaned by means of the hidden comparison. Here the entire psalm is a *māšāl.*

4. *their grandchildren.* Usually translated "their children," which seems a little odd since the "we" are presumably "their children," *bᵉnēhem* must be synonymous with second-colon *dōr 'aḥᵃrōn,* "the next generation," and hence denoting "grandchildren." Though "grandson" is generally expressed by *ben bēn,* there are several texts where *bēn* alone denotes "grandson"; cf. Gen xxix 5, xxxi 28, 43; Ruth iv 17, while in Josh xxii 24, 25, 27, *bānīm* refers to descendants in general.

will tell . . . The glorious deeds. A fine example of enjambment.

his triumph. For this nuance of the root *'zz* (here *'ᵉzūzō*), cf. *Psalms I,* p. 131, and the unpublished text RŠ 24.247, *mlkn y'zz 'l ḫpṯh,* "Our king will triumph over his *ḫ.*" Here the psalmist has in mind God's victory over the Egyptians.

5. *a decree . . . a law.* Doubtless refer to the legislation of the Pentateuch.

6. *tell them.* Namely, the glorious deeds and miracles performed by Yahweh. As in vss. 21, 28, 38 (twice), the poet forgoes the suffix one would expect after *wisappᵉrū.*

9. *Ephraim.* The most important of the northern tribes of Israel; hence here, as often, it refers to the Northern Kingdom in general.

his bowmen. Explaining the suffix of *nōšᵉqēy* as third person singular with a plural noun; cf. the first NOTE on Ps lxxvi 4. Despite their election as Yahweh's elite bowmen, the Ephraimites were later rejected by God because of their cowardice.

his treacherous archers. In the expression *rōmē qāšet* the poet plays on the verbs *rāmāh,* "to be deceitful, treacherous," and *rāmāh,* "to shoot," as in Jer iv 29, *rōmeh qešet,* "bowman."

12. *land . . . plain.* The parallelism between *'ereṣ* and *śādeh* also occurs in UT, 126:III:5–6, *larṣ mṭr b'l wlšd mṭr 'ly.* The fourth NOTE on Ps lvii 8 examines the bearing of parallel words on the classification of Ugaritic.

plain of Zoan. A city in the delta of the Nile, Zoan was the capital of Egypt at the time of the Exodus in the thirteenth century B.C. Cf. Exod i 11.

15. *He split.* The *yqtl* form *y^ebaqqa'* expresses the same time as preterit *bāqa'* in vs. 13. As observed in the introductory NOTE, the *yqtl* form in Ugaritic was the normal verb for describing an action in the past. Cf. Exod xvii 6; Num xx 11.

the rock. The LXX and *Juxta Hebraeos* translate singular "rock" (see vs. 20, *ṣūr*), so MT plural *ṣūrīm* doubtless arose from confusing *ṣūr* plus enclitic *mem* with the plural *ṣūrīm.* Hence read singular "rock" followed by the enclitic. As UT, § 13.102, rightly remarks, enclitic *mem* causes orthographic difficulties in Ugaritic, making a masculine singular noun look like a masculine dual or plural. The original account in Exod xvii 6 employs the singular *ṣūr,* and this is manifestly the preferred lection here because synonymous *sela',* "crag," in the following verse is clearly singular. Cf. also Isa xlviii 21.

the vast wasteland itself. Parsing *ki-t^ehōmōt* as the emphatic *kī* (consult the first NOTE on Ps lxxvi 11) and taking *t^ehōmōt* in the sense suggested by its parallelism with *midbār,* "wilderness." For the desert Arabs, *tihāmatu* denotes "sandy desert." Cf. also Ar. *baḥr,* "ocean," and feminine *baḥratu,* "country, region." Nor need one rely solely on Arabic to establish this sense of *t^ehōmōt,* because UT, 2001:3–5, apparently balances *mdbr,* "wilderness," and *thmt,* "wasteland," as in the psalm: *tlk bmdbr . . . tḥdṯn w hl . . . w tglṯ thmt.*

This analysis has two advantages. First, it provides transitive *wayyašq,* "watered," with a direct object, and second, it accounts for the sentence function of *rabbāh,* "vast," which now parses as a feminine adjective modifying *t^ehōmōt,* a feminine singular with the Phoenician ending, as in vs. 72.

Consult the second NOTE on Ps liii 7, and for parallel nouns, the first NOTE on vs. 12 above.

16. *the crag.* Singular *sela'* shows that its synonym in vs. 15 should also be read as singular *ṣūr* plus enclitic *mem.*

17. *to defy the Most High.* The phrase *lam^erōt 'elyōn* will prove serviceable in determining the correct reading and translation of Ps cvi 7. See Deut ix 7.

18. *their heart . . . their gullet.* The irony becomes evident when *napšām,* "their gullet," is taken in the sense discussed at Ps xxvii 12 (*Psalms I,* p. 169). This irony is less apparent in those versions rendering *napšām* "they craved" (RSV).

19. *They spoke . . . the wilderness.* The poet plays on the root *dbr* of *y^edabb^erū* and *midbār,* and by positioning the verb at the beginning of the verse and the noun at the end he forms an inclusion.

Can God prepare a table. The occurrence of *'ēl* and *šulḥān* in this colon recalls UT, 51:I:39, *ṯlḥn il.*

20. *the rock.* Singular *ṣūr* bears on the reading of vs. 15, *ṣūr-m.*

gushed forth. The assertion of Briggs, CECBP, II, p. 193, that the root *zwb* is a hapax legomenon in the Psalter may need modification in view of the etymology proposed at Ps li 9. The chiasm that occurs in all four cola of vs. 20 is noteworthy.

give bread. Comparing *leḥem . . . tēt* with UT, 52:71–72, *wtn wnlḥm,* "Then give that we might eat."

meat. The appearance of *šir,* "flesh, meat," in RŠ, 22.225, *tspi širh lbl ḥrb tšt dmh lbl ks,* "She consumes his flesh without a knife, she drinks his blood without a cup," upsets the Arabic etymology *ṯa'ru,* "blood revenge," that most lexicons proffer. It also makes serious inroads into W. A. Ward's translation in JNES 20 (1961), 36, of UT, 49:II:35–37, *ltikl 'ṣrm mnth ltkly npr* [*š*]*ir,* "The birds verily eat his remains, the fowl verily eat (*sic*) his *mnt.*" More probably *šir* here denotes "his flesh (note double-duty suffix provided by *mnth*) while *mnth* signifies "his parts/members." Cf. S. E. Loewenstamm, IEJ 13 (1963), 131.

21. *heard them.* The well-attested practice of using *šāma'* without a suffix when the context requires it (*Psalms I,* p. 24), plus the psalmist's tendency to omit suffixes in general (introductory NOTE), will sufficiently account for the lack of a suffix with *šāma'* here as well as in vs. 59.

His fire. Metaphorical for "his wrath." In keeping with his practice of slighting suffixes, the psalmist simply wrote *'ēš.* Cf. Pss xviii 9, "Smoke rose from his nostrils, and fire from his mouth devoured," and ii 12, "For his ire flares up quickly."

his anger. As noticed at Pss lvi 8 and lxxvii 10, *'ap,* being considered a part of the body, does not need a suffix. The parallel prose passage in Num xi 1 reads suffixed *'appō.*

23. *Yet he commanded . . . .* This fine example of chiasm—A+B// B́+Á—should be noted.

24. *gave . . .* 25. *sent.* The balance between *nātan* and *šālaḥ* corresponds to that occurring in UT, 2 Aqht:VI:27–28, *irš ḥym watnk blmt wašlḥk,* "Ask for life eternal and I will give it to you, immortality and I will bestow it upon you." On parallel words, see the first NOTE on vs. 12 and Moshe Held in JBL 84 (1965), 279, n. 32, who directs attention to the parallelism between *nātan* and *šālaḥ* in Gen xlix 21 and Ps cvi 15. The event mentioned here is fully described in Exod xvi 4, 14–15.

grain . . . 25. *food.* As in this passage, UT, 126:III:13–14, associates *dgn,* "grain," and *lḥm,* but with the more specific signification "wheat."

grain of heaven. See W. Herrmann, ZAW 72 (1960), 216.

the food of angels. Cf. Ps ciii 20.

25. *provisions. ṣēdāh* should be compared with UT, Krt:79, *bmṣdk,*

whose parallelism with *bdbḥk* suggests that *bmṣdk* is comprised of the longer preposition *bm* plus *ṣdk;* hence the substantive is *ṣd,* not *mṣd* as posited by UT, Glossary, No. 2151.

26. *He let loose.* The hiphil *yqtl* verb *yassa'* expresses past time; its root *ns'* appear in Ugaritic denoting both "to travel" and "to pull out." Cf. Ps cxxxv 7, "who brings forth the wind from his storehouses." Num xi 31 recounts this event.

the east wind. UT, Glossary, No. 2208, defines *qdm* in 75:I:8 as "east wind," but its apparent parallelism (the text is damaged) with *šḥr,* "dawn," suggests that Ugar. *qdm* signifies "morning" rather than "east wind." Cf. Jon iv 2, *qiddamtī librōaḥ taršīšāh,* "I arose at dawn to flee to Tarshish," and *Gregorianum* 43 (1962), 71. Michael C. Astour (*Hellenosemitica* [Leiden, 1965], p. 154) has independently reached the same conclusion.

from heaven. With *ba* of *baššāmayim,* as so frequently in Ugaritic and Hebrew (*Psalms I,* p. 319), denoting "from." Here both the LXX and *Juxta Hebraeos* render "from." One may here observe that Ps cxix 87, *kimeʿaṭ killūnī bāʾāreṣ,* "They virtually exterminated me from the earth," appears in 11QPsa as *km'ṭ klwny m'rṣ,* a rather clear indication that the men of Qumran no longer realized that *ba* could denote "from." In this they resemble Jared J. Jackson, who in *Pittsburgh Perspective* 7 (June 1966), 32, questions the meaning "from" of Heb. *be*.

from. See preceding NOTE on *be*, "from."

his fortress. Psalms I, p. 50, examines the texts with *'ōz,* "fortress"; see also the first NOTE on Ps lix 10 and below on vs. 61. As appears from the parallelism, *'ōz* is a poetic term for heaven, like *gebūrōt* in Ps xx 7. Thus *yassa',* "He let loose," pairs with *yenahēg,* "led forth," *qādīm,* "the east wind," is the opposite number of *tēmān,* "the south wind," while *šāmayim* and *'ōz* are synonymous for "heaven."

One may add here that the motif of heaven, the fortified city, which has been identified in Ps xxxi 22, appears in Deut i 28 (= ix 1), *'am gādōl wārām mimmennū 'ārīm gedōlōt ūbeṣūrōt baššāmayim,* "The people are greater and taller than we; the cities are larger and more fortified than heaven."

28. *He made them fall.* As in vss. 6, 21, 38, the psalmist omits for metrical reasons the suffix expected with *wayyappēl.*

30. *They did not desist.* Literally "They were not estranged from." For this nuance of *zār,* see Job xix 27, *'ašer 'anī 'eḥezeh lī weʿenay rāʾū welō' zār,* "When I shall gaze upon him, and my eyes will see him without cease."

their complaining. This meaning of *ta'awātām* from *'āwāh,* "to complain, lament," is examined in *Psalms I,* p. 57. The psalmist interprets Num xi 33 in the light of xi 34; after having been fed, the Israelites continued to complain and to offend God in the same manner. The paronomasia on *ta'ᵃwātām,* "what they craved" (vs. 29), and "their complaining" accords with the psalmist's fondness of puns; see introductory NOTE.

31. *their sturdiest.* Explaining *bᵉ* of *bᵉmišmannīm* as the intensifying particle examined in *Psalms I,* p. 177.

cut down. The lexical dispute whether *hikrīᵃ'* is a denominative verb from *kera',* "leg, shinbone," finds an affirmative resolution in the light of the Northwest Semitic tendency for coining verbs from names of parts of the body; see the NOTE on Ps lxxiii 6, and compare Ugar. *kr',* "to kneel."

33. *Their days . . . their years.* For the Ugaritic parallellism between *ymm* and *šnt,* see the third NOTE on Ps lxi 7.

more quickly than vapor. Analyzing *ba* of *bahebel* as the *beth comparativum* (second NOTE on Ps li 8), and comparing Pss xxxvii 20, *be'āšān kālū,* "More quickly than smoke shall they vanish," and cii 4, *kī kālū bᵉ'āšān yāmāy,* "For my days are more transitory than smoke."

vapor . . . fleeting phantom. Gunkel and others have remarked the root play in *hebel* and *behālāh.* The latter word, from *bāhal,* "to hasten," appears from the balance with *hebel* to be a synonym of Ps xxxix 7, *ṣelem,* "phantom."

34. *sought God in earnest.* The juxtaposition *šiḥᵃrū 'ēl* materially compares with the Ugaritic personal name *ilšḥr* whose interpretation, however, is ambiguous.

36. *their mouth . . . their tongue.* The second NOTE on Ps lxvi 17 cites the Ugaritic text balancing *p* and *lšn.*

37. *toward him.* Ugaritic *'m* more frequently denotes "to, toward" than "with"; UT § 10.14.

38. *the Merciful.* Understanding *rāḥūm* as a divine appellative rather than as a mere predicate adjective, "he, being merciful" (CCD).

their sin . . . destroy them. The lack of suffixes with *'āwōn* and *yašḥīt* is of a piece with the psalmist's habit of scrimping on suffixes, as remarked in the introductory NOTE.

nurtured. Deriving *yā'īr* from the root *'yr,* Ugar. *ǵyr,* "to protect, nurture," discussed in *Psalms I,* pp. 55 f., and by Raphael Serra, "Una raiz, afin a la raiz ugaritica *ǵyr* 'guardar', en algunos textos biblicos," in *Claretianum* 4 (1964), 161–76. The biblical synonyms, *nāṭar,* "to keep, guard," and *šāmar,* "to preserve, protect," are also used of cherishing one's wrath. The same etymology is valid for Isa xlii 13, *yā'īr qin'āh,* "He will nurture his rage."

39. *that never returns.* Alluding to the motif of Sheol, "the land of no return"; see Pope, *Job,* NOTE on Job vii 9–10, and R. Martin-Achard, *De la mort à la résurrection* (Neuchâtel, 1956), p. 39.

40. *they defied him . . . grieved him.* The verbs *yamrūhū* and *ya'aṣībūhū* provide further examples of *yqtl* forms expressing the past, a usage indicating an early date for this psalm, as proposed in the introductory NOTE.

42. *he ransomed them.* As noticed at Ps xxxiv 23, *pdy,* "to ransom," occurs in a juridical text from Ras Shamra (*Psalms I,* p. 207).

43. *his miracles . . . his prodigies.* The phrase *'ōtōtāyw ūmōpetāyw* suggests that Ps cv 27, *'ōtōtāyw ūmōpetīm* employs the double-duty suffix and should accordingly be rendered in the same manner as our phrase.

44. *could not drink. yištāyūn* belongs to the list of weak verbs preserving the final *yod* of the root.

45. *He sent.* Imperfect *yešallaḥ* describes past action; see NOTES on vss. 40 and 49.

against them. Better than "among them" (RSV); see vs. 49, *yešallaḥ bām,* "He sent against them."

46. *the grasshopper . . . the locust.* Though lexicographers differ in their definitions of *ḥāsīl,* "grasshopper," there is today general agreement that the word occurs in Ugaritic as *ḥsn* and that the biblical pairing of *ḥāsīl* and *'arbeh,* "locust," answers to that of UT, Krt:103–5, *kirby tškn šd km ḥsn pat mdbr,* "Like locusts they occupy the field, like the grasshoppers the corners of the desert." However, an unedited Ugaritic tablet contains the verb *yḥsl,* which Virolleaud, on the basis of El Amarna *ḫazālu,* renders "it will be destroyed"; see UT, Glossary, No. 882a.

48. *thunderbolts.* Cf. the first NOTE on Ps lxxvi 4.

49. *He sent.* The verb *yešallaḥ* is another example of the *yqtl* form describing action in the past; cf. introductory NOTE. The etymological figure in *yešallaḥ . . . mišlaḥat* further reveals the poet's penchant for playing on words and roots; see introductory NOTE.

his pestiferous angels. Usually rendered "a mission of angels of evil," *mišlaḥat mal'akēy rā'īm* reads more naturally when the final *yod* of *mal'akēy* is parsed as third person singular suffix (see vs. 9, *nōšeqēy,* "his bowmen," and *rā'īm,* "pestiferous," as an adjective.

The identification of these pestilential envoys depends in part on the translation of the following colon.

50. *to smooth his path.* An expression that is hapax legomenon, *yepallēs nātīb* becomes amenable to satisfactory analysis when its subject is understood as the escort of maleficent angels that goes before Yahweh to prepare his way, a motif discussed at Ps lxviii 5. Cf. Hab iii 5, "Pestilence went before him, and Plague followed close behind." The intervention of two words may explain the lack of gender agreement between *mišlaḥat,* "angels," and *yepallēs,* "to smooth."

From its occurrences in what are often considered late biblical compositions, *nātīb* (as opposed to feminine *netībāh*) is labeled by Briggs,

CECBP, II, p. 195, "a late word." Ugar. *ntb* throws serious doubt on the correctness of his inference.

before him. True to his style, the psalmist uses *'ap* in the sense of "anger" in the earlier part of the verse, but in *l*ᵉ*'appō* with the meaning "before him." For this usage, see I Sam xxv 25; Isa xiii 3, and Dahood in *Gregorianum* 43 (1962), 70.

Up to this point God had sent his instruments of destruction to chastise the Egyptians, but now he personally slays the first-born of the Egyptians, as explicitly stated in Exod xi 4 ff.

51. *the first fruit of their vigor.* Semantically equivalent to Gen xlix 3, *rē'šīt 'ōnī*, "the first fruit of my vigor," the present phrase *rē'šīt 'ōnīm* has been read *rē'šīt 'ōnām* by most of the ancient versions. Is this an indication of *scriptio defectiva 'nm* in the original text, or is *'ōnīm* genuinely plural as in a number of other biblical texts? The latter hypothesis finds support in UT, 49:I:22–23, *dq anm lyrẓ 'm b'l*, "One of little vigor cannot charge like Baal." The failure of UT, Glossary, No. 250, to proffer any definition of *anm* is difficult to explain.

Ham. A poetic synonym for Egypt; cf. Gen x 6.

54. *his holy mount.* Referring not only to Mount Zion, but also to the mountainous region of Judah. LXX *'óros*, "mountain," does not necessitate the emendation of *g*ᵉ*būl* to *hār*, since Ugar. *gbl*, "mount, hill," vouches for the meaning expressed by Ar. *jabal*, "hill, mountain." Other biblical occurrences are discussed in *Biblica* 45 (1964), 396; see also Ps cv 33 and A. B. Ehrlich, *Randglossen zur hebräischen Bibel* (Leipzig, 1909), II, p. 238.

that. The relative pronoun *zeh* corresponds to the Ugaritic relative *d* and Phoen. *z;* cf. Ps lxxiv 2.

his right hand. Like their Canaanite predecessors who speak of the right hand of Baal (*ymnh*, "his right hand," in 76:II:7), the biblical poets talk of the right hand of Yahweh.

55. *by lot.* Literally "with a measuring cord."

and felled them. Namely, the Canaanites residing in Palestine when the Israelites entered the land.

their upland patrimony. As proposed in the fourth NOTE on Ps cv 11, *ḥebel* is a metathetic form of Ugar. *ḫlb*, "hill."

He settled . . . in their tents. The phrase *wayyaškēn b*ᵉ*'oh*ᵒ*lēhem* juxtaposes two roots found in parallelism in UT, 128:III:18–19, *tity ilm lahlhm dr il lmšknthm*, "The gods go to their tents, the assembly of El to their dwellings." See below on vs. 60.

56. *they defiantly tempted.* Literally "they tempted and defied," a case of hendiadys. The chiastic arrangement of the verse might also be remarked.

the Most High. In disagreement with MT, I place *'elyōn* in the second colon, a fine example of the breakup of a composite divine title. Cf. Ps xlvi 5 on the composite divine title, and Ps cvii 25, where MT puts the composite phrase *rūaḥ se'ārāh* in the first colon, whereas the syllabic count shows, as in our verse, that its components belong to two different cola.

57. *a treacherous bow.* Harking back to vs. 9. Cf. Jer xlviii 10, where *remiyyāh,* an adjective with substantive meaning, denotes "a treacherous or slack bow."

58. *hillsite shrines.* Cf. W. F. Albright, "The High Place in Ancient Palestine," in VTS, IV (Leiden, 1957), pp. 242–58.

their idols. Hitherto witnessed only in Hebrew and Aramaic, the root of *pesīlēhem* appears frequently in Ugaritic.

roused his jealousy. See introductory NOTE on the frequency of *yqtl* forms to narrate past happenings. Cf. the chiasm here and in vs. 23.

59. *heard them.* For lack of accusative suffix with *šāma',* consult the first NOTE on vs. 21.

the Grand. Repointing MT *me'ōd,* "utterly," to *mā'ēd,* the divine epithet discussed in the first NOTE on Ps cix 30. See also D. N. Freedman, *Biblica* 54 (1973), 268.

60. *his dwelling . . . the tent.* See the third NOTE on vs. 56 where the Ugaritic pairing of *ahl* and *mškn* is cited.

the tent he pitched. Given the frequent parallelism and close association of the roots *'hl* and *škn* (see preceding NOTE), the phrase *'ōhel šikkēn* may be considered the semantic equivalent of the denominative verb *'ihhēl,* "to pitch a tent." Cf. John i 14, "And he pitched his tent among us."

61. *his fortress.* A poetic name for the ark of the covenant, which in Ps cxxxii 8 is called *'arōn 'uzzekā.* Just as the Israelites conceived of God's celestial abode as a "fortress" (see vs. 26), so they termed the ark, God's habitation in Israel, an *'ōz,* "fortress." For a somewhat different approach to the semantic development, see G. Henton Davies, "The Ark in the Psalms," in *Promise and Fulfilment,* Essays Presented to Professor S. H. Hooke, ed. F. F. Bruce (Edinburgh, 1963), pp. 51–61.

to the captors. Literally "to captivity," but abstract *šebī* takes on a concrete denotation by reason of its parallelism with *ṣār,* "adversary." Cf. *Psalms I,* pp. 32 f., and W. A. van der Weiden, "Abstractum pro concreto: phaenomenon stylisticum," in *Verbum Domini* 44 (1966), 43–52. The event alluded to is described in I Sam iv 21 ff.

63. *Fire.* Scholars dispute whether *'ēš* here refers to the fire of war, as suggested by Num xxi 28, or to the fire of divine wrath (cf. vs. 21) that devoured some of the men of Beth Shemesh because they looked into the ark (I Sam vi 19). The similarity between biblical

'ākelāh 'ēš and UT, 51:vi:24–25, *tikl išt,* which describes the activity of a divine fire devouring the palace, may have some bearing on the exegesis of the biblical phrase. Cf. also vs. 21.

were not praised in wedding song. Though some few moderns see in *hullālū* the verb *yālal,* "to wail, lament," the majority view that it is the pual perfect of *hālal,* "to praise," finds support in the Ugaritic designation of the *ktrt* (see the third NOTE on Ps lxviii 7), professional songstresses who assist at births and weddings, as *bnt hll,* "the daughters of joyful song."

64. *sang no dirges.* Just as *hullālū* in preceding verse evokes the *bnt hll,* so *tibkēnāh* recalls the professional mourners who in Canaanite culture are termed *bkyt,* "weeping women." As frequently in this psalm, the imperfect verb states past activity.

65. *resting after wine. Psalms I,* p. 196, cites the evidence, albeit inconclusive, for this version of *mitrōnēn miyyāyin,* while the second NOTE on Ps lxxiii 20 lists examples of *min,* "after."

66. *on the rear.* Buttenwieser, PCTNT, p. 147, has little patience with those who opt for this translation, maintaining that "He put his enemies to rout" is the only possible rendition of *wayyak ṣārāyw 'āḥōr.* He fails to appreciate, however, the psalmist's taste for words of double entendre, commented upon in the introductory NOTE. For the poet, *'āḥōr* means both the "posterior," an allusion to the boils that covered the Philistines for carrying off the ark (I Sam v 6, 9), and the rear guard of the army. Understood in a military sense, the clause in question is the semantic equivalent of *zinnēb,* literally "to smite the tail, 'detail,'" but actually "to attack or smite the rear." Consult the NOTE on Ps cx 6.

he covered them. Employing the metaphor of a garment, as in Ps xxxv 26, *yilbešū bōšet,* "Let them be clothed with shame." Cf. also Jer iii 25, xxiii 40, and Pss cix 18, cxix 22.

69. *like . . . like.* The balance between *kemō* and *ke* reverses the order of the parallelism between *k* and *km* in UT, Krt:103–5.

the high heavens. rāmīm is an adjective with the force of a substantive, a usage studied in the NOTES to Pss lxii 3 and lxxiii 10. In other terms, *rāmīm* is short for Ugar. *šmm rmm* in one of Anath's epithets, *b'lt šmm rmm,* "mistress of the high heavens," Phoen. *šmm rmm,* and *samēroumos* in Sanchunyaton. Cf. Job xvi 19 and S. E. Loewenstamm in *Leshonenu* 29 (1964), 7.

from eternity. The currency of *le,* "from," in both Ugaritic and Hebrew (*Psalms I,* p. 84) raises numerous problems of translation and interpretation. The present verse is such a case in point. But the fact that one Hebrew manuscript does read *mē'ōlām* for MT *le'ōlām* shows that someone has already felt the inadequacy of rendering *le'ōlām,* "to eternity." Cf. Ps cxix 152, *qedem yāda'tī-m 'ēdōtekā kī* *l*^{e}*'ōlām y*^{e}*sadtām,* "O Primeval One, I acknowledge your stipulations, because you established them from eternity." Here the synonymity with *qedem* clarifies the sense of *l*^{e}*'ōlām.* Cf. also *Psalms I,* p. 56, on Ps xxix 10, *l*^{e}*'ōlām.*

72. *with skillful hands.* Explaining the purported plural *t*^{e}*būnōt* as a Phoenician singular ending in *-ōt;* see vs. 15 and Prov xxviii 16. Hence the repointing to singular *t*^{e}*būnat,* as found in some manuscripts, is unnecessary. The chiastic structure of the verse also merits notice.

PSALM 79

(lxxix 1–13)

1 *A psalm of Asaph.*

O God, the heathen have invaded your patrimony,
they have defiled your holy temple,
they have made Jerusalem a heap of ruins.
2 They have given the corpses of your servants
to the birds of heaven for food,
the flesh of your devoted ones,
to the beasts of the earth.
3 They have shed their blood like water,
with no one around Jerusalem to bury them.
4 We have become the taunt of our neighbors,
the mockery and scorn of those around us.
5 How long, O Yahweh? Will you be eternally angry?
how long will your zeal burn like fire?
6 Pour out your rage, O God,
upon the nations that do not know you,
and upon the kingdoms that invoke not your name.
7 For they have devoured Jacob,
and laid waste his habitation.
8 Do not record to our debit, O Scribe,
the iniquities of our forefathers;
Let your acts of mercy come to meet us,
because we are down and out.
9 Help us, O triumphant God of ours!
because of your glorious name rescue us,
forgive us our sins for your name's sake,
10 Lest the heathen should say,
"Where is their God?"
That it may be known among the heathen before our eyes,
avenge the shed blood of your servants!

11 Let the groans of your prisoners come before you,
with your long arm preserve those condemned to die.
12 And seven times over return into our neighbors' bosoms
their taunts with which they taunted you, O Lord.
13 But we, your people and the sheep of your pasture,
will give thanks to you for ever;
From generation to generation
we will tell your praise.

Notes

lxxix. A lamentation of the people (national lament) over the havoc wrought by foreign invaders of Jerusalem. The occasion is probably the same as that of Ps lxxiv. Since vss. 2–3 are quoted somewhat freely in I Macc vii 17, many commentators have concluded that this lament describes the treacherous slaughter of sixty pious Jews in Jerusalem during the Maccabean wars (first half of second century B.C.). I Maccabees, however, quotes these verses fairly clearly as Holy Scripture; hence we must assume an earlier composition of the psalm, as venerability is one of the criteria for attaining the status of Holy Scripture.

1. *the heathen.* Cf. Ps x 16.

2. *the corpses.* Singular *niblat* with collective meaning accords with Canaanite usage in which the simple stem of a noun may be used to indicate plurality or indefinite number; UT, § 13.16. Cf. 'nt:II:9–10, *tḥth kkdrt riš 'lh kirbym kp,* "Under her are heads like balls, above her hands like locusts." In vs. 11, also, singular *'āsīr* must be understood collectively.

the birds. Comparing UT, 49:II:35–36, *širh ltikl 'ṣrm,* "The birds indeed eat his flesh."

beasts. Explaining MT *ḥayᵉtō* as a mispointing for *ḥayᵉtū* with the archaic nominative ending; cf. the first NOTE on Ps lix 10 and Albright in *Mélanges . . . A. Robert,* p. 26. Of course, the nominative is incorrect after the preposition which normally demands the genitive, but the expression is a fossilized one used by a deliberate archaizer who no longer appreciated the fine points of case endings and their function. This would point to an Exilic or post-Exilic date.

3. *shed their blood.* The expression *šāpᵉkū dāmām* compares with UT, 3 Aqht:obv.:23–24, *špk km šiy dm,* "Shed his blood like *šiy.*"

with no one. This stichometric division results from parsing the *waw* of *wᵉ'ēn* as emphatic; see the third NOTE on Ps lxxvii 2 and compare Jer x 20, *bānay yᵉṣā'ūnī wᵉ'ēnām,* "My sons who issued from me in truth are no more." In the traditional versions, the first colon numbers five Hebrew words and the second only two; the present analysis assigns three words to the first colon and four to the second.

to bury them. With *qōbēr* receiving its suffix from *dāmām,* "their blood." Since proper interment of the dead was a matter of great importance to the people of the ancient Near East, the inability to bury the slain Israelites was a poignant tragedy. Among the ancient West Semitic curses preserved in inscriptions, the lack of burial figured prominently; e.g., Phoenician Eshmunazor, line 8, *w'l yqbr bqbr,* "Nor may they be buried in a grave."

4. *the mockery and scorn.* In an unpublished Akkadian letter from Ras Shamra, the governor of Kadesh on the Orontes pleads with the king of Ugarit, "May my lord not hold me up to ridicule before my brethren!" Cf. Ernst Weidner in AfO 18 (1957–58), 169.

5. *How long . . . how long.* Recognizing in *'ad mah* of the first colon a double-duty interrogative whose force extends to the final colon, much like *mah* in Ps iii 2. Note the possible double-duty preposition in next verse.

your zeal. The root of *qin'āh* appears in UT, 52:21–22, *iqnu šmt bn šrm,* "I am zealous for the names of the princes," and 2078:1, *rišym qnum.*

6. *O God.* Most commentators describe MT *'el* as a mistake for *'al,* the construction *šāpak 'el* being elsewhere unattested. Possibly we should vocalize it as the divine name *'ēl,* which MT mispointed to *'el* as in Pss lxii 2, lxxvii 2, etc.

upon the nations. The preposition is forthcoming from the next line on the strength of the poetic usage discussed in the second Note on Ps lvii 4. The use of the double-duty interrogative in the preceding verse has been remarked.

kingdoms. Zorell, ZLH, p. 445a, defines *mamlākōt* here in the Phoenician sense of *mmlkt,* "prince, king," but the *gōyīm-mamlākōt* parallelism is replaced by the *gōyīm-mišpāḥōt* pairing in Jer x 25, which counters Zorell's definition. There are, however, a good number of biblical passages where *mamlākōt* does signify "kings" rather than "kingdoms"; see below on Ps cxxxv 11.

Given the close resemblances between this lament and Ps lxxiv, the kingdoms cursed by the psalmist are probably those governed by the "kings from the East," namely the Edomites, Ammonites, and Moabites who are denounced in Ps lxxiv 12.

7. *they have devoured.* Vocalizing infinitive absolute *'ākōl* for MT singular preterit *'ākal,* which does not agree in number with parallel *hēšammū,* "laid waste." The chiastic pattern of verb-object//object-verb should be noted.

8. *Do not record.* Vocalizing hiphil jussive *tazkēr* (MT *tizkor*) and

assigning to it the nuance preserved in the hiphil participle *mazkīr*, "recorder." In other words, *tazkēr . . . 'ᵃwōnōt* collocates the same ideas as Ezek xxi 28, xxix 16, *mazkīr 'āwōn*. The second NOTE on Ps lvi 1 lists some texts that depict God as a bookkeeper, and the NOTES on Pss lxxxvii 4 and cix 14–15 present further documentation of this motif.

to our debit. Some commentators (e.g., Briggs) would delete *lānū* as a prosaic addition making the verse too long, but this objection loses much of its force when *tazkēr* is translated "record." Compare Job xiii 26, *kī tiktōb 'ālay mᵉrōrōt*, "For you write against my account acts of violence," as rendered and explained in BCCT, p. 59.

O Scribe. Vocalizing *māhīr* (MT *mahēr*) and identifying *māhīr* alone as the equivalent of Ps xlv 2, *sōpēr māhīr*, "a skillful scribe." In the Papyrus Anastasi I, 18:4, one reads, "I am a scribe, a *mahir*," and though Egyptian scholars disagree on the precise meaning of *mahir*, a Canaanite loanword in Egyptian, its association with the scribe is here unmistakable. Cf. A Barucq, *L'expression de la louange divine et de la prière dans la Bible et en Egypte* (Cairo, 1962), 487; B. Couroyer in *Orientalia* 33 (1964), 443–53, and A. F. Rainey in JNES 26 (1967), 58–60.

the iniquities of our forefathers. Cf. Ps cix 14, "May the iniquity of his father remain recorded by the God Yahweh, and the sin of his mother not be effaced!"

come to meet us. God's merciful acts are personified as messengers, a motif cited in the fourth NOTE on Ps lxi 8.

9. *Help us . . . rescue us*. By departing from the traditional stichometric division and attaching imperative *haṣṣīlēnū* to the second colon, we uncover an inclusion begun by imperative *'ozrēnū*, "help us." What is more, this word distribution provides the second colon with the dynamism needed to vitalize the inert four words that precede. Compare vs. 10 and Ps vii 3.

rescue us. Parsing the waw of *wᵉhaṣṣīlēnū* as emphatic, not conjunctive; as noticed in the third NOTE on Ps lxxvii 2, emphatic *waw* often causes the verb to be placed at the end of the sentence.

name . . . name's sake. As in vs. 7, the word order is chiastic.

10. *Lest*. This nuance of *lammāh*, found in Ps cxv 2; Eccles v 7, vii 17, etc., also occurs in Phoenician Eshmunazor, lines 21–22, *lm ysgrnm 'lnm hqdšm 'l*, "Lest these holy gods imprison (namely, in the dungeon of the nether world) them."

That it. Namely, *šᵉmekā*, "your name," in vs. 9. The thought resembles Ps lxvii 3.

avenge. By vocalizing precative perfect *nāqamtā* (MT *niqmat*), there is no need for grammarians to worry how to reconcile the masculine verb *yiwwāda'* with the purported feminine subject *niqmat*. Furthermore, the expression *niqmat dām,* "the vengeance for blood," is a hapax legomenon, whereas *nāqam dām,* "to avenge blood," finds ample documentation; cf. Deut xxxii 44; II Kings ix 7, "And I will avenge the blood of my servants the prophets."

your prisoners. Reading pausal *'^{a}sīrekā* (MT *'āsīr k^{e}-*), with singular *'āsīr* bearing a collective meaning like vs. 2, *niblat.*

come before you. To plead on their behalf. Cf. Ps lxxxviii 3 and Job xxix 13.

with your long arm. Reading *gōdel* (MT *k^{e}gōdel*; see fourth NOTE on vs. 10) *z^{e}rō'^{a}kā* and parsing it as an accusative of means preceding the verb, a word order commented upon in the fourth NOTE on Ps lxxv 9. For the nuance "long, length," of *gōdel,* see Ezek xxxi 7 where *gōdel* balances *'ōrek,* "length."

preserve. Literally *hōtēr* denotes "to make survive." The doublet in Ps cii 21 reads *l^{e}pattē^{a}ḥ,* "to release." Cf. Ps xxxiii 19, "to preserve their lives from the Hungry One."

condemned to die. Occurring but here and in Ps cii 21, *t^{e}mūtāh* appears twice in UT, 2059:16, 22, *rb tmtt,* "the Lord of Death," an epithet of some maleficent deity such as Mot or Resheph.

12. *seven times over.* A demand for vengeance of the most thoroughgoing kind, in the spirit of Lamech, who in Gen iv 24 assures his wives Adah and Zillah, "If Cain is avenged seven times over, then Lamech seventy times seven."

into our neighbors' bosoms. Well-directed, so that it strikes to their innermost being.

13. *From generation.* Consult the third NOTE on Ps lxxviii 69 for *l^{e},* "from," and UT, 49:II:26–27, *lymm lyrḫm,* "from days to months."

PSALM 80

(lxxx 1–20)

1 *For the director; according to "Lilies." A solemn commandment, a psalm of Asaph.*

2 O Shepherd of Israel, give ear,
lead Joseph like a flock;
O Enthroned upon the Cherubim, shine forth
3 before Ephraim and Benjamin and Manasseh! [2]*
Rouse your power
and come to save us!
4 O God, return to us! [3]
and let your face shine
that we may be saved.
5 O Yahweh, God of Hosts, [4]
how long will you fume
while your people prays?
6 You have fed us tears as our food, [5]
and given us tears to drink by the bowl.
7 You made us the derision of our neighbors, [6]
and our foes made sport of us.
8 O God of Hosts, return to us! [7]
and let your face shine
that we may be saved.
9 You brought a vine from Egypt, [8]
drove out the nations and planted it.
10 You pushed aside her predecessors, [9]
and made her strike roots,
and caused her to fill the land.
11 The mountains were covered with its shadow, [10]
and with its boughs the towering cedars.

* Verse numbers in RSV.

12 You caused its branches to shoot forth to the Sea, [11]
and its tendrils to the River.
13 Why have you destroyed its hedges, [12]
so that all who pass by pluck its fruit?
14 The boar from the forest cropped it, [13]
and what moves in the field fed on it.
15 O God of Hosts, return, we pray. [14]
Look down from heaven and see,
and visit this vine.
16 Take care of what your right hand has planted, [15]
and of the son you strengthened for yourself.
17 Those who burned it with a full blazing fire— [16]
at your angry rebuke may they perish!
18 May your hand be on the man at your right, [17]
upon the son of man you strengthened for yourself.
19 We have never turned away from you! [18]
Restore us to life that we may call on your name.
20 O Yahweh, God of Hosts, return to us! [19]
let your face shine that we may be saved.

Notes

lxxx. A national lament characterized by a refrain (vss. 4, 8, 15, 20) and by a prayer for the king (vss. 16, 18). The mention of Israel and Joseph in vs. 2 and of the tribes of Ephraim, Benjamin, and Manasseh in vs. 3 shows that the psalm was composed in the Northern Kingdom that was destroyed in 721 B.C. In all probability this lament belongs to the last days of the Northern Kingdom. The striking linguistic and conceptual similarities between this psalm and Ps xliv suggest a common provenance; consult the Notes on vss. 4, 7, 9, 10, 11, 12, 19.

2. *Israel . . . Joseph.* As in Ps lxxvii 16, the poet has North Israel in mind.

lead. The proposal to emend the participle *nōhēg* to imperative $n^{e}hag$, "lead!," founders on the observation at Ps lxxiv 12 that for stylistic variation biblical poets sometimes employed the participle as a substitute for the imperative.

O Enthroned upon the Cherubim. An ancient epithet of Yahweh in I Sam iv 4, II Sam vi 2, originally referring to the divine presence above the ark.

shine forth. Cf. *Psalms I,* p. 302. The absence of God being considered the cause of the calamity that occasioned this national lament, the poet implores God to shine forth in the bright light of theophanic presence. In addition to mythological texts, the Ugaritic verb *yp'* appears in many personal names such as *yp'b'l*, "May Baal shine forth!"

3. *to save us.* Parsing *līšū'ātāh* as the equivalent of an infinitive construct expressing purpose. This analysis bears on the parsing of a disputed construction in vs. 5.

4. *return to us and let your face shine.* The present darkness that envelops North Israel is due to the absence of God. Hence *h^ašībēnū* seems to resume the prayer of vs. 3, *l^ekāh*, "Come!" In other words, the juxtaposed imperatives *h^ašībēnū w^ehā'ēr pānekā* semantically equal Ps lxvii 2, "May he cause his face to shine, and may he come to us." Like vs. 2, *hōpī'āh*, "shine forth," *h^ašībēnū* is an internal hiphil as in Ezek xiv 6, xviii 30, 32; Jon i 13; see below on Ps lxxxv 4. The suffix *-ēnū* parses as datival, a usage commented upon at Pss lxvii 2 and lxxxv 5. Here then is the first point of contact with Ps xliv, which in vs. 18 employs the dative suffix with *bā'āh*. That this grammatical analysis is sound may further be supported by vs. 15, *šūb-nā'*, "return, we pray," a qal imperative that many critics would emend to the hiphil. Such an emendation becomes superfluous with the recognition that *h^ašībēnū* articulates the same prayer. Cf. Dan ix 25 where hiphil *hāšīb* expresses the same idea as qal *tāšūb*, namely "restore."

let your face shine. With the light of divine favor, as in Pss iv 7, xxxi 17, xliv 4, lxvii 2, cxix 135; Num vi 25. Cf. UT, 1015:9–10, *wpn špš nr by mid*, "And the face of the suzerain shone greatly upon me."

that we may be saved. Explaining *w^eniwwāšē'āh* as the subjunctive mode stating purpose; cf. the NOTE on Ps lxvi 16.

5. *God of Hosts.* Gunkel's description of *'^elōhīm ṣ^ebā'ōt* as "an impossible combination" will not be endorsed today by anyone conversant with Ugaritic grammar; cf. the first NOTE on Ps lix 6, and K. A. Kitchen, *Ancient Orient and Old Testament* (London, 1966), pp. 161–62.

will you fume. Reproducing the root sense of *'āšantā;* related texts are listed at Ps lxxiv 1.

while your people prays. Syntactically difficult *bit^epillat 'ammekā* yields the best sense when *t^epillat* is understood as a noun with verbal force, much like vs. 3, *līšū'ātāl-lānū*, "to save us." In other words, *bit^epillat* serves as an infinitive construct in a temporal phrase, like UT, Krt:60, *bbk krt*, "while Kirta cried."

6. *You have fed us.* Parsing *h'kltm* as the causative verb followed by the enclitic *mem*, which balances the suffix of *tašqēmō;* this stylistic balance between the enclitic *mem* and a pronominal suffix received comment at Ps x 17.

tears as our food. Parsing *leḥem dim'āh* as two accusatives, not as a construct chain, "the bread of tears." The first, *leḥem,* parses as the predicate accusative, and *dim'āh* as the direct object. Compare Ps xlii 4, *hāyᵉtāhl lī dim'ātī leḥem,* "My tears have been my food." Gunkel (*Die Psalmen,* p. 354) argues that MT *dim'āh* should be emended to masculine *dema'* because in the parallel colon we have feminine plural *dᵉmā'ōt,* "tears." If he is correct, there is still no need to emend *dim'āh* since the final *-āh* might well represent the accusative ending, as in Ps lxviii 7.

and given us. Both LXX and *Juxta Hebraeos* took the suffix of *wattašqēmō* as first person plural, but this need not entail an emendation of *-ēmō* (if this be the correct vocalization) to *-ēnū* since *lāmō,* "at/for us" (see vs. 7), is well documented, as noticed in *Psalms I,* p. 173.

tears. Comparing Prov ix 5, *ūšᵉtū bᵉyēn* (MT *bᵉyayin*) *māsaktī,* "And drink of the wine I have poured," and, for cognate imagery, UT, 62:10, *tšt kyn udm't,* "She drank tears like wine."

by the bowl. A doubtful translation of *šālīš,* which I would derive from Ugar. *ṯlṯ,* "bronze, copper." Hence *šālīš* would be a bronze container. Cf. Isa xl 12, *wᵉkāl baššālīš 'ᵃpar hā'āreṣ,* "And (who) has measured the dust of the earth in a bowl?," and Angel Marzel, "Consideraciones sobre la raiz ugarítica *'ṯlṯ',*" in *Biblica* 44 (1963), 343–51. For the thought, Deut xxxii 14c might prove instructive: *dam 'ēnāb tišteh ḥōmer* (MT *ḥāmer*), "The blood of the grape you will drink by the bowl." Cf. also Esth i 8, *wᵉhaššᵉtiyyāh kaddōt* (MT *kaddāt*) *'ēn 'ōnēs,* "And the drinking was by flagons without restraint," as correctly interpreted by John Gray, *The Legacy of Canaan,* 2d ed., pp. 266–67.

7. *You made us.* With *tᵉśīmēnū* expressing past time as in Ps xliv 14, the most common function of *yqtl* in Ugaritic; see introductory NOTE on Ps lxxviii. Other cases of this usage recur in vss. 9 (twice), 12, 14 (twice).

the derision. Relating much-canvassed *mādōn* (pointing uncertain) to the root underlying Ugar. *dnt,* which in parallelism with *bṯt, "shame,"* and *tdmm,* "abuse," most probably derives from Ar. *dana'a,* "to be vile, disgraceful." A comparison with Ps xliv 14 reveals that *mādōn* and *ḥerpāh,* "taunt," are synonymous. Cf. Gen vi 3, *lō' yādōn rūḥī bā'ādām,* possibly to be rendered, "My spirit will not reproach man."

made sport. As in the first colon, the imperfect form (*yil'ᵃgū*) states an event of the past.

of us. See the third NOTE on vs. 6 for *lāmō.*

8. *O God of Hosts.* Consult the first NOTE on vs. 5.

return to us. See the first NOTE on vs. 4.

9. *You brought.* The yqtl form *yassīaʿ* expresses past time; cf. the first NOTE on vs. 7. The verb *nsʿ* (or *nšʿ*) occurs in connection with Egypt in UT, 2116:14–16, *l tsʿn mṣrm tmkrn,* "The merchants shall not travel to Egypt."

a vine. An allegory of Israel which re-echoes Gen xlix 22; Hos x 1; Isa v 1–7, etc.

drove out. As frequently in this psalm, the imperfect *tegārēš* expresses past narrative. The verb *grš* is widely attested in Ugaritic. Cf. Ps xliv 3, "Nations you dispossessed, but you planted them."

and planted it. Here predicated of God, the verb *nāṭaʿ* is used of Baal's activity in UT, 76:II:24.

10. *You pushed aside.* As observed at Ps xiii 4, the parallelism with *hēsīr* in Zeph iii 15 brings out clearly this denotation of piel *pinnāh.* As noted by Gunkel, there is a wordplay in the phrase *pinnītā lepānehā.* On the use of wordplay in laments, see the second NOTE on Ps lx 5. The play on the words *'āḥōr,* "back," and *'ōraḥ,* "path," in the cognate lament Ps xliv 19 might here be noticed.

her predecessors. On the basis of Phoen. *hlpnyhm,* "those who were before me"; Eccles iv 16; Job xxi 8, an attempt has been made in *Biblica* 43 (1962), 357, and 47 (1966), 411, to establish this use of the preposition as a substantive. This parsing obviates the need for assuming with many critics that *derek,* "way," has fallen out of the text after *pinnītā.* In substance, *pinnītā lepānehā* equals Zeph iii 15, *pinnāh 'ōyebēk,* since "the predecessors" refer to the foes who lived in Palestine before the entry of the Israelites, namely the Canaanites, the Amorites, and others enumerated in Deut vii 1.

and made her strike roots. Though modern versions make *gepen,* "vine," the subject of *wattašrēš,* the LXX and *Juxta Hebraeos,* in keeping God the subject of this verb, are surely to be followed here.

roots . . . land. The balance of *šorāšehā,* "roots," with *'āreṣ,* "land," recalls their juxtaposition in UT, 1 Aqht:159–60, *šršk barṣ al ypʿ,* "May your roots not flourish in the earth."

and caused her to fill the land. Retaining the same subject of the preceding two verbs in this elegant 2+2+2 line, making the suffix of *šorāšehā,* "roots," provide the suffix that *temallē'* needs. Ps xliv 11, it has been noted (*Psalms I,* p. 266), also employs a double-duty suffix.

The psalmist depicts God as the immediate cause of the heathens' expulsion from Palestine, of Israel's implantation therein, and of her subsequent expansion throughout the Holy Land.

11. *The mountains were covered with its shadow.* Comparing *kossū hārīm ṣillāh* with Prov xxiv 31, *kossū pānāyw ḥarullīm,* "Its surface was covered with nettles."

with its shadow, and with its boughs. In preceding verse the poet indulges in wordplay, here he employs chiasm, and in the next line he resorts to merism, that is, the art of dividing a whole into its parts.

the towering cedars. The longstanding explanation of *'arzē 'ēl* as an expression of the superlative is sustained by the Ugaritic usage cited in *Psalms I,* p. 220, at Ps xxxvi 7. The psalmist describes the branches of the vine as climbing to the tops of the highest cedars in Lebanon and covering their great limbs.

12. *You caused . . . to shoot forth.* As in Ps xliv 3, God is the subject of *t^ešallaḥ,* a *yqtl* form designating past history, as in vss. 7 and 8.

to the Sea . . . to the River. The use of two different prepositions (*'ad . . . 'el*) with one verb is a point of style worth noting. Other examples are listed in the second NOTE on Ps lv 11.

The "Sea," *yām,* refers to the Mediterranean, while *nāhār,* as in Ps lxxii 8, denotes the Euphrates.

13. *its hedges.* One preserves the consistency of the allegory by defining *g^edērehā* as the hedge or enclosure around a vineyard rather than as fortified walls; consult James B. Pritchard, *Hebrew Inscriptions and Stamps from Gibeon* (Philadelphia, 1959), pp. 9–10.

14. *The boar from the forest.* Comparing the phrase *ḥ^azīr miyya'ar* with Ps lxxiv 12, *malkē miqqedem,* "the kings from the East." Biblical *ḥ^azīr* appears in Ugaritic as *ḫzr* and *ḫnzr.*

Here *ḥ^azīr* is used figuratively of Israel's enemies, and it is interesting to note that in the Ugaritic tablets this word also had a metaphorical sense, designating some kind of personnel in the economic texts, while in mythological UT, 67:v:9, *ḫnzr,* parallel to *ǵlm,* "youth," describes Baal's lackeys.

cropped it. Deriving the hapax legomenon *y^ekars^emennāh* from *kāsam,* "to shear," Akk. *kasāmu,* "to cut to pieces," with the *r* a secondary addition to the root; cf. the first NOTE on Ps lxxiii 4. The *yqtl* forms in both halves of the verse relate past events.

15. *O God of Hosts.* See the first NOTE on vs. 5.

return, we pray. Qal *šūb-nā'* articulates the same prayer as hiphil *h^ašībēnū* in vss. 4, 8, 20.

and visit this vine. Namely, with restorative rain. This exegesis of imperative *p^eqōd* is prompted by precative perfect *pāqadtā* in the prayer for rain in Ps lxv 10.

16. *Take care of. kannāh* is a stubborn puzzle, but its balance with *p^eqōd,* "Visit!," and a comparison with Judg xii 6, *w^elō' yākīn l^edabbēr kēn,* "But he did not take care to speak correctly," suggests this version. In vs. 12 the psalmist employs two prepositions with the same verb, but here he makes a direct object and the preposition *'al* dependent upon the imperative *kannāh.*

the son. Not a personification of Israel (e.g., Briggs, BDB), but a reference to the king; see the following NOTE.

you strengthened. Important for the interpretation of the term *bēn* is the use of this verb in royal Ps lxxxix 22, which describes God's relationship to David: *'ap zᵉrō'ī tᵉ'ammᵉṣennū,* "And my arm shall strengthen him." The root *'mṣ* lacked counterparts in the other Semitic languages till the publication of the Ras Shamra tablets which attest *amṣ yd,* "strong of hand" (UT, 1001:14), and the possible piel participle *mamṣ* in 39:3.

17. *Those who burned it.* Repointing MT *śᵉrūpāh* to the plural participle *śōrᵉpehā*. The construction *śōrᵉpehā bā'ēš* should be compared to UT, 49:v:14, *šrp bišt,* "burning by fire."

with a full blazing fire. Reading *bā'ēš kī-sōḥāh* (MT *kᵉsūḥāh*), and parsing *kī* as an emphatic modifier of the feminine singular participle *sōḥāh,* from *sāḥāh,* "to scour." In Ezek xxvi 4 this verb is associated with *ṣāḥīḥ,* "glaring, glowing surface," whose root denotes "to be scorched."

at your angry rebuke. Literally "at the rebuke of your fury," with *pānīm* carrying the connotation discussed in *Psalms I,* pp. 133, 207. Cf. especially Lam iv 16, *pᵉnē yhwh ḥillᵉqām,* "The fury of Yahweh destroyed them."

may they perish! Comparing jussive *yō'bēdū* with the precative perfect *'ābᵉdū* in Ps x 16.

18. *your hand.* At Ps lxxiv 11 it was argued that *yād,* "hand," sometimes bore the more specific denotation "left hand." Here, because of the situation described, *yādᵉkā* probably refers to "your right hand." In view of *yᵉmīnekā,* "your right hand," in the same colon, one may surmise that the need for variety dictated this poetic usage.

the man at your right. Poetic for "the king," as recognized by, among others, Hans Schmidt, *Die Psalmen* (Tübingen, 1934), p. 154. Cf. Ps cx 1, where Yahweh commands the king, "Sit at my right hand."

the son of man. Refers to the king, as suggested by the parallelism. *ben 'ādām* now finds its semantic equivalent in Ugar. *bnš,* vocalized *bu-nu-šu,* and composed of *bun,* "son," and *nōš,* "man." As Gordon, UT, Glossary, No. 486, points out, in some texts where *bnš* is applied to a courtier, it probably meant a "somebody" with a genealogy.

19. *never.* Analyzing *wᵉlō'* into the emphatic *waw* and the negative; cf. *Psalms I,* p. 303, and the third NOTE on Ps lv 12. Apparently unable to account for its presence, the Targum simply dropped the *waw.* Cf. also Job xxiii 12. Jer iv 1–2 proves very instructive: *wᵉ'im tāsīr šiqqūṣekā mippānay wᵉlō' tānūd wᵉnišba'tā,* "And if you put your vile things aside, never stray from my presence, then might you swear. . . ."

turned away. As in vss. 7, 9, 12, 14, the imperfect form *nāsōg* states past time; cf. Ps xliv 19, "Our heart has not turned back." Since the Israelites did not turn away (*nāsōg*), they feel justified in pleading with God to return (*haššībēnū, šub-nā'*) to them.

Restore us to life . . . 20. *return to us*. The relationship between these two ideas is well illustrated by Ezek xviii 32, which, as here, employs the internal hiphil of *šūb: hāšībū wīḥyū*, "Return that you may live!"

PSALM 81

(lxxxi 1–17)

1 *For the director; upon the gittith. A psalm of Asaph.*

2 Ring out your joy to the God of our Fortress,
shout in triumph to the God of Jacob.
3 Raise a song and sound the tambour, [2]*
the sweet-sounding lyre with the harp.
4 Blow the trumpet at the new moon, [3]
at the full moon, the very day of our feast.
5 For it is a statute, O Israel, [4]
an ordinance from the God of Jacob.
6 As a command he imposed it on Joseph [5]
when he went from the land of Egypt.
"I heard the speech of one unknown to me, [6]
7 I removed the burden on his shoulder,
his hands were freed from the basket.
8 In distress you called, [7]
and I delivered you;
I answered you from the hiding place of thunder,
though I was provoked by you near Meribah's waters. *Selah*
9 Listen, my people, while I testify against you, [8]
O Israel, if you would but listen to me!
10 There shall be no strange god among you, [9]
nor shall you worship any alien god.
11 I am Yahweh your God, [10]
who brought you up out of the land of Egypt;
What is more, I filled your wide-open mouth.
12 But my people did not listen to my voice, [11]
and Israel would have none of me.
13 So I repudiated him for his stubbornness of heart, [12]
they followed their own designs.

* Verse numbers in RSV.

14 If only my people would listen to me, [13]
and Israel walk in my ways!
15 Straightway would I subdue their foes, [14]
and against their adversaries turn my hand.
16 Those who hate Yahweh would cringe before him, [15]
and their doom would be sealed forever.
17 He would feed him wheat from the hill [16]
and with honey from the mountain would I satisfy you."

Notes

lxxxi. A composite liturgy of North Israelite (see vs. 6) origin. The first section (vss. 2–6a) is a hymn composed either for the Passover or for the Feast of Tabernacles. The second part (vss. 6b–17) is a divine oracle in which God reminds his people that it was he who freed them from their slavery in Egypt, led them out of bondage and fed them in the wilderness; he commanded them to worship no strange gods and punished them for their disobedience. If they will but obey him, he will give them victory over their foes and bless them with prosperity.

As one may gather from the ensuing Notes, the application of the principles of Northwest Semitic grammar may well clear up some of the outstanding syntactic difficulties; cf. especially vss. 5, 6, 7, 8, 11. In its striking use of prepositions, this poem resembles Ps xv.

1. *the gittith.* Found in the headings of Pss viii and lxxxiv, Heb. *gittīt* is a term of unknown significance.

2. *the God of our Fortress.* Reading *'elōhē-m 'ūzzēnū,* a construct chain with an interposed enclitic *mem,* like the construction *'elōhē-m ṣebā'ōt,* "the God of Hosts," discussed at Ps lix 6. In other terms, the balance between the construct chains *'elōhē-m 'ūzzēnū* and *'elōhē ya'aqōb,* "God of Jacob," syntactically equals that between *'elōhē-m ṣebā'ōt* and *'elōhē yiśrā'ēl* in Ps lix 10.

As in Ps lxxviii 61, *'ōz,* "Fortress," is a name for the ark of the covenant. G. Henton Davies in his study "The Ark in the Psalms" (cited in the first Note on Ps lxxviii 61), p. 55, has recognized that our passage alludes to the ark, even though he translates "God, our strength."

3. *tambour.* Ugar. *tp,* "tambour," and *knr,* "lyre," in unpublished RŠ 24.252, give us a pretty good idea of where the biblical names of musical instruments came from. Consult *Psalms I,* p. 297.

the sweet-sounding lyre. The phrase *kinnōr nā'īm* appears in a context not unlike that of UT, 'nt:I:19–20, *mṣltm bd n'm yšr ǵzr ṭb ql,*

"The cymbals are in the hands of the sweet-voiced; the lad with the good voice sings," and the Ugaritic word *n'm* suffices to show that the attempt of BDB, p. 654a, to derive biblical *nā'īm* in this verse from Ar. *naĝama,* "to speak in a low voice," is badly misplaced.

4. *full moon.* A dis-legomenon in the Bible (in Prov vii 20, written *kese'*), and attested in Phoen. *ks', keseh* now appears in the unpublished Ras Shamra tablet RŠ 24.271:A:6, *yrḫ wksa,* which Comte du Mesnil in *Mélanges de l'Université Saint-Joseph* 39 (1964), 178, n. 6, renders "Yaraḫ et Pleine Lune." Cf. Dahood, *Biblica* 46 (1965), 330.

The "full moon" might be either Passover or the Feast of Tabernacles. The latter is supported by Jewish tradition, and if the psalm is considered as a whole in its composite form, the stress in vss. 9–11 on the giving of the law favors that opinion. If, however, vss. 2–6 originally formed a separate hymn, they, by reason of their content, are more appropriate to the Passover festival.

the very day. Explaining l^e of *l^eyōm* as emphatic; consult *Psalms I,* p. 143.

5. *it is a statute.* That is, celebration of the Passover festival.

O Israel. Not "for Israel" with the ancient and modern versions, since, following four imperatives in vss. 2–4, the *lamedh* parses as vocative, precisely as in Pss lxxiii 1 and cxxii 4.

from the God of Jacob. As noted by O. Loretz in BZ 2 (1958), 288, on the basis of Ugar. *l,* "from," the preposition of *lē'lōhē ya'^{a}qōb* denotes "from." The versions, it might be noted, are innocent of both the vocative *lamedh* and the meaning "from" of the preposition l^e in this verse.

6. *when he went.* At the Exodus of Israel, designating the time when the Passover was instituted; see Exod xii 37–xiii 10.

from the land. This version of *'al 'ereṣ,* required by cognate passages such as vs. 11, Ps cxiv 1, *b^eṣē't yiśrā'ēl mimmiṣrāyim,* "When Israel went out of Egypt"; Isa xi 16; Amos iii 1, and sustained by the LXX, Syr., and *Juxta Hebraeos,* becomes grammatically explicable within the framework of Northwest Semitic where *'al* sometimes denotes "from." Cf. *Psalms I,* p. 26; G. R. Driver, *Die Welt des Orients,* I, 5 (1950), 413; Dahood, CBQ 17 (1955), 19–22.

I heard. The subject of the *yqtl* verb *'ešma'* expressing past time (cf. introductory NOTE on Ps lxxviii) being God himself; he remains the speaker to the end of the psalm.

the speech. Literally "the lip" (Isa xix 18), *ś^{e}pat* is a construct governing the independent verb *lō' yāda'tī;* e.g., Exod iv 13, *b^eyad tišlaḥ,* "by the hand of him who you will send." Consult GK, § 130d, and Joüon, GHB, § 129q.

of one unknown to me. Parsing *lō' yāda'tī* as a relative clause without the relative pronoun *'ašer*, "who," that has become a substantive; its grammatical function is that of a genitive governed by the construct *śepat*. Joüon, GHB, § 158d, cites Isa xli 24, lxiii 19; Jer ii 8, and Job xviii 21, the last being the most pertinent to our purpose: *wezeh meqōm lō' yāda' 'ēl*, "Such is the home of him who knows not God." This analysis also serves to explain the translation of Ps xxxv 15. Cf. also *Psalms I*, pp. 213 f.; Job xxix 12, 16; Prov ix 13, xxiii 35, and below NOTE on Ps lxxxv 9.

The "one unknown to me" is collective Israel in Egypt before it was chosen by God as his people. Before its election Israel was "unknown" to God. Cf. Amos iii 1–2, "Hear this word that Yahweh has spoken against you, O people of Israel, against the whole family which I brought up out of the land of Egypt: 'You alone have I known of all the families of the earth.'"

7. *I removed.* Reading *hasīrōtī-m*, with enclitic *mem*, instead of MT *hasīrōtī* followed by the preposition of *missēbel* (see next NOTE).

the burden on his shoulder. Reading *sēbel šikmō* and consulting the preceding NOTE. The suffix of *šikmō* refers to Israel in bondage in Egypt under taskmasters who required them to make bricks and carry them in baskets to the public buildings being erected; cf. Exod i 11–14, ii 7–9, etc.

the basket. Heb. *dūd* equals Ugar. *dd*, Akk. *dūdu*.

8. *I answered you.* As in vs. 6 *'ešma'*, "heard," *yqtl 'e'enekā* expresses past time.

from the hiding place. With *be* in *besēter* bearing one of its normal Northwest Semitic senses "from"; cf. Ps xcix 7, *be'ammūd 'ānān yedabbēr 'alēhem*, "From the pillar of the cloud he spoke to them"; the second NOTE on Ps lx 8, and O. Loretz in BZ 2 (1958), 289. Cf. UT, 'nt:v:33–34, *y'ny il bšb't ḥdrm*, "El answers from the seven rooms," and Job ix 17, *'ašer biśe'ārāh yešūpēnī*, "He spies on me from the tempest."

The "hiding place of thunder" is Mount Sinai.

though I was provoked by you. In face of Pss lxxviii 17 ff., xcv 9, cvi 32; Exod xvii 7; Num xx 24, xxvii 14; Deut xxxiii 8, there is no alternative to this translation of consonantal *'bḥnk*, which must be pointed niphal *'ebbāḥēn*, "I was provoked," followed by the dative suffix expressing the agent. Hence vocalize *'ebbāḥēnekā* and consult *Psalms I*, p. 308, and the first NOTE on Ps lxiii 11 for other examples of the dative suffix of agency.

The traditional version, based on the Masoretic pointing, *'ebḥānekā*, "I tested you at the waters of Meribah" (RSV) contradicts all the biblical texts cited in the preceding paragraph. According to these, it was not God who tried the Israelites at Meribah, but rather the Israelites who tested God's patience. Here, then, is clear proof that the construction whereby the agent is expressed by a suffix attached to a passive verb was beyond the ken of the Masoretes and the ancient versions.

near Meribah's waters. Comparing *'al mē m^erībāh* with Ps xxiii 3 and UT, 1 Aqht:152–53, *ylkm qr mym d'lk mḫṣ aqht ġzr,* "Woe to you, O fountain of waters, since near you was struck down Aqhat the hero." Meribah is the name of two different stations of the Israelites in the wilderness; their exact location cannot be determined. "Meribah's waters" refers to the waters which sprung from the rock struck by Moses (Exod xvii 1–7; Num xx 10–13).

11. *out of the land. mē'ereṣ* is semantically akin to vs. 6, *'al 'ereṣ,* "from the land."

What is more, I filled. Explaining *wa'^amal^e'ēhū* as a verb at the end of its clause *harḥīb pīkā wa'^amal^e'ēhū* because it is preceded by the emphatic *waw;* cf. the third NOTE on Ps lxxvii 2. The suffix *-hū* is resumptive, as e.g., in Ps lxxxix 12. As in vss. 7, 8, 13, the *yqtl* verb states a past action.

your wide-open mouth. Reading hiphil infinitive construct *harḥīb* for MT hiphil imperative *harḥeb.* The construct chain *harḥīb pīkā* is the direct object of the postpositive verb.

From the context it appears reasonably clear that the event described is the feeding of the Israelites in the wilderness after their departure from Egypt; cf. Num xi 4–9, 31–34; Ps lxxviii 24–30. Since *hirḥīb* in Isa v 14 describes the opening of Sheol's massive gullet, one may propose that its use here is meant to suggest the insatiable appetite of the Israelites in the desert.

13. *So I repudiated him.* Retaining the singular suffix *-hū* of MT (cf. *Juxta Hebraeos*), which most versions emend to plural *-hem* in order to establish numerical agreement with the plural suffixes of the following words.

his stubbornness of heart. Explaining the *mem* of *lbm* as the enclitic balancing the singular suffix *'^aśall^eḥēhū,* a stylistic practice examined in *Psalms I,* pp. 16 ff. See below on Ps lxxxiv 6.

they followed. Noting in *yēl^ekū* a *yqtl* form describing a past action. This disconcerting shift between third person singular and plural forms when referring to Israel is not amenable to a satisfactory explanation. The recurrence of the same phenomenon in vss. 15–16 dissuades one from assuming textual corruption. What is more, the *Juxta Hebraeos* reading vouches for the Masoretic text.

14. *would listen to me.* The documentation at Ps lx 11 of the single writing of a *yod* where morphology requires two makes it unnecessary to assume the haplography of a *yod* in the sequence *'my šm'.* This orthography permits the reading *'ammī yišma'* that the construction with optative *lū,* "if only," prefers.

15. *foes . . . adversaries.* The frequent biblical parallelism between *'ōyēb* and *ṣār* takes its origin from Canaanite poetry which balances these two roots, as in UT, 68:9, *ht ibk tmḫṣ ht tṣmt ṣrtk,* "Behold, you will smite your foes; behold, you will annihilate your adversaries!" Cf. also the second NOTE on Ps liv 9.

16. *Those who hate Yahweh.* Comparing *m^{e}śan^e'ē yhwh* with UT, 51:VII:36, *šnu hd,* "those who hate Hadd."

before him. The plural suffixes of vs. 15 referring to Israel's foes have led many critics to conclude that singular *lō* refers to Yahweh as in Ps lxvi 3, but the playing back and forth between singular and plural suffixes in regard to Israel that has been noticed in vs. 13 supports the position of those commentators who identify the antecedent of *lō* with Israel understood collectively, as in Deut xxxiii 29. Cf. Ps xviii 45.

their doom. Recognizing in *'ittām* the nuance found in Isa xiii 22; Ezek vii 7, 12, xxi 30, 34, xxii 3, and xxx 3, *'ēt gōyīm,* "a time of doom for the nations" (RSV). Cf. the use of *yōmō* in Ps xxxvii 13, and G. A. Cooke, *The Book of Ezekiel,* p. 331.

17. *He would feed him.* The subject being Yahweh, the direct object Israel. Many critics impugn MT third person *ya'^{a}kīlēhū,* but the fact that vs. 16 speaks of Yahweh in the third person sustains the MT reading.

from the hill. E. Y. Kutscher, *Leshonenu* 32 (1967–68), 346, rightly repoints MT *ḥēleb,* "fat," to *ḥeleb,* "hill," to recover the parallelism witnessed in Ugar. *ģr,* "mountain"// *ḫlb,* "hill."

See also M. Dahood in *Ras Shamra Parallels: The Texts from Ugarit and the Hebrew Bible,* ed. L. R. Fisher (Rome, 1972), I, p. 306.

would I satisfy you. The shift from the third person subject and object in the first colon to the first person verb and second person object in the final colon may be explained as court style. The chiastic structure of the verse with suffixed verb and prepositional phrase parallel to prepositional phrase and suffixed verb is noteworthy.

PSALM 82

(lxxxii 1–8)

1 A *psalm of Asaph.*

God presides in the divine council,
    in the midst of the gods adjudicates.
2 "How long will you defend the unjust,
    and show partiality to the wicked? *Selah*
3 Defend the weak and the fatherless,
    vindicate the afflicted and the poor.
4 Rescue the weak and the poor,
    from the grip of the wicked rescue them."
5 Without knowledge and without understanding
    they wander about in darkness;
All the foundations of the earth are shaken.
6 I had thought, "You are gods,
    all of you sons of the Most High;
7 Yet you shall die as men do,
    and fall like any prince."
8 Arise, O God, govern the earth,
    rule over all the nations yourself!

NOTES

lxxxii. A prophetic liturgy of the Lord's judgment on pagan gods. The poem consists of three parts. The first section (vss. 1–4) is a depiction, or rather a vision, of the heavenly tribunal where God passes judgment on the pagan deities (vs. 1), and a summation (vss. 2–4) of the charges on which they are convicted. The second part (vss. 5–7) contains the psalmist's diatribe against the heathen gods whose moral obtuseness is responsible for the cosmic disorders and will be responsible for their loss of immortality and ejection from heaven into the nether world. In the final verse the psalmist prays for the restoration of universal justice under the sole rule of Yahweh.

Because of this psalm's similarity to Isa iii 13 and Ezek xxviii 1–10, many commentators propose a sixth-century composition, but the archaic quality of the language suggests a much earlier date. In fact, James Stokes Ackerman (*An Exegetical Study of Psalm 82* [dissertation submitted at Harvard University, 1966]) is probably correct when maintaining that this psalm originated in the pre-monarchial period.

1. *presides.* For this nuance of *niṣṣāb,* cf. I Sam xix 20 and Julian Morgenstern, "The Mythological Background of Psalm 82," in HUCA 14 (1939), 29–126, especially p. 71.

presides . . . adjudicates. Preserving the chiastic order of the Hebrew.

in . . . in the midst of. The pairing of *bᵉ* and *bᵉqereb* equals that of, e.g., UT, 51:v:75–76, *bbhtk . . . bqrb hklk.*

the divine council. *ʿᵃdat ʾēl* is highly reminiscent of Ugar. *ʿdt il,* "the council of El," as pointed out by numerous scholars; see *Psalms I,* p. 5, and A. Gonzalez, "Le Psaume LXXXII," in VT 13 (1963), 293–309, especially p. 298. The picture of God in the midst of the assembly of gods recurs again and again in the Psalter; cf. Pss xxix 1–2, lxxvii 14, lxxxix 6–9, xcv 3, xcvi 4, xcvii 7, cxlviii 2.

the gods. Namely, of the "nations" mentioned in vs. 8.

2. *How long.* The speaker in vss. 2–4 being God himself.

the unjust . . . the wicked. In balance with concrete *rᵉšāʿīm,* "the wicked," abstract *ʿāwel,* "injustice," takes on a concrete denotation in virtue of the Canaanite-Hebrew poetic practice discussed at Ps lxxviii 61. These two terms designate the pagans, such as the Canaanites and Moabites, whose gods are referred to in a general manner in vs. 1. As in vss. 1 and 3, the word order is chiastic.

3. *the weak.* The widely adopted emendation of *dal* to *dak* finds no support in the Psalms scroll from Masada (first century B.C.), which, like MT, reads *dl;* cf. IEJ 15 (1965), Pl. 19, Fig. A. In fact, such a textual alteration is positively countered by the fact that the elements of *dal wᵉyātōm* occur in sequence in UT, 127:47–50, *ltdy ṯšm ʿl dl lpnk ltšlḥm ytm,* "You do not drive out those who prey on the weak, you do not feed the fatherless before you." On the text-critical value of parallel words, see the fourth NOTE on Ps lvii 8.

vindicate the afflicted and the poor. This clear sentiment serves to elucidate the unclear reading and translation of Ps xlv 4, as exposed in *Psalms I,* p. 272.

5. *Without knowledge and without understanding.* The parallel verbs *yādᵉʿū* and *yābīnū* appear in tandem in UT, ʿnt:III:23–24, *abn brq dl tdʿ šmm rgm ltdʿ nšm wltbn hmlt arṣ,* "I understand thunderbolts which the heavens do not know, thunder which men do not know, nor the multitudes of the nether world understand."

in darkness. The semantic relationship between "darkness" and "ignorance" also comes out in the root *'lm*, "to be dark, ignorant," discussed at Ps lv 2 and at Job xxii 15 by Pope (AB, vol. 15).

foundations . . . are shaken. Consult the first NOTE on Ps lxxv 4 for this metaphor depicting injustice and lawlessness as a sapping of the earth's foundations.

6. *I had thought.* Here the speaker is the psalmist. Budde's brilliant discovery in JBL 40 (1921), 39–40, that *'āmartī*, introducing one clause, followed by *'ākēn*, introducing a second clause, must be translated, "I had thought . . . but," has been rediscovered by C. J. Labuschagne in *Die Ou Testamentiese Werkgemeenskap in Suid-Afrika* (Pretoria, 1962), pp. 29 ff. Cf. Ps xxxi 23; Isa xlix 4; Jer iii 19 f.; Zeph iii 7; Job xxxii 7 f.

The psalmist had been under the impression that the pagan deities were of some importance, but now realizes that they are nothing, because they are quite incapable of defending the poor and rescuing the downtrodden.

gods. One of whose attributes is immortality.

7. *Yet you shall die.* Because of their unconcern for the less privileged, the gods of the surrounding nations have been stripped by God of their immortality. The theme of the death of a god appears in UT, 125:20–23, apropos of the semi-divine King Kirta (or Keret): *ikm yrgm bn il krt špḥ lṭpn wqdš uilm tmtn špḥ lṭpn lyḥ*, "How can Kirta be called a god, an offspring of Lṭpn (=El) and Qdš (=Asherah)? Or do gods die? Will the offspring of Lṭpn not live?"

men . . . any prince. Expressions such as UT, 51:VII:43, *umlk ublmlk*, "either king or commoner," or Phoenician Karatepe III:19–IV:1, *hmlk h' w'yt 'dm h'*, "that king or that man," would suggest that the pair *'ādām . . . śārīm* forms a merism denoting "all mortals." Some critics suspect the reading *śārīm*, "prince," but Freedman's observation that the syllable count in vs. 6 is 10:8, while in vs. 7 it is 8:10, validates the present text and the interpretation proposed here. What is more, Ps xlix 3, *gam bᵉnē 'ādām gam bᵉnē 'īš*, "of lowly birth or high degree," illustrates the same point, especially as this phrase is followed by a clear merism, "rich and poor alike." Hence the numerous attempts to identify a mythological motif in *'aḥad haśśārīm* (e.g., John Gray, *The Legacy of Canaan*, 2d ed., p. 288, n. 1) may well turn out to be exercises in misplaced ingenuity.

and fall. Namely, into the underworld. Its apparent synonymy with *tᵉmūtūn*, "You shall die," suggests that, as in Pss v 11, xxxvi 13; Jer xxiii 12, *tippōlū* here carries a pregnant meaning. The motif of divine beings cast into the infernal abyss is well known from such passages as Isa xiv 12–15 and Ezek xxviii 1–10. Cf. Pierre Grelot, "Isaïe 14, 12–15, et son arrière-plan mythologique," *Revue de l'histoire des religions* 149 (1956), 18–48.

8. *Arise.* As in Pss vii 7, x 12, lxxvi 10, etc., *qūmāh* designates the intervention of God as judge and ruler.

govern. Psalms I, p. 13, cites some recent bibliography on this meaning of *šāpaṭ.*

rule over. Parsing *tinḥal b^e^* as a jussive form employed for stylistic reasons to avoid three imperatives in succession; cf. *Psalms I,* pp. 29 f., 65 f., 261, and the NOTES on Pss lix 8 and lxvii 2. Cf. UT, 127:42, *ištm' wtqġ udn,* "Listen and be alert of ear!," where jussive *tqġ* continues the mode of imperative *ištm'*. The present writer failed to recognize a splendid example of this stylistic variation in Ps vii 8, *wa'ᵃdat le'ummīm tesōbebekkā we'ālehā lemārōm šūbāh,* "Surround yourself with the council of peoples, and preside over it, O Exalted One!"

For this nuance of *tinḥal b^e^*, cf. *Psalms I,* p. 285, and compare the synonymous verbs *māšal b^e^*, "to reign," and *dārak b^e^*, "to have dominion over" (Ps cxxxix 24). The construction *nāḥal b^e^* does not recur elsewhere, a good indication that in such a phrase *nāḥal* assumes a nuance different from *nāḥal* plus the accusative.

all the nations. That had been under the tutelage of the gods mentioned in vss. 1 and 6.

yourself. Parsing *kī 'attāh* as emphatic *kī* and independent pronoun accentuating the subject of jussive *tinḥal,* "rule over." Which is to say that this construction semantically equals the precative perfect with *kī 'attāh* in such texts as Pss x 14, *rā'ītāh kī 'attāh,* "See for yourself!," and xxxix 10, *kī 'attāh 'āśītā,* "Oh that you would act!" Cf. also Pss xxv 7, lix 5–6, and lxix 19.

The psalmist prays God, once the pagan deities have been deposed, to govern the heathen nations himself, thus assuring an equitable governance of the universe and the stabilizing of the earth's foundations, presently threatened by the ignorance and the favoritism to the wicked of the heathen divinities.

PSALM 83

(lxxxiii 1–19)

1 *A song. A psalm of Asaph.*

2 My God, what god is like you?
Be not silent, and be not still, O El!
3 For look, your foes raise a tumult, [2]*
and your enemies lift their head.
4 Against your people they lay crafty plans, [3]
and conspire against your treasure.
5 They say, "Come, let us obliterate them as a nation, [4]
let the name 'Israel' be remembered no more."
6 Indeed, they consult together with a single mind, [5]
your assailants make an alliance:
7 The tents of Edom and the Ishmaelites, [6]
of Moab and the Hagarites;
8 Byblos and with it Amalek, [7]
Philistia with the inhabitants of Tyre.
9 Assyria, too, has joined them, [8]
has become the strong arm of Lot's children. *Selah*
10 Treat them like Midian, like Sisera, [9]
like Jabin at the river Kishon.
11 Let them be exterminated from the surface of the globe, [10]
may they become dung for the ground.
12 Make their nobles like Oreb and Zeeb, [11]
all their chiefs like Zebah and Zalmunna,
13 Who said, "Let us seize for ourselves [12]
the very finest meadows."
14 My Cod, make them like tumbleweed, [13]
like chaff before the wind.
15 As fire burns the forest, [14]
as the flame sets the mountains ablaze,

* Verse numbers in RSV.

16 So pursue them with your tempest, [15]
and with your hurricane discomfit them.
17 Fill their faces with shame, [16]
and let your Name, Yahweh, avenge itself.
18 May they be humiliated and discomfited [17]
for ever and ever
May they perish in utter disgrace.
19 Let them know that your own Name is Yahweh, [18]
that you alone are the Most High
over all the earth.

Notes

lxxxiii. A national lament in which the poet or singer prays on behalf of the nation for deliverance from the surrounding enemies who threaten its existence. History transmits no record of the national crisis when the nations enumerated in this psalm formed a league to wipe out Israel; one might conceivably interpret these names merely as a poetically free collocation. However, the mention in vs. 9 of Assyria, which some critics would expunge (unwarrantedly, of course), argues a pre-Exilic date of composition.

The impressive number of archaic spellings and forms that crop up in this lament make a notable contribution to Hebrew grammar; cf. especially the Notes to vss. 2, 4, 6, 8, 11, 13, 19.

2. *My God*. Reading *'^{e}lōhay*, as in vs. 14, and detaching the final *mem* of MT *'^{e}lōhīm*.

what god. Reading *mī* (see preceding Note) *'ēl* (MT *'al*), and comparing Ps lxxvii 14, *mī 'ēl g^{e}dōl^{e}kā '^{e}lōhīm*, "What god is greater than you, O God?"

is like you. Vocalizing *dōmey* (MT *d^{o}mīy*) *lāk* and comparing the LXX, Vulg., and Syr., which all read *mī yidmeh lāk* (cf. Ps lxxxix 7), "Who shall be like you?" Consonantal *dmy* represents an archaic spelling of the qal participle (cf. Ugar. *bny*, "the one who builds/creates"), like Gen xvi 13, *r'y=rō'ey*, "seer"; Prov xii 22, *'śy='ōśey*, "doer"; Job xxxv 10, *śy='ōśey*. Another instance of the orthographic preservation of *tertiae yod* recurs in vs. 3.

Though this reconstruction enjoys good versional support and creates a fine inclusion with vs. 19b, MT can appeal to a kindred phrase in Isa lxii 6–7.

O El. Vocative *'ēl* (see *Psalms I*, p. 64) forms an inclusion with vocative *'^{e}lōhay* at the beginning of the verse, a verse structure reminiscent of Ps lxxvii 14.

3. *For look, your foes.* As in Ps xcii 10, *kī hinnēh 'ōy^e^bekā* resembles UT, 68:8–9, *ht ibk b'lm*, and 1012:27, *w hn ibm šṣq ly*, "And look, the foes are closing in on me."

your foes . . . your enemies. The second NOTE on Ps lxviii 2 cites the Ugaritic parallelism of these two nouns.

raise a tumult . . . lift. The *yqtl* form *yeh^e^māyūn*, which preserves the third radical *yod* like vs. 2, *dmy*, is paired with *qtl nāś^e^'ū*, a stylistic variation noted at Ps lxxvii 6.

lift their head. Comparing *nāś^e^'ū rō'š* with UT, 126:III:12, *nšu riš ḥrṯm*, "The plowmen lifted their head." No suffix is required with *rō'š*, since it designates a part of the body; cf. Ps lxxv 5. This action here symbolizes arrogance and readiness for aggressive action. In Ps xxiv 7, 9, however, this gesture is a sign of joy.

4. *your treasure.* Vocalizing *ṣ^e^pūnīkā* (MT *ṣ^e^pūneykā*), a singular noun with the genitive ending; cf. the sixth NOTE on Ps lxv 6. Some of the ancient versions did see here a singular noun, which makes a better parallel to singular *'amm^e^kā*, "your people."

Just what the poet intends by this term is not certain: some understand it as referring to the temple, and in view of the pairing of "your people" with "your sanctuary" in Ps lxxiv 3, this exegesis is sound. This opinion is further sustained by Ezek vii 22, *ṣ^e^pūnī*, probably denoting "temple." If, on the other hand, the synonymy of *ṣāpūn* and *s^e^gullāh*, "possession, treasure," a term used to designate the people of Israel (Exod xix 5; Deut vii 6, etc.), is considered, then *ṣ^e^pūnīkā* might well be another designation of Israel.

6. *your assailants.* Since the construction *kārat b^e^rīt 'al* is not attested elsewhere, I propose the participial pointing *'ōlekā* (MT *'ālekā*) from *'ālāh*, "to rise up against, attack." Cf. Isa ix 10, xiv 12; Jer iv 17. In other words, it is synonymous with vs. 3, "your foes" and "your enemies." The poet considers Israel's attackers the assailants of God.

make an alliance. The *yqtl* verb *yikrōtū* balances *qtl nō'^a^ṣū*, "they consult."

7. *The tents.* A poetic phrase for the entire nation (Pss lxxviii 51, cxx 5). In the fragments of the Psalms scroll discovered at Masada in 1965 there is an interesting variant here; the scroll reads *'lhy 'dwm*, "the gods of Edom." Consult Yigael Yadin in IEJ 15 (1965), 104.

the Hagarites. A semi-nomadic people of the desert regions east of Ammon and Moab.

8. *Byblos.* Customarily conjectured to be an Arab tribe residing in the environs of Petra, the MT hapax legomenon *g^e^bāl* should rather be identified with the famous Phoenician city. With *ṣōr*, Tyre, another Phoenician city, it forms the rhetorical figure known as inclusion. In this verse, the poet moves from north to south, and then back from south to north. In Ezek xxvii 8–9, Tyre and Byblos occur in parallelism.

and with it Amalek. Reading *we'immōnnū 'amālēq* for MT *we'ammōn wa'amālēq* and identifying *'immōnū* as the preposition *'m* with the afformative ending *-n,* discussed at Ps xviii 40, followed by the third masculine suffix *-ū;* in other words *'immān-hū* becomes *'immānnū,* while the shift of *ā* to *ō* reflects a Phoenicianizing vocalization of the preposition, not surprising in a verse mentioning both Byblos and Tyre. In UHP, p. 32, I have discussed Hos xii 5, *'immānnū* (MT *'immānū*), "with him." Cf. also R. B. Coote, VT 21 (1971), 396 and n. 1.

Thus the pairing of *'mn* with *'m* in the psalm compares with UT, 'nt:III:21–22, *tant šmm 'm arṣ thmt 'mn kbkbm,* "the meeting of heaven with the nether world, of the deep with the stars." What further favors this analysis is the mention of only two places in the second colon; hence we should expect only two in the first, and this is achieved by dissociating *'mn* from Ammon and identifying it as the prepositional counterpart of *'im.* In vs. 7 likewise, there are two pairs of names.

Amalek. Throughout their entire known history, the Amalekites were primarily a nomadic desert tribe, ranging the desolate wastes from Sinai and the Negeb of southern Canaan to the Arabah north of Ezion-Geber and inner Arabia. As noticed above, the psalmist moves from Byblos in the north to Amalek in the south, and then from Philistia in the south to Tyre in the north.

9. *Lot's children.* Namely, Moab and Edom (Gen xix 36–38; Deut ii 9).

10. *Like Midian, like Sisera, like Jabin.* Gideon's decisive victory over the Midianites is recorded in chs. vi–vii of Judges, while chs. iv–v relate the defeat of Sisera and Jabin by Deborah and Barak.

11. *Let them be exterminated.* Comparing precative perfect *nišmedū* with Ps x 16, "Let the heathen perish (*'ābedū*) from his earth!" Being preceded by imperative *'aśēh,* "treat," in vs. 10 and followed by imperative *šītēmō,* "make," in vs. 12, *nišmedū* and *hāyū,* "may become," most naturally parse as precatives alternating with imperatives to forestall an oppressive monotony; see the NOTES on Pss iv 2 (*Psalms I,* p. 23) and lxxxii 8.

from the surface of the globe. Since the traditional rendition of *be'ēn dō'r,* "at En-dor," has in this context no historical or geographical propriety, we must seek a meaning more akin to apparently parallel *'adāmāh,* "ground," in the second colon. The phrase *'ēn dō'r* yields the desired meaning when compared with *'ēn hā'āreṣ,* "surface of the earth" (Exod x 5, 15; Num xxii 5, 11), and *'ēn 'ādām,* also "surface of the earth," in Zech ix 1, as proposed by me in CBQ 25 (1963), 123–24. This imprecation addressed to God that he might intervene resembles closely the threat of Deut vi 15, "Lest the anger of Yahweh your God be enkindled against you, and he exterminate you (*wehišmīdekā*) from the face of the earth." The common Semitic root *dwr,* "to turn, be circular," supplies the necessary etymology (cf. Ar. *dāru*, "land"), while the alternation between *dō'r* and *dōr* in the biblical spelling of the city-name Dor (=Tantura) may account for the spelling *dō'r* in our verse.

The widely attested meaning "from" for b^e (*Psalms I*, p. 319) can be further illustrated by Ps cxix 87, *kim*^{e}*'aṭ killūnī bā'āreṣ*, "They almost effaced me from the earth," where 11QPs^a preserves the revealing lection *m'rṣ* for *b'rṣ*, clear proof that *b*, "from," was forgotten in the first century B.C.

may they become. As remarked in the first NOTE on vs. 11, *hāyū* parses as precative perfect.

dung for the ground. Their dead bodies rotting upon the ground without burial (cf. NOTE on Ps lxxix 3) and becoming fertilizers of the soil; cf. II Kings ix 37; Jer viii 2. The alliteration in *dōmen lā'*^{a}*dāmāh* accentuates the pun on *midyān*, "Midian."

12. *Make.* The deletion of the final syllable of *šītēmō* no longer convinces; an enclitic *mem* may account for the grammatically dubious pointing of MT.

Oreb and Zeeb. Two princes of Midian captured and killed by the Ephraimites. Cf. Judg vii 25.

Zebah and Zalmunna. Two kings of Midian killed by Gideon. Cf. Judg viii 21.

13. *the very finest meadows.* Acknowledging with AT the superlative function of *'*^{e}*lōhīm* in the phrase *n*^{e}*'ōt '*^{e}*lōhīm;* cf. *Psalms I*, p. 220, and UT, 49:I:37, *wymlk barṣ il klh*, "And he rules in the vast nether world, all of it."

14. *My God.* Corresponds to vs. 2, *'*^{e}*lōhay*.

15. *As fire . . . as the flame . . .* 16. *So.* The sequence k^e . . . k^e . . . *kēn* recalls that of UT, 49:II:28–30, *k . . . k . . . km.* On the pattern in Ps cxxiii 2, cf. Dahood in CBQ 22 (1960), 73–74; *Biblica* 43 (1962), 360.

Our verse also illustrates the metrical pattern A+B+C//Á+B́+Ć with 3+3 meter, that has Canaanite antecedents in verses such as UT, 2 Aqht:v:7–8, *ydn dn almnt//yṯpṭ ṭpṭ ytm*, "He judges the case of the widow, he adjudicates the cause of the fatherless."

burns the forest. The attempts of lexicographers (e.g., GB, ZLH) to relate *bā'ar*, "to burn," to Ar. *bġr*, "to thirst," and *wġr*, "to glow," should be abandoned in view of Ugar. *b'r* in such texts as UT, 2114:8–9, *akln b grnt l b'r*, "They even burned our grain upon the threshing floors."

forest . . . mountains. The pair *ya'ar//hārīm* probably form a unit, i.e., the mountain forests. Hence this is a case of enjambment.

16. *pursue them.* As in Ps lxxxii 8, the *tqtl* form *tird*^{e}*pēm* is another alternative to the imperative. To express the imperative mode, the

psalmist employs straight imperatives in vss. 10, 12, 14; precatives in vs. 11, and the jussive form here.

with your tempest. Is there an allusion here to the rainstorm of Judg v 20–21 that was largely responsible for the defeat of Jabin and the Canaanites near the river Kishon?

discomfit them. As in Ps ii 5, *t*^{e}*bah*^{a}*lēm* carries a military nuance. The word order of the verse is chiastic.

17. *your Name.* Parsing *w*^{e} of *w*^{e}*šim*^{e}*kā* (next NOTE) as emphatic.

avenge itself. The accepted translation of the second colon, "that they may seek thy name, O Lord" (RSV) is hardly amenable to coherent exegesis within the immediate context and does not accord with the pervading spirit of this psalm.

Hence I propose to read *wibaqqēš ūšim*^{e}*kā* (MT *wibaqq*^{e}*šū šim*^{e}*kā*), with *wībaqqēš* a jussive form continuing the imperative *mallē'*, "Fill!" In several texts, e.g., Gen xxxi 39; Isa i 12, *biqqēš* denotes "to exact penalty, avenge," and in Josh xxii 23 it is used absolutely, as in the psalm, with Yahweh the subject: *yhwh hū' y*^{e}*baqqēš*, "May the Lord himself take vengeance" (RSV).

The verb *bqṯ*, "to seek," occurs twice in Ugaritic, revealing that the third radical of Heb. *bqš* derives from Proto-Semitic *ṯ*.

18. *for ever and ever.* The phrase *'*^{a}*dē 'ad* connects with both cola, and by hanging it in the middle of the verse we achieve an exact balance of 8:3:8 syllables (courtesy D. N. Freedman). Other instances of this pivot pattern are cited in the first NOTE on Ps lvii 5.

perish in utter disgrace. Literally "may they be disgraced, perish," an instance of hendiadys.

19. *your own Name.* Analyzing the independent personal pronoun *'attāh* as an intensifier of the suffix of *šim*^{e}*kā;* cf. GK, § 135e, and UT, 68:11, *šmk at,* "your own name." In Gen xlix 8, and Eccles ii 15, for example, the intensifying independent pronoun precedes the suffix it emphasizes.

that you alone. The conjunction *kī* also introduces the second colon beginning with *l*^{e}*badd*^{e}*kā* (MT reads the pausal form). The poet stresses the superiority of Yahweh over the gods of the hostile nations enumerated in vss. 7–9.

PSALM 84

(lxxxiv 1–13)

1 *For the director; upon the gittith. A psalm of the sons of Korah.*

2 How lovely is your dwelling,
        O Yahweh of Hosts!
3 My soul longs and pines aloud [2]*
        for your court, O Yahweh!
    My heart and my flesh cry out.
    O God, O living God,
4   even the sparrow has found a home, [3]
        and the swallow acquired a nest
        where she may put her young,
    O Yahweh of Hosts, my King and my God!
5 How blest are they who ever dwell in your house, [4]
        and near your altars sing your praise! *Selah*
6 How blest the man whose refuge is in you, [5]
        from whose heart are your extolments!
7 May he cause brooks to flow in the valley, [6]
        turn it into a spring;
    With a crash may the Raingiver
        cover it with pools!
8 They proceed from village to village [7]
        to see the God of gods in Zion.
9 O Yahweh, God of Hosts, [8]
        hear my prayer;
    Give ear, O God of Jacob! *Selah*
10 Our suzerain regard with favor, O God, [9]
        look upon the face of your anointed.
11 How much better is one day in your court [10]
        than a thousand in the Cemetery!
    To stand on the threshold of your house, my God,
        than to abide in the Tent of the Wicked One!

* Verse numbers in RSV.

12 Truly Sun and Suzerain [11]
Yahweh God
Favors and honors bestows.
Yahweh will not withold his rain
from those who walk with integrity.
13 O Yahweh of Hosts, [12]
how blest the man who trusts in you!

Notes

lxxxiv. A psalm of mixed literary types, containing elements of a Pilgrim Song, one of those composed on the occasion of a pilgrimage to the temple of Jerusalem, as well as of a Song of Zion (*Psalms I*, pp. 278, 289). The literary classification is further complicated by the prayer for rain in vss. 7 and 12b, and by the supplication for the king in vs. 10.

I fully endorse the strictures voiced by R. de Vaux, "Jerusalem et les prophètes," in *Revue biblique* 73 (1966), 481–509, especially pp. 508–9, of G. Wanke, *Die Zionstheologie der Korachiten* (Berlin, 1966). Wanke maintains that the Korahite psalms that glorify Jerusalem (xlvi, xlviii, lxxxiv, lxxxvii) are post-Exilic because their theology, which extends to all Jerusalem the sanctity of the temple, is post-Exilic. De Vaux is correct when insisting that the psalms in question—whatever their date—contain traditions that antedate the Exile.

1. *the gittith.* A term of unknown significance. Cf. Ps lxxxi 1.

2. *your dwelling.* Though plural in form, *miškᵉnōtekā* is singular in meaning; this poetic practice, which has Canaanite antecedents, received comment at Ps xliii 3.

3. *longs and pines . . . My heart and my flesh.* The first colon contains two verbs which chiastically balance the two nouns of the third colon.

and . . . aloud. The fused *wᵉgam,* which critics maintain should be read either *wᵉ* or *gam,* appears to present no problem when *gam* is equated with Ugar. *gam,* "aloud," discussed at Ps lii 7. Thus the presence of *gam,* "aloud," and *yᵉrannᵉnū,* "cry out," in the same verse supports this definition of *gam* in Ps lxxi 24, where it is associated with *tᵉrannēnnāh* in vs. 23. Such a definition also helps to resolve the problems attending *gam* in vs. 7.

for your court, O Yahweh. Numbering six syllables, the phrase *lᵉḥaṣᵉrōt* is suspended between the first and third cola (each totaling ten syllables) and conceptually belongs to both. Ps lxxxiii 18 illustrates the same A+B// C // Á+B́ pattern.

Like its opposite number *miškᵉnōtekā,* "your dwelling," in vs. 2, plural *ḥaṣᵉrōt* carries a singular denotation and shares the suffix of its opposite number on the principle of the double-duty suffix in a construct chain noted at Pss lxxvii 12 and lxxxix 2. Since vss. 2, 3a, 4–6 all address Yahweh in the second person, it sounds discordant to refer to him in the third person in a phrase that manifestly balances one addressing him in the second person.

O God. Reading *'ēl* for MT *'el,* and identifying *'ēl 'ēl ḥāy* as divine names forming an inclusion with vs. 4, "my King and my God." In other words, the final three words of vs. 3 belong to vs. 4.

The widespread Masoretic confusion (or is it avoidance?) of *'ēl* with *'el,* remarked also in vs. 8 and Pss xxxix 13; lix 12; lxii 2, 11; lxix 19, 34; lxxvii 2, stands forth most glaringly in Ps cxliii where MT confounds *'ēl* with *'el* in vss. 1, 9, and with *'al* in vs. 7. The vocative case of *'ēl* suggests that *lē'lōhīm* in the cognate passage of Ps xlii 3 contains the vocative particle and should be rendered "O God!"

O living God. The vocative case of *'ēl ḥāy* argues for the vocative analysis of *l^e'ēl ḥāy* in Ps xlii 3; see preceding NOTE. The proposal to emend *ḥāy to ḥayyay,* "my life," slights the allusive force of *ḥāy* which, in a context describing the pining and yearning of the psalmist, elicits an image of God such as the "Fountain of Living Water" (*m^eqōr mayīm ḥayyīm*) in Jer xvii 13; cf. *Psalms I,* p. 256.

4. *acquired a nest.* MT *qēn lāh,* "a nest for herself," may also be read *qēn nālāh* on the principle of the shared consonant, i.e., *n* is shared by both words, though written but once. Root of verb is *nyl,* "to acquire," witnessed in Job xv 29, *mnlm,* "acquisitions."

my King and my God. Comparing *malkī wē'lōhay* with Ps xliv 5, as read in *Psalms I,* pp. 263, 265. Structurally, these terms form an inclusion with *'ēl 'ēl ḥāy.*

5. *and near your altars.* Transposing *'et mizb^{e}ḥōtekā* from vs. 4 and inserting it after *'ōd,* thus forming a characteristic chiasm. For the nuance "near" of *'et,* consult Zorell, ZLH, p. 90a, and Gunkel, *Die Psalmen,* p. 370.

6. *whose refuge.* The rare *scriptio plena 'wz,* usually translated "strength," suggests rather a derivation from *'wz,* "to seek refuge." Since the only frequent substantive from this root is *mā'ōz,* "refuge," it would seem that the present reading arose from an original *'dm'wz,* where the final *-m* of *'dm* was also orthographically intended for the following word; cf. the third NOTE on Ps lx 11. Hence read *'ādām mā'ōz.*

Such a reading makes this clause synonymous with vs. 13, "How blest the man who trusts in you!"

from whose heart. Recognizing in consonantal *lbbm* the substantive *lēbāb* followed by the enclitic *mem,* that stylistically balances the suffix of *lō;* consult the discussion in *Psalms I,* pp. 66 f., at Ps x 17 where *'oznekā,* "your ear," parallels *lbm,* "your attention" (literally "your heart"), and Ps xv 2, *bil^{e}bābō,* "from his heart," for this meaning of the preposition in *blbbm.*

your extolments. Following closely upon *yᵉhalᵉlūkā*, "sing your praise" (vs. 5), *mᵉsillōt* probably retains the metaphorical sense of *sālal*, "to exalt," that is found in Prov iv 8; Exod ix 17, and Late Hebrew *silsēl*, "to esteem highly." The determinative suffix "your" comes from *bāk*, "in you"; see above on vs. 3. In order to extract sense out of the traditional translation "highways," RSV inserts "to Zion" ("in whose heart are the highways to Zion"). The attempts of Mowinckel, *The Psalms in Israel's Worship*, I, pp. 170 f., to detect the idea of the *via sacra* do not fit in with the proposed interpretation.

7. *May he cause . . . to flow.* Tentatively reading *hibbīkā'* (MT *habbakā'*), the hiphil perfect of the third person masculine with the archaic ending *-a'* (the *aleph* is probably secondary) from the root *nbk/npk*, "to pour out," examined at Ps lxix 11. Syntactically, this verb would parse as precative perfect in tandem with jussive *ya'ṭeh* in the next line.

The prayer for rain in Ps lxv 10–14 likewise begins with a precative perfect, *pāqadtā*, "visit."

brooks. On plural construct *'ibrē* (MT *'ōbᵉrē*) before the prepositional phrase *bᵉ'ēmeq*, see GK, § 130a; *Psalms I*, pp. 52, 97, and UT, 52:62–63, *'ṣr šmm wdg bym*, "the birds of heaven and the fish of the sea."

This definition of *'ibrē*, suggested by its collocation with "spring" and "pools," finds support in Hab iii 10 where *'ābār* is parallel to *tᵉhōm*, "the deep." Cf. Ps civ 10, "You make springs gush forth in the valleys."

turn it. Namely, "the valley." The verb *yᵉšītūhū* parses as the *yqtl* third person masculine singular with the archaic ending *-ū*, examined at Ps lxxii 5, 16.

a spring. Proposals based on the LXX and Syr. to read *mā'ōn*, "habitation," for MT *ma'yān* should be discountenanced by the presence of the latter in the kindred context of Ps civ 10 and by the parallelism between *brky*, "pools," and *'n*, "spring," in UT, 67:I:16–17, *hm brky tkšd rumm 'n kḏd aylt*, "Lo, the wild oxen make for the pools, the hinds make for the spring."

With a crash. Namely, with the sound of thunder, as in Ps lxxxv 13; see above in vs. 3 and the first NOTE on Ps lii 7 for this meaning of *gam*.

the Raingiver. A divine appellative parsing as hiphil participle of *yōreh*, "to cast, to rain" (Hos vi 3, x 12).

cover it. The verb *ya'ṭeh* shares the suffix of *yᵉšītūhū*, "(May he) turn it."

with pools. *bᵉrākōt* is the second accusative with the verb "to cover"; cf. GK, § 117ee, and UT, 'nt:II:39, *ṭl šmm tskh*, "With dew the heavens wash her."

8. *from village to village.* In their pilgrimage to Jerusalem. With

earlier commentators (see Baethgen, *Psalmen,* p. 263), vocalizing *mēḥēl* (MT *mēḥayil*) *'el ḥēl* (MT *ḥāyil*). Literally denoting "bulwark, moat," *ḥēl* by metonymy denotes "town" or "village"; compare *ša'ar,* "gate," which sometimes signifies "city." Ps xlviii 13–14, which connects *ḥēl* with Zion, leaves open the possibility that the procession described in our psalm might be taking place around the walls of Jerusalem.

to see. Reading *yir^e'ū* (MT *yērā'eh*), and comparing the syntax of *yēl^{e}kū . . . yir^e'ū* with UT, 8:5, *hlkt tdrš,* "She went to seek."

the God of gods. As in Ps lxxvii 2, reading *'ēl* (MT *'el*) *'^{e}lōhīm;* the same Masoretic confusion of *'el* and *'ēl* is recorded in vs. 3. "To see God" is a Hebrew idiom signifying in some contexts "to visit the temple"; see Friedrich Nötscher, *Das Angesicht Gottes schauen* (Würzburg, 1924), p. 128.

9. *Yahweh . . . God of Jacob.* The scansion of this line into 3+2+3 bears on the reading and scansion of vs. 12.

10. *Our suzerain.* Reading *m^{e}gānēnū* for MT *māginnēnū,* "our shield." D. N. Freedman in *Studia Geo Widengren* (Leiden, 1972), pp. 122–23, correctly infers from the chiastic arrangement of the words that "our suzerain" designates the Davidic king and not God himself, as interpreted in our earlier editions.

your anointed. Standing at the end of the verse, *m^{e}šīḥekā* forms an inclusion with the first word *m^{e}gānēnū,* "our Suzerain." This definition of *m^{e}gānēnū,* incidentally, reveals the true nature of "your anointed" and wreaks havoc with the note to this verse in *The Jerusalem Bible* (New York, 1966), p. 869. It reads: "Here the 'anointed' (Messiah) is probably the high priest, chief authority in the post-exilic community."

One encounters short prayers for the king in an individual lament (Ps lxi 7), or in a national lament (Ps lxxx 16, 18).

11. *How much better.* For this translation of *kī ṭōb,* see *Psalms I,* p. 197, and the third NOTE on Ps lvi 3.

one day. There is no need to insert *'eḥād,* "one," as suggested by some critics, since singular *yōm* without a numeral suffices to indicate oneness; cf. UT, § 7.3, and the expressions *qšt w ql',* "one bow and one sling," and *'glm dt šnt,* "one-year-old bullocks."

in your court. As in vs. 3, where feminine plural *ḥaṣ^{e}rōt* probably refers to a single court, so here the masculine plural *ḥ^{a}ṣērekā* should probably be understood as singular. Cf. Ps lxv 5 where plural *ḥ^{a}ṣērekā* is read as singular by some manuscripts.

court . . . house. This matching of nouns occurs in UT, 51:IV–V: 62–63, *ybn bt lb'l km ilm wḥẓr kbn aṯrt,* "Let a house be built for Baal as for the gods, and a court as for the sons of Asherah." Cf. likewise Phoen. *bt//ḥṣr* in the Arslan Tash Incantation.

in the Cemetery. A poetic name for the underworld. I analyze consonantal *bḥrty* into the preposition *b* followed by the substantive *ḥrt*

(=Akk.-Ugar. *ḫrt,* "cemetery, grave"; UT, Glossary, No. 1006), whose final *-y* preserves an archaic genitive ending, discussed at Ps lxxxiii 4. Cf. UT, 1 Aqht:140–41, *abky waqbrnh aštn bḫrt ilm arṣ,* "I shall bewail him and bury him, I shall place him in the cemetery of the nether gods." On Ugar. *ḫrt,* Akk. *ḫīrītu,* "grave, cemetery," see C. H. Gordon in *Syria* 33 (1956), 102–3.

Tent of the Wicked One. Another name for the nether regions, synonymous with *ḥrt.* Morphologically plural *'ohᵒlē,* like Ugar. *ahlm* (UT, § 13.17) and *hᵃṣērekā* (see above), carries a singular meaning. MT *reša'* should probably be vocalized *rāšā'* and identified with the figure of Death described in Isa xi 4b, *wᵉhikkāh 'ereṣ bᵉšēbeṭ pīū ūbᵉrūᵃḥ śᵉpātāyw yāmīt rāšā',* "He will smite the nether goddess (cf. Ugar. *arṣy* who is identified with Mesopotamian Allatum, the goddess of the nether world; J. Nougayrol, CRAIBL, 1957, 82–83) with the rod of his mouth, and with the breath of his lips will slay the Wicked One." Cf. also Prov xiv 32. In a number of texts the cognate terms *rā'* or *rā'āh* refer to death (*Psalms I,* pp. 168, 297), while in Job xxxviii 30, *tᵉhōm,* "the abyss," is reproduced by one Greek manuscript as *aseboús,* "the ungodly one."

12. *Truly.* Understanding *kī* as emphatic; cf. vs. 11, *kī ṭōb.* This parsing confers a full beat on *kī,* so that in *kī šemeš ūmāgān* we have three beats instead of two. Like vs. 9, this verse scans into 3+2+3. Ps lxxxvi 10 presents the same metrical pattern.

Sun. In the court style of the El Amarna correspondence *šamšu,* "Sun," was a designation of the Pharaoh, while in the Ugaritic letters *špš* (=Heb. *šemeš*) referred either to the Pharaoh or to the Hittite suzerain.

Suzerain. See vs. 10. The pair *šemeš ūmāgān* semantically equals UT, 1018:23–24, *špš mlk rb,* "the Sun, the great king," since *mlk rb* is another term for "overlord."

bestows. The concurrence of *māgān* and *yittēn* in this verse recalls the balancing of these two roots in Prov iv 9, "She will provide (*tittēn*) for your head a graceful garland / And will bestow on you (*tᵉmaggᵉnekkā*) a crown of beauty" (Scott, The Anchor Bible, vol. 18). This parallelism further proves that consonantal *mgn* must not be identified with the word for "shield," but rather with the verb *māgan,* "to confer, donate." In fact, the colon *ḥēn wᵉkābōd yittēn* fairly describes the program of the beneficent suzerain.

not withhold his rain. Consulting *Psalms I,* pp. 25 f., for *ṭōb,* "rain," and comparing *yimna' ṭōb* with Amos iv 7, *wᵉgam 'ānōkī māna'tī mikkem 'et haggešem,* "And I also withheld the rain from you," and Jer v 25, "And your sins have withheld (*mānᵉ'ū*) the rain (*haṭṭōb*) from you."

This prayer for rain links up with vs. 6 and looks forward to Ps lxxxv, also a prayer for rain, while vs. 13 harks back to vs. 5.

from those who walk. With verbs of refusing or withholding *l*[e] sometimes preserves the well-documented Ugaritic meaning "from," as remarked in *Psalms I,* pp. 246 f.; cf. also BDB, p. 515a (bottom). The meaning "from" may still be seen in the Qumran document labeled 11QPs[a] Zion, vs. 14, *'rbh b'p tšbḥtk ṣywn m'lh lkwl tbl,* "May your praise, O Zion, enter into his presence, exaltation from all the world." For a different version, see J. A. Sanders, *The Psalms Scroll of Qumrân Cave 11 (11QPs*[a]*)*, pp. 86–87, and my criticism in *Biblica* 47 (1966), 143.

13. *O Yahweh of Hosts.* Forms an inclusion with vs. 2, *yhwh ṣ*[e]*bā'ōt.*

PSALM 85

(lxxxv 1–14)

1 *For the director. A psalm of the sons of Korah.*

2 Favor your land, Yahweh,
restore the fortunes of Jacob!
3 Forgive the guilt of your people, [2]*
remit all of their sin!
4 Withdraw all your fury, [3]
abate your blazing wrath!
5 Return to us, O God of our prosperity, [4]
banish from us your indignation!
6 Forever will you be angry with us, [5]
prolong your anger to all generations?
7 You are the Victor, [6]
restore us to life again
that your people might rejoice in you.
8 Show us, O Yahweh, your kindness, [7]
and give us your prosperity.
9 Let me announce what El himself has spoken: [8]
"Yahweh indeed has promised well-being
To the devoted ones of his people,
to those who again confide in him.
10 Truly near is his prosperity [9]
to those who fear him;
Indeed his glory dwells in our land.
11 Kindness and fidelity will meet, [10]
justice and well-being embrace;
12 Fidelity shall sprout from the earth, [11]
and justice lean down from heaven.
13 With a crash will Yahweh give his rain, [12]
and our land will give its produce.
14 Justice will march before him, [13]
beauty will indeed tread in his steps."

* Verse numbers in RSV.

NOTES

lxxxv. A prayer for rain; cf. *Psalms I,* pp. xxxii, 25 f., and the introductory NOTES to Pss lxv, lxvii, lxxxiv. With the identification of vs. 13, *haṭṭōb,* as "his rain," it becomes tolerably clear that the six perfect forms in vss. 2–4, customarily rendered by the past tense, are precatives pleading with God to forgive the nation's sins believed to be responsible for the drought and for the absence of God from the land. Thus the precative perfects of vss. 2–4 stylistically and semantically balance the imperatives and jussives of vss. 5–8. The final section (vss. 9–14) contains the oracle of a priest or temple prophet assuring the people that God has heard their sustained (namely, from vss. 2 to 8) prayer and will send their land the needed rain.

The intense and austere language points to a pre-Exilic date of composition; which is to say that this psalm does not derive from Deutero-Isaiah, as maintained by many commentators.

2. *Favor.* Parsing *rāṣītā* as a precative perfect, and comparing precative *pāqadtā hā'āreṣ,* "Visit the earth," at the beginning of the prayer for rain in Ps lxv 10. Buttenwieser, PCTNT, p. 271, has also recognized that all the *qatal* forms in vss. 2–4 are precatives. These six successive precatives recall the series in Ps ix 5–7.

your land. The poet reminds Yahweh that the parched land is "yours," but once the land receives the rain in vs. 13, it becomes "our land." Freedman points out a similar and equally interesting juxtaposition of suffixes in Exod xxxii 7–14, where in dialogue Moses and God each assign responsibility for the errant people to the other; each keeps using the phrase "your people."

restore the fortunes. Parsing *šabtā* as precative perfect and noting the discussion of the phrase *šūb šᵉbūt* in *Psalms I,* NOTE on Ps xiv 7.

3. *remit.* Literally "cover," but such a rendition of precative *kissītā* would obscure the real meaning.

all of their sin. Proposals to emend MT singular *haṭṭā'tām* to a plural seem to slight the singular reading in the cognate context of II Chron vi 25 ff.

Since the Israelites judged sin to be a cause of drought, it was vital that, in a prayer for rain, they ask for the remission of sin. This point is underlined in King Solomon's inaugural prayer for the dedication of the temple: "When the heavens remain closed so that there is no rain because they have sinned against you and they pray toward this place, praise your name, turn from their sin, do answer them!" (II Chron vi 26). Cf. also I Kings xviii 3; Jer iii 3, v 25; Amos iv 7.

4. *abate your blazing wrath.* As proposed by me in *Biblica* 37 (1956),

338–40, the grammatical difficulty of MT can be eased by reading *h^{e}šībōtā-m* (with enclitic *mem*) *ḥ^{a}rōn 'appekā*. However, the use of the internal hiphil *h^{a}šībēnū*, "Return to us!" in Ps lxxx 4, 8, 20, argues the possibility of an intransitive sense here; if such be the case, our clause would read "Return from your blazing wrath!," but the parallelism with the transitive first colon discountenances such a grammatical analysis.

For the Israelites the parching heat of summer was identical with the fiery anger of God brought on by their sins. In Canaanite myth, on the other hand, the intense summer heat and the absence of rain and vitality were due to the absence of the fertility god Baal who during the summer was believed to be in the underworld. When descending into the nether regions Baal was said to have taken with him his clouds (*'rpt*) and his rain (*mṭr*). Thus the absence of clouds and rain was in the eyes of his Canaanite worshipers an indication of Baal's demise, but for the Israelites a sign of estranged Yahweh's fury with his wayward people.

5. *Return to us.* Parsing the suffix of *šūbēnū* as datival (so the Targ.) rather than accusative, as interpreted by most; e.g., RSV "Restore us again." Note too the use of the dative suffix in the rain prayer Ps lxvii 2, *'ātānū*, "May he come to us." In explaining Ugaritic personal names such as *ṯbil*, Gordon, UT, Glossary, No. 2661, writes: "In personal names, the meaning is that the god N has returned (*ṯb*) from his wrath and favored the family with a child."

God of our prosperity. That is, on whom our well-being depends. For this nuance of *yiš'ēnū* (also in vss. 8, 10), see *Psalms I*, p. 221.

banish. Deriving *hāpēr* from *prr*, "to flee," found in UT, 1 Aqht:120, *pr wdu*, "Flee and fly!," as submitted by G. R. Driver in VTS, iii (Leiden, 1955), p. 77, n. 7, and CML, p. 169a. Cf. also Ps lxxxix 34; Job xv 4, and Eccles xi 10, *hāsēr ka'as millibbekā*, "Remove indignation from your heart." From this etymology emerges the sharp contrast between the two verbs of motion in this verse: "Return to us . . . banish from us."

from us. A comparison of *hāpēr ka'as^{e}kā 'immānū* with Ps lxxxix 34, *w^{e}ḥasdī lō' 'āpīr mē'immō*, "But I will not banish my kindness from him," reveals that *'immānū* alone (i.e., without *min*) can denote "from us." This inference is borne out by UT, 2065:14–15, [*i*]*rš 'my mnm irštk*, "Request of me whatever your request might be," and by Job xxvii 13, "This is the wicked man's portion from God (*'im 'ēl*), and the inheritance tyrants receive from Shaddai (*miššadday*)." Here the parallelism with *min* appears decisive, and Pope's emendation (*Job*, § 26, NOTE on xxvii 13a) is seriously weakened. Cf. UHP, p. 32.

6. *Forever . . . to all generations.* The pairing of *'ōlām* with *dōr wādōr* corresponds to that present in UT, 68:10, *tqḥ mlk 'lmk drkt dt drdrk*, "You will take your eternal kingdom, your everlasting dominion." Consult the fourth NOTE on Ps lvii 8 for parallel words as a criterion

for classifying Ugaritic in relation to Hebrew. The psalmist skillfully uses chiasm in the well-balanced cola numbering nine syllables each.

will you be angry . . . anger. The verb *te'enap* in the first colon is denominative from *'appekā* in the second.

7. *You are the Victor.* Vocalizing *hallē'* (MT *halō'*) *'attāh,* and deriving the divine appellative *lē'* from the widely used Northwest Semitic root examined in *Psalms I,* pp. 46–47, 144, 169, and the second NOTE on Ps lxxv 7. It is interesting to notice that the LXX here read *hā'ēl 'attāh, ho theós sù,* "O God, you . . . ," while some modern critics propose *yhwh 'attāh,* "O Yahweh, you . . . ." The vocalization *hallē'* provides the desired divine name and at the same time preserves intact the consonantal text.

restore us to life again. Parsing *tāšūb teḥayyēnū* as jussives with imperative function, like *tittēn,* "give," in the next verse. *Psalms I,* pp. 144, 169, points out that the divine title *lē'* often appears in contexts that deal with life and death. Here the Israelites, brought to death's door by the longstanding drought, ask the Victor to restore them to full vigor and activity.

8. *Show us.* Cf. the prayer for rain Ps iv 7, "Who will show us rain?"

Show us . . . give us. As observed in *Psalms I,* pp. 29 f., the stylistic variation between imperative and jussive forms has Canaanite antecedents in the Ras Shamra poetic texts. To express the imperative mode, the poet employs precative perfects (vss. 2–4), jussives (vss. 7–8), as well as imperatives (vss. 5, 8).

your prosperity. Namely, the prosperity that only you can bestow; see the second NOTE on vs. 5, "God of our prosperity."

9. *Let me announce.* The only explanation of MT *'ešme'āh,* a qal cohortative first person singular, that Briggs, CECBP, II, p. 234, could offer was that such a form in the midst of first person plurals was improbable. "It is not needed for measure and is a gloss of an impassioned, impatient copyist." To extract sense from this verse there is no need to incriminate "an impassioned, impatient copyist"; it suffices to repoint *'ašmī'āh,* the hiphil cohortative first person singular. With this formula (cf. Ps xx 7, *'attāh yāda'tī*) the priest or temple prophet introduces the reply received in answer to the prayer for rain (vss. 2–8). Compare Nah ii 1, *mašmīa' šālōm,* "who announces peace."

El himself. This translation of *hā'ēl* is explained at Ps lxviii 20.

has spoken. A comparison with the related formula of Ps xx 7 indicates the *yedabbēr* expresses past time, as so frequently in the Psalter; cf. introductory NOTE to Ps lxxviii.

indeed. The function of *kī* being emphatic, as in Ps lxxvii 12.

has promised. For this nuance of *yedabbēr,* consult BDB, p. 181a.

well-being. Within this psalm's context, *šālōm* appears to be a synonym of *yešaʿ*, "prosperity," in vss. 5, 8, 10; hence traditional "peace" may be exceptionable.

To the devoted ones of his people. Literally "to his people and to his devoted ones," a compelling instance of hendiadys; otherwise there would seem to be two separate groups (courtesy D. N. Freedman).

to those who again confide in him. MT *'al yāšūbū lᵉkislāh* defies analysis (*pace* UHP, p. 29), but the reading *'el yāšūbū lᵉkislāh* (or *kislōh*) proves very amenable when the relative pronoun *'ᵃšer* is mentally supplied before *yāšūbū* (courtesy Rev. Thomas Hamill). This same elliptical usage is studied in the fifth NOTE on Ps lxxxi 6. Consonantal *kislāh* is patient of two explanations. It is either the substantive *kislāh*, "confidence," sharing the suffixes of *'ammō* and *ḥᵃsīdāyw*, or the noun *kesel*, "confidence" (Ps lxxxviii 7; Job viii 14, xxxi 24) followed by the objective genitive suffix *-ōh*, that occurs in Pss x 9, xxvii 5, lxix 27, etc. Literally *yāšūbū lᵉkislōh* reads "who return to his confidence," i.e., confidence in him.

10. *Truly near.* One might compare the divine appellative *qārōb*, "the Near One," in Ps lxxv 2, and the description of Israel as *'am qᵉrōbō*, "the people near him," in Ps cxlviii 14.

his prosperity. Consult vss. 5 and 8.

Indeed. Parsing *lᵉ* of *lᵉšākēn* (see below) as emphatic *lamedh* balancing *'āk*, "truly," as proposed by me in *Biblica* 37 (1956), 338 f., and endorsed by D. R. Hillers in CBQ 27 (1965), 125, nn. 6–7. Cf. Kitchen, *Ancient Orient and Old Testament*, p. 163, n. 40.

his glory. Suffixless *kābōd* shares the suffix of its first-colon counterpart *yišʿō*, "his prosperity," as noted in *Biblica* 37 (1956), 338 f., and supported by some 120 examples of double-duty suffixes in the Psalter. Cf. also D. N. Freedman in IEJ 13 (1963), 126.

God's glory is that of the theophany that often accompanies a thunderstorm, as poetically set forth in such passages as Judg v 4–5; Pss lxv 9–10, lxviii 8–14. In commenting on such Ugaritic texts as 51:v:68 ff., N. C. Habel (*Yahweh versus Baal*, p. 74) observes that Baal's theophany in the storm is a revelation of his control over all the waters of heaven with which he renders fertile his earthly domain.

dwells. Reading *lᵉšākēn* (MT *liškōn*), with *lᵉ* the emphatic *lamedh* and *šākēn*, a stative verbal form matching stative *qārōb*, "near," in the first colon. In other words, the components of *lᵉšākēn* syntactically counterpoise *'ak qārōb; yišʿō*, "his prosperity," and *kābōd*, "his glory," pair off, while *bē'arṣēnū*, "in our land," is matched with *lirē'āyw*, "to those who fear him." The parallelism *škn//qrb* occurs in UT, 125:43–44.

11. *Kindness and fidelity . . . justice and well-being.* These four attributes are personified as attendants of God who co-operate in the production of rain. The root of one of these, *ṣedeq*, is specifically associated with rain in Joel ii 23, *kī nātan lākem 'et hammōreh liṣᵉdāqāh*,

"For he has given you the early rain at the right time." In his study, "The God Sedeq," HUCA 36 (1965), 161–77, Roy A. Rosenberg argues that the character of Ṣedeq as a solar god in ancient Semitic religions caused him to become associated with rain, and that the root *ṣdq* implies "that which is proper," hence a "proper" rain, one that comes in its season and is not too light or too heavy. The triple occurrence of *ṣedeq* in vss. 11, 12, 14 may be a reflection of this mythical connection between *ṣedeq* and rain.

justice and well-being. The phrase *ṣedeq wešālōm* juxtaposes the two components of the Ugaritic personal name *ṣdqšlm*.

13. *With a crash*. Namely, to the sound of thunder. This meaning of *gam* is noticed at Pss liv 7 and lxxxiv 7.

his rain. *Psalms I*, pp. 25 f., considers this definition of *haṭṭōb*, whose article stylistically balances the pronominal suffix of *yebūlāh*, "its produce"; cf. Pss iii 9, xxxiii 17, lv 23 (an exact illustration), cxxxiii 3; Joüon, GHB, § 137 f., p. 422. See new evidence for this definition in *Biblica* 54 (1973), 404.

our land . . . its produce. Cf. the prayer for rain Ps lxvii 7 and Ugar. *ybl arṣ* cited there. For a similar sequence of ideas—the preparation of the rain, the springing up of verdure—see Ps cxlvii 8.

14. *Justice . . . before him*. As God appears in the theophany accompanying the storm bringing the revivifying showers. The motif of God's two attendants comes in for discussion at Pss xxiii 6, xxv 25, xl 11, lxxxix 15, etc.

beauty. Much-canvassed *yśm* (MT *yāśēm*) makes the best counterpart to *ṣedeq*, "justice," when explained as a derivative from the frequent Ugaritic root *ysm*, Ar. *wsm*, "to be pleasant, beautiful." The orthographic variation between *s* and *ś* is witnessed in such pairs of Hebrew words as *mesukkāh-meśukkāh*, "hedge," *masmēr* but *maśmerōt*, "nails," in Phoenicianizing Eccles xii 11.

Close parallels to this imagery are found in, e.g., Hab iii 5, "Before him went pestilence, and plague followed close behind"; Ps xcvi 6, *hōd wehādār lepānāyw*, rendered by the Vulg. *confessio et pulchritudo in conspectu ejus*.

will indeed tread. Vocalizing *ledōrēk*, the *lamedh emphaticum* (see the third NOTE on vs. 10), followed by the qal participle *dōrēk;* MT reads *lederek* which is syntactically difficult.

in his steps. Though usually construed with a preposition, *dārak* does govern the accusative in Job xxii 15, "Do you mark the dark path / Which worthless men have trod?" (*'ašer dārekū metē 'āwen*), and in Phoenician Arslan Tash, lines 7–8, *wḥṣr 'drk bl tdrkn*, "And the court I tread you shall not tread!" It is also possible that *pe'āmāyw* shares the preposition of its counterpart *lepānāyw*, "before him." Cf. also Prov xii 28, *wederek netībāh 'al māwet*, "And the treading of her path is immortality"; *Biblica* 41 (1960), 176–81.

PSALM 86

(lxxxvi 1–17)

1 *A prayer of David.*

Incline your ear, Yahweh, and answer me,
for I am afflicted and needy.
2 Protect my life for I am devoted to you,
save your own servant
who trusts in you, my God.
3 Have pity on me, my Lord;
it is to you I cry all day long.
4 Cheer the soul of your servant;
it is to you, my Lord,
I lift up my soul.
5 Since you, my Lord, are good and forgiving,
rich in mercy to all who invoke you,
6 Give ear to my prayer, Yahweh,
hearken to my plea for mercy.
7 When besieged I cry to you,
O that you would answer me!
8 There is none like you among the gods,
nor achievement like yours, my Lord.
9 If you act, all the pagans will come
to prostrate themselves before you, my Lord,
And they will glorify your name.
10 How great you are, O Worker of Marvels,
you, O God, alone.
11 Yahweh, teach me your way,
that I may walk faithful to you alone;
Teach my heart to revere your name.
12 I will thank you, my Lord, my God,
with all my heart
I will glorify your name, O Eternal!

13 Since your love is great, O Most High,
you will rescue me from deepest Sheol.
14 Presumptuous ones, O God, have risen against me,
and the council of barbarians seeks my life;
They do not consider you my Leader.
15 But you, my Lord, are El the Compassionate and Merciful,
slow to anger, rich in kindness and fidelity.
16 Turn to me and have pity on me.
Grant your triumph to your servant,
give your faithful son victory.
17 Work a miracle for me, O Good One,
that my enemies might see and be humiliated.
O that you yourself, Yahweh,
would help me and console me!

NOTES

lxxxvi. Modern scholars approach unanimity in classifying this psalm as the lament of an individual, but none seem to have noticed that this individual happens to be the Israelite king. Couched in terms made familiar by the El Amarna royal correspondence and the Ugaritic letters of kings in which the vassal ruler calls himself "your servant" while addressing his suzerain as "my lord," this psalm may justly be described as a royal letter addressed to God. Verse 9, moreover, shows that the psalmist is no mere private citizen. How could God's miraculous intervention on behalf of a private person be thought to produce the large-scale effects described in vs. 9? And the dangers set forth in vs. 14 are not those that beset a simple citizen. This lament, too, shows marked similarities to royal Pss xx and liv in particular.

The letter is divided into three paragraphs, so to speak. Verses 1–7 contain a sustained supplication, vss. 8–13 take the form of a hymn astutely praising God's magnanimity in the hope of rendering him benevolent, while vss. 14–17 resume the entreaty of the first paragraph.

1. *Incline your ear . . . answer me.* These two imperatives of the first colon structurally balance the two precative perfects in the final colon (vs. 17).

Yahweh. Vocative *yhwh* corresponds to vocative *yhwh* in the last line.

answer me . . . afflicted. Grave as the lamenting psalmist's condition may have been, it did not discourage him from punning on *'ᵃnēnī* and *'ānī;* see the second NOTE on Ps lx 5.

2. *Protect my life.* The same idea is encountered in the letter of the king of Ugarit to the Pharaoh: UT, 1018:21–23, *l pn il mṣrm dt tġrn npš špš*, "before the gods of Egypt who will safeguard the life of the Sun (=Pharaoh)."

devoted to you. Suffixless *ḥāsīd* shares the suffix of closely parallel *'abdᵉkā*, "your servant." As in vs. 11, "faithful to you," the suffix is objective.

your own servant. The independent pronoun *'attāh* emphasizes the suffix of *'abdᵉkā*, a usage witnessed in Ugar. *šmk at*, "your own name," and discussed in *Psalms I*, pp. 156 f. In vs. 11 the poet modifies the suffix by an adjective. On the frequent use of *'bd* in Ugaritic letters written by local kings to their overlord, consult *Psalms I*, p. 124, and for the added connotation of "vassal" in Hebrew *'ebed*, see R. de Vaux in *Mélanges Eugène Tisserant*, I, pp. 121 ff., and F. Charles Fensham in BA 27 (1964), 96–100.

trusts in you. The concurrence of *ḥāsīd*, "devoted," *'abdᵉkā*, "your own servant," and *habbōṭēᵃḥ*, "trusts in you," in this verse points to the royal character of this lament when it is compared with royal Ps xxi 7, *kī hammelek bōṭēᵃḥ bayhwh ūbᵉḥesed 'elyōn bal yimmōṭ*, "Indeed the king trusts in Yahweh/and from the love of the Most High will never swerve."

3. *Have pity on me.* The verb *ḥānan* belongs to epistolary style, as may be inferred from the Ugaritic letter 1020:3, *ḥnny lpn mlk*, "Plead for me before the king."

it is to you. Taking *kī* as emphatic rather than causal.

my Lord. Briggs, CECBP, II, p. 238, correctly notes that *'ᵃdōnāy* is characteristic of this psalm (vss. 4, 5, 8, 9, 12, 15) and probably retains its original meaning, "my Lord." The identification of the genre of this psalm as a letter seems to bear out his acute observation because the El Amarna letters are rife with its Akkadian equivalent *bēliya*, "my lord."

4. *Cheer the soul of your servant.* Namely, by sending a reply to the psalmist. In a letter to the king of Egypt, Zimriddi, the governor of Sidon, employs similar phraseology: "When he (i.e., the Pharaoh) wrote to his servant, my heart rejoiced, my head was lifted high, and my eyes sparkled at hearing the word of the king, my lord" (EA, 144:14–18).

it is to you. As in previous verse, the *kī* appears emphatic rather than causal.

my Lord. See the third NOTE on vs. 3.

5. *good and forgiving.* The adjective *ṭōb* will be substituted by the appellative *ṭōbāh* in vs. 17, and *sallāḥ*, a hapax legomenon may equal Ugar. *slḫ*, whose unclear context precludes a certain definition.

rich. Or "abounding"; for *rab*, "rich," see *Psalms I*, pp. 99, 229.

6. *Give ear . . . Yahweh.* The sequence *ha'ᵃzīnāh yhwh tᵉpillātī* helps to establish the correct reading of Ps cxliii 1, *ha'ᵃzīnāh 'ēl* (MT *'el*) *taḥᵃnūnay,* "Give ear, O El, to my plea for mercy."

7. *When besieged.* For this shade of meaning in *bᵉyōm ṣārātī,* see the comments in *Psalms I,* p. 127, on royal Ps xx 2, *bᵉyōm ṣārāh.*

O that you would answer me! The balance with imperatives *haṭ,* "Turn," and *šᵉma',* "Listen," in Ps xvii 6 and with imperatives *ha'ᵃzīnāh,* "Give ear," and *haqšībāh,* "Hearken," here shows that the *kī* of *kī ta'ᵃnēnī* is precative, not causal "because, for." Other instances of precative *kī* are discussed at Pss lvi 14, lxi 4, 6, lxiii 8, etc. This precative formula recurs in II Chron vi 26, "When the heavens remain closed so that there is no rain because they have sinned against you and pray toward this place, confess your name and turn from their sin, may you answer them (*kī ta'ᵃnēm*)!"

Rhetorically, *kī ta'ᵃnēnī* forms an inclusion with imperative *'ᵃnēnī,* "Answer me," in vs. 1, and indicates the ending of the first section of the psalm (vss. 1–7). This stylistic observation is in opposition to the views of those (e.g., Gunkel) who maintain that some words are missing in vs. 7.

8. *my Lord.* I attach *'ᵃdōnāy* to the second colon so the verse scans 3+3, and explain *wᵉ* of *wᵉ'ēn* as emphatic, exactly as in Ps lxxix 3.

9. *If you act.* Or "When you act." For the usage of *'ᵃšer,* cf. Pss lxxviii 42–43, xcv 9, and BDB, p. 83b, d, where a number of texts employing conditional *'ᵃšer* are listed. The absolute use of *'āśāh* occurs in Pss xxii 32, xxxvii 5, xxxix 10, etc.

all the pagans. God's intervention on behalf of a poor and afflicted unknown Israelite would scarcely reach the ears of the surrounding nations. If, however, the favored suppliant is the king, such a reaction becomes understandable. For example, Isa xxxix 1 records that when Merodach-baladan the son of Baladan, king of Babylon, heard that King Hezekiah had been sick and recovered, he sent envoys with letters and a present for him.

will come. Namely, to Jerusalem, the city of the Israelite king.

to prostrate themselves before you. This literal rendition of *wᵉyištaḥᵃwū lᵉpānekā* instead of "to adore you" aims to bring out the physical manner of ancient Near Eastern adoration as represented in the graphic arts.

prostrate . . . glorify. These parallel verbs follow one another in UT, 51:IV:26, *tšthwy wtkbdh,* "Prostrate yourself and honor him."

10. *How great.* Explaining *kī* of *kī gādōl* as emphatic; cf. Gen xviii 20, *kī rabbāh* and Ps lxxxiv 11, *kī ṭōb.* This parsing bestows a full beat on emphatic *kī,* so that the verse scans into 3+2+3, as at Ps lxxiv 12 (first NOTE), and not into 4+3 with most metricians.

O Worker of Marvels. Parsing *wᵉ* of *wᵉʿōśēh* as the vocative particle identified in Pss lxxiv 12, lxxv 2. This divine title paves the way for the request the psalmist will make in vs. 17. This title is found also in the very archaic poem preserved in Exod xv 11.

11. *that I may walk.* Parsing *ʾᵃhallēk* as subjunctive and comparing UT, 127:37–38, *rd lmlk amlk,* "Come down from your royal seat that I may reign"; note the lack of conjunction before *amlk.*

faithful to you. Literally "in fidelity to you," with the suffix *-kā* expressing the objective genitive, as in Ps xxvi 3.

alone. Vocalizing *yāḥīd* (MT *yaḥēd*) and parsing it as an adjective modifying immediately preceding *-kā,* the same construction commented on in the third NOTE on Ps lxix 4 and at Ps lxxxviii 9, 18. The grammatical analysis results in a metrically balanced verse scanning into 3+3+3, with precisely three words in each colon. One consequently sees the unwisdom of deleting the divine name *yhwh,* as proposed by some critics.

The king pledges fidelity to Yahweh alone since he alone is God, as affirmed in the preceding verse.

Teach. With imperative "teach" of the first colon governing accusative *lᵉbābī* in the third; notice a similar construction in vs. 2.

to revere. This uncommon form of the qal infinitive recurs under the same conditions in Deut iv 10, *yilmᵉdūn lᵉyirʾāh ʾōtī,* "that they may learn to revere me."

12. *with all my heart.* Identifying *bᵉkol lᵉbābī* as a phrase dangling between the longer cola of the verse and semantically belonging to both; see the comments at Pss lxxxiv 3 and lvii 5. This scansion serves to redress the syllabic imbalance (14:11) and restores a 9:5:10 (see next NOTE) verse. The attempt to restore syllabic equilibrium by deleting either *ʾᵃdōnāy* or *ʾᵉlōhay* in the first colon may be given up.

I will glorify. Omitting the copula as secondary; the final colon thus totals ten syllables while the first colon numbers nine.

O Eternal. Recognizing in *lᵉʿōlām* the vocative particle and the divine appellative, as proposed in UHP, p. 36, and VT 16 (1966), 310. Vocative *ʿōlām* is thus seen to balance vocative "my Lord, my God" in the first colon. Cf. the first NOTE on Ps lii 11 and the second on Ps lxxv 10.

13. *O Most High.* Vocalizing *ʿēlī,* as in Pss vii 9, xiii 6, xxxii 5, etc., and thus eliminating the hapax legomenon construction of MT *gādōl ʿālāy.* The psalmist evidently employs this appellative to contrast the Most High God with *šᵉʾōl taḥtiyyāh,* "deepest Sheol," a kind of theological wordplay noted at Ps lxxv 6 and in *Psalms I,* p. 285. Royal Ps xxi 8, it might be observed, uses the related divine title *ʿelyōn,* "the Most High."

you will rescue me. Understanding *wᵉ* of *wᵉhiṣṣaltī* as conversive or consecutive, but not conjunctive, and hence referring to future time. The psalmist is still in mortal danger, and to translate the verb as past, "You have rescued me" (*The Jerusalem Bible*), is to render the following imperatives and precatives meaningless.

14. *the council of barbarians.* Referring to the king's foreign enemies.

my Leader. See the third NOTE on Ps liv 5.

15. *But you.* In contrast to the ruthless pagan gods.

16. *your triumph . . . victory.* Cf. royal Ps xxi 2 for the parallelism of these two roots. Just as Yahweh overcame the heathen gods (vs. 8), so may he grant to his king a similar triumph over the heathens who worship the gods vanquished by Yahweh.

give your faithful son victory. Comparing *hōšī'āh l^{e}ben '^{a}mittekā* (MT *'^{a}māṭekā*) with royal Ps xxi 7, *hōšī'āh yhwh m^{e}šīḥō,* "Yahweh has given his anointed victory."

That the reading "your faithful son" (also in Ps cxvi 16) must supplant MT "the son of your handmaid" follows from the stress on fidelity in vs. 11 and from a comparison between *ben '^{a}mittekā* and EA, 107:13, *arad kittišu,* "his true servant." The expression apparently belongs to epistolary genre, much like "Faithfully yours" in English letters. Menahem Mansoor in JBL 76 (1957), 145, is correct in translating Qumran Hodayot, Pl. 40, line 29, *wkl bny '[m]tw,* "And all his true children," and remarking (n. 60) "certainly not 'the children of His maidservant.'"

17. *Work a miracle.* Usually translated "Show me a sign," *'^{a}śēh 'ōt* should be interpreted in view of the divine title in vs. 10, *'ōśeh niplā'ōt,* "Worker of Marvels." Of course, the expression *'āśāh 'ōt,* "He worked a miracle," is frequently found, especially in the Pentateuch.

O Good One. Explaining *l^{e}ṭōbāh* as the divine appellative (identified in Pss xvi 2 and cxix 122) preceded by the vocative *lamedh,* recognized in vs. 12, *l^{e}'ōlām.* In the same manner that he prepared the terrain for his request, "Work a miracle for me," by addressing God as the Worker of Marvels in vs. 10, the psalmist anticipates the appellative "Good One" by reminding God in vs. 5 that he is *ṭōb,* "good." Cf. Hos viii 3, *zānaḥ yiśrā'el ṭōb 'ōyēb $yird^{e}$pū* (MT *$yird^{e}$pō*), "Israel has rejected the Good One, followed after the Foe," where *ṭōb* designates Yahweh and *'ōyēb* refers to Yahweh's enemy, namely, Baal. If this analysis of the hapax legomenon phrase *'^{a}śēh 'immī 'ōt l^{e}ṭōbāh* does justice to the poet's intentions, we have God addressed in this lament by the following names: *yhwh* (vss. 1, 6, 11, 17), *'^{e}lōhay* (vss. 2, 12), *'^{e}lōhīm* (vss. 10, 14), *'^{a}dōnay* (vss. 3, 4, 5, 8, 9, 12, 15), *'ōśēh niplā'ōt* (vs. 10), *'ōlām* (vs. 12),. *'ēlī* (vs. 13), *'ēl rāḥūm* (vs. 15), *ṭōbāh* (vs. 17).

O that you yourself. Understanding *kī 'attāh* as the mode of address often employed with precative perfects; cf. the NOTES to Pss iii 8, x 14, xxxix 10 (*Psalms I*); and Pss lxi 6, lxxxii 8.

would help me. Parsing *ʿᵃzartanī* as precative perfect and comparing the closing of the lament Ps xliv 27, *ʿāzartāl-lanū,* "Help us!" This analysis gets rid of the problem of explaining how *yēbōšū* could immediately following *kī*. Scholars are wont to describe *yēbōšū* as subordinate to the previous verb which it qualifies with adverbial force; were this the case, we would expect the order of the verbs reversed.

console me. Another precative perfect, *niḥamtānī* along with *ʿᵃzartanī* balances the two imperatives of vs. 1, and repeats the thought of vs. 4, "Cheer the soul of your servant."

PSALM 87

(lxxxvii 1–7)

1 *A psalm of the sons of Korah. A song.*

O city founded by him on the holy mountains,
2 Yahweh loves you, O gates of Zion;
He who made perfect the glorious dwellings of Jacob
3 speaks in you, O city of God. *Selah*
4 "I shall inscribe Rahab and Babylon
among those who acknowledge me;
Even Philistia and Tyre along with Cush,
'this one was born there.'"
5 But of Zion it will be said:
"This one and that one were born in her,
and the most High will make her secure."
6 Yahweh will write down in the register of the peoples,
"this one was born there." *Selah*
7 And all who have suffered in you
will sing as well as dance.

NOTES

lxxxvii. A psalm in praise of Zion that bears marked resemblance to Pss xxiv and xlviii. The poet lauds Zion as the city of God and the mother of believers everywhere.

The contrast in vs. 4 between Egypt and Babylon, and the omission of Assyria, imply a fairly late date of composition, in the seventh or sixth century B.C. Similarly, the reference to Cush suggests the period of Ethiopian ascendancy in Egypt under the Twenty-fifth Dynasty (ca. 715–663 B.C.).

Scholars generally take a dim view of the Hebrew original of this poem, considering it one of the most mangled and disordered of the Psalter; cf. E. Beaucamp, "Le problème du Psaume 87," in *Liber annuus studii biblici Franciscani* 13 (1962–63), 53–75. I do not share this pessimism; a sober sequence of ideas flows from the consonantal text, though one may not always be able to vouch for the Masoretic vocalization. Two cases where sense seems to require a departure from MT are vs. 2, *mkl*, and vs. 7, *m'ny* (MT *ma'yānay*).

1. *O city founded by him.* Literally "she founded by him," *yᵉsūdātō* is a qal feminine passive participle whose third person masculine suffix expresses the agent, as in Pss xxxvii 22, lxxxi 8; Job xix 26; Prov vii 26, ix 18, etc. Syntactically vocative, it forms an inclusion with vs. 3, "O city of God." As Beaucamp (*op. cit.*, p. 71) points out, there is no need to posit the hapax legomenon nominal form *yᵉsūdāh*, as done by KB, p. 386b, and other lexicographers.

the holy mountains. If not a plural of majesty, to be translated singular, *harᵉrē qōdeš* then refers to the several hills on which Jerusalem was situated.

2. *loves you.* With transitive *'ōhēb* sharing the suffix of vs. 3, *bāk*, "in you."

O gates of Zion. The traditional versions make *ša'ᵃrē ṣiyyōn* the direct of *'ōhēb*, but the stichometry adopted in the present translation favors its parsing as a vocative, parallel to preceding "O city founded by him" and subsequent "O city of God." The syllable count in the first bicolon is 10:9.

He who made perfect. Vocalizing hiphil participle *mēkēl* (MT *mikkōl*) from *kll*, "to complete, perfect," used of builders in Ezek xxvii 4, *bōnayik kālᵉlū yopyēk*, "Those who built you made you perfect in beauty," and UT, 51:v:72, *bt arzm ykllnh*, "As a palace of cedars let him make it perfect." As a participle predicated of God, *mēkēl* balances the participles *'ōhēb*, "love," and (vs. 3) *mᵉdabbēr*, "speaks." Conceptually, Yahweh is the founder of Zion, the beautifier of Jacob's towns, and the one who makes Zion secure (vs. 5). Thus a unified description of Yahweh comes to light.

glorious. MT and versions generally dissociate *nikbādōt* from the second colon of vs. 2. and attach it to vs. 3, but the word and syllable count strongly suggests that it modifies feminine plural *miškᵉnōt*, "dwellings." Niphal *nkbd* is attested in Ugaritic. The following arrangement emerges:

mēkēl miškᵉnōt ya'ᵃqōb nikbādōt	(4 words—11 syllables)
mᵉdabbēr bāk 'īr hā'ᵉlōhīm	(4 words—9 syllables)

dwellings of Jacob. Just as the "gates of Zion" refer to the entire city of Zion, so the "dwellings" by metonymy designate the other towns and cities of the Holy Land. Though Yahweh himself built and beautified these towns, he did not choose them as the site of his revelation; this prerogative was Jerusalem's.

3. *speaks.* Repointing MT pual *m^e^dubbār* to piel *m^e^dabbēr,* which counterpoises hiphil participle *mēkēl* of the first colon.

city of God. The psalmist makes the three vocatives *'īr hā'^e^lōhīm, ša'^a^rē ṣiyyōn,* "O gates of Zion," and *y^e^sūdātō,* "O city founded by him," correspond to the three participles predicated of Yahweh: *'ōhēb, mēkēl,* and *m^e^dabbēr.*

4. *I shall inscribe.* For this signification of *'azkīr,* consult the first NOTE on Ps lxxix 8 and Zorell, ZLH, p. 209a, who correctly proposes the translation *"inscribam Rahab et Babel tanquam noscentes me."* The second NOTE on Ps lvi 1 documents the figure of the divine bookkeeper.

Rahab. A poetical name for Egypt (Isa xxx 7), conceived as a monster who repeatedly devoured Israel. In Ps lxxxix 10 Rahab is the name of a mythological sea dragon vanquished by Yahweh in a primordial combat.

those who acknowledge me. Namely, in a religious sense; cf. the fifth NOTE on Ps lxxxi 6.

Cush. Biblical term for the territory south of Egypt, usually identified with present-day Ethiopia.

this one was born there. Though born abroad, these converts to Yahwism will become citizens of the spiritual metropolis Zion.

5. *But of Zion.* Those born in Jerusalem are an object of divine predilection.

will make her secure. Cf. Ps xlviii 9. With vs. 1 *y^e^sūdātō, y^e^kōn^e^nehā* forms an inclusion.

6. *Yahweh.* The transference of *yhwh* to the foregoing verse would carry more conviction if its proponents would offer some documentation for the composite title *'elyōn yhwh,* "Most High Yahweh."

will write down. Comparing Ps lvi 9, "You yourself write down my lament, list my tears on your parchment." Yahweh's interest in Zion is such that he keeps a careful list of all her inhabitants.

the register. Explaining *k^e^tōb* as the Phoenician form ($\bar{a}>\bar{o}$) of Heb. *k^e^tāb,* "register, enrollment," in Ezek xiii 9; Ezra ii 62=Neh vii 67. There is a related development involving this root in Eccles xii 10 where *kātūb* is the Phoenician form ($\bar{o}>\bar{u}$) of the Hebrew infinitive absolute *kātōb;* cf. *Biblica* 47 (1966), 281, and the second NOTE on Ps liii 7.

7. *who have suffered.* With the Syriac, vocalizing *m^e^'unnēy* for MT *ma'yānay,* "my springs," which is rather distant from the contents of the poem.

in you. Namely, in Zion, harking back to vs. 3, *bāk,* "in you."

will sing as well as dance. Literally "will be singers as well as dancers."

PSALM 88

(lxxxviii 1–19)

1 *A song. A psalm of the sons of Korah. For the director; according to Mahalath Leannoth. A maskil of Heman the native-born.*

2 O Yahweh, my God, my Savior,
day and night I cry to you.
3 May my prayer come before you; [2]*
incline your ear to my cry.
4 For my soul is full of troubles, [3]
and my life has reached Sheol.
5 I am reckoned as one gone down to the Pit, [4]
I have become like a strengthless man.
6 In Death is my cot [5]
like the slaughtered
My couch is in the Grave,
Where you remember them no longer,
cut off as they are from your love.
7 You have plunged me into the lowest Pit, [6]
into the regions dark and deep.
8 Your rage weighs heavy upon me, [7]
and with all your outbursts you afflict me. *Selah*
9 You have removed my companions far from me, [8]
made me an abomination to them;
Imprisoned, I cannot escape,
10 my eyes grow dim through affliction. [9]
Daily, O Yahweh, I invoke you,
I spread out my hands to you.
11 Do you work marvels for the dead, [10]
do the shades rise up to praise you? *Selah*

* Verse numbers in RSV.

12 Is your kindness declared in the Grave, [11]
your fidelity in Abaddon?
13 Are your marvels made known in the Darkness, [12]
your generosity in the Land of Forgetfulness?
14 But I, O Yahweh, am calling to you; [13]
at dawn let my prayer come before you.
15 Why, O Yahweh, do you rebuff me, [14]
why do you turn your face from me?
16 Afflicted and groaning, I die, [15]
I suffer the terrors of your wheel.
17 Your furies have swept over me, [16]
your dread assaults have annihilated me.
18 They surround me like a flood [17]
all day long
They close in on me alone.
19 You have removed my friendly neighbors far from me; [18]
my chief companion is the Darkness.

Notes

lxxxviii. This lament of a desolate man in mortal illness is especially notable for its numerous names of the nether world and its tone of hopelessness.

1. *Mahalath Leannoth.* Words whose meaning is uncertain, though the first looks like a derivative from *ḥwl,* "to circle, dance," and the second a derivative from *'ny,* "to sing an antiphonal song."

Heman the native-born. According to I Kings v 11, Heman was one of the wise men of Israelite tradition and a member of an orchestral guild. As shown by Albright, *Archaeology and the Religion of Israel,* pp. 127, 210, the term *'ezrāḥī* designates originally "aborigine" and then "member of a pre-Israelite family."

2. *my God.* Reading *'^{e}lōhay* for MT *'^{e}lōhēy.*

my Savior. See the second Note on Ps li 16.

day and night I cry to you. The Hebrew literally reads "By day I cry, at night to you." As an accusative of time, *yōm* balances the prepositional phrase *ballaylāh.*

to you. For this nuance of *negdekā,* see Ps lii 11. The customary translation "before you," implying the nearness of God, does not accord with the tenor of this lament; the psalmist pictures himself in deepest Sheol and hence at the greatest possible distance from God.

3. *come before you.* Cf. Ps xviii 7, where a prayer uttered in Sheol

was heard in God's heavenly palace. A similar situation obtains in Jon ii 8. The pairing of a jussive with an imperative (*haṭṭēh*, "incline") is frequent in the Psalter.

4. *full of*. The expression *śābeʿāh bᵉ* illustrates the interchangeability of *bᵉ* and *min*, "from," since this verb governs both these prepositions with no palpable difference in meaning.

has reached. The journey of life is over for the psalmist. Similar imagery underlies Isa xxxviii 10, "I have marched my days. I have been consigned to Sheol for the rest of my years" (CBQ 22 [1960], 401), and Job iii 22, "and happy to reach the grave."

5. *I am reckoned*. In the census list of Sheol's citizens. As proposed in *Biblica* 40 (1959), 164–66, *neḥšabtī ʿim* is synonymous with Jer xvii 13, *bāʾāreṣ yikkātēbū*, "They shall be enrolled in the nether world," and UT, 51:VIII:8–9, *tspr byrdm arṣ*, "Be numbered among those gone down to the nether world." In recently published economic texts from Ras Shamra *ḥṯbn* denotes "an account"; cf. Dahood, *Biblica* 45 (1964), 409; 47 (1966), 277.

gone down to the Pit. A poetic expression for those who have died, *yōrᵉdē bōr* is synonymous with Ugar. *yrdm arṣ*, cited in the preceding NOTE; Eccles iii 21, *yōredet . . . lāʾāreṣ*; Ps xxx 10, *ridtī ʾel šaḥat*, "my descent to the Pit." Cf. Tromp, *Primitive Conceptions of Death in the Old Testament, and the Nether World*, pp. 19, 33, 69–71.

a strengthless man. In view of Ugar. *ul*, "army, host," in Krt:88, 178, and *ulny*//*ʿẓmy*, "strength," in 68:5, one may no longer follow older commentators (e.g., Briggs, Gunkel) who label *ʾᵉyal* an Aramaism.

Cf. A. E. Housman, "To an Athlete Dying Young," "And round that early-laurelled head / Will flock to gaze the strengthless dead."

6. *In Death . . . in the Grave*. A line of fifteen syllables, vs. 6a scans into a tricolon chiastically arranged in an A+B//C//B́+Ć pattern, in which the C member is suspended between the first and third members (cf. Ps lxxxvi 12), and conceptually modifies both. This pattern recurs in vs. 18. The restructured line would read:

bammētīm ḥopšī	(5 syllables+2 beats)
kᵉmō ḥᵃlālīm	(5 syllables+2 beats)
miškābī qeber	(5 syllables+2 beats)

Like *māwet*, "Death," which in Pss vi 6 (*Psalms I*, p. 38), lv 14, etc., signifies the realm of death, so here *mētīm*, parallel to *qeber*, "Grave," denotes a place rather than its inhabitants. Similarly in Job xxxiii 22, *wattiqrab laššaḥat napšō wᵉḥayyātō lᵉmō mētīm* (MT *lamᵉmītīm*), "And his soul draws near to the Pit, his life to Death." The balance with "Pit" points to a locative meaning for *mōtīm;* the reading *l^{e}mō mētīm,* it should be observed, produces a balanced line with eight syllables in each colon, as well as uncovering the parallelism between *l^e* and *l^{e}mō* (Ugar. *l//lm*), discussed at Ps xc 8 and in UHP, p. 27.

my cot. Relating *ḥpšy* (MT pointing *ḥopšī* is dubious) to Ugar. *ḥpṯt* in 51:VIII:7–8, *wrd bt ḫpṯt arṣ,* "And go down to the nether house of cots," which evidently equals II Kings xv 5 (=II Chron xxvi 21), *bēt haḥopšīt.* Scholars dispute over the precise meaning of Ugar. *bt ḫpṯt,* but Gordon's tentative definition "infirmary" coincides with the sense proposed for *ḥpšy* in the psalm and with the motif of Sheol as a place of beds in such texts as Ps cxxxix 8, "If I make Sheol my bed, you are there"; Job xvii 13, "If I call Sheol my house, spread my couch in Darkness"; Prov vii 27, "the rooms of Death." In support of this definition of *ḥpš* one may cite the difficult phrase in Ezek xxvii 20, *bigdē ḥōpeš l^{e}rikbāh,* "bedspreads for riding." Tromp, *Primitive Conceptions,* pp. 192–94, reviews the recent etymologies proposed for this vocable.

My couch. The single writing of a consonant where morphology requires two like consonants (cf. the third NOTE on Ps lx 11) permits the reading *ḥ^{a}lālīm miškābī* (MT *šōk^{e}bē*). Cf. Ezek xxxii 25, *b^{e}tōk ḥ^{a}lālīm nāt^{e}nū miškāb lāh,* "Among the slaughtered they put a couch for her," and Phoen. *mškb 't rp'm,* "a couch among the shades" (Eshmunazor, line 8, Tabnit, line 8).

in the Grave. qeber shares the preposition of *bammētīm,* an example of double-duty preposition as in vs. 8, Ps lxxii 6, etc. As in vs. 12, *qeber* is a poetic name for the underworld.

where. This locative meaning of *'^{a}šer* can also be observed in Pss lxxviii 42, 43, lxxxiv 4; Num xx 13.

them. Referring to the dead, especially "the slaughtered."

your love. Numerous versions (e.g., *The Jerusalem Bible*) translate *ydk* as "your protecting hand," but a much more viable explanation simply equates *ydk* with Ugar. *yd,* "love," a noun in parallelism with *ahbt,* "affection," in 'nt:III:3–4. Hence I prefer to dissociate *ydk* from *yād,* "hand," since the dead cannot be said to be cut off from Yahweh's power (cf. Pss xcv 4, cxxxix 8; Amos ix 2), and to derive it from *ydd,* "to love." Cf. Deut xxxiii 3; Lam iii 3.

8. *weighs heavy.* Comparing Ps xxxii 4, "your hand was oppressive," and Ezek v 13, *wah^{a}nīḥōtī ḥ^{a}mātī bām,* "And I shall bring my rage to rest on them." Whether *sām^{e}kāh* relates to UT, 125:35, *smkt* cannot be made out, though an equation of roots appears likely since both occur in laments.

with all your outbursts. Usually rendered "breakers" or "waves," *mišbārekā,* an accusative of means preceding its verb, better accords with its counterpart "your rage" if related to the Ugaritic expression *ṯbr aphm,* "their nostrils," in UT, 137:13; cf. WuS, No. 2834. We assume, of course, that this phrase underwent the same semantic development as *'ap,* "nostril, anger."

you afflict me. Suffixless *'innītā* shares the suffix of *'ālay,* "upon me," on the principle of the double-duty suffix which enables the poet to match two cola of nine syllables each. Cf. the fifth NOTE on vs. 6. The structure of the verse is chiastic.

9. *You have removed.* The phrase *hirḥaqtā mᵉyuddā'ay mimmenni* is reminiscent of UT, 'nt:IV:84, *šrḥq aṯt lpnnh,* "He removed the women far from his presence."

an abomination. Parsing *tō'ēbōt* as the Phoenician feminine singular ending *-ōt,* commented upon in the second NOTE on Ps liii 7. The same explanation is valid in Prov vi 16 where, Ketiv *tw'bwt* has been mistakenly pointed *tō'ᵃbat* by MT.

Imprisoned. The passive participle *kālū'* depends upon the suffix of *šattanī,* the construction examined at Ps lxix 4. A similar usage will be noticed at vs. 18.

This poetic allusion to Sheol as a prison (cf. Job xii 14; Lam iii 7; Rev i 18, xx 1–2, 7) makes it possible to improve the translation of Ps xxxi 9, *wᵉlō' hisgartanī bᵉyad 'ōyēb,* "And you did not imprison me in the hand of the Foe," as pointed out by Tromp, *Primitive Conceptions,* pp. 155–56. Cf. Job xii 14 and below on Ps cxlii 8, cited in the NOTE on vs. 11.

10. *my eyes grow dim.* Though most versions translate plural "eyes," MT reads singular *'ēnī,* "my eye." Perhaps this less felicitous pointing was induced by the misconstruing of the verb *dā'ᵃbāh,* "grow dim," as feminine singular. However, the texts cited in the fourth NOTE on Ps lxviii 14 suggest that dual *'ēnay* would be a better reading with *dā'ᵃbāh* parsing as feminine dual or plural.

through affliction. The wordplay on *'ēnay,* "my eyes," and *'ōnī* evokes the pun in Lam i 16, *'ēnē 'ēnay yōrᵉdāh mayim,* "The fountains of my eyes stream with water," and that in vs. 16. Cf. the second NOTE on Ps lx 5.

I invoke you. Namely, from the nether world where the psalmist pictures himself. Cf. Ecclus li 9, *w'rym m'rṣ qwly wmš'ry š'wl šw'ty,* "And I sent up my voice from the City (=Sheol), and my cry from the gates of Sheol."

11. *rise up to praise you.* The lack of the conjunction in the phrase *yāqūmū yōdūkā* is syntactically identical with that examined at Ps xxxix 5. The inability to praise God in Sheol (cf. Pss vi 6, xxx 10) represents one of the nether world's most poignant sorrows. In fact, in Ps cxlii 8 the psalmist entreats God to release him from the prison of Sheol precisely to praise his name.

12. *the Grave.* Cf. the fifth NOTE on vs. 6.

Abaddon. From *'ābad,* "to perish," this name for the underworld is semantically akin to Ps lxxiii 18, *ḥ^{a}lāqōt,* "Perdition," from *ḥlq,* "to die, perish." As in vs. 8, the word order is chiastic.

13. *the Land of Forgetfulness.* A poetic term unknown elsewhere in the Bible (compare Greek Lethe, a river in Hades whose water caused forgetfulness of the past in those who drank of it). Ps vi 6 also associates the loss of memory and the inability to praise Yahweh as features of existence in Sheol. Not only do the dead lose their memory; they in turn are forgotten by the living as Ecclesiastes sadly observes (i 11, ii 16, ix 5).

14. *at dawn.* The phrase *babbōqer* literally means this since it was at dawn that God came to the aid of the *orante;* cf. Ps lvii 9 and Joseph Ziegler, "Die Hilfe 'am Morgen'," in *Alttestamentliche Studien F. Nötscher gewidmet,* pp. 281–88. *The Jerusalem Bible* strays afar with "But I am here, calling for your help, praying to you every morning."

come before you. The denominative verb *t^{e}qadd^{e}mekkā* repeats the prayer of vs. 3; in fact, it might also repeat the thought of *babbōqer* insofar as *qedem* denotes "dawn" in UT, 75:I:7–8, *km šḥr . . . km qdm;* cf. Dahood, *Gregorianum* 43 (1962), 71; M. C. Astour, *Hellenosemitica,* p. 154, and James D. Muhly, JAOS 85 (1965), 586. Hence the psalmist employs a verb evoking the nuance found in Ps cxix 147 and Jon iv 2, *qiddamtī librō^{a}ḥ taršīšāḥ,* "I rose at dawn to flee to Tarshish." Cf. also the second NOTE on Ps xlviii 8.

15. *you turn your face.* Parsing *tastīr* as an infixed *-t-* form of *sūr,* as proposed in *Psalms I,* p. 64.

16. *Afflicted.* *'ānī '^{a}nī* (cf. Ps lxix 30) represents the second pun of this lament (see vs. 10).

groaning I die. Vocalizing *gō'ē-m* (enclitic *mem*) *nō'ēr* (MT *nō'ar*) The usual derivation of MT *nō'ar* from the root signifying "youth" gives rise to serious misgivings. More consonant with the language of lament would be its identification with *nġr,* "to roar, bleat, groan," found in UT, 68:6–7, *wttn gh yġr tḥt ksi zbl ym,* "And his voice was given forth, he groaned under the throne of Prince Sea"; *Le palais royal d'Ugarit,* V, 124:1–2, *arḫ td rgm bġr,* "The wild cow throws her voice by mooing"; Jer li 38, *yaḥdāyw kakk^{e}pīrīm yiš'āgū nā'^{a}rū k^{e}gōrē '^{a}rāyōt,* "Like lions they roar in unison, like lion cubs they growl." The balance with *šā'ag,* "to roar," pinpoints the sense of *nā'ar,* while *šā'agtī* in the lament Ps xxxviii 9 shows that synonymous *nā'ar* also belongs to the vocabulary of lament. Cf. UHP, p. 68, and for similar concepts, Pss vi 7 and lxix 4.

the terrors of your wheel. An admittedly desperate attempt to wrench sense out of that ancient puzzle *'ēmekā 'āpūnāh.* By pointing *'ōpānāh* (cf. Ugar. *apn, apnm, apnt*) and comparing Prov xx 26 where the wheel is an instrument of torture, a description coherent with the first colon emerges. Syntactically, the phrase belongs to that group of construct chains with interposed pronominal suffixes discussed at Pss lxi 5, lxxi 7, etc. Another possible reading is *'epneh*, "I pass away," from *pānāh*, discussed at Ps lxxii 5.

17. *have annihilated me*. Often discarded as an impossible form, consonantal *ṣmtwtny* has a claim to further attention in view of Isa li 9, *mḥṣbt*, evidently a quadriliteral verb formed from *mḥṣ* and *ḥṣb*, both denoting "to smite"; cf. Dahood, BCCT, p. 56. Hence *ṣmtwtny* may well be a blend of *ṣmt*, "to annihilate," and *mwtt*, "to slay."

18. *all day long*. Scanning the phrase *kol hayyōm* as a link between the first and third cola, semantically belonging with both; consult the first NOTE on vs. 6. The syllable count thus becomes 6:3:7 instead of 9:7.

on me alone. Reading *'ālay yāḥīd* (MT *yaḥad*) whose syntax is identical with that of the phrase examined in the third NOTE on vs. 9. This vocalization results in a description that dramatically ties in with the burden of vs. 19.

19. *my friendly neighbors*. Explaining *'ōhēb wārēᵃ'* as hendiadys, whose suffix is forthcoming from *mᵉyuddā'ay*, "my chief companion."

my chief companion. Used with its normal denotation in vs. 9, plural *mᵉyuddā'ay* here seems to be a plural of majesty, stressing that the psalmist's one and only colleague is the Darkness. God's abandonment of the psalmist is complete.

the Darkness. In a lament thick with terms designating the realm of the dead, *maḥšāk* forms a fitting close to a lament unredeemed by any note of hope.

PSALM 89

(lxxxix 1–53)

1 *A maskil of Ethan the native-born.*

2 Your love, Yahweh, for ever shall I sing,
age after age I shall proclaim your fidelity.
3 With my mouth I clearly admit: [2]*
"Eternal One, your love created the heavens,
but you made your fidelity more steadfast than these."
4 "I have made a covenant with my chosen, [3]
I have sworn to David my servant:
5 'I will establish your line for ever, [4]
and build up your throne for all generations.'" *Selah*
6 In the heavens they praise your promise, Yahweh, [5]
and your fidelity in the congregation of holy ones.
7 For who in the skies can compare with Yahweh? [6]
Who resembles Yahweh among the gods?
8 An El too dreadful for the council of holy ones, [7]
too great and awesome for all around him.
9 Yahweh God of Hosts, who is like you? [8]
Mighty Yah, your faithful ones surround you.
10 You rule upon the back of the sea, [9]
when its waves surge, you check them.
11 You crushed Rahab like a carcass, [10]
with your strong arm you scattered your foes.
12 Yours are the heavens and yours is the earth, [11]
the world and all it holds—you founded them.
13 You created Zaphon and Amanus, [12]
Tabor and Hermon sing with joy in your presence.
14 Yours is a powerful arm, O Warrior! [13]
your left hand is triumphant,
your right hand raised in victory!

* Verse numbers in RSV.

15 Justice and right are the foundation of your throne, [14]
love and truth stand before you.
16 Happy the people who know your radiance, [15]
who walk, Yahweh, in the light of your face.
17 They rejoice in your presence all day, [16]
and are jubilant over your generosity.
18 Indeed, you are our glorious triumph, [17]
and by your favor you give us victory.
19 Truly Yahweh is our Suzerain, [18]
the Holy One of Israel our King!
20 Once you spoke in a vision, [19]
to your devoted one indeed you said:
"I made a lad king in preference to a warrior,
I exalted a youth above a hero.
21 I have found David my servant, [20]
with my holy oil I anointed him.
22 My hand shall supply his power, [21]
and my arm shall keep him strong.
23 No foe shall rise up against him, [22]
nor son of iniquity overcome him.
24 But I will hammer his adversaries before him, [23]
and strike down those who hate him.
25 My fidelity and love shall be with him, [24]
and through my Name he shall be victorious.
26 And I will put his left hand on the sea, [25]
and his right hand on the river.
27 He shall cry to me: [26]
'You are my father, my God,
the Mountain of my salvation.'
28 And I will make him my first-born, [27]
the highest of earthly kings.
29 I will keep my love for him eternal, [28]
and my covenant shall endure for him.
30 I will put his offspring on his seat, [29]
and his throne will be like heaven's days.
31 Should his children forsake my law, [30]
refuse to follow my decrees,
32 Should they violate my statutes, [31]
and not keep my commandments,

33 I will punish their rebellion with the rod, [32]
and their malice with whiplashes.
34 But I will never banish from him my love, [33]
or be false to my fidelity.
35 I will not violate my covenant, [34]
nor alter my given word.
36 Once for all I have sworn on my holiness, [35]
I cannot lie to David.
37 His dynasty shall last to eternity, [36]
his throne as the sun before me.
38 Like the moon will his descendants live on, [37]
and his seat will be stabler than the sky." *Selah*
39 And yet you spurned in your anger, [38]
you raged at your anointed;
40 You repudiated the covenant with your servant, [39]
you utterly desecrated his crown.
41 You breached all his walls, [40]
reduced his fortifications to rubble.
42 All who pass by despoil him, [41]
he has become the taunt of his neighbors.
43 You exalted the right hand of his adversaries, [42]
raised high both hands of his foes.
44 In your wrath you turned back his blade, [43]
and did not sustain his sword.
45 Among his troops you made his splendor cease, [44]
and hurled his throne upon the ground.
46 You cut short the days of his youth, [45]
robed his young manhood with sterility. *Selah*
47 How long, O Yahweh, will you estrange yourself? [46]
How long, O Conqueror, must your rage burn like fire?
48 Remember my sorrow, [47]
the few days of my life.
For what void did you create all mankind?
49 What man alive will not see death? [48]
What man can rescue self from the hand of Sheol? *Selah*
50 Where are those earlier acts of love, [49]
O Lord,
Which you promised on your fidelity to David?
51 Remember, Lord, the insults to your servant, [50]
how in my breast I bear all the shafts of pagans;

52 That your foes, Yahweh, insult me, [51]
insultingly malign your anointed.
53 Praised be Yahweh for ever! [52]
Amen and Amen.

Notes

lxxxix. A royal psalm in which the Israelite king prays for deliverance from his enemies. The prelude (vss. 2–5) is followed by a hymn to the Creator (vss. 6–19) in phrases reminiscent of ancient poems such as Exod xv. This hymn in turn introduces a messianic oracle (vss. 20–38) rehearsing the glorious promises to David (cf. II Sam vii 8–16) that sharply contrast with the king's defeat and humiliation set forth in vss. 39–46. In the final strophe (vss. 47–52), the king pleads with God to remember his sorrow and sufferings at the hands of heathen adversaries. The doxology (vs. 53—not part of the psalm) marks the end of Book III of the Psalter.

The question of this psalm's date invariably sparks lively debate, but the language and conceptions comport well with a dating in the post-Davidic monarchic period. The covenant with David is a matter of the past, and dynastic considerations are uppermost. Though the psalm contains much archaic material, which may have been subsequently reworked, attempts at precise dating become rather precarious.

From its many mythological phrases and allusions a number of Scandinavian scholars (e.g., Engnell, Pedersen, Bentzen, Ahlström) conclude that the psalm is a cultic liturgy with no historical content; the philological and exegetical notes that follow often counter their conclusion.

1. *Ethan.* One of the traditional wise men of Israel mentioned in I Kings v 11 (iv 31) and I Chron ii 6; on the morphology of the name, see Albright, *Archaeology and the Religion of Israel,* p. 127.

2. *Your love, Yahweh.* Suffixless *ḥasdē yhwh* is served by the suffix of closely parallel "your fidelity" in the second colon. A similar usage is noticed at Pss lxxvii 12 and lxxxiv 2–3; here attention may be directed to Prov v 16 where *palgē māyim,* by grace of its parallelism with *ma'yenōtekā,* "your fountains," is correctly rendered "your streams of water." Cf. further Ps cii 16 where *šēm yhwh,* "your name, Yahweh," is paired with *kebōdekā,* "your glory."

Your love . . . shall I sing. The syntax (*ḥasdē* is direct object of the verb) and thought of *ḥasdē . . . 'āšīrāh* resemble those of RŠ 24.245, *tšr dd al*[*iyn*] *b'l,* "She sings the affection of Victor Baal."

for ever. The standard explanation of *'ōlām* as an accusative of time is unobjectionable; however, the linguistic instinct which induced some scribes to insert *l* before *'ōlām* counsels appeal to the poetic practice (see preceding NOTE) of double-duty preposition, with *'ōlām* sharing *l^{e}* of *l^{e}dōr wādōr,* "age after age." See the first NOTE on vs. 6.

3. *With my mouth. b^{e}pī* was falsely attached to vs. 2 when the emphatic nature of *kī* at the beginning of vs. 3 was forgotten. Of course, *b^{e}pī* may also be rendered as an adverb "explicitly," much like Prov viii 3, *l^{e}pī,* "loudly, expressly."

I clearly admit. In the clause *b^{e}pī kī 'āmartī,* the final position of the verb finds its explanation in emphatic *kī* which often produces such an effect; cf. *Psalms I,* p. 301, and UHP, p. 22. Its balance with *'āšīrāh,* "shall I sing," and *'ōdī^{a}',* "I shall proclaim," makes *'āmartī* temporally present.

Eternal One. The NOTES on Pss lxvi 7 and lxxv 10 cite further evidence for the divine appellative *'ōlām,* which can now probably be verified in UT, 76:III:6–7, *kqnyn 'l[m] kdrd<r> dyknn,* "For our creator is the Eternal, for the Everlasting One is he who brought us into being." For the restoration of the text, see Herdner, *Corpus de tablettes,* p. 50.

your love. As in vs. 2, suffixless *ḥesed* shares the suffix of its counterpart, "your fidelity."

created. Repointing to qal *yibneh* (MT niphal *yibbāneh*) with the *yqtl* form expressing action in the past; cf. the introductory NOTE on Ps lxxviii.

you made . . . more steadfast. Retaining MT hiphil *tākīn* (cf. vs. 5, *'ākīn*) against LXX, Symm. niphal *tikkōn;* cf. Prov viii 27, *bah^{a}kīnō šāmayim,* "when he made the heavens firm."

than these. Namely, than the heavens which were considered made of bronze and to be a fortified city, as appears from the proverbial comparison in Deut i 28 (cf. ix 1), "It is a people taller and stronger than we are; their cities are larger and more fortified than the heavens (*b^{e}ṣūrōt baššāmayim*)."

Gunkel and others have seen the rapport between the present diction and Ps cxix 89, though Gunkel (*Die Psalmen,* p. 390) considered both texts corrupt. Both passages turn out to be quite sound when critics recognize the *beth* of comparison in each. Cf. the second NOTE on Ps li 8 and *Biblica* 44 (1963), 299 f. Thus Ps cxix 89, *l^{e}'ōlām yhwh d^{e}bār^{e}kā niṣṣāb baššāmāyim,* may be rendered "Yahweh, your word is eternal, more stable than the heavens," an unexceptionable statement that has a fine companion in Matt xxiv 35. Other instances of comparative *beth* may be seen in vss. 8, 38.

5. *for ever . . . for all generations.* For the Ugaritic pair *'lm//dr dr,* see the first NOTE on Ps lxxxv 6.

6. *In the heavens. šāmayim* shares the preposition of parallel *biqhal,* "in the congregation," on the strength of double-duty prepositions noticed in vs. 2 and in the fourth NOTE on Ps lxxxviii 6. Gunkel's

(*Die Psalmen,* p. 391) insertion of *ba* before *šāmayim* is both unnecessary and disruptive, since each colon is now perfectly balanced with eleven syllables.

they praise. The implied subject being the denizens of heaven. Since God's fidelity to his promises is a theme of praise among his celestial courtiers, it would be most unseemly, so the psalmist reasons, for him to go back on his word.

your promise. In a context that speaks of covenant, oath, and faithfulness to one's word, *pil'ᵃkā* is evidently intended in the sense preserved in Lev xxii 21, xxvii 2; Num xv 3, 8, and possibly in UT, 128:III:25–26, *wtḫss aṯrt ndrh wilt p[lah],* "And Asherah remembers his vow, and the Goddess his promise." Virolleaud in *Syria* 23 (1942–43), 156, and Ginsberg, LKK, p. 41, restore plural *plih,* but this difference of number does not affect the present argument. What makes the restoration particularly suasive is the collocation of *ndr* and *pl'* in the biblical phrase *yaplī' neder* (Lev xxvii 2). Cf. Gaster, *Thespis,* 1950, p. 457. The current translation of *pil'ᵃkā* looks to Ps lxxxviii 13 for support.

holy ones. The divine beings who comprise the court of Yahweh. The most recent study of *qᵉdōšīm* is that of C. H. W. Brekelmans, "The Saints of the Most High and Their Kingdom," in *Oudtestamentische Studiën* 14 (1965), 305–29.

7. *can compare with Yahweh.* Cf. C. J. Labuschagne, *The Incomparability of Yahweh in the Old Testament* (Leiden, 1966).

Who resembles. Consult the second and third NOTES to Ps lxxxiii 2. Interrogative *mī* of the first colon extends its force to the second, as recognized by *The Jerusalem Bible.* Cf. *Psalms I,* p. 16. The chiastic arrangement of the verse should be noted.

8. *too dreadful for the council.* Parsing *bᵉ* of *bᵉsōd* as comparative (cf. vs. 3) and comparing Pss lxviii 35–36 and xcix 2, *yhwh bᵉṣiyyōn gādōl wᵉrām hū' 'al kol hā'ammīm,* "Yahweh is too great for Zion, exalted is he beyond all the Strong Ones."

For the psalmist, Yahweh has no peers in the divine assembly.

too great. Explaining *rabbāh* as the archaic *qatala* form, here probably preserved for the sake of assonance with following *nōrā';* cf. *Psalms I,* p. 26; UHP, p. 20; Pss xciii 5 and ciii 19.

9. *Yah.* Heb. *yāh* is a shortened form of *Yahweh.*

your faithful ones. Another term for the members of Yahweh's celestial court. By reason of its chiastic parallelism with concrete *qᵉdōšīm,* "holy ones," in vs. 8, abstract *'ᵉmūnātᵉkā* takes on a concrete denotation, cf. Ps xxxi 24 and the second NOTE on ps lxxxii 2. Contrast Job iv 18 and xv 15, "Even his holy ones he distrusts, the heavens are not pure in his sight." Another instance of this poetic practice recurs in vs. 14.

10. *the back of the sea.* See *Psalms I,* p. 279; Job ix 8.

surge. The intransitive force of the infinitive construct *śō'* (cf. BDB, pp. 670–71; Nah i 5) bears on the translation of vs. 23.

you check them. The first NOTE on Ps lxv 8 examines this meaning of *tᵉšabbᵉḥēm,* Ugar. *šbḥ.*

11. *Rahab.* A mythological monster representing the restless waters of the ocean. In Ps lxxiv 14 he is called Leviathan.

with your strong arm. Cf. the first NOTE on Ps lxxvii 16.

13. *Zaphon.* O. Eissfeldt (*Baal Zaphon, Zeus Kasios und der Durchzug der Israeliten durchs Meer* [Halle, 1932], pp. 13 ff.) has rightly argued that here and in Job xxvi 7 (see Pope, *Job,* § 25, NOTE on xxvi 7a) *ṣāpōn* carries its original meaning as the name of the sacred mountain of Baal, the Canaanite weather-god. Since this mountain, now called Jebel el 'Aqra, lay some thirty miles north of Ras Shamra-Ugarit and hence directly north of Palestine, we now understand why in the OT *ṣāpōn* came to mean "north."

Amanus. Explaining purely consonantal *ymn* (MT *yāmīn*) as an alternate spelling of *'mn,* found in Song of Sol iv 8 and in UT, 1012:16, *ġr 'amn,* "Mount Amanus," a lofty mountain, today known as Alma Dag, in southern Turkey. For a full discussion with bibliography, cf. Oswald Mowan, "Quattuor montes sacri in Ps 89, 13?," in *Verbum Domini* 41 (1963), 11–20, and M. H. Pope in *Wörterbuch der Mythologie,* ed. H. W. Haussig, p. 258. R. de Vaux in *Revue biblique* 73 (1966), 506, accepts this identification.

From this analysis and translation springs the motif of the four sacred mountains (note Tabor and Hermon in the second colon) in Phoenician religion mentioned by Philo Byblius: Casius, Libanus, Antilibanus, Brathy.

Tabor. An isolated hill with a maximum elevation of 1843 feet situated in the Valley of Jezreel, some six miles E-SE of Nazareth. Albright in *The Bible and the Ancient Near East,* p. 352, n. 7, appears to be correct when deriving *tābōr* from **taburru,* "brightness" (cf. Ugar. *tbrrt,* "brightness, freedom"). This etymology upsets the conclusions drawn from an Akkadian etymology by G. W. Ahlström, *Psalm 89; Eine Liturgie aus dem Ritual des leidenden Königs* (Lund, 1959), p. 186. Ahlström derives Tabor from Akk. *ti-bi-ra, ta-bu-ra,* which signifies a "metal worker," but was also an epithet of Tammuz. He concludes that Tabor was probably a site of Tammuz worship.

in your presence. For this nuance of *šēm,* see Zorell, ZLH, 856b, who cites I Kings viii 29; II Kings xxiii 27, etc., and G. A. Cooke, *A Text-Book of North-Semitic Inscriptions* (Oxford, 1903), p. 37, on Phoen. *šm,* "presence." Ps xcviii 8–9 expresses a sentiment akin to that of our verse; cf. also Isa xviii 7.

14. *a powerful arm.* Cf. the first NOTE on Ps lxxvii 16.

O Warrior. Identifying *gᵉbūrāh* as an abstract noun with a concrete meaning, as noticed at vs. 9. Cf. Isa iii 25, 'Your men will fall by the sword, your warriors (abstract *gebûrātēk*) in the battle." The motif of *'ēl gibbōr* is found in Ps xxiv 8; Deut x 17; Isa x 21; Ezek xxxiii 21.

your left hand. As pointed out in *Psalms I*, p. 163, and the first NOTE on Ps lxxiv 11, *yādekā* denotes "left hand" when paired with "right hand."

is triumphant. For this nuance of *tā'ōz*, see *Psalms I*, p. 131, and below on vs. 18.

15. *Justice and right . . . love and truth.* These four personified attributes recall Ps lxxxv 11 and the four personified sacred mountains in vs. 13; they probably stem from the same Canaanite tradition. Hence it is difficult to accept the view of Hellmut Brunner, "Gerechtigkeit als Fundament des Thrones," VT 8 (1958), 426–28, that we must seek in Egypt the direct ancestry of this motif.

foundation of your throne. The expression *mekōn kise'ekā* illumines the meaning of UT, 51:I:31, *kt il*, "dais of El"; cf. Albright in BASOR 91 (1943), 40.

stand before you. The phrase *yeqaddemū pānekā* juxtaposes two roots that occur in parallelism at UT, 51:v:107–8, *št alp qdmh mra wtk pnh*, "Put an ox before him, a fatling right in front of his face."

16. *your radiance.* That is, the radiance of your presence. Usually rendered "festal shout" or something similar, *terū'āh*, because of the parallel colon, more probably equates with Num xxiii 21, *yhwh 'elōhāyw 'immō ūtōr'at* (MT *terū'at*) *melek bō*, "Yahweh his God is with him, and the radiance (cf. LXX, Onkelos) of the King upon him." Cf. Albright in JBL 63 (1944), 215, n. 43, who derives *tōrā'āh* from *yr'*, Ar. *wr'*, "to fear." The lack of suffix with *tōrā'āh*, which receives its determination from *pānekā*, "your face," may plausibly be accounted for. As the verse now reads, the first colon numbers ten syllables and the second eleven; were a suffix to be attached to *tōrā'āh*, the first colon would total twelve syllables, thus overloading the first half-verse.

17. *in your presence.* Cf. vs. 13.

are jubilant. The verb *yārūmū*, literally "They are high," also signifies "to jubilate," as observed in *Psalms I*, pp. 77, 134 f. Cf. vs. 43, *hiśmaḥtā* and English "high," which can also denote "elated, hilarious."

18. *Indeed.* Parsing *kī* as emphatic rather than causal.

our glorious triumph. Given that suffixed *-āmō* often refers to the first person plural (*Psalms I*, p. 173), there is no need to emend *'uzzāmō* to *'uzzēnū*, "our strength."

you give us victory. Literally "You raise high our horn."

19. *Truly.* As observed by Gaster, *Thespis*, 1950, p. 457, *kī la* at the beginning of the verse is the *kī lā*, "truly, verily," of the El Amarna letters. The same explanation is probably valid for Ps xxii 29.

our Suzerain . . . our King. Cf. the first NOTE on Ps lxxxv 10, and *Psalms I,* p. 143.

the Holy One. As noticed in *Psalms I,* p. 143, the *lamedh* preceding this divine title is emphatic; cf. Patton, CPBP, and more recently O. Eissfeldt, *Die Welt des Orients,* III, 1–2 (1964), 29, n. 1. Contrast Ahlström, *Psalm 89,* p. 96, n. 8.

20. *to your devoted one.* Namely, David; for full discussion concerning the identification, consult Ahlström, *Psalm 89,* pp. 99 f. Though many manuscripts read singular *lḥsdk,* consonantal *lḥsdyk* can be defended and read either as the singular with the archaic genitive ending, as in Ps cxxxviii 6, or a plural of majesty referring to the king, like plural *'ᵃbādekā* in vs. 51.

indeed you said. This stichometric arrangement results from the identification of *wa* in *wattō'mer* as emphatic with the consequent post-position of the verb; cf. the third NOTE on Ps lxxvii 2 and UHP, p. 40. The same phenomenon may be seen in vs. 44.

I made a lad king. Ugaritic is the key to this translation of *šiwwītī 'ezer* (MT *'ēzer*). Scholars have long equated *'ezer* with Ugar. *ǵzr,* "lad, hero" (*Psalms I,* pp, 173, 210), while Ugar. *ṯwy,* "to rule, govern," has well served A. A. Wieder in JBL 84 (1965), 160–62, who recognized that in Gen xiv 17, *šāwēh=melek,* and that piel *šiwwītī* stems from this root. Hence it is difficult to endorse Milik's view in *Revue biblique* 73 (1966), 99, that 4QPs89, *št, šattī,* "I placed," is surely superior to MT *šiwwītī* which Milik labels Aramaizing.

to a warrior. God rejected the warrior Saul and chose David in his stead. Freedman observes that here the use in parallel of the prepositions *'al* and *min* answers to vs. 8 where *bᵉ* and *'al* fulfill the same comparative function; this observation points up once again the interchangeability of *bᵉ* and *min.*

a youth. Namely, David.

a hero. As in verses 14 and 22, deriving *'ām* from *'mm,* "to be strong," examined in *Psalms I,* p. 112, and identifying him with Saul, the *gibbōr* of the first colon. In Judg v 13–14 and Ecclus xlvii 4 these two roots probably occur in parallelism. From this grammatical analysis emerges the perfect balance of the corresponding members: A+B+C//Á+B́+Ć. Cf. also vs. 43.

22. *shall supply.* Vocalizing hiphil *tākīn* for MT niphal *tikkōn.* 4QPs89 reads *tknm* which Milik, *loc. cit.,* p. 100, would also vocalize as hiphil. Though the 4QPs89 reading may not be the preferable one (see following NOTE), it does point to a defectively written original.

his power. Reading *'ammō* (MT *'immō*) from *'mm,* "to be powerful," attested in vss. 14 and 20. Since *tākīn 'ammō* makes such an excellent semantic counterpart to *tᵉ'ammᵉṣennū,* there is no need to adopt with Milik, *loc. cit.,* p. 100, the 4QPs89 lection *tknm.*

23. *No foe shall rise up*. Reading *yiśśā'* (MT *yaššī'*) and comparing the intransitive use of this verb in vs. 10. A very interesting semantic parallel appears in UT, 'nt:IV:49–50, *lib yp' lb'l*, "No foe has risen up against Baal." What is meant is that no adversary shall mount a successful rebellion against the king.

iniquity. 4QPs89 has the arresting reading *'l* (MT *'awlāh*), *'ōl*, to be compared with the Phoenician feminine form *'ōlōt* discussed at Ps lviii 3. See M. Dahood, *Bibbia e Oriente* 15 (1973), 253–54, on Prov x 12, and cf. Eccles i 13, where *'al*, "upon," should be repointed *'ōl*, "iniquity."

overcome him. On *ye'annennū*, see *Psalms I*, pp. 116, 128 f.

25. *he shall be victorious*. Literally "His horn shall be raised high."

26. *left hand*. See the third NOTE on vs. 14. 4QPs89 preserves the remarkable defective spelling *yd* (=*yādō*), where the third person suffix is graphically zero. On the other hand, the omission of *waw* at the end of *ydw* may merely represent the orthographic option of writing a letter but once when the same letter ends one word and begins the next, as documented at Ps lx 11. The next letter, it will be observed, is *waw*.

the sea . . . the river. Usually identified with the Mediterranean and the Euphrates, respectively, *yām* and *nehārōt* may well be mythical terms expressing worldwide dominion. In UT text 68, Baal achieved his eternal dominion by vanquishing *ym*, "Sea," and *nhr*, "River." Cf. Ahlström, *Psalm 89*, pp. 108 ff., and contrast Mowinckel, *The Psalms in Israel's Worship*, I, p. 155, who stoutly asserts that "the river" here, as everywhere in the Bible, denotes the Euphrates.

the river. Apparently plural *nehārōt* (cf. *behēmōt*) is really the feminine singular of the Phoenician type examined at Pss liii 7, lviii 3, etc. So also Milik in *Revue biblique* 73 (1966), 101.

27. *He shall cry to me*. Parsing the suffix of *yiqrā'ēnī* as datival; cf. Bogaert, *Biblica* 45 (1964), 229–30, and D. R. Hillers, *Treaty-Curses and the Old Testament Prophets* (Rome, 1964), p. 73, for examples of dative suffixes with verbs of speaking. Failure to recognize the datival nature of the suffix led Briggs to delete *'attāh* as secondary.

my father . . . the Mountain. The balance between *'ābī* and *ṣūr* is reminiscent of their juxtaposition in UT, 125:6–7, *ab ǵr b'l ṣpn*.

30. *on his seat*. For this definition of *'d* (vocalization uncertain), which recurs in vs. 38, see the fourth NOTE on Ps lx 11 and UHP, p. 67. The necessary suffix is forthcoming from its parallel synonym *kise'ō*, "his throne." In UT, 127:22–23, it is the suffix of *'dh* that supplies for parallel *ksi*: *yṯb krt l'dh yṯb lksi mlk*, "Kirta sits upon his seat, he sits upon his royal throne." The traditional version, "I shall establish his line forever" (RSV), assumes a meaning of *śamtī*, "I shall put," elsewhere unwitnessed, as observed by BDB, p. 963b. On the thought, cf. Ps cxxxii 11.

heaven's days. Recurring in Ecclus xlv 15, the phrase *kīmē šāmayim* has its Aramaic counterpart in a late seventh-century B.C. Aramaic papyrus from Saqqara in Egypt; cf. KAI, II, pp. 312 ff. In this inscription King Adon of Ashkelon, whose native language was Phoenician, has one of his scribes write a letter in Aramaic to the Pharaoh in which he prays the gods to render the Pharaoh's throne *kywmy šmyn,* "like the days of heaven."

34. *banish.* Cf. the third NOTE on Ps lxxxv 5.

be false. For the construction *'ašaqqēr b^e,* cf. *Psalms I,* p. 267.

35. *alter.* Comparing *'ašanneh* with UT, 128:III:29, *uṯn ndr,* "or alter vows?"

37. *to eternity . . . the sun.* The sequence *'ōlām . . . šemeš* evokes the phrase *špš 'lm* in UT, 2008:7, *šmš 'lm* in Karatepe III:19, and EA, 155:6, 47, *šamaš daritum.*

38. *his descendants.* Reading *'ūlīm* (MT *'ōlām*), the plural of *'ūl,* "suckling, infant," whose determination lies in the suffix of synonymous *zar'ō,* "his dynasty," in vs. 37. The same confusion between these two words can also be seen in Prov xxiii 10 and Ecclus iv 23 (courtesy T. Penar). Cf. also Job xxiv 9 and viii 6, *kī 'attāh yā'īr 'ūlekā* (MT *'ālekā*) *w^ešillam n^ewat ṣidqekā,* "Even now he would be safeguarding your little ones and prospering your lawful abode." See below on vs. 46. It is also possible to read singular *'ūl,* with the enclitic *mem* balancing the suffix of *zar'ō,* a stylistic balance noted at Ps x 17.

his seat. Cf. the first NOTE on vs. 30 for this definition of *'d* (MT *'ēd,* "witness"), which shares the suffix of its counterpart *kis^e'ō,* "his throne," in vs. 37.

than the sky. Cf. the seventh NOTE on vs. 3 and Deut i 28 cited there.

39. *you spurned in your anger.* Explaining *zānaḥtā* (cf. Ps lx 3) *wattim'ās* as hendiadys.

40. *utterly.* This sense of *lā'āreṣ* is noted as Ps lxxiv 7.

43. *raised high.* Just as the psalmist employs *yārūmū,* literally "to be high," in vs. 17 to signify "jubilate," so here he uses hiphil *hiśmaḥtā,* literally "to gladden," to denote "raise high." Cf. Jonas C. Greenfield in HUCA 30 (1959), 141–51, especially p. 148.

his adversaries . . . his foes. For this parallelism see the second NOTE on Ps lxxxi 15.

both hands. Reading *kele'* (MT *kol*), a lection that does not necessarily assume the haplography of an *aleph* since the following word begins with an *aleph;* cf. the third NOTE on Ps lx 11 and *Biblica* 47 (1966), 141–42, on Ps cxxxix 14 and Jer viii 13. I would identify *kele'* with Ugar. *klat,* "both hands," in Krt:68 (cf. 161) where it is parallel to *ymn,* precisely as in our verse. From this lexical analysis springs to light the metrical sequence (cf. vs. 20) A+B+C//Á+B́+Ć.

In Prov xxii 2, LXX *amphotérous* justifies the emendation of MT *kullām* to *kil'ēhem,* "both of them."

44. *In your wrath.* For the lack of suffix with *'ap,* consult the third NOTE on Ps lvi 8.

you turned back. The *yqtl* form *tāšīb* expresses past action.

his blade. In Exod iv 25; Josh v 2, 3, *ṣūr* denotes a "knife of flint" (GB, p. 694b), but the present association with *ḥarbō,* "his sword," rather recalls Job xvi 9, *ṣūrī* (MT *ṣārī*) *yilṭōš,* "He (namely Yahweh) sharpens his blade" (*Psalms I,* p. 46). Cf. Akk. *ṣurru, ṣurtu,* "flint, blade."

As in vss. 30, 37–38, *ṣūr* may share the suffix of its counterpart *ḥarbō,* or it might be vocalized *ṣūrō,* a case of defective spelling. Metrical considerations favor the second alternative.

did not. Parsing *w*^{e} of *w*^{e}*lō'* as emphatic, which helps explain why the verb is placed last; cf. vs. 20 and Ps lxxvii 2. The proposed stichometric division of vs. 44:

'ap tāšīb ṣūrō
ḥarbō w^e*lō' h*^{a}*qēmōtā*

sustain. Reading *h*^{a}*qēmōtā* (MT *h*^{a}*qēmōtō*) and attaching the final *waw* to the following verse.

45. *Among his troops.* Peter Nober has called to my attention that here *milḥāmāh* bears the sense found in Ps xxvii 3 rather than "battle," as translated by me in *Biblica* 47 (1966), 417. He noted that the two cola of vs. 44 describe the reduction of the king's weapons to complete inefficacy against the foe, while the two cola of vs. 45 relate the king's loss of authority among his rebellious troops.

his splendor. The hapax legomenon *miṭhār* (cf. Ugar. *ṭhr,* "gem") expresses the radiance that enveloped the king in battle and struck terror into his opponents, a theme discussed at Ps xlv 4. Cf. also Ps xxi 6 and Num xxiii 21, *tōra'at melek,* "royal majesty," as rightly pointed and explained by Albright in JBL 63 (1944), 215, n. 43; 224.

There remains, however, the possibility that the text should be read *hišbattā-m* (enclitic *mem*) *ṭoh*^{o}*rō;* in this case the substantive would be *ṭōhar,* "splendor, purity," that occurs in other texts.

46. *his youth.* *'*^{a}*lūmāyw* equals Phoen. *'lmy,* "his youth." The king probably laments the lack of offspring during his vigorous period.

his young manhood. Since hiphil *he'*^{e}*ṭāh* in Ps lxxxiv 7 and Isa lxi 10 governs two accusatives, whereas the construction *he'*^{e}*ṭītā 'ālāyw* is elsewhere unattested, I suspect that consonantal *'lyw* conceals the plural abstract substantive from the root discussed in the first NOTE on vs. 38. Hence vocalize *'ūlāyw,* an impeccable counterpart to *'*^{a}*lūmāyw,* "his youth."

with sterility. Literally "with dryness," if *būšāh* derives from **būš,* a byform of *yābēš,* "to be dry," exactly as *šūbāh,* "sitting still," in Isa xxx 15 stems from **šwb,* an alternate form of *yšb,* "to sit"; cf. *Psalms I,* pp. 44, 148, and PNWSP, p. 7. Such an etymology renders needless Gunkel's otherwise good emendation of *bûšāh* to *śēbāh*, "greyness, old age," which is what the context desires.

Having been promised numerous progeny that would endure forever (vss. 30, 37), the king finds himself cursed with sterility.

47. *will you estrange yourself*. Parsing *tstr* as an infixed *-t-* form of *swr*, "to turn aside"; cf. *Psalms I*, p. XXXVIII.

How long. Interrogative *'ad-māh* in the first colon probably extends its force to the second; cf. the second NOTE on Ps lxxiv 1.

O Conqueror. Analyzing *lāneṣaḥ* into vocative *lamedh* followed by the divine appellative studied in the fourth NOTE on Ps lxxiv 10; cf. Thaddaeus Penar in *Verbum Domini* 45 (1967), 37–39. Cf. Ps lxxix 5 and Lam v 2.

48. *Remember my sorrow*. Some of the obscurity befogging this verse can be cleared away by vocalizing *zᵉkōr 'ōnī* (whose final *yod* also functions as the first consonant of the next word; cf. first NOTE on vs. 26). As noticed at Ps xxxviii 18, suffixed forms of *'āwēn*, "iniquity, sorrow," presented difficulties for MT.

the few days of my life. Reading *yᵉmē* (see preceding NOTE) *hāḥāled* (MT *meh ḥāled*). The article of *haḥāled* stylistically substitutes for the first person suffix of *'ōnī;* cf. the second NOTE on Ps lxxxv 13 and Ps xc 16, the first NOTE. The proposed pointing of the first two cola: *zᵉkor 'ōnī yᵉmē haḥāled*. For related concepts, cf. Ps xxxix 6.

50. *O Lord*. The fourth word of a seven-unit line, vocative *'ᵃdōnay* hinges on both cola and semantically belongs to both; this metrical pattern is discussed in the NOTES to Ps lvii 5, 8.

51. *to your servant*. Explaining plural *'ᵃbādekā* as a plural of majesty referring to the king, on a par with vs. 20 *ḥᵃsīdekā*, "your devoted one." The king considered himself *servus servorum*.

in my breast. Not "in his bosom" (*Psalms I*, p. 19), since this verse is an illustration of epistolary style, discussed in *Psalms I*, pp. 124, 190.

the shafts of pagans. Reading *rabbē-m* (MT *rabbīm*) *'ammīm* and consulting *Psalms I*, pp. 19, 117, for this definition of *rabbē-m*. I suspect that Ps xxxi 14 and Jer xx 10 may have to submit to a similar analysis.

52. *insultingly malign*. Consult *Psalms I*, p. 252. As noted at Ps liv 7, the king was the favorite target of foreign abuse.

53. *Praised be Yahweh*. This doxology terminates the third Book of the Psalter; cf. Pss xli 14, lxxii 19. It was added later by a liturgist when the Psalter was divided into five Books; cf. *Psalms I*, pp. XXXI f.

PSALM 90

(xc 1–17)

1 *A prayer of Moses, the man of God.*

O Lord, our mainstay, come!
Be ours from age to age!
2 Before the mountains were born,
or the earth and the world came to birth—
From eternity to eternity you are!
3 Do not send man back to the Slime,
nor say, "Back, you sons of men!"
4 For a thousand years just pass
before your eyes like yesterday,
like a watch in the night.
5 If you pluck them at night,
with the dawn they become like cut grass;
6 Should it sprout and be cut in the morning,
toward evening it withers and dries.
7 Indeed we are consumed by your wrath
and worn out by your rage.
8 You have kept our iniquities before you,
the sins of our youth in the light of your face.
9 All our days have passed away under your fury,
we end our years like a sigh.
10 Our life, then, lasts seventy years,
and if heaven wills, eighty.
And so arrogance is mischief and iniquity,
pleasure is fleeting, and we too vanish.
11 Who can understand the violence of your wrath,
or that those who fear you
can be the object of your fury?
12 So teach us to number our days
that we might gain the heart of wisdom.

13 Return, Yahweh! How long?
Have pity on your servants.
14 Fill us at daybreak with your love
that we may shout for joy and happiness all our days.
15 Make our happiness equal the days you afflicted us,
the years we saw disaster.
16 Let your achievement be manifest to your servants,
and your dominion to their children.
17 And may the loveliness of the Lord our God
be upon us;
For our sake may he sustain the work of our hands,
and for his good sustain the work of our hands.

Notes

xc. A meditation on the brevity and misery of human life occasioned by an unspecified crisis into which the nation has been plunged. The poet contrasts the precariousness of individual and national existence with God's eternal dominion, and concludes that the essence of Wisdom lies in recognizing the transience of human life.

The psalmist's terse style often makes the sense elusive and causes the text to bristle with grammatical and stylistic difficulties. The use of ellipsis in vss. 1, 3, 4, 12, 15 is a case in point. The resemblances with Deut xxxii (see Notes on vss. 10, 13, 15), and Gen ii 4 and iii 19 (cf. Note on vs. 3), and the numerous instances of archaic language clearly point to an early (ninth-century?) composition.

1. *Moses.* The only poem of the Psalter attributed to Moses; cf., however, Exod xv 1; Deut xxxi 19, 30, xxxii 1 ff., xxxiii 1.

O Lord. *'ᵃdōnāy* begins the inclusion with vs. 17, *'ᵃdōnay;* hence proposals to read *yhwh* with many manuscripts seem ill-founded.

our mainstay. Consult the first Note on Ps lxxi 3 for this definition of *mā'ōn,* whose suffix is supplied by *lānū.* A similar instance of double-duty suffix recurs in vs. 12. The concept underlying *mā'ōn* comes out more clearly as we observe that this word relates by the rhetorical medium of inclusion to vs. 17, *kōnᵉnāh,* "sustain," which suggests the idea of foundation, support, mainstay. Hence it becomes difficult to fit in S. D. Goitein's idea in JSS 10 (1965), 52–53, that *mā'ōn* is somehow connected with *'āwōn,* "sin."

come! Pointing *'ᵃtēh* (MT *'attāh*), an imperative to balance vs. 13, *šūbāh,* "Return!" and precative *kōnᵉnēhū* in vs. 17. Cf. the sixth Note on Ps lxvii 2 and the fourth Note on Ps lxxiv 9 for other occurrences of this verb.

Be ours. Parsing *hāyītāl-lānū* as precative perfect to be compared with a similar prayer in Ps lxxi 3, *hᵉyēh lī lᵉṣūr mā'ōn,* "Be mine, O mountain of succor!" Cf. also Ps lxi 4, *kī hāyītā maḥseh lī,* "O that you would be my refuge!" Stylistically, precative *hāyītā* forms an inclusion with the jussive and two precatives in the final verse.

from age. bᵉdōr balances vs. 2, *mē'ōlām,* "from eternity."

2. *mountains . . . earth.* See the fourth NOTE on Ps lxxii 16.

were born . . . came to birth. The verbs *yullādū* and *tᵉḥōllal* (see next NOTE) belong to the list of 240 parallel pairs of words found in Ugaritic and Hebrew; cf. the fourth NOTE on Ps lvii 8; UT, 75:I: 25–26, *ḫl ld aklm,* and Phoen. *ḥl w ld* in the Arslan Tash magical text.

came to birth. With most ancient versions reading polal *tᵉḥōlal* for MT polel *tᵉḥōlēl.*

you are. That is, you exist. MT reads *'attāh 'ēl,* "you are God," but with LXX I point the second word as negative *'al* and attach it to the next verse. *Juxta Hebraeos* omits *'l* altogether. Cf. Ps xciii 2, *mē'ōlām 'attāh.*

3. *Do not.* Transposing *'l* from vs. 2 and vocalizing it as negative *'al,* which will account for the hiphil jussive punctuation of *tāšēb;* so the LXX and the Vulg., which, however, seems to have read both *'ēl* and *'al: "Tu es Deus, ne avertas. . . ." Juxta Hebraeos,* on the other hand, reads neither *'ēl* nor *'al,* simply omitting them both. The opposite mistake of pointing *'al* for *'ēl* is noted at Pss lix 12 and lxii 11.

to the Slime. Cf. Gen iii 19. The root of Heb. *dakkā'* appears in the Ugaritic by-form *dkk,* "to crush, pulverize." Being synonymous with *'āpār,* which in some texts (e.g., Ps xxx 10) connotes the underworld, *dakkā'* too refers to the nether regions whence man was originally taken. In Ps cxliii 3 the subject of piel *dikkā'* is the "Foe," namely, Death. Cf. Tromp, *Primitive Conceptions,* p. 89.

nor say. The difficulties bedeviling the second colon may be resolved by recognizing the ellipsis of the negative particle *'al;* the second colon shares the negating force of *'al* in the first. Consult Joüon, GHB, § 160q; *Psalms I,* p. 188, and the third NOTE on Ps lxxv 6. As observed in the introductory NOTE, ellipsis is a characteristic of the psalmist's style.

Back. Namely, to the mud from which you came (Gen iii 19).

4. *a thousand years.* Since in God's everlasting existence a millennium is no more than a day, the psalmist urges God to allow men to remain upon the earth at least a short while.

just pass. I propose reading *kī ya'ᵃbōrū* (MT *ya'ᵃbōr wᵉ*) whose subject is *'elep šānīm,* "a thousand years," an example of enjambment.

The *kī* parses as emphatic with the consequent final position of the verb; cf. the second NOTE on Ps lxxxix 3 and the fifth NOTE on Ps lx 4.

like yesterday, like a watch. The sequence *keyōm . . . 'ašmūrāh* illustrates the use of the double-duty preposition, as noted by Baethgen, *Psalmen,* p. 282, and others. Cf. Pss xxxvi 7, xlviii 8, lviii 9; Job xxvii 20; UT, 49:II:22–23. Hence Gordon's insertion of *k* before *imr* is unnecessary in UT, 49:II:22–23, *'dbnn ank imr bpy klli bṯbr nt'y ḫtu hw,* "I put him like a lamb in my mouth, like a lambkin he was crushed by my grinding teeth." For the reading *ṯbr nt'y,* see CBQ 17 (1955), 302–3.

5. *If you pluck them.* A doubtful version of *zeramtām,* a verb that probably occurs in Eshmunazor, lines 3, 13, as argued by G. R. Driver, BZAW 77 (1958), 44. I understand the verb as conditional without the morphological indicator *'im* or *kī; Psalms I,* pp. 19, 168.

at night. Literally "sleep," *šēnāh* is an accusative of time (cf. Ps lxxxviii 2) denoting the period of sleep, as indicated by its chiastic parallelism with vs. 6, *'ereb,* "evening, dusk." Analogous is *'īšōn,* "sleep," but also "time of sleep" in Prov vii 9, as maintained in PNWSP, pp. 14 f.

like cut grass. Reading *keḥāṣīr yuḥlāp* (MT *yaḥalōp*), a relative clause without the corresponding pronoun. The qal passive verbal form is tentatively derived from *ḥlp,* "to cut," Syriac *ḥalap,* "to shear," preserved in the Ugaritic substantive *ḫlpn,* "knife," Heb. *maḥalāpāh,* "knife"; cf. N. Tromp, "De radice *ḥlp* in lingua hebraica," *Verbum Domini* 41 (1963), 299–304, which also discusses Judg v 26; Job xiv 7, xx 24; Isa ii 18; Ezra i 9.

6. *and be cut.* Vocalizing qal passive *weḥūlāp* for MT qal active; for the signification "be cut," consult the preceding NOTE. The sequence of *yqtl* (*yḥlp*) and *qtl* (*ḥlp*) forms of the same root is a feature of Ugaritic and Hebrew poetry noted in *Psalms I,* p. 236.

7. *Indeed.* Understanding *kī* as emphatic.

are consumed. Just as grass is seared by the torrid sun, so the Israelites are wasted by the scorching heat of divine wrath. The verse provides a typical case of chiasm.

worn out. Usually rendered "troubled" or "overwhelmed," *nibhālnū* makes a better parallel to *kālīnū,* "consumed," and more fittingly accords with the current metaphor when explained as a secondary form of *bālāh,* "to wear out." In fact, the acute emendation to *nābalnū,* "we have withered up," has already been proposed. Cf. Ps vi 3, *'umlal 'ānī . . . nibhalū 'aṣāmay,* where the apparent synonymy with *'umlal,* "I am spent," suggests a cognate meaning for *nibhalū.* Predicated of "hands" in Ezek vii 27, *tibbāhalenāh* is rightly rendered by the LXX *paralythēsontai,* "are exhausted." Cf. also Ps civ 29. For the use of *h* as a formative element of roots, see UHP, p. 9, and Albright in VTS, iv, pp. 255–57.

8. *You have kept our iniquities.* Probably inscribed on a tablet (Ps li 11; Isa lxv 6; Jer ii 22) which Yahweh read by the light issuing from his face.

sins of our youth. By following the Targum's understanding of *ʻᵃlūmēnū* (*Psalms I,* p. 124; Briggs, CECBP, II, p. 274), we are better able to explain *kol yāmēnū,* "all our days," in the next verse. Cf. Ps xxv 7; Job xiii 26, and BCCT, pp. 59–60.

the light of your face. Reading *lᵉmō ʼōr* (MT *limᵉʼōr*) *pānekā* and comparing Ps lxxxix 16, *ʼōr pānekā.* MT *mᵉʼōr pānekā,* it should be noted, is hapax legomenon, whereas our reading uncovers the poetic balance between *lᵉ* and *lᵉmō* (*kᵉmō* occurs in next verse) discussed in the fifth NOTE on Ps lxxvi 12. Cf. A. Herdner, *Syria* 46 (1969), 131.

9. *All our days.* Consult the second NOTE on vs. 8; the poet stresses that in their youth as well as now the Israelites incurred the wrath of God. Hence the proposed deletion of *kol* need not enlist our further attention.

days . . . years. For the Ugaritic parallelism, cf. third NOTE on Ps lxi 7.

like a sigh. AT translates it "cobweb," though on what philological basis is not immediately evident. I am nonplused by the remarks of Ely E. Pilchik, "How the Spider Got into the Psalm," *Science* 151 (January 28, 1966), 404–5, who claims that none of the great translations (he includes the LXX and Syr.) hints of a spider in Ps xc. But both the LXX (*aráchnēn*) and Syr. (*gwāgay*) render *hgh* by "spider." Heb. *hegeh* equals Ugar. *hg,* "number, reckoning," and the simile recalls UT, 3 Aqht:24–25, *tṣi km rḥ npšh km iṯl brlth km qṭr baph,* "Let his soul go out like the wind, like a breath, his spirit; like smoke out of his nose!"

10. *then.* As a consequence of God's fury. For this definition of *bāhem,* see *Psalms I,* p. 122.

seventy . . . eighty. Cf. UT, 128:IV:6–7, *ṣḥ šbʻm ṯry ṯmnym* [*ẓ*]*byy,* "Invite my seventy bulls (=princes), my eighty gazelles (=nobles)."

if heaven wills. A doubtful translation of the perplexing expression *bigᵉbūrōt.* Perhaps *gᵉbūrōt* is the divine appellative cited at Ps lxxxix 14 (cf. also Job xxvi 14) with the Phoenician singular ending *-ōt* (Ps liii 7), or the metaphorical name for heaven examined at Ps xx 7.

arrogance. Vocalizing *rᵉhābīm* (MT *rohbām*), an instance of defective spelling (cf. introductory NOTE on Ps lxxxix). Given the brevity and precariousness of human life, arrogance ill becomes mortal man.

pleasure. Relating hapax legomenon *ḥīš* (this MT pointing not necessarily correct) to the root *ḥšš,* "to rejoice," Ugar. *ḫšt,* "joy, pleasure," found in Eccles ii 25, as proposed by me in *Biblica* 39 (1958), 307–8;

47 (1966), 269, and endorsed by H. W. Hertzberg, *Der Prediger* (Gütersloh, 1963), p. 81. Cf. Scott (AB, vol. 18), NOTE to Eccles ii 18–26, and Wolf Leslau, JAOS 84 (1964), 117, on Ge'ez (the Semitic language of ancient Ethiopia, now used only as the liturgical language of the Ethiopian Church) (*ta*)*ḫašaya*, "to rejoice."

11. *that those who fear you.* Pointing *kī* (defectively written *k*) *yir'ātekā*, and consulting *Psalms I*, pp. 32–33, for this sense of latter; cf. CCD, "those who should fear you."

can be the object of your fury. Literally "are your fury."

12. *teach us.* Imperative *hōda'* shares the suffix of *yāmēnū*, "our days"; cf. introductory NOTE. To have used a suffix with *hōda'* would have made the first colon much too long for its counterpart.

our days. Cf. Pss xxxix 5 and lxxxix 48.

the heart of wisdom. Which consists in realizing how few are man's days upon the earth. Cf. Ps lxxxi 17, *ṣūr debaš*, "the essence of honey," and Prov xv 33 as interpreted in PNWSP, p. 34.

13. *Return.* As noticed at Ps lx 3, when God is angry with his people he leaves them. Cf. Ps lxxxv 5, "Return to us!," a prayer directly following the request asking God to withdraw his anger.

your servants. '*abādekā* is a synonym of vs. 11 "those who fear you." This identification tells against those who describe vss. 13–17 as originally independent of vss. 1–12.

14. *at daybreak.* Cf. the second NOTE on Ps lxxxviii 14.

15. *the days . . . the years.* The rare plural form *yemōt* (Deut xxxii 7) was doubtless dictated by the desire of assonance with *šenōt*. Both may concur in unpublished RŠ 24.252:rev:11–12, *lymt špš wyrḫ wn'mt šnt il.*

the days you afflicted us. Construct *yemōt* depends upon the verb *'innītānū* which equivalently stands in the genitive case; the same usage appears in Ugaritic as noted at Ps lxv 5. Cf. above on vs. 5 for lack of relative pronoun, a further indication that the entire psalm is the work of one poet.

the years. The fact that the same psalm employs both masculine and feminine plurals *šānīm* (vss. 4, 9) and *šānōt* (vss. 10, 15) bears on the translation of the Ugaritic divine epithet *ab šnm* which some scholars decline to render "Father of Years" because elsewhere the Ugaritic plural is till now *šnt*.

16. *your dominion.* The consonantal cluster *hdrk* is amenable to several punctualizations and consequently to different translations. The LXX saw the idea of "govern, direct" (*hadrēk*) in this grouping while RSV proposes a conflate translation, "glorious power." I propose reading *hadderek*, "your dominion" (cf. *Psalms I*, pp. 2, 63, 70; first NOTE on Ps lxvii 3), whose article serves as the stylistic balance to the suffix of its

opposite number *po'olekā*. This point of style is noticed at Ps lxxxix 48, while the confusion between the roots *hdr* and *drk* is instanced at Ps xlv 4.

to . . . to. The use of two different prepositions (*'el . . . 'al*) with one verb is commented upon at Pss lv 11 and lxxx 12. UT, § 10.13, p. 100, directs attention to the possible substitution of *'l* and *l*, like *'al* and *'el* in Hebrew.

17. *the loveliness.* Rather than his fury. Cf. Ps xxvii 4 and the soon-to-be-published Ras Shamra tablet, discovered during the twenty-second campaign, in which *n'm* is predicated of the Canaanite god Baal.

may he sustain. Parsing *kōnenāh* as precative (notice jussive in first colon) third person masculine singular of the archaic *qatala* type, noticed most recently in Ps lxxxix 8. The conception underlying the verb forms an inclusion with vs. 1, *mā'ōn,* "mainstay," while the precative mode balances the imperative and precative of vs. 1. This double inclusion argues unity of authorship.

and for his good sustain. Yahweh's prestige among the surrounding nations is tied up with the fortunes of his peoples. The troublesome reading *kōnenēhū* submits to reasonable analysis when the suffix is understood as datival, expressing the dative of advantage; cf. the second NOTE on Ps lxxviii 55.

PSALM 91

(xci 1–16)

1 Let him who sits enthroned in the shelter of the Most High,
passes the night in the shadow of Shaddai,
2 Say: "O Yahweh, my refuge and my mountain fastness,
My God, in whom I trust!"
3 He alone will free you from the snare,
shield you against the venomous substance.
4 With his pinions he will cover you,
and under his wings will you find refuge;
his arm will be buckler and shield.
5 You need not fear the pack of night,
the arrow that flies by day,
6 The plague that prowls in the dark,
the scourge that stalks at noon.
7 Though a thousand fall on your left,
ten thousand at your right hand,
It will not approach you.
8 Your eyes will behold decay,
you will see the requital of the wicked.
9 If you consider Yahweh himself your refuge,
the Most High your mainstay,
10 No evil shall meet you,
no plague approach your tent.
11 For he will send you his angels
to guard you in all your marches;
12 On their hands they will bear you
lest your foot stub against a stone.
13 On lion and adder you will tread
and trample young lion and serpent.
14 "If he clings to me,
I will rescue him;
I will be his bulwark,
if he acknowledges my Name.

15 If he cries to me, I will answer him;
I will be with him in time of trouble;
I will rescue him and feast him.
16 With length of days will I content him,
and make him drink deeply of my salvation."

NOTES

xci. A royal psalm of trust or confidence composed by a court poet who here recites it before the king. Once the *Sitz im Leben* (cf. the introductory NOTE on royal Ps xlv) is established, the dramatic nature of the psalm with its frequent change of persons becomes readily intelligible.

In recent decades, three scholars (H. Birkeland, A. Bentzen, B. Gemser) have suggested in passing that the worshiper in this psalm might be the king. In his phraseological study, "Le Psaume XCI," in *Semitica* 8 (1958), 21–37, André Caquot lent some substance to this idea, and the subsequent identification of other royal psalms (e.g., lvii, lviii, lxi 2–6, lxxxvi) makes it possible nearly to double the phrasal evidence that will be recorded in the following NOTES.

In the last century, F. Hitzig (*Die Psalmen* [Heidelberg, 1836], II, p. 154) pointed out some arresting verbal similarities between the psalm and the ancient poem in Deut xxxii. While these resemblances do not of themselves argue an early date of composition for the psalm, since both may be indebted to a common source, there is nothing in the psalm which militates against an early composition.

1. *Let him who sits enthroned.* For this pregnant meaning of *yōšēb,* cf. *Psalms I,* pp. 8–9, as well as Ezek xxvii 8 where the kings (*yōšᵉbē*) of Sidon and Arvad are listed with the wise men of Tyre and the elders of Byblos (vs. 9). In keeping with court style (cf. Pss lxxiii 28, cx 1), the poet formally addresses the king in the third person before turning to the second person in vs. 2.

the shelter. sēter recurs in royal Ps lxi 5.

Most High . . . Shaddai. This breakup of the composite divine name *'elyōn šadday* might be compared with the separation of the components of *yhwh 'elyōn* in royal Pss xviii 14, xxi 8, xcii 2; cf. also the psalm celebrating God's kingship xcvii 9. This sequence—*'elyōn . . . šadday* —resembles more closely, however, the breakup of the composite name *'ēlī šadday* in Ps xxxii 4.

passes the night. Both day and night the king enjoys divine protection.

The predication of this same form *yitlōnān* of an eagle in Job xxxix 28 suggests that the poet likens the king to an eaglet safeguarded by the Great Eagle; cf. *Psalms I,* pp. 96, 107 ff. For the parallelism between the roots *yšb,* "to sit," and *lyn,* "to pass the night," in Isa lxv 4, see CBQ 22 (1960), 408 f.

Shaddai. This poetic divine name is probably based on the ancient poems Gen xlix 25; Deut xxxii 8; Ps xviii 14.

2. *Say.* Vocalizing imperative *'ᵉmōr* for the MT imperfect *'ōmar.* This imperative stands outside the meter so that this verse scans into 3+3, the prevailing beat of the other verses.

O Yahweh. The psalmist's careful balance of the components of composite divine names in vss. 1 and 9 suggests that vocative *'ᵉlōhay* in the second colon has a vocative counterpart in *lyhwh;* hence parse the *lamedh* as vocative. For other instances of vocative *lamedh* after *'āmar,* see Pss xvi 2, xlii 10, cxl 7, and the present writer in VT 16 (1966), 309.

my refuge. maḥsī occurs in royal Ps lxi 4 (*maḥseh*).

my mountain fastness. In a metaphor likening God to an eagle and the king to an eaglet, consistency is better maintained when *mᵉṣūdātī* is given the nuance found in Job xxxix 28 where the author employs both *yitlōnān* (occurring elsewhere only in our psalm) and *mᵉṣūdāh* in his description of an eagle's habitat. This latter substantive also recurs in royal Pss xviii 3, cxliv 2.

My God. Vocative *'ᵉlōhay* balances vocative *yhwh* in first colon.

in whom I trust. A similar formula may be seen in royal Ps lxxxvi 2, while the verb *bāṭaḥ* is found in royal Pss xxi 8, lvi 4, 5.

3. *He alone.* Parsing *kī* of the phrase *kī hū'* (also in Ps cxlviii 5) as emphatic, and comparing *kī 'attāh,* "you yourself," in Pss lxxxii 8, lxxxvi 17, etc. See Briggs, CECBP, II, p. 279.

from the snare. Metrical considerations (3+3) indicate that the first colon ends with *mippaḥ;* consequently, the sequence *paḥ yāqūš,* must be dissociated from Hos ix 8 and Prov vi 5 where commentators have vainly sought a solution to this puzzling collocation.

shield you. The needs of parallelism suggest that *yāqūš* is a verb balancing *yaṣṣīlᵉkā;* accordingly I postulate a root *qwš* signifying "to shield, protect," which may also serve to explain the unexplained personal names *qūšāyāhū,* "Shield, O Yahu" (I Chron xv 17), and *qīšī,* "my shielded one" (I Chron vi 29). Cf. M. Noth, *Die Israelitische Personennamen* (Stuttgart, 1928), p. 32, and T. C. Vriezen, "The Edomitic Deity Qaus," in *Oudtestamentische Studiën* 14 (1965), 330–53, especially p. 352. On this hypothesis, *yāqūš* would share the accusative suffix of the parallel verb. A connection with the Ugaritic verb *qṯ,* "draw, drag," is also possible.

venomous substance. Pointing *d^e^bar* (MT *deber*) *hawwōt,* and comparing Pss xli 9, *d^e^bar b^e^liyya'al,* "a lethal substance," and lxiv 4, *dābār mār,* "a poisonous substance." The fourth NOTE on Ps lii 3 discusses the different nuances of *hawwōt.*

God will safeguard the king against the poisoned arrows that were used in ancient hunting and warfare. Cf. Ps cxli 9 where *paḥ* and *q^e^šōt,* "bows," are the instruments of the chase.

4. *With . . . under.* For the pairing of the prepositions *b^e^* and *taḥat,* cf. UT, 2 Aqht:v:6–7, *yṯb bap ṯġr tḥt adrm dbgrn,* "He sits at the edge of the gate, among the nobles who are on the threshing floor," as well as Isa x 16, lvii 5; Job xl 21.

his pinions. Consonantal *'brtw* is a fine example of defective spelling, to be vocalized as plural (cf. the versions) *'ebrōtāw;* exactly as in Deut xxxii 11.

his wings. Cf. royal Pss lvii 2, lxi 5, lxiii 8.

will you find refuge. The verb *ḥāsāh* is frequent in royal psalms; cf., e.g., ii 12, xviii 3, 32, lvii 2, lxi 5. This fact makes it difficult to credit the reading *tškwn,* "You will dwell," of 11QPsAp published by J. van der Ploeg, "Le Psaume XCI dans une recension de Qumran," *Revue biblique* 72 (1965), 210–17.

his arm. Caquot, *loc. cit.,* p. 29, is singularly ill-advised when rejecting Immanuel Löw's repointing of MT *'^a^mittō,* "his fidelity," to *'ammātō;* cf. *Ignace Goldziher Memorial Volume* (Budapest, 1948), I, p. 328. Pinions, wings, and fidelity make a strange combination, whereas a consistent metaphor requires that *'mtw* denote a part of the body. Ugar. *amt,* "arm," and biblical *'ammāh* in Job ix 34, xiii 21, xxxiii 7; cf. Dahood, *Biblica* 44 (1963), 295, and for cognate conception, Wisd of Sol v 16, "And with his arm he will shield them."

5. *the pack of night.* Namely, the pack of wild dogs that marauds at night. Identifying *paḥad* with Ugar. *pḫd,* "flock," and consulting *Psalms I,* pp. 81–82, for other examples. Cf. also Isa xxiv 18, *hannās miqqōl happaḥad yippōl 'el happaḥat,* "He who escapes the howling pack will fall into the Pit" (cf. Job xv 21); Song of Sol iii 8, "Each man has his sword at his side against packs marauding at night"; Hab i 8, "fiercer than wolves at night" (=Zeph iii 3); Ps lix 7, 15.

the arrow. Since "arrow" in OT usage has symbolic meaning beyond its literal sense as an instrument of hunting or war, it is difficult to determine what the poet has in mind. If *paḥad* in the first colon refers to a pack of hunting dogs as in Isa xxiv 18, then *ḥēṣ* probably denotes the hunter's arrow. This would fall in with the metaphor of vss. 1–3 comparing the king to a young eagle. If, however, it looks forward to *deber,* "pestilence," in vs. 6, the "arrow" designates the symbol of Resheph, the god of pestilence, who in Ugaritic is termed *b'l ḥẓ ršp* (UT, 1001:3), and in Phoenician *ršp ḥṣ.* The obscure text UT, 'nt:Pl.

X:IV:11, apparently associates the concepts "night" and "arrow," as in our verse: *km ll kḥṣ tus*, "like the night, like the arrow. . . ."

6. *The plague . . . the scourge.* On *deber* and *qeṭeb*, see A. Caquot, "Sur quelques démons de l'Ancien Testament:Reshep, Qeṭeb, Deber," in *Semitica* 6 (1956), 53–68.

in the dark . . . at noon. Cf. the first NOTE on Ps xlii 9.

that stalks. Deriving consonantal *yšwd* from *'šd*, with the elision of initial *aleph* (cf. GK, § 69h–k; Milik in *Biblica* 38 [1957], 251), from Ugar. *'šd*, "leg," discussed in UHP, pp. 52–53, in connection with Deut xxxii 2. Cf. Ugar. *yitmr* and, without *aleph*, *ytmr*. Hence vocalize *yēšōd* and cf. *Psalms I*, pp. 84, 118, 164, for other examples of denominative verbs from names of parts of the body.

7. *Though. Psalms I*, pp. 19, 168, cites Hebrew, Ugaritic, and Phoenician instances of conditional sentences without the morphological indicator.

a thousand . . . ten thousand. The pairing of *'elep* with *rᵉbābāh* is one of the 240 pairs of parallel words attested in Hebrew and Ugaritic. Cf. e.g., UT, 51:I:27–29, *yṣq ksp lalpm ḫrṣ yṣqm lrbbt*, "He pours silver by thousands (of shekels), gold he pours by ten thousands," and S. Gevirtz, *Patterns in the Early Poetry of Israel*, (Chicago, 1963), pp. 15–17. The occurrence of this pair in Deut xxxii 30 points up further the connections between the psalm and this ancient poem.

Who are the "thousand" and the "ten thousand"? Since this sequence occurs in the military context of I Sam xviii 7, one may propose that the psalmist intends the military foes of the king who were struck down by a plague that broke out in their camp; cf. II Kings xix 35, "And that night the angel of Yahweh went forth and slew five thousand, one hundred and eighty in the camp of the Assyrians."

on your left. Cf. *Psalms I*, p. 163, I Sam xx 25. Gevirtz, *op. cit.*, proposes to emend *ṣad* to *yād*, "hand," but this orthographically improbable emendation is made more unlikely by the 11QPsApᵃ reading *ṣd*.

It will not approach. Namely, the plague that frequently broke out during military campaigns. In UT, 49:II:21, *ngš* (in the psalm *yiggaš*) is significantly used of Mot (=Death): *ngš ank aliyn b'l*, "I approached Victor Baal." Is *dbr* in line 20 the *deber* of our vs. 6?

8. *Your eyes.* Reading *'ēnēkā* with the initial *bᵉ* of MT attached to preceding word.

will behold. Reading *tabbīṭū* for MT *tabbīṭ wᵉ* and comparing *'ēnēkā tabbīṭū* with Job xxxix 29, where this phrase describes the sharp vision of an eagle.

decay. Namely, the rotting bodies of the king's adversaries decimated by the plague. I propose reading *rāqāb* (MT *raq* b^e); cf. Prov x 7 where this root is predicated of the offspring of the wicked.

9. *If you consider.* This verse yields its content only after some coaxing; compare the earlier attempt in *Psalms I*, p. 162. As MT now reads, there are seven syllables in the first colon and eight in the second, a normal balance. Were the psalmist to employ a separate verb in the first half-verse, it would become too long. Hence *śamtā*, "consider," of the second colon was also intended for the first; for other examples of double-duty verbs, cf. Pss xviii 42, lxvii 5, cxix 144; Eccles v 9, and Dahood, *Biblica* 47 (1966), 272.

Yahweh himself. Reading *'ōtōh* (MT *'attāh*) *yhwh*, and consulting the second NOTE on Ps lxix 27.

your refuge. Explaining consonantal *mḥsy* as archaic spelling with the preservation of the final *-y;* compare Ugar. *arby*, "locusts," with Heb. *'arbeh*. In royal Ps lvii 2, it will be noted, *ḥāsāyāh* preserves the original third radical *-y*. The suffix of *mḥsy* is provided by its opposite number *me'ōnekā*, "your mainstay."

the Most High. The breakup of the composite divine name *yhwh 'elyōn* is also witnessed in royal Pss xviii 14, xxi 8, and xcii 2.

your mainstay. See the first NOTE on Ps lxxi 3 and for similar concepts, Pss liii 9 and xc 1.

10. *No evil.* Indefinite *rā'āh* can partially be specified by comparing Job xviii 12 which employs the verb *'ānāh* (here piel) of Death as rendered in *Psalms I*, p. 203. Cf. Prov xii 21.

your tent. Referring to the king's tent in the military camp. The frequent interpretation of this term as an allusion to nomadic life (cf. *La Bible de la Pléiade*, II, p. 1103), does not commend itself.

11. *he will send.* For this meaning of *yeṣawweh*, consult *Psalms I*, p. 259, and the first NOTE on Ps lxviii 29.

his angels. Cf. royal Ps lxi 8 for a similar motif.

12. *your foot.* The subject of *tiggōp* being *raglekā*, "your foot," as in Prov iii 23.

13. *lion.* Recent discussions of *šaḥal* include S. Mowinckel, *Hebrew and Semitic Studies Presented to G. R. Driver*, eds. D. W. Thomas and W. D. McHardy (Oxford, 1963), pp. 95–103; Pope, *Job*, § 27, NOTE on xxviii 8b. The word probably occurs in the Ugaritic place name *šḥl mmt;* cf. WuS, No. 2589.

adder . . . serpent. The parallelism between *peten* and *tannīn* (also in Deut xxxii 33) corresponds to the Ugaritic brace in UT, 'nt:III:37–38, *lištbm tnn išbḥnh mḫšt btn 'qltn*, "Indeed I muzzled Tannin, I silenced him; I smote the winding serpent."

14. *If he clings to me.* Conditional *kī* (see vs. 9) begins the divine oracle recited by the court poet or priest; cf. the divine oracle in royal

Ps xx 7, as well as Ps lxxv 3, *kī 'eqqaḥ,* the opening words of the oracle. Royal Ps lxiii 9 expresses a similar conception.

I will be his bulwark. Comparing royal Ps xx 2, "The Name of Jacob's God be your bulwark."

15. *If he cries to me.* Cf. royal Ps lxxxix 27. Conditional *kī* of preceding verse extends its governing power to present verse.

I will rescue him. Namely, from the clutch of Death; the king is assured of immortality if he remains loyal to Yahweh. Cf. Ps xxi 5 and the king's prayer for eternal life in Ps lxi 7–8.

I will feast him. Cf. *Psalms I,* pp. 308, 310. The messianic banquet awaits the faithful king.

16. *length of days.* As in royal Ps xxi 5, *'ōrek yāmīm* denotes an everlasting afterlife; cf. *Psalms I,* p. 149, on Ps xxiii 6. In Isa liii 10 the Servant of Yahweh is promised immortality for his fulfillment of the divine will.

drink deeply. The existence of the root studied in *Psalms I,* pp. 206 and 310 f. renders superfluous Gunkel's emendation, *'arwēhū,* "I will make him drink his fill."

of my salvation. In an eschatological sense. As in vs. 15, *b^eṣārāh,* *b^e* denotes "from," a meaning still preserved in first-century B.C. 1QS 3:19, *bm'wn 'wr twldwt h'mt wmmqwr ḥwšk twldwt h'wl,* "From the habitation of light are the origins of truth, but from the wellspring of darkness are the origins of perversity."

PSALM 92

(xcii 1–16)

1 *A psalm. A song for the Sabbath.*

2 It is good to give thanks, O Yahweh,
and celebrate your Name in song, Most High;
3 To proclaim your love at daybreak, [2]*
and your fidelity through the watches of the night,
4 To the music of the zither and harp, [3]
to the melody of the lyre.
5 Because you, Yahweh, made me happy by your work, [4]
at your handiwork I sang for joy.
6 How great your works, [5]
Yahweh the Grand,
How deep your thoughts!
7 The stupid man is unaware, [6]
and the fool cannot appreciate this:
8 When the wicked sprouted like weeds, [7]
and all the evildoers thrived,
He completely destroyed them for all time!
9 But you, Yahweh, are the Exalted from eternity: [8]
10 For see how your foes, Yahweh, [9]
For see how your foes have perished,
how all evildoers have been scattered!
11 But you exalted my horn as if I were a wild ox, [10]
I have been anointed with fresh oil.
12 My eyes have seen the rout of my defamers, [11]
of my evil assailants.
My ears have heard:
13 "The just will flourish like the palm tree, [12]
and grow like the cedar of Lebanon;
14 Transplanted to the house of Yahweh, [13]
they will richly flourish in the court of our God.

* Verse numbers in RSV.

15 Still full of sap in old age, [14]
they will remain fresh and green,
16 To proclaim how upright is Yahweh, [15]
my Mountain in whom there is no iniquity."

NOTES

xcii. A royal song of thanksgiving to be classified with Ps xviii. The reasons for the royal classification appear in the following NOTES.

2. *to give thanks.* For the absolute use of *hōdōt,* cf. II Chron xxxi 2; Neh xi 17, xii 24.

O Yahweh. In the traditional version, "It is good to give thanks to the Lord, to sing praises to thy name, O Most High" (RSV), we have Yahweh being addressed in the third person in the first colon, but directly in the second colon. This incongruity can effectively be eliminated by parsing the *lamedh* preceding the Tetragrammaton as the vocative particle, as proposed by me in VT 16 (1966), 300–1.

celebrate . . . in song. Cf. royal Ps xviii 50.

your Name. The divine Name also appears in royal Pss xviii 50, xx 2, liv 8–9, lxxxvi 9, 11, xci 14, etc.

O Yahweh . . . Most High. As noticed at Ps xci 9, the components of the divine name *yhwh 'elyōn* are separated and placed in the parallel cola in royal Pss xviii 14 and xxi 8.

3. *your love . . . your fidelity.* These are key concepts in royal Ps lxxxix.

watches of the night. Cf. *Psalms I,* p. 90.

5. *you . . . made me happy . . . I sang for joy.* The transition from the second person subject, Yahweh, to the first person subject, the king, bears on the grammatical analysis of vs. 11. The *Jerusalem Bible*'s rendition of causative *śimmaḥtanī,* "I am happy," is indefensible. For other instances of *qtl* balancing *yqtl,* see Ps lxxiii 3, 9, 18.

by your work. Probably referring to God's intervention on the psalmist's behalf.

6. *How deep.* An instance of double-duty interjection; cf. the first NOTE on Ps lxxix 5. In JBL 84 (1965), 163, A. A. Wieder has remarked that the balancing of the roots *gdl* and *'mq* takes on added significance in view of Ugar. *'mq,* "strength."

7. *The stupid man . . . the fool.* Since *ba'ar* and *kᵉsīl* belong to the vocabulary of Wisdom Literature, Briggs describes this verse as a gloss. His inference is invalidated, however, by the identification of the psalmist as the king, who was especially trained in the precepts of Wisdom Literature.

is unaware . . . cannot appreciate. For the Ugaritic pairing of *yd'* and *byn,* consult the first NOTE on Ps lxxxii 5.

8. *When . . . sprouted . . . thrived.* The syntax of *biprōaḥ . . . wayyāṣīṣū* closely resembles that of Ps ix 4, *bešūb . . . yikkāšelū.*

He completely destroyed them. In this sentence position a finite verb rather than an infinitive construct is required; hence vocalize *lehišmīdām* with the emphatic *lamedh,* noted at Pss lxxxi 4, lxxxix 19, etc.

9. *the Exalted.* Cf. the fourth NOTE on royal Ps lvi 3. With vs. 11, *wattārem,* "But you exalted," *mārōm* forms a theological wordplay much like Ps lxxv 6.

from eternity. See *Psalms I,* p. 180. Yahweh is uniquely exalted because of his victory over the gods of chaos in primeval times.

10. *For see how your foes. . . .* The tricolon of standard pattern A+B+C//A+B+D//E+F+G has its Canaanite antecedent in UT, 68:8–9, *ht ibk b'lm ht ibk tmḫṣ ht tṣmt ṣrtk,* as noted by Albright in CBQ 7 (1945), 21. This identification is lost on both the *Bible de Jérusalem* and the *New English Bible* which simply delete the first colon!

your foes. Probably the rival divinities of the Canaanites.

have perished. yō'bēdū is a *yqtl* form expressing something that happened in the primordial period; the Masoretes recognized this, as is evident from their pointing in vs. 11, *wattārem,* with consecutive *waw* indicating that the preceding verbs state punctual past action. Note also the *yqtl* forms in vss. 5 and 12 expressing past events.

the evildoers. Most likely these are the worshipers of pagan gods defeated and reduced to impotence by Yahweh.

11. *But you exalted.* Once the preceding *yqtl* verbs are taken as past, MT *wattārem* proves to be the correct pointing.

I have been anointed. Vocalizing qal passive *bullōtī* and comparing Ps xxiii 6. The transition from a second person subject in opening colon to a first person subject in the final part tallies with vs. 5. The action described is a sign of the festivity after the psalmist's victory over his enemies.

12. *My eyes have seen.* Cf. royal Pss liv 9 and xci 8.

my defamers. See the fourth NOTE on Ps liv 7.

my evil assailants. In royal Ps xviii 49 *qāmay,* the military assailants of the king, precedes *'īš ḥāmās,* "calumniators," in the list of the king's enemies.

My ears have heard. Since this particular use of *šāma' be* is not instanced elsewhere, I prefer to dissociate this phrase from the preceding colon and make it introduce the following verses. The *yqtl* form *tišma'nāh* expresses past time, like vss. 5, *'arannēn,* and 10, *yō'bēdū.* With this formula the poet introduces what must have been traditional teaching in Israel, namely, that the just will be transplanted like the palm and the cedar, symbols of immortality, to the celestial court of Yahweh.

13. *the palm tree . . . the cedar of Lebanon.* The tree of life is here presented both as a palm, as in I Enoch xxiv 4, and as a cedar. The just will become as immortal as these trees of life.

the cedar of Lebanon. Parsing *'erez ballᵉbānōn* as a construct chain with the interposed preposition, the type discussed in *Psalms I,* p. 52, and at Ps lxxxiv 7. Hence RSV's "cedar in Lebanon" appears less likely.

14. *Transplanted.* For this meaning of *šᵉtūlīm,* see *Psalms I,* pp. 3–4, and Julian Morgenstern in HUCA 16 (1941), p. 81, n. 222. As in Pss i 3, lxxiii 18, it carries an eschatological connotation. In vs. 13 the two verbs are in the singular, with *ṣaddīq,* "the just," as their subject, while in vss. 14–15 all four verbs are in the plural, with *tāmār,* "the palm tree," and *'erez,* "cedar," as their subject.

to the house . . . in the court. As in Pss xxiii 6, xxvii 4, xxxi 3, xxxvi 9, lxv 5, texts which speak of immortality, they refer to the heavenly palace and courtyard of Yahweh. For the Ugaritic and Phoenician parallelism between *bēt,* "house" and *ḥāṣēr,* "court," see the fifth NOTE on Ps lxxxiv 11, while the third NOTE on Ps lxv 5 examines plural forms of names of habitations to express a singular concept.

they will richly flourish. Though he employed qal *yiprāḥ* in vs. 13, the poet here uses hiphil *yaprīḥū* with an elative denotation; see *Psalms I,* p. 271, and cf. Prov xiv 11. The second NOTE on Ps lxix 15 cites other instances of the same root being used in different conjugations in the same context.

16. *upright. yāšār* forms with vs. 13 *ṣaddīq* the rhetorical figure of inclusion. Because Yahweh is upright, the just will eternally participate in the festivities of the divine court. For the Ugaritic-Phoenican balance of *ṣdq* and *yšr,* cf. *Psalms I,* pp. 56 f.

my Mountain. The divine appellative *ṣūrī* evokes vs. 9, *mārōm,* "the Exalted." In Ps lxxv 6 both these epithets occur together. It is significant that *ṣūrī* also occurs in royal Pss xviii, xxviii, lxxxix, and cxliv.

iniquity. For the contraction of the diphthong in *'ōlātāh,* see UHP, p. 8, and the second NOTE on Ps lxxxix 23.

PSALM 93

(xciii 1–5)

1 Yahweh reigns, in majesty robed,
Robed is Yahweh, belted with victory.
Surely established is the world,
no more shall it totter.
2 Your throne was established of old,
you are from eternity!
3 Ocean currents raised, Yahweh,
Ocean currents raised their thunderous roar,
Ocean currents raised their pounding waves.
4 Stronger than thundering waters,
Mightier than breakers of the sea,
Mightier than high heaven was Yahweh.
5 Your enthronement was confirmed of old;
in your temple the holy ones will laud you,
Yahweh, for days without end.

NOTES

xciii. A hymn celebrating Yahweh's victory over the primordial forces of chaos (vs. 3, *n^{e}hārōt,* "ocean currents," 4, *yām,* "the sea") the consolidation of his royal power over the world (vs. 1, *tēbēl,* "the world") and heaven (vs. 4, *mārōm,* "high heaven," 5, *qōdeš,* "holy ones"), and his enthronement (vs. 5, *'idt^{e}kā*). This hymn perhaps finds its closest counterpart in Ps xxix, a tenth-century hymn with similar motifs of victory, kingship, and praise of Yahweh by his celestial court.

This short poem exhibits a clear structure: introduction (vs. 1a–b), body of the poem (vss. 1c–4), and conclusion (vs. 5).

The arguments for a tenth-century date of composition advanced by James D. Shenkel, "An Interpretation of Ps 93, 5," in *Biblica* 46 (1965), 401–16, especially pp. 401–2, and E. Lipiński, *La royauté de Yahwé dans la poésie et le culte de l'ancien Israël* (Brussel, 1965), pp. 163–72, are convincing.

1. *Yahweh reigns . . . with victory.* The 2+2//2+2 metrical structure of the introductory cola contrasts noticeably with the 3+3+3 pattern in vss. 3–5.

Yahweh reigns. For the most recent defense of this rendition of *yhwh mālāk,* see Kitchen, *Ancient Orient and Old Testament,* p. 103, and n. 63, with bibliography and comments, and A. G. Gelston, "A Note on *yhwh mlk,*" in VT 16 (1966), 507–12. By placing *yhwh* before the verb, the psalmist appears to stress that Yahweh, and no other deity, exercises kingship. Though no firm conclusion can be based on the word order, the inference drawn is supported by the contents of the psalm, especially by the statement in the middle colon of vs. 5.

in majesty robed, Robed is Yahweh. The chiastic arrangement *gē'ūt lābēš lābēš yhwh* suggests an A+B//B+C pattern, which bears on the interpretation of *'ōz,* "victory"; see next NOTE.

belted with victory. Being chiastically paired with *yhwh mālāk, 'ōz hit'azzār* should be interpreted in a manner designed to bring out more clearly the logical nexus between *'ōz* and Yahweh's kingship. Hence I take *'ōz* in the sense found at Ps xxix 11 and elsewhere; cf. the first NOTE on Ps lxxxvi 17.

Surely. Lipiński errs when he asserts, in *La royauté de Yahwé,* p. 95, that in the phrase *'ap tikkōn, 'ap* has no bearing on the sense. In Ugaritic, *ap* is an emphatic conjunction, and when scholars point out that the lack of the copula *wa* in this psalm resembles Ugaritic poetry where it is infrequent, they might at the same time indicate that the infrequency of *w* is partially compensated by the fairly numerous instances of *ap,* "also, surely, and."

established. Though the reading *tikkēn,* accepted by many modern scholars largely on the authority of the ancient versions, finds new support in 11QPs[a], col. xxii, 17, [*t*]*kn,* its adoption would diminish the assonance in *tikkōn-timmōṭ-nākōn;* hence MT *tikkōn* is best preserved.

2. *Your throne . . . of old.* This colon forms an inclusion with vs. 5, "Your enthronement was confirmed of old."

of old. Prepositional *mē'āz* corresponds to vs. 5, *m'd,* which should be vocalized *mē'ād* and explained as a Canaanite form. In fact, *m'd* may also have been the original consonants here before they were redacted into the Jerusalem dialect.

from eternity. For a similar concept, Pss ix 8, xxix 10. Patton, CPBP, p. 30, has directed attention to the association of the roots of *nākōn* and *'ōlām* that one encounters in UT, 76:III:6–7, *kqnyn 'l*[*m*] *kdrd*[*r*] *dyknn,* "Indeed our creator is the Eternal, indeed the Everlasting is he who brought us into being" (my translation).

3. *Ocean currents. Psalms I,* p. 151, documents this nuance of *n*[e]*hārōt,* endorsed by Lipiński, *op. cit.,* p. 122, and n. 3.

As noticed by Albright in *Studies in Old Testament Prophecy,* pp. 6–7, the stylized pattern of this tricolon, A+B+C//A+B+D//A+B+E, has Canaanite origins. Each of the carefully structured cola, it will be noticed, numbers eight syllables; in the next verse the syllable count is 7:7:7.

raised . . . raised . . . raised. The *qtl-qtl-yqtl* sequence corresponds to Ugaritic stylistic practice, and the frequently proposed emendation of final imperfect *yiśᵉʾû* to perfect *nāśᵉʾû* founders on this fact; cf. M. Held in *Studies and Essays in Honor of Abraham A. Neuman* (Leiden, 1962), p. 286, and Lipiński, *op. cit.*, p. 97.

their thunderous roar. As noticed in *Psalms I*, p. 281, *qōl,* like Ugar. *ql,* sometimes signifies "thunder."

their pounding waves. The hapax legomenon *dokyām* remains an unresolved puzzle, though the new interpretation of *rabbīm*, "strong," in vs. 4 and a re-examination of Ugar. *dkym* combine to produce some new possibilities. Thus the concurrence of *dokyām* and *rabbīm* in the biblical description of chaotic waters upholds the judgment of those identifying *dokyām* with Ugar. *dkym* in UT, 49:v:1–3, *yiḫd bʿl bn aṯrt rbm ymḫṣ bktp dkym ymḫṣ bṣmd,* "Baal seized the sons of Asherah, the Strong One smote with a cudgel, the Pounder smote with a club." The controverted terms *rbm* and *dkym* I would parse as plurals of majesty serving as epithets of Baal. The latter derives from *dky*, Heb. *dākāh,* "to pound, crush," a fitting description of the storm-god whose alternate name *hd/hdd* denotes "the Crasher." Hence biblical *dokyām* would be a common noun analogous to *hēdād,* "noise, roar," from the root found in the divine name *hd/hdd.* A similar phenomenon is present in the Canaanite divine name *dgn,* "Dagan," which in biblical Hebrew denotes "wheat."

4. *Stronger.* The usual identification of *mayim rabbīm* with a similar phrase in Ps xviii 17 and elsewhere produces in our verse a grammatically non-viable colon. Moreover, the chiastic arrangement of the first two cola (compare the second and third cola of vs. 1) indicates that *rabbīm* is the opposite number of *'addīrīm* and accordingly should be dissociated from *mayim:*

miqqōlōt mayim rabbīm (A+B)
'addīrīm mišbᵉrē yām (B́+Á)

Thus *rabbīm* parses as a plural adjective referring to God; since the syllable count of this verse is 7:7:7, the reason for employing the plural of majesty is at hand. BDB, p. 913b, cites II Chron xiv 10; Isa liii 12, lxiii 1, where "strong" is the nuance carried by *rab.*

Mightier. Like its counterpart *rabbīm, 'addīrīm* is a plural adjective describing Yahweh. Again, metrical considerations seem to have dictated the choice of the plural form. In Job xxi 22, the plural adjective *rāmīm,* "the High One," designates God, while in Hos xii 1, Prov ix 10 and xxx 3, Yahweh is called *qᵉdōšîm*, "the Holy One."

than breakers of the sea. Balancing *miqqōlōt mayim*, "than thundering waters" (literally "the thunders of waters"), *mišbᵉrê yām* shares its comparative preposition *min* by grace of the principle examined in the second NOTE on Ps lvii 4; hence MT needs no *remaniement.*

Mightier. To keep the syllable count to seven in the third colon, the psalmist employs the singular adjective *'addîr.*

than high heaven. Explaining the preposition of *bammārōm* as comparative, in parallelism with comparative *min* of the first colon. Other instances of comparative *b//min* are listed at Pss li 8–9 and lxviii 35. The psalmist states that Yahweh overcame the marine-god Yamm and his unruly waters, and implies that he also conquered the celestial deity Baal who, in Ugaritic mythology, was the archenemy of Yamm (about whom cf. NOTES to Ps lxxiv 13). In the next verse the psalmist again alludes to this motif. Cf. Ps lxviii 35, "whose majesty and might are too great for heaven."

5. *Your enthronement.* Since the first colon, purely consonantal *'dtk n'mn m'd*, structurally balances vs. 2, *nākōn kis'ᵃkā mē'āz*, it follows that *'dtk* contains the root of Ugar. *'d//ksu* in UT, 127:22–24, cited in the fourth NOTE to Ps lx 11. Shenkel in *Biblica* 46 (1965), 408–9, explains *'dt* as a lexical variant of *'d*, "seat, throne," from *'dd*, but the analogy of Ugaritic-Hebrew infinitive construct *ṯbt/šebet*, "(throne) sitting," suggests that *'dt* too is an infinitive construct, from *y'd* (*w'd*), "to appoint, assemble." Since *y'd* connotes jurisdiction, derivatives from this root denoting "seat, throne," appear reasonable. Hence vocalize infinitive construct *'idtᵉkā* for MT *'ēdōtekā*, "your decrees."

As will be seen below, the psalmist is describing Yahweh's enthronement in heaven.

was confirmed. Reading niphal singular *ne'ᵉman* (MT *ne'emᵉnū*) to achieve agreement with its subject and to balance it with singular *nākōn*, "was established," in vs. 2.

of old. Vocalizing *mē'ād* (MT *mᵉ'ōd*), a dialectal form which answers to vs. 2, *mē'āz*; cf. *Psalms I*, p. 278. Unlike *mē'āz*, the Canaanite form *mē'ād* escaped the redactor's attention. Albright has somewhere pointed out that the redaction or updating of archaic poems is seldom free of oversights.

in your temple. For euphonic reasons the psalmist used *lᵉbētᵉkā* for *bᵉbētᵉkā*, just as Jer lii 17, for reasons of style employs *lᵉbēt yhwh*, "in Yahweh's house," to balance *bᵉbēt yhwh*, "in Yahweh's house," in the same verse. Overlooking the niceties of style, some scribes altered *lᵉbēt* to *bᵉbēt*, "in the house." Cf. Ps li 12 where *lī*, "in me," balances *bᵉqirbī*, "within me."

Commentators assume that the temple mentioned here was situated in Jerusalem, an assumption which may be challenged. Just as in closely cognate Ps xxix 9, *hēkālō* refers to Yahweh's heavenly palace, so here *byt* designates his celestial temple. In Ugaritic mythology Baal, victorious over Yamm, could not fully exercise his royal powers until he had his own palace. Text 51 describes the construction of this palace from which Baal sends his rain and snow to earth and discharges his thunderbolts. Hence it is a palace in heaven; see UT, 51:v:68:81, and Habel, *Yahweh versus Baal,* p. 76, who writes: "Baal's theophany as the storm god is apparent from the spectacular weather phenomena in the heavens above and the temple of Baal is that specific location of the heavens from which this royal self-expression emanates. Thus, to that extent, the terms 'temple' and 'heavens' can be considered parallel. In brief, a heavenly residential palace, a location for the exercise of kingship in cosmic proportions, and not merely some earthly shrine, appear to be the nature of this *hkl.*"

The context of our psalm is very similar. Verse 4 states that Yahweh subdued the sea and its waves; the first colon of vs. 5 mentions the first result of this victory, namely, the consolidation of his royal power. In referring to Yahweh's *bayit,* "temple," the second colon adheres to the Canaanite description in which the construction of a palace follows a victory and acquisition of kingship. *Psalms I,* pp. 148 f., and the fifth NOTE on Ps lxv 5 list other texts in which *bayit* designates God's abode in the heavens.

the holy ones. Namely, the gods or divine beings composing Yahweh's celestial council; they are the *b^{e}nē 'ēlīm* of Ps xxix 1 who are invited to sing Yahweh's praises. For this definition of *qōdeš,* which is thick with Canaanite associations, consult the third NOTE on Ps lxxvii 14. This identification of *qōdeš* verifies the exegesis of *bayit* in the preceding NOTE. And while Shenkel, *Biblica* 46 (1965), 412–13, correctly defines *qōdeš,* he is hardly consistent when concluding (pp. 402, 409) that *bytk* is Yahweh's temple on earth.

will laud you. In *Psalms I,* p. 200, *na'^{a}wāh* was parsed as a piel infinitive construct, as in Ps cxlvii 1, but the 4QPs^{b} reading *nwh,* to be vocalized *nāwāh,* the third person qal singular, may prove to be a more satisfactory reading and grammatically more feasible. Hence P. W. Skehan's description of *nwh* as a phonetic, anti-etymological spelling is unacceptable, assuming as he does that "beauty" is the sense desiderated by the context; cf. CBQ 26 (1964), 313–22, especially p. 315.

The object "you" is borrowed from the suffix of *bēt^{e}kā,* "your temple," on the principle of the double-duty suffix; meter may account for its omission since this colon with nine syllables already overbalances the first with eight syllables and the third that counts but seven syllables. Thus the verse's twenty-four syllables are divided into 8:9:7 cola, whereas vs. 4 balances perfectly with 7:7:7 and vs. 3 with 8:8:8.

for days without end. For Ugar. *urk ymm* and Phoen. *'rk ymm,* see *Psalms I,* p. 149. In her article "Psalm 93," JBL 71 (1952), 155–60, H. G. Jefferson pointed out that, prescinding from the name Yahweh, only nine words of Ps xciii had not been attested in the Ras Shamra tablets: *g'wt, tbl, mwṭ, 'z, mn, dky, 'dwt, 'mn, n'wh.* The identification of *'z, mn, dky* and *'dwt* in Ugaritic now reduces the number of missing words to five.

PSALM 94

(xciv 1–23)

1 The God of vindication, Yahweh,
The God of vindication shone forth!
2 Rise, judge of the world,
give the presumptuous their deserts!
3 How much longer shall the wicked, O Yahweh,
How much longer shall the wicked exult?
4 How much longer shall they pour forth defiant words,
shall all the evildoers flaunt themselves?
5 Your people, Yahweh, they crushed,
and your patrimony they afflicted.
6 Widow and stranger they killed,
the fatherless they murdered,
7 Thinking, "Yah does not see,
Jacob's God takes no notice."
8 Learn some sagacity, you dolts,
O fools, when will you understand?
9 Is the planter of the ear unable to hear?
The cultivator of the eye unable to see?
10 Is the instructor of nations unable to punish?
Is the teacher of mankind without knowledge?
11 Yahweh knows how vapid are men's thoughts.
12 Blest the man whom you have instructed,
Yah,
Whom you have taught from your law,
13 Giving him respite after the evil days,
while a pit is being dug for the wicked.
14 Surely Yahweh will not desert his people,
and his patrimony he will not abandon.
15 But the tribunal of justice will restore equity,
and with it all upright hearts.

16 Who rose up for me against the wicked?
who took a stand for me against evildoers?
17 If Yahweh had not been my help
I would have directly dwelt in the Fortress.
18 When I said, "My foot is sinking,"
your love, Yahweh, supported me.
19 When my cares grew rife within me,
your consolations delighted my soul.
20 Can the seat of iniquity associate with you,
the architect of disorder receive your protection?
21 They banded together against the life of the just,
and secretly condemned the innocent.
22 But Yahweh became a bulwark for me,
and my God my mountain of refuge.
23 He made their malice recoil upon them,
and for their wickedness annihilated them;
Yahweh our God annihilated them.

NOTES

xciv. Conventionally labeled a lament, this complex poem is more properly classified as a psalm of thanksgiving. The verbs in vs. 1 and in the final two lines express past tense, describing the divine intervention on behalf of the psalmist and his people. The interposed verses, however, do contain the text of the individual and group lament which elicited a favorable response from God, who delivered the suppliants from corrupt oppressors.

The frequency of the *yqtl* verb form to express past time (first NOTE on vs. 5) definitely suggests a pre-Exilic date of composition; see the introductory NOTE to Ps lxxviii.

1. *The God of vindication.* Though in some other texts the stress of the root *nqm* lies on the idea of "salvation" or "deliverance," the contents of this psalm show that "vindication" is the keynote. By rescuing the oppressed and punishing the wicked, Yahweh has vindicated his law.

shone forth. Some ancient versions and most modern translations emend hiphil preterit *hōpī*^{a}*ʿ* of MT to hiphil imperative *hōpīʿāh,* but this is not sustained by the LXX nor by 4QPs^{b} (CBQ 26 [1964], 317), which reads a clear *hwpyʿ*. Hence we are obliged to retain MT and translate it in the same manner as Ps l 2, where it describes Yahweh's theophanic approach when he arrives to hold court and pass judgment on wayward men. This verb fits equally well the present passage which relates Yahweh's decisive intervention and punishment of the psalmist's adversaries. The past tense of *hōpīaʿ* is further confirmed by the observation that the verbs in the final two verses also describe completed action and thus form an inclusion with the opening verse.

The roots of the juxtaposed words *neqāmōt hōpīaʿ* are probably combined in the Ugaritic royal name *nqmpʿ*.

2. *Rise . . . give.* These imperatives begin the prayer for deliverance from wicked tyrants and unjust judges. The lament, which runs from vss. 2–21, is distinguished from traditional laments by a passage (vss. 8–15) composed in the style of the Wisdom writers.

judge of the world. Whose judicial chair is termed *ʿad ṣedeq,* "tribunal of justice," in vs. 15.

the presumptuous. Usually translated "the proud," *gēʾīm* seems rather to bear the nuance witnessed in UT, 2 Aqht:VI:44, *ntb gan,* "the path of presumption," as correctly interpreted by Albright in BASOR 94 (1944), 34, n. 24, and Ginsberg, BASOR 98 (1945), 23, n. 74. Cf. *Psalms I,* p. 186, for the translation of Ps xxxi 19. The sin of unjust judges lies in their presuming that Yahweh will not right wronged justice.

3. *How much longer.* The A+B+C//A+B+D pattern is familiar from the Ras Shamra texts such as UT, 127:54–56, *yṯbr ḥrn ybn yṯbr ḥrn rišk,* "May Ḥoron break, O son, may Ḥoron break your head!"

4. *How much longer.* The force of interrogative *ʿad mātay* extends from vs. 3 to the present verse; cf. *Psalms I,* p. 16, for a similar usage in Ps iii 2–3.

pour forth . . . words. The two verbs *yabbīʿū yedabberū* are an example of hendiadys, a figure well documented among nouns but biblically less frequent with verbs.

flaunt themselves. To give the root of *yitʾammerū* its common meaning "to say" would be bathetic here, coming as it does after the forceful hendiadys. This consideration obliges one to recognize in the hithpael verb a form of *ʾāmar,* "to see," examined in *Psalms I,* pp. 16, 24, 69, and the NOTE on Ps lxxi 10. Compare *mitʿaššēr,* "flaunting one's riches," in Prov xiii 7 and *mitkabbēd,* "one who plays the great man," in Prov xii 9.

5. *they crushed . . . they afflicted.* The *yqtl* verbs *yedakkeʾū* and *yeʿannū* express past events; cf. the third NOTE on Ps xcii 10. The same usage recurs in vss. 6, 12, 18, 19, 21, 23, and its frequency points to a pre-Exilic date.

7. *Thinking.* Consult the first NOTE on Ps liii 2 for this nuance of *ʾāmar* when introducing an *Hoffartsmonolog.*

Yah. As in Ps lxxxix 9, *yāh* is a shortened form of *yahweh.*

8. *some sagacity.* Identifying the root of the phrase *bāʿām* with *ʿmm,* "to be wise/strong," studied in *Psalms I,* pp. 112 f. Compare Ecclus x 1, *šwpṭ ʿm ywsr ʿmw,* "A sagacious ruler instructs his people,"

where the LXX and Syr. translate *'m*, if this was in their *Vorlage*, by "wise." This definition likewise produces a clearer translation of UT, 51:IV:41–43, *tḥmk il ḥkm ḥkmt 'm 'lm ḥyt ḥẓt tḥmk*, "Your message, O El, is wise: your wisdom is eternal sagacity, a felicitous life your message."

O fools. The particle *ū-* of *ūkᵉsīlīm* is parsed as the vocative *waw* discussed in the second NOTE on Ps lxxiv 12. The same expression recurs in Prov viii 5, "Learn shrewdness, you simple-minded, O fools (*ūkᵉsīlīm*), acquire understanding."

9. *the cultivator of the eye.* Its parallelism with *nōṭa' 'ōzen*, "the planter of the ear," and the growing evidence that biblical poets used their metaphors consistently (cf. Ps li 9) leave little doubt that hapax legomenon *yōṣēr 'ayin* continues the metaphor begun in the first colon. In fact, Gordon, Glossary, No. 1142, may prove correct when translating *yṣr š'rm*, "cultivator of barley," and the demurral of O. Loretz and M. Dietrich in BO 23 (1966), 130, unfounded.

10. *without knowledge.* Reading *'ādām middā'at* for MT *'ādām dā'at*. The final *mem* of *'ādām* is also connected with the following word *dā'at*, where it stands for the preposition *min*. This single writing of a consonant where morphology and syntax require two is discussed in the third NOTE on Ps lx 11. A new instance of this textual ambivalence of Hebrew consonants has turned up in Isa xiii 17 where MT *yḥšbw wzhb* (*yaḥšōbū wᵉzāhāb*) appears in 1QIsᵃ as *yḥšwb wzhb*, where the singly written *w* of *wzhb* also serves as the final letter of *yḥšwb*. Hence the Qumran reading can be vocalized in the same manner as MT, namely, *yaḥšōbū wᵉzāhāb*, "They consider, and gold . . . ."

12. *you have instructed . . . you have taught.* The *yqtl* verbs *tᵉyassᵉrennū* and *tᵉlammᵉdennū* express past time.

Yah. This shortened form of *yahweh* is a vocative that belongs both to the first and to the third cola, a metrical pattern discussed at Ps lxxxviii 6 and elsewhere (courtesy D. N. Freedman).

whom. Explaining *waw* as a relative pronoun, a usage examined at Ps lxxii 12.

13. *Giving him respite.* Parsing *lᵉhašqīṭ* as a circumstantial infinitive (cf. the third NOTE on Ps lxiii 3). The interpretation of *hašqīṭ*, which Gunkel describes as "inner composure," depends on one's understanding of the next phrase *mīmē rā'* and of vs. 15.

after the evil days. As in Ps xlix 6 (*Psalms I*, p. 297), "the evil days" probably refer to a man's last days on earth. The psalmist suggests that the oppressed Israelite who remains faithful to the law will find eternal repose after death. But this interpretation depends in large measure upon the precise force of *min* in *mīmē*. Some commentators understand *mīmē rā'* as "(To give him rest) from days of evil," and explain the "days of evil" as the days of discipline. When they have accomplished their purpose such days will pass away and Israel will be given rest and quietness. I, however, understand *min* as in Ps lxxviii 20. Cf. especially Hos vi 2, *yeḥayyēnū miyyōmāyim*, "He will restore us to life after two days," and Ps xxx 4, *ḥiyyītanī miyyōredī bōr*, "You restored me to life after my descent to the Pit." The analysis of consonantal *mywrdy* into *min*, "after," plus the construct infinitive *ywrdy* (cf. UHP, p. 62) must replace the explication in *Psalms I*, p. 182.

This exegesis serves to explain the nature of the "pit" in the second colon of the verse.

a pit. Namely, in Sheol. A special pit will be dug in the underworld for the oppressors of Israel.

15. *the tribunal of justice*. Crucial for the interpretation of the immediately preceding verses, vs. 15 is unfortunately the thorniest line of the entire psalm, grammatically and lexically. What is proposed here is at least syntactically feasible.

A comparison with vs. 20, *kissē' hawwōt*, "the seat of injustice," reveals that *'ad ṣedeq* is its antonym, and that *'ad* equals Ugar.-Heb. *'d* discussed at Ps lx 11. Note the association of *ṣedeq* with *kissē'* in Ps lxxxix 15 and elsewhere.

As in Ps i 5, the tribunal refers to the day of final judgment when the just will be vindicated and the wicked condemned to a special pit in Sheol.

will restore. For the transitive meaning of qal *yāšūb*, see Pss xiv 7, liii 7, cxxvi 1; Isa lii 8; Nah ii 3. Tainted justice will be restored to full vigor on the day of final judgment.

and with it. This meaning of *'aḥarāyw* is discussed in *Psalms I*, pp. 275, 302, and the third NOTE on Ps lxxiii 24. Ps xlv 15 supplies the most instructive parallel.

16. *rose up . . . took a stand*. The content of the next three verses indicates that the *yqtl* verbs *yāqūm* and *yityaṣṣēb* describe something that happened in the past. Suffice it to read, for example, the RSV's rendition of vss. 16–18 to be convinced that these two verbs do not refer to future or present time.

17. *the Fortress*. Meaning and morphology will be better served when the current translation and dictionary definition of *dūmāh* as "silence," from the root *dmm* (*dūmāh* would be an improbable formation from *dmm*) yield to new evidence. LXX "hades" and *Juxta Hebraeos* "inferno" bespeak no familiarity with modern translation of *dūmāh*. What is more, biblical parlance demands a place rather than a condition as the object of *šākan*, "dwell." Hence an identification of *dūmāh* with Akk.-Ugar. *dmt*, "tower, fortress" (cf. Mari place name *dumtan*), appears more satisfactory and significant. In *Biblica* 45

(1964), 83–84, I have proposed this identification in Ezek xxvii 32, which has been endorsed by F. L. Moriarty in *Gregorianum* 46 (1965), 87. Cf. also Ps cxv 17, *yōrᵉdē dūmāh*, "those that go down to the Fortress," and the place name *dūmāh* in Josh xv 52 and Isa xxi 11.

Cognate motifs of Sheol as a walled city (Ps ix 14; Ecclus li 9, etc.) and a prison (e.g., Pss lxxxviii 9, cxlii 8) show the proposed translation to be consonant with biblical imagery and reveal a proleptic touch because in vs. 22 the poet relates that Yahweh was his citadel. Had Yahweh not aided him, the psalmist would have become a denizen of the nether fortress.

18. *My foot is sinking.* The poet probably means "My foot is sinking into the nether world," because in Ps lxvi 9, *mōṭ*, from the same root as *māṭāh*, is a poetic name for Sheol. Cf. the third NOTE on Ps lxvi 9.

supported me. yis'ādēnī is another example of *yqtl* verb expressing past action.

19. *my cares.* The morphology of *śar'appay*, with epenthetic or secondary *r* (cf. *śᵉ'ippīm*), resembles that of synonymous *ḥarṣubbōt*, "struggles," in Ps lxxiii 4.

delighted. The poet again employs the *yqtl* form to describe his past experience.

20. *the seat of iniquity.* The poet contrasts *kissē' hawwōt* with vs. 15, *'ad, ṣedeq*, "the tribunal of justice." Of course, the phrase is metonymic for iniquitous rulers.

associate with you. Parsing the suffix of *yᵉḥābrᵉkā* as datival; cf. Ps v 5, *lō' yᵉgūrᵉkā rā'*, "No evil man can be your guest." For the condemnation of unjust judges, see Ps lviii 2–3.

the architect. Pointing *'ōmēl* (MT *'āmāl*), literally "the worker." Grammatically, *'ōmēl* is the construct (balancing *kissē'*) of a construct chain.

of disorder. The structure of the verse points to *'ᵃlē ḥōq* as the genitive of a construct chain corresponding to first-colon *hawwōt*, "iniquity." The growing number of recognizable composite nouns (*Psalms I*, p. 30; second NOTE on Ps lxi 4) authorizes the assignment of *'ᵃlē ḥōq* to this class. This parsing helps explain *'al yōšer* in Prov xvii 26, *gam 'ᵃnōš laṣṣaddīq lō'-ṭōb lᵉhakkōt nᵉdībīm 'al yōšer*, "Claiming a fine from the innocent is indeed a crime (*lō'-ṭōb* being a composite noun), to strike the noble an injustice."

receive your protection. Unexplained MT *yōṣēr* can be made meaningful if vocalized as qal passive *yuṣṣār* from *nāṣar*, "to protect"; its suffix derives from the parallel verb. Literally, *yuṣṣār* would be rendered "be protected by you." From this reading and parsing emerges an A+B//Á+B́ pattern in the verse.

21. *They banded together.* Deriving *yāgōddū* from the root *gdd* that underlies the noun *gedūd,* "band, troop of marauders."

secretly. Comparison with Prov i 11, *ne'erebāh ledām,* "Let us wait in secret," and Prov i 18, *wehēm ledāmām ye'erōbū,* "And these men secretly waited," favors the analysis of *dām* as an adverbial accusative from *dmm,* "to be silent." The judges had reached a secret agreement among themselves to condemn the unjustly accused.

condemned. From their vocalization of the next verb with consecutive *waw,* it appears that the Masoretes understood *yaršī'ū* as referring to past action.

22. *became.* Proposals to emend *wayehī* to *wīhī,* "became," should be scouted in view of the preceding NOTE.

23. *He made . . . recoil.* With the awareness that the verbs in vs. 21 state preterit action, MT *wayyāšeb* proves to be correct pointing and the proposed emendation *weyāšēb* misguided.

annihilated them . . . annihilated them. Parallelism with past *wayyāšeb* indicates that once again the psalmist employs the *yqtl* verb form to state completed action, as normally in Ugaritic, and that the three verbs in this verse express the same time as *qtl hōpīaʻ,* "shone forth," in vs. 1, thereby forming a type of inclusion. Cf. Ps xviii 41, where *yqtl 'aṣmītēm,* "I exterminated," is paired with *qtl nātattāh,* "you gave."

From this analysis of the verbs, the present psalm emerges as a psalm of thanksgiving for favors received rather than a lament imploring divine intervention.

PSALM 95

(xcv 1–11)

1 Come, let us sing joyfully to Yahweh,
let us hail the Rock who saved us.
2 Let us enter his presence with songs of praise,
with hymns let us hail him.
3 For Yahweh is the great El,
the Great King over all the gods.
4 In his hand are the recesses of the nether world,
and the mountaintops are his.
5 His is the sea, since he made it,
and the dry land his hands molded.
6 Come in, let us worship and bow down,
let us kneel before Yahweh our Maker,
7 For he is our God,
and we are the people of his pasture,
the flock of his grazing plot.
Today hear the Awesome One when he proclaims:
8 "Harden not your hearts as at Meribah,
as on the day at Massah in the wilderness,
9 Where your forefathers tested me,
provoking me, though they had seen my work.
10 Forty years I loathed a generation
until I said:
'They are a people whose hearts go astray,
who do not know my ways.'
11 Then I took an oath in my anger:
'Never shall they enter my rest.'"

Notes

xcv. This psalm divides into two parts, the first (vss. 1–7a), a hymn celebrating God's kingship, while the second (vss. 7b–11) contains an admonition or prophetic oracle warning the congregation not to disobey the laws of Yahweh. The structure and genre thus closely resemble those of Ps lxxxi. From the text itself there are few clues as to its date of composition.

1. *the Rock.* A probable allusion to the rock that yielded water in the desert, according to Exod xvii 1 ff. The facts related in this passage underlie vss. 8–11 of the psalm.

2. *enter his presence.* This psalm was evidently sung during the procession toward the temple.

3. *the great El.* In contrast to El, the head of the Canaanite pantheon, who was deposed by Yahweh.

the Great King. melek gādōl is the equivalent of the Ugaritic expression *mlk rb,* "the great king."

over all the gods. The not infrequent contrasting of God's supreme power with the ineffectiveness of foreign deities (cf. Pss lxxvii 17, lxxxix 7–8) makes it difficult to credit Lipiński's contention, *La royauté de Yahwé,* p. 283, n. 2, that the Israelite scribes suppressed the plural ending of *qdšm,* "gods," in Exod xv 11 and Ps lxxiv 14. As noticed in the third Note to Ps lxxvii 14, singular *qōdeš* bears the collective meaning "gods, holy ones."

4. *recesses.* Frequently rendered "depths," *meḥqār* from *ḥāqor,* "to search," probably denotes a region yet to be explored. Comparison with Job xxxviii 16, *ḥēqer t^ehōm,* "the recesses of the abyss," raises the question whether hapax legomenon *mḥqr* is a genuine substantive; its preformative *m-* may well belong to the preceding word as an enclitic.

of the nether world. Job xxxviii 16, *ḥēqer t^ehōm* and the antithesis to "the mountaintops" in our verse suggest that *'ereṣ* carries this well-established meaning here. In other terms, the parallelism in both vss. 4–5 is antithetic. The proposed translation, it may be noted, bears on the translation of Ps lxxxviii 6.

6. *bow . . . kneel.* The denominative verbs *nikrā'āh* and *nibr^ekāh* from names of parts of the body (*Psalms I,* pp. 84, 118, 164) are both attested in Ugaritic; on the latter, see *Psalms I,* p. 62. Some critics (e.g., Gunkel) find it difficult to accept three synonymous verbs in one verse and accordingly recommend the deletion of *nibr^ekā* as a variant of *nikrā'āh,* but such reasoning scarcely commands assent in view of, for example, UT, 76:II:17–18, *lpnnh ydd wyqm lp'nh ykr'*

wyql, or 51:VIII:26–29, *lp'n mt hbr wql tšthwy wkbd hwt*, "At the feet of Mot bow down and be prostrate, worship and honor him."

7. *his grazing plot*. Though many commentators question *yādō*, its synonymy with *mar'ītō*, "his pasture," comes across from such texts as Jer vi 3, "To her the shepherds come with their flocks; they shall pitch their tents around her, (*rā'ū 'īš yādō*) each shall pasture on his grazing plot," and Job i 14, "The oxen were plowing and the she-asses (*rō'ōt 'al yedēhem*) were pasturing on their grazing plots." Thus *ṣō'n yādō* does not essentially differ from Jer xxiii 1, *ṣō'n mar'ītī*, "the flock of my pasture." The semantic transition from *yād* "portion, part" (e.g., II Sam xix 44; II Kings xi 7) to "plot, portion of ground," is illuminated by *ḥēleq*, "portion, share," but also "tract, territory." In UT, Krt:127, *yd* may mean "portion," as proposed by Gordon, Glossary, No. 1072.

the Awesome One. On the strength of Ps lxxxi 9, *yiśrā'ēl 'im tišme'ū lī*, "O Israel, if you would but listen to me," commentators can make out a good case for rendering *'im beqōlō tišmā'ū*, "O that you would hearken to his voice." On the other hand, such an analysis results in a case of aposiopesis in the present context, since the following clause begins with a negative jussive. Hence I tentatively explain our phrase in the light of Num xii 6, *šime'ū-nā' dibrē 'ēm* (MT *debāray 'im*) *yihyeh nebī'akem yhwh*, "Hear the words of the Awesome One, Yahweh will be your prophet." Morphologically, *'ēm* would be a stative participle from *'ym*, "to be awesome," just as Ugar. *ib*, "foe," a stative form, corresponds to transitive Heb. *'ōyēb*. On *'āyōm* as a divine appellative, see Ps cxxxix 14.

when he proclaims. Parsing *beqōlō* as preposition followed by infinitive construct *qōlō*, from **qwl*, "to voice." Perhaps this is the better way to parse Ps lxviii 34, *yittēn beqōlō qōl 'ōz*, "He gives forth in his pealing a mighty voice."

8. *Meribah*. Literally "contention," this is the place where the Israelites quarreled with Yahweh; see Num xx 13.

Massah. The place of testing where the Israelites tried Yahweh's patience; cf. Exod xvii 7.

9. *provoking me*. The bearing of *beḥānūnī* on the translation and exegesis of Ps lxxxi 8 is discussed there.

10. *I loathed*. With the *yqtl* verb form *'āqūṭ* stating an historical fact. As at Ps xciv 22–23, the Masoretes were familiar with this usage since they pointed the succeeding verb *wā'ōmar*, with consecutive *waw*.

go astray . . . do not know my ways. The psalmist resumes the metaphor of sheep in vs. 7 since both *tō'ē* (Jer l 6) and *yāde'ū derākāy* are elsewhere predicated of sheep; cf. Prov iii 6, *bekol derākekā dā'ēhū*,

"In all your ways know him," a phrase occurring in the longer metaphor of shepherd and sheep (vss. 5–6), as pointed out by W. van der Weiden (in a paper as yet unpublished), who relates this use of *yāda'* to John x 14.

The resumption of the flock metaphor in the second part of the psalm indicates a unity of authorship for both the hymn and the prophetic oracle.

my rest. Namely, the Promised Land. Considerable subtlety lies in the choice of the term *m^{e}nūḥātī*. Because of their behavior at *m^{e}rībāh* and *massāh*, the wilderness generation was denied entry into Yahweh's *m^{e}nūḥāh*.

PSALM 96

(xcvi 1–13)

1 Sing to Yahweh a song that is new,
Sing to Yahweh, all the earth
2 Sing to Yahweh, bless his name!
Proclaim from sea to sea his victory,
3 Declare among the nations his glory,
among all the peoples his marvels!
4 For great is Yahweh and worthy of praise the Grand,
to be feared is he beyond all gods,
5 while all the gods of the peoples are but rags.
Yahweh himself made the heavens;
6 splendor and majesty are before him,
strength and beauty at his side.
7 Give Yahweh, you clans of the peoples,
Give Yahweh glory and praise,
8 Give Yahweh the glory due to his name.
Bring an offering and enter his court,
9 bow down to Yahweh when the Holy One appears,
tremble before him, all the earth!
10 Say among the nations, "Yahweh reigns,
surely established is the world, no more to totter;
he will judge the peoples with equity."
11 Let the heavens rejoice and earth be glad,
the sea and what fills it thunder,
12 the highland and everything on it exult.
Then all the woodland trees will shout for joy
13 before Yahweh when he comes,
when he comes to govern the earth.
He will govern the world with his justice,
and the peoples with his truth.

NOTES

xcvi. A hymn celebrating Yahweh's sovereignty, this psalm is characteristic for its several tricola arranged in a stairlike A+B+C//A+B+D//A+B+E sequence. It is cited in part by I Chron xvi 23–33 with some interesting variants none of which, however, in view of the principles of double transmission stated in the introductory NOTE to Ps liii, warrant the correction or emendation of the present transmission. The psalm divides into two strophes: vss. 1–9 and 10–13.

The verbal and phrasal similarities between this hymn and Second Isaiah, and the clear-cut universalism of the psalm, have led some scholars to conclude that the psalmist is indebted to the prophet both for his language and for his ideas. Such a conclusion must be re-examined in view of the strong possibility that both psalmist and prophet were heir to a common literary tradition long existent in Canaan (see *Biblica* 43 [1962], 535). Further it is widely recognized that universalism, namely, the rule of God over the known world as well as over one people, was current in the ancient Near East from the third millennium onward. Cf. Albright, *From the Stone Age to Christianity*, 2d ed., (Anchor Books, 1957), pp. 213–17, and the first NOTE on Ps lxvi 4. The recovery, moreover, of several archaic phrases in vss. 4, 6, 9, 10, that doubtless antedate Second Isaiah, partially neutralizes the arguments upholding the dependence of the psalmist on the prophet.

1. *Sing . . . Sing . . .* 2. *Sing.* This A+B+C//A+B+D sequence, noticed at Ps xciii 3, is repeated in vss. 7–8.

a song that is new. Namely, this psalm. In Ps xl 4 the motive for the *šīr ḥādāš* was the psalmist's recovery from illness, but here and in Ps xxxiii 3 the reason for the new composition seems to be the fresh appreciation of Yahweh the Creator's control of the world and its historical developments. What concrete event induced this insight cannot be determined from the psalm text.

2. *Proclaim.* The six occurrences of the root *bšr* in the Ras Shamra tablets prevent the simple ascription of the psalmist's use of *baśśᵉrū* to Isaianic influence. Many commentators argue for a dependency of this psalm on Second Isaiah where the root *bśr* is frequent.

from sea to sea. The apparent synonymy with *baggōyīm*, "among the nations," and *bᵉkol hā'ammīm*, "among all peoples," in the following members of the tricolon favors the reading *miyyām lᵉyām* or the explanation of MT *miyyōm lᵉyōm* as the Phoenician pronunciation of "from sea to sea." In Phoenician both "day" and "sea" were written simply *ym*, and a defectively written Hebrew original may account for MT and the ancient versions that follow its reading. The proposed reading yields a translation that better accords with the stress on universalism that characterizes this tricolon; cf. the phrase *miyyām 'ad yām* in the universalist contexts of Ps lxxii 8 and Zech ix 10.

his victory. Over the heathen deities, as in Pss xxix 11, xcviii 1, etc.

5. *rags*. Usually translated "naught" or "idols," Heb. *'ᵉlīlīm*, which is still lacking an etymology, may find one in Ugar. *all*, a type of garment whose sense comes through from its pairing with *lbš*, "clothes, garment." This etymology is of a piece with Albright's possible explanation of biblical *tᵉrāpīm*, a type of idol and object of reverence as literally denoting "old rags," since Canaanite *trp* is now known to have meant "to wear out"; cf. *Archaeology and the Religion of Israel*, 2d ed., p. 207, n. 63.

6. *strength and beauty*. There is related imagery also in Ps lxxxv 14 where justice and beauty are the pages who accompany Yahweh.

at his side. Comparison with such standard theophanic descriptions as Pss lxxxv 14, xcvii 3; Deut xxxiii 2, and Hab iii 5 leaves little doubt that the conventional rendition of *bᵉmiqdāšō*, "in his sanctuary" (I Chron xvi 27 reads *bimᵉqōmō*, "in his place"), does not meet the requisites of biblical parallelism. After *lᵉpānāyw*, "before him," one expects "behind him," or "at his side." A return to the primitive meaning of *qdš*, which probably expressed the idea of "separation" or "withdrawal," facilitates the definition of *mqdš* as "side." Thus Bright (*Jeremiah*, The Anchor Bible, vol. 21) justly translates Jer i 5, *hiqdaštīkā*, "I set you apart." Cf. below on Ps xcviii 1.

7. *Give . . . Give . . .* 8. *Give*. See first NOTE on vs. 1 and Ps xxix 1–2.

8. *his court*. On morphologically plural *ḥaṣᵉrōtāyw* with singular meaning, consult the second NOTE on Ps lxxxiv 3.

9. *when the Holy One appears*. Cf. *Psalms I*, p. 176, on *hadrat qōdeš*, and P. R. Ackroyd in JTS 17 (1966), 393–96, who also identifies biblical *hadrat*, "vision," with Ugar. *hdrt*, "dream." He stresses that though their meanings are not identical, they do belong to the same realm of ideas.

all the earth. *kol hā'āreṣ* forms an inclusion with this same phrase in vs. 1, and at the same time closes the first strophe of the poem.

11. *heavens . . . earth*. *šāmayim//'āreṣ* answer to the Ugaritic pair *šmm//arṣ* in UT, 52:61–62. Cf. the fourth NOTE on Ps lvii 8.

rejoice . . . be glad. cf. *Psalms I*, p. 90, for the parallelism of Ugar. *šmḫ//gl*, and also the fourth NOTE on Ps lvii 8.

the sea . . . what fills it. Comparing *hayyām ūmᵉlō'ō* with Ugar. *ym mlat*, "the full sea," mentioned by Virolleaud in CRAIBL, 1962, 97.

12. *the highland*. The archaic spelling *śāday* of the psalm is normalized to *śādeh* in I Chron xvi 32. For the meaning "highland, mountain," cf. J. P. Peters in JBL 12 (1893), 54–56, and Driver, CML, p. 148a.

exult. I Chron xvi 32 reads the variant form *ya'ᵃlōṣ* (MT *ya'lōz*) that appears in Ugaritic as *'lṣ*. The author of Ps lxviii 4–5, on the other hand, employs both forms to create an inclusion.

Then. Namely, when Yahweh comes to govern the world himself, thus ushering in a new era of justice. That *'āz* should not be emended to *'ap*, "also, and," is clear from I Chron xvi 33, where the stichometric division helps establish the proper distribution of the cola in the psalm.

13. *his justice. ṣedeq* shares the suffix of its counterpart *'ᵉmūnātō*, "his truth." These two concepts form an inclusion with vs. 10, *mēšārīm*, "equity," and close the second strophe (vss. 10–13).

PSALM 97

(xcvii 1–12)

1 Yahweh reigns, let the earth be glad,
the many isles rejoice.
2 Cloud and storm cloud surround him,
justice and right are the foundation of his throne.
3 A fire goes before him,
and blazes round his back.
4 His lightning bolts light up the world,
the earth sees and trembles;
5 The mountains melt like wax
at the sight of Yahweh,
At the sight of the Master of all the earth.
6 The heavens announce his just claim,
all the peoples see his glory.
7 Let all who serve images be humiliated,
those who boast of their rags;
Bow down to him, all you gods!
8 Let Zion hear and rejoice;
let the daughters of Judah be glad
because of your acts of providence, Yahweh.
9 Because you are Yahweh Most High,
over all the earth the Grand One;
you are high above all gods.
10 Yahweh, who loves those who hate evil,
who protects the lives of his devoted,
Will rescue them from the hand of the wicked.
11 A sown field awaits the just,
and upright hearts, happiness
12 Rejoice, you just, in Yahweh,
and give thanks to his holy name.

Notes

xcvii. An eschatological hymn of three parts portraying the coming of Yahweh as universal judge. The first stanza (vss. 1–6) describes the theophany in terms reminiscent of Pss. xviii 9, 13, 14, l 3, lxxvii 19; Hab iii 10, etc.; the next strophe (vss. 7–9) tells of Israel's joy at paganism's defeat, and the last section (vss. 10–12) betrays kinship to Ps xxxvi 10–11 in depicting what God holds in store for those who worship him.

1. *isles.* Heb. *'iyyīm* designates not only the islands in the Mediterranean, but also the coastlands of southern Europe and northern Africa that were explored by Phoenician mariners and traders.

2. *storm cloud.* As noted in *Psalms I,* p. 107, *'ᵃrāpel* equals Ugar. *ǵrpl.*

justice and right. These personified attributes of God recur in Ps lxxxix 15.

3. *round his back. Psalms I,* p. 306, presents the evidence for this rendition of *sābīb ṣryw,* to be pointed *ṣūrāyw.* Further examples of *ṣūr,* "back," Ugar. *ẓr* and *ẓhr,* can be seen in Amos iii 11; Job xxii 24; xli 7. For the imagery, compare Ps l 3 and Joel ii 3, *lᵉpānāyw 'ākᵉlāh 'ēš wᵉ'aḥᵃrāyw tᵉlahēṭ lehābāh,* "Before him fire devours, and behind him blazes a flame." Cf. also 11QPsᵃ Creation, vss. 2–3 (lines 9–11) in Sanders, *The Psalms Scroll of Qumrân Cave 11,* p. 89. John Gray, *The Legacy of Canaan,* 2d ed., p. 270, appeals to Ugar. *ṣrrt,* "cliffs," translating, "Fire goes before him and lights up his crags." But this proposal disregards the parallelism that characterizes the theophanic decriptions cited in *Psalms I,* p. 281. Our proposal has been adopted by F. M. Cross, *Canaanite Myth and Hebrew Epic* (Cambridge, Mass., 1973), p. 162 and n. 75.

4. *the earth.* Depicted as a person losing control of self at an unexpected sight, a motif documented in *Psalms I,* p. 281.

5. *Master of all the earth.* Unpublished RŠ 24.274, *ymǵy adn ilm rbm,* "The master of the great gods arrived," provides interesting background on *'ᵃdōn kol hā'āreṣ,* an appellative found again in Zech vi 5. In noncanonical 11QPsᵃ 151:8, the phrase *'dwn hkwl,* "the Master of all," completely lacking in the Bible, bespeaks a late date of composition according to Avi Hurwitz, *Tarbiẓ* 34 (1965), 224–27.

6. *see.* MT has placed the conjunction *wᵉ,* "and," before *rā'ū,* but from an examination of the parallelistic structure of the verse a good case can be made for branding the *wᵉ* as secondary. With *wᵉ* omitted, the verse numbers nine syllables in each colon whose elements correspond to their counterparts in an A+B+C//Á+B́+Ć pattern and whose rhythm is marked by assonance:

higgīdū haššāmayim ṣidqō
rā'ū kol-hā'ammīm k^ebōdō

A similar instance of punctilious structuring is noted at vs. 11.

his just claim. For this nuance of *ṣidqō,* see *Psalms I,* p. 322, and the last NOTE on Ps xcviii 2. The Lord of Israel has claims which he upholds against the would-be usurpers.

7. *who boast.* The alliteration *hammithal^{e}līm bā'^{e}līlīm* and the theological wordplay (cf. Ps lxxv 5) are effective.

their rags. Cf. the first NOTE on Ps xcvi 5.

8. *Let Zion hear.* Explaining *šām^e'āh* as precative perfect which modally corresponds to jussive *yēbōšū,* "be humiliated," that describes the reaction of the polytheists in the preceding verse.

and rejoice. Repointing to jussive *w^{e}tiśmaḥ* (MT *wattiśmaḥ*) and comparing Ps xlviii 12, "Let Mount Zion rejoice; let the daughters of Judah be glad."

daughters of Judah. Hebraic for the towns and villages of Judah.

be glad. Repointing to jussive *w^{e}tāgēlnāh* (MT *wattāgēlnāh*), and comparing Ps xlviii 12, cited in second NOTE on this verse.

acts of providence. Cf. *Psalms I,* p. 293. In the present context, these acts probably refer to the election of Israel to participate in the worship of the one true God.

9. *Most High . . . are high.* The theological wordplay with the breakup of the composite title *'elyōn na'^{a}lētā* is noted in *Psalms I,* p. 285, NOTE on Ps xlvii 6.

10. *who loves.* There is no need to drop the final *-y* of *'hby* (MT *'ōh^{a}bēy*), as proposed by many commentators, since it can be explained as a third person singular suffix expressing *dativus commodi.* Compare Prov viii 35, *mōṣ^e'ī m^{e}ṣā'ī* (MT *māṣā'y*) *ḥayyīm,* "Who finds me finds to his benefit life eternal," and xxviii 16, where the final *-y* of *śn'y* expresses dative of advantage.

who loves . . . who protects. Ps cxlvi 8–9 also make Yahweh the subject of the parallel participles *'ōhēb* and *šōmēr.*

those who hate evil. Reading *śān^e'ū* (MT *śin^e'ū*) and parsing *śān^e'ū rā'* as a relative clause without the relative pronoun, an ellipsis studied in the fifth NOTE on Ps lxxxi 6 and in *Psalms I,* pp. 213 f.

11. *A sown field.* Since *'ōr,* "light," and *zārūa'*, "sowing," do not blend into a congruent metaphor and, as was discussed at Ps li 9, it may be assumed that the psalmists chose their metaphors with care, we should repoint MT *'ōr* to *'ūr* and identify the latter with the noun documented in *Psalms I,* pp. 222 f. As in Ps xxxvi 10, *'ūr* refers to the field of Paradise, an interpretation fully consonant with the eschatological nature of the hymn. To suggest, however, that in his choice of terms the psalmist wished to evoke the motif of "the Desert and the Sown" (see

the fourth NOTE on Ps lxxii 6), since the nether world is termed "scorched land" in Ps lxviii 7, would be to go beyond the immediate evidence.

The A+B//B́+Á chiastic arrangement of the verse merits comment. The line contains six elements, three in each colon, and numbers fourteen syllables with seven in each colon. The two words of A (*'ūr zārūaʻ*, "sown field") balance the single word of Á (*śimḥāh*, "happiness"), while the prepositional phrase of B (*laṣṣaddīq*, "the just"), is counterpoised by the two nouns of the prepositional phrase in B́, *leyišrē lēb*, "the upright hearts." For another example of careful literary carpentry, see first NOTE on vs. 6.

happiness. As in Ps xvi 11, *śimḥāh* pregnantly connotes eternal beatitude with Yahweh in the sown field of Paradise.

12. *Rejoice.* Imperative *śimeḥū* forms an inclusion with jussive *yiśmeḥū* in vs. 1.

PSALM 98

(xcviii 1–9)

1 A *psalm.*

Sing to Yahweh a song that is new,
because he has worked marvels;
His right hand brought him victory,
and his arm set him apart.
2 Yahweh made known his victory
before the eyes of the nations
He revealed his vindication.
3 Remember his love and his fidelity,
O house of Israel!
all you ends of the earth,
See the victory of our God!
4 Sing to Yahweh with joy, all the earth,
burst into joyous song and make music.
5 Make music to Yahweh with the lyre,
with the lyre and melodious voice.
6 With trumpets and sound of horns
joyfully sing before King Yahweh!
7 Let the sea and what fills it thunder,
the world with all who live in it.
8 Let the ocean currents clap their hands,
the mountains shout for joy together
9 Before Yahweh
when he comes
To govern the earth.
He will govern the world with justice,
and the peoples with equity.

Notes

xcviii. A hymn praising Yahweh's kingship, similar to Ps xcvi, extolling him for his triumph over heathen gods both in primordial and in historical times, and foretelling his return to re-establish the universal reign of justice. The opening two verses describe Yahweh's victory, vss. 3–8 are a summons to worship him, while vs. 9 announces Yahweh's coming to inaugurate the messianic era of worldwide justice.

1. *marvels.* Biblical poets use *niplā'ōt* to designate cosmic wonders worked by God as well as his historical achievements on behalf of his people Israel. Both senses may be intended here.

brought him victory. As in Ps xcvi 2, the psalmist has in mind Yahweh's triumph over the forces of chaos in primeval times.

his arm. Heb. $z^{e}r\bar{o}^{a'}$ either shares the suffix of parallel $y^{e}m\bar{\imath}n\bar{o}$, "his right hand," or, denoting a part of the body, it may dispense with the suffix; cf. *kāp* in vs. 8.

set him apart. Repointing MT *qodšō* to piel preterit *qiddēšō* and assigning the verb its primitive meaning discussed at Ps xcvi 6. This reading results in two chiastically placed cola of verb-subject//subject-verb, each of which contains seven syllables. Cf. the first NOTE to Ps xcvii 6 on utility of counting syllables.

This victory over the gods of the other nations set Yahweh apart from all other divinities or, in the words of Ps xcvii 9, "exalted far beyond all gods."

2. *made known his victory.* Yahweh gave historical proof of his conquest over his cosmic rivals by giving Israel victory over the nations which were still under the tutelage of gods long since vanquished by Yahweh.

before the eyes of the nations. By scanning the verse as A+B//C//Á+B́ (cf. Ps lxxxvi 12), we find three cola numbering 7:6:5 syllables instead of two unbalanced cola of 7:11 syllables. The proposed scansion, moreover, yields a line conceptually richer than the conventional versions.

his vindication. As recognized by RSV and others, this is here the precise nuance of *ṣidqātō*, often translated "his justice." Cf. the comment on *ṣidqō* in Ps xcvii 6. Yahweh has not only vindicated his supremacy over other deities, but he has also manifested his sovereignty to heathens by exalting the house of Israel.

3. *Remember.* Vocalizing imperative $z^{e}k\bar{o}r$ instead of MT preterit *zākar*, "He remembered"; cf. Dahood, VT 16 (1966), 310.

O house of Israel! Departing from the versions in identifying l^{e} of *l^{e}bēt yiśrā'ēl* as the vocative *lamedh;* cf. the same usage in Ps lxxiii 1, *l^{e}yiśrā'ēl,* "O Israel!" This analysis bears on the parsing and translation of Pss cxxxii 1, *z^{e}kōr yhwh l^{e}dāwīd,* "Remember Yahweh, O David!" (RSV "Remember, O Lord, in David's favor"), and cxxxvii 7, *z^{e}kōr yhwh libnē '^{e}dōm,* "Remember Yahweh, O sons of Edom!" (RSV "Remember, O Lord, against the Edomites!") Cf. Jer xxi 11–12, *l^{e}bēt melek y^{e}hūdāh šim^e'ū d^{e}bar yhwh bēt dāwīd kōh 'āmar yhwh,* "O royal house of Judah, hear Yahweh's word; house of David, thus speaks Yahweh!"

See. Repointing MT *rā'ū* to imperative *r^e'ū,* as in Pss lxviii 25 and lxix 33.

5. *Make music . . . with the lyre.* The phrase *zamm^{e}rū . . . b^{e}kinnōr* might be compared with RŠ 24.252:4, *wyḏmr bknr,* "And he sings with the lyre."

6. *trumpets.* On the nature of the *ḥ^{a}ṣōṣ^{e}rōt,* see J. M. Myers, *I Chronicles,* § 16, COMMENT on I Chron xv 16–24.

8. *their hands.* Being the name of a part of the body, *kāp* need not be determined by a suffix; cf. the third NOTE on vs. 1.

9. *when he comes.* Comparison with Ps xcvii 13 has convinced some critics that one *kī bā'* has dropped out by haplography, but the metrical pattern A+B//C//Á+B́ employed in vs. 2 suggests that the psalmist may have availed himself of a similar sequence here with *kī bā'* suspended between the first and third phrases of the verse and belonging to both.

PSALM 99

(xcix 1–9)

1 Yahweh reigns, let the peoples tremble,
O Enthroned upon the Cherubim, let the earth quake.
2 Yahweh is too great for Zion,
exalted is he beyond all the Strong Ones.
3 Let them praise your name,
O Great and Awesome One!
Holy is he!
4 The strongest king, the lover of justice,
you yourself established equity;
Right and justice in Jacob
you yourself wrought.
5 Exalt Yahweh our God,
prostrate yourselves at his footstool.
Holy is he!
6 Moses and Aaron were among his priests,
and Samuel among those invoking his name,
invoking El Yahweh.
He himself answered them
7 from the pillar of the cloud
He spoke to them.
They observed his commands,
the law he gave them.
8 Yahweh our God, you yourself answered them.
For them you became El the Forgiver,
who cleansed them of their evil deeds.
9 Exalt Yahweh our God,
and prostrate yourselves at his holy mountain,
for holy is Yahweh our God.

Notes

xcix. A hymn in praise of God's kingship, as well as of his holiness, since each of the three strophes ends with a refrain acclaiming Yahweh's sanctity (vss. 3, 5, 9).

1. *let the peoples tremble.* Though many versions take *yirgᵉzū* as indicative, the jussive forms following *yhwh mālak* in Ps xcvii 1, permit one to interpret *yirgᵉzū* in the same manner. Cf. *Juxta Hebraeos, "Commoveantur populi."* A stylistic characteristic of this psalmist is his use of the independent pronoun to underscore the subject of the verb; cf. vss. 4 bis, 6, 8. Doubtless "the peoples" refers to all peoples of the known world.

O Enthroned upon the Cherubim. Cf. Ps lxxx 2. Like vs. 3, *šimᵉkā*, "your name," second person *yōšēb*, coming on the heels of third person *yhwh*, has proved troublesome to scholars. If, however, we ascribe this usage to court style (cf. Ps lxi 5–9) in which shifting from third to second person is not uncommon, we have a satisfactory explanation at hand.

quake. Proposals to emend *tānūṭ* to synonymous *tāmūṭ* or *tāmūg*, "to melt, faint," founder upon the by-form *nṭṭ*, "to wobble," attested in the Ugaritic descriptions of a person's reaction upon receiving alarming news; cf. Ps lx 4. Moreover, some scholars (e.g., Gaster, Aistleitner, Lipiński) would restore UT, 51:vii:34–35 to read *bmt a*[*rṣ*] *ṭṭn*, "The high places of earth quaked," where *arṣ ṭṭn* collocates the ideas expressed in biblical *tānūṭ hā'āreṣ*. Cf. Herdner, *Corpus de tablettes*, p. 29. The close kinship between medial *waw* and double *'ayin* verbs is well known; cf. GK, § 77, who cites *mwk-mkk, mwš-mšš, nwd-ndd, dwk-dkk*. The pair *nwṭ-nṭṭ* can be added to the list.

2. *too great for Zion.* The comparison expressed by *'al*, "beyond, above," in the second colon points to the comparative function of *bᵉ* in *bᵉṣiyyōn;* cf. the first Note on Ps lxxxix 8. The psalmist states the reason why earth and all nations should cringe before Yahweh; even Mount Zion cannot contain his cosmic power.

exalted. By omitting the connecting link *wᵉ* before *rām* one recovers a syllabically balanced line of 7:7.

the Strong Ones. The identification of the root *'mm*, "to be strong, wise," at royal Pss xviii 28 and xlvii 2, uncovers a name for the pagan deities, and at the same time renders the emendation to *'ᵉlōhīm*, "gods," based on Pss xcv 3, xcvi 4, and the reading of three manuscripts less compelling. Thus there is a theological wordplay (see Ps xcvii 9) in the use of *'ammīm*, "peoples," and *'ammīm*, "Strong Ones," in successive verses.

3. *them.* Namely, all nations, together with their gods.

praise. With *Juxta Hebraeos, confiteantur,* understanding *yōdū* as jussive.

your name. As noticed at vs. 1, the juxtaposition of third and second person characterizes court style.

O Great and Awesome One! Many commentators see in *gādōl wenōrā'* adjectives modifying "your name," but by parsing them as appellatives of Yahweh in the vocative case, we find the counterpart to vocative "O Enthroned upon the Cherubim" in vs. 1. Cf. Ps lxxxviii 8, *rabbāh wenōrā',* "too great and awesome."

Holy is he! This refrain, repeated in vss. 5, 9, closes the first strophe.

4. *The strongest king.* For the syntax of *'ōz melek,* consult *Psalms I,* p. 289. In addition to the explication given there, one may propose the reading *'ōz melākīm mišpāṭ,* a reading that does not necessarily assume the haplography of a *mem* since, as pointed out at Pss lxxxviii 6 and xciv 10, a singly written *mem* can orthographically suffice for two. Nor is there any need to repoint adjectival *'ōz to 'āz,* "strong," since the former may represent the Phoenician pronunciation as in Prov xxiv 5; Eccles viii 1; cf. Job vi 27 on possible *tōm* for *tām.*

the lover of justice. Comparing *mišpāṭ 'āhēb* with Ps xi 7, *ṣedāqōt 'āhēb,* "who loves just actions."

5. *footstool.* Unwitnessed in the other Semitic languages, *hadōm* recurs repeatedly in the Ras Shamra texts. Egyptian *hdmw* is probably a Canaanite loanword; cf. A. Gardiner, *Ancient Egyptian Onomastica* (Oxford, 1947), I, p. 68. Scholars dispute whether, in the present context, "footstool" metaphorically refers to the ark on Mount Zion or to Mount Zion itself. The corresponding phrase in vs. 9 suggests that *hadōm raglāyw* is synonymous with *lehar qōdšō,* "at his holy mountain."

6. *El Yahweh.* This composite divine name results from repointing MT *'el,* "to," to *'ēl,* "El," which recurs in vs. 8.

He himself. The use of the independent pronoun before the verb seems to indicate a certain emphasis on the subject.

answered them. The *yqtl* form *ya'anēm* expresses past time; cf. the introductory NOTE on Ps lxxviii.

7. *from the pillar.* Consult *Psalms I,* p. 83, and the second NOTE on Ps lx 8 for *be,* "from." The inaccessible God spoke to Moses and Aaron out of the pillar of cloud, which hid him from the presumptuous glances of men but was nevertheless also the sign of his presence. Cf. Exod xxxlii 9; Num xii 5. Stylistically, "from the pillar of the cloud" scans as a double-duty modifier, looking both to what precedes and to what follows. This literary technique is also termed "the two-way middle."

8. *you . . . answered them.* Preterit *'anītām* forms an inclusion with vs. 6, *ya'anēm,* which also describes past events.

who cleansed them. With C. F. Whitley, ZAW 85 (1973), 227–30, analyzing *nōqēm* into the particle of *nāqāh*, "to cleanse," and the plural pronominal suffix. Though qal in form, *nōqēm* has the force of the piel "to cleanse," thus joining the ranks of qal participles with the signification of the piel. For other instances, see Dahood, PNWSP, p. 38, and GK, § 113w. The resultant parallelism of *nōśē'*, "the Forgiver," and *nōqēm,* "who cleansed them," may be compared with the concurrence of these two roots in Job x 14–15.

of their evil deeds. Whitley, ZAW 85 (1973), 227–30, correctly identifies the separative force of *'al.* In the present writer's notes this possibility was listed but was then discarded in favor of a coin of baser metal. He happily returns to the earlier possibility. Thus the balance in this line of *lāhem,* "for them," and *'al 'alîlōtām,* "of their evil deeds," has a counterpart in Hos xi 4, *lāhem,* "for them" // *'al leḥehem,* "from their cheeks."

PSALM 100

(c 1–5)

1 *A psalm for giving thanks.*

Hail Yahweh, all the earth,
2 serve Yahweh in happiness,
enter his presence with joyful song.
3 Know that Yahweh is God:
he made us and is the Omnipotent;
We are his people
and the sheep of his pasture.
4 Enter his gates giving thanks,
his court with song of praise;
give thanks to him, bless his name.
5 For Yahweh is good:
from eternity is his love,
to every generation his faithfulness.

NOTES

c. A hymn sung at the solemn entry into the court of the temple, probably in connection with a thanksgiving ceremony. Though this hymn does not specifically refer to God as king, its phraseology sufficiently resembles that of the preceding psalms celebrating Yahweh's kingship (especially xcv 1–7) as to justify classifying it among them.

3. *he . . . we.* With *'anaḥnū* attached to the second colon instead of to the third (cf. the versions), the syllable count results in 9:9:7, a more balanced sequence than 9:6:10. This scansion brings out, moreover, both the inclusion and the contrast formed by the two independent pronouns.

the Omnipotent. Repointing MT negative *lō'* to *lē'*, "the Omnipotent," discussed in the second NOTE on Ps lxxv 7, where *lē'* balances *'elōhīm,* "God," just as in our verse. Another text connecting this title with creation is Mal ii 15, as read and interpreted by L. Sabottka, *Zephaniah* (Rome, 1972), pp. 17–18. The proposal of J. O. Lewis, JBL 86 (1967), 216, to take *l'* as the asservative particle "indeed"—He has made us, and, indeed, we are his people—leaves the *aleph* of *l'* unaccounted for; hence it must be declined as a less probable solution.

4. *his court.* On this singular meaning of plural *ḥ^{a}ṣērōtāyw,* see the second NOTE on Ps lxxxiv 3.

5. *from eternity*. Cf. *Psalms I,* pp. 56, 180, 271, and Jer xlii 8.

eternity . . . generation after generation. For the Ugaritic brace *'lm //dr dr,* cf. the first NOTE on Ps lxxxv 6.

INDEX OF BIBLICAL PASSAGES

INDEX OF HEBREW WORDS

INDEX OF SUBJECTS